STUDENT'S SOLUTIONS MANUAL

TO ACCOMPANY TERRY SINCICH'S

BUSINESS STATISTICS BY EXAMPLE

**THIRD
EDITION**

NANCY J. SHAFER

Bowling Green State University

DELLEN PUBLISHING COMPANY
San Francisco

COLLIER MACMILLAN PUBLISHERS
London

Divisions of Macmillan, Inc.

Permissions: Dellen Publishing Company
              400 Pacific Avenue
              San Francisco, California 94133

Orders: Dellen Publishing Company
         c/o Macmillan Publishing Company
         Front and Brown Streets
         Riverside, New Jersey 08075

Collier Macmillan Canada, Inc.

ISBN 0-02-411002-7

Printing: 1 2 3 4 5 6 7   Year: 9 0 1 2 3 4 5 6

PREFACE

This solutions manual is designed to accompany the text, *Business Statistics By Example,* Third Edition, by Terry Sincich (Dellen Publishing Company, 1988). It provides answers to most odd-numbered exercises for each chapter in the text. Other methods of solution may also be appropriate; however, the author has presented one that she believes to be most instructive to the beginning Statistics student. The student should first attempt to solve the assigned exercises without help from this manual. Then, if unsuccessful, the solution in the manual will clarify points necessary to the solution. The student who successfully solves an exercise should still refer to the manual's solution. Many points are clarified and expanded upon to provide maximum insight into and benefit from each exercise.

Instructors will also benefit from the use of this manual. It will save time in preparing presentations of the solutions and possibly provide another point of view regarding their meaning.

Some of the exercises are subjective in nature and thus omitted from the Answer Key at the end of *Business Statistics by Example,* Third Edition. The subjective decisions regarding these exercises have been made and are explained by the author. Solutions based on these decisions are presented; the solution to this type of exercise is often most instructive. When an alternative interpretation of an exercise may occur, the author has often addressed it and given justification for the approach taken.

ACKNOWLEDGMENTS

I would like to thank Phyllis Curtiss, Peggy Kintner, Rajesh Bandekar, and Betty Jackson for their help in preparing this manual. I would also like to thank Brenda Dobson for her assistance and for typing this work.

CONTENTS

ONE   INTRODUCTION

1.1   a.   The collection of the recorded dollar values of all items held in inventory (Population A) characterizes the believed or assessed dollar values of all items stocked by the hospital.

b.   The collection of the actual dollar values of all items held in inventory (Population B) characterizes the actual value of all items stocked by the hospital that are actually on hand.

c.   The auditor can compare the assessed values to the actual values of items stocked by the hospital to determine discrepancies due to failure to record the use or destruction of an item or the theft of an item.

d.   The actual values may be different from the assessed values of items due to failure to record the use or destruction of an item or the theft of an item.

e.   The total of the sample values can be adjusted to estimate the total value of all items by multiplying the sample value by N/50, where N is the total number of items stocked by the hospital. This method assumes that all items in the inventory are of approximately equal value. If this is not the case, error may result.

1.3   a.   The annual incomes of the households characterize the amount of money that will be available to spend on the fried chicken at the new franchise.

b.   These 30 incomes represent a sample of the annual incomes of the town. The population would be the incomes of all the households in the town.

c.   No, the average of the 30 incomes is an estimate of the population average. The sample average probably will not be equal to the population average because there is variability in the sample.

1.5　a.　Population A would be the job performance ratings of all Type A workers. Population B would be the job performance of all Type B workers.

b.　Yes, if the sample is chosen appropriately, it will represent the population from which it is taken.

c.　To estimate the difference in average performance ratings for the two populations, the researchers could calculate the difference in average performance ratings for the two samples.

d.　No, the sample difference is an estimate of the population difference. The sample difference probably will not equal the population difference because there is variability in the samples.

1.7　a.　The population of interest is the deferred-payment plan status of all residential customers served by the company.

b.　The sample is the deferred-payment plan status of the 200 selected customers.

c.　The inference desired is an estimate of the percentage of residential customers who qualify for the deferred-payment plan. The chosen sample could be used to estimate this percentage.

1.9　a.　The population of interest is the responses of all smokers of low-tar, low-nicotine cigarettes concerning whether or not each smoker is aware of the U.S. Surgeon General's report on low-tar, low-nicotine cigarettes.

b.　No, the Surgeon General would have to interview all smokers of low-tar, low-nicotine cigarettes to determine the true fraction who are aware of the report. This would be a very difficult, if not, impossible task.

c.　The manufacturer could obtain an estimate of the true fraction by taking a sample of low-tar, low-nicotine cigarette smokers and computing from this sample the fraction who are aware of the report.

CASE STUDIES

1.1 a. The daily closing prices characterize the daily value of Standard & Poor's common stocks from 1982 to 1986.

   b. The daily changes in closing prices characterize the changes in daily value of Standard & Poor's common stocks from 1982 to 1986.

   c. The five populations would characterize the daily value of Standard & Poor's common stocks for 1982, for 1983, for 1984, for 1985, and for 1986.

   d. Yes, the selected values would be a sample of 10 observations from the daily values of Standard & Poor's common stock for 1986.

   e. No, the sample average is an estimate of the population average value. The sample average probably will not equal the population average because there is variability in the sample.

1.3 a. The supermarket A checkout times characterize the customer checkout times at a supermarket operating manual cash registers. The supermarket B checkout times characterize the customer checkout times at a supermarket operating automated cash registers.

   b. The data sets are subsets of the populations described above; therefore, they are samples.

   c. No, the sample average is an estimate of the population average. The sample average probably will not equal the population average because there is variability in the sample.

TWO GRAPHICAL METHODS FOR DESCRIBING DATA SETS

2.1   a.   Quantitative. The *number* of acres can be measured on a *numerical scale* from zero upward (for example, 2.3 acres).

       b.   Qualitative. Zoning for a property cannot be measured on a numerical scale; it is *nonnumerical data* (for example, residential, business, etc.).

       c.   Qualitative. *Type* of residential water heating system cannot be measured on a numerical scale; it is nonnumerical data (for example, gas, electric, etc.).

2.3   Some examples are:

       COLOR (qualitative) - because it *cannot* be measured on a numerical scale; it is nonnumerical data (for example, red, blue, etc.).

       COST (quantitative) - because it *can* be measured on a numerical scale, from a few thousand dollars upward (for example, $8,900).

       TYPE OF TRANSMISSION (qualitative) - because it is nonnumerical and *cannot* be measured on a numerical scale (for example, manual, automatic, etc.).

       GAS MILEAGE (quantitative) - because it *can* be measured on a nonnumerical scale (for example, 25 MPG).

2.5   Some examples are:

       SALARY (quantitative) - because it *can* be measured on a numerical scale (for example, $30,000).

       JOB HISTORY (qualitative) - because it is nonnumerical data and *cannot* be measured on a numerical scale (for example, auto mechanic, lawyer, etc.).

CREDIT REFERENCE (qualitative) - because it *cannot* be measured on a numerical scale; it is nonnumerical data (for example, good risk, bad risk, etc.)

2.7 a. To find frequencies, one must count the number of observations within each of the 4 categories. The relative frequencies are found by dividing the frequency by the total number of observations.

CATEGORY	FREQUENCY	RELATIVE FREQUENCY
6 day, 48 hr	3	3/25 = .12
5 day, 40 hr	10	.40
4 day, 40 hr	8	.32
3 day, 40 hr	4	.16
	25	1.00

The relative frequency bar graph is drawn by making the vertical axis an appropriate length so as to be long enough to accommodate the largest bar (.40). Then the bars are drawn of length according to the scale of the vertical axis.

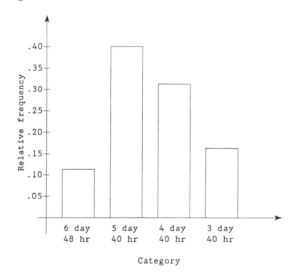

  b. From the table above, the relative frequency of workers who prefer a 5-day, 40-hour work week is .40.

  c. From the table above, the relative frequency of workers who prefer a 3-day, 40-hour work week is .16.

2.9   a.   A relative frequency bar graph has been used to describe the
             survey results.

       b.   The percentage of companies who offer no group-life coverage is
             16%.

       c.   Twenty percent of the companies offer $10,000 as the lowest group-
             life benefit. If 1,000 companies were surveyed, that means that
             1000(.20) = 200 of them offer $10,000 as the lowest group-life
             benefit.

       d.   The survey results are probably based on a sample of companies as
             it would be very difficult to survey all U.S. companies.

2.11   a.

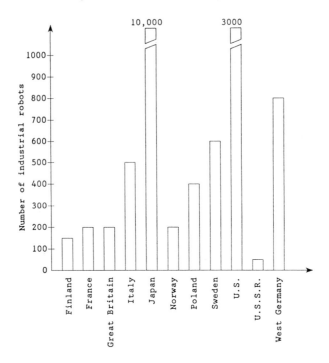

The bar graph is constructed by forming a vertical axis to an
appropriate scale. Since the U.S. and Japan have many more than
all other countries, the scale is based on the remaining nine.
Since 800 is the largest of the remaining nine, the top of the
scale is chosen as 1000. All other countries' amounts are drawn
as bars of a proportionate length. Since Japan's and the U.S.'s
numbers go off the scale, their bars were left open and the
numbers of robots were placed at the openings.

b. Japan has more industrial robots than all of the other countries listed combined. All other listed countries combined have 6050 industrial robots compared to Japan's 10,000. The U.S. has about as many as all other listed countries, except Japan, combined-- 3050 for the others versus 3000 for the U.S. The U.S.S.R. has the fewest, less than 20% of the next smallest country's total:

$$(25 \div 130) \times 100 = 19.2\%$$

2.13 a. The relative frequencies are found by dividing the frequency by the total number of observations.

SUPERMARKET	NUMBER OF STORES	RELATIVE FREQUENCY
Safeway	1,712	1,712/8,524 = .2008
Kroger	1,273	.1493
Winn-Dixie	1,271	.1491
A & P	1,200	.1408
American Stores	958	.1124
Lucky Stores	579	.0679
Albertson's	452	.0530
Food Lion	404	.0474
Grand Union	368	.0432
Publix	307	.0360
	8,524	.9999

The relative frequency bar graph is drawn by making the vertical axis an appropriate length so as to be long enough to accommodate the largest bar (.2008). Then, the bars are drawn of length according to the scale of the vertical axis.

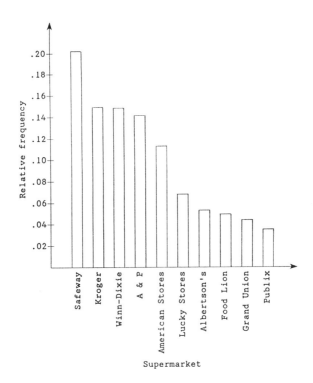

b. The percentage of stores operated by supermarket chains based in Florida is

$$\frac{1271 + 307}{8524}(100) = 18.512\%$$

2.15   a.   The first two digits, in order, which form the stems are:

21, 22, 23, 24, 25, 26, 27, 28, 29, 30, 31, and 32

b. The stem-and-leaf display is:

STEMS	LEAVES
21	3, 5
22	4, 8, 7, 6
23	4, 7
24	1
25	4
26	7, 8, 6, 5
27	4, 0
28	8, 5
29	1
30	3, 3
31	6, 9
32	0

2.17 a. The first digit forms the stems and ranges from 1 through 9.

STEMS	LEAVES
1.	6, 6, 1, 1, 2
2.	1
3.	5, 3
4.	0, 3, 5
5.	9, 3, 0
6.	5, 7, 3, 4
7.	6, 3, 4
8.	2, 4, 9, 6, 4
9.	7, 4

b. The frequency distribution is found by first tallying the number of leaves that correspond to each stem.

STEMS	FREQUENCY
1.	5
2.	1
3.	2
4.	3
5.	3
6.	4
7.	3
8.	5
9.	2

A graph is as follows:

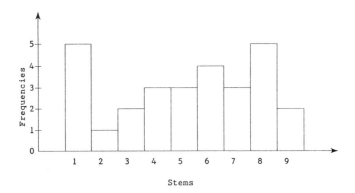

2.19   a.   The first digit forms the stems and ranges from 0 through 8.

STEMS	LEAVES
0	76, 52
1	96, 86, 36, 37, 00
2	82, 64, 80, 05, 83, 57, 50
3	17, 84, 03, 73, 25, 45, 13
4	17, 02, 22, 00, 08, 80, 72
5	
6	93, 43
7	50, 91, 49, 32
8	91

CHAPTER 2

b. The first two digits form the stems and range from 5 through 89.

STEMS	LEAVES	STEMS	LEAVES	STEMS	LEAVES
05	2	27		49	
06		28	2, 0, 3	//	
07	6	29		64	3
08		30	3	65	
09		31	7, 3	66	
10	0	32	5	67	
11		33		68	
12		34	5	69	3
13	6, 7	35		70	
14		36		71	
15		37	3	72	
16		38	4	73	2
17		39		74	9
18	6	40	8, 0, 2	75	0
19	6	41	7	76	
20	5	42	2	77	
21		43		78	
22		44		79	1
23		45		80	
24		46		81	
25	0, 7	47	2	//	
26	4	48	0	89	1

c. The figure in part (a) provides more information about the yearly per-bed rental costs. The figure in part (b) breaks down too finely, not allowing a picture of the data as a whole.

2.21 a. The digits to the left of the decimal point form the stems and range from 0 through 13.

STEMS	LEAVES	STEMS	LEAVES
0.	95, 70, 63, 63, 63	7.	75, 50, 33, 30
1.	55, 53, 05	8.	30, 25
2.	45, 10	9.	40, 00
3.	65, 00, 00	10.	
4.	25	11.	50
5.		12.	
6.		13.	10

b. Kirby Puckett's salary of $365,000 is the item with stem 3. and leaf 65.

c. Salaries of $1 million or more would be represented by stems of 10 or larger. Only 2 out of the 24 players have salaries of $1 million or more for a percentage of 2/24(100) = 8.333%.

2.23   a.   The lower boundary of the first interval is 10.5. The upper boundary of the first interval is 10.5 + 5 (the class interval width) = 15.5. The other class interval boundaries are found in a similar way and are 15.5 - 20.5, 20.5 - 25.5, 25.5 - 30.5, 30.5 - 35.5 and 35.5 - 40.5.

b.	CLASS	CLASS INTERVAL	TALLY	CLASS FREQUENCY	CLASS RELATIVE FREQUENCY
	1	10.5 - 15.5	|	1	1/20 = .05
	2	15.5 - 20.5	||	2	.10
	3	20.5 - 25.5	||||	4	.20
	4	25.5 - 30.5	ꟷꟷꟷ	5	.25
	5	30.5 - 35.5	||||	4	.20
	6	35.5 - 40.5	||||	4	.20
			TOTALS	20	1.00

c.

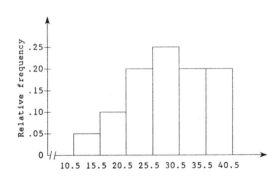

Class Intervals

2.25   a.   First, we must find the class interval width so that we get the desired ten classes. The range is 930 - 99 = 831. The class interval width is approximately equal to the range divided by the number of classes: 831/10 ≈ 85. To ensure that no data point falls on a class boundary, we will choose 98.5 for the lower limit of our first interval. The upper limit of the first interval will be 98.5 + 85 = 183.5. This process is continued until we have our ten intervals.

CLASS	CLASS INTERVAL	TALLY	CLASS FREQUENCY	CLASS RELATIVE FREQUENCY
1	98.5 – 183.5	⊬⊬ ||	7	7/54 = .1296
2	183.5 – 268.5	⊬⊬ ⊬⊬ ⊬⊬	15	.2778
3	268.5 – 353.5	⊬⊬ ⊬⊬ ||||	14	.2593
4	353.5 – 438.5	⊬⊬	5	.0926
5	438.5 – 523.5	⊬⊬ ||	7	.1296
6	523.5 – 608.5	||||	4	.0741
7	608.5 – 693.5		0	0
8	693.5 – 778.5	|	1	.0185
9	778.5 – 863.5		0	0
10	863.5 – 948.5	|	1	.0185
		TOTALS	54	1.0000

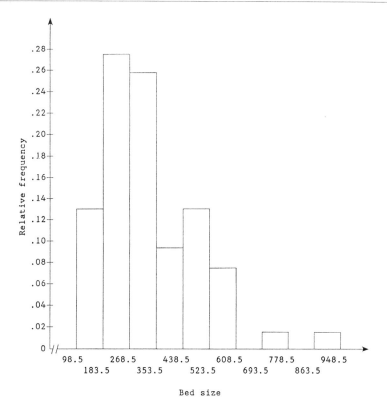

Bed size

b. Using the same process as above, the class interval width is
    approximately equal to 831/3 ≈ 280. The lower limit of the first
    class is 98.5. The upper limit of the first class will be
    98.5 + 280 = 378.5. This process is continued until we have our
    three classes.

CLASS	CLASS INTERVAL	TALLY	CLASS FREQUENCY	CLASS RELATIVE FREQUENCY
1	98.5 – 378.5	⊬⊬⊬ ⊬⊬⊬ ⊬⊬⊬ ⊬⊬⊬ ⊬⊬⊬ ⊬⊬⊬ ⊬⊬⊬ |||	38	38/54 = .7037
2	378.5 – 658.5	⊬⊬⊬ ⊬⊬⊬ ||||	14	.2593
3	659.5 – 938.5	||	2	.0370
		TOTALS	54	1.0000

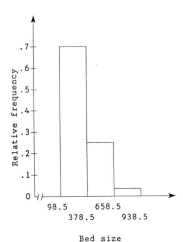

Bed size

The relative frequency distribution in part (a) is more
informative because it gives a finer breakdown of the data,
especially in the lower classes. Note that the breakdown is not
so fine that too few data points fall in the intervals. The use
of too few classes tends to lump too much data together and
distorts the "shape" of the distribution.

c. As before,

$$\text{class interval width} \approx \frac{831}{25} \approx 35$$

CLASS	CLASS INTERVAL	TALLY	CLASS FREQUENCY	CLASS RELATIVE FREQUENCY
1	98.5 - 133.5	|	1	1/54 = .0185
2	133.5 - 168.5	||	2	.0370
3	168.5 - 203.5	̸H̸t̸ ||||	9	.1667
4	203.5 - 238.5	||||	4	.0741
5	238.5 - 273.5	̸H̸t̸ |	6	.1111
6	273.5 - 308.5	̸H̸t̸ |	6	.1111
7	308.5 - 343.5	̸H̸t̸ ||	7	.1296
8	343.5 - 378.5	|||	3	.0556
9	378.5 - 413.5	||	2	.0370
10	413.5 - 448.5	|	1	.0185
11	448.5 - 483.5	|||	3	.0556
12	483.5 - 518.5	|||	3	.0556
13	518.5 - 553.5	|||	3	.0556
14	553.5 - 588.5	|	1	.0185
15	588.5 - 623.5	|	1	.0185
16	623.5 - 658.5		0	0
17	658.5 - 693.5		0	0
18	693.5 - 728.5	|	1	.0185
19	728.5 - 763.5		0	0
20	763.5 - 798.5		0	0
21	798.5 - 833.5		0	0
22	833.5 - 868.5		0	0
23	868.5 - 903.5		0	0
24	903.5 - 938.5	|	1	.0185
25	938.5 - 973.5		0	0
		TOTALS	54	1.0000

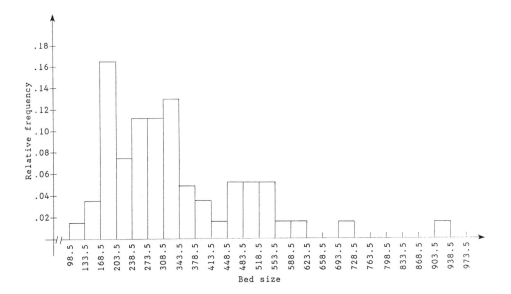

The relative frequency distribution in part (a) is more informative because there are fewer "useless" classes. The breakdown is too fine so that too few data points fall in the intervals.

2.27   a.   The number of brands with an ad awareness index of 40 or less will be the sum of the frequencies in the classes with boundaries of 40 or less, i.e., 2 + 3 + 4 = 9.

        b.   The number of brands with a sales effectiveness index of 70 or more will be the sum of the frequencies in the classes with boundaries of 70 or more i.e., 2 + 2 + 1 = 5.

        c.   The relative frequency of a class is found by dividing the frequency of that class by the total number of observations.

CLASS	CLASS FREQUENCY	CLASS RELATIVE FREQUENCY
1	0	0/18 = 0
2	2	.111
3	3	.167
4	4	.222
5	5	.278
6	1	.056
7	1	.056
8	1	.056
9	0	0
10	1	.056
TOTALS	18	1.002

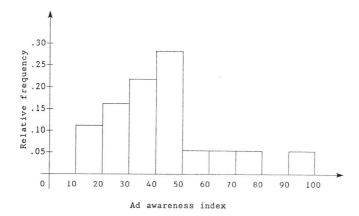

Notice that the relative frequency distribution has the same shape
as the frequency distribution. Most (i.e., 14/18 = 77.8%) of the
brands had an ad awareness index of 10-50. Only 22.2% of the
brands had an awareness index of 50 or more.

d.	CLASS	CLASS FREQUENCY	CLASS RELATIVE FREQUENCY
	1	2	2/18 = .111
	2	1	.056
	3	2	.111
	4	3	.167
	5	4	.222
	6	1	.056
	7	0	0
	8	2	.111
	9	2	.111
	10	1	.056
	TOTALS	18	1.001

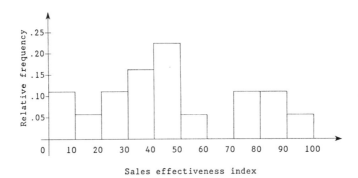

Sales effectiveness index

2.29 a. TOTAL = 3 + 11 + 21 + 20 + 18 + 11 + 9 + 4 + 2 + 1 = 100%

  b. The percentage of NFIB members starting their businesses between the ages of 26 and 30 is 21%.

  c. The percentage of NFIB members starting their businesses between the ages of 21 and 30 will be the sum of the percentages in the 21-25 class and the 26-30 class, i.e., 11 + 21 = 32%.

2.31 a. From the second bar down, the percentage of adults who believe Japanese companies are better managed is 56%.

  b. From the third bar down, the percentage of adults who believe that U.S. products sell poorly in Japan because they are too expensive is 75%.

2.33 a. To construct the bar graph, a rectangular bar for each product category is drawn with height proportional to the percentage of consumers who mentioned the rebated product as being most frequently bought.

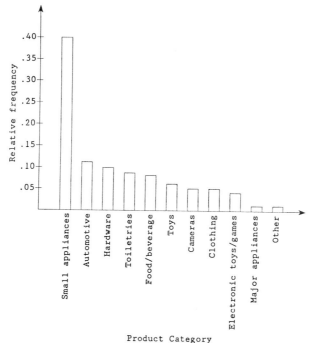

b. The percentage of consumers who purchase rebated appliances most frequently is the sum of the percentages in the small appliances category and the major appliances category, i.e., 40 + 1 = 41%.

c. The percentage of consumers who did not mention food or beverage as the most frequently purchased rebated item is the sum of the percentages in all categories except the food/beverage category. Since the sum of all the percentages is 100%, the desired percentage can be more simply found by taking 100% minus the percentage who do most frequently purchase rebated food or beverage, i.e., 100 - 8 = 92%.

2.35   a. The left most digit forms the stems and ranges from 0 through 8.

STEMS	LEAVES
0	2, 1
1	6, 3, 8, 5
2	7, 6, 0, 2, 6, 8, 0, 4, 5, 0, 3, 2, 3, 8, 3
3	2, 1, 1, 2, 7, 1, 8
4	2, 2, 2, 8, 8, 9, 6
5	4, 1, 7, 5
6	6, 2, 1, 2, 5, 7, 6, 1
7	1, 0
8	5

    b. The proportion of money funds with an average maturity greater than or equal to 40 days will be the number of leaves with stems of 4 or more divided by the total number of observations, 22/50 = .44.

    c. The proportion of money funds with an average maturity less than 10 days will be the number of leaves with a stem of 0 divided by the total number of observations, 2/50 = .04.

2.37   a. The digit to the right of the decimal point forms the stems and ranges from .3 through .9.

STEMS	LEAVES
.3	3, 9
.4	1, 8, 3
.5	3, 5, 2, 8, 9
.6	8, 7, 8, 6, 0, 0, 2, 9, 7
.7	1, 7, 0
.8	0, 1, 2, 5
.9	3, 2, 1

    b. The stem with the largest relative frequency is .6 containing 10/30 = 33.3% of the data. Thus, one-third of the Miami hotels and motels had a room occupancy between .60 and .70 during a particular day in August.

    c. Since there are 30 observations, we will use a small number of classes (6) to describe the data. The class interval width is:

$$\frac{\text{Largest measurement} - \text{smallest measurement}}{\text{Number of class intervals}} = \frac{.93 - .33}{6}$$

$$= \frac{.6}{6} = .10 \approx .11$$

Thus, the first class interval is from .325 to (.325 + .11) = .435, the second from .435 to (.435 + .11) = .545, and so on.

To obtain the class frequency, count the number of observations that fall within each class interval. The class relative frequency is the class frequency divided by the total number of observations (30).

CLASS	CLASS INTERVAL	TALLY	CLASS FREQUENCY	CLASS RELATIVE FREQUENCY
1	.325 – .435	||||	4	.13
2	.435 – .545	|||	3	.10
3	.545 – .655	⎢⎢⎢⎢ ||	7	.23
4	.655 – .765	⎢⎢⎢⎢ |||	8	.27
5	.765 – .875	⎢⎢⎢⎢	5	.17
6	.875 – .985	|||	3	.10
			30	1.00

The relative frequency distribution bar graph is constructed by:

1) marking off the class intervals along the horizontal line; and
2) drawing a bar over each class interval whose height is proportional to the class relative frequency.

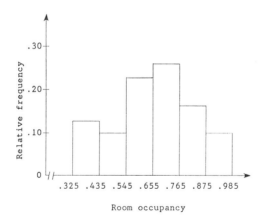

Room occupancy

d. The same basic shape is found in the two graphs, but the histogram contains less information. More of the data are combined in classes when using a histogram.

2.39 a. The data are described using a frequency bar graph.

b. The graph conveys the number of tasters giving each of the seven possible responses.

c. There is no bar over -3 (terrible). Therefore, the proportion of the 50 tasters who rated the new chocolate peanut butter as "terrible" is 0/50 = 0.

2.41 a. The data are qualitative. They cannot be measured on a numerical scale.

b. We will use a bar graph to describe the data, where the bars correspond to frequency.

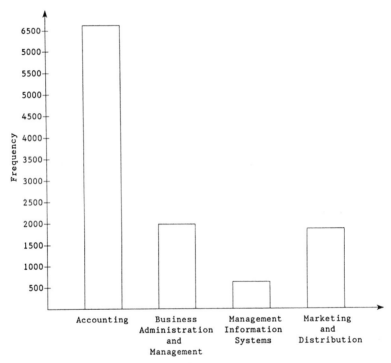

c. Most job offers were made to accounting majors who received 6575/10,951 = 60% of the offers. The fewest job offers were made to management information systems majors.

2.43 Appropriate graphs would be a stem-and-leaf display or a frequency distribution for this set of quantitative data.

The left most digit forms the stems and ranges from 0 through 6.

STEMS	LEAVES
0	49, 82, 90, 47, 91, 85, 70, 93, 79
1	56, 94, 81, 74, 62, 63, 61, 24, 92, 01, 20, 88, 62, 75, 33, 35, 74
2	22, 15, 05, 56, 14, 69, 38, 19
3	73, 49, 43
4	05
5	97
6	74

Most of the business publications run fewer than 300 full-run display pages during the third quarter with many of the publications running between 100 and 200 full-run display pages.

2.45 a. The variable, hardware vendor, is nonnumeric; therefore, it is qualitative.

b. A bar graph or a pie chart would be appropriate for summarizing these data.

c. We will use a bar graph to describe the data, where the bars correspond to relative frequency.

HARDWARE VENDOR	NUMBER OF HOSPITALS	RELATIVE FREQUENCY
Burroughs	45	45/341 = .132
Data General	6	.018
Digital Equipment	8	.023
Honeywell	8	.028
IBM	188	.551
NCR	50	.147
Others	36	.106
TOTALS	341	1.005

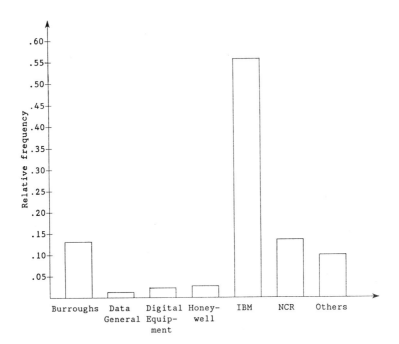

Hardware vendor

d. The percentage of hospitals surveyed who purchased Burroughs hardware is 13.2%.

e. The percentage of hospitals surveyed who did not purchase their hardware from IBM is 100 − 55.1 = 44.9%.

2.47 TAR

Since there are so few data points, we should use fewer classes, perhaps 5. To find the class interval width, we find:

Range = 29.8 − 1.0 = 28.8

and Width $\approx \dfrac{28.8}{5} \approx 6$

To ensure that no data points fall on a class boundary, we will choose 0.95 for the lower limit of our first interval.

CLASS	CLASS INTERVAL	TALLY	CLASS FREQUENCY	CLASS RELATIVE FREQUENCY
1	0.95 – 6.95	|||	3	3/25 = .12
2	6.95 – 12.95	⊬⊬⊬ ⊬⊬⊬	10	.40
3	12.95 – 18.95	⊬⊬⊬ ⊬⊬⊬		11	.44
4	18.95 – 24.95		0	0
5	24.95 – 30.95			1	.04
		TOTALS	25	1.00

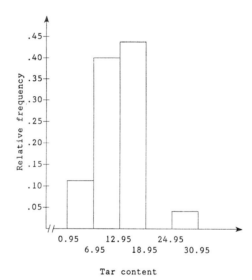

Tar content

NICOTINE

Using the same techniques as above:

$$Range = 2.03 - .13 = 1.90$$

and $Width \approx \dfrac{1.90}{5} \approx 4$

CLASS	CLASS INTERVAL	TALLY	CLASS FREQUENCY	CLASS RELATIVE FREQUENCY
1	.125 – .525	|||	3	3/25 = .12
2	.525 – .925	||||| |||||	10	.40
3	.925 – 1.325	||||| |||||		11	.44
4	1.325 – 1.725		0	0
5	1.725 – 2.125			1	.04
		TOTALS	25	1.00

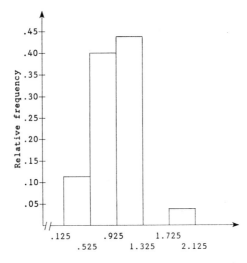

Nicotine content

CARBON MONOXIDE

Range = 23.5 – 1.5 = 22

and Width $\approx \dfrac{22}{5} \approx 5$

CLASS	CLASS INTERVAL	TALLY	CLASS FREQUENCY	CLASS RELATIVE FREQUENCY
1	1.45 – 6.45	|||	3	3/25 = .12
2	6.45 – 11.45	⊬⊬ ||	7	.28
3	11.45 – 16.45	⊬⊬ ⊬⊬		11	.44
4	16.45 – 21.45	|||	3	.12
5	21.45 – 26.45			1	.04
		TOTALS	25	1.00

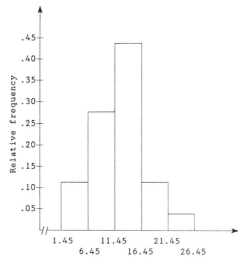

Carbon monoxide content

The same basic shape is found in the frequency distributions and their corresponding stem-and-leaf displays. The histograms will contain less information because more of the data are combined into classes.

CASE STUDIES

2.1   a. The percentage of preschool children who are cared for in their own or another's home is 31 + 37 = 68%.

    b. The number of these children will be approximately 8 million × .23 = 1.84 million who are cared for at an organized child-care facility.

    c. The percentage of school-age children for whom school is the primary source of child care is 75%.

    d. The number of children who require secondary care who are responsible for taking care of themselves is approximately 5 million × .20 = 1 million.

2.3   a. The data are measured on a numerical scale; therefore, the data are quantitative.

    b. A frequency distribution is used to describe the data.

    c. From the height of the two bars over 1.003 and 1.004, the frequency between 1.0025 and 1.0045 is about 80 + 65 = 145.

    d. From the height of the bars over 0.996, 0.997, 0.998 and 0.999, the frequency less than .9995 is about 0 + 15 + 30 + 0 = 45.

    e. The percentage of bars with diameters less than the LSL is approximately 45/500 = 9%. The process does not appear to be out of control.

    f. Yes. There were no rods recorded with a diameter between .9985 and .9995 and more than expected between .9995 and 1.0005. Notice that the maximum frequency is at the interval 1.0015 - 1.0025 and the frequencies decrease to the right. One might expect the same trend to the left, but the two intervals, .9985 - .9995 (too low) and .9995 - 1.0005 (too high), do not fit the expected trend. Inspectors passing rods with diameters that were barely below the LSL is a possible explanation for this observation.

    g. The percentage of defectives is 105/500 = 21%, indicating the process was out of control.

THREE NUMERICAL METHODS FOR DESCRIBING QUANTITATIVE DATA

3.1   a. $\sum x = 5 + 1 + 3 + 2 + 1 = 12$

      b. $\sum x^2 = (5)^2 + (1)^2 + (3)^2 + (2)^2 + (1)^2$
$$= 25 + 1 + 9 + 4 + 1 = 40$$

      c. $\sum(x - 1) = (5 - 1) + (1 - 1) + (3 - 1) + (2 - 1) + (1 - 1)$
$$= 4 + 0 + 2 + 1 + 0 = 7$$

      d. $\sum(x - 1)^2 = (5 - 1)^2 + (1 - 1)^2 + (3 - 1)^2 + (2 - 1)^2 + (1 - 1)^2$
$$= (4)^2 + (0)^2 + (2)^2 + (1)^2 + (0)^2$$
$$= 16 + 0 + 4 + 1 + 0 = 21$$

      e. $(\sum x)^2 = (5 + 1 + 3 + 2 + 1)^2 = (12)^2 = 144$

3.3   a. $\sum x^2 - \dfrac{(\sum x)^2}{5}$

$$= (5)^2 + (1)^2 + (3)^2 + (2)^2 + (1)^2 - \frac{(5 + 1 + 3 + 2 + 1)^2}{5}$$

$$= 40 - \frac{144}{5}$$

$$= 40 - 28.8 = 11.2$$

      b. $\sum(x - 2)^2 = (5 - 2)^2 + (1 - 2)^2 + (3 - 2)^2 + (2 - 2)^2 + (1 - 2)^2$
$$= (3)^2 + (-1)^2 + (1)^2 + (0)^2 + (-1)^2$$
$$= 9 + 1 + 1 + 0 + 1 = 12$$

      c. $\sum x^2 - 10 = (5)^2 + (1)^2 + (3)^2 + (2)^2 + (1)^2 - 10$
$$= 40 - 10 = 30$$

3.5   a. $\sum x = 6 + 0 + (-2) + (-1) + 3 = 6$

      b. $\sum x^2 = (6)^2 + (0)^2 + (-2)^2 + (-1)^2 + (3)^2$
$$= 36 + 0 + 4 + 1 + 9 = 50$$

c. $\sum x^2 - \dfrac{(\sum x)^2}{5}$

$$= (6)^2 + (0)^2 + (-2)^2 + (-1)^2 + (3)^2 - \dfrac{(6 + 0 - 2 - 1 + 3)^2}{5}$$

$$= 50 - \dfrac{36}{5}$$

$$= 50 - 7.2 = 42.8$$

3.7   The mean is calculated using Definition 3.1 as

$$\bar{x} = \dfrac{\sum x}{n} = \dfrac{3 + 9 + 0 + 7 + 4}{5} = \dfrac{23}{5} = 4.6$$

The median is found by ordering the observations and selecting the middle number because n = 5 is odd. The ordered sample is: 0, 3, 4, 7, 9. The median is the middle number, 4.

3.9   a.   The mean is $\bar{x} = \dfrac{\sum x}{n} = \dfrac{3 + 4 + 4 + 5 + 5 + 5 + 6 + 6 + 7}{9} = \dfrac{45}{9} = 5$

The numbers are already arranged in order. Because n = 9 is odd, the median is the middle number, 5.

The mode is the most frequently occurring value, 5.

     b.   The mean is $\bar{x} = \dfrac{\sum x}{n} = \dfrac{3 + 4 + 4 + 5 + 5 + 5 + 6 + 6 + 70}{9} = \dfrac{108}{9} = 12$

The numbers are already arranged in order. Because n = 9 is odd, the median is the middle number, 5.

The mode is the most frequently occurring value, 5.

     c.   The mean is $\bar{x} = \dfrac{\sum x}{n} = \dfrac{(-50) + (-49) + 0 + 0 + 49 + 50}{6} = \dfrac{0}{6} = 0$

The numbers are already arranged in order. Because n = 6 is even, the median is the average of the two middle numbers,

$$\dfrac{0 + 0}{2} = \dfrac{0}{2} = 0$$

The mode is the most frequently occurring value, 0.

     d.   The mean is $\bar{x} = \dfrac{\sum x}{n} = \dfrac{(-50) + (-49) + 0 + 9 + 9 + 81}{6} = \dfrac{0}{6} = 0$

The numbers are already arranged in order. Because n = 6 is even, the median is the average of the two middle numbers,

$$\frac{0 + 9}{2} = \frac{9}{2} = 4.5$$

The mode is the most frequently occurring value, 9.

3.11　The modal class is that with the most observations, 55,050 - 65,050 (from Figure 2.13). The midpoint of this interval is

$$\frac{55,050 + 65,050}{2} = 60,050$$

The mean (62,502), median (59,750), and mode (60,050) are similar in value. This is because the distribution is relatively symmetric.

3.13　a.　The left most digit forms the stems and ranges from 0 through 3.

STEMS	LEAVES
0	5, 5, 8, 4, 8, 7, 5, 9, 4, 0, 0
1	0, 6
2	
3	6

b.　The mean is $\bar{x} = \dfrac{\sum x}{n} = \dfrac{5 + 5 + 8 + 10 + \ldots + 16 + 0 + 36}{14} = \dfrac{117}{14}$

$$\approx 8.357$$

The median is found by ordering the observations and, since n = 14 is even, taking the average of the two middle numbers. The ordered sample is: 0, 0, 4, 4, 5, 5, 5, 7, 8, 8, 9, 10, 16, 36. The median is

$$\frac{5 + 7}{2} = 6$$

The mode is the most frequently occurring value, 5.

Since the data are skewed to the right, the mean is too large to be a representative measure of the center of the distribution. In situations such as this when the data are skewed, the median provides the best measure of the center.

3.15　a.　To form a relative frequency distribution, we must first decide on the number of intervals. Since there are only 20 observations, we will use 5 intervals. To find the class interval width, divide the range (9.11 - 0.72 = 8.39) by the number of intervals (5). The width is 8.39/5 ≈ 1.7. To ensure no data points fall on the class boundaries, we will use .705 as the lower limit of the first interval. The upper limit is .705 + 1.7 = 2.405. The other class interval boundaries are found in a similar fashion.

CLASS	CLASS INTERVAL	TALLY	CLASS FREQUENCY	CLASS RELATIVE FREQUENCY
1	.705 - 2.405	⊬⊬ ⎮⎮⎮	8	8/20 = .40
2	2.405 - 4.105	⊬⊬ ⎮	6	.30
3	4.105 - 5.805	⎮⎮⎮	3	.15
4	5.805 - 7.505	⎮⎮	2	.10
5	7.505 - 9.205	⎮	1	.05
		TOTALS	20	1.00

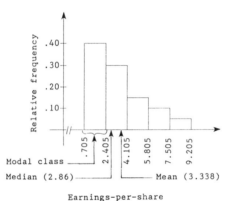

Earnings-per-share

b. The mean is $\bar{x} = \dfrac{\sum x}{n} = \dfrac{66.76}{20} \approx 3.338$

To find the median, we must first arrange the data in order: .72, .75, 1.12, 1.35, 1.72, 1.85, 1.96, 2.01, 2.75, 2.80, 2.92, 3.27, 3.54, 3.75, 4.40, 4.65, 5.23, 6.28, 6.58, 9.11. Since n = 20 is even, the median is the average of the two middle numbers:

$$\frac{2.80 + 2.92}{2} = 2.86$$

The modal is the class interval with the greatest frequency, .705 - 2.405.

The median appears to be the best measure of the center of the distribution since the data are skewed.

3.17 a. $s^2 = \dfrac{\sum x^2 - \dfrac{(\sum x)^2}{n}}{n-1} = \dfrac{301 - \dfrac{(50)^2}{10}}{10 - 1} = \dfrac{81}{9} = 9$

$s = \sqrt{s^2} = \sqrt{9} = 3$

b. $s^2 = \dfrac{\sum x^2 - \dfrac{(\sum x)^2}{n}}{n-1} = \dfrac{163456 - \dfrac{(2000)^2}{25}}{25 - 1} = \dfrac{3456}{24} = 144$

$s = \sqrt{s^2} = \sqrt{144} = 12$

c. $s^2 = \dfrac{\sum x^2 - \dfrac{(\sum x)^2}{n}}{n-1} = \dfrac{26.46 - \dfrac{(11.5)^2}{5}}{5 - 1} = \dfrac{.01}{4} = .0025$

$s = \sqrt{s^2} = \sqrt{.0025} = .05$

3.19 The range is the largest measurement minus the smallest measurement: $7 - 1 = 6$. The variance is

x	x^2
7	49
3	9
4	16
1	1
5	25
6	36
26	136

$s^2 = \dfrac{\sum x^2 - \dfrac{(\sum x)^2}{n}}{n-1}$

$= \dfrac{136 - \dfrac{(26)^2}{6}}{6 - 1} = \dfrac{23.333}{5} \approx 4.667$

$s = \sqrt{s^2} = \sqrt{4.667} \approx 2.160$

3.21 The range is the largest number minus the smallest number: $9 - 1 = 8$.

In order to use the shortcut formula to calculate the variance, $\sum x$ and $\sum x^2$ must first be computed.

$\sum x = 2 + 1 + \ldots + 5 = 116$

and

$\sum x^2 = 2^2 + 1^2 + \ldots + 5^2 = 4 + 1 + \ldots + 25 = 626$

The variance is

$s^2 = \dfrac{\sum x^2 - \dfrac{(\sum x)^2}{n}}{n-1} = \dfrac{626 - \dfrac{(116)^2}{25}}{25 - 1} = \dfrac{87.76}{24} \approx 3.657$

The standard deviation is $s = \sqrt{s^2} = \sqrt{3.657} \approx 1.912$

3.23 From Exercise 3.22, the mean, $\bar{x}$, was

$$\frac{\sum x}{n} = \frac{2 + 1 + \ldots + 5}{25} = \frac{116}{25} = 4.64$$

The intervals $\bar{x} \pm s$, $\bar{x} \pm 2s$, and $\bar{x} \pm 3s$ were

4.64 ± 1.91, 4.64 ± 2(1.91), and 4.64 ± 3(1.91)

4.64 ± 1.91, 4.64 ± 3.82, and 4.64 ± 5.73

2.73 - 6.55, 0.82 - 8.46, and -1.09 - 10.37

The class frequencies and class relative frequencies are tabulated below. The class intervals were obtained by using s = 1.91 as the class width and beginning at $\bar{x} - 3s = -1.09$.

CLASS	CLASS INTERVAL	TALLY	CLASS FREQUENCY	CLASS RELATIVE FREQUENCY
1	-1.09 to 0.82		0	.00
2	0.82 to 2.73	|||	3	.12
3	2.73 to 4.64	⊬⊬ ||||	9	.36
4	4.64 to 6.55	⊬⊬ ||||	9	.36
5	6.55 to 8.46	|||	3	.12
6	8.46 to 10.37			1	.04
TOTALS			25	1.00

Sketching from the relative frequencies above yields the relative frequency distribution bar graph shown as follows.

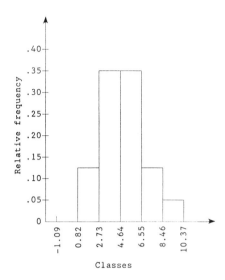

The frequencies and relative frequencies calculated form the class intervals 0.5 - 1.5, 1.5 - 2.5, ... , 8.5 - 9.5 are given in the following table.

CLASS	CLASS INTERVAL	TALLY	CLASS FREQUENCY	CLASS RELATIVE FREQUENCY
1	0.5 - 1.5	|	1	.04
2	1.5 - 2.5	||	2	.08
3	2.5 - 3.5	||||	4	.16
4	3.5 - 4.5	⊬⊬	5	.20
5	4.5 - 5.5	⊬⊬ |	6	.24
6	5.5 - 6.5	|||	3	.12
7	6.5 - 7.5	||	2	.08
8	7.5 - 8.5	|	1	.04
9	8.5 - 9.5	|	1	.04
TOTALS			25	1.00

The relative frequency distribution from these data is shown in the vertical bar graph below. The sketched distribution above, approximates the shape of the distribution below.

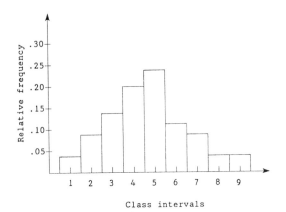

Class intervals

3.25 Since the data are not mound shaped, we must use Tchebysheff's Theorem to determine the proportions of observations falling within the intervals:

   a) $\bar{x} \pm s$ is at least 0%,
   b) $\bar{x} \pm 2s$ is at least 75%,
and c) $\bar{x} \pm 3s$ is at least 89%.

3.27 a. By the Empirical Rule, $\bar{x} \pm s$ contains nearly 70% of the observations, assuming a bell-shaped distribution. This means that 35% will fall in the interval from $\bar{x} - s$ to $\bar{x}$ and 35% in $\bar{x}$ to $\bar{x} + s$. The intervals $\bar{x} - 2s$ to $\bar{x} - s$ and $\bar{x} + s$ to $\bar{x} + 2s$ will contain 95% - 70% = 25% or about 12.5% each because $\bar{x} \pm 2s$ contains about 95% of the observations. Likewise, $\bar{x} - 3s$ to $\bar{x} - 2s$ and $\bar{x} + 2s$ to $\bar{x} + 3s$ will contain 2.5% each, since $\bar{x} \pm 3s$ contains nearly 100% of the observations. Thus, the relative frequencies are as given in the following table:

		CLASS INTERVAL			CLASS RELATIVE FREQUENCY
CLASS		PACKAGING	ASSEMBLY	MAINTENANCE	
1	$\bar{x} - 3s$ to $\bar{x} - 2s$	9.6 – 19.48	1.90 – 7.06	-6.08 – 0.80	.025
2	$\bar{x} - 2s$ to $\bar{x} - s$	19.48 – 29.36	7.06 – 12.22	0.80 – 7.68	.125
3	$\bar{x} - s$ to $\bar{x}$	29.36 – 39.24	12.22 – 17.38	7.68 – 14.56	.350
4	$\bar{x}$ to $\bar{x} + s$	39.24 – 49.12	17.38 – 22.54	14.56 – 21.44	.350
5	$\bar{x} + s$ to $\bar{x} + 2s$	49.12 – 59.00	22.54 – 27.70	21.44 – 28.32	.125
6	$\bar{x} + 2s$ to $\bar{x} + 3s$	59.00 – 68.88	27.70 – 32.86	28.32 – 35.20	.025

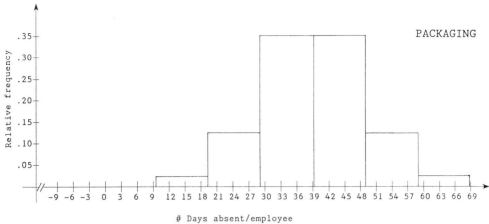

PACKAGING

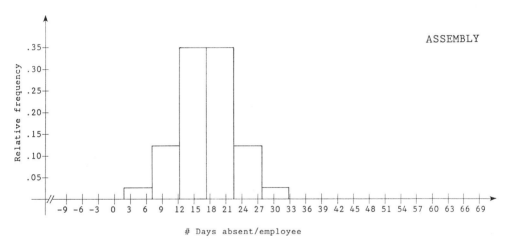

ASSEMBLY

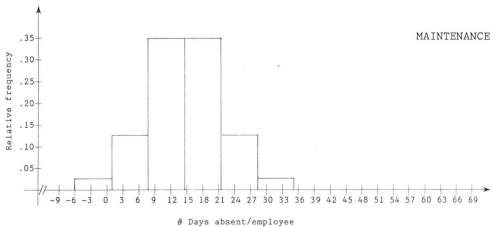

MAINTENANCE

b. The interval (19.48, 59.00) is the interval $\bar{x} \pm 2s$ for the packaging department. The Empirical Rule states that about .95 of the observations will fall in this interval.

c. Using the Empirical Rule, we expect about 95% of the observations to fall in the interval $\bar{x} \pm 2s$. Thus, for the assembly department, we expect between $17.38 - 2(5.16)$ to $17.38 + 2(5.16)$ or 7.06 to 27.70 unanticipated absences per 100 workers in a typical week.

d. Similarly, for the maintenance department, we expect between $14.56 - 2(6.88)$ to $14.56 + 2(6.88)$ or 0.80 to 28.32 unanticipated absences per 100 workers in a typical week.

3.29 a. $\bar{x} = \dfrac{\sum\limits_{i=1}^{n} x_i}{n} = \dfrac{216,000}{46} \approx 4695.65$

$s^2 = \dfrac{\sum\limits_{i=1}^{n} x_i^2 - \dfrac{\left(\sum\limits_{i=1}^{n} x_i\right)^2}{n}}{n-1} = \dfrac{2,240,100,000 - \dfrac{(216,000)^2}{46}}{46 - 1}$

$= \dfrac{1,225,839,130}{45} = 27,240,869.56$

$s = \sqrt{s^2} = \sqrt{27,240,869.56} \approx 5219.28$

b. According to Tchebysheff's Theorem for interpreting a standard deviation, we know at least 75% of the measurements will fall in the interval $\bar{x} \pm 2s$. According to the Empirical Rule, about 95% of the measurements will fall in the interval $\bar{x} \pm 2s$.

c. $\bar{x} \pm 2s \Rightarrow 4695.65 \pm 2(5219.28) \Rightarrow 4695.65 \pm 10,4348.56$

or $(-5742.91, 15134.21)$

Forty-four of the 46 observations, or $44/46 \times 100\% = 95.7\%$, fall within the interval. This agrees with both the Empirical Rule and Tchebysheff's Theorem.

d. We would expect $\bar{x}$ to decrease since an extremely large observation has been removed. The standard deviation would also decrease since we are removing an extreme value (one that differs greatly from the mean of the observations.)

e. Notice: The sums can be obtained simply by subtracting the unwanted General Motors data, i.e.,

$$\sum_{i=1}^{45} x_i = \sum_{i=1}^{46} x_i - 31{,}000$$

$$\text{and} \quad \sum_{i=1}^{45} x_i^2 = \sum_{i=1}^{46} x_i^2 - (31{,}000)^2$$

$$\bar{x} = \frac{\sum_{i=1}^{n} x_i}{n} = \frac{185{,}000}{45} \approx 4111.11$$

$$s^2 = \frac{\sum_{i=1}^{n} x_i^2 - \frac{\left(\sum_{i=1}^{n} x_i\right)^2}{n}}{n - 1} = \frac{1{,}279{,}100{,}000 - \frac{(185{,}000)^2}{45}}{45 - 1}$$

$$= \frac{518{,}544{,}444.4}{44} = 11{,}785{,}101.01$$

$$s = \sqrt{s^2} = \sqrt{11{,}785{,}101.01} \approx 3432.94$$

The mean and standard deviation are both smaller than those in (a).

f. The answer to part (b) remains the same.

$$\bar{x} \pm 2s \Rightarrow 4111.11 \pm 2(3432.94) \Rightarrow 4111.11 \pm 6865.88$$

$$\text{or} \quad (-2754.77,\ 10976.99)$$

Forty-three out of 45 observations, or $43/45 \times 100\% = 95.6\%$, fall within the interval.

3.31 a. 20th percentile - 20% of the measurements are below the 20th percentile, while 80% of the measurements are above it.

b. Median (50th percentile) - 50% of the measurements are below the 50th percentile, while 50% of the measurements are above it.

c. 76th percentile - 76% of the measurements are below the 76th percentile, while 24% of the measurements are above it.

d. Lower quartile (25th percentile) - 25% of the measurements are below the 25th percentile, while 75% of the measurements are above it.

e. Upper quartile (75th percentile) – 75% of the measurements are below the 75th percentile, while 25% of the measurements are above it.

3.33   a. Using Definition 3.11:

$$z = \frac{x - \bar{x}}{s} = \frac{12 - 20}{5} = \frac{-8}{5} = -1.60$$

b. $$z = \frac{x - \bar{x}}{s} = \frac{13 - 20}{5} = \frac{3}{5} = .60$$

c. $$z = \frac{x - \bar{x}}{s} = \frac{28 - 20}{5} = \frac{8}{5} = 1.60$$

3.35   Since there are 28 observations in the data set, the lower quartile, Q_L, will be the smallest observation that exceeds at least 1/4 (7) of the 28 observations. This is the 8th observation when the data are arranged from smallest to largest, or Q_L = 3.5. The median is the number such that half are greater than it and half are smaller. Since the number of observations is even, this is the average of the 14th and 15th observations,

$$M = \frac{(5.9 + 6.3)}{2} = 6.1$$

The upper quartile, Q_U, will be selected so that 3/4 (21) of the 28 observations are below it. This is the 22nd observation, or Q_U = 8.2.

3.37   This means that 75% (about 1688) of the 2251 residential sale prices lie below $78,500 and the remaining 25% (about 563) lie above $78,500.

3.39   a. The left most digit forms the stems and ranges from 0 through 2.

STEMS	LEAVES
0	9
1	8, 5, 4, 6, 9, 4, 6, 7, 6, 2 4, 0, 8, 8, 0, 3, 6, 2, 5, 8, 4, 3, 4, 8, 5, 9, 2, 9
2	0

b. Since there are 30 observations in the data set, the lower quartile, Q_L, will be the smallest observation that exceeds at least 1/4 (7.5) of the 28 observations. This is the 8th observation when the data are arranged from smallest to largest, or Q_L = 13. Twenty-five percent of the observations are below 13 and 75% are above 13. The median is the number such that half of the observations are greater than it and half are smaller. Since the number of observations is even, this is the average of the 15th and 16th observations,

$$M = \frac{(15 + 15)}{2} = 15.$$

Fifty percent of the observations are below 15 and 50% are above 15. The upper quartile, Q_U, will be selected so that 3/4 (22.5) of the 30 observations are below it. This is the 23rd observation, or $Q_U = 18$. Seventy-five percent of the observations are below 18 and 25% are above 18.

3.41 a. By the Empirical Rule, $\bar{x} \pm s$ contains nearly 70% of the observations, assuming a bell-shaped distribution. This means 35% will fall in the interval $\bar{x} - s$ to $\bar{x}$ and 35% will fall in the interval $\bar{x}$ to $\bar{x} + s$. The intervals $\bar{x} - 2s$ to $\bar{x} - s$ and $\bar{x} + s$ to $\bar{x} + 2s$ will contain 95% - 70% = 25% or about 12.5% each, because $\bar{x} \pm 2s$ contains about 95% of the observations. Likewise, $\bar{x} - 3s$ to $\bar{x} - 2s$ and $\bar{x} + 2s$ to $\bar{x} + 3s$ will contain 2.5% each, since $\bar{x} \pm 3s$ contains nearly 100% of the observations. Thus, the relative frequencies for the zero-coupon bonds is:

CLASS	CLASS INTERVAL	CLASS RELATIVE FREQUENCY
1	-49.92 to -29.12	.025
2	-29.12 to -8.32	.125
3	-8.32 to 12.48	.350
4	12.48 to 33.28	.350
5	33.28 to 54.08	.125
6	54.08 to 74.88	.025

The relative frequency distribution is:

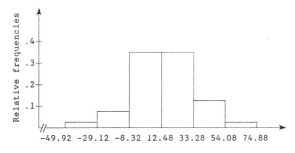

Rates of Return for Zero-Coupon Bonds

For the coupon-attached bonds, the relative frequencies are:

CLASS	CLASS INTERVAL	CLASS RELATIVE FREQUENCY
1	-31.20 to -16.64	.025
2	-16.64 to -2.08	.125
3	-2.08 to 12.48	.350
4	12.48 to 27.04	.350
5	27.04 to 41.60	.125
6	41.60 to 56.16	.025

The relative frequency distribution is:

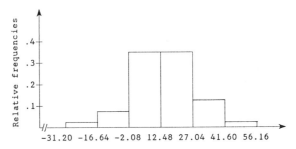

Rates of Return for Coupon-Attached Bonds

b. The z-score for the zero-coupon bond is

$$z = \frac{x - \bar{x}}{s} = \frac{-20 - 12.48}{20.80} = -1.56$$

A rate of return of -20% for a zero-coupon bond is 1.56 standard deviations below the mean. Since this is less than 2 standard deviations from the mean, it is not unusual.

c. The z-score for the coupon-attached bond is

$$z = \frac{x - \bar{x}}{s} = \frac{-20 - 12.48}{14.56} = -2.23$$

A rate of return of -20% for a coupon-attached bond is 2.23 standard deviations below the mean. Since this is more than 2 standard deviations from the mean, it is rather unusual.

3.43 From Exercise 3.34, $Q_U = 288$ and $Q_L = 228$.

The IQR = $Q_U - Q_L = 288 - 228 = 60$

The inner fences of a distribution lie 1.5(IQR) below the lower quartile and above the upper quartile.

$Q_L - (1.5)IQR = 228 - (1.5)(60) = 138$
$Q_U + (1.5)IQR = 288 + (1.5)(60) = 378$

The outer fences lie 3 (IQR) below Q_L and above Q_U.

$Q_L - 3IQR = 228 - 3(60) = 48$
$Q_U + 3IQR = 288 + 3(60) = 468$

The box plot is shown below:

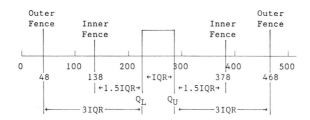

3.45 The observation, 874, has a z-score of:

$$z = \frac{x - \bar{x}}{s} = \frac{874 - 630}{80} = 3.05$$

Both the Empirical Rule and Tchebysheff's Theorem tell us that almost all the observations in a data set will have z-scores between -3 and 3. A z-score of 3.05 indicates this observation is an outlier. We would not expect an observation of 874 kwh in this data set. Either the mean or standard deviation have been reported incorrectly or we have observed a rare event.

3.47 a. To construct a box plot for the data, we must first calculate the quartiles. Since there are 29 observations in the data set, the lower quartile, Q_L, will be the smallest observation that exceeds at least 1/4 (7.25) of the 29 observations. This is the 8th observation when the data are arranged from smallest to largest, or $Q_L = 2433$. The upper quartile, Q_U, will be selected so that 3/4 (21.75) of the 28 observations are below it. This is the 22nd observation, or $Q_U = 3764$. The IQR = $Q_U - Q_L = 3764 - 2433 = 1331$.

The inner fences are 1.5(IQR) below the lower quartile and above the upper quartile.

$$Q_L - (1.5)IQR = 2433 - (1.5)(1331) = 436.5$$
$$Q_U + (1.5)IQR = 3764 + (1.5)(1331) = 5760.5$$

The outer fences lie 3(IQR) below Q_L and above Q_U.

$$Q_L - 3(IQR) = 2433 - 3(1331) = -1560$$
$$Q_U + 3(IQR) = 3764 + 3(1331) = 7757$$

The box plot is shown below:

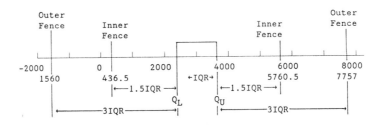

b. Any observations between the inner and outer fences are suspect outliers. There are no observations that are suspect outliers.

   Any observations outside the outer fences are highly suspect outliers. There are no observations that are highly suspect outliers.

c. An outlier would be a value with a z-score less than -3 or greater than 3 or, in other words, an observation that lies outside the interval, $\bar{x} \pm 3s$. From Exercise 3.28, this is the interval 3,033.5 ± 2,743.6 or (289.9, 5,777.1). There are no observations outside this interval; thus, there are no outliers. This is consistent with the results in part (b).

3.49 a. MINITAB uses an asterisk (*) to locate suspect outliers and small circles (0) to locate highly suspect outliers. The MINITAB plot shows there is one suspect outlier, 6355 and three highly suspect outliers, 8,400, 13,063, and 20,542.

   b. From Exercise 3.16, $\bar{x} = 5277.96$.

   The variance is

$$s^2 = \frac{\sum x^2 - \frac{(\sum x)^2}{n}}{n - 1} = \frac{1,050,326,887 - \frac{(131,949)^2}{25}}{25 - 1} = 14,746,056$$

   The standard deviation is $s = \sqrt{s^2} = \sqrt{14,746,056} = 3840.0594$

The observation, 6355, has a z-score of

$$z = \frac{x - \bar{x}}{s} = \frac{6355 - 5277.96}{3840.0594} = 0.28$$

The observation, 8400, has a z-score of

$$z = \frac{x - \bar{x}}{s} = \frac{8400 - 5277.96}{3840.0594} = 0.81$$

The observation, 13,063, has a z-score of

$$z = \frac{x - \bar{x}}{s} = \frac{13063 - 5277.96}{3840.0594} = 2.03$$

The observation, 20,542, has a z-score of

$$z = \frac{x - \bar{x}}{s} = \frac{20542 - 5277.96}{3840.0594} = 3.97$$

Using the rule that observations with z-scores greater than 3 in absolute value are outliers, the observation 20,542 is the only one of the four which would be considered an outlier using the z-score approach.

3.51   The mean for grouped data is

$$\bar{x} = \frac{\sum x_i f_i}{n}$$

where x_i is the midpoint of the ith class interval, f_i is the frequency in the ith class interval, and n is the sample size. The mean is:

$$\bar{x} = \frac{\sum x_i f_i}{n}$$

$$= \frac{1.415(8) + 2.815(7) + 4.215(5) + 5.615(4) + 7.015(3) + 8.415(3)}{30}$$

$$= \frac{120.85}{30} = 4.03$$

The variance for grouped data is

$$s^2 = \frac{\sum x_i^2 f_i - \frac{(\sum x_i f_i)^2}{n}}{n - 1}$$

$$= \frac{(1.415)^2(8) + (2.815)^2(7) + \ldots + (8.415)^2(3) - \frac{(120.85)^2}{30}}{30 - 1}$$

$$= \frac{159.675}{29} = 5.51$$

The standard deviation $= s = \sqrt{5.51} \approx 2.346$

3.53   a.   Using the following class intervals, the frequency distribution is:

CLASS	CLASS INTERVAL	MIDPOINT x_i	CLASS FREQUENCY f_i
1	7.5 - 9.5	8.5	1
2	9.5 - 11.5	10.5	2
3	11.5 - 13.5	12.5	5
4	13.5 - 15.5	14.5	8
5	15.5 - 17.5	16.5	5
6	17.5 - 19.5	18.5	8
7	19.5 - 21.5	20.5	1
			30

b.   The mean for grouped data is:

$$\bar{x} = \frac{\sum x_i f_i}{n}$$

$$= \frac{(8.5)1 + (10.5)2 + (12.5)5 + (14.5)8 + (16.5)5 + (18.5)8 + (20.5)1}{30}$$

$$= \frac{459}{30} = 15.3$$

The variance for grouped data is

$$s^2 = \frac{\sum x_i^2 f_i - \frac{(\sum x_i f_i)^2}{n}}{n-1}$$

$$= \frac{(8.5)^2(1) + (10.5)^2(2) + \ldots + (20.5)^2(1) - \frac{(459)^2}{30}}{29}$$

$$= \frac{252.8}{29} \approx 8.717$$

The standard deviation is $s = \sqrt{s^2} = \sqrt{8.717} \approx 2.952$

From Exercise 3.26, when using the raw data, $\bar{x} = 15.13$ and $s = 2.945$. The values of $\bar{x}$ and s in this exercise are not exactly equal to the values using the raw data because we have grouped the data into classes. Every observation within a class is approximated using the midpoint of that class when finding $\bar{x}$ and s for grouped data.

3.55 a. The mean for grouped data is

$$\bar{x} = \frac{\sum x_i f_i}{n}$$

$$= \frac{0(13) + 1(2) + 2(10) + 3(19) + 4(12) + 5(9) + \ldots + 15(0)}{69}$$

$$= \frac{201}{69} \approx 2.913$$

The variance for grouped data is

$$s^2 = \frac{\sum x_i^2 f_i - \dfrac{(\sum x_i f_i)^2}{n}}{n - 1}$$

$$= \frac{(0)^2(13) + (1)^2(2) + (2)^2(10) + \ldots + (15)^2(0) - \dfrac{(201)^2}{69}}{68}$$

$$= \frac{259.47826}{68} \approx 3.816$$

The standard deviation is $s = \sqrt{s^2} = \sqrt{3.816} \approx 1.953$

b. The mean for grouped data is

$$\bar{x} = \frac{\sum x_i f_i}{n}$$

$$= \frac{0(9) + 1(11) + 2(20) + \ldots + 15(1)}{93}$$

$$= \frac{279}{93} = 3.000$$

The variance for grouped data is

$$s^2 = \frac{\sum x_i^2 f_i - \dfrac{(\sum x_i f_i)^2}{n}}{n - 1}$$

$$= \frac{(0)^2(9) + (1)^2(1) + (2)^2(20) + \ldots + (15)^2(1) - \dfrac{(279)^2}{93}}{92}$$

$$= \frac{394}{92} \approx 4.283$$

The standard deviation $= s = \sqrt{s^2} = \sqrt{4.283} \approx 2.070$

c. The mean for grouped data is

$$\bar{x} = \frac{\sum x_i f_i}{n}$$

$$= \frac{0(22) + 1(13) + 2(30) + \ldots + 15(1)}{162}$$

$$= \frac{480}{162} \approx 2.963$$

The variance for grouped data is

$$s^2 = \frac{\sum x_i^2 f_i - \frac{(\sum x_i f_i)^2}{n}}{n - 1}$$

$$= \frac{(0)^2(22) + (1)^2(13) + (2)^2(30) + \ldots + (15)^2(1) - \frac{(480)^2}{162}}{161}$$

$$= \frac{653.77778}{161} \approx 4.061$$

The standard deviation is $s = \sqrt{s^2} = \sqrt{4.061} \approx 2.015$

3.57 a. Using only the means compares only the center of the distributions. We also need to consider the variability of the distributions to compare them adequately. We could use the range, variance, or standard deviation as a measure of variation.

b. By the Empirical Rule, $\bar{x} \pm s$ contains nearly 70% of the observations assuming a bell-shaped distribution. This means that 35% will fall in the interval from $\bar{x} - s$ to $\bar{x}$ and 35% in $\bar{x}$ to $\bar{x} + s$. The intervals $\bar{x} - 2s$ to $\bar{x} - s$ and $\bar{x} + s$ to $\bar{x} + 2s$ will contain 95% - 70% = 25% or about 12.5% each because $\bar{x} + 2s$ contains about 95% of the observations. Likewise, $\bar{x} - 3s$ to $\bar{x} - 2s$ and $\bar{x} + 2s$ to $\bar{x} + 3s$ will contain 2.5% each since $\bar{x} \pm 3s$ contains nearly 100% of the observations. Thus, the relative frequencies are as given in the following table:

CLASS		CHICAGO	TOKYO	PARIS	DUSSELDORF	LONDON	CLASS RELATIVE FREQUENCY
1	$\bar{x} - 3s$ to $\bar{x} - 2s$	(32, 42)	(55, 63)	(93, 108)	(71, 83)	(111, 122)	.025
2	$\bar{x} - 2s$ to $\bar{x} - s$	(42, 52)	(63, 71)	(108, 123)	(83, 95)	(122, 133)	.125
3	$\bar{x} - s$ to $\bar{x}$	(52, 62)	(71, 79)	(123, 138)	(95, 107)	(133, 144)	.350
4	$\bar{x}$ to $\bar{x} + s$	(62, 72)	(79, 87)	(138, 153)	(107, 119)	(144, 155)	.350
5	$\bar{x} + s$ to $\bar{x} + 2s$	(72, 82)	(87, 95)	(153, 168)	(119, 131)	(155, 166)	.125
6	$\bar{x} + 2s$ to $\bar{x} + 3s$	(82, 92)	(95, 103)	(168, 183)	(131, 143)	(166, 177)	.025

CLASS INTERVAL

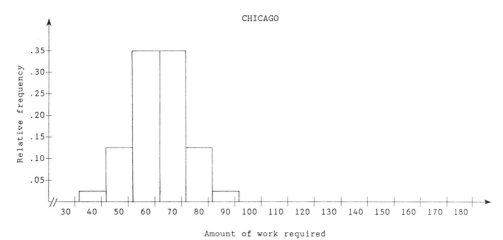

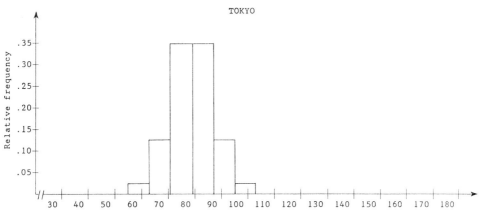

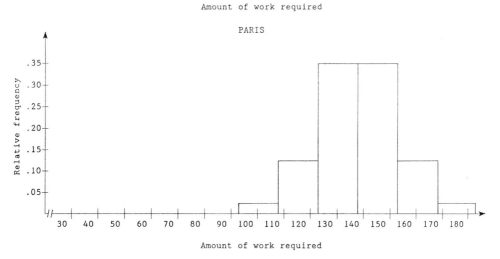

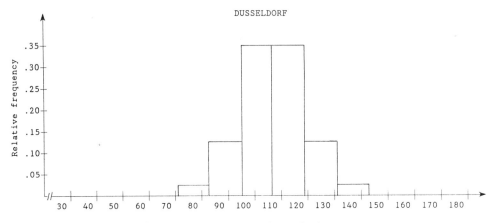

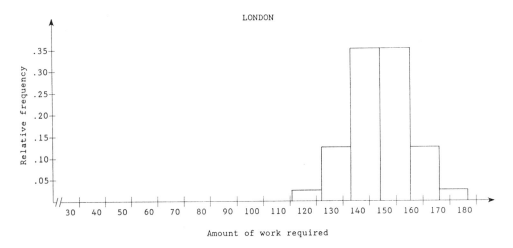

c. The interval (42, 82) is the interval $\bar{x} \pm 2s$ for Chicago drivers. The Empirical Rule states that about 95% of the observations will fall in this interval.

d. The interval (122, 166) is the interval $\bar{x} \pm 2s$ for London drivers. The Empirical Rule states that about 95% of the observations will fall in this interval.

3.59 From Exercise 3.13, $\bar{x} = 8.357$.

The variance is

$$s^2 = \frac{\sum x^2 - \frac{(\sum x)^2}{n}}{n-1} = \frac{2017 - \frac{(117)^2}{14}}{13} = \frac{1039.2143}{13} \approx 79.9396$$

The standard deviation is $s = \sqrt{s^2} = \sqrt{79.9396} \approx 8.9409$

Using Definition 3.11:

$$z = \frac{x - \bar{x}}{s} = \frac{36 - 8.357}{8.9409} = 3.09$$

From the Empirical Rule, almost all of the observations are within three standard deviations of the mean. Thus, a z-score of 3.09 is very unlikely. This indicates that the MGM Grand observation is unlikely to occur if the mean of the distribution is 8.357 and the standard deviation is 8.9409. The MGM Grand observation is an outlier; hence, there is support for treating this observation differently than the other measurements in the sample.

3.61   a.   The mean is $\bar{x} = \frac{\sum x}{n} = \frac{156 + 49 + \ldots + 79}{40} = \frac{7960}{40} = 199$

The median is found by ordering the observations and, since n = 40 is even, taking the average of the two middle numbers. The median is

$$\frac{174 + 174}{2} = 174$$

The mode is the most frequently occurring value. Since both 162 and 174 occur twice, both of these values are modes.

b.   The range is the largest number minus the smallest number: $674 - 47 = 627$.

The variance is

$$s^2 = \frac{\sum x^2 - \frac{(\sum x)^2}{n}}{n - 1} = \frac{2,272,838 - \frac{(7960)^2}{40}}{39} = \frac{668,798}{39} \approx 17661.487$$

The standard deviation is $s = \sqrt{s^2} = \sqrt{17661.487} \approx 132.897$

c.   The intervals, counts, and proportions are given below. The proportions are calculated by count ÷ 40, the total number of observations.

	INTERVAL		TALLY	COUNT	PROPORTIONS
$\bar{x} \pm s$	199 ± 132.897	$(66.103, 331.897)$	⊞ ⊞ ⊞ ⊞ ⊞ ⊞ ‖	32	.80
$\bar{x} \pm 2s$	$199 \pm 2(132.897)$	$(-66.794, 464.794)$	⊞ ⊞ ⊞ ⊞ ⊞ ⊞ ⊞ ‖‖	38	.95
$\bar{x} \pm 3s$	$199 \pm 3(132.897)$	$(-199.691, 597.691)$	⊞ ⊞ ⊞ ⊞ ⊞ ⊞ ⊞ ‖‖‖	39	.975

The proportions of observations falling in the intervals are very close to the proportions expected by the Empirical Rule. We found .80, .95, and .975 for the intervals $\bar{x} \pm s$, $\bar{x} \pm 2s$, and $\bar{x} \pm 3s$, respectively, while the Empirical Rule expects .60 – .80, .95 and almost 1.00. Tchebysheff's Theorem expects at least 0%, at least 75%, and at least 89% in the intervals $\bar{x} \pm s$, $\bar{x} \pm 2s$, and $\bar{x} \pm 3s$, respectively. The proportions we obtained fit this rule, but the Empirical Rule gives a closer estimate. This indicates that the data are probably mound-shaped.

d. The 10th percentile is the number such that 10% of the measurements fall below it and 90% fall above it. The 10th percentile will be selected so that 10% (4) of the 40 observations are below it. This is the 5th observation, or 10th percentile = 82.

e. To construct a box plot for the data, we must first calculate the quartiles. Since there are 40 observations in the data set, the lower quartile, Q_L, will be the smallest observation that exceeds at least 1/4 (10) of the 40 observations. This is the 11th observation when the data are arranged from smallest to largest, or $Q_L = 120$. The upper quartile, Q_U, will be selected so that 3/4 (30) of the 40 observations are below it. This is the 31st observation, or $Q_U = 222$. The IQR = $Q_U - Q_L = 222 - 120 = 102$.

The inner fences are 1.5(IQR) below Q_L and above Q_U and are:

$Q_L - 1.5(IQR) = 120 - 1.5(102) = -33$
$Q_U + 1.5(IQR) = 222 + 1.5(102) = 375$

The outer fences are 3(IQR) below Q_L and above Q_U and are:

$Q_L - 3(IQR) = 120 - 3(102) = -186$
$Q_U + 3(IQR) = 222 + 3(102) = 528$

The box plot is given below:

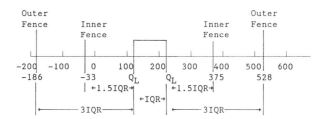

Any observations between the inner and outer fences are suspect outliers. There is one suspect outlier, that is 405. Any observations outside the outer fences are highly suspect outliers. There are two highly suspect outliers; they are 597 and 674.

Using Definition 3.11, the z-scores for these numbers are:

$$z = \frac{x - \bar{x}}{s} = \frac{405 - 199}{132.897} = 1.55$$

$$z = \frac{x - \bar{x}}{s} = \frac{597 - 199}{132.897} = 2.99$$

$$z = \frac{x - \bar{x}}{s} = \frac{674 - 199}{132.897} = 3.57$$

The z-score approach confirms that the two highly suspect outliers are, indeed, outliers. (The observation, 597, has a z-score less than 3.00, but, for practical purposes, may be considered an outlier.)

3.63 b. For Neighborhood A:

	INTERVAL		PROPORTION
$\bar{x} \pm s$	112,497 ± 53,272	(59,225, 165,769)	.856
$\bar{x} \pm 2s$	112,497 ± 2(53,272)	(5,953, 219,041)	.967
$\bar{x} \pm 3s$	112,497 ± 3(53,272)	(-47,319, 272,313)	.978

For Neighborhood B:

	INTERVAL		PROPORTION
$\bar{x} \pm s$	90,803 ± 47,007	(43,796, 137,810)	.9375
$\bar{x} \pm 2s$	90,803 ± 2(47,007)	(-3,211, 184,817)	.975
$\bar{x} \pm 3s$	90,803 ± 3(47,007)	(-50,218, 231,824)	.975

For Neighborhood C:

	INTERVAL		PROPORTION
$\bar{x} \pm s$	72,506 ± 17,743	(54,763, 90,249)	.876
$\bar{x} \pm 2s$	72,506 ± 2(17,743)	(37,020, 107,992)	.944
$\bar{x} \pm 3s$	72,506 ± 3(17,743)	(19,277, 125,735)	.978

For Neighborhood D:

	INTERVAL		PROPORTION
$\bar{x} \pm s$	43,876 ± 14,823	(29,053, 58,699)	.85
$\bar{x} \pm 2s$	43,876 ± 2(14,823)	(14,230, 73,522)	.95
$\bar{x} \pm 3s$	43,876 ± 3(14,823)	(-593, 88,345)	.979

For Neighborhood E:

	INTERVAL		PROPORTION
$\bar{x} \pm s$	61,027 ± 12,074	(48,953, 73,101)	.728
$\bar{x} \pm 2s$	61,027 ± 2(12,074)	(36,879, 85,175)	.956
$\bar{x} \pm 3s$	61,027 ± 3(12,074)	(24,805, 97,249)	.978

For Neighborhood F:

	INTERVAL		PROPORTION
$\bar{x} \pm s$	75,753 ± 31,104	(44,649, 106,857)	.750
$\bar{x} \pm 2s$	75,753 ± 2(31,104)	(13,545, 137,961)	.966
$\bar{x} \pm 3s$	75,753 ± 3(31,104)	(-17,559, 169,065)	.991

The Empirical Rule states that 60% to 80% of the observations should be within one standard deviation of the mean, about 95% should be within two standard deviations of the mean, and nearly 100% should be within three standard deviations of the mean if the data are mound-shaped. Neighborhoods E and F fit this distribution. More conservatively, Tchebysheff's Theorem states that at least 0%, at least 75%, and at least 89% of the observations should lie within one, two, and three standard deviations of the mean, respectively, for any distribution. All neighborhoods follow Tchebysheff's Theorem.

3.65 a. First, find the midpoint of each class interval by averaging the class boundaries of each interval.

CLASS	CLASS INTERVAL	MIDPOINT x_i	CLASS FREQUENCY f_i
1	0 – 3.5	1.75	12
2	3.5 – 7.0	5.25	11
3	7.0 – 10.5	8.75	7
4	10.5 – 14.0	12.25	15
5	14.0 – 17.5	15.75	6
6	17.5 – 21.0	19.25	3
7	21.0 – 24.5	22.75	1
			n = 55

$$\bar{x} = \frac{\sum x_i f_i}{n} = \frac{1.75(12) + 5.25(11) + \ldots + 22.75(1)}{55} = \frac{498.75}{55} \approx 9.068$$

$$s^2 = \frac{\sum x_i^2 f_i - \frac{(\sum x_i f_i)^2}{n}}{n - 1}$$

$$= \frac{(1.75)^2(12) + (5.25)^2(11) + \ldots + (22.75)^2(1) - \frac{(498.75)^2}{55}}{54}$$

$$= \frac{1721.6818}{54} \approx 31.883$$

$$s = \sqrt{s^2} = \sqrt{31.883} \approx 5.647$$

b. The interval $\bar{x} \pm 2s$ is $9.068 \pm 2(5.647)$ => (-2.226, 20.362). This interval encloses classes 1 through 6, approximately; therefore, the number of patients with waiting times within this interval is about 54.

c. The Empirical Rule states that about 95% of the observations should lie within the interval $\bar{x} \pm 2s$. We observed approximately 54/55 => 98.18% of the observations within this interval.

3.67 a. The mean is $\bar{x} = \frac{\sum x}{n} = \frac{128 + 113 + \ldots + 122}{50} = \frac{5891}{50} = 117.82$

The median is found by ordering the observations and, since n = 50 is even, taking the average of the two middle numbers. The median is

$$\frac{117 + 118}{2} = 117.5$$

The mode is the most frequently occurring value. Since 97, 112, 124, 128, and 131 all appear three times, all of these values are modes.

b. The range is the largest number minus the smallest number: 150 - 88 = 62.

The variance is

$$s^2 = \frac{\sum x^2 - \frac{(\sum x)^2}{n}}{n-1} = \frac{705,119 - \frac{(5891)^2}{50}}{49} = \frac{11,041.38}{49} \approx 225.334$$

The standard deviation is $s = \sqrt{s^2} = \sqrt{225.334} \approx 15.011$

c. The intervals, counts, and proportions are given below. The proportions are calculated by count ÷ 50, the total number of observations.

INTERVAL			COUNT	PROPORTION
$\bar{x} \pm s$	117.82 ± 15.011	(102.809, 132.831)	31	.62
$\bar{x} \pm 2s$	117.82 ± 2(15.011)	(87.798, 147.842)	49	.98
$\bar{x} \pm 3s$	117.82 ± 3(15.011)	(72.787, 162.853)	50	1.00

The proportions of observations falling in the intervals are very close to the proportions expected by the Empirical Rule. We found .62, .98, and 1.00 for the intervals $\bar{x} \pm s$, $\bar{x} \pm 2s$, and $\bar{x} \pm 3s$, respectively, while the Empirical Rule expects .60 - .80, .95, and almost 1.00.

An outlier would be an observation outside the interval $\bar{x} \pm 3s$. There are no outliers.

d. To construct a box plot for the data, we must first calculate the quartiles. Since there are 50 observations in the data set, the lower quartile, Q_L, will be the smallest observation that exceeds at least 1/4 (12.5) of the 50 observations. This is the 13th observation when the data are arranged from smallest to largest, or Q_L = 109. The upper quartile, Q_U, will be selected so that 3/4 (37.5) of the 50 observations are below it. This is the 38th observation, or Q_U = 131. The IQR = $Q_U - Q_L$ = 131 - 109 = 22.

The inner fences are 1.5(IQR) below Q_L and above Q_U and are:

$$Q_L - 1.5(IQR) = 109 - 1.5(22) = 76$$
$$Q_U + 1.5(IQR) = 131 + 1.5(22) = 164$$

The outer fences are 3(IQR) below Q_L and above Q_U and are:

$$Q_L - 3(IQR) = 109 - 3(22) = 43$$
$$Q_U + 3(IQR) = 131 + 3(22) = 197$$

The box plot is given below:

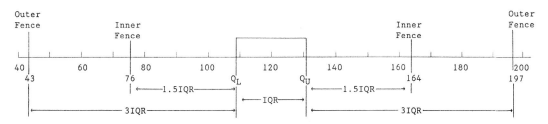

Any observations between the inner and outer fences are suspect outliers. There are no suspect outliers. Any observations outside the outer fences are highly suspect outliers. There are no highly suspect outliers.

e. The 70th percentile is the number such that 70% of the measurements fall below it and 30% fall above it. The 70th percentile will be selected so that 70% (35) of the 50 observations are below it. This is the 36th observation, or 70th percentile = 128. Seventy percent of total man-hours required have values less than or equal to 128 man-hours.

3.69

$$\bar{x} = \frac{\sum x_i f_i}{n} = \frac{580(38) + 750(34) + \ldots + 3000(1)}{117} = \frac{118620}{117} \approx 1013.846$$

$$s^2 = \frac{\sum x_i^2 f_i - \frac{(\sum x_i f_i)^2}{n}}{n - 1}$$

$$= \frac{(580)^2(38) + (750)^2(34) + \ldots + (3000)^2(1) - \frac{(118620)^2}{117}}{116}$$

$$= \frac{35,882,569.24}{116} \approx 309,332.493$$

$$s = \sqrt{s^2} = \sqrt{309,332.493} \approx 556.177$$

CASE STUDIES

3.1   a. $\bar{x} = \dfrac{\sum x}{n} = \dfrac{1277.8}{25} = 51.112$

$$s^2 = \frac{\sum x^2 - \dfrac{(\sum x)^2}{n}}{n-1} = \frac{169,925.98 - \dfrac{(1277.8)^2}{25}}{24} = \frac{104615.07}{24} \approx 4358.961$$

$s = \sqrt{s^2} = \sqrt{4358.961} \approx 66.022$

   b. $\bar{x} = \dfrac{\sum x}{n} = \dfrac{551.48}{13} = 42.42$

$$s^2 = \frac{\sum x^2 - \dfrac{(\sum x)^2}{n}}{n-1} = \frac{31,166.4258 - \dfrac{(551.48)^2}{13}}{12} = \frac{8771.7958}{12} \approx 730.983$$

$s = \sqrt{s^2} = \sqrt{730.983} \approx 27.037$

   c.   We can find both the z-score and the percentile ranking for the Miller Lite observation. From Definition 3.11:

$$z = \frac{x - \bar{x}}{s} = \frac{70.9 - 51.112}{66.022} = .30$$

The Miller Lite observation is only .30 standard deviations above the mean in terms of television advertising budget.

When these observations are ranked from smallest to largest, Miller Lite is ranked 20th out of the 25 observations. This means that Miller Lite is the 20/25 = .8 => 80th percentile. Eighty percent of the top 25 agencies have an advertising budget less than or equal to Miller Lite's.

   d.   From Definition 3.11:

$$z = \frac{x - \bar{x}}{s} = \frac{42.89 - 42.42}{27.037} = .02$$

The Miller Lite observation is only .02 standard deviations above the mean in terms of cost efficiency.

Miller Lite is ranked 7th out of 13 observations. This means that Miller Lite is the 7/13 ≈ .538 => approximately 54th percentile. Fifty-four percent of the top 25 agencies have cost efficiency less than or equal to Miller Lite's.

e. From Definition 3.11:

$$z = \frac{x - \bar{x}}{s} = \frac{72.1 - 51.112}{66.022} = .32$$

The Coor's observation is only .32 standard deviations above the mean in terms of television advertising budget.

Coor's is ranked 22nd out of the 25 observations. This means that Coor's is the 22/25 = .88 => 88th percentile. Eight-eight percent of the top 25 agencies have an advertising budget less than or equal to Coor's.

f. From Definition 3.11:

$$z = \frac{x - \bar{x}}{s} = \frac{73.00 - 42.42}{27.037} = 1.13$$

The Coor's observation is 1.13 standard deviations above the mean in terms of cost efficiency.

Coor's is ranked 12th out of the 13 observations. This means that Coor's is the 12/13 ≈ .923 => 92nd percentile. Ninety-two percent of the top 25 agencies have cost efficiency less than or equal to Coor's.

Although Coor's does not spend much more than average on television advertising, its cost efficiency is worse than most of the companies.

3.3 a. From Definition 3.11:

$$z = \frac{x - \bar{x}}{s} = \frac{93.12 - 26.01}{11.28} = 5.95$$

b. This z-score implies that the observation, 93.12 complaints per 10,000 bottles sold, is 5.95 standard deviations above the mean. It is extremely unlikely that this event is a chance occurrence.

c. Since the observed complaint rate is more than 2 standard deviations above the mean rate, the problem is deemed to be due to a specific problem in the production or distribution of the product.

FOUR PROBABILITY: BASIC CONCEPTS

4.1 a. From Figure 4.3, there are 15 outcomes that result in a sum less than 7. They are:

(1,1) (2,1) (3,1) (4,1) (5,1)
(1,2) (2,2) (3,2) (4,2)
(1,3) (2,3) (3,3)
(1,4) (2,4)
(1,5)

Since each outcome is equally likely and there are 36 possible outcomes,

$$P(\text{sum is less than 7}) = \frac{15}{36} = \frac{5}{12}$$

b. We mean that, in a very long series of tosses, we believe that approximately 5/12 would result in a sum of less than seven. Therefore, the number 5/12 measures the likelihood of observing a sum less than seven on a single toss of the dice.

4.3 The probability of event A is the proportion of times that A is observed when the experiment is repeated a very large number of times.

$$P(A) \approx \frac{\text{number of times PCB exceeds standard}}{\text{number of days PCB recorded}} = \frac{2}{365} = .0054795$$

4.5 Define the event A as follows:

A: An eligible worker is unemployed

$$P(A) = \frac{5.9}{100} = .059$$

4.7 Since the 5 outcomes are mutually exclusive,

$$
\begin{aligned}
P(A) &= P(\text{outcome 1, 2, or 4 occurs}) \\
&= P(1 \text{ occurs}) + P(2 \text{ occurs}) + P(4 \text{ occurs}) \\
&= \quad .15 \quad + \quad .20 \quad + \quad .25 \\
&= .60
\end{aligned}
$$

```
P(B) = P(outcome 2, 3, or 5 occurs)
     = P(2 occurs) + P(3 occurs) + P(5 occurs)
     =     .20     +     .20     +     .20
     = .60

P(C) = P(outcome 4 does not occur)
     = 1 - P(outcome 4 occurs)
     = 1 - .25
     = .75
```

4.9   a. $P(A) = P(1) + P(2) + P(3)$

$$= \frac{1}{6} + \frac{1}{6} + \frac{1}{6}$$

$$= \frac{3}{6} = \frac{1}{2}$$

$P(B) = P(1) + P(3) + P(5)$

$$= \frac{1}{6} + \frac{1}{6} + \frac{1}{6}$$

$$= \frac{3}{6} = \frac{1}{2}$$

$P(C) = P(2) + P(4) + P(6)$

$$= \frac{1}{6} + \frac{1}{6} + \frac{1}{6}$$

$$= \frac{3}{6} = \frac{1}{2}$$

b.   The complement of event A, denoted $\bar{A}$, is the event that A does not occur. This means that 4, 5, or 6 must occur since the number is not less than 4. Thus,

$\bar{A} = \{4, 5, 6\}$

$\bar{B} = \{2, 4, 6\}$ because if it is not odd, it is even.

$\bar{C} = \{1, 3, 5\}$ because if it is not even, it is odd.

c. $P(\bar{A}) = 1 - P(A) = 1 - \frac{1}{2} = \frac{1}{2}$

$P(\bar{B}) = 1 - P(B) = 1 - \frac{1}{2} = \frac{1}{2}$

$P(\bar{C}) = 1 - P(C) = 1 - \frac{1}{2} = \frac{1}{2}$ (Refer to part (a).)

d. A and B are not complementary events since all numbers that are not less than 4 are not odd.

   A and C are not complementary events since all numbers that are not less than 4 are not even.

   B and C are complementary events since all the numbers that are not odd are even.

4.13 Property 3 for probability says that the sum of the probabilities of all possible mutually exclusive events associated with an experiment always equals one.

Ex. 4.6: $P(H_1H_2) + P(H_1T_2) + P(T_1H_2) + P(T_1T_2)$

$$= \frac{1}{4} + \frac{1}{4} + \frac{1}{4} + \frac{1}{4}$$

$$= 1$$

Ex. 4.7: $P(A) + P(B) + P(C) + P(D)$

$$= .05 + .20 + .30 + .45$$

$$= 1.00$$

4.15 Events A and B are mutually exclusive. If the monthly inventory shows 30,310 bearings, the monthly inventory level cannot be less than 30,000 bearings.

   Events A and C are not mutually exclusive. If the monthly inventory level shows 30,310 bearings, then it exceeds 30,000 bearings.

   Events B and C are mutually exclusive. The monthly inventory level cannot be less than 30,000 bearings and exceed 30,000 bearings at the same time.

4.17 a. There are 9 possible outcomes for this experiment. The outcomes are:

   (40,300) (40,350) (40,400)
   (45,300) (45,350) (45,400)
   (50,300) (50,350) (50,400)

   b. The different outcomes for this experiment that are listed above are probably not equally likely to yield the highest electrical resistivity. There are many different factors that affect the electrical resistivity.

4.19   Let A = outcome "item was shoplifted."
            B = outcome "item was stolen by an employee."
            C = outcome "item was victim of poor paper-work."

    a. P(stolen) = P(A) + P(B) = .30 + .50 = .80

    b. P(not stolen) = 1 - P(stolen) = 1 - .80 = .20

4.21   a. Let L_1, L_2 and L_3 represent the large corporation applicants and
            S_1 and S_2 represent the small business applicants. The sample
            space for choosing two from the five is:

        L_1, L_2 L_1, S_2 L_2, S_2 S_1, S_2
        L_1, L_3 L_2, L_3 L_3, S_1
        L_1, S_1 L_2, S_1 L_3, S_2

        Thus, M = 10.

        Of the 10 events, three have both large corporations, so m = 3.

        P(awarding grants to two large corporations) = $\frac{m}{M} = \frac{3}{10}$ = .30

    b. The probability of the grants being given to two corporations was
        .30. Such a probability is not small enough to cause us to doubt
        the agency's claim that the selection was random.

4.23   a. .21 + .07 + .13 + .15 + .44 = 1.00

    b. P(Courageous act occurred prior to 1975)
        = .21 + .07 = .28

    c. P(courageous act did not occur during 1981-1983)
        = 1 - P(courageous act occurred during 1981-1983)
        = 1 - .44 = .56

4.25   Letting P_i represent player i, the 28 possible outcomes are:

    (P_1, P_2) (P_1, P_3) (P_1, P_4) (P_1, P_5) (P_1, P_6) (P_1, P_7) (P_1, P_8)
            (P_2, P_3) (P_2, P_4) (P_2, P_5) (P_2, P_6) (P_2, P_7) (P_2, P_8)
                    (P_3, P_4) (P_3, P_5) (P_3, P_6) (P_3, P_7) (P_3, P_8)
                            (P_4, P_5) (P_4, P_6) (P_4, P_7) (P_4, P_8)
                                    (P_5, P_6) (P_5, P_7) (P_5, P_8)
                                            (P_6, P_7) (P_6, P_8)
                                                    (P_7, P_8)

4.27   a. Outcomes associated with event D: AA   AB   AC

            P(D) = $\frac{3}{9}$

b. Outcomes associated with event E: AB BB CB

$$P(E) = \frac{3}{9}$$

c. The event E|D is the event E occurs given event D has occurred.
Event D has only three outcomes--AA, AB, AC. Since it is given
that D has occurred, one of these three outcomes has occurred. Of
these three events, only one, AB, is in E. Therefore, P(E|D) =
1/3.

d. D and E are independent if

$$P(E|D) = P(E)$$

From (b) and (c), P(E) = 1/3 and P(E|D) = 1/3
=> P(E) = P(E|D).

Therefore, D and E are independent events.

e. Since D and E are independent events,

$$P(\text{both D and E}) = P(D)P(E) = (\frac{1}{3})(\frac{1}{3}) = \frac{1}{9}$$

4.29   P(A) = .6   P(B) = .4   P(C) = .5
P(A|B) = .15   P(A|C) = .5   P(B|C) = .3

a. P(A|B) = .15 ≠ .6 = P(A); therefore, events A and B are not
independent.

b. P(A|C) = .5 ≠ .6 = P(A); therefore, events A and C are not
independent.

c. P(B|C) = .3 ≠ .4 = P(B); therefore, events B and C are not
independent.

4.31   Let A = employee favors a buyout
B = employee will retire within the next 15 years

a. $P(A) = \frac{397}{1040} = .382$

b. $P(B) = \frac{394}{1040} = .379$

c. $P(A|B) = \frac{P(A \text{ and } B)}{P(B)} = \frac{\frac{215}{1040}}{\frac{394}{1040}} = \frac{215}{394} = .546$

d. If events A and B are independent,

$$P(A) = P(A|B)$$

From (a) and (c), $P(A) = .382$ and $P(A|B) = .546$
=> $.382 \neq .546$ => $P(A) \neq P(A|B)$

The employee favoring a buyout and an employee retiring within the next 15 years are not independent. Therefore, an employee's attitude toward the buyout is not independent of his or her retirement plans.

4.33   Define the following events:

A: Observe a 4 on a single die
B: Observe a 4 on another single die

Events A and B are independent and $P(A) = P(B) = 1/6$. The probability of observing two 4's, that is, observing both events A and B is:

$$P(\text{both A and B}) = P(A)P(B) = (\tfrac{1}{6})(\tfrac{1}{6}) = \tfrac{1}{36}$$

From Figure 4.3, $P(\text{both A and B}) = \tfrac{1}{36}$

4.35   Let A = win the grand prize in the Publishing Clearing House sweepstakes
        B = win the grand prize in the American Family Publishers sweepstakes
        C = win the grand prize in the Reader's Digest sweepstakes

From 4.34, $P(A) = .0000000055$, $P(B) = .000000005$, and $P(C) = .0000000119$.

a. $P(A \text{ and } B \text{ and } C) = P(A)P(B)P(C)$ (using independence)
    $= (.00000000055)(.000000005)(.0000000119)$
    $= 3.27 \times 10^{-25}$

b. $P(\overline{A} \text{ and } \overline{B} \text{ and } \overline{C}) = P(\overline{A})P(\overline{B})P(\overline{C})$ (using independence)
    $= (1 - P(A))(1 - P(B))(1 - P(C))$
    $= (1 - .0000000055)(1 - .000000005)(1 - .0000000119)$
    $= (.9999999945)(.999999995)(.9999999881)$
    $= .9999999776$

c. P(winning at least one of the three grand prizes)
    $= 1 - P(\overline{A} \text{ and } \overline{B} \text{ and } \overline{C})$
    $= 1 - .9999999776$ (Refer to part (b).)
    $= .0000000224$

4.37   Define the following events:

A: Battery one fails
B: Battery two fails
C: Battery three fails

Since all three events are independent,

$$P(A \text{ and } B \text{ and } C) = P(A)P(B)P(C) = (\frac{1}{20})(\frac{1}{20})(\frac{1}{20}) = \frac{1}{8000} = .000125$$

4.39   Define the following events:

A: Customer 1 replaces needle after 5 years
B: Customer 2 replaces needle after 5 years
C: Customer 3 replaces needle after 5 years
D: Customer 4 replaces needle after 5 years

a. Since each of these events is independent,

$$P(A \text{ and } B \text{ and } C \text{ and } D) = P(A)P(B)P(C)P(D)$$

$$= (\frac{1}{100})(\frac{1}{100})(\frac{1}{100})(\frac{1}{100}) = \frac{1}{100,000,000}$$

$$= .00000001$$

b. Since this probability is so small and it did occur, the claim is probably false.

4.41   a. Let A = throwing a sum of 7
            B = throwing a sum of 11

Using Figure 4.3, there are six outcomes that result in a sum of seven and 2 outcomes that result in a sum of eleven.

A = {(1,6), (2,5), (3,4), (4,3), (5,2), (6,1)}
B = {(5,6), (6,5)}

Each outcome is equally likely and has a probability of $\frac{1}{36}$.

Therefore, the probability of throwing a "natural" is

$$P(A) + P(B) = \frac{6}{36} + \frac{2}{36} = \frac{8}{36}$$

b. Let C = throwing a sum of 2
        D = throwing a sum of 3
        E = throwing a sum of 12

Using Figure 4.3,

$$C = \{(1,1)\}$$
$$D = \{(1,2), (2,1)\}$$
$$E = \{(6,6)\}$$

Therefore, the probability of throwing "craps" is

$$P(C) + P(D) + P(E) = \frac{1}{36} + \frac{2}{36} + \frac{1}{36} = \frac{4}{36}$$

c. The outcome of each throw is independent of what happened on previous throws. Thus, the probability of a "hot" player throwing a "natural" given that he has thrown five "naturals" in a row is

$$P(\text{throwing a "natural"} | \text{thrown 5 "naturals" in a row})$$

$$= P(\text{throwing a "natural"}) = \frac{8}{36}$$

d. Since each throw of the dice is independent of any other throw, the probability of a "cold" player throwing "craps" after having thrown five "craps" in a row is

$$P(\text{throwing "craps"} | \text{thrown 5 "craps" in a row})$$

$$= P(\text{throwing "craps"}) = \frac{4}{36}$$

4.43 $$P(\text{either A or B or both}) = P(A) + P(B) - P(\text{both A and B})$$
$$= .3 + .5 - .2$$
$$= .6$$

4.45 Let A = driver resides in a state with a mandatory seat belt law
 B = driver resides in a state with a pending mandatory seat belt law
 C = driver resides in a state with no mandatory seat belt law
 D = driver always uses seat belts
 E = driver uses seat belts frequently
 F = driver uses seat belts infrequently
 G = driver never uses seat belts

a. $$P(C) = \frac{181}{387} = .468$$

b. $$P(F) = \frac{79}{387} = .204$$

c. $$P(\text{both B and G}) = \frac{8}{387} = .021$$

d. P(either A or D or both) = P(A) + P(D) - P(both A and D)

$$= \frac{128}{387} + \frac{157}{387} - \frac{67}{387}$$

$$= \frac{218}{387} = .563$$

e. $P(C|G) = \frac{P(\text{both C and G})}{P(G)} = \frac{\frac{38}{387}}{\frac{65}{387}} = \frac{38}{65} = .585$

f. $P(E|B) = \frac{P(\text{both E and B})}{P(B)} = \frac{\frac{20}{387}}{\frac{78}{387}} = \frac{20}{78} = .256$

4.47 a. From the table, we see that the probability that a person believes that his or her retirement income will be adequate is

$$P(A) = \frac{63}{100} = .63$$

b. From the table, the probability that the major source of income will be a Social Security pension is

$$P(B) = \frac{57}{100} = .57$$

c. The probability that the major source of income will be a job pension is

$$P(C) = \frac{21}{100} = .21$$

d. From the table, we see that 41% of the people will have Social Security as their major source of retirement (B) income and believe this will be inadequate (A). Therefore,

$$P(\text{both A and B}) = \frac{41}{100} = .41$$

e. A person cannot have both Social Security and a job pension as their major source of retirement income. Therefore,

$$P(\text{both B and C}) = 0$$

f. The probability that either A or B or both occur is given by the Additive Law of Probability. From parts (a), (b), and (d), we know

P(A) = .63   P(B) = .57   P(both A and B) = .41

Thus,

$$P(\text{either A or B or both}) = P(A) + P(B) - P(\text{both A and B})$$
$$= .63 + .57 - .41$$
$$= .79$$

g. Using the Multiplicative Law of Probability,

$$P(\text{both A and B}) = P(A)P(B|A)$$

Solving for $P(B|A)$ yields

$$P(B|A) = \frac{P(\text{both A and B})}{P(A)} = \frac{.41}{.63} = \frac{41}{63}$$

4.49 Define the following events:

A: A woman has a sewing machine
B: A woman has used a sewing pattern in the past 12 months

We know $P(A) = .58$ and $P(B|A) = .36$. We want to find P(both A and B occur).

Using the Multiplicative Law of Probability:

$$P(\text{both A and B occur}) = P(A)P(B|A)$$
$$= (.58)(.36) = .2088$$

4.51 Define the following events:

A: A strike of craft employees will be called
B: The telephone craft employees will agree to strike

We know $P(A) = .75$ and $P(B|A) = .90$. We want to find P(both A and B occur).

Using the Multiplicative Law of Probability:

$$P(\text{both A and B occur}) = P(A)P(B|A)$$
$$= .75(.90) = .675$$

4.53 a. A A A A   B A A A   A B B B   B A B B
         A A A B   B A A B   A B B A   B B A B
         A A B A   B A B A   A A B B   B B B A
         A B A A   B B A A   A B A B   B B B B

b. There is only m = 1 way out of M = 16 that all four customers will prefer style A. Therefore, the probability that all four customers will prefer style A is

$$P(AAAA) = \frac{m}{M} = \frac{1}{16}$$

c. If this event did occur, we could infer that either the public prefers style A or this is a rare event since the probability is so small.

4.55 This is incorrect. The woman who called has an equally likely chance of being selected as anyone else whose name is in the directory, regardless of what letter of the alphabet the last name begins with. So, if there were 1000 names in the directory, the woman who called would have a 1/1000 chance of being selected.

4.57 a. P(no answer, busy signal, or out-of-service number)
= .347 + .020 + .203 = .570.

b. P(eligible person at home to take call)
= P(eligible person at home--refusal) + P(eligible person at home--completed interview)
= .014 + .084 = .098.

c. By the Multiplicative Law of Probability,

P(refuse to participate|eligible person at home)

$$= \frac{\text{P(both person refuses to participate and eligible person at home)}}{\text{P(eligible person at home)}}$$

= .014/.098 = .143.

4.59 a. P(white homeowner will default on a loan above $20,705|located in the city) = .0344.

b. P(black homeowner will default on a loan above $20,705|located in the city) = .1250.

c. P(black homeowner will default on a loan above $20,750)
= P(black homeowner will default on a loan above $20,750|located in the city) • P(located in the city) + P(black homeowner will default on a loan above $20,750|located in the suburbs) • P(located in the suburbs) = .125(.7) + .1695(.3)
= .0875 + .05085 = .1384.

4.61 There are 16 (2^4) possible ways that the four transactions with two choices can occur. Letting H be a "hit" and M be a "miss," there are:

```
H H H H     M H H H     H M M M     M H M M
H H H M     M H H M     H M M H     M M H M
H H M H     M H M H     H H M M     M M M H
H M H H     M M H H     H M H M     M M M M
```

a. Of the 16 possible outcomes, 6 have exactly 2 matches. They are:

     M H H M   M M H H   H H M M
     M H M H   H M M H   H M H M

P(exactly 2 matches) = $\dfrac{6}{16}$

b. Of the 16 possible outcomes, 15 have at least 1 match. They are:

     H H H H   M H H H   H M M M   M H M M
     H H H M   M H H M   H M M H   M M H M
     H H M H   M H M H   H H M M   M M M H
     H M H H   M M H H   H M H M

P(at least 1 match) = $\dfrac{15}{16}$

c. The assumption of equally likely outcomes implies that for any one
    unusual cash transaction, the probability of a "hit" is P(H) = .5.
    Since probably very few of the unusual cash transactions are
    actually illegal transactions, it is very unlikely that the name
    will match one of the names of convicted criminals 50% of the
    time.

4.63   Define the following event:

       A: Correctly predicts an increase or decrease in Stock 1 price
       B: Correctly predicts an increase or decrease in Stock 2 price
       C: Correctly predicts an increase or decrease in Stock 3 price

If the "witch's" claim is true,

       P(A) = P(B) = P(C) = .60

and the three events are independent.

a. P(A and B and C) = P(A)P(B)P(C) = (.6)(.6)(.6) = .216

b. P($\overline{A}$ and $\overline{B}$ and $\overline{C}$) = P($\overline{A}$)P($\overline{B}$)P($\overline{C}$) = (.4)(.4)(.4) = .064

    [Remember, P($\overline{A}$) = 1 - P(A) = 1 - .6 = .4.]

c. Either we have observed a rare event (probability of occurrence of
    only .064) or the claimed accuracy rate of 60% is too high. A
    value of P(A) less than .60 would increase the probability of the
    observed event (i.e., three incorrect predictions). Thus, it is
    probably true that P(A) < .60.

4.65   a.   We are interested in the probability that both the first and
            second machines break down. From the Multiplicative Rule,

            P(both first and second machines break down)

            = P(first breaks down)P(second breaks down|first breaks down)

            We know that the probability that the first machine breaks down is
            .20 and the probability that the second machine breaks down given
            that the first machine breaks down is .30. Therefore,

            P(both machines break down) = (.2)(.3) = .06

       b.   The complement of the event (A), the system is working during
            operating hours, is the event (Ā), the system is not working
            during operating hours. From part (a), we saw that P(Ā) = .06.
            Therefore,

            P(A) = 1 - .06 = .94

4.67   a.   P(either A or B or both occur)
            = P(A) + P(B) - P(both A and B occur)
            = P(A) + P(B) - P(C)
            = .20 + .08 - .03
            = .25

       b.   The probability that either A or B or both occurs is the
            probability that a consumer views a typical television show or
            reads a typical magazine issue in the schedule or does both.

       c.   D̄ is the complement of D. This is the event that a consumer views
            a typical television show or a typical magazine issue in the
            schedule. Note: the event either A or B or both occur is the
            same as the event D̄.

       d.   Since the events either A or B or both and D̄ are the same,

            P(D) = 1 - P(D̄)
                 = 1 - P(either A or B or both)
                 = 1 - .25 (Refer to part (a).)
                 = .75

4.69   a.   The probability that a craps player wins is .493. Therefore, if
            he plays the game 1000 times, he would win about 493 times.

       b.   Since the probability of winning at the game of craps is less than
            .5, you would expect to lose more money than you win if you bet
            repeatedly.

CASE STUDIES

4.1 a. The first digit could be a 0, 1, 2, 3, 4, 5, 6, 7, 8, or 9. The digit is randomly selected; therefore, the probability that the winning first digit will be a one is 1/10.

b. The second and third digits could also be a 0, 1, 2, 3, 4, 5, 6, 7, 8, or 9. The digits are randomly selected. Therefore,

$$P(\text{second digit is a 3}) = \frac{1}{10}$$

$$P(\text{third digit is a 9}) = \frac{1}{10}$$

c. Since there are 1000 possible three-digit numbers (000-999) which all have an equal chance of occurring, the probability that a person selecting one three-digit number will win is 1/1000.

d. Since the probability of winning is 1/1000, a player would expect to receive $500 for every $1000 he puts into the game. Therefore, the payoff rate is not reasonable for the player.

4.3 a. First, we find M, the number of distinctly different samples that can be selected from the remaining 50 cards.

$$M = C^N_n = \frac{N!}{n!(N-n)!} = \frac{50!}{2!48!} = \frac{(50)(49)(48)\ \ldots\ (3)(2)(1)}{(2)(1)(48)(47)(46)\ \ldots\ (3)(2)(1)}$$

$$= \frac{(50)(49)}{2} = 1,225$$

Next, we determine the number m of samples that result in a blackjack (21).

There are 15 cards that are valued at 10 points and 3 aces left in the deck. Therefore, there are m = (3)(15) = 45 pairs of cards that could result in a blackjack.

Applying Probability Rule #2,

$$P(\text{blackjack}) = \frac{m}{M} = \frac{45}{1225} = .0367$$

b. Let D_1 = dealer gets blackjack on the first hand
    D_2 = dealer gets blackjack on the second hand
    D_3 = dealer gets blackjack on the third hand

$P(D_1) = P(D_2) = P(D_3) = .04826546$ (Refer to the case study.)

D_1, D_2, and D_3 are independent events since the deck of cards is shuffled between hands. Therefore, what occurs on one hand will not affect the outcome on the next hand.

Since D_1, D_2, and D_3 are independent,

$$P(D_1 \text{ and } D_2 \text{ and } D_3) = P(D_1)P(D_2)P(D_3)$$
$$= (.04826546)^3$$
$$= .0001124$$

c. Either we have observed a rare event (probability of occurrence is only .0001124) or the cards were not shuffled very well. Therefore, the cards were probably not shuffled very well.

FIVE   DISCRETE PROBABILITY DISTRIBUTIONS

5.1   a.   x can be -5, 0, 2, or 5

         b.   P(x = 2) = p(2) = .4. Since this is a larger value than the probabilities for the other values, x = 2 is most probable.

         c.   P(x > 0) = p(2) + p(5) = .4 + .1 = .5

         d.   P(x = -5) = p(-5) = .2

         e.   .2 + .3 + .4 + .1 = 1.0

5.3   a.   The two requirements for a valid discrete probability distribution are:

            1. $0 \leq p(x) \leq 1$

            2. $\sum\limits_{\text{all } x} p(x) = 1$

         For this distribution, none of the rectangles are higher than 1 and none are below 0. Thus, $0 \leq p(x) \leq 1$ holds.

         From the graph p(7) = .10, p(8) = .10, p(9) = .15, p(10) = .20, p(11) = .20, p(12) = .15, and p(13) = .10.

         $\sum\limits_{\text{all } x} p(x) = .10 + .10 + .15 + .20 + .20 + .15 + .10 = 1.00$

         Therefore, this is a valid probability distribution.

b.

x	p(x)
7	.10
8	.10
9	.15
10	.20
11	.20
12	.15
13	.10

$$\sum_{\text{all } x} p(x) = 1.00$$

c. $P(x = 9) = p(9) = .15$

d. $P(x < 12) = p(7) + p(8) + p(9) + p(10) + p(11)$
$$= .10 + .10 + .15 + .20 + .20 = .75$$

5.5 $\mu = \sum xp(x)$
$$= -5(.2) + 0(.3) + 2(.4) + 5(.1)$$
$$= -1 + 0 + .8 + .5$$
$$= .3$$

$\sigma^2 = \sum (x - \mu)^2 p(x)$ where $\mu = .3$
$$= (-5 - .3)^2 p(-5) + (0 - .3)^2 p(0) + (2 - .3)^2 p(2) + (5 - .3)^2 p(5)$$
$$= (-5 - .3)^2(.2) + (0 - .3)^2(.3) + (2 - .3)^2(.4) + (5 - .3)^2(.1)$$
$$= 5.618 + .027 + 1.156 + 2.209$$
$$= 9.01$$

$\sigma = \sqrt{\sigma^2} = \sqrt{9.01} = 3.0017$

5.7 From Exercise 5.3, part (b),

x	7	8	9	10	11	12	13
p(x)	.10	.10	.15	.20	.20	.15	.10

a. $\mu = \sum xp(x)$
$$= 7(.10) + 8(.10) + 9(.15) + 10(.20) + 11(.20) + 12(.15)$$
$$+ 13(.10)$$
$$= .7 + .8 + 1.35 + 2 + 2.2 + 1.8 + 1.3$$
$$= 10.15$$

$\sigma^2 = \sum (x - \mu)^2 p(x)$ where $\mu = 10.15$
$$= (7 - 10.15)^2(.10) + (8 - 10.15)^2(.10) + (9 - 10.15)^2(.15)$$
$$+ (10 - 10.15)^2(.20) + (11 - 10.15)^2(.20)$$
$$+ (12 - 10.15)^2(.15) + (13 - 10.15)^2(.10)$$
$$= .99225 + .46225 + .198375 + .0045 + .1445 + .513375 + .81225$$
$$= 3.1275$$

$\sigma = \sqrt{\sigma^2} = \sqrt{3.1275} = 1.7685$

b. $(\mu - 2\sigma, \mu + 2\sigma) = (10.15 - 2(1.77), 10.15 + 2(1.77))$
$$= (10.15 - 3.54, 10.15 + 3.54)$$
$$= (6.61, 13.69)$$

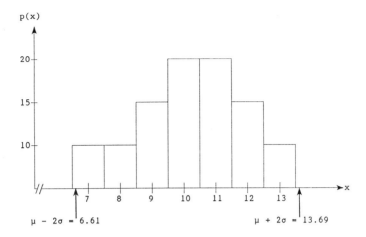

c. $P(6.61 < x < 13.69)$
$$= p(7) + p(8) + p(9) + p(10) + p(11) + p(12) + p(13)$$
$$= .10 + .10 + .15 + .20 + .20 + .15 + .10$$
$$= 1$$

According to the Empirical Rule, the probability that x falls within the interval $(\mu - 2\sigma, \mu + 2\sigma)$ is approximately .95 for mound-shaped distributions. This distribution is mound-shaped, and the probabilities are comparable.

5.9   a.   For a parcel worth $25,000,   For a parcel worth $150,000

$25,000(\frac{1}{5,000}) = \$5$ to $150,000(\frac{1}{5,000}) = \$30$

The expected gain is between $5 and $30 for a single $10 entry.

b. Let x equal the number of wins. Let W be the event you won the parcel of land and L be the event you did not win. If you enter the lottery for three parcels of land, the sample space and the value of x for each simple event are listed below.

WWW	x = 3
WWL	x = 2
WLW	x = 2
WLL	x = 1
LWW	x = 2
LWL	x = 1
LLW	x = 1
LLL	x = 0

$$p(0) = P(x = 0) = P(LLL) = P(L)P(L)P(L) \text{ (by independence)}$$

$$= (1 - \frac{1}{5000})^3$$

$$= .99940012$$

$$p(1) = P(x = 1) = P(WLL) + P(LWL) + P(LLW)$$
$$= 3P(W)P(L)P(L)$$

$$= 3(\frac{1}{5000})(1 - \frac{1}{5000})(1 - \frac{1}{5000})$$

$$= .00059976$$

$$p(2) = .000000119976$$

$$p(3) = .000000000008$$

Then the expected number of wins is:

$$E(x) = \sum xp(x) = 0(.9940012) + 1(.00059976)$$
$$+ 2(.000000119976) + 3(.000000000008)$$
$$= .0006$$

Let y equal your gain. Then y = \$25,000x

Therefore, $E(y) = 25{,}000\ E(x) = 25000(.0006)$
$$= \$15$$

5.11 The toss of a coin is an example of a binomial experiment because it meets the five conditions required:

1. A sample of n = 10 tosses is selected from a population of all coin tosses.
2. There are two possible outcomes: heads and tails--which can be considered "success" and "failure."
3. The probability of tossing a head is p = 1/2, and this probability is the same for each toss.
4. The outcome for any toss does not depend on previous or future tosses.
5. The random variable x counts the number of heads tossed in a sample of size n = 10.

5.13 The binomial probability distribution is

$$p(x) = C_x^n p^x q^{n-x} = \frac{n!}{x!(n-x)!}p^x q^{n-x}$$

In this example, $n = 4$, $p = .2$, and $x = 0, 1, 2, 3$, and 4. Substituting these values into the formula, we get:

$$P(x = 0) = p(0) = C_0^4(.2)^0(.8)^4 = \frac{4!}{0!4!}(.2)^0(.8)^4$$

$$= (1)(1)(.4096) = .4096$$

$$P(x = 1) = p(1) = C_1^4(.2)^1(.8)^3 = \frac{4!}{1!3!}(.2)^1(.8)^3$$

$$= (4)(.2)(.5120) = .4096$$

$$P(x = 2) = p(2) = C_2^4(.2)^2(.8)^2 = \frac{4!}{2!2!}(.2)^2(.8)^2$$

$$= (6)(.04)(.64) = .1536$$

$$P(x = 3) = p(3) = C_3^4(.2)^3(.8)^1 = \frac{4!}{3!1!}(.2)^3(.8)^1$$

$$= (4)(.008)(.8) = .0256$$

$$P(x = 4) = p(4) = C_4^4(.2)^4(.8)^0 = \frac{4!}{4!0!}(.2)^4(.8)^0$$

$$= (1)(.2)^4(1) = .0016$$

The graph is given below.

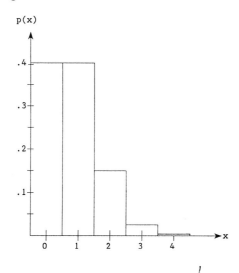

5.15   From Exercise 5.13, the probability distribution of x is:

x	0	1	2	3	4
p(x)	.4096	.4096	.1536	.0256	.0016

a. $P(x < 2) = p(0) + p(1) = .4096 + .4096 = .8192$

b. $P(x \geq 2) = p(2) + p(3) + p(4) = .1536 + .0256 + .0016 = .1808$

c. $P(x < 2) = 1 - P(x \geq 2) = 1 - .1808 = .8192$

The two events are complements of each other.

d. Since the 2 events are complements of each other, the probabilities must sum to 1.

$P(x < 2) + P(x \geq 2) = .8192 + .1808 = 1$

5.17 a. The probability that $x \leq 8$ is

$$P(x \leq 8) = P(x = 0 \text{ or } x = 1 \text{ or } ... \text{ or } x = 8)$$
$$= p(0) + p(1) + ... + p(8)$$

From Table 1 (Appendix E in the text), looking in the column corresponding to $p = .4$ and the row corresponding to $x = 8$, we read

$$p(x \leq 8) = .9983$$

b. The probability that $x < 8$ is the probability that $x \leq 7$. From Table 1, looking in the column corresponding to $p = .4$ and the row corresponding to $x = 7$, we read:

$$P(x < 8) = P(x \leq 7) = .9877$$

c. $P(x > 8) = 1 - P(x \leq 8)$
$= 1 - .9983$
$= .0017$

5.19 a. $\mu = np = 10(.1) = 1$

$\sigma = \sqrt{npq} = \sqrt{10(.1)(.9)} = \sqrt{.9} = .95$

b. $\mu = np = 15(.1) = 1.5$

$\sigma = \sqrt{npq} = \sqrt{15(.1)(.9)} = \sqrt{1.35} = 1.16$

c. $\mu = np = 20(.1) = 2$

$\sigma = \sqrt{npq} = \sqrt{20(.1)(.9)} = \sqrt{1.8} = 1.34$

d. $\mu = np = 25(.1) = 2.5$

$\sigma = \sqrt{npq} = \sqrt{25(.1)(.9)} = \sqrt{2.25} = 1.5$

5.21   This is a binomial experiment because it meets the five conditions
        required:

        1. A sample of n = 3 experimental units (lotteries) is selected from
            the population of all lotteries.
        2. Each unit has two outcomes: Win, Lose.
        3. P(Win) = 1/20 for each lottery, according to Case Study 4.2.
        4. The lotteries are independent, because the choices of parcels are
            made at random, independently.
        5. The random variable x = the number of winners out of n = 3
            lotteries.

5.23   a. By checking the five characteristics of a binomial experiment, we
            see that x is a binomial random variable.

            1. A random sample of 100 persons was selected.
            2. Each person's choice could result in a "success," choosing
                floor wax A, or a "failure," choosing floor wax B.
            3. The probability of a person choosing floor wax A, p, is the
                same for each trial.
            4. The choice of any person is independent of what any other
                person selected.
            5. The random variable x counts the number of "successes," that
                is, the number of persons preferring floor wax A.

        b. This implies that p > .5, since majority means more than 50 of 100
            chose floor wax A. An estimate of p would be x/100 and since
            x > 50, p > .5.

        c. If the two waxes are identical, p = .5, since the evaluators would
            be equally likely to choose A or B.

5.25   a. By checking the five characteristics of a binomial experiment, we
            see that x is close to a binomial random variable with n = 20 and
            p = .60.

            1. A sample of n = 20 adults is selected from the population of
                2,052 surveyed adults.
            2. There are two possible outcomes: believe the federal income
                tax is unfair and believe it is fair--which can be considered
                "success" and "failure."
            3. The probability of an adult thinking the federal income tax is
                unfair, p = .60, is the same for each adult. (Since n is
                small compared to the population size, p ≈ .6 for each trial.)
            4. The adults are randomly selected from a somewhat large
                population. Therefore, the thoughts of any adult is almost
                independent of what any other adult thinks.
            5. The random variable x = the number who think the federal
                income tax is unfair out of n = 20 adults.

b. Using Table 1 of Appendix E,

$P(x \leq 15)$ is the entry beside row 15 and under column $.6(p = .6)$:

$$P(x \leq 15) = p(0) + p(1) + \ldots + p(15)$$
$$= .9490$$

c. $P(x > 10) = 1 - P(x \leq 10)$

$P(x \leq 10)$ is found in row 10 under column $.6(p = .6)$ in Table 1 of Appendix E: $P(x \leq 10) = .2447$.

$P(x > 10) = 1 - P(x \leq 10) = 1 - .2447 = .7553$

5.27   A sample of n = 20 independent ventures was chosen. The two outcomes are "wining in a single venture" and "not winning in a single venture." Let a "success" be the first outcome listed above. $P(S) = p = .6$. Then x = the number of independent ventures out of 20 that you win. The random variable x is a binomial random variable with n = 20 and p = .6.

a. $P(x \geq 10) = 1 - P(x \leq 9)$
$$= 1 - .1275 \quad \text{(Table 1, Appendix E)}$$
$$= .8725$$

b. $P(x \geq 12) = 1 - P(x \leq 11)$
$$= 1 - .4044 \quad \text{(Table 1, Appendix E)}$$
$$= .5956$$

c. If you win at least 80% of the ventures, you win at least $.8(20) = 16$ of the ventures.

$P(x \geq 16) = 1 - P(x \leq 15)$
$$= 1 - .9490 \quad \text{(Table 1, Appendix E)}$$
$$= .0510$$

5.29   A sample of n = 25 adults was chosen. A "success" is when the adult believes that business executives possess either low or very low honesty and ethical standards. $P(S) = p = .2$. The random variable x is a binomial random variable with n = 25 and p = .20.

a. $P(x \geq 10) = 1 - P(x \leq 9)$
$$= 1 - .9827 \quad \text{(Table 1, Appendix E)}$$
$$= .0173$$

b. $P(x \leq 5) = .6167 \quad \text{(Table 1, Appendix E)}$

c. $P(x \geq 7) = 1 - P(x \leq 6)$
$$= 1 - .7800 \quad \text{(Table 1, Appendix E)}$$
$$= .2200$$

5.31 A sample of n = 150 business executives was randomly selected. The
two outcomes are "the business executive will develop symptoms of
stress-induced problems" and "the business executive will not develop
symptoms of stress-induced problems." Let a "success" be the first
outcome listed above. $P(S) = p = .4$. Then x = the number of business
executives who develop stress-related problems. The random variable x
is a binomial random variable with n = 150 and p = .40.

a. $\mu = np = (150)(.4) = 60$

b. $\sigma = \sqrt{npq} = \sqrt{(150)(.4)(.6)} = 6$

c. From the Empirical Rule, approximately 95% of the observations lie
within the interval $\mu \pm 2\sigma$.

   $\mu \pm 2\sigma \Rightarrow 60 \pm 2(6) \Rightarrow 60 \pm 12 \Rightarrow (48, 72)$

d. Since the value x = 80 is not in the interval of values we would
expect x to fall, we would infer that p is probably not really .4.
The real value of p is probably larger than .4 since such a large
value of x was found.

5.33 a. $e^{-4.5} = .011109$

b. $e^{-2.0} = .135335$

c. $e^{-6.0} = .002479$

d. $e^{-1.3} = .272532$

e. $\dfrac{(8.2)^3 e^{-8.2}}{3!} = \dfrac{551.368(.000275)}{3 \cdot 2 \cdot 1} = \dfrac{551.368(.000275)}{6} = .025$

f. $\dfrac{(1.5)^4 e^{-1.5}}{4!} = \dfrac{5.0625(.223130)}{4 \cdot 3 \cdot 2 \cdot 1} = \dfrac{5.0625(.223130)}{24} = .047$

g. $\dfrac{(3.0)^2 e^{-3.0}}{2!} = \dfrac{9(.049787)}{2 \cdot 1} = .224$

5.35 a. $p(x) = \dfrac{\mu^x e^{-\mu}}{x!} = \dfrac{2.5^x e^{-2.5}}{x!} = \dfrac{(2.5)^x (.082085)}{x!}$ (using Table 3 of Appendix E)

$p(0) = \dfrac{(2.5)^0 (.082085)}{0!} = .082085$ $p(5) = \dfrac{(2.5)^5 (.082085)}{5!} = .0668$

$p(1) = \dfrac{(2.5)^1 (.082085)}{1!} = .2052$ $p(6) = \dfrac{(2.5)^6 (.082085)}{6!} = .0278$

$p(2) = \dfrac{(2.5)^2 (.082085)}{2!} = .2565$ $p(7) = \dfrac{(2.5)^7 (.082085)}{7!} = .0099$

$$p(3) = \frac{(2.5)^3(.082085)}{3!} = .2138 \qquad p(8) = \frac{(2.5)^8(.082085)}{8!} = .0031$$

$$p(4) = \frac{(2.5)^4(.082085)}{4!} = .1336 \qquad p(9) = \frac{(2.5)^9(.082085)}{9!} = .00086$$

$$p(10) = \frac{(2.5)^{10}(.082085)}{10!} = .00022$$

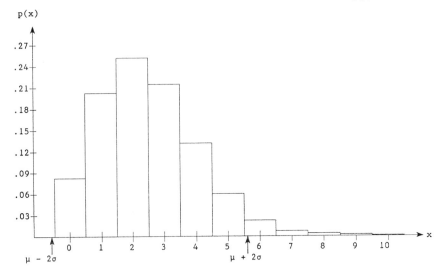

b. Mean = μ = 2.5

$\sigma = \sqrt{\mu} = \sqrt{2.5} = 1.58$

c. $\mu \pm 2\sigma \Rightarrow 2.5 \pm 2(1.58) \Rightarrow 2.5 \pm 3.16 \Rightarrow (-.66, 5.66)$

$$\begin{aligned} P(-.66 < x < 5.66) &= p(0) + p(1) + p(2) + p(3) + p(4) + p(5) \\ &= .082085 + .2052 + .2565 + .2138 + .1336 \\ &\quad + .0668 \\ &= .958 \end{aligned}$$

5.37 x has a binomial probability distribution with n = 100, p = .02, and q = 1 - p = .98. We can get an adequate approximation of the binomial by using the Poisson distribution since n is somewhat large, p is small, and μ = np = 100(.02) = 2 < 7.

The Poisson probability distribution is:

$$p(x) = \frac{\mu^x e^{-\mu}}{x!} = \frac{2^x e^{-2}}{x!} = \frac{2^x(.135335)}{x!} \quad \text{(using Table 3 of Appendix E)}$$

a. $P(x \geq 3) = 1 - P(x < 3) = 1 - [p(0) + p(1) + p(2)]$

$$= 1 - \left[\frac{(2^0)(.135335)}{0!} + \frac{(2^1)(.135335)}{1!} + \frac{(2^2)(.135335)}{2!} \right]$$

$$= 1 - [.135335 + .27067 + .27067]$$

$$= 1 - .6767 = .3233$$

b. $P(x = 5) = \dfrac{(2^5)(.135335)}{5!} = \dfrac{32(.135335)}{120} = .0361$

c. $P(x = 0) = \dfrac{(2^0)(.135335)}{0!} = .135335$

d. $P(x < 2) = p(0) + p(1) = .135335 + .27067 = .4060$

5.39 Let x equal the number of vehicles that use the acceleration lane in the next minute. The random variable x is a Poisson random variable with $\mu = 1.1$.

$$p(x) = \frac{\mu^x e^{-\mu}}{x!} = \frac{1.1^x e^{-1.1}}{x!} = \frac{1.1^x(.332871)}{x!} \quad \text{(using Table 3 of Appendix E)}$$

a. $P(x > 2) = 1 - P(x \leq 2)$

$$= 1 - [p(0) + p(1) + p(2)]$$

$$= 1 - \left[\frac{1.1^0(.332871)}{0!} + \frac{1.1^1(.332871)}{1!} + \frac{1.1^2(.332871)}{2!} \right]$$

$$= 1 - [.332871 + .366158 + .201387]$$

$$= 1 - .900 = .10$$

b. $P(x = 3) = p(3) = \dfrac{1.1^3(.332871)}{3!} = \dfrac{1.331(.332871)}{6} = .074$

5.41 The probability distribution of x, the number of breakdowns per 8-hour shift, can be approximated by a Poisson distribution with $\mu = 1.5$.

$$p(x) = \frac{\mu^x e^{-\mu}}{x!} = \frac{1.5^x e^{-1.5}}{x!} = \frac{1.5^x(.223130)}{x!} \quad \text{(using Table 3 of Appendix E)}$$

a. $P(x = 2) = p(2) = \dfrac{1.5^2(.223130)}{2!} = \dfrac{2.25(.223130)}{2 \cdot 1} = .2510$

b. $P(x < 2) = p(0) + p(1) = \dfrac{(1.5)^0(.223130)}{0!} + \dfrac{(1.5)^1(.223130)}{1!}$

$$= .223130 + .3347 = .5578$$

c. The probability of no breakdowns on one shift is

$$P(x = 0) = .223130 \quad \text{(Refer to part (b).)}$$

Therefore, the probability of no breakdowns for 3 consecutive 8-hour shifts

$$
\begin{aligned}
&= P(x = 0 \text{ and } x = 0 \text{ and } x = 0) \\
&= P(x = 0)P(x = 0)P(x = 0) \quad \text{(by independence)} \\
&= p(0)p(0)p(0) \\
&= (.223130)^3 \\
&= .0111
\end{aligned}
$$

5.43 The probability distribution of x, the demand for new tractor-trailer rigs, can be approximated by a Poisson probability distribution with $\mu = 1.6$.

$$p(x) = \frac{\mu^x e^{-\mu}}{x!} = \frac{1.6^x e^{-1.6}}{x!} = \frac{1.6^x(.201897)}{x!} \quad \begin{array}{l}\text{(using Table 3 of} \\ \text{Appendix E)}\end{array}$$

a. $P(x < 3) = p(0) + p(1) + p(2) = \dfrac{(1.6)^0(.201897)}{0!} + \dfrac{(1.6)^1(.201897)}{1!}$

$$+ \frac{(1.6)^2(.201897)}{2!}$$

$$= .201897 + .323035 + .258428$$

$$= .7834$$

b. $P(x > 5) = 1 - P(x \leq 5)$

$$= 1 - [p(0) + p(1) + p(2) + p(3) + p(4) + p(5)]$$

$$= 1 - \left[.7834 + \frac{(1.6)^3(.201897)}{3!} + \frac{(1.6)^4(.201897)}{4!} \right.$$

$$\left. + \frac{(1.6)^5(.201897)}{5!} \right]$$

(Refer to part (a).)

$$= 1 - \left[.7834 + \frac{(4.096)(.201897)}{3 \cdot 2 \cdot 1} + \frac{(6.5536)(.201897)}{4 \cdot 3 \cdot 2 \cdot 1} \right.$$

$$\left. + \frac{(10.48576)(.201897)}{5 \cdot 4 \cdot 3 \cdot 2 \cdot 1} \right]$$

$$= 1 - [.7834 + .13783 + .05513 + .01764]$$

$$= 1 - .9940 = .0060$$

5.45 The probability distribution of x, the number of industrial accidents per month, can be approximated by a Poisson probability distribution with $\mu = 4.1$.

$$p(x) = \frac{\mu^x e^{-\mu}}{x!} = \frac{4.1^x e^{-4.1}}{x!} = \frac{4.1^x(.016573)}{x!} \qquad \text{(using Table 3 of Appendix E)}$$

a. $P(x = 2) = p(2) = \dfrac{4.1^2(.016573)}{2!} = \dfrac{(16.81)(.016573)}{2 \cdot 1} = .1393$

b. $P(x \geq 4) = 1 - P(x \leq 3)$

$= 1 - [p(0) + p(1) + p(2) + p(3)]$

$= 1 - \left[\dfrac{(4.1)^0(.016573)}{0!} + \dfrac{(4.1)^1(.016573)}{1!} + \dfrac{(4.1)^2(.016573)}{2!} \right.$

$\left. + \dfrac{(4.1)^3(.016573)}{3!} \right]$

$= 1 - [.016573 + .067949 + .139296 + .190371]$

$= 1 - .4142 = .5858$

5.47 a. $p(x) = \dfrac{C_x^r C_{n-x}^{N-r}}{C_n^N} = \dfrac{C_x^2 C_{4-x}^{6-2}}{C_4^6}$

$p(0) = \dfrac{C_0^2 C_4^4}{C_4^6} = \dfrac{\left(\frac{2!}{0!2!}\right)\left(\frac{4!}{4!0!}\right)}{\frac{6!}{4!2!}} = \dfrac{(1)(1)}{15} = \dfrac{1}{15}$

$p(1) = \dfrac{C_1^2 C_3^4}{C_4^6} = \dfrac{\left(\frac{2!}{1!1!}\right)\left(\frac{4!}{3!1!}\right)}{\frac{6!}{4!2!}} = \dfrac{(2)(4)}{15} = \dfrac{8}{15}$

$p(2) = \dfrac{C_2^2 C_2^4}{C_4^6} = \dfrac{\left(\frac{2!}{2!0!}\right)\left(\frac{4!}{2!2!}\right)}{\frac{6!}{4!2!}} = \dfrac{(1)(6)}{15} = \dfrac{6}{15}$

b.

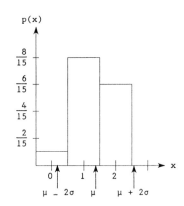

c. $\mu = \dfrac{nr}{N} = \dfrac{(4)(2)}{6} = 1.33$

$\sigma = \sqrt{\dfrac{r(N - r)n(N - n)}{N^2(N - 1)}} = \sqrt{\dfrac{(2)(6 - 2)(4)(6 - 4)}{6^2(6 - 1)}} = \sqrt{\dfrac{64}{180}} = .596$

d. $\mu \pm 2\sigma \Rightarrow 1.33 \pm 2(.596) \Rightarrow 1.33 \pm 1.192 \Rightarrow (.138, 2.522)$

$P(\mu - 2\sigma < x < \mu + 2\sigma) = P(.138 < x < 2.522)$

$$= p(1) + p(2)$$

$$= \dfrac{8}{15} + \dfrac{6}{15}$$

$$= \dfrac{14}{15}$$

5.49 $p(x) = \dfrac{C_x^r C_{n-x}^{N-r}}{C_n^N} = \dfrac{C_x^5 C_{7-x}^{12-5}}{C_7^{12}}$

a. $P(x = 3) = \dfrac{C_3^5 C_4^7}{C_7^{12}} = \dfrac{\left(\dfrac{5!}{3!2!}\right)\left(\dfrac{7!}{4!3!}\right)}{\dfrac{12!}{7!5!}} = \dfrac{(10)(35)}{792} = \dfrac{350}{792}$

b. $P(x \le 2) = p(0) + p(1) + p(2)$

$$= \dfrac{C_0^5 C_7^7}{C_7^{12}} + \dfrac{C_1^5 C_6^7}{C_7^{12}} + \dfrac{C_2^5 C_5^7}{C_7^{12}}$$

$$= \dfrac{\left(\dfrac{5!}{0!5!}\right)\left(\dfrac{7!}{7!0!}\right)}{\dfrac{12!}{7!5!}} + \dfrac{\left(\dfrac{5!}{1!4!}\right)\left(\dfrac{7!}{6!1!}\right)}{\dfrac{12!}{7!5!}} + \dfrac{\left(\dfrac{5!}{2!3!}\right)\left(\dfrac{7!}{5!2!}\right)}{\dfrac{12!}{7!5!}}$$

$$= \dfrac{(1)(1)}{792} + \dfrac{(5)(7)}{792} + \dfrac{(10)(21)}{792} = \dfrac{1}{792} + \dfrac{35}{792} + \dfrac{210}{792} = \dfrac{246}{792}$$

c. $P(x = 5) = \dfrac{C_5^5 C_2^7}{C_7^{12}} = \dfrac{\left(\dfrac{5!}{5!0!}\right)\left(\dfrac{7!}{2!5!}\right)}{\dfrac{12!}{7!5!}} = \dfrac{(1)(21)}{792} = \dfrac{21}{792}$

d. $P(x > 3) = 1 - P(z \leq 3) = 1 - [p(0) + p(1) + p(2) + p(3)]$

$$= 1 - (\dfrac{1}{792} + \dfrac{35}{792} + \dfrac{210}{792} + \dfrac{350}{792})$$

$$= 1 - \dfrac{596}{792} \quad \text{(Refer to parts (a) and (b).)}$$

$$= \dfrac{196}{792}$$

e. $\mu = \dfrac{nr}{N} = \dfrac{(7)(5)}{12} = 2.92$

f. $\sigma = \sqrt{\dfrac{r(N - r)n(N - n)}{N^2(N - 1)}} = \sqrt{\dfrac{(5)(7)(7)(5)}{(12^2)(11)}} = \sqrt{\dfrac{1225}{1584}} = .88$

g. $\mu \pm 2\sigma \Rightarrow 2.92 \pm 2(.88) \Rightarrow 2.92 \pm 1.76 \Rightarrow (1.16, 4.68)$

$P(\mu - 2\sigma \leq x \leq \mu + 2\sigma) = P(1.16 \leq x \leq 4.68) = P(2 \leq x \leq 4)$

$$= p(2) + p(3) + P(4)$$

$$= \dfrac{210}{792} + \dfrac{350}{792} + \dfrac{C_4^5 C_3^7}{C_7^{12}} \quad \text{(Refer to parts (a) and (b).)}$$

$$= \dfrac{210}{792} + \dfrac{350}{792} + \dfrac{\left(\dfrac{5!}{4!1!}\right)\left(\dfrac{7!}{3!4!}\right)}{\dfrac{12!}{7!5!}}$$

$$= \dfrac{210}{792} + \dfrac{350}{792} + \dfrac{175}{792}$$

$$= \dfrac{735}{792} = .928$$

5.51   For this problem, the number of elements in the population is N = 7, and the sample size is n = 3. Define a "success" as finding a defective. Then x is the number of defectives found in the sample. We will accept the lot only if no "successes" (defectives) are found (i.e., if x = 0).

We use the hypergeometric probability distribution:

$$p(x) = \dfrac{C_x^r C_{n-x}^{N-r}}{C_n^N}$$

a. Since there is r = 1 defective in the lot,

$$p(0) = \frac{C_0^1 C_{3-0}^{7-1}}{C_3^7} = \frac{\left(\frac{1!}{0!0!}\right)\left(\frac{6!}{3!3!}\right)}{\frac{7!}{3!4!}} = \frac{(1)(20)}{35} = \frac{4}{7}$$

b. For r = 3, $p(0) = \frac{C_0^3 C_{3-0}^{7-3}}{C_3^7} = \frac{\left(\frac{3!}{0!3!}\right)\left(\frac{4!}{3!1!}\right)}{\frac{7!}{3!4!}} = \frac{(1)(4)}{35} = \frac{4}{35}$

5.53 For this problem, the number of elements in the population is N = 20 and the sample size is n = 5. Define a "success" as finding a defective switch. Then x is the number of defective switches in the sample. There are r = 2 defective switches in the lot.

We use the hypergeometric probability distribution:

$$p(x) = \frac{C_x^r C_{n-x}^{N-r}}{C_n^N}$$

a. $p(2) = \frac{C_2^2 C_{5-2}^{20-2}}{C_5^{20}} = \frac{\left(\frac{2!}{2!0!}\right)\left(\frac{18!}{3!15!}\right)}{\frac{20!}{5!15!}} = \frac{(1)(816)}{15,504} = \frac{1}{19}$

b. $P(x \geq 1) = 1 - P(x < 1) = 1 - p(0)$

$$= 1 - \frac{C_0^2 C_{5-0}^{20-2}}{C_5^{20}} = 1 - \frac{\left(\frac{2!}{0!2!}\right)\left(\frac{18!}{5!13!}\right)}{\frac{20!}{5!15!}} = 1 - \frac{8568}{15,504}$$

$$= 1 - \frac{21}{38} = \frac{17}{38}$$

c. $\mu = \frac{nr}{N} = \frac{(5)(2)}{20} = \frac{10}{20} = \frac{1}{2}$

5.55 For this problem, the number of elements in the population is N = 22, the number of "successes" is r = 6, and the sample size is n = 3. Define a "success" as finding a firm operating in violation of regulations. Then x is the number of firms operating in violation of regulations in the sample.

We use the hypergeometric probability distribution:

$$p(x) = \frac{C_x^r C_{n-x}^{N-r}}{C_n^N}$$

a. $p(0) = \dfrac{C_0^6 C_{3-0}^{22-6}}{C_3^{22}} = \dfrac{\left(\dfrac{6!}{0!6!}\right)\left(\dfrac{16!}{3!13!}\right)}{\dfrac{22!}{3!19!}} = \dfrac{(1)(560)}{1540} = \dfrac{4}{11}$

b. $p(3) = \dfrac{C_3^6 C_{3-3}^{22-6}}{C_3^{22}} = \dfrac{\left(\dfrac{6!}{3!3!}\right)\left(\dfrac{16!}{0!16!}\right)}{\dfrac{22!}{3!19!}} = \dfrac{(20)(1)}{1540} = \dfrac{1}{77}$

c. $P(x \geq 1) = 1 - P(x < 1) = 1 - p(0) = 1 - \dfrac{4}{11} = \dfrac{7}{11}$

5.57   a. $p(x) = pq^{x-1} = (.3)(.7)^{x-1}$ $x = 1, 2, 3, \ldots$

$p(1) = (.3)(.7)^0 = .3$ $p(5) = (.3)(.7)^4 = .072$

$p(2) = (.3)(.7)^1 = .21$ $p(6) = (.3)(.7)^5 = .050$

$p(3) = (.3)(.7)^2 = .147$ $p(7) = (.3)(.7)^6 = .035$

$p(4) = (.3)(.7)^3 = .103$ $p(8) = (.3)(.7)^7 = .025$

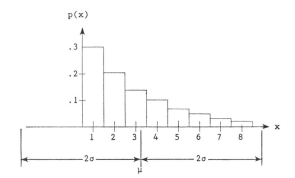

b. $\mu = \dfrac{1}{p} = \dfrac{1}{.3} = 3.33$ $\sigma = \sqrt{\dfrac{q}{p^2}} = \sqrt{\dfrac{.7}{.3^2}} = 2.79$

c. $\mu \pm 2\sigma \Rightarrow 3.33 \pm 2(2.79) \Rightarrow 3.33 \pm 5.58 \Rightarrow (-2.25, 8.91)$;

$P(\mu - 2\sigma \leq x \leq \mu + 2\sigma) = P(-2.25 \leq x \leq 8.91) = P(1 \leq x \leq 8)$

$= p(1) + p(2) + \ldots + p(8)$

$= .3 + .21 + \ldots + .025 = .942$

(Refer to part (a).)

5.59 $p(x) = pq^{x-1} = (.4)(.6)^{x-1}$ $x = 1, 2, 3, \ldots$

a. $P(x = 2) = (.4)(.6)^{2-1} = (.4)(.6) = .24$

b. $P(x \geq 4) = 1 - P(x < 4) = 1 - [p(1) + p(2) + p(3)]$

$$= 1 - [(.4)(.6)^0 + (.4)(.6)^1 + (.4)(.6)^2]$$

$$= 1 - [.4 + .24 + .144] = .216$$

c. $P(x < 3) = p(1) + p(2) = .4 + .24 = .64$ (Refer to part (b).)

d. $P(x = 5) = (.4)(.6)^{5-1} = (.4)(.6)^4 = .052$

e. $P(x > 1) = 1 - P(x \leq 1) = 1 - p(1) = 1 - .4 = .6$ (Refer to part (b).)

f. $\mu = \dfrac{1}{p} = \dfrac{1}{.4} = 2.5$

g. $\sigma = \sqrt{\dfrac{q}{p^2}} = \sqrt{\dfrac{.6}{(.4)^2}} = 1.94$

5.61 a. Let x be the number of prices read before the first misreading. The random variable x is a geometric random variable with $p = .001$.

$p(x) = (.001)(.999)^{x-1}$ $x = 1, 2, 3, \ldots$

b. $P(x > 5) = 1 - P(x \leq 5) = 1 - [p(1) + p(2) + p(3) + p(4) + p(5)]$

$$= 1 - [(.001)(.999)^0 + (.001)(.999)^1$$

$$+ (.001)(.999)^2 + (.001)(.999)^3$$

$$+ (.001)(.999)^4]$$

$$= 1 - [.001 + .000999 + .000998 + .000997$$

$$+ .000996]$$

$$= 1 - .004954 = .995$$

c. $P(x \leq 5) = 1 - P(x > 5) = 1 - .995 = .005.$

Since this probability is so small, it is very unlikely that we would observe a misread price on or before the 5th price. Since the third price was misread, we could infer that the manufacturer's claim is probably false.

5.63 Let x be the number of jobs surveyed before you find a job filled by a local resident. The random variable x is a geometric random variable with p = .40.

$$p(x) = (.40)(.60)^{x-1} \qquad x = 1, 2, 3, \ldots$$

a. The mean for the geometric distribution is

$$\mu = \frac{1}{p} = \frac{1}{.40} = 2.5$$

b. $P(x > 4) = 1 - P(x \leq 4) = 1 - [p(1) + p(2) + p(3) + p(4)]$

$$= 1 - [(.4)(.6)^0 + (.4)(.6)^1 + (.4)(.6)^2$$
$$+ (.4)(.6)^3]$$
$$= 1 - [.4 + .24 + .144 + .0864]$$
$$= 1 - .8704 = .1296$$

5.65 Let x be the number of fuses tested before the first defective is found. The random variable x is a geometric random variable with p = .05.

$$p(x) = (.05)(.95)^{x-1} \qquad x = 1, 2, 3, \ldots$$

a. $P(1 \leq x \leq 5) = p(1) + p(2) + p(3) + p(4) + p(5)$

$$= (.05)(.95)^0 + (.05)(.95)^1 + (.05)(.95)^2$$
$$+ (.05)(.95)^3 + (.05)(.95)^4$$
$$= .05 + .0475 + .045125 + .04287 + .04072 = .226$$

b. $\mu = \dfrac{1}{p} = \dfrac{1}{.05} = 20 \qquad \sigma^2 = \dfrac{q}{p^2} = \dfrac{.95}{(.05)^2} = 380$

$\sigma = \sqrt{\sigma^2} = \sqrt{380} = 19.49$

c. We would expect x to fall within 2 standard deviations of the mean.

$$\mu \pm 2\sigma \Rightarrow 20 \pm 2(19.49)$$
$$\Rightarrow 20 \pm 38.98$$
$$\Rightarrow (-18.98, 58.98)$$

5.67 Let x be the number of years before a nuclear war occurs. The random variable x is a geometric random variable with p = .01.

$$p(x) = (.01)(.99)^{x-1} \qquad x = 1, 2, 3, \ldots$$

The probability of a nuclear war occurring in the next 5 years is:

$$P(x \leq 5) = p(1) + p(2) + p(3) + p(4) + p(5)$$
$$= (.01)(.99)^0 + (.01)(.99)^1 + (.01)(.99)^2$$
$$+ (.01)(.99)^3 + (.01)(.99)^4$$
$$= .01 + .0099 + .009801 + .009703 + .009606$$
$$= .049$$

In the next 10 years:

$$P(x \leq 10) = P(x \leq 5) + p(6) + p(7) + p(8) + p(9) + p(10)$$
$$= .049 + (.01)(.99)^5 + (.01)(.99)^6 + (.01)(.99)^7$$
$$+ (.01)(.99)^8 + (.01)(.99)^9$$
$$= .049 + .0095099 + .0094148 + .0093207 + .0092274$$
$$+ .0091352$$
$$= .0956$$

In the next 15 years:

$$P(x \leq 15) = P(x \leq 10) + p(11) + p(12) + p(13) + p(14) + p(15)$$
$$= .0956 + .0090438 + .0089534 + .0088638 + .0087752$$
$$+ .0086875$$
$$= .1399$$

In the next 20 years:

$$P(x \leq 20) = P(x \leq 15) + p(16) + p(17) + p(18) + p(19) + p(20)$$
$$= .1399 + .0086006 + .0085146 + .0084294 + .0083451$$
$$+ .0082617$$
$$= .1821$$

5.69   The random variable x is a binomial random variable with n = 15 and p = .20. Using Table 1 in Appendix E:

a. $P(x > 10) = 1 - P(x \leq 10)$
$$\approx 1 - 1$$
$$= 0$$

b. $P(x \leq 2) = .3980$

c. $P(x = 0) = .0352$

d. Since the probability of none of the fifteen employees being a "troubled employee" is small (.0352), either the percentage of "troubled employees" is really less than 20%, or at least one of the sampled employees is not being entirely honest, or we have seen a rare event.

5.71 Let x be the number of the 100 sampled transactions that are in error. The random variable x has a binomial probability distribution with n = 100, p = .06, and q = 1 - p = .94.

a. We can get an adequate approximation of the binomial by using the Poisson distribution since n is somewhat large, p is small, and $\mu = np = 100(.06) = 6 < 7$.

The Poisson probability distribution is:

$$p(x) = \frac{\mu^x e^{-\mu}}{x!} = \frac{6^x e^{-6}}{x!}$$

$P(x \geq 1) = 1 - p(0)$

$$= 1 - \frac{(6)^0 e^{-6}}{0!} = 1 - \frac{(6)^0(.002479)}{0!} \quad \text{(using Table 3 in Appendix E)}$$

$$= 1 - .002479 = .9975$$

b. We can get an adequate approximation of the binomial by using the Poisson distribution since $\mu = np = 100(.03) = 3 < 7$.

$$p(x) = \frac{\mu^x e^{-\mu}}{x!} = \frac{3^x e^{-3}}{x!}$$

$P(x \geq 1) = 1 - p(0)$

$$= 1 - \frac{(3)^0 e^{-3}}{0!} = 1 - \frac{(3)^0(.049787)}{0!} \quad \text{(using Table 3 in Appendix E)}$$

$$= 1 - .049787 = .9502$$

c. Since the two events in parts (a) and (b) are independent, we know

$$P(\text{both (a) and (b) occurring}) = P(\text{a occurs})P(\text{b occurs})$$
$$= .9975(.9502)$$
$$= .9478$$

5.73 The probability distribution of x, the number of maintenance-related shutdowns of the elevated rail system, can be approximated by the Poisson distribution with $\mu = 6.5$.

$$p(x) = \frac{\mu^x e^{-\mu}}{x!} = \frac{6.5^x e^{-6.5}}{x!} = \frac{6.5^x(.001503)}{x!} \quad \text{(using Table 3 in Appendix E)}$$

DISCRETE PROBABILITY DISTRIBUTIONS   95

a. $P(x \geq 5) = 1 - P(x < 5) = 1 - [p(0) + p(1) + p(2) + p(3) + p(4)]$

$$= 1 - \left[\frac{(6.5)^0(.001503)}{0!} + \frac{(6.5)^1(.001503)}{1!} \right.$$

$$+ \frac{(6.5)^2(.001503)}{2!} + \frac{(6.5)^3(.001503)}{3!}$$

$$\left. + \frac{(6.5)^4(.001503)}{4!} \right]$$

$$= 1 - [.001503 + .00977 + .03175 + .06879 + .11179]$$

$$= 1 - .2236 = .7764$$

b. $P(x = 4) = \dfrac{(6.5)^4(.001503)}{4!} = .1118$

5.75   a. The expected value, μ, for this binomial distribution with
n = 2000 and p = .98 is μ = np = 2000(.98) = 1960.

b. $\sigma = \sqrt{npq} = \sqrt{2000(.98)(1 - .98)} = \sqrt{39.2} \approx 6.26$

c. By the Empirical Rule, about 95% would fall between $\mu \pm 2\sigma$, that
is, 1960 ± 2(6.26) => 1960 ± 12.52 => (1947.48, 1972.52). For
this distribution, which can only take on whole number values,
about 95% would fall between 1948 and 1972 inclusive.

d. Yes, because it falls

$$z = \frac{x - \mu}{\sigma} = \frac{1850 - 1960}{6.26} = -17.57$$

standard deviations from the mean μ. This is a contradiction to
the Empirical Rule based on the 98% assumption.

5.77   Let x equal the number of employed heads of household in 1983 that
make over $16,200. Then x is a binomial random variable with
n = 1000, p = .5, and q = 1 - p = .5.

a. .5, by definition of "median" as stated in the "Hint" to the
exercise.

b. Since x is a binomial random variable,

$$\mu = np = 1000(.5) = 500$$

$$\sigma = \sqrt{npq} = \sqrt{1000(.5)(1 - .5)} = \sqrt{250} \approx 15.81$$

c. By the Empirical Rule, about 95% of the observations should fall
within $\mu \pm 2\sigma$, which, for this distribution, is:

$$500 \pm 2(15.81) => 500 \pm 31.62 => (468.38, 531.62)$$

Since x can only assume whole number values, about 95% should be between 469 and 531 inclusive.

5.79 Let x be the number of new U.S. corporations formed until the first corporation to survive to age 5 years is observed. The random variable x is a geometric random variable with p = .38.

$$p(x) = (.38)(.62)^{x-1} \qquad x = 1, 2, 3, \ldots$$

a. $P(x \leq 3) = p(1) + p(2) + p(3)$

$$= (.38)(.62)^0 + (.38)(.62)^1 + (.38)(.62)^2 = .7617$$

b. $\mu = \dfrac{1}{p} = \dfrac{1}{.38} = 2.63$

$\sigma^2 = \dfrac{q}{p^2} = \dfrac{.62}{(.38)^2} = 4.29 \qquad \sigma = \sqrt{\sigma^2} = \sqrt{4.29} = 2.07$

5.81 The probability distribution of x can be approximated by a Poisson distribution with $\mu = 4.5$.

$$p(x) = \frac{\mu^x e^{-\mu}}{x!} = \frac{4.5^x e^{-4.5}}{x!} = \frac{4.5^x (.011109)}{x!} \quad \text{(using Table 3 in Appendix E)}$$

a. $P(x = 2) = p(2) = \dfrac{(4.5)^2(.011109)}{2!} = .1125$

b. $P(x \geq 5) = p(5) + p(6) + \ldots = 1 - [p(0) + p(1) + p(2) + p(3) + p(4)]$

$$= 1 - \left[\frac{(4.5)^0(.011109)}{0!} + \frac{(4.5)^1(.011109)}{1!} \right.$$

$$+ \frac{(4.5)^2(.011109)}{2!} + \frac{(4.5)^3(.011109)}{3!}$$

$$\left. + \frac{(4.5)^4(.011109)}{4!} \right]$$

$$= 1 - [.011109 + .04999 + .1125 + .1687 + .1898]$$

$$= 1 - .5321 = .4679$$

c. $P(x = 0) = p(0) = \dfrac{4.5^0 e^{-4.5}}{0!} = \dfrac{(4.5)^0(.011109)}{0!} = .011109$

5.83 Let x equal the number of helicopters that succeed on the day of the mission out of 8. We can assume that the random variable x has a binomial distribution with n = 8, p = .99, and q = 1 − p = .01.

$$p(x) = C_x^n p^x q^{n-x} = C_x^8 .99^x .01^{8-x} \qquad x = 0, 1, 2, \ldots, 8$$

DISCRETE PROBABILITY DISTRIBUTIONS

The probability that 3 or more helicopters fail is the same as the probability that 5 or fewer succeed.

$$P(x \le 5) = p(0) + p(1) + p(2) + p(3) + p(4) + p(5)$$

$$= 1 - [p(6) + p(7) + p(8)]$$

$$= 1 - [C_6^8(.99)^6(.01)^2 + C_7^8(.99)^7(.01)^1 + C_8^8(.99)^8(.01)^0]$$

$$= 1 - \left[\frac{8!}{6!2!}(.99)^6(.01)^2 + \frac{8!}{7!1!}(.99)^7(.01)^1\right.$$

$$\left. + \frac{8!}{8!0!}(.99)^8(.01)^0\right]$$

$$= 1 - [28(.99)^6(.01)^2 + 8(.99)^7(.01)^1 + 1(.99)^8(.01)^0]$$

$$= 1 - (.002636144 + .074565227 + .922744694)$$

$$= 1 - .999946$$

$$= .000054$$

Therefore, if p = .99, then P(at least 3 failures out of 8) = .000054. since this did occur and the probability of it occurring was so small, the true value for p is probably less than .99.

CASE STUDIES

5.1   a.   The random variable x is a binomial random variable with n equal to the number of insider transactions and $p = p_1$.

According to the Empirical Rule, approximately 95% of the time, x will fall within 2 standard deviations of the mean. Since x is a binomial random variable,

$$\mu = np = np_1 \text{ and } \sigma = \sqrt{npq} = \sqrt{np_1q_1}.$$

$$\mu \pm 2\sigma \Rightarrow np_1 \pm 2\sqrt{np_1q_1}$$

$$\Rightarrow (np_1 - 2\sqrt{np_1q_1}, \; np_1 + 2\sqrt{np_1q_1}$$

b.   If the number of buys next month, x, falls in the above range $(np_1 - 2\sqrt{np_1q_1}, \; np_1 + 2\sqrt{np_1q_1})$, there would be no indication that p_2 is different from p_1. However, if x is greater than $np_1 + 2\sqrt{np_1q_1}$, we would infer that p_2 is probably greater than p_1. This would indicate the market is likely to rise. If x is less than $np_1 - 2\sqrt{n_1pq_1}$, we would infer that p_2 is probably less than p_1. This would indicate the market is likely to fall.

5.3   a.   The binomial distribution is not a good model since the sample size ($n = 5$) is too large relative to the population size ($N = 14$). When sampling is performed without replacement and the sample size is large relative to the population size, the random variable x has a hypergeometric probability distribution.

$$p(x) = \frac{C_x^r C_{n-x}^{N-r}}{C_n^N} = \frac{C_x^{10} C_{5-x}^{14-10}}{C_5^{14}}$$

b. $P(x = 5) = \dfrac{C_5^{10} C_0^4}{C_5^{14}} = \dfrac{\dfrac{10!}{5!5!}\left(\dfrac{4!}{0!4!}\right)}{\dfrac{14!}{5!9!}} = \dfrac{252(1)}{2002} = \dfrac{18}{143} = .126$

c. $P(x \leq 2) = p(1) + p(2)$

$$= \frac{C_1^{10} C_4^4}{C_5^{14}} + \frac{C_2^{10} C_3^4}{C_5^{14}}$$

$$= \frac{\dfrac{10!}{1!9!}\left(\dfrac{4!}{4!0!}\right)}{\dfrac{14!}{5!9!}} + \frac{\dfrac{10!}{2!8!}\left(\dfrac{4!}{3!1!}\right)}{\dfrac{14!}{5!9!}}$$

$$= \frac{10(1)}{2002} + \frac{45(4)}{2002}$$

$$= \frac{10 + 180}{2002} = \frac{190}{2002} = \frac{95}{1001} = .095$$

d.   Let x be the number of years in which the November Indicator correctly predicts market performance. The random variable x has a hypergeometric probability distribution.

$$p(x) = \frac{C_x^r C_{n-x}^{N-r}}{C_n^N} = \frac{C_x^{10} C_{5-x}^{14-10}}{C_5^{14}}$$

$$P(x = 5) = \frac{C_5^{10} C_0^4}{C_5^{14}} = \frac{18}{143} = .126 \quad \text{(Refer to part (b).)}$$

$$P(x \leq 2) = p(1) + p(2)$$

$$= \frac{C_1^{10} C_4^4}{C_5^{14}} + \frac{C_2^{10} C_3^4}{C_5^{14}}$$

$$= \frac{95}{1001} = .095 \quad \text{(Refer to part (c).)}$$

e. Let x be the number of years in which the September Indicator correctly predicts market performance. The random variable x has a hypergeometric probability distribution.

$$p(x) = \frac{C_x^r C_{n-x}^{N-r}}{C_n^N} = \frac{C_x^3 C_{5-x}^{14-3}}{C_5^{14}}$$

$P(x = 5) = 0$ since there cannot be more than 3 successes out of 3

$P(x \leq 2) = p(0) + p(1) + p(2)$

$$= \frac{C_0^3 C_5^{11}}{C_5^{14}} + \frac{C_1^3 C_4^{11}}{C_5^{14}} + \frac{C_2^3 C_3^{11}}{C_5^{14}}$$

$$= \frac{\frac{3!}{0!3!}\left(\frac{11!}{5!6!}\right)}{\frac{14!}{5!9!}} + \frac{\frac{3!}{1!2!}\left(\frac{11!}{4!7!}\right)}{\frac{14!}{5!9!}} + \frac{\frac{3!}{2!1!}\left(\frac{11!}{3!8!}\right)}{\frac{14!}{5!9!}}$$

$$= \frac{1(462)}{2002} + \frac{3(330)}{2002} + \frac{3(165)}{2002}$$

$$= \frac{462 + 990 + 495}{2002} = \frac{1947}{2002} = \frac{177}{182} = .973$$

f. Let x be the number of years which the September Contrary-Opinion Indicator correctly predicts market performance. The random variable x has a hypergeometric probability distribution.

$$p(x) = \frac{C_x^r C_{n-x}^{N-r}}{C_n^N} = \frac{C_x^{11} C_{5-x}^{14-11}}{C_5^{14}}$$

$$P(x = 5) = \frac{C_5^{11} C_0^3}{C_5^{14}} = \frac{\frac{11!}{5!6!}\left(\frac{3!}{0!3!}\right)}{\frac{14!}{5!19!}} = \frac{462(1)}{2002} = \frac{3}{13} = .231$$

$$P(x \leq 2) = p(2) = \frac{C_2^{11} C_3^3}{C_5^{14}} = \frac{\frac{11!}{2!9!}\left(\frac{3!}{3!0!}\right)}{\frac{14!}{5!19!}} = \frac{55(1)}{2002} = \frac{5}{182} = .027$$

6.1   a.

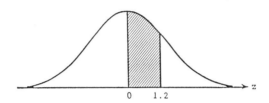

Table 4 (Appendix E in the text: throughout this section, we will refer to this table) gives this area in the row marked 1.2 under the column .00 (1.2 + .00 = 1.20) as .3849.

b.

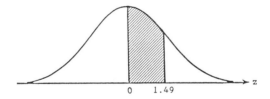

Table 4 gives this area in the row marked 1.4 under the column .09 (1.4 + .09 = 1.49) as .4319.

c.

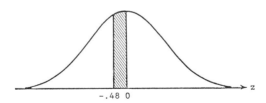

This area is equal to the area between 0 and .48 because of symmetry. It can be found in Table 4 in the row marked 0.4 under the column marked .08 (0.4 + .08 = 0.48) as .1844.

d.

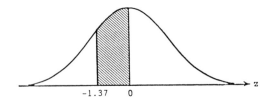

This area is equal to the area between 0 and 1.37 because of symmetry. It can be found in Table 4 (Appendix E) in row 1.3, column .07 (1.3 + .07 = 1.37) as .4147.

e.

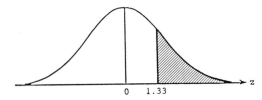

This area is found by first finding the area between 0 and 1.33. It is, from Table 4, row 1.3, column .03, .4082. Since the area to the right of 0 is .5, the area to the right of 1.33 is .5 − .4082 = .0918.

6.3   a.

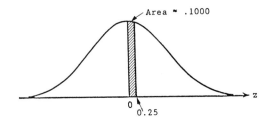

Area ≈ .1000

This process is the opposite of that explained in the solutions to Exercise 6.1. First, .1000 is found in the body of the table. Notice that it cannot be found, but is between .0987 and .1026 in row 0.2 of Table 4. .0987 is closer to .1000 than .1026, so it is used to find z = 0.25 because .0987 is in row 0.2 and column .05: 0.2 + .05 = 0.25.

b.

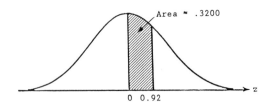

Area ≈ .3200

.3200 is not found in the body of Table 4. The two closest numbers are .3186 and .3212 in row 0.9. Since .3212 is closer to .3200, it is used to find z = 0.92. Because .3212 is in row 0.9 and column .02: 0.9 + .02 = 0.92.

c.

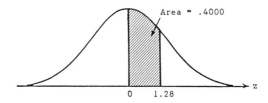

.4000 is not found in Table 4; the closest number is .3997 in row 1.2 under column .08. Thus, z = 1.2 + .08 = 1.28.

d.

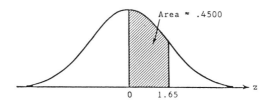

.4500 is not found in Table 4, but two numbers are found to be equally close to .4500. These are .4495 and .4505 in row 1.6 under columns .04 and .05, respectively. Using the midpoint of these, .045, z is found to be 1.6 + .045 = 1.645. Since only two decimal places are required, z = 1.65.

e.

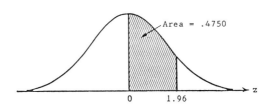

.4750 is found in Table 4 in row 1.9 under column .06. Thus, z = 1.9 + .06 = 1.96.

6.5   The random variable x has mean μ = 20 and standard deviation σ = 4.

a. If x = 23,

$$z = \frac{x - \mu}{\sigma} = \frac{23 - 20}{4} = \frac{3}{4} = .75$$

b. If x = 16,

$$z = \frac{x - \mu}{\sigma} = \frac{16 - 20}{4} = \frac{-4}{4} = -1.00$$

c. If x = 13.5,

$$z = \frac{x - \mu}{\sigma} = \frac{13.5 - 20}{4} = \frac{-6.5}{4} = -1.625$$

d. If x = 28.0,

$$z = \frac{x - \mu}{\sigma} = \frac{28 - 20}{4} = \frac{8}{4} = 2.00$$

e. If x = 12.0,

$$z = \frac{x - \mu}{\sigma} = \frac{12 - 20}{4} = \frac{-8}{4} = -2.00$$

6.7 $P(z < z_0)$ corresponds to finding z_0 that cuts off $P(z < z_0)$ in the lower tail. (Recall that the area in an interval under the distribution is equal to the probability that the random variable falls in that interval.)

a. Area = $P(z < -1.28)$ = .10

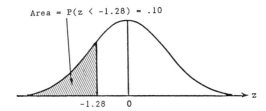

Since $P(z < z_0)$ = .10 is required in the lower tail, there must be .5 - .10 = .40 between z_0 (< 0) and 0. .40 is found in Table 4, in row 1.2 between .3997 and .4015 under columns .08 and .09, respectively. Since .3997 is closer to .40, z_0 = 1.2 + .08 = 1.28. But since $z_0 < 0$, $z_0 = -1.28$.

b. Area = $P(z < -1.04)$ = .15

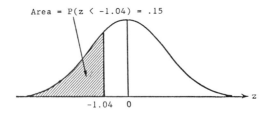

Since $P(z < z_0)$ = .15 is required in the lower tail, there must be .5 - .15 = .35 between z_0 (< 0) and 0. .35 is found in Table 4, in row 1.0, column .04. Thus, $-z_0$ = 1.0 + .04 = 1.04 => $z_0 = -1.04$.

c. Area = P(z < -0.52) = .30

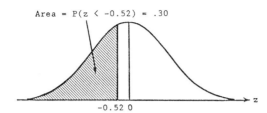

Area = P(z < -0.52) = .30

Since P(z < z_0) = .30 is required in the lower tail, there must be
.5 - .30 = .20 between z_0 (< 0) and 0. .20 is found in Table 4 to
be closer to .1985 in row 0.5, column .02. Thus,
$-z_0$ = 0.5 + .02 = 0.52 => z_0 = -0.52.

d. Area = P(z < 0) = .5

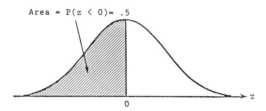

Area = P(z < 0)= .5

Since the normal distribution is symmetric about zero, .5 is below
zero and .5 is above. Thus, z_0 = 0.

6.9 Let x = advertising revenue of a weekly professional newsletter. The
     random variable x is normally distributed with μ = \$7,800 and
     σ = \$620.

a.

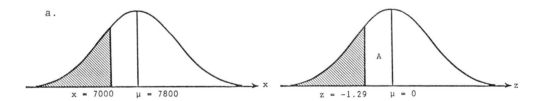

The probability we are interested in is the shaded portion of the
graphs above. To find this proportion, we need to find this
z-value for x = 7000.

$$z = \frac{x - \mu}{\sigma} = \frac{7000 - 7800}{620} = -1.29$$

The area to the left of x = 7000 is the same as the area to the
left of z = -1.29. Because of symmetry, this is the same as the
area to the right of z = 1.29. From Table 4, we get

$$P(x < 7000) = P(z < -1.29) = P(z > 1.29)$$
$$= .5 - A = .5 - .4015 = .0985$$

b.

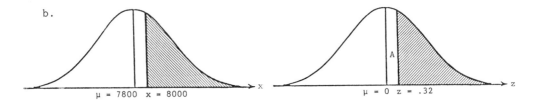

$\mu = 7800 \quad x = 8000$ $\mu = 0 \quad z = .32$

The probability we are interested in is the shaded portion of the graphs above. To find this proportion, we need to find this z-value for x = 8000.

$$z = \frac{x - \mu}{\sigma} = \frac{8000 - 7800}{620} = .32$$

The area to the right of x = 8000 is the same as the area to the right of z = .32. From Table 4, we get

$$P(x > 8000) = P(z > .32) = .5 - A = .5 - .1255 = .3745$$

c.

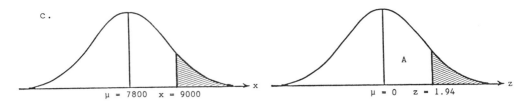

$\mu = 7800 \quad x = 9000$ $\mu = 0 \quad z = 1.94$

The probability we are interested in is the shaded portion of the graphs above. To find this proportion, we need to find this z-value for x = 9000.

$$z = \frac{x - \mu}{\sigma} = \frac{9000 - 7800}{620} = 1.94$$

The area to the right of x = 9000 is the same as the area to the right of z = 1.94. From Table 4, we get

$$P(x > 9000) = P(z > 1.94) = .5 - A = .5 - .4738 = .0262$$

6.11   Let x = current returns on a class of municipal tax-free bonds. The random variable x is normally distributed with $\mu = 9\%$ and $\sigma = .4\%$.

a.

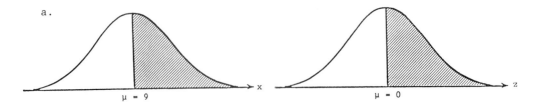

$\mu = 9$ $\mu = 0$

The probability we are interested in is the shaded portion of the graphs above. To find this proportion, we need to find this z-value for x = 9.

$$z = \frac{x - \mu}{\sigma} = \frac{9 - 9}{.4} = 0$$

Thus, $P(x > 9) = P(z > 0) = .5$.

b.

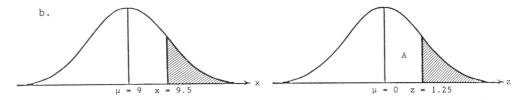

The probability we are interested in is the shaded portion of the graphs above. To find this proportion, we need to find this z-value for x = 9.5.

$$z = \frac{x - \mu}{\sigma} = \frac{9.5 - 9}{.4} = 1.25$$

The area to the right of x = 9.5 is the same as the area to the right of z = 1.25. Using Table 4 of Appendix E, we get:

$$P(x > 9.5) = P(z > 1.25) = .5 - A = .5 - .3944 = .1056$$

c.

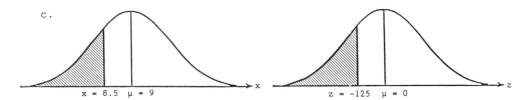

The probability we are interested in is the shaded portion of the graphs above. To find this proportion, we need to find this z-value for x = 8.5.

$$z = \frac{x - \mu}{\sigma} = \frac{8.5 - 9}{.4} = -1.25$$

The area to the left of x = 8.5 is the same as the area to the left of z = -1.25. Because of symmetry, this is the same as the area to the right of z = 1.25.

$$P(x < 8.5) = P(z < -1.25) = P(z > 1.25) = .1056$$
$$\text{(Refer to part (b).)}$$

6.13 Let x = monthly CB sales in the late 1970's. The random variable x is approximately normally distributed with $\mu = 40$ and $\sigma = 10$.

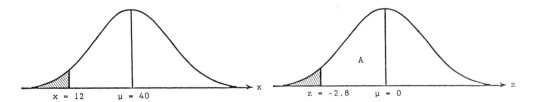

We want to find P(x < 12). This is seen in the shaded portion of
the graphs above. To find this proportion, we need to find the
z-value for x = 12.

$$z = \frac{x - \mu}{\sigma} = \frac{12 - 40}{10} = -2.8$$

The area to the left of x = 12 is the same as the area to the left
of z = -2.8. Because of symmetry, this is the same as the area to
the right of z = 2.8. From Table 4, we get

P(x < 12) = P(z < -2.8) = P(z > 2.8) = .5 - A = .5 - .4974
= .0026

b. If the distribution of 1983 monthly CB sales is the same as the
distribution of monthly CB sales in the 1970's, then the observed
number of sales (12) is a rare event since, from part (a),
P(x < 12) = .0026. Such a small probability leads us to believe
that the distribution of 1983 CB sales is not the same as that in
the 1970's. A distribution with a mean less than 40 or standard
deviation greater than 10 of both would yield a more reasonable
probability for the observed event.

6.15 Let x = bid received on a 110-mile highway construction project in
millions of dollars. The random variable x is normally distributed
with μ = 290 and σ = 40.

a.

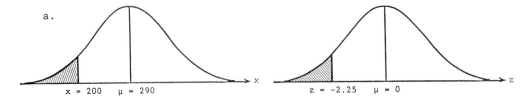

We want to find the P(x ≤ 200). This proportion is shown in the
shaded portion of the graph above. First, we must find the
z-value for x = 200.

$$z = \frac{x - \mu}{\sigma} = \frac{200 - 290}{40} = -2.25$$

The area to the left of x = 200 is the same as the area to the
left of z = -2.25. By symmetry, this is the same as the area to
the right of z = 2.25. From Table 4, we get

$$P(x < 200) = P(z < -2.25) = .5 - .4878 = .0122$$

b.

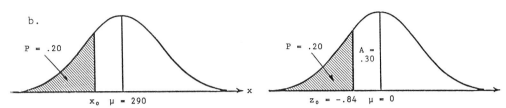

We want to find the value of x_0 such that $P(x < x_0) = .20$. First,
we find z_0, the z-value corresponding to x_0. This would be the
z-score from Table 4 in Appendix E associated with the area
A = .5000 - .2000 = .3000, z_0 = -0.84 (z_0 is negative since it is
to the left of the mean).

To compute x_0,

$$\begin{aligned}
x_0 &= \mu + z_0(\sigma) \\
&= 290 + (-0.84)(40) \\
&= 256.4
\end{aligned}$$

Therefore, 20% of the bids will fall below $256.4 million.

6.17   From Exercise 6.16, x = the length of time a caller is on hold in
minutes. The random variable x is normally distributed with μ = 3.1
and σ = .9.

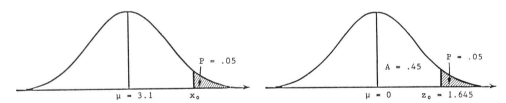

We want to find the value of x_0, such that $P(x > x_0) = .05$. First, we
find z_0, the z-value corresponding to x_0. This would be the value of
z from Table 4 associated with the area A = .5000 - .05 = .4500, which
is z_0 = 1.645.

To compute x_0,

$$\begin{aligned}
x_0 &= \mu + z_0(\sigma) \\
&= 3.1 + 1.645(.9) \\
&= 4.58
\end{aligned}$$

6.19 The normal distribution provides a good approximation to the binomial distribution if both $\mu - 2\sigma = np - 2\sqrt{npq}$ and $\mu + 2\sigma = np + 2\sqrt{npq}$ lie between 0 and n.

a. When n = 25 and p = .30,

$\mu \pm 2\sigma \Rightarrow np \pm 2\sqrt{npq} \Rightarrow 25(.30) \pm 2\sqrt{25(.30)(1 - .30)}$
$\Rightarrow 7.5 \pm 2\sqrt{5.25}$
$\Rightarrow 7.5 \pm 4.5826$
$\Rightarrow (2.9174, 12.0826)$

Since both $\mu - 2\sigma = 2.9174$ and $\mu + 2\sigma = 12.0826$ lie between 0 and 25, the normal distribution will give a good approximation.

b. When n = 3 and p = .01,

$\mu \pm 2\sigma \Rightarrow np \pm 2\sqrt{npq} \Rightarrow 3(.01) \pm 2\sqrt{3(.01)(1 - .01)}$
$\Rightarrow .03 \pm 2\sqrt{.0297}$
$\Rightarrow .03 \pm .3447$
$\Rightarrow (-0.3147, 0.3747)$

Since $\mu - 2\sigma = -0.3147$ does not lie between 0 and 3, the normal distribution will not give a good approximation.

c. When n = 100 and p = .97,

$\mu \pm 2\sigma \Rightarrow np \pm 2\sqrt{npq} \Rightarrow 100(.97) \pm 2\sqrt{100(.97)(1 - .97)}$
$\Rightarrow 97 \pm 2\sqrt{2.91}$
$\Rightarrow 97 \pm 3.4117$
$\Rightarrow (93.5883, 100.4117)$

Since $\mu + 2\sigma = 100.4117$ does not lie between 0 and 100, the normal distribution will not give a good approximation.

d. When n = 15 and p = .45,

$\mu \pm 2\sigma \Rightarrow np \pm 2\sqrt{npq} \Rightarrow 15(.45) \pm 2\sqrt{15(.45)(1 - .45)}$
$\Rightarrow 6.75 \pm 2\sqrt{3.7125}$
$\Rightarrow 6.75 \pm 3.8536$
$\Rightarrow (2.8964, 10.6036)$

Since both $\mu - 2\sigma = 2.8964$ and $\mu + 2\sigma = 10.6036$ lie between 0 and 15, the normal distribution will give a good approximation.

6.21 The random variable x is a binomial random variable with n = 20 and p = .6.

a. $P(x > 13) = 1 - P(x \leq 13) = 1 - .7500 = .2500$

b.

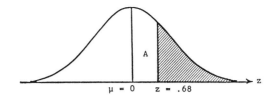

To find the approximate probability with the normal approximation for $P(x > 13) = P(x \geq 14)$,

$$z = \frac{(a - .5) - np}{\sqrt{npq}} = \frac{(14 - .5) - 20(.6)}{\sqrt{20(.6)(1 - .6)}}$$

$$= \frac{13.5 - 12}{2.19} = .68$$

$P(x > 13) \approx P(z > .68) = .5 - A = .5 - .2517 = .2483.$

(Using Table 4 of Appendix E)

6.23   a.   Let x = the number of systems analysts that are women in the sample of 20. The random variable x is a binomial random variable with n = 20 and p = .30.

To find the approximate probability with the normal distribution for $P(x > 10) = P(x \geq 11)$,

$$z = \frac{(a - .5) - np}{\sqrt{npq}} = \frac{(11 - .5) - 20(.30)}{\sqrt{20(.30)(1 - .30)}}$$

$$= \frac{10.5 - 6}{2.05} = 2.20$$

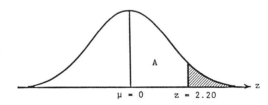

$P(x > 10) \approx P(z > 2.20) = .5 - A = .5 - .4861 = .0139$

(Using Table 4 of Appendix E)

b.   To find the approximate probability with the normal distribution for $P(x \leq 5)$,

$$z = \frac{(a + .5) - np}{\sqrt{npq}} = \frac{(5 + .5) - 20(.3)}{\sqrt{20(.3)(1 - .3)}}$$

$$= \frac{5.5 - 6}{2.05} = -.24$$

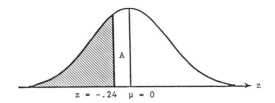

$$P(x \leq 5) \approx P(z \leq -.24) = .5 - A = .5 - .0948 = .4052$$

(Using Table 4 of Appendix E)

c. Using Table 1 in Appendix E,

$$P(x > 10) = 1 - P(x \leq 10) = 1 - .9829 = .0171$$

$$P(x \leq 5) = .4164$$

The answers in parts (a) and (b) are slightly off, but they do provide good approximations to the probabilities.

Note: $\mu \pm 2\sigma \Rightarrow np \pm 2\sqrt{npq} \Rightarrow 20(.3) \pm 2\sqrt{20(.3)(1 - .3)}$
$\Rightarrow 6 \pm 2\sqrt{4.2}$
$\Rightarrow 6 \pm 4.099$
$\Rightarrow (1.901, 10.099)$

Since $\mu - 2\sigma = 1.901$ and $\mu + 2\sigma = 10.099$ both lie between 0 and 20, the normal distribution will provide a good approximation to this binomial distribution.

6.25 The random variable x is a binomial random variable with n = 200 and p = .08.

$\mu \pm 2\sigma \Rightarrow np \pm 2\sqrt{npq} \Rightarrow 200(.08) \pm 2\sqrt{200(.08)(1 - .08)}$
$\Rightarrow 16 \pm 2\sqrt{14.72}$
$\Rightarrow 16 \pm 7.673$
$\Rightarrow (8.327, 23.673)$

Since $\mu - 2\sigma = 8.3267$ and $\mu + 2\sigma = 23.6733$ lie between 0 and 200, the normal distribution will give a good approximation for this binomial distribution.

6% of 200 circuits = .06(200) = 12

We want to find the approximate probability that the lot will be rejected (more than 6% of the circuits are defective):

$$P(x > 12) = P(x \geq 13)$$

$$z = \frac{(a - .5) - np}{\sqrt{npq}} = \frac{(13 - .5) - 200(.08)}{\sqrt{200(.08)(1 - .08)}}$$

$$= \frac{12.5 - 16}{3.837} = -.91$$

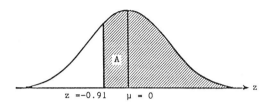

z = -0.91   μ = 0

Using Table 4 in Appendix E,

$$P(x > 12) \approx P(x \geq 13) \approx P(z \geq -.91) = .5 + A = .5 + .3186 = .8186$$

6.27   a.   When a = 2 and b = 10,

$$\mu = \frac{a + b}{2} = \frac{2 + 10}{2} = 6$$

$$\sigma = \frac{(b - a)}{\sqrt{12}} = \frac{(10 - 2)}{\sqrt{12}} = 2.31$$

The height of the rectangle is $\dfrac{1}{b - a} = \dfrac{1}{10 - 2} = \dfrac{1}{8}$

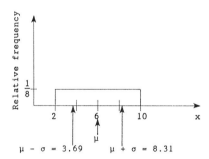

b.   When a = -5 and b = 5,

$$\mu = \frac{a + b}{2} = \frac{-5 + 5}{2} = 0$$

$$\sigma = \frac{(b - a)}{\sqrt{12}} = \frac{5 - (-5)}{\sqrt{12}} = 2.89$$

The height of the rectangle is $\dfrac{1}{b - a} = \dfrac{1}{5 - (-5)} = \dfrac{1}{10}$

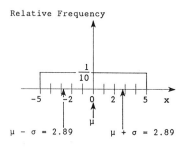

Relative Frequency

$\mu - \sigma = 2.89$ $\mu + \sigma = 2.89$

c. When a = 0 and b = 1,

$$\mu = \frac{a + b}{2} = \frac{0 + 1}{2} = \frac{1}{2} = .5$$

$$\sigma = \frac{(b - a)}{\sqrt{12}} = \frac{(1 - 0)}{\sqrt{12}} = .29$$

The height of the rectangle is $\dfrac{1}{b - a} = \dfrac{1}{1 - 0} = 1$

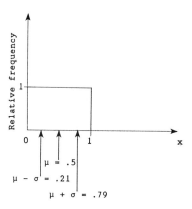

Relative frequency

$\mu = .5$
$\mu - \sigma = .21$
$\mu + \sigma = .79$

d. When a = 60 and b = 75,

$$\mu = \frac{a + b}{2} = \frac{60 + 75}{2} = 67.5$$

$$\sigma = \frac{(b - a)}{\sqrt{12}} = \frac{75 - 60}{\sqrt{12}} = 4.33$$

The height of the rectangle is $\dfrac{1}{b - a} = \dfrac{1}{75 - 60} = \dfrac{1}{15}$

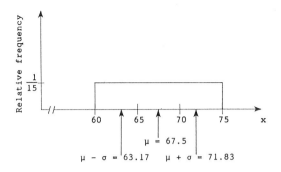

6.29 a. When x is uniformly distributed with a = 100 and b = 200,

$$\mu = \frac{a + b}{2} = \frac{100 + 200}{2} = 150$$

$$\sigma = \frac{b - a}{\sqrt{12}} = \frac{200 - 100}{\sqrt{12}} = 28.87$$

b. $\mu \pm 2\sigma \Rightarrow 150 \pm 2(28.87)$
$\Rightarrow 150 \pm 57.74$
$\Rightarrow (92.26, 207.74)$

The height of the rectangle is $\dfrac{1}{b - a} = \dfrac{1}{200 - 100} = \dfrac{1}{100} = .01$

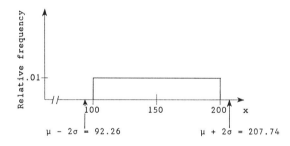

c. $P(\mu - 2\sigma \leq x \leq \mu + 2\sigma) = P(92.26 \leq x \leq 207.74) = 1$

According to the Empirical Rule, the probability should be close to .95.

Using Tchebyscheff's Theorem, we would expect the probability to be at least $1 - \dfrac{1}{2^2} = .75$.

Therefore, the probability compares well with both the Empirical Rule and Tchebyscheff's Theorem.

6.31 a. When x is uniformly distributed with a = .5 and b = 2.25,

$$\mu = \frac{a + b}{2} = \frac{.5 + 2.25}{2} = 1.375$$

$$\sigma = \frac{b - a}{\sqrt{12}} = \frac{2.25 - .5}{\sqrt{12}} = .5052$$

$$\sigma^2 = (.5052)^2 = .2552$$

b. $\mu \pm 2\sigma \Rightarrow 1.375 \pm 2(.51)$
$\Rightarrow 1.375 \pm 1.02$
$\Rightarrow (.355, 2.395)$

The height of the rectangle is $\dfrac{1}{b - a} = \dfrac{1}{2.25 - .5} = \dfrac{1}{1.75} = .57$

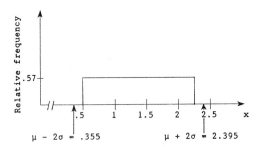

$P(\mu - 2\sigma < x < \mu + 2\sigma) = P(.355 < x < 2.395) = 1$

According to the Tchebyscheff's Theorem, we would expect the probability to be at least $1 - \dfrac{1}{2^2} = .75$. This compares very well with our answer.

c. $P(x < 1) = \dfrac{c - a}{b - a} = \dfrac{1 - .5}{2.25 - .5} = \dfrac{.5}{1.75} = .286$

6.33 Using Table 2 in Appendix E and interpolation or a calculator:

a. $P(x > 3) = e^{-c/\beta} = e^{-3/7} = .6514$

b. $P(x \leq 10) = 1 - e^{-c/\beta} = 1 - e^{-10/7} = 1 - .2397 = .7603$

c. $P(4 < x < 12) = P(x > 4) - P(x > 12)$

$$= e^{-4/7} - e^{-12/7}$$

$$= .5647 - .1801$$

$$= .3846$$

d. $P(x \geq 5.5) = e^{-c/\beta} = e^{-5.5/7} = .4558$

e. $P(x < 7) = 1 - e^{-c/\beta} = 1 - e^{-7/7} = 1 - .367879 = .6321$

6.35 a. $P(x > 2) = e^{-c/\beta} = e^{-2/.5} = .018316$ (using Table 2 in Appendix E)

 b $P(x \leq .75) = 1 - e^{-c/\beta} = 1 - e^{-.75/.5} = 1 - e^{-1.15} = 1 - .223130$
$$= .776870$$

 (using Table 2 in Appendix E)

 c. $\mu = \beta = .5, \sigma = \beta = .5$

6.37 Let x = the time between breakdowns of a particular electrical generator. The random variable x can be approximated by an exponential distribution with $\mu = \beta = 10$.

 a. $\sigma = \beta = 10$

 b. $P(x \leq 14) = 1 - e^{-c/\beta} = 1 - e^{-14/10} = 1 - .246597 = .753403$

 (using Table 2 in Appendix E)

 c. $P(x > 20) = e^{-c/\beta} = e^{-20/10} = e^{-2} = .135335$

 (using Table 2 in Appendix E)

6.39 $P(x \geq 15) = e^{-c/\beta} = e^{-15/4} = e^{-3.75} = .023518$

 (using Table 2 in Appendix E)

 Since the probability of this occurring is quite small but it did occur, this does suggest the mean time between major customer complaints may have increased.

6.41 The random variable x has a normal distribution with $\mu = 6$ and $\sigma = 50$.

 a.

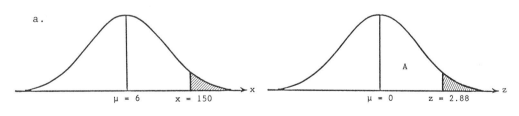

$$z = \frac{x - \mu}{\sigma} = \frac{150 - 6}{50} = 2.88$$

Using Table 4 in Appendix E,

$$P(x > 150) = P(z > 2.88) = .5 - A = .5 - .4980 = .0020$$

b.

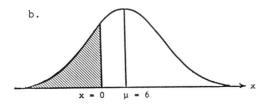 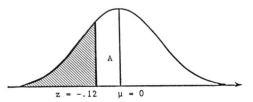

$$z = \frac{x - \mu}{\sigma} = \frac{0 - 6}{50} = -.12$$

Using Table 4 in Appendix E,

$$P(x < 0) = P(z < -.12) = .5 - A = .5 - .0478 = .4522$$

6.43   Let x = time a passenger at concourse B must wait for a monorail car. The random variable has a uniform distribution with a = 0 and b = 10.

a. $\mu = \dfrac{a + b}{2} = \dfrac{0 + 10}{2} = 5$

$\sigma^2 = \left(\dfrac{b - a}{\sqrt{12}}\right)^2 = \left(\dfrac{10 - 0}{\sqrt{12}}\right)^2 = 8.33$

b.   Since it will take 1 minute to get to concourse A, we need to find the probability that the passenger waits for less than 3 minutes for the next car.

$$P(x < 3) = \frac{c - a}{b - a} = \frac{3 - 0}{10 - 0} = .3$$

(We are assuming x is the time a passenger at concourse B must wait for a monorail car going from B to A.)

6.45   Let x = the life of a certain steel-belted radial tire. The random variable x is normally distributed with μ = 60,000 and σ = 2500.

a.

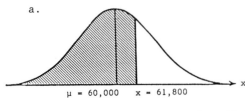 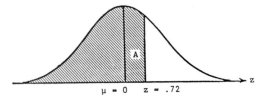

$$z = \frac{x - \mu}{\sigma} = \frac{61,800 - 60,000}{2,500} = .72$$

Using Table 4 in Appendix E,

$$P(x \le 61{,}800) = P(z < .72) = .5 + A = .5 + .2642 = .7642$$

b.

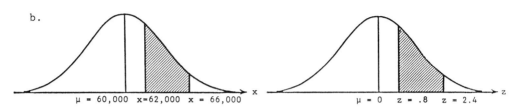

$$z = \frac{x - \mu}{\sigma} = \frac{62{,}000 - 60{,}000}{2{,}500} = .8$$

$$z = \frac{x - \mu}{\sigma} = \frac{66{,}000 - 60{,}000}{2{,}500} = 2.4$$

Using Table 4 in Appendix E,

$$
\begin{aligned}
P(62{,}000 < x < 66{,}000) &= P(.8 < z < 2.4) \\
&= P(0 < z < 2.4) - P(0 < z < .8) \\
&= .4918 - .2881 \\
&= .2037
\end{aligned}
$$

c.

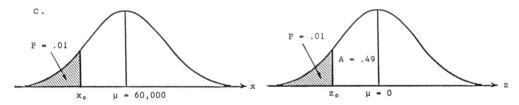

We want to find the value of x_0 such that $P(x < x_0) = .01$. First, we find z_0, the z-value corresponding to x_0. This would be the z-score from Table 4 in Appendix E associated with the area $A = .5000 - .0100 = .4900$, $z_0 = -2.33$ (z_0 is negative since it is to the left of the mean).

To compute x_0,

$$
\begin{aligned}
x_0 &= \mu + z_0\sigma \\
&= 60{,}000 + (-2.33)(2{,}500) \\
&= 54{,}175
\end{aligned}
$$

6.47   Let x = weekly sales of extra large eggs. The random variable x has a normal distribution with $\mu = 743$ and $\sigma = 254$.

a.

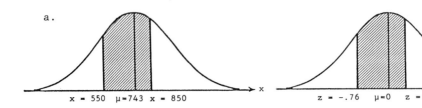

$$z = \frac{x - \mu}{\sigma} = \frac{550 - 743}{254} = -.76$$

$$z = \frac{x - \mu}{\sigma} = \frac{850 - 743}{254} = .42$$

Using Table 4 in Appendix E,

$$
\begin{aligned}
P(550 < x < 850) &= P(-.76 < z < .42) \\
&= P(-.76 < z < 0) + P(0 < z < .42) \\
&= P(0 < z < .76) + P(0 < z < .42) \\
&\qquad\qquad\qquad\qquad \text{(due to symmetry)} \\
&= .2764 + .1628 \\
&= .4392
\end{aligned}
$$

b.

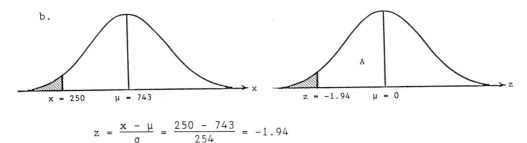

$$z = \frac{x - \mu}{\sigma} = \frac{250 - 743}{254} = -1.94$$

Using Table 4 in Appendix E,

$$P(x < 250) = P(z < -1.94) = .5 - A = .5 - .4738 = .0262$$

c.

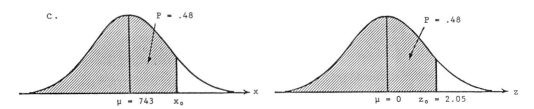

We want to find the value of x_0 such that $P(x < x_0) = .98$. First, we find z_0, the z-value corresponding to x_0. This would be the z-score from Table 4 in Appendix E associated with the area $P = .9800 - .5000 = .4800$, $z_0 = 2.05$.

To compute x_0,

$$x_0 = \mu + z_0(\sigma)$$
$$= 743 + (2.05)(254)$$
$$= 1263.7$$

Since we cannot stock .7 of a carton of eggs, the manager should stock 1264 cartons of eggs.

6.49 Let x = the number of push-button terminal switches demanded daily. The random variable x has a normal distribution with $\mu = 200$ and $\sigma = 50$.

a.

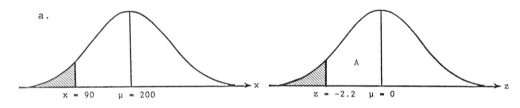

$$z = \frac{x - \mu}{\sigma} = \frac{90 - 200}{50} = -2.2$$

Using Table 4 in Appendix E,

$$P(x < 90) = P(z < -2.2) = .5 - A = .5 - .4861 = .0139$$

b.

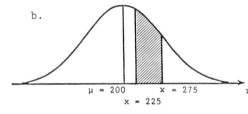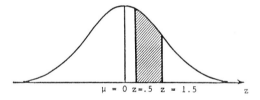

$$z = \frac{x - \mu}{\sigma} = \frac{225 - 200}{50} = .5$$

$$z = \frac{x - \mu}{\sigma} = \frac{275 - 200}{50} = 1.5$$

Using Table 4 in Appendix E,

$$P(225 < x < 275) = P(.5 < z < 1.5)$$
$$= P(0 < z < 1.5) - P(0 < z < .5)$$
$$= .4332 - .1915$$
$$= .2417$$

c.

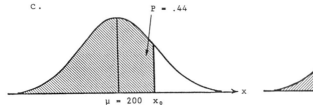 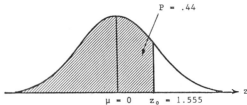

We want to find the value of x_0 such that $P(x < x_0) = .94$. First, we find z_0, the z-value corresponding to x_0. This would be the z-score from Table 4 in Appendix E associated with the area $P = .9400 - .5000 = .4400$, $z_0 = 1.555$.

To compute x_0,

$$x_0 = \mu + z_0(\sigma)$$
$$= 200 + (1.555)(50)$$
$$= 277.75$$

Since we cannot produce .75 of a switch, we should produce 278 switches per day.

6.51   a.   The random variable x is a binomial random variable with n = 2,052 and p = .60.

$$\mu \pm 2\sigma \Rightarrow np \pm 2\sqrt{npq} \Rightarrow 2,052(.60) \pm 2\sqrt{2,052(.60)(1 - .60)}$$
$$\Rightarrow 1231.2 \pm 2\sqrt{492.48}$$
$$\Rightarrow 1231.2 \pm 44.3839$$
$$\Rightarrow (1,186.8161, 1,275.5839)$$

Since both $\mu - 2\sigma = 1,186.8161$ and $\mu + 2\sigma = 1,275.5839$ lie between 0 and 2,052, the normal distribution will give a good approximation for this binomial distribution.

We want to find the approximate probability that x is greater than 1300, $P(x > 1300) = P(x \geq 1301)$:

$$z = \frac{(a - .5) - np}{\sqrt{npq}} = \frac{(1301 - .5) - 2052(.60)}{\sqrt{2052(.60)(1 - .60)}}$$
$$= \frac{1300.5 - 1231.2}{22.19} = 3.12$$

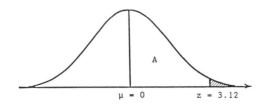

CHAPTER 6

Using Table 4 in Appendix E,

$$P(x > 1300) = P(x \geq 1301) \approx P(z \geq 3.12) = .5 - A \approx .5 - .5 = 0$$

b. Since the probability of more than 1300 adults in the survey believing the tax is unfair is approximately zero, it looks like the percentage of adults that believe the tax is unfair is greater than 60%.

6.53 Let x = the miles per gallon under "ideal" conditions for all Dodge Aries-K wagons. The random variable x is approximately normal with $\mu = 28$ and $\sigma = 2$.

a.

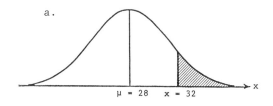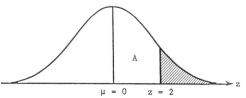

$$z = \frac{x - \mu}{\sigma} = \frac{32 - 28}{2} = 2$$

Using Table 4 in Appendix E,

$$P(x \geq 32) = P(z \geq 2) = .5 - A = .5 - .4772 = .0228$$

b.

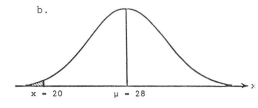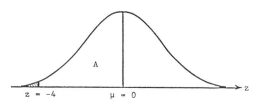

$$z = \frac{x - \mu}{\sigma} = \frac{20 - 28}{2} = -4$$

$$P(x < 20) = P(z < -4) = .5 - A \approx .5 - .5 = 0$$

c.

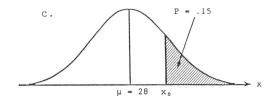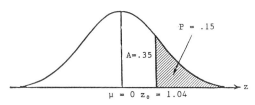

We want to find the value of x_0 such that $P(x > x_0) = .15$. First, we find z_0, the z-value corresponding to x_0. This would be the

z-score from Table 4 in Appendix E associated with the area
A = .5000 − .1500 = .3500, z_0 = 1.04.

To compute x_0,

$$x_0 = \mu + z_0(\sigma)$$
$$= 28 + 1.04(2)$$
$$= 30.08$$

d. If the true mean is 28 mpg, we found in part (b) that the
    probability that a Dodge Aries-K wagon tested under "ideal"
    conditions will obtain less than 20 mpg is approximately zero.
    Therefore, if this occurs, it is very likely that the EPA
    estimated mpg figure of 28 is too high.

CASE STUDIES

6.1   a.

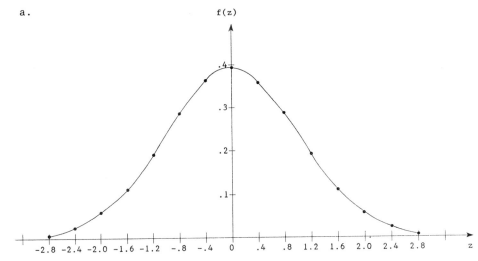

b. To graph the normal curve with μ = 10 and σ = 2, we need to find
    the x values that correspond with the z values given in the table
    in part (a).

$$z = \mu = 0, \ x = \mu = 10, \ f(x) = .3989$$

$$z = .4, \ x = 10.8, \ f(x) = .3683$$

$$z = .8, \ .8 = \frac{x - 10}{2} \Rightarrow x = 11.6, \ f(x) = .2897$$

$z = 1.2, \ 1.2 = \dfrac{x - 10}{2} \Rightarrow x = 12.4, \ f(x) = .1942$

$z = 1.6, \ 1.6 = \dfrac{x - 10}{2} \Rightarrow x = 13.2, \ f(x) = .1109$

$z = 2.0, \ 2.0 = \dfrac{x - 10}{2} \Rightarrow x = 14, \ f(x) = .0540$

$z = 2.4, \ 2.4 = \dfrac{x - 10}{2} \Rightarrow x = 14.8, \ f(x) = .0224$

$z = 2.8, \ 2.8 = \dfrac{x - 10}{2} \Rightarrow x = 15.6, \ f(x) = .0079$

$z = -.4, \ -.4 = \dfrac{x - 10}{2} \Rightarrow x = 9.2, \ f(x) = .3683$

$z = -.8, \ -.8 = \dfrac{x - 10}{2} \Rightarrow x = 8.4, \ f(x) = .2897$

$z = -1.2, \ -1.2 = \dfrac{x - 10}{2} \Rightarrow x = 7.6, \ f(x) = .1942$

$z = -1.6, \ -1.6 = \dfrac{x - 10}{2} \Rightarrow x = 6.8, \ f(x) = .1109$

$z = -2.0, \ -2.0 = \dfrac{x - 10}{2} \Rightarrow x = 6.0, \ f(x) = .0540$

$z = -2.4, \ -2.4 = \dfrac{x - 10}{2} \Rightarrow x = 5.2, \ f(x) = .0224$

$z = -2.8, \ -2.8 = \dfrac{x - 10}{2} \Rightarrow x = 4.4, \ f(x) = .0079$

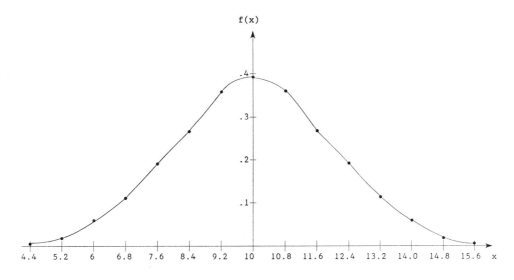

To graph the normal curve with $\mu = 10$ and $\sigma = 4$, we need to find the x values that correspond with the z values given in the table in part (a).

$z = \mu = 0$, $x = \mu = 10$, $f(x) = .3989$

$z = .4$, $.4 = \dfrac{x - 10}{4}$ => $x = 11.6$, $f(x) = .3683$

$z = .8$, $.8 = \dfrac{x - 10}{4}$ => $x = 13.2$, $f(x) = .2897$

$z = 1.2$, $1.2 = \dfrac{x - 10}{4}$ => $x = 14.8$, $f(x) = .1942$

$z = 1.6$, $1.6 = \dfrac{x - 10}{4}$ => $x = 16.4$, $f(x) = .1109$

$z = 2.0$, $2.0 = \dfrac{x - 10}{4}$ => $x = 18$, $f(x) = .0540$

$z = 2.4$, $2.4 = \dfrac{x - 10}{4}$ => $x = 19.6$, $f(x) = .0224$

$z = 2.8$, $2.8 = \dfrac{x - 10}{4}$ => $x = 21.2$, $f(x) = .0079$

$z = -.4$, $-.4 = \dfrac{x - 10}{4}$ => $x = 8.4$, $f(x) = .3683$

$z = -.8$, $-.8 = \dfrac{x - 10}{4}$ => $x = 6.8$, $f(x) = .2897$

$z = -1.2$, $-1.2 = \dfrac{x - 10}{4}$ => $x = 5.2$, $f(x) = .1942$

$z = -1.6$, $-1.6 = \dfrac{x - 10}{4}$ => $x = 3.6$, $f(x) = .1109$

$z = -2.0$, $-2.0 = \dfrac{x - 10}{4}$ => $x = 2.0$, $f(x) = .0540$

$z = -2.4$, $-2.4 = \dfrac{x - 10}{4}$ => $x = 0.4$, $f(x) = .0224$

$z = -2.8$, $-2.8 = \dfrac{x - 10}{4}$ => $x = -1.2$, $f(x) = .0079$

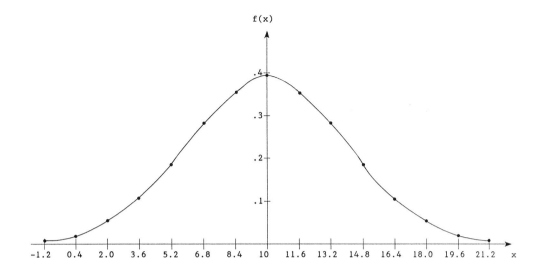

6.3   Let **x** = demand D for a certain type of ceiling fan this year. The
        random variable **x** follows a normal distribution with $\mu = 4,000$ and
        $\sigma = 500$. The break-even point is BE = 3,500 units.

    a. According to Decision Rule A, we should market the new product if
        the chance is better than 50% that the demand D will exceed the
        break-even point BE, i.e., $P(D > BE) > .5$. We know the mean
        demand is $\mu = 4000$, thus, $P(D > 4000) = 1/2$. Also,
        $P(D > 3500) > P(D > 4000) = 1/2$. Therefore, the company should
        market the new fans.

    b.

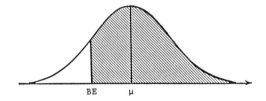

        If $P(D \geq BE) > .5$, then BE must be to the left of μ. Therefore,
        $\mu \geq BE$.

    c. According to Decision Rule B, we should market the product if
        $P(D \geq BE) > p$.

First way of implementing Decision Rule B:

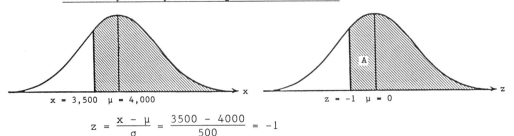

$$x = 3,500 \quad \mu = 4,000 \qquad\qquad z = -1 \quad \mu = 0$$

$$z = \frac{x - \mu}{\sigma} = \frac{3500 - 4000}{500} = -1$$

Using Table 4 in Appendix E:

$$P(D \geq BE) = P(x \geq 3,500) = P(z \geq -1) = .5 + A = .5 + .3413$$
$$= .8413$$

Since $P(D \geq BE) = .8413 > .8$, we should market the ceiling fan.

Second way of implementing Decision Rule B:

Compute $M = BE - z_p\sigma$ where $P(z > z_0) = p$, if $\mu \geq M$, we should market the product.

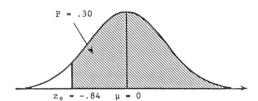

$$P = .30$$

$$z_0 = -.84 \quad \mu = 0$$

We want to find the value of z_0 such that $P(z > z_0) = .8$. This would be the z-score from Table 4 in Appendix E associated with the area $P = .8000 - .5000 = .3000$, $z_0 = -.84$ (z_0 is negative since it is to the left of the mean).

Then $M = BE - z_p\sigma = 3500 - (-.84)(500) = 3920$

Since $\mu = 4000 > M = 3920$, we should market the ceiling fan.

SEVEN   SAMPLING AND SAMPLING DISTRIBUTIONS

7.1   Step 1. The observations have already been numbered from 0001 to 2251 in the listing of the data in Appendix A of the text. This labeling implies that we will obtain random numbers of 4 digits from the table. Therefore, only the first 4 digits of each number are used.

Step 2. Let us begin in row 36, column 5, of Table 5, Appendix E and proceed horizontally to the right across rows until we have selected n = 15 observations. The first element selected is numbered 0402.

Step 3. The next elements to be included in the sample are those numbered 8638(skip), 2988(skip), 9973(skip), 5553(skip), 8485(skip), 2908(skip), 0925, 7965(skip), 7321(skip), 1795, 5634(skip), 9099(skip)... . The random numbers and the associated observations on the ratio of sale price to total appraised values are shown in the table below.

RANDOM NUMBER OBTAINED	RATIO OF SALE PRICE TO TOTAL APPRAISED VALUE FOR CORRESPONDING POPULATION ELEMENT
402	1.32017
925	1.23808
1795	1.33088
2004	1.40498
611	1.19535
2054	2.26176
1805	1.18554
200	1.51943
1858	1.62387
1884	1.91608
230	1.83593
2065	1.23712
1547	1.20752
2056	1.43000
992	1.27009

7.3   Step 1. The observations have already been numbered from 501 to 1000
               in the listing of the data in Appendix D in the text. This
               means we can obtain random numbers of three digits from the
               table (allowing the number 500 to represent 1000). Therefore,
               only the first 3 digits of each number in the table are used.

       Step 2. Let us begin in row 9, column 7 of Table 5, Appendix E, and
               proceed horizontally to the right across rows until we have
               selected n = 10 numbers from 500 to 999 from the table. The
               first element selected is numbered 577.

       Step 3. The next elements to be included in the sample are 843,
               253(skip), 125(skip), 586... . The random numbers and the
               associated observations on the checkout times are shown in the
               following table.

RANDOM NUMBER OBTAINED	CHECKOUT TIME FOR CORRESPONDING POPULATION ELEMENT
577	93
843	10
586	27
569	47
854	15
533	18
539	7
530	65
595	25
623	7
649	71
695	120
882	80
709	40
799	35

7.5   Not all people will respond to this type of survey. For example, if
       someone had strong feelings (either negative or positive) about the
       subject being surveyed, he/she would tend to reply to the poll more
       frequently than someone who either did not care, had no opinion, or
       had no knowledge of what was being surveyed.

7.7   The relative frequency distribution for the sample should be similar
       to that of the population and should produce reliable inferences about
       the population. However, a sample size of more than 20 will produce a
       more reliable frequency distribution.

7.9 a. $\bar{x} = \dfrac{\sum x_i}{5}$ for each of the fifty samples.

The fifty means are:

4.2	3.2	3.0	4.8	4.2
4.2	5.8	3.8	5.6	2.8
4.8	5.0	4.0	3.6	3.0
3.8	4.0	4.0	3.6	5.2
6.8	5.8	4.6	6.4	2.4
6.0	5.2	4.0	7.0	7.0
7.4	5.6	4.6	5.8	6.2
5.6	4.4	4.6	4.0	2.2
4.6	4.4	5.4	6.8	6.0
5.6	3.0	3.0	5.0	5.0

b. Since there are 50 sample means, we shall use a small number of classes to describe the data (6). The class interval width is:

$$\dfrac{\text{Largest mean - smallest mean}}{\text{Number of class intervals}} = \dfrac{7.4 - 2.2}{6} = \dfrac{5.2}{6} = .87 \Rightarrow 1$$

The class intervals, frequencies, and relative frequencies are given in the following table:

CLASS	CLASS INTERVAL	TALLY	CLASS FREQUENCY	CLASS RELATIVE FREQUENCY
1	2.15 – 3.15	⦀⦀ ‖	7	.14
2	3.15 – 4.15	⦀⦀ ⦀⦀	10	.20
3	4.15 – 5.15	⦀⦀ ⦀⦀ ‖‖	14	.28
4	5.15 – 6.15	⦀⦀ ⦀⦀ ‖	12	.24
5	6.15 – 7.15	⦀⦀		6	.12
6	7.15 – 8.15			1	.02
			n = 50	1.00

The relative frequency distribution for the 50 sample means is given as follows.

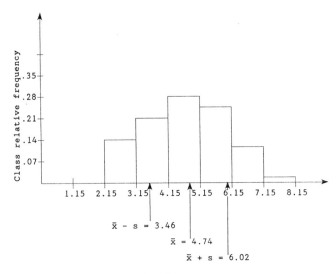

$$\bar{x} - s = 3.46$$

$$\bar{x} = 4.74$$

$$\bar{x} + s = 6.02$$

Sample means

c. $\bar{x} = \dfrac{\sum x}{n} = \dfrac{4.2 + 4.2 + \ldots + 6.0 + 5.0}{50} = \dfrac{237.0}{50} = 4.74$

$s^2 = \dfrac{\sum x^2 - \dfrac{(\sum x)^2}{n}}{n - 1} = \dfrac{1203.08 - \left(\dfrac{237^2}{50}\right)}{49} = 1.627$

$s = \sqrt{s^2} = \sqrt{1.627} = 1.28$

7.11　a.　The parameter of interest is μ, the mean of the ratios of sale price to total appraised value. We would expect this value to be close to 1 if the residential property appraisers are doing a good job by giving an appraisal that is close to the sale price.

　　　b.　The steps for generating 50 random samples of size n = 10 and constructing the approximate sampling distribution will be explained without going through the mechanics and calculations.

　　　　　We will use Table 5 (Appendix E in the text) to generate random numbers. Since our data are labeled from 0001 to 2251, we will obtain random numbers of 4 digits.

　　　　　Choose any arbitrary starting point, for example, row 8, column 3, and proceed horizontally to the right across rows. (We could also proceed horizontally left, vertically up, vertically down, or diagonally). The first random number selected is 0546, which corresponds to observation 546 of the data with a ratio of 1.25639. The next random number is 0797, corresponding to observation 797, which has a ratio of 1.34655. Continue in this manner until 10 observations and their corresponding ratios are selected for sample 1.

Repeat the entire procedure (from choosing an arbitrary starting point) 49 times for a total of 50 samples.

The next step is to calculate the mean ($\bar{x}$) and standard deviation (s) for each of the 50 samples using the formulas:

$$\bar{x} = \frac{\sum x}{n} \quad \text{and} \quad s = \sqrt{\frac{\sum x^2 - \frac{(\sum x)^2}{n}}{n - 1}}$$

Now, use the 50 $\bar{x}$'s obtained and construct a relative frequency distribution as described in Chapter 2 of the text, which would be the approximate sampling distribution of the sample mean $\bar{x}$.

When comparing the relative frequency distribution for $\bar{x}$ with the relative frequency distribution for the population (see Figure 3.8, page 88 of the text), notice that the values of $\bar{x}$ in the figure cluster around the population mean and that the values of the sample means have less variability than the population values shown in Figure 3.8.

7.13 Each random sample is obtained from Table 5 following the method described on page 270 of the text. From the n = 500 checkout times for supermarket B, random samples of size n = 5 are to be chosen. The n = 500 times are labeled 501-1000 under the OBS column. So, from Table 5, we will choose 3-digit, random numbers, allowing the number 500 to represent 1000. The first sample chosen is described below. The other 29 were chosen in a similar manner. Note that these are just 30 of the total C_5^{500} possible samples. ($C_5^{500} = 255 \times 10^{11}$.)

The first random sample is obtained starting (arbitrarily) in row 2, column 3 of Table 5. The following random numbers are obtained and the five corresponding OBS and times are chosen as the random sample. Note that only the first 3 digits of the random number are used and that numbers 0-499 are skipped.

RANDOM NUMBER	OBS	TIME
25595	skip	--
85393	853	25
30995	skip	--
89198	891	10
27982	skip	--
53402	534	12
93965	939	50
34095	skip	--
52666	526	18

Random numbers for each of the 30 samples are given below.

SAMPLE		RANDOM	NUMBERS			SAMPLE		RANDOM	NUMBERS		
1	853	891	534	939	526	16	587	569	533	873	921
2	535	713	570	749	977	17	875	700	706	888	777
3	534	706	906	818	995	18	587	800	961	606	595
4	632	963	919	945	568	19	764	543	627	922	911
5	533	539	530	595	623	20	888	710	729	574	807
6	901	855	916	781	635	21	859	982	523	692	827
7	927	889	841	749	611	22	763	533	644	647	753
8	977	859	744	907	510	23	528	738	731	886	889
9	540	949	715	850	511	24	967	952	578	897	974
10	912	858	902	591	616	25	869	603	885	925	669
11	876	873	587	924	609	26	919	560	827	709	653
12	767	870	796	957	680	27	546	531	627	953	786
13	639	661	754	665	904	28	642	516	641	625	591
14	599	861	579	886	679	29	994	686	552	934	613
15	863	997	555	848	796	30	997	851	963	979	807

RANDOM SAMPLE	ARBITRARY TABLE STARTING POINTS	OBTAINED USING RANDOM NUMBERS	$\bar{x}$
1	Row 2, Col 3	25, 10, 12, 50, 18	23.0
2	4, 7	18, 24, 36, 228, 4	62.0
3	6, 2	12, 40, 57, 110, 70	57.8
4	7, 9	45, 13, 40, 30, 16	28.8
5	10, 3	18, 7, 65, 25, 7	24.4
6	11, 8	30, 40, 50, 110, 6	47.2
7	13, 4	75, 100, 3, 228, 22	85.6
8	15, 9	4, 5, 40, 26, 67	28.4
9	18, 1	27, 100, 350, 30, 13	104.0
10	21, 6	52, 10, 50, 142, 17	54.2
11	24, 2	50, 8, 12, 80, 8	31.6
12	26, 9	103, 30, 8, 10, 85	47.2
13	29, 3	16, 40, 40, 25, 2	24.6
14	33, 7	66, 4, 96, 48, 60	54.8
15	36, 5	70, 10, 73, 45, 8	41.2
16	38, 8	12, 47, 18, 8, 70	31.0
17	42, 6	15, 53, 40, 30, 130	53.6
18	45, 2	12, 50, 23, 165, 25	55.0
19	49, 6	33, 51, 10, 80, 23	39.4
20	53, 7	30, 25, 90, 60, 50	51.0
21	56, 2	5, 13, 65, 50, 100	46.6
22	59, 1	85, 18, 13, 39, 135	58.0
23	62, 6	57, 50, 63, 48, 100	63.6
24	66, 3	38, 25, 20, 7, 60	30.0
25	68, 7	90, 45, 21, 100, 110	73.2
26	72, 6	40, 8, 100, 40, 13	40.2
27	77, 4	43, 124, 10, 80, 35	58.4
28	82, 5	28, 69, 81, 20, 142	68.0
29	88, 8	45, 40, 7, 125, 78	59.0
30	93, 6	10, 35, 13, 50, 50	31.6

a. $\bar{x}$ was calculated for each sample (see above). The relative frequency distribution is constructed as described in Chapter 2 of the text. Note that the class intervals are chosen so that none of the observations fall on the boundaries.

$$\frac{\text{Largest mean } - \text{ smallest mean}}{\text{Number of class intervals}} = \frac{104 - 23}{6} = 13.5 \Rightarrow 15$$

CLASS INTERVAL	TALLY	CLASS FREQUENCY	CLASS RELATIVE FREQUENCY
20-35	~~||||~~ ||||	9	.30
35-50	~~||||~~		6	.20
50-65	~~||||~~ ~~||||~~		11	.37
65-80	||	2	.07
80-95			1	.03
95-110			1	.03
		30	1.00

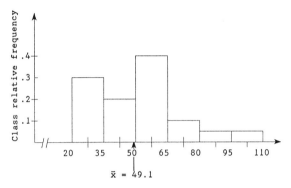

Sample means

b. $\bar{x}$ for the 30 sample means is:

$$\bar{x} = \frac{\sum x}{n} = \frac{23.0 + 62.0 + \ldots + 31.6}{30} = \frac{1473.4}{30} = 49.11$$

c. $s = \sqrt{\dfrac{\sum x^2 - \dfrac{(\sum x)^2}{n}}{n-1}} = \sqrt{\dfrac{82751.6 - \dfrac{(1473.4)^2}{30}}{29}} = 18.94$

7.15   The sampling distribution for the statistic $\bar{x}$, based on a random
sample of $n = 15$ observations, would be generated in this manner:
First, number the observations in the data set from 1 to 1264; select
a random sample of 15 measurements and record $\bar{x}$ for this sample;
return these 15 measurements and repeat the procedure, that is, draw
another random sample of $n = 15$ measurements and record $\bar{x}$. If this
sampling procedure could be repeated an infinite number of times, the

infinite number of values of $\bar{x}$ so obtained could be summarized in a relative frequency distribution, called the "sampling distribution of $\bar{x}$."

7.17 $\mu_{\bar{x}} = \mu$ $\sigma_{\bar{x}} = \dfrac{\sigma}{\sqrt{n}}$

   a. $\mu_{\bar{x}} = 10$ $\sigma_{\bar{x}} = \dfrac{20}{\sqrt{100}} = 2$

   b. $\mu_{\bar{x}} = 20$ $\sigma_{\bar{x}} = \dfrac{10}{\sqrt{100}} = 1$

   c. $\mu_{\bar{x}} = 50$ $\sigma_{\bar{x}} = \dfrac{300}{\sqrt{100}} = 30$

   d. $\mu_{\bar{x}} = 100$ $\sigma_{\bar{x}} = \dfrac{200}{\sqrt{100}} = 20$

7.19 $\mu_{\bar{x}} = \mu = 21$ $\sigma_{\bar{x}} = \dfrac{\sigma}{\sqrt{n}} = \dfrac{6}{\sqrt{50}} = .85$

   a.

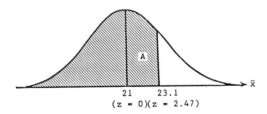

$$21 \qquad 23.1$$
$$(z = 0)(z = 2.47)$$

$$z = \dfrac{\bar{x} - \mu_{\bar{x}}}{\sigma_{\bar{x}}} = \dfrac{231 - 21}{.85} = 2.47$$

$$P(\bar{x} < 23.1) = P(z < 2.47) = .5 + A$$
$$= .5 + .4932 = .9932 \quad \text{(using Table 4 in Appendix E)}$$

b.

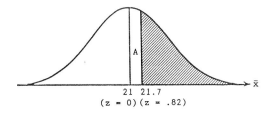

$$z = \frac{\bar{x} - \mu_{\bar{x}}}{\sigma_{\bar{x}}} = \frac{21.7 - 21}{.85} = .82$$

$P(\bar{x} > 21.7) = P(z > .82) = .5 - A$
$\qquad\qquad\qquad = .5 - .2939 = .2061 \quad$ (using Table 4 in Appendix E)

c.

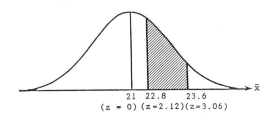

$$z_1 = \frac{\bar{x} - \mu_{\bar{x}}}{\sigma_{\bar{x}}} = \frac{22.8 - 21}{.85} = 2.12 \qquad z_2 = \frac{\bar{x} - \mu_{\bar{x}}}{\sigma_{\bar{x}}} = \frac{23.6 - 21}{.85} = 3.06$$

$P(22.8 < \bar{x} < 23.6) = P(2.12 < z < 3.06) = .4989 - .4830 = .0159$

(using Table 4 in Appendix E)

7.21 a. Although we have no information about the shape of the relative
frequency distribution of the building permits, we can apply the
Central Limit Theorem to conclude that the sampling distribution
of the sample mean building permits, based on 40 observations, is
approximately normally distributed. In addition, the mean, $\mu_{\bar{x}}$,
and the standard deviation, $\sigma_{\bar{x}}$, of the sampling distribution are

$$\mu_{\bar{x}} = \mu = 8000 \quad \text{and} \quad \sigma_{\bar{x}} = \frac{\sigma}{\sqrt{n}} = \frac{1500}{\sqrt{40}} = 237.17$$

b.

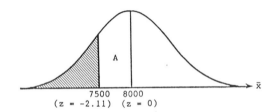

$$z = \frac{\bar{x} - \mu_{\bar{x}}}{\sigma_{\bar{x}}} = \frac{7500 - 8000}{237.17} = -2.11$$

$$P(\bar{x} < 7500) = P(z < -2.11) = .5 - A = .5 - .4826 = .0174$$

(using Table 4 in Appendix E)

c.

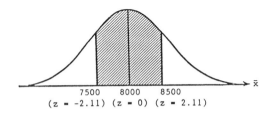

$$z = \frac{\bar{x} - \mu_{\bar{x}}}{\sigma_{\bar{x}}} = \frac{7500 - 8000}{237.17} = -2.11 \qquad z = \frac{\bar{x} - \mu_{\bar{x}}}{\sigma_{\bar{x}}} = \frac{8500 - 8000}{237.17} = 2.11$$

$$P(7500 < \bar{x} < 8500) = P(-2.11 < z < 2.11) = .4826 + .4826$$
$$= .9652$$

(using Table 4 in Appendix E)

7.23 $\mu_{\bar{x}} = \mu = 3.00$ $\sigma_{\bar{x}} = \dfrac{\sigma}{\sqrt{n}} = \dfrac{1.03}{\sqrt{30}} = .188$

Though we do not know the relative frequency distribution of the sampled population, we know by the Central Limit Theorem that the sampling distribution of $\bar{x}$ will be approximately normal.

a.

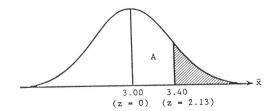

$$z = \frac{\bar{x} - \mu_{\bar{x}}}{\sigma_{\bar{x}}} = \frac{3.40 - 3.00}{.188} = 2.13$$

$$P(\bar{x} > 3.40) = P(z > 2.13) = .5 - A$$
$$= .5 - .4834 = .0166 \quad \text{(using Table 4 in Appendix E)}$$

b. If the population mean is really 3.00, then the probability of getting a sample mean of 3.55 is very small. In part (a), we found $P(\bar{x} > 3.40) = .0166$, thus $P(\bar{x} > 3.55)$ would be even smaller. Therefore, there is strong evidence that μ is really larger than 3.00 under these circumstances.

7.25   a. If the sample size was decreased from n = 50 to n = 20, the sampling distribution of $\bar{x}$ would still be approximately normal by the Central Limit Theorem. The mean would remain the same when n = 20 but the standard deviation of $\bar{x}$ would increase.

$$\mu_{\bar{x}} = \mu = 9.8 \qquad \sigma_{\bar{x}} = \frac{.55}{\sqrt{20}} = .123$$

b. If the sample size was increased from n = 50 to n = 100, the sampling distribution of $\bar{x}$ would still be approximately normal by the Central Limit Theorem. The mean would remain the same when n = 100 but the standard deviation would decrease.

$$\mu_{\bar{x}} = \mu = 9.8 \qquad \sigma_{\bar{x}} = \frac{\sigma}{\sqrt{n}} = \frac{.55}{\sqrt{100}} = .055$$

7.27   Let $\bar{x}$ = mean tar content of the sample. Assuming that the tobacco company's claim is true, $\bar{x}$ is approximately normally distributed by the Central Limit Theorem.

$$\mu_{\bar{x}} = \mu = 3.9 \qquad \sigma_{\bar{x}} = \frac{\sigma}{\sqrt{n}} = \frac{1}{\sqrt{100}} = .1$$

a.

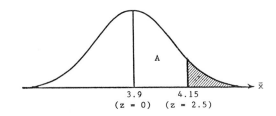

3.9   4.15
(z = 0)   (z = 2.5)

$$z = \frac{\bar{x} - \mu_{\bar{x}}}{\sigma_{\bar{x}}} = \frac{4.15 - 3.9}{.1} = 2.5$$

$$P(\bar{x} > 4.15) = P(z > 2.5) = .5 - A$$
$$= .5 - .4938 = .0062 \quad \text{(using Table 4 in Appendix E)}$$

b. Yes, because either a rare event occurred [$\bar{x} = 4.18$ and $P(\bar{x} > 4.15) = .0062$] or the assumptions on which $P(\bar{x} > 4.15)$ was calculated are in error. The latter explanation is more likely.

c. One explanation is that manufacturing process is not properly adjusted. Another is that the 100 measurements were incorrectly measured. A third is that an extremely rare event occurred.

7.29   a. By the Central Limit Theorem, the sampling distribution of $\bar{x}_{25}$ is approximately normally distributed with mean $\mu_{\bar{x}_{25}} = \mu = 17$ and standard deviation

$$\sigma_{\bar{x}_{25}} = \frac{\sigma}{\sqrt{n}} = \frac{10}{\sqrt{25}} = 2$$

b. Similarly, the sampling distribution of $\bar{x}_{100}$ is approximately normally distributed with mean $\mu_{\bar{x}_{100}} = \mu = 17$ and standard deviation

$$\sigma_{\bar{x}_{100}} = \frac{\sigma}{\sqrt{n}} = \frac{10}{\sqrt{100}} = 1$$

c. $P(15 < \bar{x}_{100} < 19) > P(15 < \bar{x}_{25} < 19)$ because $\sigma_{\bar{x}_{100}} < \sigma_{\bar{x}_{25}}$, which means that the distribution of $\bar{x}_{100}$ is more tightly "bunched" than that of $\bar{x}_{25}$. Thus, more area under the curve (and, therefore, more probability) will be inside this interval under the distribution of $\bar{x}_{100}$ than under that of $\bar{x}_{25}$.

d.

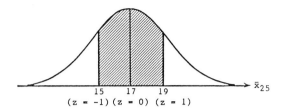

$$z = \frac{\bar{x}_{25} - \mu_{\bar{x}_{25}}}{\sigma_{\bar{x}_{25}}} = \frac{15 - 17}{2} = -1 \qquad z = \frac{\bar{x}_{25} - \mu_{\bar{x}_{25}}}{\sigma_{\bar{x}_{25}}} = \frac{19 - 17}{2} = 1$$

$$P(15 < \bar{x}_{25} < 19) = P(-1 < z < 1) = P(-1 < z < 0) + P(0 < z < 1)$$
$$= .3413 + .3413$$
$$= .6826$$

(using Table 4 in Appendix E)

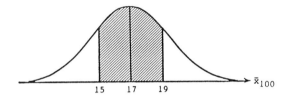

$$z = \frac{\bar{x}_{100} - \mu_{\bar{x}_{100}}}{\sigma_{\bar{x}_{100}}} = \frac{15 - 17}{1} = -2 \qquad z = \frac{\bar{x}_{100} - \mu_{\bar{x}_{100}}}{\sigma_{\bar{x}_{100}}} = \frac{19 - 17}{1} = 2$$

$$P(15 < \bar{x}_{100} < 17) = P(-2 < z < 2) = P(-2 < z < 0) + P(0 < z < 2)$$
$$= .4772 + .4772$$
$$= .9544$$

(using Table 4 in Appendix E)

Note: The $P(15 < \bar{x}_{100} < 17) = .9544 > P(15 < \bar{x}_{25} < 17) = .6826$ as expected.

7.31   Step 1. The observations would already be numbered from 001 to 500. This labeling implies that we will obtain random numbers of 3 digits from the table. Therefore, only the first 3 digits of each number are used.

Step 2. Pick a row and column in Table 5, Appendix E, to start in and decide upon a direction.

Step 3. Record the starting number and continue until n = 10 elements have been selected, ignoring numbers larger than N = 500 and repeats of numbers previously obtained. These numbers can then be matched to the list in order to obtain the names of 10 companies from the list.

7.33 Let $\bar{x}$ = mean job satisfaction ratings of the 27 sampled flextime workers. The random variable $\bar{x}$ is approximately normally distributed by the Central Limit Theorem with

$$\mu_{\bar{x}} = \mu = 35 \qquad \sigma_{\bar{x}} = \frac{\sigma}{\sqrt{n}} = \frac{10}{\sqrt{27}} = 1.9245$$

a.

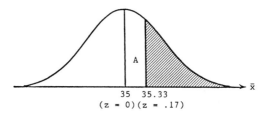

$$z = \frac{\bar{x} - \mu_{\bar{x}}}{\sigma_{\bar{x}}} = \frac{35.33 - 35}{1.9245} = .17$$

$P(\bar{x} \geq 35.33) = P(z > .17) = .5 - A$
$\qquad\qquad\qquad = .5 - .0675 = .4325 \qquad$ (using Table 4 in Appendix E)

b.

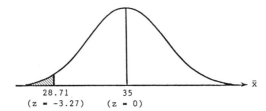

$$z = \frac{\bar{x} - \mu_{\bar{x}}}{\sigma_{\bar{x}}} = \frac{28.71 - 35}{1.9245} = -3.27$$

$P(\bar{x} \leq 28.71) = P(z \leq -3.27) \approx .5 - .5 = 0$

c. A sample mean of $\bar{x}$ = 35.33 does not represent a rare event since $P(\bar{x} \geq 35.33)$ = .4325 (part (a)). A rare event has a very small probability.

d. A sample mean of $\bar{x}$ = 28.71 does represent a rare event since $P(\bar{x} \leq 28.71) \approx 0$ (part (b)). A rare event has a very small probability of occurring which is the case when $\bar{x}$ = 28.71.

e. Since $\bar{x} = 28.71$ is a rare event when $\mu = 35$, the true mean satisfaction rating of workers on a fixed schedule is most likely smaller than 35.

7.35 Let $\bar{x}$ = sample mean amount of alkali in soap. The random variable $\bar{x}$ is approximately normally distributed by the Central Limit Theorem.

$$\mu_{\bar{x}} = \mu = 2\% \qquad \sigma_{\bar{x}} = \frac{\sigma}{\sqrt{n}} = \frac{1\%}{\sqrt{30}} = .1826$$

a. Lower control limit: $\mu - 3\sigma_{\bar{x}} = 2\% - 3(.1826) = 2 - .548 = 1.452\%$

Upper control limit: $\mu + 3\sigma_{\bar{x}} = 2\% + 3(.1826) = 2 + .548 = 2.548\%$

b.

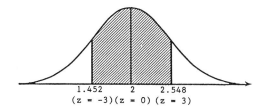

$$1.452 \qquad 2 \qquad 2.548$$
$$(z = -3)(z = 0)(z = 3)$$

$$z = \frac{\bar{x} - \mu_{\bar{x}}}{\sigma_{\bar{x}}} = \frac{1.452 - 2}{.1826} = -3 \qquad z = \frac{\bar{x} - \mu_{\bar{x}}}{\sigma_{\bar{x}}} = \frac{2.548 - 2}{.1826} = 3$$

$$1 - P(\text{Process is in control}) = 1 - P(\mu - 3\sigma_{\bar{x}} < \bar{x} < \mu + 3\sigma_{\bar{x}})$$

$$= 1 - P(1.452 < \bar{x} < 2.548)$$

$$= 1 - P(-3 < z < 3)$$

$$= 1 - [P(-3 < z < 0) + P(0 < z < 3)]$$

$$= 1 - [.4987 + .4987]$$

$$= 1 - .9974$$

$$= .0026$$

7.37 Let $\bar{x}$ = sample mean depreciation time of the copy machines. The random variable $\bar{x}$ is approximately normally distributed by the Central Limit Theorem.

$$\mu_{\bar{x}} = \mu = 45 \qquad \sigma_{\bar{x}} = \frac{\sigma}{\sqrt{n}} = \frac{10}{\sqrt{25}} = 2$$

a.

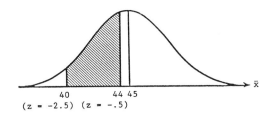

$$z = \frac{\bar{x} - \mu_{\bar{x}}}{\sigma_{\bar{x}}} = \frac{40 - 45}{2} = -2.5 \qquad z = \frac{\bar{x} - \mu_{\bar{x}}}{\sigma_{\bar{x}}} = \frac{44 - 45}{2} = -.5$$

$$\begin{aligned} P(40 < \bar{x} < 44) &= P(-2.5 < z < -.5) \\ &= P(0 < z < 2.5) - P(0 < z < .5) \\ &= .4938 - .1915 = .3023 \end{aligned}$$

b.

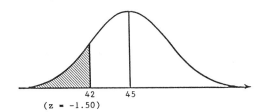

$$z = \frac{\bar{x} - \mu_{\bar{x}}}{\sigma_{\bar{x}}} = \frac{42 - 45}{2} = -1.50$$

$$\begin{aligned} P(\bar{x} < 42) = P(z < -1.50) &= .5 - P(0 < z < 1.50) \\ &= .5 - .4332 = .0668 \end{aligned}$$

c. If the 25 photocopiers were sold during a deep recession, the price might have been below that which would have been charged if they were sold at a time other than a deep recession. Thus, the depreciation time would be reduced. Thus, this sample information could be biased.

7.39 a. Let $\bar{x}$ = sample mean number of sick days used. The random variable $\bar{x}$ is approximately normal by the Central Limit Theorem. If the compensation program is not effective,

$$\mu_{\bar{x}} = \mu = 9.2 \qquad \sigma_{\bar{x}} = \frac{\sigma}{\sqrt{n}} = \frac{1.8}{\sqrt{81}} = .2$$

a.

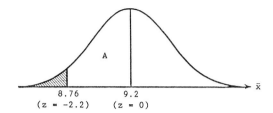

$$z = \frac{\bar{x} - \mu_{\bar{x}}}{\sigma_{\bar{x}}} = \frac{8.76 - 9.2}{.2} = -2.2$$

$P(\bar{x} < 8.76) = P(z < -2.2) = .5 - A = .5 - .4861 = .0139$

b. From part (a), we have $P(\bar{x} < 8.76) = .0139$; thus, it is very unlikely to observe a sample mean of $\bar{x} = 8.76$ or smaller if the population mean is $\mu = 9.2$. Since we actually observed $\bar{x} = 8.76$, the true mean number of sick days used after implementation of the compensation program is unlikely to be 9.2.

CASE STUDIES

7.1 The ABC-TV survey could have produced a biased forecast of the debate "winner" since the responses were taken from people that were willing to pay the $.50 for the phone call. As a result, the responses were probably from those in higher income brackets.

7.3 a. The sample mean $\bar{x}$ is approximately normal by the Central Limit Theorem with

$$\mu_{\bar{x}} = \mu = 26 \qquad \sigma_{\bar{x}} = \frac{\sigma}{\sqrt{n}} = \frac{2.7}{\sqrt{30}} = .493$$

b. Using Rule 1 with $p = .10$ and $\mu = 24$,

LCL $= \mu - p\mu = 24 - .10(24) = 24 - 2.4 = 21.6$
UCL $= \mu + p\mu = 24 + .10(24) = 24 + 2.4 = 26.4$

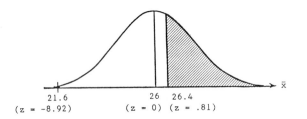

$$z = \frac{\bar{x} - \mu_{\bar{x}}}{\sigma_{\bar{x}}} = \frac{21.6 - 26}{.493} = -8.92 \qquad z = \frac{\bar{x} - \mu_{\bar{x}}}{\sigma_{\bar{x}}} = \frac{26.4 - 26}{.493} = .81$$

$P(\bar{x}$ falls outside the control limits)

$= 1 - P(LCL \leq \bar{x} \leq UCL)$

$= 1 - P(21.6 \leq \bar{x} \leq 26.4)$

$= 1 - P(-8.92 \leq z \leq .81)$

$= 1 - [P(-8.92 \leq z \leq 0) + P(0 \leq z \leq .81)]$

$\approx 1 - [.5 + .2910]$ (using Table 4 in Appendix E)

$= 1 - .7910$

$= .2090$

c.   Using Rule 2 with $\mu = 24$ and $\sigma = 2.7$,

    LCL $= \mu - 2\sigma = 24 - 2(2.7) = 24 - 5.4 = 18.6$
    UCL $= \mu + 2\sigma = 24 + 2(2.7) = 24 + 5.4 = 29.4$

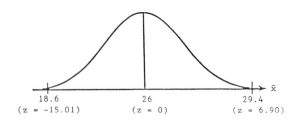

$$z = \frac{\bar{x} - \mu_{\bar{x}}}{\sigma_{\bar{x}}} = \frac{18.6 - 26}{.493} = -15.01 \qquad z = \frac{\bar{x} - \mu_{\bar{x}}}{\sigma_{\bar{x}}} = \frac{29.4 - 26}{.493} = 6.90$$

P($\bar{x}$ falls outside the control limits)

$= 1 - P(\text{LCL} \le \bar{x} \le \text{UCL})$

$= 1 - P(18.6 \le \bar{x} \le 29.4)$

$= 1 - P(-15.01 \le z \le 6.90)$

$= 1 - [P(-15.01 \le z \le 0) + P(0 \le z \le 6.90)]$

$\approx 1 - [.5 + .5]$

$= 1 - 1$

$= 0$

d. Using Rule 3 with $\mu = 24$ and $\sigma = 2.7$, and $n = 30$,

$$\text{LCL} = \mu - \frac{2\sigma}{\sqrt{n}} = 24 - \frac{2(2.7)}{\sqrt{30}} = 24 - .986 = 23.014$$

$$\text{UCL} = \mu + \frac{2\sigma}{\sqrt{n}} = 24 + \frac{2(2.7)}{\sqrt{30}} = 24 + .986 = 24.986$$

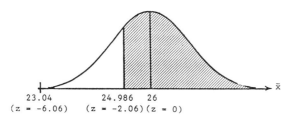

$$\begin{array}{cc} 23.04 & 24.986 \quad 26 \\ (z = -6.06) & (z = -2.06)(z = 0) \end{array}$$

$$z = \frac{\bar{x} - \mu_{\bar{x}}}{\sigma_{\bar{x}}} = \frac{23.014 - 26}{.493} = -6.06 \qquad z = \frac{\bar{x} - \mu_{\bar{x}}}{\sigma_{\bar{x}}} = \frac{24.986 - 26}{.493} = -2.06$$

P($\bar{x}$ falls outside the control limits)

$= 1 - P(\text{LCL} \le \bar{x} \le \text{UCL})$

$= 1 - P(23.014 \le \bar{x} \le 24.986)$

$= 1 - P(-6.06 \le z \le -2.06)$

$= 1 - [P(-6.06 \le z \le 0) - P(-2.06 \le z \le 0)]$

$\approx 1 - [.5 - .4803]$

$= 1 - .0197$

$= .9803$

e. I would recommend Rule 3 since it has the larger probability. If the process is out of control, we would want a large probability of $\bar{x}$ falling outside of the control limits.

EIGHT   ESTIMATION OF MEANS AND PROPORTIONS

8.1   As Definition 8.3 (page 312 in the text) states, the confidence coefficient is the proportion of times that a confidence interval encloses the true value of the population parameter if the confidence interval procedure is used repeatedly a very large number of times.

8.3   For each of the problems, we will use the following formula to construct a $(1 - \alpha)$ 100% confidence interval:

$$\bar{x} \pm z_{\alpha/2}\left(\frac{\sigma}{\sqrt{n}}\right) \approx \bar{x} \pm z_{\alpha/2}\left(\frac{s}{\sqrt{n}}\right) = 81 \pm z_{\alpha/2}\left(\frac{12}{\sqrt{100}}\right) = 81 \pm z_{\alpha/2}(1.2)$$

a.   Confidence coefficient .90 = 1 - α => α = 1 - .90 = .10; $\alpha/2$ = .10/2 = .05. From Table 4, Appendix E, $z_{.05}$ = 1.645. The 90% confidence interval for μ is:

$$81 \pm 1.645(1.2) => 81 \pm 1.974 => (79.026, 82.974)$$

b.   Confidence coefficient .95 = 1 - α => α = 1 - .95 = .05; $\alpha/2$ = .05/2 = .025. From Table 4, Appendix E, $z_{.025}$ = 1.96. The 95% confidence interval for μ is:

$$81 \pm 1.96(1.2) => 81 \pm 2.352 => (78.648, 83.352)$$

c.   Confidence coefficient .99 = 1 - α => α = 1 - .99 = .01; $\alpha/2$ = .01/2 = .005. From Table 4, Appendix E, $z_{.005}$ = 2.58. The 99% confidence interval for μ is:

$$81 \pm 2.58(1.2) => 81 \pm 3.096 => (77.904, 84.096)$$

8.5 $\bar{x} = \dfrac{\sum x}{n} = \dfrac{2280}{400} = 5.7$

$$s^2 = \frac{\sum x^2 - \dfrac{(\sum x)^2}{n}}{n - 1} = \frac{38,532 - \dfrac{(2280)^2}{400}}{399} = 64 \qquad s = \sqrt{s^2} = \sqrt{64} = 8$$

a. Confidence coefficient .90 = 1 − α => α = 1 − .90 = .10; α/2 = .10/2 = .05. From Table 4, Appendix E, $z_{.05}$ = 1.645. The 90% confidence interval for μ is:

$$\bar{x} \pm z_{\alpha/2}\left(\frac{\sigma}{\sqrt{n}}\right) \approx \bar{x} \pm z_{\alpha/2}\left(\frac{s}{\sqrt{n}}\right)$$

$$=> 5.7 \pm 1.645\left(\frac{8}{\sqrt{400}}\right)$$

$$=> 5.7 \pm .658$$

$$=> (5.042, 6.358)$$

b. Confidence coefficient .99 = 1 − α => α = 1 − .99 = .01; α/2 = .01/2 = .005. From Table 4, Appendix E, $z_{.005}$ = 2.58. The 99% confidence interval for μ is:

$$\bar{x} \pm z_{\alpha/2}\left(\frac{\sigma}{\sqrt{n}}\right) \approx \bar{x} \pm z_{\alpha/2}\left(\frac{s}{\sqrt{n}}\right)$$

$$=> 5.7 \pm 2.58\left(\frac{8}{\sqrt{400}}\right)$$

$$=> 5.7 \pm 1.032$$

$$=> (4.668, 6.732)$$

8.7   If repeated random samples were selected and a 95% confidence interval for μ ($\bar{x} \pm 1.96\sigma/\sqrt{n}$) was constructed for each sample, then approximately 95% of the intervals so constructed would contain μ.

8.9   a. Confidence coefficient .98 = 1 − α => α = 1 − .98 = .02; α/2 = .02/2 = .01. From Table 4, Appendix E, $z_{.01}$ = 2.33. The 98% confidence interval for μ is:

$$\bar{x} \pm z_{\alpha/2}\left(\frac{\sigma}{\sqrt{n}}\right) \approx \bar{x} \pm z_{\alpha/2}\left(\frac{s}{\sqrt{n}}\right)$$

$$=> 3,412 \pm 2.33\left(\frac{580}{\sqrt{36}}\right)$$

$$=> 3,412 \pm 225.23$$

$$=> (3,186.77, 3,637.23)$$

b. In order to reduce the width of the confidence interval in part (a), you could increase the sample size (n) or decrease the confidence level which would decrease the size of $z_{\alpha/2}$.

8.11   Confidence coefficient .95 = 1 - α => α = 1 - .95 = .05;
α/2 = .05/2 = .025.   From Table 4, Appendix E, $z_{.025}$ = 1.96.   The 95%
confidence interval for μ is:

$$\bar{x} \pm z_{\alpha/2}\left(\frac{\sigma}{\sqrt{n}}\right) \approx \bar{x} \pm z_{\alpha/2}\left(\frac{s}{\sqrt{n}}\right)$$

$$=> 29.07 \pm 1.96\left(\frac{4.68}{\sqrt{115}}\right)$$

$$=> 29.07 \pm .855$$

$$=> (28.215, 29.925)$$

We can be 95% confident that the interval (28.215, 29.925) encloses
the true mean "perceived unit effectiveness" rating of all purchasing
agents.

8.13   a.   To select a random sample of 30 checkout service times from
Appendix D, follow the procedure used in Exercise 7.3.

b.   Confidence coefficient .97 = 1 - α => α = 1 - .97 = .03;
α/2 = .03/2 = .015.   From Table 4, Appendix E, $z_{.015}$ = 2.17.   The
form of the 97% confidence interval for μ is:

$$\bar{x} \pm z_{\alpha/2}\left(\frac{\sigma}{\sqrt{n}}\right) \approx \bar{x} \pm z_{\alpha/2}\left(\frac{s}{\sqrt{n}}\right) => \bar{x} \pm 2.17\left(\frac{s}{\sqrt{n}}\right)$$

c.   The confidence coefficient for the interval in part (b) is .97.
If we used the confidence interval procedure a large number of
times, approximately .97 of the intervals formed would enclose the
true average customer service time at the supermarket.

8.15   a.   1 - α = .99   α = .01   α/2 = .005

We thus require the value of $t_{.005}$ for a t distribution based on
n - 1 = 18 - 1 = 17 degrees of freedom.   In Table 6, at the
intersection of the column labeled $t_{.005}$ and the row corresponding
to df = 17, we find the entry 2.898.

b.   1 - α = .95   α = .05   α/2 = .025

We thus need the value of $t_{.025}$ for a t distribution based on
n - 1 = 10 - 1 = 9 df.   In Table 6, at the intersection of the
column labeled $t_{.025}$ and the row corresponding to df = 9, we find
the entry 2.262.

c.   1 - α = .90   α = .10   α/2 = .05

We thus need the value of $t_{.05}$ for a t distribution based on
n - 1 = 15 - 1 = 14 df.   In Table 6, at the intersection of the

column labeled $t_{.05}$ and the row corresponding to df = 14, we find the entry 1.761.

8.17 Confidence coefficient .95 = 1 - α => α = 1 - .95 = .05; $\alpha/2$ = .05/2 = .025. For each of the problems, we will use the following formula to construct a (1 - α)100% confidence interval:

$$\bar{x} \pm t_{\alpha/2}\left(\frac{s}{\sqrt{n}}\right) \Rightarrow 33 \pm t_{.025}\left(\frac{4}{\sqrt{n}}\right)$$

a. From Table 6, Appendix E, with df = n - 1 = 5 - 1 = 4, $t_{.025}$ = 2.776. The 95% confidence interval for μ is:

$$33 \pm 2.776\left(\frac{4}{\sqrt{5}}\right)$$

=> 33 ± 4.97 => (28.03, 37.97)

b. From Table 6, Appendix E, with df = n - 1 = 15 - 1 = 14, $t_{.025}$ = 2.145. The 95% confidence interval for μ is:

$$33 \pm 2.145\left(\frac{4}{\sqrt{15}}\right)$$

=> 33 ± 2.22 => (30.78, 35.22)

c. From Table 6, Appendix E, with df = n - 1 = 25 - 1 = 24, $t_{.025}$ = 2.064. The 95% confidence interval for μ is:

$$33 \pm 2.064\left(\frac{4}{\sqrt{25}}\right)$$

=> 33 ± 1.65 => (31.35, 34.65)

8.19 The z and t distributions are alike in that they are both symmetric, bell-shaped distributions centered at 0. They differ in variability, though. The z distribution always has σ^2 = 1, where the variance of the t distribution is always larger and depends on the degrees of freedom.

8.21 a. $\bar{x} = \frac{\sum x}{n} = \frac{131,949}{25} = 5,277.96$

$$s^2 = \frac{\sum x^2 - \frac{(\sum x)^2}{n}}{n - 1} = \frac{1,050,326,887 - \frac{(131,949)^2}{25}}{25 - 1} = 14,746,055.96$$

$s = \sqrt{s^2} = 3840.06$

b. Confidence coefficient .95 = 1 − α => α = 1 − .95 = .05;
α/2 = .05/2 = .025. From Table 6, Appendix E, with df = n − 1 =
25 − 1 = 24, $t_{.025}$ = 2.064. The 95% confidence interval for μ is:

$$\bar{x} \pm t_{\alpha/2}\left(\frac{s}{\sqrt{n}}\right)$$

$$=> 5{,}277.96 \pm 2.064\left(\frac{3840.06}{\sqrt{25}}\right)$$

$$=> 5{,}277.96 \pm 1585.18$$

$$=> (3{,}692.78,\ 6{,}863.14)$$

c. Assumption: The population from which the sample is selected
(total 1986 compensation for the highest-paid corporate executives
in the United States) has an approximate normal distribution.

8.23 a. Confidence coefficient .95 = 1 − α => α = 1 − .95 = .05;
α/2 = .05/2 = .025. From Table 6, Appendix E, with
df = n − 1 = 10 − 1 = 9, $t_{.025}$ = 2.262. The small sample
confidence interval for μ is:

$$\bar{x} \pm t_{.025}\left(\frac{s}{\sqrt{n}}\right) => .604 \pm 2.262\left(\frac{.163}{\sqrt{10}}\right)$$

$$=> .604 \pm .117 => (.487,\ .721)$$

b. If the sample size was increased from n = 10 to n = 20, the
standard error (s/√n) would decrease. Therefore, the interval
would be narrower if the sample size was increased. Also, the
degrees of freedom would increase which would cause the value of
$t_{.025}$ to decrease, again decreasing the interval width.

c. The procedure requires the assumption that the relative frequency
distribution of all farebox recovery rates for LRT systems in
North American cities is approximately normal.

8.25 a. Confidence coefficient .95 = 1 − α => α = 1 − .95 = .05;
α/2 = .05/2 = .025. From Table 6, Appendix E, with
df = n − 1 = 19 − 1 = 18, $t_{.025}$ = 2.101. The small-sample
confidence interval for μ is:

$$\bar{x} \pm t_{.025}\left(\frac{s}{\sqrt{n}}\right) => 51.75 \pm (2.101)\left(\frac{5.50}{\sqrt{19}}\right)$$

$$=> 51.75 \pm (2.101)(1.26) => 51.75 \pm 2.65 => (49.10,\ 54.40)$$

b. The procedure requires the assumption that the relative frequency
distribution of the price of designer jeans in the New York City
area is approximately normal.

c. No, the prices obtained form the 19 stores in New York City do not represent a random sample of retail outlets across the U.S.

8.27 Confidence coefficient $.95 = 1 - \alpha \Rightarrow \alpha = 1 - .95 = .05$; $\alpha/2 = .05/2 = .025$. From Table 4, Appendix E, $z_{.025} = 1.96$.

For each of the following problems, substitute the proper values into the equation:

$$\hat{p} \pm z_{\alpha/2}\sqrt{\frac{\hat{p}\hat{q}}{n}} \Rightarrow \hat{p} \pm 1.96\sqrt{\frac{\hat{p}\hat{q}}{n}} \text{ where } \hat{q} = 1 - \hat{p}$$

a. $.38 \pm 1.96\sqrt{\frac{(.38)(.62)}{50}} \Rightarrow .38 \pm .135 \text{ or } (.245, .515)$

b. $.45 \pm 1.96\sqrt{\frac{(.45)(.55)}{100}} \Rightarrow .45 \pm .098 \text{ or } (.352, .548)$

c. $.43 \pm 1.96\sqrt{\frac{(.43)(.57)}{1000}} \Rightarrow .43 \pm .031 \text{ or } (.399, .461)$

8.29 Confidence coefficient $.95 = 1 - \alpha \Rightarrow \alpha = 1 - .95 = .05$; $\alpha/2 = .05/2 = .025$. From Table 4, Appendix E, $z_{.025} = 1.96$. We know $\hat{p} = .20$ and $\hat{q} = 1 - \hat{p} = 1 - .20 = .80$.

a. $\hat{p} \pm z_{\alpha/2}\sqrt{\frac{\hat{p}\hat{q}}{n}} \Rightarrow .20 \pm 1.96\sqrt{\frac{(.20)(.80)}{50}}$

$$\Rightarrow .20 \pm .111 \text{ or } (.089, .311)$$

b. $\hat{p} \pm z_{\alpha/2}\sqrt{\frac{\hat{p}\hat{q}}{n}} \Rightarrow .20 \pm 1.96\sqrt{\frac{(.20)(.80)}{500}}$

$$\Rightarrow .20 \pm .035 \text{ or } (.165, .235)$$

8.31 The estimate of proportion of families who tuned in to the certain program is:

$$\hat{p} = \frac{\text{Number of sampled families tuned in}}{\text{Total number of families sampled}} = \frac{101}{165} = .61$$

and $\hat{q} = 1 - \hat{p} = 1 - .61 = .39$. Confidence coefficient $.90 = 1 - \alpha \Rightarrow \alpha = 1 - .90 = .10$; $\alpha/2 = .10/2 = .05$. From Table 4, Appendix E, $z_{.05} = 1.645$. The 90% confidence interval for p is:

$$\hat{p} \pm z_{\alpha/2} \sqrt{\frac{\hat{p}\hat{q}}{n}} \Rightarrow .61 \pm 1.645 \sqrt{\frac{(.61)(.39)}{165}}$$

$$\Rightarrow .61 \pm .062 \Rightarrow (.548, .672)$$

8.33   The estimate of the proportion of working adults who regularly use computer equipment on the job is:

$$\hat{p} = \frac{\text{Number of working adults using computer equipment}}{\text{Total number of working adults sampled}} = \frac{184}{616} = .299$$

and $\hat{q} = 1 - \hat{p} = 1 - .299 = .701$. Confidence coefficient $.90 = 1 - \alpha \Rightarrow \alpha = 1 - .90 = .10$; $\alpha/2 = .10/2 = .05$. From Table 4, Appendix E, $z_{.05} = 1.645$. The large-sample confidence interval for p, the population proportion of working adults who regularly use computer equipment on the job is:

$$\hat{p} \pm z_{\alpha/2} \sqrt{\frac{\hat{p}\hat{q}}{n}} \Rightarrow .299 \pm 1.645 \sqrt{\frac{(.299)(.701)}{616}}$$

$$\Rightarrow .299 \pm .030 \Rightarrow (.269, .329)$$

8.35   The estimate of the proportion of U.S. design engineers who consider the shear wall of the building too lightly reinforced is:

$$\hat{p} = \frac{\text{Number of U.S. design engineers who consider the shear wall too lightly reinforced}}{\text{Total number of U.S. design engineers sampled}}$$

$$= \frac{36}{48} = .75 \quad \text{and} \quad \hat{q} = 1 - \hat{p} = .25$$

Confidence coefficient $.95 = 1 - \alpha \Rightarrow \alpha = 1 - .95 = .05$; $\alpha/2 = .05/2 = .025$. From Table 4, Appendix E, $z_{.025} = 1.96$.

The large-sample confidence interval for p, the population proportion of U.S. design engineers who consider the shear wall too lightly reinforced is:

$$\hat{p} \pm z_{\alpha/2} \sqrt{\frac{\hat{p}\hat{q}}{n}} \Rightarrow .75 \pm 1.96 \sqrt{\frac{(.75)(.25)}{48}}$$

$$\Rightarrow .75 \pm .1225 \Rightarrow (.6275, .8725)$$

8.37   a.   The estimate of $\mu_{(\bar{x}_1 - \bar{x}_2)}$ is $\bar{x}_1 - \bar{x}_2 = 150 - 140 = 10$.

Since $n_1 \geq 30$ and $n_2 \geq 30$, the estimate of $\sigma_{(\bar{x}_1 - \bar{x}_2)}$ is

$$\sqrt{\frac{s_1^2}{n_1} + \frac{s_2^2}{n_2}} = \sqrt{\frac{36}{35} + \frac{24}{35}} = 1.31$$

b. The estimate of $\mu_{(\bar{x}_1 - \bar{x}_2)}$ is $\bar{x}_1 - \bar{x}_2 = 125 - 112 = 13$.

Since $n_1 \geq 30$ and $n_2 \geq 30$, the estimate of $\sigma_{(\bar{x}_1 - \bar{x}_2)}$ is

$$\sqrt{\frac{s_1^2}{n_1} + \frac{s_2^2}{n_2}} = \sqrt{\frac{225}{90} + \frac{90}{60}} = 2$$

8.39 The two populations must have:

1) relative frequency distributions that are approximately normal, and
2) variances σ_1^2 and σ_2^2 that are equal.

The two samples must both have been randomly and independently chosen.

8.41 $s_p^2 = \dfrac{(n_1 - 1)s_1^2 + (n_2 - 1)s_2^2}{n + n - 2} = \dfrac{(14 - 1)96.8 + (7 - 1)102.0}{14 + 7 - 2} = 98.44$

a. Confidence coefficient $.90 = 1 - \alpha \Rightarrow \alpha = 1 - .90 = .10$; $\alpha/2 = .10/2 = .05$. From Table 6, Appendix E, with df = $n_1 + n_2 - 2 = 14 + 7 - 2 = 19$, $t_{.05} = 1.729$. The 90% confidence interval is:

$$(\bar{x}_1 - \bar{x}_2) \pm t_{.05}\sqrt{s_p^2\left(\frac{1}{n_1} + \frac{1}{n_2}\right)}$$

$$\Rightarrow (53.2 - 43.4) \pm 1.729\sqrt{98.44\left(\frac{1}{14} + \frac{1}{7}\right)} \Rightarrow 9.8 \pm 7.94$$

$$\Rightarrow (1.86, 17.74)$$

b. Confidence coefficient $.95 = 1 - \alpha \Rightarrow \alpha = 1 - .95 = .05$; $\alpha/2 = .05/2 = .025$. From Table 6, Appendix E, with df = 19, $t_{.025} = 2.093$. The 95% confidence interval is:

$$(\bar{x}_1 - \bar{x}_2) \pm t_{.025}\sqrt{s_p^2\left(\frac{1}{n_1} + \frac{1}{n_2}\right)}$$

$$\Rightarrow (53.2 - 43.4) \pm 2.093\sqrt{98.44\left(\frac{1}{14} + \frac{1}{7}\right)} \Rightarrow 9.8 \pm 9.61$$

$$\Rightarrow (.19, 19.41)$$

c. Confidence coefficient $.99 = 1 - \alpha \Rightarrow \alpha = 1 - .99 = .01$; $\alpha/2 = .01/2 = .005$. From Table 6, Appendix E, with df = 19, $t_{.005} = 2.861$. The 99% confidence interval is:

$$(\bar{x}_1 - \bar{x}_2) \pm t_{.005}\sqrt{s_p^2\left(\frac{1}{n_1} + \frac{1}{n_2}\right)}$$

$$\Rightarrow (53.2 - 43.4) \pm 2.861\sqrt{98.44\left(\frac{1}{14} + \frac{1}{7}\right)} \Rightarrow 9.8 \pm 13.14$$

$$\Rightarrow (-3.34, 22.94)$$

8.43   a. Confidence coefficient $.99 = 1 - \alpha \Rightarrow \alpha = 1 - .99 = .01$; $\alpha/2 = .01/2 = .005$. From Table 4, Appendix E, $z_{.005} = 2.58$. The 99% confidence interval is:

$$(\bar{x}_1 - \bar{x}_2) \pm z_{\alpha/2}\sqrt{\frac{s_1^2}{n_1} + \frac{s_2^2}{n_2}}$$

$$\Rightarrow (85.7 - 90.7) \pm 2.58\sqrt{\frac{13.2^2}{1076} + \frac{14.3^2}{1782}}$$

$$\Rightarrow -5 \pm 1.36 \Rightarrow (-6.36, -3.64)$$

b. We are 99% confident that $(-6.36, -3.64)$ contains the mean difference in Machiavellian scores between marketing professionals and college students. In other words, we estimate that the mean Machiavellian score for marketing professionals is anywhere from 6.36 to 3.64 less than the mean score for college students.

8.45   a. The random samples will be chosen by labeling each checkout time using the OBS number. The random numbers will be chosen starting arbitrarily from row 24, column 13 of Table 5 (Appendix E in the text) and reading across. Only the first three digits of random numbers are needed because the checkout times are labeled from 1 through 1000 (000 = 1000).

The random numbers taken from the table are:

361, 185, 24, 330, 288, 73, 197, 924, 609, 612, 500, 676, 325, 866, and 507.

The first six numbers from 1 - 500 are chosen from supermarket A (361, 185, 24, 330, 288, and 73) and the first six numbers from 501 - 999 (and 000) are chosen from supermarket B (924, 609, 612, 676, 866, and 507).

The corresponding checkout times are:

Supermarket A: 75, 35, 90, 125, 60, 80
Supermarket B: 80, 8, 17, 40, 15, 65

For supermarket A:

$$\bar{x}_1 = \frac{\sum x_1}{n_1} = \frac{465}{6} = 77.5$$

$$s_1^2 = \frac{\sum x_1^2 - \frac{(\sum x_1)^2}{n_1}}{n_1 - 1} = \frac{40575 - \frac{(465)^2}{6}}{6 - 1} = 907.5$$

$$s_1 = \sqrt{s_1^2} = \sqrt{907.5} = 30.125$$

For supermarket B:

$$\bar{x}_2 = \frac{\sum x_2}{n_2} = \frac{225}{6} = 37.5$$

$$s_2^2 = \frac{\sum x_2^2 - \frac{(\sum x_2)^2}{n_2}}{n_2 - 1} = \frac{12803 - \frac{(225)^2}{6}}{6 - 1} = 873.1$$

$$s_2 = \sqrt{s_2^2} = \sqrt{873.1} = 29.548$$

b. $s_p^2 = \dfrac{(n_1 - 1)s_1^2 + (n_2 - 1)s_2^2}{n_1 + n_2 - 2} = \dfrac{(6 - 1)907.5 + (6 - 1)873.1}{6 + 6 - 2} = 890.3$

Confidence coefficient $.90 = 1 - \alpha \Rightarrow \alpha = 1 - .90 = .10$; $\alpha/2 = .10/2 = .05$. From Table 6, Appendix E, with $df = n_1 + n_2 - 2 = 6 + 6 - 2 = 10$, $t_{.05} = 1.812$. The small-sample 90% confidence interval is:

$$(\bar{x}_1 - \bar{x}_2) \pm t_{\alpha/2}\sqrt{s_p^2 \left(\frac{1}{n_1} + \frac{1}{n_2}\right)}$$

$$\Rightarrow (77.5 - 37.5) \pm 1.812\sqrt{890.3\left(\frac{1}{6} + \frac{1}{6}\right)} \Rightarrow 40 \pm 31.22$$

$$\Rightarrow (8.78, \ 71.22)$$

Since all the values in the interval are positive, there is sufficient evidence that the mean checkout service time at supermarket B is less than the mean checkout service time at supermarket A by 8.78 to 71.22 seconds.

c. The assumptions are three:

1) The populations of checkout times for supermarkets A and B each have relative frequency distributions that are approximately normal.

2) The variances σ_1^2 and σ_2^2 of the two supermarket checkout times are equal.

3) The two samples were randomly and independently obtained.

d. The 2 random samples can be chosen in the same way as described in part (a).

e. The increase in sample sizes should give a narrower confidence interval.

f. I would recommend the interval in part (e) since it was formed using larger sample sizes than the one in part (b).

8.47 a. Point estimate for $\mu_1 - \mu_2$, the difference in mean sales before and after the campaign, is $\bar{x}_1 - \bar{x}_2 = 487 - 548 = -61$.

b. Confidence coefficient $.93 = 1 - \alpha \Rightarrow \alpha = 1 - .93 = .07$; $\alpha/2 = .07/2 = .035$. From Table 4, Appendix E, $z_{.035} = 1.81$. The large-sample confidence interval for $\mu_1 - \mu_2$ is:

$$(\bar{x}_1 - \bar{x}_2) \pm z_{\alpha/2}\sqrt{\frac{\sigma_1^2}{n_1} + \frac{\sigma_2^2}{n_2}}$$

Substituting s_1^2 and s_2^2 for σ_1^2 and σ_2^2, we obtain:

$$(487 - 548) \pm 1.81\sqrt{\frac{(23)^2}{50} + \frac{(31)^2}{40}} \Rightarrow -61 \pm 10.65$$

$$\Rightarrow (-71.65, -50.35)$$

c. 1) The two random samples must have been selected in an independent manner.

2) The sample sizes, n_1 and n_2, must be sufficiently large for the Central Limit Theorem to be effective.

d. The 93% confidence interval shows $\mu_1 - \mu_2 < -50.35$ $\Rightarrow \mu_2 > \mu_1 + 50.4$ Thus, the advertising campaign is worth it based on the information given by the 93% confidence interval.

8.49 a. $s_p^2 = \dfrac{(n_1 - 1)s_1^2 + (n_2 - 1)s_2^2}{n_1 + n_2 - 2} = \dfrac{(28 - 1)(.038)^2 + (28 - 1)(.030)^2}{28 + 28 - 2}$

$$= .0012$$

Confidence coefficient $.99 = 1 - \alpha \Rightarrow \alpha = 1 - .99 = .01$; $\alpha/2 = .01/2 = .005$. From Table 6, Appendix E, with $df = n_1 + n_2 - 2 = 28 + 28 - 2 = 54$, $t_{.005} \approx 2.66$. The small-sample confidence interval for $(\mu_1 - \mu_2)$ is:

$$(\bar{x}_1 - \bar{x}_2) \pm t_{\alpha/2}\sqrt{s_p^2\left(\frac{1}{n_1} + \frac{1}{n_2}\right)}$$

$$\Rightarrow (.540 - .330) \pm 2.66\sqrt{.0012\left(\frac{1}{28} + \frac{1}{28}\right)}$$

$$\Rightarrow .21 \pm .025 \text{ or } (.185, .235)$$

b. The following assumptions must be satisfied:

1) The relative frequency distribution for the market share is approximately normal for both brands of biscuits.

2) The variance in the market share is the same for both brands.

3) The samples are randomly and independently selected from the two target populations.

8.51 a.

PAIR	A	B	d(Difference)	d^2
1	2	0	2	4
2	5	7	-2	4
3	10	6	4	16
4	8	5	3	9
			$\sum d = 7$	$\sum d^2 = 33$

$$\bar{d} = \frac{\sum d}{n} = \frac{7}{4} = 1.75$$

$$s_d^2 = \frac{\sum d^2 - \frac{(\sum d)^2}{n}}{n-1} = \frac{33 - \frac{(7)^2}{4}}{3} = 6.92 \qquad s_d = \sqrt{s_d^2} = 2.63$$

b. $\mu_d = \mu_1 - \mu_2$ since $d = x_1 - x_2$

c. Confidence coefficient $.95 = 1 - \alpha \Rightarrow \alpha = 1 - .95 = .05$; $\alpha/2 = .05/2 = .025$. From Table 6, Appendix E, with df $= n - 1 = 4 - 1 = 3$, $t_{.025} = 3.182$. The 95% confidence interval is:

$$\bar{d} \pm t_{.025}\left(\frac{s_d}{\sqrt{n}}\right) \Rightarrow 1.75 \pm 3.182\left(\frac{2.63}{\sqrt{4}}\right)$$

$$\Rightarrow 1.75 \pm 4.18 \Rightarrow (-2.43, 5.93)$$

8.53

PAIR	POP. 1	POP. 2	$d = x_1 - x_2$	d^2
1	83	78	5	25
2	69	65	4	16
3	87	88	-1	1
4	93	91	2	4
5	78	72	6	36
6	59	59	0	0
			$\sum d = 16$	$\sum d^2 = 82$

The mean, variance, and standard deviation of the differences are:

$$\bar{d} = \frac{\sum d}{n} = \frac{16}{6} = 2.67$$

$$s_d^2 = \frac{\sum d^2 - \frac{(\sum d)^2}{n}}{n-1} = \frac{82 - \frac{(16)^2}{6}}{5} = 7.866 \qquad s_d = \sqrt{s_d^2} = 2.80$$

Confidence coefficient .95 = 1 - α => α = 1 - .95 = .05;
α/2 = .05/2 = .025. From Table 6, Appendix E, with
df = n - 1 = 6 - 1 = 5, $t_{.025}$ = 2.571. The 95% confidence interval
is:

$$\bar{d} \pm t_{.025}\left(\frac{s_d}{\sqrt{n}}\right) => 2.67 \pm 2.571\left(\frac{2.80}{\sqrt{6}}\right)$$

$$=> 2.67 \pm 2.94 => (-.27, 5.61)$$

8.55 a.

BUY Signal	4 WEEKS AFTER BUY	13 WEEKS AFTER BUY	(4 weeks-13 weeks) d	d^2
1	0.0	11.1	-11.1	123.21
2	3.0	4.7	-1.7	2.89
3	18.4	13.5	4.9	24.01
4	1.5	5.4	-3.9	15.21
5	5.5	11.9	-6.4	40.96
6	7.0	22.1	-15.1	228.01
7	2.5	-2.5	5.0	25.00
8	-4.6	19.9	-24.5	600.25
			$\sum d$ = -52.8	$\sum d^2$ = 1059.54

$$\bar{d} = \frac{\sum d}{n} = \frac{-52.8}{8} = -6.6$$

$$s_d^2 = \frac{\sum d^2 - \frac{(\sum d)^2}{n}}{n - 1} = \frac{1059.54 - \frac{(-52.8)^2}{8}}{8 - 1} = 101.58$$

$$s_d = \sqrt{s_d^2} = 10.08$$

Confidence coefficient .95 = 1 - α => α = 1 - .95 = .05;
α/2 = .05/2 = .025. From Table 6, Appendix E, with
df = n - 1 = 8 - 1 = 7, $t_{.025}$ = 2.365. The 95% confidence
interval is:

$$\bar{d} \pm t_{.025}\left(\frac{s_d}{\sqrt{n}}\right) => -6.6 \pm 2.365\left(\frac{10.08}{\sqrt{8}}\right)$$

$$=> -6.6 \pm 8.43$$

$$=> (-15.03, 1.83)$$

b. Since one endpoint of the interval is negative and the other is
positive, there is no evidence of a difference in selling the
stock in 4 weeks or 13 weeks on the average.

8.57 a.

PAIR	SEPT. 30	DEC. 31	d(Sept.-Dec.)	d^2
1	8.70	8.90	-.20	.04
2	8.75	8.50	.25	.0625
3	9.35	9.75	-.40	.16
4	7.80	6.00	1.80	3.24
5	9.25	8.75	.50	.25
6	8.25	8.00	.25	.0625
7	9.25	10.00	-.75	.5625
8	7.70	7.90	-.20	.04
9	8.50	8.15	.35	.1225
10	8.50	8.50	0.00	0.0000
11	9.50	8.50	1.00	1.00
12	8.50	8.15	.35	.1225
13	8.50	9.00	-.50	.25
14	9.00	8.50	.50	.25
15	9.15	9.30	-.15	.0225
16	9.25	9.25	0.00	0.0000
17	10.00	9.00	1.00	1.00
			$\sum d = 3.8$	$\sum d^2 = 7.185$

$$\bar{d} = \frac{\sum d}{n} = \frac{3.8}{17} = .22$$

$$s_d^2 = \frac{\sum d^2 - \frac{(\sum d)^2}{n}}{n - 1} = \frac{7.185 - \frac{(3.8)^2}{17}}{16} = .396$$

$$s_d = \sqrt{s_d^2} = \sqrt{.396} = .6293$$

Confidence coefficient .95 = 1 - α => α = 1 - .95 = .05; α/2 = .05/2 = .025. From Table 6, Appendix E, with df = n - 1 = 17 - 1 = 16, $t_{.025}$ = 2.120. The 95% confidence interval is:

$$\bar{d} \pm t_{.025}\left(\frac{s_d}{\sqrt{n}}\right) => .22 \pm 2.120\left(\frac{.6293}{\sqrt{17}}\right)$$

$$=> .22 \pm .324$$

$$=> (-.104, .544)$$

b. The following assumptions must be met:

1) The sampled paired differences are randomly selected from the target population of paired differences.

2) The population of paired differences is normally distributed.

The seventeen economists should be randomly selected from all economists in order for the assumptions to be met.

PAIR	1986	1987	d(1986-1987)	d²
1	1.4243	1.3504	.0739	.0055
2	.6002	.6623	-.0621	.0039
3	1.3372	1.3798	-.0426	.0018
4	2.0210	2.5085	-.4875	.2377
5	5.9725	7.0820	-1.1095	1.2310
6	7.8020	7.7885	.0135	.0002
7	1.5826	1.4770	.1056	.0112
8	6.7170	7.0800	-.363	.1318
9	6.2720	7.0900	-.818	.6691
10	1.4670	1.8620	-.395	.1560
11	1.7890	2.2220	-.433	.1875
			$\sum d = -3.5177$	$\sum d^2 = 2.6357$

$$\bar{d} = \frac{\sum d}{n} = \frac{-3.5177}{11} = -.3198$$

$$s_d^2 = \frac{\sum d^2 - \frac{(\sum d)^2}{n}}{n - 1} = \frac{2.6357 - \frac{(-3.5177)^2}{11}}{11 - 1} = .1511$$

$$s_d = \sqrt{s_d^2} = .3887$$

Confidence coefficient .90 = 1 - α => α = 1 - .90 = .10; α/2 = .10/2 = .05. From Table 6, Appendix E, with df = n - 1 = 11 - 1 = 10, $t_{.05}$ = 1.812. The 90% confidence interval is:

$$\bar{d} \pm t_{.05}\left(\frac{s_d}{\sqrt{n}}\right) => -.3198 \pm 1.812\left(\frac{.3887}{\sqrt{11}}\right)$$

$$=> -.3198 \pm .2124$$

$$=> (-.5322, -.1074)$$

We estimate, with 90% confidence, that the mean difference in foreign currency per dollar for 1986 and 1987 is between -.5322 and -.1074. Since all the values within the interval are negative, the mean foreign currency per dollar in 1987 was substantially higher than the mean foreign currency per dollar in 1986.

8.61 a. $\hat{q}_1 = 1 - \hat{p}_1 = 1 - .3 = .7$, $\hat{q}_2 = 1 - \hat{p}_2 = 1 - .4 = .6$

The point estimate of $\mu_{(\hat{p}_1 - \hat{p}_2)}$ is $\hat{p}_1 - \hat{p}_2 = .3 - .4 = -.1$

The estimate of $\sigma_{\hat{p}_1 - \hat{p}_2}$ is $\sqrt{\dfrac{\hat{p}_1 \hat{q}_1}{n_1} + \dfrac{\hat{p}_2 \hat{q}_2}{n_2}} = \sqrt{\dfrac{.3(.7)}{50} + \dfrac{.4(.6)}{30}} = .11$

b. $\hat{q}_1 = 1 - \hat{p}_1 = 1 - .10 = .90$, $\hat{q}_2 = 1 - \hat{p}_2 = 1 - .05 = .95$

The point estimate of $\mu_{(\hat{p}_1 - \hat{p}_2)}$ is $\hat{p}_1 - \hat{p}_2 = .10 - .05 = .05$

The estimate of $\sigma_{(\hat{p}_1 - \hat{p}_2)}$ is $\sqrt{\dfrac{\hat{p}_1 \hat{q}_1}{n_1} + \dfrac{\hat{p}_2 \hat{q}_2}{n_2}} = \sqrt{\dfrac{.10(.90)}{100} + \dfrac{.05(.95)}{100}}$

$$= .037$$

c. $\hat{q}_1 = 1 - \hat{p}_1 = 1 - .76 = .24$, $\hat{q}_2 = 1 - \hat{p}_2 = 1 - .96 = .04$

The point estimate of $\mu_{(\hat{p}_1 - \hat{p}_2)}$ is $\hat{p}_1 - \hat{p}_2 = .76 - .96 = -.20$

The estimate of $\sigma_{(\hat{p}_1 - \hat{p}_2)}$ is $\sqrt{\dfrac{\hat{p}_1 \hat{q}_1}{n_1} + \dfrac{\hat{p}_2 \hat{q}_2}{n_2}} = \sqrt{\dfrac{.76(.24)}{25} + \dfrac{.96(.04)}{25}}$

$$= .094$$

8.63 $\hat{p}_1 = \dfrac{100}{250} = .40$, $\hat{q}_1 = 1 - \hat{p}_1 = 1 - .40 = .60$

$\hat{p}_2 = \dfrac{75}{250} = .30$, $\hat{q}_2 = 1 - \hat{p}_2 = 1 - .30 = .70$

a. Confidence coefficient $.90 = 1 - \alpha \Rightarrow \alpha = 1 - .90 = .10$; $\alpha/2 = .10/2 = .05$. From Table 4, Appendix E, $z_{.05} = 1.645$. The 90% confidence interval for $(p_1 - p_2)$ is:

$$(\hat{p}_1 - \hat{p}_2) \pm z_{\alpha/2} \sqrt{\dfrac{\hat{p}_1 \hat{q}_1}{n_1} + \dfrac{\hat{p}_2 \hat{q}_2}{n_2}}$$

$$\Rightarrow (.40 - .30) \pm 1.645 \sqrt{\dfrac{.40(.60)}{250} + \dfrac{.30(.70)}{250}}$$

$$\Rightarrow .10 \pm .070 \Rightarrow (.03, .17)$$

b. Confidence coefficient $.99 = 1 - \alpha \Rightarrow \alpha = 1 - .99 = .01$; $\alpha/2 = .01/2 = .005$. From Table 4, Appendix E, $z_{.005} = 2.58$. The 99% confidence interval for $(p_1 - p_2)$ is:

$$(\hat{p}_1 - \hat{p}_2) \pm z_{\alpha/2}\sqrt{\frac{\hat{p}_1\hat{q}_1}{n_1} + \frac{\hat{p}_2\hat{q}_2}{n_2}}$$

$$\Rightarrow (.40 - .30) \pm 2.58\sqrt{\frac{.40(.60)}{250} + \frac{.30(.70)}{250}}$$

$$\Rightarrow .10 \pm .109 \Rightarrow (-.009, .209)$$

8.65   a. $\hat{p}_1 = \dfrac{\text{Number of males that feel shopping is unpleasant}}{\text{Total number of males}} = \dfrac{425}{1012}$

$$= .420$$

b. $\hat{p}_2 = \dfrac{\text{Number of females that feel shopping is unpleasant}}{\text{Total number of females}} = \dfrac{283}{1013}$

$$= .279$$

c. $\hat{q}_1 = 1 - \hat{p}_1 = 1 - .420 = .580$, $\hat{q}_2 = 1 - \hat{p}_2 = 1 - .279 = .721$

Confidence coefficient $.98 = 1 - \alpha \Rightarrow \alpha = 1 - .98 = .02$; $\alpha/2 = .02/2 = .01$. From Table 4, Appendix E, $z_{.01} = 2.33$. The 98% confidence interval is:

$$(\hat{p}_1 - \hat{p}_2) \pm z_{\alpha/2}\sqrt{\frac{\hat{p}_1\hat{q}_1}{n_1} + \frac{\hat{p}_2\hat{q}_2}{n_2}}$$

$$\Rightarrow (.420 - .279) \pm 2.33\sqrt{\frac{.420(.580)}{1012} + \frac{.279(.721)}{1013}}$$

$$\Rightarrow .141 \pm .049 \Rightarrow (.092, .19)$$

d.   Since all the values in the interval are positive, we can be 98% confident that a larger proportion of males than females feel shopping is unpleasant.

8.67   Let p_1 = proportion of database search reruns performed by ENSTINET in 1982 and p_2 = proportion of database search reruns performed by ENSTINET in 1985.

$$\hat{p}_1 = x_1/n_1 = 40/342 = .117 \text{ and } \hat{q}_1 = 1 - \hat{p}_1 = 1 = .117 = .883$$

$$\hat{p}_2 = x_2/n_2 = 83/2117 = .039 \text{ and } \hat{q}_2 = 1 - \hat{p}_2 = 1 = .039 = .961$$

For confidence coefficient $.95$, $\alpha = 1 - .95 = .05$; $\alpha/2 = .05/2 = .025$. From Table 4, Appendix E, $z_{.025} = 1.96$. The 95% confidence interval for $(p_1 - p_2)$ is:

$$(\hat{p}_1 - \hat{p}_2) \pm z_{\alpha/2} \sqrt{\frac{\hat{p}_1 \hat{q}_1}{n_1} + \frac{\hat{p}_2 \hat{q}_2}{n_2}}$$

$$\Rightarrow (.117 - .039) \pm 1.96 \sqrt{\frac{.117(.883)}{342} + \frac{.039(.961)}{2117}}$$

$$\Rightarrow .078 \pm .035 \Rightarrow (.043, .113)$$

We estimate with 95% confidence that the interval (.043, .113) contains the difference between the true proportion of database search reruns performed in 1982 and 1985. Since all the values in the interval are positive, there is evidence that the proportion of database search reruns performed is larger in 1982 than in 1985.

8.69 a. The proportion of sampled workers with fewer than 5 years of experience that were satisfied with their job is

$$\hat{p}_1 = \frac{165}{206} = .801; \quad \hat{q}_1 = 1 - \hat{p}_1 = 1 - .801 = .199$$

The proportion of sampled workers with 5 or more years of experience that were satisfied with their job is

$$\hat{p}_2 = \frac{1179}{1352} = .872; \quad \hat{q}_2 = 1 - \hat{p}_2 = 1 - .872 = .128$$

Confidence coefficient $.90 = 1 - \alpha \Rightarrow \alpha = 1 - .90 = .10$; $\alpha/2 = .10/2 = .05$. From Table 4, Appendix E, $z_{.05} = 1.645$. The 90% confidence interval is:

$$(\hat{p}_1 - \hat{p}_2) \pm z_{\alpha/2} \sqrt{\frac{\hat{p}_1 \hat{q}_1}{n_1} + \frac{\hat{p}_2 \hat{q}_2}{n_2}}$$

$$\Rightarrow (.801 - .872) \pm 1.645 \sqrt{\frac{.801(.199)}{206} + \frac{.872(.128)}{1352}}$$

$$\Rightarrow -.071 \pm .048 \Rightarrow (-.119, -.023)$$

b. We estimate with 90% confidence that the interval (-.119, -.023) contains the difference between the true proportion of workers that are satisfied with their jobs in the 2 groups. Since all the values in the interval are negative, there is sufficient evidence that between 11.9% and 2.3% more workers with 5 or more years experience are satisfied with their job than those with less than 5 years experience.

8.71 To determine the sample size needed to estimate μ,

$$n = \left(\frac{z_{\alpha/2} \sigma}{d}\right)^2$$

a. $.95 = 1 - \alpha \Rightarrow \alpha = 1 - .95 = .05$; $\alpha/2 = .05/2 = .025$.
    $z_{.025} = 1.96$ from Table 4, Appendix E.

$$n = \left(\frac{1.96(40)}{3}\right)^2 = (26.1333)^2 = 682.95$$

Rounding upward to assure probability of at least .95, n = 683.

b. The confidence coefficient is the same as in part (a).

$$n = \left(\frac{1.96(40)}{5}\right)^2 = (15.68)^2 = 245.86$$

Rounding upward to assure probability of at least .95, n = 246.

c. $.99 = 1 - \alpha \Rightarrow \alpha = 1 - .99 = .01$; $\alpha/2 = .01/2 = .005$.
    $z_{.005} = 2.58$ from Table 4, Appendix E.

$$n = \left(\frac{2.58(40)}{5}\right)^2 = (20.64)^2 = 426.01$$

Rounding upward to assure probability of at least .99, n = 427.

8.73   To determine the sample size needed to estimate $\mu_1 - \mu_2$,

$$n_1 = n_2 = \left(\frac{z_{\alpha/2}}{d}\right)^2 (\sigma_1^2 + \sigma_2^2)$$

a. $.95 = 1 - \alpha \Rightarrow \alpha = 1 - .95 = .05$; $\alpha/2 = .05/2 = .025$.
    $z_{\alpha/2} = z_{.025} = 1.96$ from Table 4, Appendix E.

$$n_1 = n_2 = \left(\frac{1.96}{5}\right)^2 (12^2 + 15^2) = (.153664)(369) = 56.7$$

So, rounding upward to assure at least probability of .95, we need $n_1 = n_2 = 57$.

b. $.99 = 1 - \alpha \Rightarrow \alpha = 1 - .99 = .01$; $\alpha/2 = .01/2 = .005$.
    $z_{\alpha/2} = z_{.005} = 2.58$ from Table 4, Appendix E.

$$n_1 = n_2 = \left(\frac{2.58}{5}\right)^2 (12^2 + 15^2) = (.266256)(369) = 98.2$$

So, rounding upward to assure at least probability of .99, we need $n_1 = n_2 = 99$.

c. $.90 = 1 - \alpha \Rightarrow \alpha = 1 - .90 = .10$; $\alpha/2 = .10/2 = .05$.
    $z_{\alpha/2} = z_{.05} = 1.645$ from Table 4, Appendix E.

$$n_1 = n_2 = \left(\frac{1.645}{1}\right)^2 (100 + 120) = (2.706025)(220) \approx 595.3$$

So, rounding upward to assure at least probability of .90, we need $n_1 = n_2 = 596$.

Note that the increase in probability from (a) to (b) results in a greater required sample size. Despite decreased probability, a reduction in width, d, and increased variability from (a) and (b) to (c) results in a much greater required sample size.

8.75   To determine the sample size needed to estimate μ,

$$n = \left(\frac{z_{\alpha/2}\sigma}{d}\right)^2$$

From Exercise 8.20, $\sigma \approx \$95,000$.

$.90 = 1 - \alpha \Rightarrow \alpha = 1 - .90 = .10;$ $\alpha/2 = .10/2 = .05.$
$z_{.05} = 1.645$ from Table 4, Appendix E.

$$n = \left(\frac{1.645(95,000)}{10,000}\right)^2 = (15.6275)^2 = 244.22$$

Therefore, in order to estimate μ to within $10,000 with probability equal to .90, we will have to sample approximately n = 245 "successful" trade promotions.

8.77   To determine the sample size needed to estimate $p_1 - p_2$,

$$n_1 = n_2 = \left(\frac{z_{\alpha/2}}{d}\right)^2 (p_1 q_1 + p_2 q_2)$$

Since we have no information about the values of p_1 and p_2, we will approximate both p_1 and p_2 with the value .5.

$.95 = 1 - \alpha \Rightarrow \alpha = 1 - .95 = .05;$ $\alpha/2 = .05/2 = .025.$ $z_{.025} = 1.96$ from Table 4, Appendix E.

$$n_1 = n_2 = \left(\frac{1.96}{.02}\right)^2 [(.5)(.5) + (.5)(.5)] = 4,802$$

Therefore, in order to estimate $p_1 - p_2$ to within .02 with probability equal to .95, we will have to sample approximately 4,802 stalks from each section of the field.

8.79   To determine the sample size needed to estimate p,

$$n = \left(\frac{z_{\alpha/2}}{d}\right)^2 pq$$

Since we have no prior information about the value of p, we will estimate this value with .5.

$.90 = 1 - \alpha \Rightarrow \alpha = 1 - .90 = .10;$ $\alpha/2 = .10/2 = .05.$ $z_{.05} = 1.645$ from Table 4, Appendix E.

$$n = \left(\frac{1.645}{.03}\right)^2 (.5)(.5) = 751.67$$

Therefore, in order to estimate p to within .03 with probability equal to .90, we will have to sample approximately n = 752 people.

8.81   a. Confidence coefficient $.99 = 1 - \alpha \Rightarrow \alpha = 1 - .99 = .01$; $\alpha/2 = .01/2 = .005$. From Table 4, Appendix E, $z_{.005} = 2.58$. The 99% confidence interval is:

$$(\bar{x}_1 - \bar{x}_2) \pm z_{\alpha/2}\sqrt{\frac{s_1^2}{n_1} + \frac{s_2^2}{n_2}}$$

$$(526 - 312) \pm 2.58\sqrt{\frac{(214)^2}{101} + \frac{(170)^2}{101}} \Rightarrow 214 \pm (2.58)(27.195)$$

$$\Rightarrow 214 \pm 70.16$$

$$\Rightarrow (143.84, 284.16)$$

     b. We can be 99% confident that the difference in the mean cost of living in Stockholm and New York is between \$143.84 and \$284.16. Since all the values in the interval are positive, we have sufficient evidence that the mean cost of living in Stockholm is larger than in New York.

     c. The data could be matched by item for each city.

     d. A matched-pairs experiment might yield more information since it would reduce the variability.

8.83 Confidence coefficient $.90 = 1 - \alpha \Rightarrow \alpha = 1 - .90 = .10$; $\alpha/2 = .10/2 = .05$. From Table 4, Appendix E, $z_{.05} = 1.645$. The general form of a 90% confidence interval for $(p_1 - p_2)$ based on large samples is given by:

$$(\hat{p}_1 - \hat{p}_2) \pm z_{\alpha/2}\sqrt{\frac{\hat{p}_1\hat{q}_1}{n_1} + \frac{\hat{p}_2\hat{q}_2}{n_2}}$$

     a. $\hat{p}_1 = .06$ = proportion of males sampled that earn money babysitting
        $\hat{p}_2 = .51$ = proportion of females sampled that earn money babysitting

$$\Rightarrow (.06 - .51) \pm 1.645\sqrt{\frac{(.06)(.94)}{271} + \frac{(.51)(.49)}{271}}$$

$$\Rightarrow -.45 \pm .055 \Rightarrow (-.505, -.395)$$

     b. $\hat{p}_1 = .36$ = proportion of males sampled that earn money doing yardwork
        $\hat{p}_2 = .08$ = proportion of females sampled that earn money doing yardwork

$$\Rightarrow (.36 - .08) \pm 1.645\sqrt{\frac{(.36)(.64)}{271} + \frac{(.08)(.92)}{271}}$$

$$\Rightarrow .28 \pm .055 \Rightarrow (.225, .335)$$

8.85   Confidence coefficient .99 = 1 − α => α = 1 − .99 = .01;
        α/2 = .01/2 = .005. From Table 4, Appendix E, $z_{\alpha/2}$ = 2.58. The 99%
        confidence interval is:

$$\bar{x} \pm z_{\alpha/2}\left(\frac{\sigma}{\sqrt{n}}\right) \approx \bar{x} \pm z_{\alpha/2}\left(\frac{s}{\sqrt{n}}\right)$$

$$=> 8.5 \pm 2.58\left(\frac{5.7}{\sqrt{200}}\right)$$

$$=> 8.5 \pm 1.04$$

$$=> (7.46, \ 9.54)$$

We can be 99% confident that the interval (7.46, 9.54) encloses the
true mean increase in savings account values over the past year.

8.87 $\hat{p} = \dfrac{\text{Number children sampled prefer toy trucks to toy trains}}{\text{Total number of children sampled}} = \dfrac{615}{1000}$

$$= .615$$

$\hat{q} = 1 − \hat{p} = 1 − .615 = .385$

Confidence coefficient .97 = 1 − α => α = 1 − .97 = .03;
α/2 = .03/2 = .015. From Table 4, Appendix E, $z_{.015}$ = 2.17. The 97%
confidence interval is:

$$\hat{p} \pm z_{\alpha/2}\sqrt{\frac{\hat{p}\hat{q}}{n}} => .615 \pm 2.17\sqrt{\frac{(.615)(.385)}{1000}}$$

$$=> .615 \pm .033 => (.582, .648)$$

We can be 97% confident that the interval (.582, .648) encloses the
true proportion of children 6-10 years old who prefer toy trucks to
toy trains.

8.89   a. $\hat{p} = \dfrac{\text{Number defective}}{\text{Number sampled}} = \dfrac{4}{200} = .02, \quad \hat{q} = 1 − \hat{p} = 1 − .02 = .98$

Confidence coefficient .95 = 1 − α => α = 1 − .95 = .05;
α/2 = .05/2 = .025. From Table 4, Appendix E, $z_{.025}$ = 1.96. The
95% confidence interval is:

$$\hat{p} \pm z_{.025}\sqrt{\frac{\hat{p}\hat{q}}{n}} => .02 \pm 1.96\sqrt{\frac{(.02)(.98)}{200}}$$

$$=> .02 \pm (1.96)(.0099) => .02 \pm .019$$

$$=> (.001, .039)$$

b. Since all the values in the interval are no more than .05, the retailer can be 95% confident that no more than 5% of the blenders in the shipment are defective.

8.91 a. Confidence coefficient .90 = 1 − α => α = 1 − .90 = .10; α/2 = .10/2 = .05. From Table 4, Appendix E, $z_{.05} = 1.645$. The 90% confidence interval is:

$$(\bar{x}_1 - \bar{x}_2) \pm z_{\alpha/2}\sqrt{\frac{s_1^2}{n_1} + \frac{s_2^2}{n_2}}$$

$$(2115 - 2003) \pm 1.645\sqrt{\frac{(450)^2}{60} + \frac{(388)^2}{45}}$$

$$=> 112 \pm 134.85 => (-22.85,\ 246.85)$$

b. Since the interval contains both negative and positive values, we cannot conclude that the revised pricing policy is effective.

c. To determine the sample size needed to estimate $\mu_1 - \mu_2$,

$$n_1 = n_2 = \left(\frac{z_{\alpha/2}}{d}\right)^2 (\sigma_1^2 + \sigma_2^2)$$

We can estimate σ_1^2 and σ_2^2 with s_1^2 and s_2^2 that were found in the sample.

.95 = 1 − α => α = 1 − .95 = .05; α/2 = .05/2 = .025. From Table 4, Appendix E, $z_{.025} = 1.96$.

$$n_1 = n_2 = \left(\frac{1.96}{50}\right)^2 (450^2 + 388^2) = 542.50$$

Therefore, in order to estimate $\mu_1 - \mu_2$ to within 50 kilowatt-hours with probability equal to .95, we will have to sample approximately n = 543 customers from each group.

CASE STUDIES

8.1 a. Point estimate of p is:

$$\hat{p} = \frac{\text{Number of women sampled who prefer the Daisy to Lady Bic}}{\text{Number of women sampled}} = \frac{9}{13}$$

$$= .692$$

b. Confidence coefficient $.98 = 1 - \alpha \Rightarrow \alpha = 1 - .98 = .02$; $\alpha/2 = .02/2 = .01$. From Table 4, Appendix E, $z_{.01} = 2.33$. The 98% confidence interval is:

$$\hat{p} \pm z_{\alpha/2}\sqrt{\frac{\hat{p}\hat{q}}{n}} \Rightarrow .692 \pm 2.33\sqrt{\frac{(.692)(.308)}{13}}$$

$$\Rightarrow .692 \pm .298 \Rightarrow (.394, .99)$$

c. The sample size was quite small in this problem (n = 13). It would be more reliable if a larger sample was taken.

d. To reduce the width of the interval found in part (b), we could 1) lower the confidence level or 2) increase the sample size, n.

It would be better to increase the sample size. The interval would tend to be more reliable and we can still be 98% confident in our answer.

e. To determine the sample size needed to estimate p,

$$n = \left(\frac{z_{\alpha/2}}{d}\right)^2 pq$$

We know from this sample that $p \approx .692$ and $q \approx 1 - .692 = .308$.

$.99 = 1 - \alpha \Rightarrow \alpha = 1 - .99 = .01$; $\alpha/2 = .01/2 = .005$. From Table 4, Appendix E, $z_{.005} = 2.58$.

$$n = \left(\frac{2.58}{.05}\right)^2 (.692)(.308) = 567.49$$

Therefore, in order to estimate p to within .05 with probability equal to .99, we will have to sample approximately n = 568 women.

Note: This is a much larger sample than the one used in this problem (n = 13) since we want to be more confident and have a narrower interval.

8.3 a. $\hat{p} = .60$ = proportion of sampled voters that favored Reagan in USA Today poll

$\hat{q} = 1 - \hat{p} = 1 - .60 = .40$

Confidence coefficient $.95 = 1 - \alpha \Rightarrow \alpha = 1 - .95 = .05$; $\alpha/2 = .05/2 = .025$. From Table 4, Appendix E, $z_{.025} = 1.96$. The 95% confidence interval is:

$$\hat{p} \pm z_{\alpha/2}\sqrt{\frac{\hat{p}\hat{q}}{n}} \Rightarrow .60 \pm 1.96\sqrt{\frac{.60(.40)}{1500}}$$

$$\Rightarrow .60 \pm .025 \Rightarrow (.575, .625)$$

b. $\hat{p}$ = .525 = proportion of sampled voters that favored Reagan in PBS poll

$\hat{q} = 1 - \hat{p} = 1 - .525 = .475$

$z_{.025} = 1.96$ (same as part (a))

The 95% confidence interval is:

$$\hat{p} \pm z_{\alpha/2} \sqrt{\frac{\hat{p}\hat{q}}{n}} \Rightarrow .525 \pm 1.96 \sqrt{\frac{.525(.475)}{1500}}$$

$$\Rightarrow .525 \pm .025 \Rightarrow (.500, .550)$$

c. I would not expect to see such a difference in the two confidence intervals in parts (a) and (b). The two intervals do not have any values in common; therefore, at least one of them cannot contain the true proportion of voters that favored Reagan despite the fact that we were 95% confident that each of them contained p.

NINE   INTRODUCTION TO SAMPLE SURVEY METHODS (OPTIONAL)

9.1 $N = 300$, $n = 30$, $\bar{x} = 680$, $s = 22$

An approximate 95% confidence interval for μ is

$$\bar{x} \pm 1.96\left(\frac{s}{\sqrt{n}}\right)\sqrt{\frac{N-n}{N}} \Rightarrow 680 \pm 1.96\left(\frac{22}{\sqrt{30}}\right)\sqrt{\frac{300-30}{300}}$$

$$\Rightarrow 680 \pm 7.47 \Rightarrow (672.53, 687.47)$$

9.3 $N = 5000$, $n = 800$, $\hat{p} = .81$

An approximate 95% confidence interval for p is

$$\hat{p} \pm 1.96\sqrt{\frac{\hat{p}(1-\hat{p})}{n}}\sqrt{\frac{N-n}{N}} \Rightarrow .81 \pm 1.96\sqrt{\frac{(.81)(.19)}{800}}\sqrt{\frac{5000-800}{5000}}$$

$$\Rightarrow .81 \pm .025 \Rightarrow (.785, .835)$$

9.5   For this example, we have $n = 32$, $N = 95$, $\bar{x} = 779,030$, and $s = 1,083,162$. The approximate 95% confidence interval for μ is

$$\bar{x} \pm 1.96\left(\frac{s}{\sqrt{n}}\right)\sqrt{\frac{N-n}{N}} \Rightarrow 779,030 \pm 1.96\left(\frac{1,083,162}{\sqrt{32}}\right)\sqrt{\frac{95-32}{95}}$$

$$\Rightarrow 779,030 \pm 305,620.84$$

$$\Rightarrow (473,409.16, 1,084,650.84)$$

9.7   For this example, we have $n = 40$, $N = 272$, $\bar{x} = 371$, and $s = 66$.

a.   An approximate 95% confidence interval for μ is

$$\bar{x} \pm 1.96\left(\frac{s}{\sqrt{n}}\right)\sqrt{\frac{N-n}{N}} \Rightarrow 371 \pm 1.96\left(\frac{66}{\sqrt{40}}\right)\sqrt{\frac{272-40}{272}}$$

$$\Rightarrow 371 \pm 18.89 \Rightarrow (352.11, 389.89)$$

b. $\hat{\tau} = N\bar{x} = 272(371) = 100,912$

An approximate 95% confidence interval for τ is

$$\hat{\tau} \pm 1.96\left(\frac{Ns}{\sqrt{n}}\right)\sqrt{\frac{N-n}{N}} \Rightarrow 100,912 \pm 1.96\left(\frac{272(66)}{\sqrt{40}}\right)\sqrt{\frac{272-40}{272}}$$

$$\Rightarrow 100,912 \pm 5,138.05$$

$$\Rightarrow (95,773.95, \ 106,050.05)$$

9.9 $N = 2000, \ d = 6, \ \sigma^2 \approx 225$

$$D = \frac{d^2}{4} = \frac{6^2}{4} = 9$$

$$n = \frac{N\sigma^2}{(N-1)D + \sigma^2} \approx \frac{2000(225)}{(1999)(9) + 225} = 24.7 \approx 25$$

Therefore, to estimate the population mean to within 6 units with 95% confidence, we need a sample of size n = 25.

9.11 $N = 800, \ d = .10, \ p \approx .33$

$$D = \frac{d^2}{4} = \frac{(.10)^2}{4} = .0025$$

$$n = \frac{Npq}{(N-1)D + pq} \approx \frac{(800)(.33)(.67)}{(799)(.0025) + (.33)(.67)} = 79.73 \approx 80$$

Therefore, to estimate the population proportion to within .10 with 95% confidence, we need a sample of size n = 80.

9.13   From Exercise 9.6, N = 50,840 and $p \approx .62$.

We also have d = .02.

Therefore, $D = \frac{d^2}{4} = \frac{(.02)^2}{4} = .0001$

$$n = \frac{Npq}{(N-1)D + pq} \approx \frac{(50,840)(.62)(.38)}{(50,839)(.0001) + (.62)(.38)} = 2251.697 \approx 2252$$

Therefore, to estimate the population proportion to within .02 with 95% confidence, we need to sample n = 2,252 voters.

9.15 $N = N_1 + N_2 + N_3 + N_4 = 4000 + 3000 + 5000 + 10,000 = 22,000$

The point estimate of μ is:

$$\bar{x}_{ST} = \frac{1}{N}(N_1\bar{x}_1 + N_2\bar{x}_2 + N_3\bar{x}_3 + N_4\bar{x}_4)$$

$$= \frac{1}{22,000}[4000(23.4) + 3000(29.5) + 5000(18.6) + 10,000(20.2)]$$

$$= 21.69$$

The approximate 95% confidence interval is:

$$\bar{x}_{ST} \pm 1.96 \sqrt{\frac{1}{N^2} \sum N_i^2 \frac{s_i^2}{n_i} \left(\frac{N_i - n_i}{N_i}\right)}$$

$$\Rightarrow 21.69 \pm 1.96 \sqrt{\frac{1}{22,000^2} \left[(4000)^2 \frac{3.3^2}{80}\left(\frac{4000 - 80}{4000}\right) + (3000)^2 \frac{4.8^2}{60}\left(\frac{3000 - 60}{3000}\right)\right.}$$
$$\overline{\left. + (5000)^2 \frac{9.1^2}{100}\left(\frac{5000 - 100}{5000}\right) + (10,000)^2 \frac{2.7^2}{200}\left(\frac{10,000 - 200}{10,000}\right)\right]}$$

$$\Rightarrow 21.69 \pm .48 \Rightarrow (21.21, 22.17)$$

9.17 In Exercise 9.15, we found the population size to be N = 22,000.
The point estimate of p is:

$$\hat{p}_{ST} = \frac{1}{N}(N_1\hat{p}_1 + N_2\hat{p}_2 + N_3\hat{p}_3 + N_4\hat{p}_4)$$
$$= \frac{1}{22,000}[4000(.6) + 3000(.5) + 5000(.7) + 10,000(.3)] = .473$$

The approximate 95% confidence interval is:

$$\hat{p}_{ST} \pm 1.96 \sqrt{\frac{1}{N^2} \sum N_i^2 \frac{\hat{p}_i\hat{q}_i}{n_i - 1}\left(\frac{N_i - n_i}{N_i}\right)}$$

$$\Rightarrow .473 \pm 1.96 \sqrt{\frac{1}{22,000^2} \left[(4000)^2 \frac{(.6)(.4)}{79}\left(\frac{4000 - 80}{4000}\right)\right.}$$
$$+ (3000)^2 \frac{(.5)(.5)}{59}\left(\frac{3000 - 60}{3000}\right)$$
$$+ (5000)^2 \frac{(.7)(.3)}{99}\left(\frac{5000 - 100}{5000}\right)$$
$$\overline{\left. + (10,000)^2 \frac{(.3)(.7)}{199}\left(\frac{10,000 - 200}{10,000}\right)\right]}$$

$$\Rightarrow .473 \pm .044 \Rightarrow (.429, .517)$$

9.19 $N = N_1 + N_2 + N_3 = 320 + 716 + 1025 = 2061$
The point estimate of p is:

$$\hat{p}_{ST} = \frac{1}{N}(N_1\hat{p}_1 + N_2\hat{p}_2 + N_3\hat{p}_3)$$
$$= \frac{1}{2061}[320(.013) + 716(.020) + 1025(.025) = .0214$$

The approximate 95% confidence interval is:

$$\hat{p}_{ST} \pm 1.96 \sqrt{\frac{1}{N^2} \sum N_i^2 \frac{\hat{p}_i \hat{q}_i}{n_i - 1} \left(\frac{N_i - n_i}{N_i}\right)}$$

$$\Rightarrow .0214 \pm 1.96 \sqrt{\frac{1}{2061^2} \left[(320)^2 \frac{(.013)(.987)}{149} \left(\frac{320 - 150}{320}\right) \right.}$$

$$+ (716)^2 \frac{(.02)(.98)}{299} \left(\frac{716 - 300}{716}\right)$$

$$\left. + (1025)^2 \frac{(.025)(.975)}{399} \left(\frac{1025 - 400}{1025}\right) \right]$$

$$\Rightarrow .0214 \pm .0076 \Rightarrow (.0138, .0290)$$

9.21 $d = 2$

$D = d^2/4 = 2^2/4 = 1$

$N = N_1 + N_2 + N_3 = 2000 + 1000 + 5000 = 8000$

$$n = \frac{\sum \left(\frac{N_i^2 \sigma_i^2}{w_i}\right)}{N^2 D + \sum N_i \sigma_i^2}$$

$$= \frac{\frac{(2000)^2(225)}{.25} + \frac{(1000)^2(300)}{.10} + \frac{(5000)^2(170)}{.65}}{(8000)^2(1) + [(2000)(225) + (1000)(300) + (5000)(170)]}$$

$$= 200.28 \approx 201$$

Applying the strata weights, we should sample:

$n_1 = w_1 n = .25(201) = 50$

$n_2 = w_2 n = .10(201) = 20$

$n_3 = w_3 n = .65(201) = 131$

9.23   From Exercise 9.21, $N = 8000$

$d = .05$

$D = \frac{d^2}{4} = \frac{(.05)^2}{4} = .000625$

$$n = \frac{\sum\left(\frac{N_i^2 p_i q_i}{w_i}\right)}{N^2 D + \sum N_i p_i q_i}$$

$$= \frac{\frac{(2000)^2(.3)(.7)}{.25} + \frac{(1000)^2(.5)(.5)}{.10} + \frac{(5000)^2(.45)(.55)}{.65}}{(8000)^2(.000625) + [2000(.3)(.7) + 1000(.5)(.5) + 5000(.45)(.55)]}$$

$$= 366.98 \approx 367$$

Applying the strata weights, we should sample:

$n_1 = w_1 n = (.25)(367) = 91.75 \approx 92$

$n_2 = w_2 n = (.10)(367) = 36.7 \approx 37$

$n_3 = w_3 n = (.65)(367) = 238.55 \approx 239$

9.25   From Exercise 9.19,

$N_1 = 320$, $N_2 = 716$, $N_3 = 1025$, $N = 2061$

$\hat{p}_1 = .013$, $\hat{p}_2 = .020$, $\hat{p}_3 = .025$

For this example, we have

$w_1 = .10$, $w_2 = .30$, $w_3 = .60$, $d = .005$

$$D = \frac{d^2}{4} = \frac{(.005)^2}{4} = .00000625$$

$$n = \frac{\sum\left(\frac{N_i^2 p_i q_i}{w_i}\right)}{N^2 D + \sum N_i p_i q_i}$$

$$= \frac{\frac{(320)^2(.013)(.987)}{.10} + \frac{(716)^2(.02)(.98)}{.30} + \frac{(1025)^2(.025)(.975)}{.60}}{(2061)^2(.00000625) + 320(.013)(.987) + 716(.02)(.98) + 1025(.025)(.975)}$$

$$= 1281.92 \approx 1282$$

Applying the strata weights, we should sample:

$n_1 = w_1 n = (.1)(1282) = 128.2 \approx 128$

$n_2 = w_2 n = (.3)(1282) = 384.6 \approx 385$

$n_3 = w_3 n = (.6)(1282) = 769.2 \approx 769$

9.27   For this example, $N = 300$, $n = 8$, and $m = 1280$.

$\sum m_i = 2 + 4 + 2 + 2 + 5 + 3 + 4 + 3 = 25$

$\sum x_i = 6.0 + 5.2 + 8.1 + 16.7 + 28.0 + 3.4 + 15.5 + 12.6 = 95.5$

$$\bar{m} = \frac{\sum m_i}{n} = \frac{25}{8} = 3.125 \qquad \bar{M} = \frac{M}{N} = \frac{1280}{300} = 4.267 \qquad \bar{x} = \frac{\sum x_i}{\sum m_i} = \frac{95.5}{25} = 3.82$$

To find the approximate 95% confidence interval, we should first obtain the sample estimate of the variance of the cluster totals.

$$\frac{\sum(x_i - \bar{x}m_i)^2}{n - 1} = \frac{1}{8 - 1}\{[6.0 - (3.82)(2)]^2 + [5.2 - (3.82)(4)]^2 + \ldots$$
$$+ [12.6 - (3.82)(3)]^2\}$$

$$= \frac{332.11}{7} = 47.44$$

The approximate 95% confidence interval is:

$$\bar{x} \pm 1.96 \sqrt{\frac{N - n}{Nn\bar{M}^2} \sum \frac{(x_i - \bar{x}m_i)^2}{n - 1}}$$

$$\Rightarrow 3.82 \pm 1.96 \sqrt{\frac{(300 - 8)}{300(8)(4.267)^2}(47.44)}$$

$$\Rightarrow 3.82 \pm 1.10 \Rightarrow (2.72, 4.92)$$

9.29 $N = 100$, $n = 10$, $M = 2500$

$\sum m_i = 20 + 30 + 31 + 22 + 25 + 16 + 44 + 27 + 22 + 25 = 262$

$\sum a_i = 6 + 10 + 12 + 7 + 4 + 1 + 15 + 10 + 11 + 9 = 85$

$$\bar{M} = \frac{M}{N} = \frac{2500}{100} = 25 \qquad \hat{p} = \frac{\sum a_i}{\sum m_i} = \frac{85}{262} = .324$$

To find the approximate 95% confidence interval, we should first obtain the sample estimate of the variance of the cluster totals.

$$\frac{\sum(a_i - \hat{p}m_i)^2}{n - 1} = \frac{1}{10 - 1}\{[6 - (.324)(20)]^2 + [10 - (.324)(30)]^2 + \ldots$$
$$+ [9 - (.324)(.25)]^2\}$$

$$= \frac{56.3904}{9} = 6.2656$$

The approximate 95% confidence interval is:

$$\hat{p} \pm 1.96 \sqrt{\frac{N - n}{Nn\bar{M}^2} \sum \frac{(a_i - \hat{p}m_i)^2}{n - 1}}$$

$$\Rightarrow .324 \pm 1.96 \sqrt{\frac{(100 - 10)}{100(10)(25)^2}(6.2656)} \Rightarrow .324 \pm .059$$

$$\Rightarrow (.265, .383)$$

9.31 In this example, $N = 15$, $n = 5$, $M = 75$.

$$\sum m_i = 6 + 2 + 8 + 3 + 2 = 21$$

$$\sum x_i = 16.2 + 3.4 + 5.0 + 10.7 + 12.8 = 48.1$$

$$\bar{x} = \frac{\sum x_i}{\sum m_i} = \frac{48.1}{21} = 2.29 \qquad M\bar{x} = M\frac{\sum x_i}{\sum m_i} = 75\left(\frac{48.1}{21}\right) = 171.79$$

To find the approximate 95% confidence interval, we should first obtain the sample estimate of the variance of the cluster totals.

$$\frac{\sum(x_i - \bar{x}m_i)^2}{n - 1} = \frac{1}{5 - 1}\{[16.2 - (2.29)(6)]^2 + [3.4 - (2.29)(2)]^2$$
$$+ [5.0 - (2.29)(8)]^2 + [10.7 - (2.29)(3)]^2$$
$$+ [12.8 - (2.29)(2)]^2\}$$

$$= \frac{267.1037}{4} = 66.78$$

The approximate 95% confidence interval for τ is:

$$M\bar{x} \pm 1.96\sqrt{N^2\left(\frac{N - n}{Nn}\right)\sum\frac{(x_i - \bar{x}m_i)^2}{n - 1}}$$

$$\Rightarrow 171.79 \pm 1.96\sqrt{(15)^2\left(\frac{15 - 5}{15(5)}\right)(66.78)}$$

$$\Rightarrow 171.79 \pm 87.73 \text{ or } (84.06, 259.52)$$

9.33 $N = 200$, $M = 1500$, $\sigma_c^2 \approx 96$, $d = 1$

$$\bar{M} = \frac{M}{N} = \frac{1500}{200} = 7.5$$

$$D = \frac{d^2\bar{M}^2}{4} = \frac{(1)^2(7.5)^2}{4} = 14.0625$$

$$n = \frac{N\sigma_c^2}{ND + \sigma_c^2} \approx \frac{200(96)}{200(14.0625) + 96} = 6.6 \approx 7$$

Therefore, to find a 95% confidence interval for μ to within 1, we need to sample approximately 7 clusters.

9.35 $N = 100$, $M = 2500$, $\sigma_c^2 \approx 6$, $d = .06$

$$\bar{M} = \frac{M}{N} = \frac{2500}{100} = 25$$

$$D = \frac{d^2\bar{M}^2}{4} = \frac{(.06)^2(25)^2}{4} = .5625$$

$$n = \frac{N\sigma_c^2}{ND + \sigma_c^2} = \frac{100(6)}{100(.5625) + 6} = 9.64 \approx 10$$

Therefore, to find a 95% confidence interval for p to within .06, we need to sample approximately 10 clusters.

9.37   From Exercise 9.31, $N = 15$ and $\sigma_c^2 \approx 66.78$.

For this exercise, $d = 60$.

$$D = \frac{d^2}{4N^2} = \frac{(60)^2}{4(15)^2} = 4$$

$$n = \frac{N\sigma_c^2}{ND + \sigma_c^2} = \frac{(15)(66.78)}{15(4) + 66.78} = 7.9 \approx 8$$

Therefore, in order to estimate the total number of bushels to within 60 with 95% confidence, we need to sample approximately 8 markets.

9.39 $N = 4000$, $n = 50$, $\bar{x} = 461.7$, $s = 98.8$, $\hat{p} = .44$

a.   An approximate 95% confidence interval for μ is:

$$\bar{x} \pm 1.96\left(\frac{s}{\sqrt{n}}\right)\sqrt{\frac{N - n}{N}} \Rightarrow 461.7 \pm 1.96\left(\frac{98.8}{\sqrt{50}}\right)\sqrt{\frac{4000 - 50}{4000}}$$

$$\Rightarrow 461.7 \pm 27.21 \Rightarrow (434.49, 488.91)$$

b.   An approximate 95% confidence interval for τ is

$$\hat{\tau} \pm 1.96\left(\frac{Ns}{\sqrt{n}}\right)\sqrt{\frac{N - n}{N}} \Rightarrow 4000(461.7) \pm 1.96\left(\frac{4000(98.8)}{\sqrt{50}}\right)\sqrt{\frac{4000 - 50}{4000}}$$

$$\Rightarrow 1,846,800 \pm 108,857.05$$

$$\Rightarrow (1,737,942.95, 1,955,657.05)$$

where $\hat{\tau} = N\bar{x}$

c.   An approximate 95% confidence interval for p is:

$$\hat{p} \pm 1.96\sqrt{\frac{\hat{p}\hat{q}}{n}}\sqrt{\frac{N - n}{N}} \Rightarrow .44 \pm 1.96\sqrt{\frac{(.44)(.56)}{50}}\sqrt{\frac{4000 - 50}{4000}}$$

$$\Rightarrow .44 \pm .137 \Rightarrow (.303, .577)$$

d. $D = \dfrac{d^2}{4} = \dfrac{(15)^2}{4} = 56.25$

$$n = \frac{N\sigma^2}{(N-1)D + \sigma^2} \approx \frac{4000(98.8)^2}{(3999)(56.25) + 98.8^2} = 166.36 \approx 167$$

Therefore, to estimate μ to within 15 with 95% confidence, we need to sample $n = 167$.

9.41 $N = 900$, $n = 5$, and $M = 5400$

a. $\sum m_i = 4 + 10 + 3 + 6 + 5 = 28$

$\sum x_i = 181 + 363 + 107 + 310 + 294 = 1255$

$\bar{M} = \frac{M}{N} = \frac{5400}{900} = 6$ $\bar{x} = \frac{\sum x_i}{\sum m_i} = \frac{1225}{28} = 44.82$

To find the approximate 95% confidence interval, we should first obtain the sample estimate of the variance of the cluster totals.

$$\frac{\sum(x_i - \bar{x}m_i)^2}{n-1} = \frac{1}{4}\{[181 - 44.82(4)]^2 + [363 - 44.82(10)]^2$$
$$+ [107 - 44.82(3)]^2 + [310 - 44.82(6)]^2$$
$$+ [294 - 44.82(5)]^2\}$$
$$= \frac{14589.63}{4} = 3647.41$$

The approximate 95% confidence interval is:

$$\bar{x} \pm 1.96\sqrt{\frac{N-n}{Nn\bar{M}^2} \sum \frac{(x_i - \bar{x}m_i)^2}{n-1}}$$

$$\Rightarrow 44.82 \pm 1.96\sqrt{\frac{900-5}{900(5)(6)^2}(3647.41)}$$

$$\Rightarrow 44.82 \pm 8.80 \Rightarrow (36.02,\ 54.62)$$

b. The approximate 95% confidence interval τ is:

$$M\bar{x} \pm 1.96\sqrt{N^2\left(\frac{N-n}{Nn}\right) \sum \frac{(x_i - \bar{x}m_i)^2}{n-1}}$$

$$\Rightarrow 5400\left(\frac{1255}{28}\right) \pm 1.96\sqrt{(900)^2\frac{(900-5)}{900(5)}(3647.41)}$$

$$\Rightarrow 242,035.71 \pm 47511.21 \Rightarrow (194,524.5,\ 289,546.92)$$

c. $\sum a_i = 1 + 4 + 1 + 2 + 2 = 10$

$$\hat{p} = \frac{\sum a_i}{\sum m_i} = \frac{10}{28} = .357$$

To find the approximate 95% confidence interval, we should first obtain the sample estimate of the variance of the cluster totals.

$$\frac{\sum(a_i - \hat{p}m_i)^2}{n - 1} = \frac{1}{4}\{[1 - .357(4)]^2 + [4 - .357(10)]^2 + [1 - .357(3)]^2$$
$$+ [2 - .357(6)]^2 + [2 - .357(5)]^2\}$$
$$= \frac{.4395}{4} = .11$$

The approximate 95% confidence interval for p is:

$$\hat{p} \pm 1.96\sqrt{\frac{N - n}{Nn\bar{M}^2}\sum\frac{(a_i - \hat{p}m_i)^2}{n - 1}}$$

$$\Rightarrow .357 \pm 1.96\sqrt{\frac{900 - 5}{900(5)(6)^2}(.11)} \Rightarrow .357 \pm .048 \Rightarrow (.309, .405)$$

d. $D = \frac{d^2\bar{M}^2}{4} = \frac{(.03)^2(6)^2}{4} = .0081 \qquad \sigma_C^2 = \frac{\sum(a_i - \hat{p}m_i)^2}{n - 1} = .11$

$$n = \frac{N\sigma_C^2}{ND + \sigma_C^2} \approx \frac{900(.11)}{900(.0081) + .11} = 13.38 \approx 14$$

Therefore, to find a 95% confidence interval for p with a half-width of .03, we need to sample approximately 14 clusters.

9.43   From Exercise 9.42, $n_1 = n_2 = n_3 = 400$

$N = N_1 + N_2 + N_3 = 20,800 + 6400 + 12,600 = 39,800$

$\hat{p}_1 = \frac{28}{400} = .07 \qquad \hat{p}_2 = \frac{17}{400} = .0425 \qquad \hat{p}_3 = \frac{45}{400} = .1125$

$\hat{q}_1 = 1 - \hat{p}_1 = 1 - .07 = .93 \qquad \hat{q}_2 = 1 - \hat{p}_2 = 1 - .0425 = .9575$

$\hat{q}_3 = 1 - \hat{p}_3 = 1 - .1125 = .8875$

$\hat{p}_{ST} = \frac{1}{N}(N_1\hat{p}_1 + N_2\hat{p}_2 + N_3\hat{p}_3)$

$= \frac{1}{39,800}[20,800(.07) + 6400(.0425) + 12,600(.1125)] = .079$

The approximate 95% confidence interval for p is:

$$\hat{p}_{ST} \pm 1.96 \sqrt{\frac{1}{N} \sum N_i^2 \frac{\hat{p}_i \hat{q}_i}{n_i - 1}\left(\frac{N_i - n_i}{N_i}\right)}$$

$$\Rightarrow .079 \pm 1.96 \sqrt{\frac{1}{(39,800)^2}\left[(20,800)^2\frac{(.07)(.93)}{399}\left(\frac{20,800 - 400}{20,800}\right)\right.}$$
$$+ (6,400)^2\frac{(.0425)(.9575)}{399}\left(\frac{6,400 - 400}{6,400}\right)$$
$$\left.+ (12,600)^2\frac{(.1125)(.8875)}{399}\left(\frac{12,600 - 400}{12,600}\right)\right]$$

$\Rightarrow .079 \pm .016 \Rightarrow (.063, .095)$

9.45 For this example, n = 25 and N = 100.

$$\bar{x} = \frac{\sum x}{n} = \frac{131,949}{25} = 5,277.96$$

$$s^2 = \frac{\sum x^2 - \frac{(\sum x)^2}{n}}{n - 1} = \frac{1,050,326,887 - \frac{(131,949)^2}{25}}{25 - 1} = 14,746,055.96$$

$$s = \sqrt{s^2} = 3,840.059$$

An approximate 95% confidence interval for μ is:

$$\bar{x} \pm 1.96\left(\frac{s}{\sqrt{n}}\right)\sqrt{\frac{N - n}{N}}$$

$$\Rightarrow 5,277.96 \pm 1.96\left(\frac{3,840.059}{\sqrt{25}}\right)\sqrt{\frac{100 - 25}{100}}$$

$\Rightarrow 5,277.96 \pm 1,303.63$

$\Rightarrow (3,974.33, 6,581.59)$

9.47 In this example, M = 1500, N = 96, and n = 6.

$$\sum x_i = 36 + 25 + 16 + 24 + 15 + 20 = 136$$
$$\sum m_i = 20 + 10 + 18 + 18 + 10 + 16 = 92$$

$$\bar{x} = \frac{\sum x_i}{\sum m_i} = \frac{136}{92} = 1.4783 \qquad M\bar{x} = 1500\left(\frac{136}{92}\right) = 2217.39$$

To find the approximate 95% confidence interval, we should first obtain the sample estimate of the variance of the cluster totals.

$$\frac{\sum(x_i - \bar{x}m_i)^2}{n - 1} = \frac{1}{6 - 1}\{[36 - 1.4783(20)]^2 + \ldots + [20 - 1.4783(16)]^2\}$$

$$= \frac{278.5418}{5} = 55.7084$$

The approximate 95% confidence interval τ is:

$$M\bar{x} \pm 1.96\sqrt{N^2\left(\frac{N - n}{Nn}\right)\sum\frac{(x_i - \bar{x}m_i)^2}{n - 1}}$$

$$\Rightarrow 2217.39 \pm 1.96\sqrt{(96)^2\left(\frac{96 - 6}{96(6)}\right)(55.7084)}$$

$$\Rightarrow 2217.39 \pm 555.13 \Rightarrow (1,662.26, \ 2,772.52)$$

CASE STUDIES

9.1   a.   For Question one, $N = 500$, $n = 172$.

$$\sqrt{\frac{N - n}{N}} = \sqrt{\frac{500 - 172}{500}} = .810$$

b. $\hat{p} = \frac{95}{172} = .552$

An approximate 95% confidence interval for p is

$$\hat{p} \pm 1.96\sqrt{\frac{\hat{p}(1 - \hat{p})}{n}}\sqrt{\frac{N - n}{N}}$$

$$\Rightarrow .552 \pm 1.96\sqrt{\frac{.552(1 - .552)}{172}}(.810)$$

$$\Rightarrow .552 \pm .060 \Rightarrow (.492, .612)$$

c.   For Question two, $N = 500$ and $n = 177$.

$$\sqrt{\frac{N - n}{N}} = \sqrt{\frac{500 - 177}{500}} = .804$$

d. $\hat{p} = \frac{74}{177} = .418$

An approximate 95% confidence interval for p is

$$\hat{p} \pm 1.96 \sqrt{\frac{\hat{p}(1 - \hat{p})}{n}} \sqrt{\frac{N - n}{N}}$$

$$\Rightarrow .418 \pm 1.96 \sqrt{\frac{.418(1 - .418)}{177}} (.804)$$

$$\Rightarrow .418 \pm .058 \Rightarrow (.36, .476)$$

e. For Question three, N = 500 and n = 183.

$$\sqrt{\frac{N - n}{N}} = \sqrt{\frac{500 - 183}{500}} = .796$$

f. $\hat{p} = \frac{38}{183} = .208$

An approximate 95% confidence interval for p is

$$\hat{p} \pm 1.96 \sqrt{\frac{\hat{p}(1 - \hat{p})}{n}} \sqrt{\frac{N - n}{N}}$$

$$\Rightarrow .208 \pm 1.96 \sqrt{\frac{.208(1 - .208)}{183}} (.796)$$

$$\Rightarrow .208 \pm .047 \Rightarrow (.161, .255)$$

TEN COLLECTING EVIDENCE TO SUPPORT A THEORY: GENERAL CONCEPTS OF HYPOTHESIS TESTING

10.1   a.   The null hypothesis (H_0) is that which is hoped to be disproved or rejected, whereas the alternative hypothesis (H_a) is that about which supportive evidence is to be gathered.

10.3   We define the following parameter:

μ = true mean price of a pair of straight-leg jeans at all retail outlets in New York City

Since we want to test whether this mean price is greater than \$35.00, the null and alternative hypotheses would be

H_0: $\mu = \$35.00$
H_a: $\mu > \$35.00$

10.5   The breeder/seller wishes to gather evidence that p, the proportion of chicken mortality due to cannibalism is less than .04. Thus,

H_0: $p = .04$
H_a: $p < .04$

10.7   The tests in Exercises 10.2, 10.3, and 10.5 are one-tailed since the alternative hypothesis in each is directional and includes either the symbol "<" or ">". Exercises 10.4 and 10.6 have two-tailed tests since the alternative hypothesis does not specify departure from H_0 in a particular direction.

10.9   a. α is the probability of rejecting a null hypothesis when it is true.

        b.   If the null hypothesis is rejected, the probability that the alternative hypothesis is not correct is α. By rejecting H_0, there is evidence to support H_a, but we cannot absolutely prove H_a.

c. If $\alpha + \beta = 1$, then $\alpha = 1 - \beta = 1 - P(\text{Fail to reject } H_0 | H_0 \text{ false})$
    $= P(\text{Reject } H_0 | H_0 \text{ false})$. But, we know $\alpha = P(\text{Reject } H_0 | H_0 \text{ true})$.
    However, it is true that as α increases, β decreases and as α
    decreases, β increases.

10.11 If we were to accept H_0, then the reliability of the conclusions would
       be measured by β, the probability of a Type II error--which is usually
       unknown.

10.13 For this two-sided alternative, we would reject the null hypothesis
       for "sufficiently small" or "sufficiently large" values of the
       standardized test statistic

$$z = \frac{\bar{x} - 65}{s/\sqrt{n}}$$

Thus, $\alpha/2 = .02/2 = .01$ is required in each tail of the normal
distribution. $z_{\alpha/2} = z_{.01}$ must be found such that $P(z > z_{.01}) = .01$
$\Rightarrow P(0 < z < z_{.01}) = .5 - .01 = .4900$, which yields $z_{.01} = 2.33$
(Table 4, Appendix E).

We noted that the chance of observing a sample mean $\bar{x}$ more than 2.33
standard deviations above 65, when in fact H_0 is true, is only
$\alpha/2 = .02/2 = .01$. Thus, the rejection region consists of two sets of
values. We will reject H_0 if z is either less than -2.33 or greater
than 2.33. For this rejection rule, the probability of a Type I error
is .02.

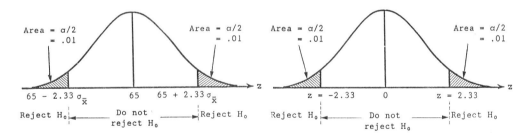

Rejection region in terms of $\bar{x}$.   Rejection region in terms of z.

10.15 α = probability of rejecting H_0 when it is true or the probability
       that the test statistic will fall in the rejection region when H_0 is
       true.

a. $\alpha = P(z < -1.96) = .5 - P(-1.96 < z < 0)$
    $= .5 - .4750 = .025$ (Table 4, Appendix E)

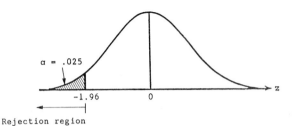

b. $\alpha = P(z > 1.645) = .5 - P(0 < z < 1.645)$
    $= .5 - .45 = .05$ (Table 4, Appendix E)

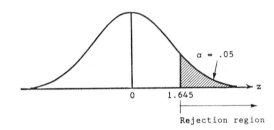

c. $\alpha = P(z < -2.58) + P(z > 2.58)$
    $= 1 - P(-2.58 < z < 0) - P(0 < z < 2.58)$
    $= 1 - .4951 - .4951$
    $= .0098$
    $\approx .01$

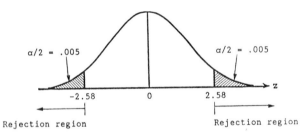

10.17 From Exercise 10.12, we want to test:

       $H_o:$ $\mu = 16$
       $H_a:$ $\mu < 16$

a. $z = \dfrac{\bar{x} - \mu_{\bar{x}}}{\sigma_{\bar{x}}} - \dfrac{\bar{x} - 16}{\sigma/\sqrt{n}} \approx \dfrac{\bar{x} - 16}{s/\sqrt{n}} = \dfrac{15.7 - 16}{.8/\sqrt{50}} = -2.65$

b. Since the alternative hypothesis is $\mu < 16$, the test is one-tailed. Thus, $\alpha = .01$ is required in the lower tail of the normal distribution. $z_\alpha = z_{.01}$ must be found so that $P(z < -z_{.01})$

$= P(z > z_{.01}) = .01 \Rightarrow P(0 < z < z_{.01}) = .5 - .01 = .4900$, which yields $z_{.01} = 2.33$ (Table 4, Appendix E). Thus, the rejection region is $z < -2.33$.

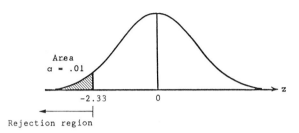

Area
$\alpha = .01$

-2.33

0

Rejection region

c. Since the calculated value of $z = -2.65$ is less than -2.33, we can reject H_0 at the $\alpha = .01$ level. There is sufficient evidence to indicate the mean weight of a bag of this particular brand of potato chips is less than 16 ounces at $\alpha = .01$.

10.19 The power of a test is equal to $1 - \beta$. Therefore, β and the power of a test are complements of each other.

10.21 We want to test:

$H_0:$ $\mu = \mu_0$
$H_a:$ $\mu > \mu_0$

a. $\alpha = .01$ is required in the upper tail of the normal distribution. $z_\alpha = z_{.01}$ must be found so that $P(z > z_{.01}) = .01$ $\Rightarrow P(0 < z < z_{.01}) = .5 - .01 = .4900$, which yields $z_{.01} = 2.33$ (Table 4, Appendix E). Thus, the rejection region in terms of z is $z > 2.33$.

$$\bar{x}_0 = \mu_0 + z_\alpha \left(\frac{\sigma}{\sqrt{n}}\right) = 1,000 + 2.33\left(\frac{42}{\sqrt{36}}\right) = 1016.31$$

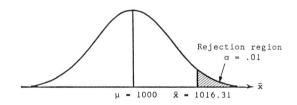

Rejection region
$\alpha = .01$

$\mu = 1000$ $\bar{x} = 1016.31$

b. $\alpha = .05$ is required in the upper tail of the normal distribution. $z_\alpha = z_{.05}$ must be found so that $P(z > z_{.05}) = .05$ $\Rightarrow P(0 < z < z_{.05}) = .5 - .05 = .4500$, which yields $z_{.05} = 1.645$ (Table 4, Appendix E). Thus, the rejection region in terms of z is $z > 1.645$.

$$\bar{x}_0 = \mu_0 + z_\alpha\left(\frac{\sigma}{\sqrt{n}}\right) = 68 + 1.645\left(\frac{42}{\sqrt{100}}\right) = 74.909$$

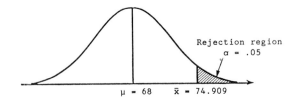

c. $\alpha = .10$ is required in the upper tail of the normal distribution. $z_\alpha = z_{.10}$ must be found so that $P(z > z_{.10}) = .10$ => $P(0 < z < z_{.10}) = .5 - .10 = .4000$, which yields $z_{.10} = 1.28$ (Table 4, Appendix E). Thus, the rejection region in terms of z is $z > 1.28$.

$$\bar{x}_0 = \mu_0 + z_\alpha\left(\frac{\sigma}{\sqrt{n}}\right) = 7.8 + 1.28\left(\frac{42}{\sqrt{85}}\right) = 13.63$$

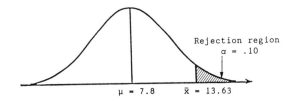

10.23 We want to test:

$H_0: \quad \mu = 25$
$H_a: \quad \mu \neq 25$

a. $\alpha/2 = .10/2 = .05$ is required in each tail of the normal distribution. $z_{\alpha/2} = z_{.05}$ must be found such that $P(z > z_{.05}) = .05$ => $P(0 < z < z_{.05}) = .5 - .05 = .4500$, which yields $z_{.05} = 1.645$ (Table 4, Appendix E). Thus, the rejection region in terms of z is $z < -1.645$ or $z > 1.645$.

$$\bar{x}_{0,U} \approx \mu_0 + z_{\alpha/2}\left(\frac{s}{\sqrt{n}}\right) = 25 + 1.645\left(\frac{12}{\sqrt{100}}\right) = 26.974$$

$$\bar{x}_{0,L} \approx \mu_0 - z_{\alpha/2}\left(\frac{s}{\sqrt{n}}\right) = 25 - 1.645\left(\frac{12}{\sqrt{100}}\right) = 23.026$$

Thus, the rejection region in terms of $\bar{x}$ is $\bar{x} < 23.026$ or $\bar{x} > 26.974$.

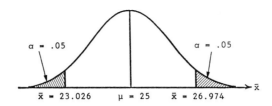

$$\beta = P(\text{Type II error})$$
$$= P(\text{Accept } H_0 \text{ when } H_0 \text{ is false})$$
$$= P(23.026 < \bar{x} < 26.974 \text{ when } \mu_a = 23)$$

$$= P\left(\frac{23.026 - 23}{12/\sqrt{100}} < \frac{\bar{x} - \mu}{s/\sqrt{n}} < \frac{26.974 - 23}{12/\sqrt{100}}\right)$$

$$= P(.02 < z < 3.31)$$
$$\approx .5 - .0080 = .4920 \qquad \text{(Table 4, Appendix E)}$$

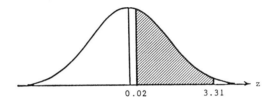

Power of the test = $1 - \beta = 1 - .492 = .508$

b. $\alpha/2 = .05/2 = .025$ is required in each tail of the normal
distribution. $z_{\alpha/2} = z_{.025}$ must be found such that
$P(z > z_{.025}) = .025 \Rightarrow P(0 < z < z_{.025}) = .5 - .025 = .475$, which
yields $z_{.025} = 1.96$ (Table 4, Appendix E). Thus, the rejection
region in terms of z is $z < -1.96$ or $z > 1.96$.

$$\bar{x}_{0,U} \approx \mu_0 + z_{\alpha/2}\left(\frac{s}{\sqrt{n}}\right) = 25 + 1.96\left(\frac{12}{\sqrt{100}}\right) = 27.352$$

$$\bar{x}_{0,L} \approx \mu_0 - z_{\alpha/2}\left(\frac{s}{\sqrt{n}}\right) = 25 - 1.96\left(\frac{12}{\sqrt{100}}\right) = 22.648$$

Thus, the rejection region in terms of $\bar{x}$ is $\bar{x} < 22.648$ or
$\bar{x} > 27.352$.

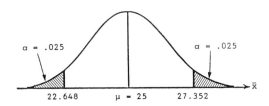

β = P(Type II error)

  = P(Accept H_0 when H_0 is false)

  = P(22.648 < $\bar{x}$ < 27.352 when μ_a = 23)

  = $P\left(\dfrac{22.648 - 23}{12/\sqrt{100}} < \dfrac{\bar{x} - \mu}{s/\sqrt{n}} < \dfrac{27.352 - 23}{12/\sqrt{100}}\right)$

  = P(-.29 < z < 3.63)

  $\approx$ .5 - .1141 = .3859   (Table 4, Appendix E)

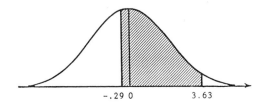

Power of the test = 1 - β = 1 - .3859 = .6141

c. $\alpha/2$ = .01/2 = .005 is required in each tail of the normal distribution. $z_{\alpha/2}$ = $z_{.005}$ must be found such that P(z > $z_{.005}$) = .005 => P(0 < z < $z_{.005}$) = .5 - .005 = .495, which yields $z_{.005}$ = 2.58 (Table 4, Appendix E). Thus, the rejection region in terms of z is z < -2.58 or z > 2.58.

$$\bar{x}_{0,U} \approx \mu_0 + z_{\alpha/2}\left(\frac{s}{\sqrt{n}}\right) = 25 + 2.58\left(\frac{12}{\sqrt{100}}\right) = 28.096$$

$$\bar{x}_{0,L} \approx \mu_0 - z_{\alpha/2}\left(\frac{s}{\sqrt{n}}\right) = 25 - 2.58\left(\frac{12}{\sqrt{100}}\right) = 21.904$$

Thus, the rejection region in terms of $\bar{x}$ is $\bar{x}$ < 21.904 or $\bar{x}$ > 28.096.

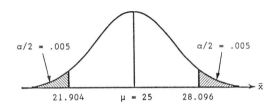

β = P(Type II error)

= P(Accept H_0 when H_0 is false)

= P(21.904 < $\bar{x}$ < 28.096 when μ_a = 23)

= P$\left(\dfrac{21.904 - 23}{12/\sqrt{100}} < \dfrac{\bar{x} - \mu}{s/\sqrt{n}} < \dfrac{28.096 - 23}{12/\sqrt{100}}\right)$

= P(-.91 < z < 4.25)

$\approx$ .5 - .3186 = .1814   (Table 4, Appendix E)

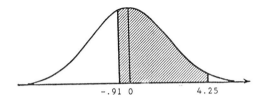

Power of the test = 1 - β = 1 - .1814 = .8186

10.25   In Examples 10.3 and 10.16, we want to test:

H_0: μ = .5
H_a: $\mu \neq$ .5

From Example 10.16, the rejection region in terms of z is z < -1.96 or z > 1.96.

$$\bar{x}_{0,U} \approx \mu_0 + z_{\alpha/2}\left(\dfrac{s}{\sqrt{n}}\right) = .5 + 1.96\left(\dfrac{.075}{\sqrt{50}}\right) = .5208$$

$$\bar{x}_{0,L} \approx \mu_0 - z_{\alpha/2}\left(\dfrac{s}{\sqrt{n}}\right) = .5 - 1.96\left(\dfrac{.075}{\sqrt{50}}\right) = .4792$$

Thus, the rejection region in terms of $\bar{x}$ is $\bar{x}$ < .4792 or $\bar{x}$ > .5208.

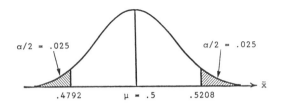

$\beta = P(\text{Type II error})$
$\quad = P(\text{Accept } H_0 \text{ when } H_0 \text{ is false})$
$\quad = P(.4792 < \bar{x} < .5208 \text{ when } \mu_a = .495)$

$\quad = P\left(\dfrac{.4792 - .495}{.075/\sqrt{50}} < \dfrac{\bar{x} - \mu}{s/\sqrt{n}} < \dfrac{.5208 - .495}{.075/\sqrt{50}}\right)$

$\quad = P(-1.49 < z < 2.43)$
$\quad = .4319 + .4925 \qquad (\text{Table 4, Appendix E})$
$\quad = .9244$

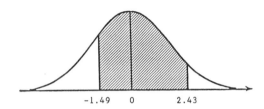

Power of the test $= 1 - \beta = 1 - .9244 = .0756$

10.27   In a statistical test of hypothesis, we either (1) reject H_0 or (2) do not reject H_0.

10.29   We risk making a Type I error when we reject a null hypothesis. We risk making a Type II error when we accept a null hypothesis.

10.31   As α decreases, β increases. As β increases, the power of the test (Power $= 1 - \beta$) decreases.

10.33   a. $\alpha/2 = .01/2 = .005$ is required in each tail of the normal distribution. $z_{\alpha/2} = z_{.005}$ must be found such that $P(z > z_{.005}) = .005 \Rightarrow P(0 < z < z_{.005}) = .5 - .005 = .495$, which yields $z_{.005} = 2.58$ (Table 4, Appendix E). Thus, the rejection region is $z < -2.58$ or $z > 2.58$.

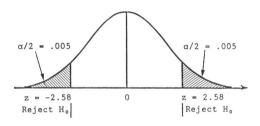

b. $\alpha/2 = .02/2 = .01$ is required in each tail of the normal
    distribution. $z_{\alpha/2} = z_{.01}$ must be found such that
    $P(z > z_{.01}) = .01 \Rightarrow P(0 < z < z_{.01}) = .5 - .01 = .49$, which
    yields $z_{.01} = 2.33$ (Table 4, Appendix E). Thus, the rejection
    region is $z < -2.33$ or $z > 2.33$.

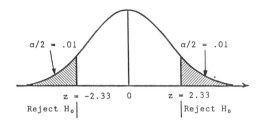

c. $\alpha/2 = .04/2 = .02$ is required in each tail of the normal
    distribution. $z_{\alpha/2} = z_{.02}$ must be found such that
    $P(z > z_{.02}) = .02 \Rightarrow P(0 < z < z_{.02}) = .5 - .02 = .48$, which
    yields $z_{.02} = 2.05$ (Table 4, Appendix E). Thus, the rejection
    region is $z < -2.05$ or $z > 2.05$.

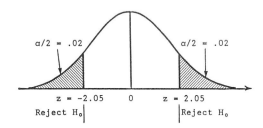

10.35 Define the following parameter:

μ = true mean breaking strength of the competitor's 22-pound line

If $\mu < 22$, then the competitor's line is not as advertised. The null
and alternative hypotheses are:

H_0: $\mu = 22$ (the competitor's claim is true)
H_a: $\mu < 22$ (the competitor's claim is not true)

10.37 Define the following parameters:

μ_1 = true mean starting salary for male graduates
μ_2 = true mean starting salary for female graduates

The college placement center wants to determine if μ_1 is greater than μ_2. The null and alternative hypotheses are:

H_0: $\mu_1 - \mu_2 = 0$ (that is, $\mu_1 = \mu_2$; there is no difference between the two means)
H_a: $\mu_1 - \mu_2 > 0$ (that is, $\mu_1 > \mu_2$; the mean salary for males exceeds the mean salary for females)

10.39 Define the following parameter:

p = proportion of "sevens" occurring in many tosses of two dice

The craps player wishes to test whether this proportion is different from 1/6. Thus, the null and alternative hypotheses are:

H_0: $p = 1/6$ (the dice are not loaded)
H_a: $p \neq 1/6$ (the dice are loaded)

10.41 The dealer wishes to test:

H_0: $\mu = 24,000$
H_a: $\mu > 24,000$

a. $\alpha = .01$ is required in the upper tail of the normal distribution. $z_\alpha = z_{.01}$ must be found so that $P(z > z_{.01}) = .01$
=> $P(0 < z < z_{.01}) = .5 - .01 = .4900$, which yields $z_{.01} = 2.33$ (Table 4, Appendix E). Thus, the rejection region is $z > 2.33$.

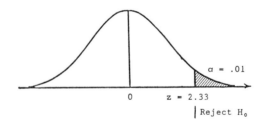

b. $z = \dfrac{\bar{x} - \mu_{\bar{x}}}{\sigma_{\bar{x}}} = \dfrac{\bar{x} - \mu_{\bar{x}}}{\sigma/\sqrt{n}} \approx \dfrac{\bar{x} - \mu}{s/\sqrt{n}} = \dfrac{24,517 - 24,000}{1866/\sqrt{32}} = 1.57$

c. Since the calculated value of $z = 1.57$ is not greater than 2.33, do not reject H_0. There is insufficient evidence to indicate the true mean number of miles driven by Fiat owners in 2 years is greater than 24,000 miles at $\alpha = .01$.

d. A Type I error would be to reject H_0 when it is true, that is, to consider that the true mean number of miles driven by Fiat owners is greater than 24,000 when in fact it is less than or equal to 24,000 miles.

e. A Type II error would be to accept H_0 when it is false, that is, to say that the true mean number of miles driven by Fiat owners is less than or equal to 24,000 miles when in fact it is more than 24,000 miles.

f. From part (a), the rejection region in terms of z is $z > 2.33$.

$$\bar{x}_0 \approx \mu_0 + z_\alpha\left(\frac{s}{\sqrt{n}}\right) = 24,000 + 2.33\left(\frac{1866}{\sqrt{32}}\right) = 24,768.586$$

Thus, the rejection region in terms of $\bar{x}$ is $\bar{x} > 24,768.586$.

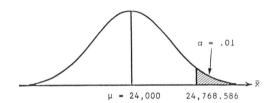

$$\begin{aligned}
\beta &= P(\text{Type II error})\\
&= P(\text{Accept } H_0 \text{ when } H_0 \text{ is false})\\
&= P(\bar{x} \leq 24,768.586 \text{ when } \mu_a = 25,000)\\
&= P\left(\frac{\bar{x} - \mu}{s/\sqrt{n}} \leq \frac{24,768.586 - 25,000}{1866/\sqrt{32}}\right)\\
&= P(z \leq -.70)\\
&= .5 - .2580 = .2420
\end{aligned}$$

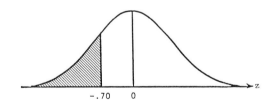

g. From part (a), the rejection region in terms of z is $z > 2.33$.

From part (f), the rejection region in terms of $\bar{x}$ is $\bar{x} > 24,768.586$.

$$\beta = P(\text{Type II error})$$
$$= P(\text{Accept } H_0 \text{ when } H_0 \text{ is false})$$
$$= P(\bar{x} \leq 24,768.586 \text{ when } \mu_a = 26,000)$$

$$= P\left(\frac{\bar{x} - \mu}{s/\sqrt{n}} \leq \frac{24,768.586 - 26,000}{1866/\sqrt{32}} \right)$$

$$= P(z \leq -3.73)$$
$$\approx .5 - .5 = 0$$

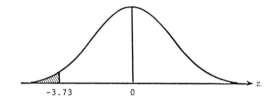

Power of the test $= 1 - \beta \approx 1 - 0 = 1$

CASE STUDIES

10.1   a.   Define the following parameter:

p = proportion of all "loyal" Budweiser drinkers who would prefer Schlitz over Budweiser in a similar taste test.

The null and alternative hypotheses are:

$$H_0: \quad p = .40$$
$$H_a: \quad p > .40$$

b. $\alpha = .05$ is required in the upper tail of the normal distribution. $z_{\alpha/2} = z_{.05}$ must be found so that $P(z > z_{.05}) = .05$ => $P(0 < z < z_{.05}) = .5 - .05 = .4500$, which yields $z_{.05} = 1.645$ (Table 4, Appendix E).   Thus, the rejection region is $z > 1.645$.

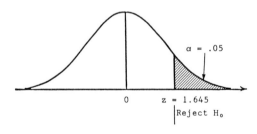

c. $\hat{p} = \dfrac{46}{100} = .46$

$z = \dfrac{\hat{p} - p_0}{\sqrt{\dfrac{p_0 q_0}{n}}} = \dfrac{.46 - .40}{\sqrt{\dfrac{.40(.60)}{100}}} = 1.22$

d.   Since the calculated value of z = 1.22 is not greater than 1.645, do not reject H_0. There is insufficient evidence to indicate the true proportion of all "loyal" Budweiser drinkers who prefer Schlitz over Budweiser in a similar taste test is larger than .40 at α = .05.

10.3 a.   Since the drug will be provisionally accepted if μ_1 is significantly less than μ_2, the null and alternative hypotheses are:

H_0: $\mu_1 - \mu_2 = 0$ (that is, $\mu_1 = \mu_2$; there is no difference between the two means.)

H_a: $\mu_1 - \mu_2 < 0$ (that is, $\mu_1 < \mu_2$; the mean tumor weight for mice treated with the drug is less than the mean tumor weight for untreated mice.)

b.   A Type I error would be to reject H_0 when it is true. In this case, we would decide the mean tumor weight for mice treated with the drug is less than the mean tumor weight for untreated mice, when it really is not. This would be a false positive result.

A Type II error would be to accept H_0 when it is really false. In this case, we would decide the mean tumor weight is the same for treated and untreated mice when it is really lower for treated mice. This would be a false negative result.

c.   α = .01 is required in the lower tail of the normal distribution. $z_\alpha = z_{.01}$ must be found so that $P(z < -z_{.01}) = .01$ => $P(0 < z < z_{.01}) = .5 - .01 = .4900$, which yields $z_{.01} = 2.33$ (Table 4, Appendix E). Thus, the rejection region is z < -2.33.

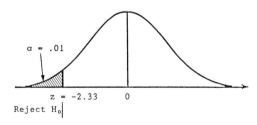

α = .01

z = -2.33   0

Reject H_0

d. $\bar{x}_1 - \bar{x}_2 = 1.23 - 1.37 = -.14$.

We should not base our decision on this value alone. Some consideration should be given to the variability of the responses and the number of responses taken. Also, these are just sample means. If we took another sample, the values of $\bar{x}_1$ and $\bar{x}_2$ will change.

e. $z = \dfrac{(\bar{x}_1 - \bar{x}_2) - (\mu_1 - \mu_2)}{\sqrt{\dfrac{\sigma_1^2}{n_1} + \dfrac{\sigma_2^2}{n_2}}} \approx \dfrac{(\bar{x}_1 - \bar{x}_2) - (\mu_1 - \mu_2)}{\sqrt{\dfrac{s_1^2}{n_1} + \dfrac{s_2^2}{n_2}}}$

$= \dfrac{(1.23 - 1.37) - 0}{\sqrt{\dfrac{(.55)^2}{50} + \dfrac{(.21)^2}{50}}} = -1.68$

f. Since the calculated value of $z = -1.68$ is not less than -2.33, do not reject H_0. There is insufficient evidence to indicate the mean tumor weight for mice treated with the drug is less than the mean tumor weight of untreated mice at $\alpha = .01$. The pharmaceutical company should not provisionally accept the drug, but should subject it to further testing at $\alpha = .01$.

ELEVEN   HYPOTHESIS TESTING: APPLICATIONS

11.1   a.   The test statistic is $z \approx \dfrac{\bar{x} - \mu_0}{s/\sqrt{n}} = \dfrac{10 - 9.8}{4.3/\sqrt{30}} = \dfrac{.2}{.785} = .25$

    b.   The test statistic is $z \approx \dfrac{\bar{x} - \mu_0}{s/\sqrt{n}} = \dfrac{75 - 80}{\sqrt{19}/\sqrt{36}} = \dfrac{-5}{.7264} = -6.88$

    c.   The test statistic is $z \approx \dfrac{\bar{x} - \mu_0}{s/\sqrt{n}} = \dfrac{8.2 - 8.3}{.79/\sqrt{175}} = \dfrac{-.1}{.0597} = -1.67$

11.3   a.   The rejection region for the two-tailed, small-sample test requires $\alpha/2 = .05/2 = .025$ in each tail of the t distribution with df = n - 1 = 15 - 1 = 14. From Table 6, Appendix E, $t_{.025} = 2.145$. The rejection region is t < -2.145 or t > 2.145.

    b.   The rejection region for the two-tailed, small-sample test requires $\alpha/2 = .01/2 = .005$ in each tail of the t distribution with df = n - 1 = 15 - 1 = 14. From Table 6, Appendix E, $t_{.005} = 2.977$. The rejection region is t < -2.977 or t > 2.977.

    c.   The rejection region for the one-tailed, small-sample test requires $\alpha = .05$ in the lower tail of the t distribution with df = n - 1 = 15 - 1 = 14. From Table 6, Appendix E, $t_{.05} = 1.761$. The rejection region is t < -1.761.

    d.   The rejection region for the one-tailed, small-sample test requires $\alpha = .10$ in the upper tail of the t distribution with df = n - 1 = 5 - 1 = 4. From Table 6, Appendix E, $t_{.10} = 1.533$. The rejection region is t > 1.533.

    e.   The rejection region for the one-tailed, small-sample test requires $\alpha = .10$ in the upper tail of the t distribution with df = n - 1 = 25 - 1 = 24. From Table 6, Appendix E, $t_{.10} = 1.318$. The rejection region is t > 1.318.

11.5 Some preliminary calculations are:

$$\bar{x} = \frac{\sum x}{n} = \frac{50.3}{49} \approx 1.0265$$

$$s^2 = \frac{\sum x^2 - \frac{(\sum x)^2}{n}}{n - 1} = \frac{68 - \frac{(50.3)^2}{49}}{49 - 1} \approx .34095$$

$$s = \sqrt{s^2} \approx \sqrt{.34095} \approx .5839$$

a. H_0: $\mu = 1.18$
    H_a: $\mu < 1.18$

The rejection region for the one-tailed, large-sample test requires $\alpha = .01$ in the lower tail of the normal distribution. From Table 4, Appendix E, $z_{.01} = 2.33$. The rejection region is $z < -2.33$.

The test statistic is $z \approx \dfrac{\bar{x} - \mu_0}{s/\sqrt{n}} = \dfrac{1.0265 - 1.18}{.5839/\sqrt{49}} \approx -1.84$

Since the observed value of the test statistic does not fall in the rejection region ($z \approx -1.84 \not< -2.33$), H_0 cannot be rejected. There is insufficient evidence at $\alpha = .01$ that $\mu < 1.18$.

b. H_0: $\mu = 1.18$
    H_a: $\mu < 1.18$

The rejection region for the one-tailed, large-sample test requires $\alpha = .10$ in the lower tail of the normal distribution. From Table 4, Appendix E, $z = 1.28$. The rejection region is $z < -1.28$.

The test statistic is $z \approx -1.84$. (Refer to part (a).)

Since the observed value of the test statistic falls in the rejection region ($z \approx -1.84 < -1.28$), H_0 is rejected. There is sufficient evidence at $\alpha = .10$ that $\mu < 1.18$.

Note that H_a was rejected in part (b), not in part (a), because of the increased α-level. That is, a greater chance of Type I error.

11.7 a. Since it is desired to determine if the average abnormal rate of return exceeds 0, we test:

H_0: $\mu = 0$
H_a: $\mu > 0$

The rejection region for the one-tailed, large sample test requires $\alpha = .05$ in the upper tail of the normal distribution. From Table 4, Appendix E, $z_{.05} = 1.645$. The rejection region is $z > 1.645$.

The test statistic is $z = \dfrac{\bar{x} - \mu_0}{\sigma_{\bar{x}}} \approx \dfrac{\bar{x} - \mu_0}{s/\sqrt{n}} = \dfrac{.005 - 0}{.0233/\sqrt{112}} = 2.27$

Since the observed value of the test statistic falls in the rejection region ($z = 2.27 > 1.645$), H_0 is rejected. There is sufficient evidence to conclude at $\alpha = .05$ that the average abnormal rate of return 2 days after the recall announcement exceeds 0.

b. H_0: $\mu = 0$
   H_a: $\mu > 0$

The rejection region for the one-tailed, small-sample test requires $\alpha = .05$ in the upper tail of the t distribution with df $= n - 1 = 25 - 1 = 24$. From Table 6, Appendix E, $t_{.05} = 1.711$ with 24 df. The rejection region is $t > 1.711$.

The test statistic is $t = \dfrac{\bar{x} - \mu_0}{s/\sqrt{n}} = \dfrac{.005 - 0}{.0233/\sqrt{25}} = 1.07$

Since the observed value of the test statistic does not fall in the rejection region ($t = 1.07 \not> 1.711$), H_0 is not rejected. There is insufficient evidence to conclude at $\alpha = .05$ that the average abnormal rate of return 2 days after the recall announcement exceeds 0.

11.9 Since it is desired to determine if the mean trigger price differs from \$358.31, we test:

   H_0: $\mu = 358.31$
   H_a: $\mu \neq 358.31$

The rejection region for the large-sample, two-tailed test requires $\alpha/2 = .10/2 = .05$ in each tail of the normal distribution. From Table 4, Appendix E, $z_{.05} = 1.645$. The rejection region is $z < -1.645$ or $z > 1.645$.

The test statistic is $z = \dfrac{\bar{x} - \mu_0}{\sigma_{\bar{x}}} \approx \dfrac{\bar{x} - \mu_0}{s/\sqrt{n}} = \dfrac{390.88 - 358.31}{106.19/\sqrt{40}} = 1.94$

Since the observed test statistic falls in the rejection region ($z = 1.94 > 1.645$), H_0 is rejected. There is sufficient evidence to conclude at $\alpha = .10$ that the mean trigger price is different from \$358.31.

11.11   As the city building inspector, we would like to be very confident
        that the manufacturer's sewer pipes meet the requirements. This would
        be very important to the people living in the city and to the
        inspector's job. He might, therefore, use a smaller value of α to
        have a smaller probability of deciding the pipes meet the
        specifications when they really do not.

11.13   Since the manager suspects the mean number of overtime pay hours
        worked per month exceeds the national average of 9 hours, we test:

$$H_0: \quad \mu = 9$$
$$H_a: \quad \mu > 9$$

The rejection region for a one-tailed, large-sample test requires
$\alpha = .05$ in the upper tail of the normal distribution. From Table 4,
Appendix E, $z_{.05} = 1.645$. The rejection region is $z > 1.645$.

The test statistic is $z = \dfrac{\bar{x} - \mu_0}{\sigma_{\bar{x}}} \approx \dfrac{\bar{x} - \mu_0}{s/\sqrt{n}} = \dfrac{12.3 - 9}{4.1/\sqrt{50}} = 5.69$

Since the observed value of the test statistic falls in the rejection
region ($z = 5.69 > 1.645$), H_0 is rejected. There is sufficient
evidence at $\alpha = .05$ to support the manager's hypothesis.

11.15   Since we want to determine if the dispensing machines are in need of
        adjustment, we test:

$$H_0: \quad \mu = 32 \text{ (i.e., no adjustment needed)}$$
$$H_a: \quad \mu \neq 32 \text{ (i.e., machines are in need of adjustment)}$$

The rejection region for the small-sample, two-tailed test requires
$\alpha/2 = .05/2 = .025$ in each tail of the t distribution with
$df = n - 1 = 10 - 1 = 9$. From Table 6, Appendix E, $t_{.025} = 2.262$.
The rejection region is $t < -2.262$ or $t > 2.262$.

The test statistic is $t = \dfrac{\bar{x} - \mu_0}{s/\sqrt{n}} = \dfrac{31.55 - 32}{.48/\sqrt{10}} = -2.96$

Since the observed value of the test statistic falls in the rejection
region ($t = -2.96 < -2.262$), H_0 is rejected. There is sufficient
evidence at $\alpha = .05$ to conclude the machines are in need of
adjustment.

11.17   a. $H_0: \quad p = .10$
             $H_a: \quad p > .10$

        The rejection region for a one-tailed test requires $\alpha = .10$ in the
        upper tail of the normal distribution. From Table 4, Appendix E,
        $z_{.10} = 1.28$. The rejection region is $z > 1.28$.

The test statistic is $z = \dfrac{\hat{p} - p_0}{\sqrt{\dfrac{p_0 q_0}{n}}} = \dfrac{.13 - .10}{\sqrt{\dfrac{.10(1 - .10)}{200}}} = 1.41$

Since the observed value of the test statistic falls in the rejection region ($z = 1.41 > 1.28$), H_0 is rejected. There is sufficient evidence to conclude at $\alpha = .10$ that $p > .10$.

b. H_0: $p = .05$
    H_a: $p < .05$

The rejection region for a one-tailed test requires $\alpha = .05$ in the lower tail of the normal distribution. From Table 4, Appendix E, $z_{.05} = 1.645$. The rejection region is $z < -1.645$.

The test statistic is $z = \dfrac{\hat{p} - p_0}{\sqrt{\dfrac{p_0 q_0}{n}}} = \dfrac{.04 - .05}{\sqrt{\dfrac{.05(1 - .05)}{1124}}} = -1.54$

Since the observed value of the test statistic does not fall in the rejection region ($z = -1.54 \nless -1.645$), H_0 is not rejected. There is insufficient evidence to conclude at $\alpha = .05$ that $p < .05$.

c. H_0: $p = .90$
    H_a: $p \neq .90$

The rejection region for a two-tailed test requires $\alpha/2 = .01/2 = .005$ in each tail of the normal distribution. From Table 4, Appendix E, $z_{.005} = 2.58$. The rejection region is $z < -2.58$ or $z > 2.58$.

The test statistic is $z = \dfrac{\hat{p} - p_0}{\sqrt{\dfrac{p_0 q_0}{n}}} = \dfrac{.73 - .90}{\sqrt{\dfrac{.90(1 - .90)}{49}}} = -3.97$

Since the observed value of the test statistic falls in the rejection region ($z = -3.97 < -2.58$), H_0 is rejected. There is sufficient evidence to conclude at $\alpha = .01$ that $p \neq .90$.

11.19   Since we want to determine if the proportion of job applicants preferring the computer interview is not .85, we test:

H_0: $p = .85$
H_a: $p \neq .85$

The rejection region for a two-tailed test with $\alpha = .01$ requires $\alpha/2 = .01/2 = .005$ in each tail of the normal distribution. From Table 4, Appendix E, $z_{.005} = 2.58$. The rejection region is $z < -2.58$ or $z > 2.58$.

Since $\hat{p} = \dfrac{162}{200} = .81$, the test statistic is

$$z = \frac{\hat{p} - p_0}{\sqrt{p_0 q_0/n}} = \frac{.81 - .85}{\sqrt{(.85)(.15)/200}} = -1.58$$

Since the observed value of the test statistic does not fall in the rejection region ($z = -1.58 \not< -2.58$), H_0 is not rejected. There is insufficient evidence to dispute the spokesman's claim at $\alpha = .01$.

Note that the interval

$$\hat{p} \pm 2\sqrt{\hat{p}\hat{q}/n} \Rightarrow .81 \pm 2\sqrt{\frac{.81(1 - .81)}{200}}$$

$$\Rightarrow .81 \pm .0555$$

$$\Rightarrow (.7545, .8655)$$

does not contain 0 or 1. Thus, the sample size is large enough to guarantee the validity of the hypothesis test.

11.21   Since we want to determine if the proportion of food retailers in rural areas who are members of FMI is less than the national proportion, we test:

H_0: $p = .55$
H_a: $p < .55$

The rejection region for the one-tailed test requires $\alpha = .05$ in the lower tail of the normal distribution. From Table 4, Appendix E, $z_{.05} = 1.645$. The rejection region is $z < -1.645$.

$$\hat{p} = \frac{\text{Number of sampled rural food retailers belonging to FMI}}{\text{Number of rural food retailers sampled}}$$

$$= \frac{18}{40} = .45$$

Note that $q_0 = 1 - p_0 = 1 - .55 = .45$. We can obtain the test statistic:

$$z = \frac{\hat{p} - p_0}{\sqrt{p_0 q_0/n}} = \frac{.45 - .55}{\sqrt{(.55)(.45)/40}} = \frac{-.10}{.079} = -1.27$$

Since the value of the test statistic does not fall in the rejection region ($z = -1.27 \nless -1.645$), H_0 is not rejected. There is insufficient evidence to conclude that the proportion of rural food retailers belonging to FMI is less than the national average at $\alpha = .05$.

Note that the interval

$$\hat{p} \pm 2\sqrt{\hat{p}\hat{q}/n} \Rightarrow .45 \pm 2\sqrt{.45(.55)/100}$$

$$\Rightarrow .45 \pm .099 \Rightarrow (.351, .549)$$

does not contain 0 or 1; thus, the test is valid.

11.23   Since it is desired to determine if the proportion of surviving trees is less than .95, we test:

H_0: $p = .95$
H_a: $p < .95$

The rejection region for the one-tailed, large-sample test requires $\alpha = .01$ in the lower tail of the normal distribution. From Table 4, Appendix E, $z_{.01} = 2.33$. The rejection region is $z < -2.33$.

The test statistic is

$$z = \frac{\hat{p} - p_0}{\sqrt{p_0 q_0/n}} = \frac{\frac{46}{50} - .95}{\sqrt{(.95)(1 - .95)/50}} = \frac{-0.03}{.0308} = -0.97$$

Since the observed value of the test statistic does not fall in the rejection region ($z = -0.97 \nless -2.33$), H_0 is not rejected. There is insufficient evidence at $\alpha = .01$ to conclude the proportion of surviving trees is less than .95.

11.25   a.   The rejection region for a two-tailed, large-sample test requires $\alpha/2 = .01/2 = .005$ in each tail of the normal distribution. From Table 4, Appendix E, $z_{.005} = 2.58$. The rejection region is $z < -2.58$ or $z > 2.58$.

b.   The rejection region for a two-tailed, large-sample test requires $\alpha/2 = .10/2 = .05$ in each tail of the normal distribution. From Table 4, Appendix E, $z_{.05} = 1.645$. The rejection region is $z < -1.645$ or $z > 1.645$.

c.   The rejection region for a one-tailed, large-sample test requires $\alpha = .05$ in the upper tail of the normal distribution. From Table 4, Appendix E, $z_{.05} = 1.645$. The rejection region is $z > 1.645$.

d.   The rejection region for a one-tailed, large-sample test requires $\alpha = .05$ in the lower tail of the normal distribution. From Table 4, Appendix E, $z_{.05} = 1.645$. The rejection region is $z < -1.645$.

11.27 a. H_0: $(\mu_1 - \mu_2) = 0$
           H_a: $(\mu_1 - \mu_2) \neq 0$

The rejection region for a two-tailed, large-sample test requires $\alpha/2 = .05/2 = .025$ in each tail of the normal distribution. From Table 4, Appendix E, $z_{.025} = 1.96$. The rejection region is $z < -1.96$ or $z > 1.96$.

The test statistic is

$$z \approx \frac{(\bar{x}_1 - \bar{x}_2) - D_0}{\sqrt{\dfrac{s_1^2}{n_1} + \dfrac{s_2^2}{n_2}}} = \frac{(7.0 - 6.0) - 0}{\sqrt{\dfrac{3^2}{40} + \dfrac{1^2}{60}}} = 2.03$$

Since the test statistic falls in the rejection region ($z = 2.03 > 1.96$), H_0 is rejected. There is sufficient evidence to conclude $(\mu_1 - \mu_2) \neq 0$ at $\alpha = .05$.

       b. H_0: $(\mu_1 - \mu_2) = .5$
           H_a: $(\mu_1 - \mu_2) \neq .5$

The rejection region is $z < -1.96$ or $z > 1.96$. (Refer to part (a).)

The test statistic is

$$z \approx \frac{(\bar{x}_1 - \bar{x}_2) - D_0}{\sqrt{\dfrac{s_1^2}{n_1} + \dfrac{s_2^2}{n_2}}} = \frac{(7.0 - 6.0) - .5}{\sqrt{\dfrac{3^2}{40} + \dfrac{1^2}{60}}} = 1.02$$

Since the test statistic does not fall in the rejection region ($z = 1.02 \not> 1.96$), H_0 is not rejected. There is insufficient evidence to conclude $(\mu_1 - \mu_2) \neq .5$ at $\alpha = .05$.

11.29 Some preliminary calculations are:

$$\bar{x}_1 = \frac{\sum x_1}{n_1} = \frac{4.8 + 5.2 + 5.0 + 4.9 + 5.1}{5} = \frac{25}{5} = 5$$

$$s_1^2 = \frac{\sum x_1^2 - \dfrac{(\sum x_1)^2}{n_1}}{n_1 - 1} = \frac{125.1 - \dfrac{(25)^2}{5}}{4} = .025$$

$$\bar{x}_2 = \frac{\sum x_2}{n_2} = \frac{5.0 + 4.7 + 4.9 + 4.8}{4} = \frac{19.4}{4} = 4.85$$

$$s_2^2 = \frac{\sum x_2^2 - \dfrac{(\sum x_2)^2}{n_2}}{n_2 - 1} = \frac{94.14 - \dfrac{(19.4)^2}{4}}{3} = .0167$$

$$s_p^2 = \frac{(n_1 - 1)s_1^2 + (n_2 - 1)s_2^2}{n_1 + n_2 - 2} = \frac{(5 - 1)(.025) + (4 - 1)(.0167)}{5 + 4 - 2} = .0214$$

We wish to test the following hypotheses:

H_0: $(\mu_1 - \mu_2) = 0$
H_a: $(\mu_1 - \mu_2) > 0$

The rejection region for a one-tailed, small-sample test requires $\alpha = .05$ in the upper tail of the t distribution with df = $n_1 + n_2 - 2$ = 5 + 4 - 2 = 7. From Table 6, Appendix E, $t_{.05}$ = 1.895. The rejection region is t > 1.895.

The test statistic is

$$t = \frac{(\bar{x}_1 - \bar{x}_2) - D_0}{\sqrt{s_p^2\left(\frac{1}{n_1} + \frac{1}{n_2}\right)}} \quad \frac{(5 - 4.85) - 0}{\sqrt{.0214\left(\frac{1}{5} + \frac{1}{4}\right)}} = 1.53$$

Since the calculated value of the test statistic does not fall in the rejection region (t = 1.53 ≯ 1.895), H_0 is not rejected. There is insufficient evidence to conclude $(\mu_1 - \mu_2) > 0$ at $\alpha = .05$.

11.31 a. Let μ_1 = mean initial performance rating of stayers and μ_2 = mean initial performance rating of leavers.

Since we wish to determine if there is a difference between the mean initial performance ratings of stayers and leavers, we test:

H_0: $(\mu_1 - \mu_2) = 0$
H_a: $(\mu_1 - \mu_2) \neq 0$

The rejection region for this two-tailed, large-sample test requires $\alpha/2 = .01/2 = .005$ in each tail of the normal distribution. From Table 4, Appendix E, $z_{.005}$ = 2.58. The rejection region is z < -2.58 or z > 2.58.

The test statistic is

$$z \approx \frac{(\bar{x}_1 - \bar{x}_2) - D_0}{\sqrt{\frac{s_1^2}{n_1} + \frac{s_2^2}{n_2}}} \quad \frac{(3.51 - 3.24) - 0}{\sqrt{\frac{(.51)^2}{174} + \frac{(.52)^2}{355}}} = 5.68$$

Since the computed value of the test statistic falls in the rejection region (z = 5.68 > 2.58), H_0 is rejected. There is sufficient evidence to indicate there is a difference in the mean initial performance ratings of stayers and leavers at $\alpha = .01$.

b. Let μ_1 = mean rate of career advancement for stayers and μ_2 = mean rate of career advancement for leavers. Since we wish to determine if the mean rate of career advancement differs for stayers and leavers, we test:

$$H_0: \ (\mu_1 - \mu_2) = 0$$
$$H_a: \ (\mu_1 - \mu_2) \neq 0$$

The rejection region is $z < -2.58$ or $z > 2.58$. Refer to part (a).)

The test statistic is

$$z \approx \frac{(\bar{x}_1 - \bar{x}_2) - D_0}{\sqrt{\dfrac{s_1^2}{n_1} + \dfrac{s_2^2}{n_2}}} = \frac{(.43 - .31) - 0}{\sqrt{\dfrac{.20^2}{174} + \dfrac{.31^2}{355}}} = 5.36$$

Since the computed value of the test statistic falls in the rejection region ($z = 5.36 > 2.58$), H_0 is rejected. There is sufficient evidence to conclude the mean rate of career advancement differs for stayers and leavers at $\alpha = .01$.

11.33 Let μ_1 = mean ethic rating of male executives and μ_2 = mean ethic rating of female executives. Since we wish to determine if the mean ethic ratings of the two groups differ, we test:

$$H_0: \ (\mu_1 - \mu_2) = 0$$
$$H_a: \ (\mu_1 - \mu_2) \neq 0$$

The rejection region for a two-tailed, large-sample test requires $\alpha/2 = .05/2 = .025$ in each tail of the normal distribution. From Table 4, Appendix E, $z_{.025} = 1.96$. The rejection region is $z < -1.96$ or $z > 1.96$.

The test statistic is

$$z \approx \frac{(\bar{x}_1 - \bar{x}_2) - D_0}{\sqrt{\dfrac{s_1^2}{n_1} + \dfrac{s_2^2}{n_2}}} = \frac{(2.44 - 3.06) - 0}{\sqrt{\dfrac{2.2}{50} + \dfrac{2.2}{50}}} = -2.09$$

Since the computed value of the test statistic falls in the rejection region ($z = -2.09 < -1.96$), H_0 is rejected. There is sufficient evidence to conclude the mean ethic ratings of the two groups differ at $\alpha = .05$.

11.35 Let μ_1 = mean monthly return before the merger and μ_2 = mean monthly return after the merger. Since it is desired to determine if a difference exists between the means of the monthly returns before and after the merger, we test:

H_0: $\mu_1 - \mu_2 = 0$
H_a: $\mu_1 - \mu_2 \neq 0$

The rejection region for a two-sided, small-sample test requires $\alpha/2 = .01/2 = .005$ in each tail of the t distribution with df $= n_1 + n_2 - 2 = 10 + 6 - 2 = 14$. From Table 6, Appendix E, $t_{.005} = 2.977$. The rejection region is $t < -2.977$ or $t > 2.977$.

Our pooled estimate of the common variance is given by

$$s_p^2 = \frac{(n_1 - 1)s_1^2 + (n_2 - 1)s_2^2}{n_1 + n_2 - 2} = \frac{(10 - 1)(4.3)^2 + (6 - 1)(4.8)^2}{10 + 6 - 2} = 20.115$$

The test statistic is

$$t = \frac{(\bar{x}_1 - \bar{x}_2) - D_0}{\sqrt{s_p^2\left(\frac{1}{n_1} + \frac{1}{n_2}\right)}} = \frac{(8.5 - 7.1) - 0}{\sqrt{20.115\left(\frac{1}{10} + \frac{1}{6}\right)}} = .60$$

Since the computed value of the test statistic does not fall in the rejection region (t = .60 $\not>$ 2.977), H_0 is not rejected. There is insufficient evidence to conclude that there is a difference in the means of the monthly returns before and after the merger at $\alpha = .01$.

11.37 a. Let μ_1 = mean ratio for small banks and μ_2 = mean ratio for large banks. Since we wish to detect a difference between the mean ratios, we test:

H_0: $(\mu_1 - \mu_2) = 0$
H_a: $(\mu_1 - \mu_2) \neq 0$

   b. The rejection region for a two-sided, large-sample test requires $\alpha/2 = .05/2 = .025$ in each tail of the normal distribution. From Table 4, Appendix E, $z_{.025} = 1.96$. The rejection region is $z < -1.96$ or $z > 1.96$.

The test statistic is z = 1.50.

Since the computed value of the test statistic does not fall in the rejection region (z = 1.50 $\not>$ 1.96), H_0 is not rejected. There is insufficient evidence to conclude there is a difference in mean ratios for small and large banks at $\alpha = .05$.

11.39 a. H_0: $(\mu_1 - \mu_2) = 0$
          H_a: $(\mu_1 - \mu_2) \neq 0$

The rejection region for a two-sided, small-sample test requires $\alpha/2 = .01/2 = .005$ in each tail of the t distribution with n - 1 = 10 - 1 = 9. From Table 6, Appendix E, $z_{.005} = 3.250$. The rejection region is $t < -3.250$ or $t > 3.250$.

The test statistic is $t = \dfrac{\bar{d} - D_0}{s_d/\sqrt{n}} = \dfrac{400 - 0}{435/\sqrt{10}} = 2.91$

Since the computed value of the test statistic does not fall in the rejection region (t = 2.91 ≯ 3.250), H_0 is not rejected. There is insufficient evidence to indicate μ_1 is different from μ_2 at α = .01.

b. H_0: $(\mu_1 - \mu_2) = 0$
   H_a: $(\mu_1 - \mu_2) > 0$

The rejection region for a one-sided, small-sample test requires α = .05 in the upper tail of the t distribution with n - 1 = 5 - 1 = 4. From Table 6, Appendix E, $t_{.05}$ = 2.132. The rejection region is t > 2.132.

The test statistic is $t = \dfrac{\bar{d} - D_0}{s_d/\sqrt{n}} = \dfrac{.48 - 0}{.08/\sqrt{5}} = 13.42$

Since the computed value of the test statistic falls in the rejection region (t = 13.42 > 2.132), H_0 is rejected. There is sufficient evidence to indicate μ_1 is greater than μ_2 at α = .05.

c. H_0: $(\mu_1 - \mu_2) = 0$
   H_a: $(\mu_1 - \mu_2) < 0$

The rejection region for a one-sided, small-sample test requires α = .10 in the lower tail of the t distribution with n - 1 = 6 - 1 = 5. From Table 6, Appendix E, $t_{.10}$ = 1.476. The rejection region is t < -1.476.

The test statistic is $t = \dfrac{\bar{d} - D_0}{s_d/\sqrt{n}} = \dfrac{-1.3 - 0}{.95/\sqrt{6}} = -3.27$

Since the computed value of the test statistic falls in the rejection region (t = -3.27 < -1.476), H_0 is rejected. There is sufficient evidence to indicate μ_1 is less than μ_2 at α = .10.

11.41 a. The first step in conducting the test is to calculate the difference d between each pair in the sample.

PAIR	SAMPLE 1	SAMPLE 2	d
1	6	4	2
2	2	1	1
3	5	8	-3
4	10	7	3
5	8	6	2
6	4	2	2

Next we calculate the mean $\bar{d}$ and standard deviation s_d for this sample of n = 6 differences.

$$\bar{d} = \frac{\sum d}{n} = \frac{2 + 1 - 3 + 3 + 2 + 2}{6} = \frac{7}{6} = 1.167$$

$$\sum d^2 = 2^2 + 1^2 + (-3)^2 + 3^2 + 2^2 + 2^2 = 31$$

$$s_d^2 = \frac{\sum d^2 - \frac{(\sum d)^2}{n}}{n - 1} = \frac{31 - \frac{(7)^2}{6}}{5} = 4.567$$

$$s_d = \sqrt{s_d^2} = \sqrt{4.567} = 2.14$$

The hypotheses we want to test are:

$$H_0: \ (\mu_1 - \mu_2) = 0$$
$$H_a: \ (\mu_1 - \mu_2) \neq 0$$

The rejection region for this two-tailed, small-sample test requires $\alpha/2 = .05/2 = .025$ in each tail of the t distribution with df = n - 1 = 6 - 1 = 5. From Table 6, Appendix E, $t_{.025} = 2.571$. The rejection region is t < -2.571 or t > 2.571.

The test statistic is $t = \dfrac{\bar{d} - D_0}{s_d/\sqrt{n}} = \dfrac{1.167 - 0}{2.14/\sqrt{6}} = 1.34$

Since the calculated value of the test statistic does not fall in the rejection region (t = 1.34 $\not>$ 2.571), H_0 is not rejected. There is insufficient evidence to conclude $(\mu_1 - \mu_2) \neq 0$ at $\alpha = .05$.

b. These assumptions must be met:

1) The relative frequency distribution of the population of differences is approximately normal.
2) The paired differences are randomly selected from the population of differences.

11.43 The first step in conducting the test is to calculate the difference d between each pair in the sample and calculate d^2.

CONTRACT	WINNING BID – DOT ESTIMATE (d)	d^2
1	227	51,529
2	319	101,761
3	2	4
4	626	391,876
5	-7	49
6	61	3,721
7	82	6,724
8	5	25
	$\sum d = 1315$	$\sum d^2 = 555,689$

Next we calculate the mean $\bar{d}$ and standard deviation s_d for the sample differences.

$$\bar{d} = \frac{\sum d}{n} = \frac{1315}{8} = 164.375$$

$$s_d^2 = \frac{\sum d^2 - \frac{(\sum d)^2}{n}}{n - 1} = \frac{555,689 - \frac{(1315)^2}{8}}{7} = 48,505.125$$

$$s_d = \sqrt{s_d^2} = \sqrt{48,505.125} = 220.239$$

We want to test:

$$H_0: \quad \mu_1 - \mu_2 = 0$$
$$H_a: \quad \mu_1 - \mu_2 > 0$$

where μ_1 = population mean winning bid price and μ_2 = population DOT estimated mean bid price. H_a included ">" because it is desired to test that μ_1 exceeds μ_2.

The rejection region for this one-tailed, small-sample test requires $\alpha = .05$ in the upper tail of the t distribution with df = n - 1 = 8 - 1 = 7. From Table 6, Appendix E, $t_{.05} = 1.895$. The rejection region is t > 1.895.

The test statistic is $t = \dfrac{\bar{d} - D_0}{s_d/\sqrt{n}} = \dfrac{164.375 - 0}{220.239/\sqrt{8}} = 2.11$

Since the observed value of the test statistic falls in the rejection region (t = 2.11 > 1.895), H_0 is rejected. There is sufficient evidence to conclude that the mean winning bid exceeds the mean DOT estimate for road construction contracts at $\alpha = .05$.

11.45 The first step in conducting the test is to calculate the difference d between each pair in the sample and calculate d^2.

BRAND	TRADITIONAL - WEEKEND (d)	d^2
1	-1.0	1.00
2	-2.0	4.00
3	.4	.16
4	1.6	2.56
5	-.8	.64
6	.4	.16
	$\sum d = -1.4$	$\sum d^2 = 8.52$

Next we calculate the mean $\bar{d}$ and standard deviation s_d for the sample differences.

$$\bar{d} = \frac{\sum d}{n} = \frac{-1.4}{6} = -.233$$

$$s_d^2 = \frac{\sum d^2 - \frac{(\sum d)^2}{n}}{n - 1} = \frac{8.52 - \frac{(-1.4)^2}{6}}{5} = 1.64$$

$$s_d = \sqrt{s_d^2} = 1.28$$

Let μ_1 = mean estimate of beer brand market share produced by the traditional audit method and μ_2 = mean estimate of beer brand market share produced by the weekend selldown audit method. Since we wish to determine if there is a difference in the mean estimates produced by the two methods, we test:

$H_0: \; (\mu_1 - \mu_2) = 0$
$H_a: \; (\mu_1 - \mu_2) \neq 0$

The rejection region for this two-tailed, small-sample test requires $\alpha/2 = .05/2 = .025$ in each tail of the t distribution with df = n - 1 = 6 - 1 = 5. From Table 6, Appendix E, $t_{.025} = 2.571$. The rejection region is t < -2.571 or t > 2.571.

The test statistic is t $= \dfrac{\bar{d} - D_0}{s_d/\sqrt{n}} = \dfrac{-.233 - 0}{1.28/\sqrt{6}} = -.45$

Since the calculated value of the test statistic does not fall in the rejection region (t = -.45 ≮ -2.571), H_0 is not rejected. There is insufficient evidence to conclude that a difference exists in the mean estimates of beer brand market shares produced by the two auditing methods at $\alpha = .05$.

11.47 The first step in conducting the test is to calculate the difference d between each pair in the sample and d^2.

DOG	DRUG A – DRUG B (d)	d^2
1	.04	.0016
2	.02	.0004
3	-.01	.0001
4	.07	.0049
5	0	0
6	.04	.0016
7	.03	.0009
	$\sum d = .19$	$\sum d^2 = .0095$

Next we calculate the mean $\bar{d}$ and standard deviation s_d for the sample differences.

$$\bar{d} = \frac{\sum d}{n} = \frac{.19}{7} = .0271$$

$$s_d^2 = \frac{\sum d^2 - \frac{(\sum d)^2}{n}}{n - 1} = \frac{.0095 - \frac{(.19)^2}{7}}{6} = .0007238$$

$$s_d = \sqrt{s_d^2} = \sqrt{.007238} = .0269$$

Let μ_1 = mean pressure reading for Drug A and μ_2 = mean pressure reading for Drug B. Since we wish to determine if there is a difference in the mean pressure readings for the two drugs, we test:

H_0: $(\mu_1 - \mu_2) = 0$
H_a: $(\mu_1 - \mu_2) \neq 0$

The rejection region for this two-sided, small-sample test requires $\alpha/2 = .05/2 = .025$ in each tail of the t distribution with df = n - 1 = 7 - 1 = 6. From Table 6, Appendix E, $t_{.025} = 2.447$. The rejection region is t < -2.447 or t > 2.447.

The test statistic is t = $\dfrac{\bar{d} - D_0}{s_d/\sqrt{n}} = \dfrac{.0271 - 0}{.0269/\sqrt{7}} = 2.67$

Since the observed value of the test statistic falls in the rejection region (t = 2.67 > 2.447), H_0 is rejected. There is sufficient evidence to conclude that there is a difference between the two drugs in mean pressure readings at $\alpha = .05$.

11.49 a. H_0: $(p_1 - p_2) = 0$
           H_a: $(p_1 - p_2) > 0$

The rejection region for a one-tailed, large-sample test requires $\alpha = .05$ in the upper tail of the normal distribution. Using Table 4, Appendix E, $z_{.05} = 1.645$. The rejection region is $z > 1.645$.

$$\hat{p}_1 = \frac{82}{100} = .82 \qquad \hat{p}_2 = \frac{76}{100} = .76$$

$$\hat{p} = \frac{82 + 76}{100 + 100} = .79, \; \hat{q} = 1 - \hat{p} = 1 - .79 = .21$$

The test statistic is

$$z = \frac{(\hat{p}_1 - \hat{p}_2) - D_0}{\sqrt{\hat{p}\hat{q}\left(\frac{1}{n_1} + \frac{1}{n_2}\right)}} = \frac{(.82 - .76) - 0}{\sqrt{(.79)(.21)\left(\frac{1}{100} + \frac{1}{100}\right)}} = 1.04$$

Since the observed value of the test statistic does not fall in the rejection region ($z = 1.04 \not> 1.645$), H_0 is not rejected. There is insufficient evidence to indicate p_1 is greater than p_2 at $\alpha = .05$.

In order for the above test to be valid, the following 2 intervals must not contain 0 or 1:

$$\hat{p}_1 \pm 2\sqrt{\frac{\hat{p}_1\hat{q}_1}{n_1}} \qquad\qquad \hat{p}_2 \pm 2\sqrt{\frac{\hat{p}_2\hat{q}_2}{n_2}}$$

$$\Rightarrow .82 \pm 2\sqrt{\frac{.82(.18)}{100}} \qquad \Rightarrow .76 \pm 2\sqrt{\frac{.76(.24)}{100}}$$

$$\Rightarrow .82 \pm .077 \qquad\qquad \Rightarrow .76 \pm .085$$

$$\Rightarrow (.743, .897) \qquad\qquad \Rightarrow (.675, .845)$$

The above intervals do not contain 0 or 1, so the test is valid.

b. H_0: $(p_1 - p_2) = 0$
    H_a: $(p_1 - p_2) > 0$

The rejection region is $z > 1.645$. (Refer to part (a).)

The test statistic is

$$z = \frac{(\hat{p}_1 - \hat{p}_2) - D_0}{\sqrt{\hat{p}\hat{q}\left(\frac{1}{n_1} + \frac{1}{n_2}\right)}} = \frac{(.82 - .76) - 0}{\sqrt{(.79)(.21)\left(\frac{1}{1000} + \frac{1}{1000}\right)}} = 3.29$$

Since the observed value of the test statistic falls in the rejection region ($z = 3.29 > 1.645$), H_0 is rejected. There is sufficient evidence to indicate p_1 is greater than p_2 at $\alpha = .05$.

In order for the above test to be valid, the following 2 intervals must not contain 0 or 1:

$$\hat{p}_1 \pm 2\sqrt{\frac{\hat{p}_1\hat{q}_1}{n_1}} \qquad\qquad \hat{p}_2 \pm 2\sqrt{\frac{\hat{p}_2\hat{q}_2}{n_2}}$$

$$\Rightarrow .82 \pm 2\sqrt{\frac{.82(.18)}{1000}} \qquad\qquad \Rightarrow .76 \pm 2\sqrt{\frac{.76(.24)}{1000}}$$

$$\Rightarrow .82 \pm .024 \qquad\qquad\qquad \Rightarrow .76 \pm .027$$

$$\Rightarrow (.796, .844) \qquad\qquad\qquad \Rightarrow (.733, .787)$$

The above intervals do not contain 0 or 1, so the test is valid.

11.51   Let p_1 = proportion of women who rate American products "high" in quality and p_2 = proportion of men who rate American products "high" in quality. Since we wish to determine if the proportion of women exceeds the proportion of men, we test:

$$H_0: \quad (p_1 - p_2) = 0$$
$$H_a: \quad (p_1 - p_2) > 0$$

The rejection region for a one-tailed, large-sample test requires $\alpha = .01$ in the upper tail of the normal distribution. Using Table 4, Appendix E, $z_{.01} = 2.33$. The rejection region is $z > 2.33$.

$$\hat{p}_1 = .58 \qquad \hat{p}_2 = .43$$

$$\hat{p} = \frac{500(.58) + 500(.43)}{500 + 500} = .505, \quad \hat{q} = 1 - \hat{p} = 1 - .505 = .495$$

The test statistic is

$$z = \frac{(\hat{p}_1 - \hat{p}_2) - D_0}{\sqrt{\hat{p}\hat{q}\left(\frac{1}{n_1} + \frac{1}{n_2}\right)}} = \frac{(.58 - .43) - 0}{\sqrt{(.505)(.495)\left(\frac{1}{500} + \frac{1}{500}\right)}} = 4.74$$

Since the observed value of the test statistic falls in the rejection region ($z = 4.74 > 2.33$), H_0 is rejected. There is sufficient evidence to conclude the proportion of women who rate American products "high" in quality exceeds the proportion of men who rate the American products "high" in quality at $\alpha = .01$.

In order for the above test to be valid, the following 2 intervals
must not contain 0 or 1:

$$\hat{p}_1 \pm 2\sqrt{\frac{\hat{p}_1\hat{q}_1}{n_1}} \qquad\qquad \hat{p}_2 \pm 2\sqrt{\frac{\hat{p}_2\hat{q}_2}{n_2}}$$

$$\Rightarrow .58 \pm 2\sqrt{\frac{.58(.42)}{500}} \qquad \Rightarrow .43 \pm 2\sqrt{\frac{.43(.57)}{500}}$$

$$\Rightarrow .58 \pm .044 \qquad\qquad \Rightarrow .43 \pm .044$$

$$\Rightarrow (.536,\ .624) \qquad\qquad \Rightarrow (.386,\ .474)$$

The above intervals do not contain 0 or 1, so the test is valid.

11.53 a. Let p_1 = proportion of MFWS users who rely on the computer
and p_2 = proportion of non-MFWS users who rely on the computer.
Since we wish to determine if there is a difference in the
proportions, we test:

$$H_0:\ (p_1 - p_2) = 0$$
$$H_a:\ (p_1 - p_2) \neq 0$$

The rejection region for a two-tailed, large-sample test requires
$\alpha/2 = .10/2 = .05$ in each tail of the normal distribution. Using
Table 4, Appendix E, $z_{.05} = 1.645$. The rejection region is
$z < -1.645$ or $z > 1.645$.

$$\hat{p}_1 = \frac{4}{12} = .333 \qquad \hat{p}_2 = \frac{2}{25} = .08$$

$$\hat{p} = \frac{x_1 + x_2}{n_1 + n_2} = \frac{4 + 2}{12 + 25} = \frac{6}{37} = .162, \quad \hat{q} = 1 - \hat{p} = 1 - .162 = .838$$

The test statistic is

$$z = \frac{(\hat{p}_1 - \hat{p}_2) - D_0}{\sqrt{\hat{p}\hat{q}\left(\frac{1}{n_1} + \frac{1}{n_2}\right)}} = \frac{(.333 - .08) - 0}{\sqrt{(.162)(.838)\left(\frac{1}{12} + \frac{1}{25}\right)}} = 1.96$$

Since the observed value of the test statistic falls in the
rejection region ($z = 1.96 > 1.645$), H_0 is rejected. There is
sufficient evidence to indicate a difference in the proportions of
MFWS users and non-MFWS users that rely on the computer as their
major information source at $\alpha = .05$.

b. The samples are sufficiently large if the following 2 intervals do not contain 0 or 1.

$$\hat{p}_1 \pm 2\sqrt{\frac{\hat{p}_1\hat{q}_1}{n_1}} \qquad\qquad \hat{p}_2 \pm 2\sqrt{\frac{\hat{p}_2\hat{q}_2}{n_2}}$$

$$\Rightarrow .333 \pm 2\sqrt{\frac{.333(.667)}{12}} \qquad\qquad \Rightarrow .08 \pm 2\sqrt{\frac{.08(.92)}{25}}$$

$$\Rightarrow .333 \pm .272 \qquad\qquad\qquad \Rightarrow .08 \pm .109$$

$$\Rightarrow (.061, .605) \qquad\qquad\qquad \Rightarrow (-.029, .189)$$

Since the second interval contains 0, n_2 is not large enough to run the test. Therefore, the test run in part (a) is not necessarily valid.

11.55 Let p_1 = proportion of the experimental group (false advertisement) who perceive the coffee as having "no bitterness" and p_2 = proportion of the control group (no advertisement) who perceive the coffee as having "no bitterness." To determine if the proportion in the experimental group is larger than that in the control group, we test:

H_0: $(p_1 - p_2) = 0$
H_a: $(p_1 - p_2) > 0$

$\hat{p}_1 = 32/100 = .32$, $\hat{p}_2 = 11/100 = .11$,

$\hat{p} = (32 + 11)/(100 + 100) = .215$, $\hat{q} = 1 - \hat{p} = 1 - .215 = .785$

The rejection region for a one-tailed, large-sample test requires $\alpha = .10$ in the upper tail of the normal distribution. Using Table 4, Appendix E, $z_{.10} = 1.28$. The rejection region is $z > 1.28$.

The test statistic is

$$z = \frac{(\hat{p}_1 - \hat{p}_2) - D_0}{\sqrt{\hat{p}\hat{q}\left(\frac{1}{n_1} + \frac{1}{n_2}\right)}} = \frac{(.32 - .11) - 0}{\sqrt{.215(.785)\left(\frac{1}{100} + \frac{1}{100}\right)}} = \frac{.21}{.0581} = 3.61$$

Since the observed value of the test statistic falls in the rejection region ($z = 3.61 > 1.28$), H_0 is rejected. There is sufficient evidence to indicate the proportion of the experimental subjects who perceive "no bitterness" is greater than that of the control group ($p_1 - p_2 > 0$) at $\alpha = .10$.

In order for the above test to be valid, the following 2 intervals must not contain 0 or 1.

$$\hat{p}_1 \pm 2\sqrt{\frac{\hat{p}_1\hat{q}_1}{n_1}} \qquad\qquad \hat{p}_2 \pm 2\sqrt{\frac{\hat{p}_2\hat{q}_2}{n_2}}$$

$$=> .32 \pm 2\sqrt{\frac{.32(.68)}{100}} \qquad => .11 \pm 2\sqrt{\frac{.11(.89)}{100}}$$

$$=> .32 \pm .093 \qquad\qquad => .11 \pm .063$$

$$=> (.227, .413) \qquad\qquad => (.047, .173)$$

The above intervals do not contain 0 or 1, so the test is valid.

11.57 For these large-sample, upper-tailed tests, the p-value is $P(z \geq z_c)$. Use Table 4, Appendix E to find the p-values.

a. $P(z \geq z_c) = P(z \geq 1.96) = .5 - .4750 = .025$

b. $P(z \geq z_c) = P(z \geq 1.645) = .5 - .4500 = .05$

c. $P(z \geq z_c) = P(z \geq 2.67) = .5 - .4962 = .0038$

d. $P(z \geq z_c) = P(z \geq 1.25) = .5 - .3944 = .1056$

11.59 For these small-sample, two-tailed tests, the p-value is $2P(t \geq |t_c|)$. Use Table 6, Appendix E to find the p-values.

a. $2P(t \geq |t_c|) = 2P(t \geq 3.25)$ with df = n − 1 = 10 − 1 = 9. Thus, the p-value is 2(.005) = .01.

b. $2P(t \geq |t_c|) = 2P(t \geq 1.58)$ with df = n − 1 = 15 − 1 = 14. The p-value is between 2(.10) = .20 and 2(.05) = .10. Using the conservative approach, the p-value is .20.

c. $2P(t \geq |t_c|) = 2P(t \geq 2.20)$ with df = n − 1 = 12 − 1 = 11. The t value is very close to $t_{.025}$ = 2.201. Thus, the p-value is 2(.025) = .05.

d. $2P(t \geq |t_c|) = 2P(t \geq 2.97)$ with df = n − 1 = 5 − 1 = 4. The p-value is between 2(.025) = .05 and 2(.01) = .02. Using the conservative approach, the p-value is .05.

11.61 For Exercise 11.15, the hypotheses are

H_0: $\mu = 32$
H_a: $\mu \neq 32$

The test statistic is t = −2.96 with df = n − 1 = 10 − 1 = 9.

The p-value for this small-sample, two-tailed test is $2P(t \geq |t_c|)$ = $2P(t \geq 2.96)$ with df = 9. Using Table 6, Appendix E, the p-value is between $2(.01) = .02$ and $2(.005) = .01$. Using the conservative approach, the p-value is .02.

We would reject H_0 if the p-value is less than α. Since the p-value is not less than α (.02 $\nless$ .01), H_0 is not rejected.

11.63 For Exercise 11.37, the hypotheses are

H_0: $(\mu_1 - \mu_2) = 0$
H_a: $(\mu_1 - \mu_2) \neq 0$

The test statistic is z = 1.50.

The p-value for this large-sample, two-tailed test is $2P(z \geq |z_c|)$ = $2P(z \geq 1.50) = 2(.5 - .4332) = 2(.0668) = .1336$. (Using Table 4, Appendix E.)

We would reject H_0 if the p-value is less than α. Since the p-value is not less than α (.1336 $\nless$ .10), H_0 is not rejected.

11.65 Using Table 8, Appendix E,

a. For $\nu_1 = 7$ and $\nu_2 = 25$, $F_{.05} = 2.40$

b. For $\nu_1 = 10$ and $\nu_2 = 8$, $F_{.05} = 3.35$

c. For $\nu_1 = 30$ and $\nu_2 = 60$, $F_{.05} = 1.65$

d. For $\nu_1 = 15$ and $\nu_2 = 4$, $F_{.05} = 5.86$

11.67 a. $F = \dfrac{s_1^2}{s_2^2} = \dfrac{1.75}{1.23} = 1.42$

b. $F = \dfrac{s_2^2}{s_1^2} = \dfrac{5.90}{1.52} = 3.88$

c. $F = \dfrac{\text{Larger sample variance}}{\text{Smaller sample variance}} = \dfrac{s_2^2}{s_1^2} = \dfrac{4009}{2264} = 1.77$

11.69 Let σ_1^2 = variance in the ME content for canned food and σ_2^2 = variance in the ME content for dry food. To determine if a difference exists between the 2 variances, we test:

H_0: $\dfrac{\sigma_1^2}{\sigma_2^2} = 1$

H_0: $\dfrac{\sigma_1^2}{\sigma_2^2} \neq 1$

The test statistic is $F = \dfrac{\text{Larger sample variance}}{\text{Smaller sample variance}} = \dfrac{s_2^2}{s_1^2} = \dfrac{.48^2}{.26^2} = 3.41$

The rejection region for this two-tailed test requires $\alpha/2 = .10/2$
$= .05$ in the upper tail of the F distribution with $v_1 = n_2 - 1$
$= 29 - 1 = 28$ and $v_2 = n_1 - 1 = 28 - 1 = 27$. From Table 8, Appendix
E, $F_{.05} \approx 1.90$. The rejection region is $F > 1.90$.

Since the observed value of the test statistic falls in the rejection
region ($F = 3.41 > 1.90$), H_0 is rejected. There is sufficient
evidence to conclude the variation in the ME content of cats fed
canned food differs from the variation in the ME content of cats fed
dry food at $\alpha = .10$.

11.71   Let σ_1^2 = population variance of the cost of running jobs using TSO
and σ_2^2 = population variance of the cost of running job using TCP.

Since it is desired to determine if there is a difference in the
variability of costs of TSO and TCP jobs, we test:

H_0: $\sigma_1^2/\sigma_2^2 = 1$ $(\sigma_1^2 = \sigma_2^2)$
H_a: $\sigma_1^2/\sigma_2^2 \neq 1$ $(\sigma_1^2 \neq \sigma_2^2)$

The test statistic is

$$F = \frac{\text{Larger sample variance}}{\text{Smaller sample variance}} = \frac{s_1^2}{s_2^2} = \frac{1.02^2}{.89^2} = \frac{1.0404}{.7921} = 1.31$$

The rejection region for a two-tailed test with $\alpha = .05$ requires
$\alpha/2 = .05/2 = .025$ in the upper tail of the F distribution with
$v_1 = n_1 - 1 = 20 - 1 = 19$ and $v_2 = n_2 - 1 = 15 - 1 = 14$. From Table
9, Appendix E, $F_{.025} \approx 2.86$. The rejection region is $F > 2.86$.

Since the observed value of the test statistic does not fall in the
rejection region ($F = 1.31 \not> 2.84$), H_0 is not rejected. There is
insufficient evidence to indicate a difference in the variability of
costs of TSO and TCP jobs at $\alpha = .05$.

11.73   Since we wish to determine if more than one-half of the adult
population favors higher taxes for schools, we test:

H_0: $p = .5$
H_a: $p > .5$

The rejection region for a one-tailed test requires $\alpha = .01$ in the
upper tail of the normal distribution. From Table 4, Appendix E,
$z_{.01} = 2.33$. The rejection region is $z > 2.33$.

$$\hat{p} = \frac{\text{Number of American adults in favor of paying higher taxes}}{\text{Number sampled}}$$

$$= \frac{1078}{1658} = .6502$$

The value of the test statistic is

$$z = \frac{\hat{p} - p_0}{\sqrt{p_0 q_0 / n}} = \frac{.6502 - .50}{\sqrt{(.5)(.5)/1658}} = 12.23$$

Since the computed value of the test statistic falls in the rejection region ($z = 12.23 > 2.33$), H_0 is rejected. There is sufficient evidence to indicate that more than half the population favors higher taxes for schools at $\alpha = .01$.

Note that the interval

$$\hat{p} \pm 2\sqrt{\frac{\hat{p}\hat{q}}{n}} \Rightarrow .65 \pm 2\sqrt{\frac{.65(.35)}{1658}}$$

$$\Rightarrow .65 \pm .027$$

$$\Rightarrow (.623, .677)$$

does not contain 0 or 1. Thus, the sample size is large enough to guarantee the validity of the hypothesis test.

11.75   Some preliminary calculations are:

$$\bar{x} = \frac{\sum x}{n} = \frac{118.5}{8} = 14.8$$

$$s^2 = \frac{\sum x^2 - \frac{(\sum x)^2}{n}}{n - 1} = \frac{3723.25 - \frac{(118.5)^2}{8}}{7} = 281.14$$

$$s = \sqrt{s^2} = \sqrt{281.14} = 16.77$$

Since we wish to determine if the mean percentage gain is greater than 0, we test:

$$H_0: \quad \mu = 0$$
$$H_a: \quad \mu > 0$$

The rejection region for a one-tailed, small-sample test requires $\alpha = .05$ in the upper tail of the t distribution with df $= n - 1 = 8 - 1 = 7$. From Table 6, Appendix E, $t_{.05} = 1.895$. The rejection region is $t > 1.895$.

The value of the test statistic is $t = \dfrac{\bar{x} - \mu_0}{s/\sqrt{n}} = \dfrac{14.8 - 0}{16.77/\sqrt{8}} = 2.50$

Since the calculated value of the test statistic falls in the rejection region ($t = 2.50 > 1.895$), H_0 is rejected. There is sufficient evidence to conclude the mean percentage gain for the 26-week holding period is greater than 0% at $\alpha = .05$.

11.77　a.　Let μ_1 = mean score for organizational climate before the program and μ_2 = mean score for organizational climate after the program. Since we wish to determine if the mean score increased after implementation of the program ($\mu_2 > \mu_1$), we test:

$$H_0: \quad (\mu_1 - \mu_2) = 0$$
$$H_a: \quad (\mu_1 - \mu_2) < 0$$

The rejection region for a one-tailed, large-sample test requires $\alpha = .01$ in the lower tail of the normal distribution. From Table 4, Appendix E, $z_{.01} = 2.33$. The rejection region is $z < -2.33$.

The test statistic is

$$z \approx \frac{(\bar{x}_1 - \bar{x}_2) - D_0}{\sqrt{\dfrac{s_1^2}{n_1} + \dfrac{s_2^2}{n_2}}} = \frac{(2.70 - 3.45) - 0}{\sqrt{\dfrac{3.91^2}{455} + \dfrac{3.91^2}{455}}} = -2.89$$

Since the computed value of the test statistic falls in the rejection region ($z = -2.89 < -2.33$), H_0 is rejected. There is sufficient evidence to conclude that the mean score for organizational climate increased after implementation of the supervisory development program at $\alpha = .01$.

b.　Let μ_1 = mean score for leadership behavior before the program and μ_2 = mean score for leadership behavior after the program. Since we wish to determine if the mean score increased after implementation of the program ($\mu_2 > \mu_1$), we test:

$$H_0: \quad (\mu_1 - \mu_2) = 0$$
$$H_a: \quad (\mu_1 - \mu_2) < 0$$

The rejection region is $z < -2.33$. (Refer to part (a).)

The test statistic is

$$z \approx \frac{(\bar{x}_1 - \bar{x}_2) - D_0}{\sqrt{\dfrac{s_1^2}{n_1} + \dfrac{s_2^2}{n_2}}} = \frac{(3.45 - 3.94) - 0}{\sqrt{\dfrac{4.74^2}{455} + \dfrac{4.74^2}{455}}} = -1.56$$

Since the computed value of the test statistic does not fall in the rejection region ($z = -1.56 \not< -2.33$), H_0 is not rejected. There is insufficient evidence to conclude that the mean score for leadership behavior increased after implementation of the supervisory development program at $\alpha = .01$.

c. The experiment described was actually a matched-pairs experiment. To perform the tests described in parts (a) and (b), the difference d of before and after scores should be calculated for each of the 455 employees. The mean and standard deviation used in testing would be calculated using the differences d. Then, a one-sample test should be done using the differences.

11.79 The first step in conducting the test is to calculate the difference d between each pair in the sample and calculate d^2.

WEEK	LIVE OAK - GAINESVILLE d	d^2
1	-0.82	.6724
2	-2.16	4.6656
3	-0.09	.0081
4	-1.24	1.5376
	$\sum d = -4.31$	$\sum d^2 = 6.8837$

Next we calculate the mean $\bar{d}$ and standard deviation s_d for the sample differences.

$$\bar{d} = \frac{\sum d}{n} = \frac{-4.31}{4} = -1.0775$$

$$s_d^2 = \frac{\sum d^2 - \frac{(\sum d)^2}{n}}{n - 1} = \frac{6.8837 - \frac{(-4.31)^2}{4}}{4 - 1} = .74656$$

$$s_d = \sqrt{.74656} = .86404$$

Let μ_1 = average weekly selling price of live hogs in Live Oak and μ_2 = average weekly selling price of live hogs in Gainesville. Since we wish to determine if there is a difference in the average weekly selling prices, we test:

H_0: $(\mu_1 - \mu_2) = 0$
H_a: $(\mu_1 - \mu_2) \neq 0$

The rejection region for this two-sided, small-sample test requires $\alpha/2 = .05/2 = .025$ in each tail of the t distribution with df = n - 1 = 4 - 1 = 3. From Table 6, Appendix E, $t_{.025} = 3.182$. The rejection region is t < -3.182 or t > 3.182.

The test statistic is $t = \dfrac{\bar{d} - D_0}{s_d/\sqrt{n}} = \dfrac{-1.0775 - 0}{.86404/\sqrt{4}} = -2.49$

Since the observed value of the test statistic does not fall in the rejection region (t = -2.49 ≮ -3.182), H_0 is not rejected. There is insufficient evidence to conclude the average selling price of live hogs is different for the two Florida markets at $\alpha = .05$.

11.81 The first step in conducting the test is to calculate the difference d between each pair in the sample and calculate d^2.

MONTH	SEEDED - UNSEEDED d	d^2
1	.13	.0169
2	.29	.0841
3	.13	.0169
4	.35	.1225
5	-.01	.0001
6	.09	.0081
	$\sum d = .98$	$\sum d^2 = .2486$

Next we calculate the mean $\bar{d}$ and standard deviation s_d for the sample differences.

$$\bar{d} = \frac{\sum d}{n} = \frac{.98}{6} = .1633$$

$$s_d^2 = \frac{\sum d^2 - \frac{(\sum d)^2}{n}}{n - 1} = \frac{.2486 - \frac{(.98)^2}{6}}{6 - 1} = .017707$$

$$s_d = \sqrt{.017707} = .1331$$

Let μ_1 = mean precipitation for seeded farm areas and μ_2 = mean precipitation for unseeded farm areas. Since we wish to determine if the mean difference in precipitation for the two farm areas is greater than 0, we test:

H_0: $(\mu_1 - \mu_2) = 0$
H_a: $(\mu_1 - \mu_2) > 0$

The rejection region for this one-sided, small-sample test requires $\alpha = .05$ in the upper tail of the t distribution with df = n - 1 = 6 - 1 = 5. From Table 6, Appendix E, $t_{.05} = 2.015$. The rejection region is t > 2.015.

The test statistic is $t = \dfrac{\bar{d} - D_0}{s_d/\sqrt{n}} = \dfrac{.1633 - 0}{.1331/\sqrt{6}} = 3.01$

Since the computed value of the test statistic falls in the rejection region (t = 3.01 > 2.015), H_0 is rejected. There is sufficient evidence to conclude the mean difference between the monthly precipitation in the seeded and unseeded farm areas is greater than 0 at $\alpha = .05$.

11.83   Let p_1 = proportion of passive solar-heated homes that required less than 200 gallons of oil last year and p_2 = proportion of active solar-heated homes that required less than 200 gallons of oil last year. Since we want to determine if there is a difference in the 2 proportions, we test:

$$H_0: \quad (p_1 - p_2) = 0$$
$$H_a: \quad (p_1 - p_2) \neq 0$$

The rejection region for this two-sided, large-sample test requires $\alpha/2 = .02/2 = .01$ in each tail of the normal distribution. From Table 4, Appendix E, $z_{.01} = 2.33$. The rejection region is $z < -2.33$ or $z > 2.33$.

$$\hat{p}_1 = \frac{37}{50} = .74 \qquad \hat{p}_2 = \frac{46}{50} = .92$$

$$\hat{p} = \frac{x_1 + x_2}{n_1 + n_2} = \frac{37 + 46}{50 + 50} = .83, \ \hat{q} = 1 - \hat{p} = 1 - .83 = .17$$

The test statistic is

$$z = \frac{(\hat{p}_1 - \hat{p}_2) - D_0}{\sqrt{\hat{p}\hat{q}\left(\frac{1}{n_1} + \frac{1}{n_2}\right)}} = \frac{(.74 - .92) - 0}{\sqrt{.83(.17)\left(\frac{1}{50} + \frac{1}{50}\right)}} = -2.40$$

Since the observed value of the test statistic falls in the rejection region ($z = -2.40 < -2.33$), H_0 is rejected. There is sufficient evidence to conclude the proportions of passive and active solar-heated homes that required less than 200 gallons of oil in fuel consumption last year differ at $\alpha = .02$.

In order for the above test to be valid, the following 2 intervals must not contain 0 or 1.

$$\hat{p}_1 \pm 2\sqrt{\frac{\hat{p}_1\hat{q}_1}{n_1}} \qquad\qquad \hat{p}_2 \pm 2\sqrt{\frac{\hat{p}_2\hat{q}_2}{n_2}}$$

$$\Rightarrow .74 \pm 2\sqrt{\frac{.74(.26)}{50}} \qquad\qquad \Rightarrow .92 \pm 2\sqrt{\frac{.92(.08)}{50}}$$

$$\Rightarrow .74 \pm .124 \qquad\qquad\qquad \Rightarrow .92 \pm .077$$

$$\Rightarrow (.616, .864) \qquad\qquad\quad \Rightarrow (.843, .997)$$

The above intervals do not contain 0 or 1, so the test is valid.

CASE STUDIES

11.1 a. Since we wish to determine if over 50% of all college students would prefer a Colonel Potter type to be their superior, we test:

H_0: $p = .5$
H_a: $p > .5$

The rejection region for a one-sided, large-sample test requires $\alpha = .01$ in the upper tail of the normal distribution. From Table 4, Appendix E, $z_{.01} = 2.33$. The rejection region is $z > 2.33$.

The test statistic is

$$z = \frac{\hat{p} - p_0}{\sqrt{p_0 q_0/n}} = \frac{.55 - .5}{\sqrt{.5(.5)/1082}} = 3.29$$

Since the observed value of the test statistic falls in the rejection region ($z = 3.29 > 2.33$), H_0 is rejected. There is sufficient evidence to indicate over 50% of all college students would prefer a Colonel Potter type as a superior at $\alpha = .01$.

Note that the interval

$$\hat{p} \pm 2\sqrt{\frac{\hat{p}\hat{q}}{n}} \Rightarrow .55 \pm 2\sqrt{\frac{.55(.45)}{1082}}$$

$$\Rightarrow .55 \pm .03$$

$$\Rightarrow (.52, .58)$$

does not contain 0 or 1. Therefore, the test is valid.

b. Since we wish to determine if over 50% of all college students would prefer a Hawkeye Pierce type to be their peer, we test:

H_0: $p = .5$
H_a: $p > .5$

The rejection region is $z > 2.33$. (Refer to part (a).)

The test statistic is

$$z = \frac{\hat{p} - p_0}{\sqrt{p_0 q_0/n}} = \frac{.51 - .50}{\sqrt{.5(.5)/1082}} = .66$$

Since the observed value of the test statistic does not fall in the rejection region (z = .66 $\not>$ 2.33), H_0 is not rejected. There is insufficient evidence to indicate that over 50% of all college students would prefer a Hawkeye Pierce type to be their peer at α = .01.

Note that the interval

$$\hat{p} \pm 2\sqrt{\frac{\hat{p}\hat{q}}{n}} \Rightarrow .51 \pm 2\sqrt{\frac{.51(.49)}{1082}}$$

$$\Rightarrow .51 \pm .03$$

$$\Rightarrow (.48, .54)$$

does not contain 0 or 1. Therefore, the test is valid.

c. Since we wish to determine if over 50% of all college students would prefer a Radar O'Reilly type to be a subordinate, we test:

H_0: p = .5
H_a: p > .5

The rejection region is z > 2.33. (Refer to part (a).)

The test statistic is

$$z = \frac{\hat{p} - p_0}{\sqrt{p_0 q_0/n}} = \frac{.36 - .5}{\sqrt{.5(.5)/1082}} = -9.21$$

Since the observed value of the test statistic does not fall in the rejection region (z = -9.21 $\not>$ 2.33), H_0 is not rejected. There is insufficient evidence to indicate over 50% of all college students would prefer a Radar O'Reilly type to be a subordinate at α = .01.

Note that the interval

$$\hat{p} \pm 2\sqrt{\frac{\hat{p}\hat{q}}{n}} \Rightarrow .36 \pm 2\sqrt{\frac{.36(.64)}{1082}}$$

$$\Rightarrow .36 \pm .029$$

$$\Rightarrow (.331, .389)$$

does not contain 0 or 1. Therefore, the test is valid.

d. Let p_1 = proportion of college students with lower GPA's that choose Hawkeye as a desirable superior and p_2 = proportion of college students with higher GPA's that choose Hawkeye as a desirable superior. Since we wish to determine if college students with lower GPA's are more likely to select Hawkeye as a desirable superior than college students with higher GPA's, we test:

$$H_0: \quad (p_1 - p_2) = 0$$
$$H_a: \quad (p_1 - p_2) > 0$$

The rejection region is $z > 2.33$. (Refer to part (a).)

$$\hat{p}_1 = \frac{222}{411} = .54 \qquad \hat{p}_2 = \frac{23}{76} = .303$$

$$\hat{p} = \frac{x_1 + x_2}{n_1 + n_2} = \frac{222 + 23}{411 + 76} = .503, \quad \hat{q} = 1 - \hat{p} = 1 - .503 = .497$$

The test statistic is

$$z = \frac{(\hat{p}_1 - \hat{p}_2) - D_0}{\sqrt{\hat{p}\hat{q}\left(\frac{1}{n_1} + \frac{1}{n_2}\right)}} = \frac{(.54 - .303) - 0}{\sqrt{.503(.497)\left(\frac{1}{411} + \frac{1}{76}\right)}} = 3.80$$

Since the observed value of the test statistic falls in the rejection region ($z = 3.80 > 2.33$), H_0 is rejected. There is sufficient evidence to indicate that college students with lower GPA's are more likely to select Hawkeye as a desirable superior than college students with higher GPA's at $\alpha = .01$.

In order for the above test to be valid, the following intervals must not contain 0 or 1.

$$\hat{p}_1 \pm 2\sqrt{\frac{\hat{p}_1\hat{q}_1}{n_1}} \qquad\qquad \hat{p}_2 \pm 2\sqrt{\frac{\hat{p}_2\hat{q}_2}{n_2}}$$

$$\Rightarrow .54 \pm 2\sqrt{\frac{.54(.46)}{411}} \qquad\qquad \Rightarrow .303 \pm 2\sqrt{\frac{.303(.697)}{76}}$$

$$\Rightarrow .54 \pm .049 \qquad\qquad\qquad \Rightarrow .303 \pm .105$$

$$\Rightarrow (.491, .589) \qquad\qquad\qquad \Rightarrow (.198, .408)$$

Since the intervals do not contain 0 or 1, the test is valid.

11.3 a. In order for the hypothesis-testing procedure to be valid, the following intervals must not contain 0 or 1:

$$\hat{p}_1 \pm 2\sqrt{\frac{\hat{p}_1\hat{q}_1}{n_1}} \qquad \text{and} \qquad \hat{p}_2 \pm 2\sqrt{\frac{\hat{p}_2\hat{q}_2}{n_2}}$$

For Brand 1

$$\hat{p}_1 = \frac{17}{25} = .68 \quad \hat{q}_1 = 1 - .68 = .32 \quad \hat{p}_2 = \frac{30}{75} = .40 \quad \hat{q}_2 = 1 - .40 = .60$$

$$\hat{p}_1 \pm 2\sqrt{\frac{\hat{p}_1\hat{q}_1}{n_1}} \qquad\qquad \hat{p}_2 \pm 2\sqrt{\frac{\hat{p}_2\hat{q}_2}{n_2}}$$

$$\Rightarrow .68 \pm 2\sqrt{\frac{.68(.32)}{25}} \qquad \Rightarrow .40 \pm 2\sqrt{\frac{.40(.60)}{75}}$$

$$\Rightarrow .68 \pm .187 \qquad\qquad \Rightarrow .40 \pm .113$$

$$\Rightarrow (.493, .867) \qquad\qquad \Rightarrow (.287, .513)$$

The above intervals do not contain 0 or 1, so the procedure is valid.

For Brand 2

$$\hat{p}_1 = \frac{34}{46} = .739 \quad \hat{q}_1 = 1 - .739 = .261 \quad \hat{p}_2 = \frac{33}{54} = .611 \quad \hat{q}_2 = 1 - .611 = .389$$

$$\hat{p}_1 \pm 2\sqrt{\frac{\hat{p}_1\hat{q}_1}{n_1}} \qquad\qquad \hat{p}_2 \pm 2\sqrt{\frac{\hat{p}_2\hat{q}_2}{n_2}}$$

$$\Rightarrow .739 \pm 2\sqrt{\frac{.739(.261)}{46}} \qquad \Rightarrow .611 \pm 2\sqrt{\frac{.611(.389)}{54}}$$

$$\Rightarrow .739\ .130 \qquad\qquad \Rightarrow .611 \pm .133$$

$$\Rightarrow (.609, .869) \qquad\qquad \Rightarrow (.478, .744)$$

The above intervals do not contain 0 or 1, so the procedure is valid.

For Brand 3

$$\hat{p}_1 = \frac{1}{34} = .029 \quad \hat{q}_1 = 1 - .029 = .971 \quad \hat{p}_2 = \frac{2}{66} = .03 \quad \hat{q}_2 = 1 - .03 = .97$$

$$\hat{p}_1 \pm 2\sqrt{\frac{\hat{p}_1\hat{q}_1}{n_1}} \qquad\qquad \hat{p}_2 \pm 2\sqrt{\frac{\hat{p}_2\hat{q}_2}{n_2}}$$

$$\Rightarrow .029 \pm 2\sqrt{\frac{.029(.971)}{34}} \qquad \Rightarrow .03 \pm 2\sqrt{\frac{.03(.97)}{66}}$$

$$\Rightarrow .029 \pm .058 \qquad\qquad \Rightarrow .03 \pm .042$$

$$\Rightarrow (-.029, .087) \qquad\qquad \Rightarrow (-.012, .072)$$

Since both intervals contain 0, the procedure is not valid.

For Brand 4

$$\hat{p}_1 = \frac{26}{40} = .65 \quad \hat{q}_1 = 1 - .65 = .35 \quad \hat{p}_2 = \frac{39}{60} = .65 \quad \hat{q}_2 = 1 - .65 = .35$$

$$\hat{p}_1 \pm 2\sqrt{\frac{\hat{p}_1\hat{q}_1}{n_1}} \qquad\qquad \hat{p}_2 \pm 2\sqrt{\frac{\hat{p}_2\hat{q}_2}{n_2}}$$

$$\Rightarrow .65 \pm 2\sqrt{\frac{.65(.35)}{40}} \qquad\qquad \Rightarrow .65 \pm 2\sqrt{\frac{.65(.35)}{60}}$$

$$\Rightarrow .65 \pm .151 \qquad\qquad\qquad \Rightarrow .65 \pm .123$$

$$\Rightarrow (.499, .801) \qquad\qquad\qquad \Rightarrow (.527, .773)$$

The above intervals do not contain 0 or 1, so the procedure is valid.

For Brand 5

$$\hat{p}_1 = \frac{7}{40} = .175 \quad \hat{q}_1 = 1 - .175 = .825 \quad \hat{p}_2 = \frac{0}{60} = 0 \quad \hat{q}_2 = 1 - 0 = 1$$

$$\hat{p}_1 \pm 2\sqrt{\frac{\hat{p}_1\hat{q}_1}{n_1}} \qquad\qquad \hat{p}_2 \pm 2\sqrt{\frac{\hat{p}_2\hat{q}_2}{n_2}}$$

$$\Rightarrow .175 \pm 2\sqrt{\frac{.175(.825)}{40}} \qquad\qquad \Rightarrow 0 \pm 2\sqrt{\frac{0(1)}{60}}$$

$$\Rightarrow .175 \pm .120 \qquad\qquad\qquad \Rightarrow 0 \pm 0$$

$$\Rightarrow (.055, .295) \qquad\qquad\qquad \Rightarrow (0, 0)$$

Since the second interval contains 0, the procedure is not valid.

For Brand 6

$$p_1 = \frac{13}{34} = .382 \quad \hat{q}_1 = 1 - .382 = .618 \quad \hat{p}_2 = \frac{20}{66} = .303 \quad \hat{q}_2 = 1 - .303 = .697$$

$$\hat{p}_1 \pm 2\sqrt{\frac{\hat{p}_1\hat{q}_1}{n_1}} \qquad\qquad \hat{p}_2 \pm 2\sqrt{\frac{\hat{p}_2\hat{q}_2}{n_2}}$$

$$\Rightarrow .382 \pm 2\sqrt{\frac{.382(.618)}{34}} \qquad\qquad \Rightarrow .303 \pm 2\sqrt{\frac{.303(.697)}{66}}$$

$$\Rightarrow .382 \pm .167 \qquad\qquad\qquad \Rightarrow .303 \pm .113$$

$$\Rightarrow (.215, .549) \qquad\qquad\qquad \Rightarrow (.190, .416)$$

The above intervals do not contain 0 or 1, so the procedure is valid.

b.   For Brand 1

$$\hat{p} = \frac{17 + 30}{25 + 75} = .47 \qquad \hat{q} = 1 - .47 = .53$$

The test statistic is $z = \dfrac{\hat{p}_1 - \hat{p}_2 - D_0}{\sqrt{\hat{p}\hat{q}\left(\frac{1}{n_1} + \frac{1}{n_2}\right)}} = \dfrac{.68 - .40 - 0}{\sqrt{.47(.53)\left(\frac{1}{25} + \frac{1}{75}\right)}}$

$$= \frac{.28}{.1153} = 2.43$$

For Brand 2

$$\hat{p} = \frac{34 + 33}{46 + 54} = .67 \qquad \hat{q} = 1 - .67 = .33$$

The test statistic is $z = \dfrac{\hat{p}_1 - \hat{p}_2 - D_0}{\sqrt{\hat{p}\hat{q}\left(\frac{1}{n_1} + \frac{1}{n_2}\right)}} = \dfrac{.739 - .611 - 0}{\sqrt{.67(.33)\left(\frac{1}{46} + \frac{1}{54}\right)}}$

$$= \frac{.128}{.0943} = 1.36$$

For Brand 4

$$\hat{p} = \frac{26 + 39}{40 + 60} = .65 \qquad \hat{q} = 1 - .65 = .35$$

The test statistic is $z = \dfrac{\hat{p}_1 - \hat{p}_2 - D_0}{\sqrt{\hat{p}\hat{q}\left(\frac{1}{n_1} + \frac{1}{n_2}\right)}} = \dfrac{.65 - .65 - 0}{\sqrt{.65(.65)\left(\frac{1}{40} + \frac{1}{60}\right)}} = 0$

For Brand 6

$$\hat{p} = \frac{13 + 20}{34 + 66} = .33 \qquad \hat{q} = 1 - .33 = .67$$

The test statistic is $z = \dfrac{\hat{p}_1 - \hat{p}_2 - D_0}{\sqrt{\hat{p}\hat{q}\left(\frac{1}{n_1} + \frac{1}{n_2}\right)}} = \dfrac{.382 - .303 - 0}{\sqrt{.33(.67)\left(\frac{1}{34} + \frac{1}{66}\right)}}$

$$= \frac{.079}{.0993} = .80$$

c.   For Brand 1

The p-value = $P(z \geq 2.43) = .5 - .4925 = .0075$

For Brand 2

The p-value = $P(z \geq 1.36) = .5 - .4131 = .0869$

For Brand 4

The p-value = $P(z \geq 0) = .5$

For Brand 6

The p-value = $P(z \geq .80) = .5 - .2881 = .2119$

d. We will reject H_0 for any test that has the p-value less than $\alpha = .05$. The only brand with a p-value less than $\alpha = .05$ is Brand 1 (p-value = .0075). Thus, the proportion of physicians who prescribe the product is significantly greater for those aware of the ad than for those unaware of the ad for Brand 1 at $\alpha = .05$.

TWELVE   COMPARING MORE THAN TWO POPULATION MEANS: AN ANALYSIS OF VARIANCE

12.1   a.   The line plot is given below where o indicates a sample 1 value and ● indicates a sample 2 value.

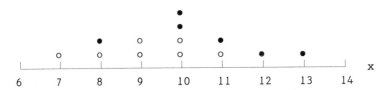

Notice that the difference between the sample means is small relative to the variability within the sample observations. The difference between $\bar{x}_1$ and $\bar{x}_2$ is probably not large enough to indicate a difference between μ_1 and μ_2.

   b.   From page 520 of the test:

$$MST = \frac{n_1(\bar{x}_1 - \bar{x})^2 + n_2(\bar{x}_2 - \bar{x})^2}{2 - 1}$$

First compute the means:

$$\bar{x}_1 = \frac{\sum x_1}{n_1} = \frac{10 + 7 + \ldots + 9}{7} = \frac{64}{7} = 9.1429$$

$$\bar{x}_2 = \frac{\sum x_2}{n_2} = \frac{12 + 8 + \ldots + 11}{7} = \frac{64}{6} = 10.6667$$

$$\bar{x} = \frac{\sum x}{n} = \frac{10 + 7 + \ldots + 9 + 12 + 8 + \ldots + 11}{13} = \frac{128}{13} = 9.8462$$

$$MST = \frac{7(9.1429 - 9.8462)^2 + 6(10.6667 - 9.8462)^2}{1}$$

$$= \frac{7.502}{1} = 7.502$$

The mean square for treatments measures the variability among the three population means.

c. From page 520 of the text:

$$MSE = s^2 = \frac{\sum_{i=1}^{n_1} (x_{i1} - \bar{x}_1)^2 + \sum_{i=1}^{n_2} (x_{i2} - \bar{x}_2)^2}{n_1 + n_2 - 2}$$

$$= \frac{[(10 - 9.1429)^2 + ... + (9 - 9.1429)^2] + [(12 - 10.6667)^2 + ... + (11 - 10.6667)^2]}{7 + 6 - 2}$$

$$= \frac{[10.8571 + 15.3333]}{11} = 2.381$$

The mean square for error measures the variability within samples.

d. The degrees of freedom associated with MST is the numerator df $= \nu_1 = k - 1 = 2 - 1 = 1$.

e. The degrees of freedom associated with MSE is the denominator df $= \nu_2 = n - k = 13 - 2 = 11$.

f. The test statistic is $F = \frac{MST}{MSE} = \frac{7.502}{2.381} = 3.15$, which has 1 and 11 df.

g. The ANOVA (ANALYSIS OF VARIANCE) table is merely a structured presentation of the results of the calculations for an analysis of variance. It lists, in tabular form, the sources of variability, degrees of freedom, sums of squares for each source, mean squares for those sources in the F test and the F statistic. The table is:

SOURCE	df	SS	MS	F
Treatments	1	7.502	7.502	3.15
Error	11	26.190	2.381	
Total	12	33.692		

h. The rejection region is $F > F_\alpha = F_{.05}$ with 1 and 11 df, which is $F > 4.84$ (see Table 8 of Appendix E).

i. The conclusion is to fail to reject H_0 at $\alpha = .05$ because $F = 3.15$ does not fall in the rejection region ($F = 3.15 \not> F_\alpha = 4.84$). Our intuitive decision in part (a) is consistent with this statistical decision.

j. The form of the confidence interval for μ_i is $\bar{x}_i \pm t_{\alpha/2} s/\sqrt{n_i}$ where $s = \sqrt{MSE}$. For confidence coefficient .95, $\alpha = 1 - .95 = .05$ and

$\alpha/2 = .05/2 = .025$. From Table 6 of Appendix E, $t_{.025} = 2.201$ with df $= n - k = 13 - 2 = 11$. The point estimate for μ_1 is

$$\bar{x}_1 = \frac{\sum x_1}{n_1} = \frac{10 + 7 + \ldots + 9}{7} = \frac{64}{7} = 9.14$$

From part (c), MSE $= 2.381 \Rightarrow s = \sqrt{2.381} = 1.543$. The 95% confidence interval for μ_1 is

$$9.14 \pm 2.201\frac{(1.543)}{\sqrt{7}}$$

$$\Rightarrow 9.14 \pm 1.284$$

$$\Rightarrow (7.856,\ 10.424)$$

The point estimate for μ_2 is

$$\bar{x}_2 = \frac{\sum x_2}{n} = \frac{12 + 8 + \ldots + 11}{6} = \frac{64}{6} = 10.667$$

The 95% confidence interval for μ_2 is

$$10.667 \pm 2.201\frac{(1.543)}{\sqrt{6}}$$

$$\Rightarrow 10.667 \pm 1.386$$

$$\Rightarrow (9.281,\ 12.053)$$

k. The form of the confidence interval for $\mu_2 - \mu_1$ is

$$(\bar{x}_2 - \bar{x}_1) \pm t_{\alpha/2}\, s\sqrt{\frac{1}{n_1} + \frac{1}{n_2}}, \text{ where } s = \sqrt{MSE} = 1.543.$$

The $t_{\alpha/2}$ value is the same as for part (j). The 95% confidence interval for $\mu_2 - \mu_1$ is

$$\Rightarrow (10.667 - 9.14) \pm 2.201(1.543)\sqrt{\frac{1}{7} + \frac{1}{6}}$$

$$\Rightarrow 1.527 \pm 1.889$$

$$\Rightarrow (-.362,\ 3.416)$$

12.3   a.   df(Total) = df(Treatments) + df(Error)
$$\Rightarrow \text{df(Error)} = \text{df(Total)} - \text{df(Treatments)} = 34 - 4 = 30$$

SSE = SS(Total) $-$ SST $= 62.4 - 24.7 = 37.7$

$$MST = \frac{SST}{k - 1} = \frac{24.7}{4} = 6.175$$

$$MSE = \frac{SSE}{n - k} = \frac{37.7}{30} = 1.257$$

$$F = \frac{MST}{MSE} = \frac{6.175}{1.257} = 4.91$$

The completed table is:

SOURCE	df	SS	MS	F
Treatments	4	24.7	6.175	4.91
Error	30	37.7	1.257	
Total	34	62.4		

b. Since there are $k - 1 = 4$ df for treatments, there are $k = 5$ treatments involved in the experiment.

c. It is desired to determine if there is a difference among the five population means, which implies:

H_0: $\mu_1 = \mu_2 = \mu_3 = \mu_4 = \mu_5$
H_a: At least two treatment means differ

The test statistic is $F = \frac{MST}{MSE} = 4.91$

The rejection region requires $\alpha = .10$ in the upper tail of the F distribution with $\nu_1 = k - 1 = 4$ and $\nu_2 = n - k = 30$. From Table 7, Appendix E, $F_{.10} = 2.14$. The rejection region is $F > 2.14$.

Since the observed value of the test statistic falls in the rejection region ($F = 4.91 > 2.14$), H_0 is rejected. There is sufficient evidence to indicate at least two of the treatment means differ at $\alpha = .10$.

12.5 a. $df(\text{Industry}) = k - 1 = 3 - 1 = 2$
$df(\text{Error}) = n - k = 24 - 3 = 21$
$df(\text{Total}) = n - 1 = 24 - 1 = 23$

$$MST = \frac{SST}{k - 1} \Rightarrow SST = MST(k - 1) = 342,564.67(2)$$
$$= 685,129.34$$

$$MSE = \frac{SSE}{n - k} = \frac{1,115,232.50}{21} = 53,106.31$$

$$F = \frac{MST}{MSE} = \frac{342,564.67}{53,106.31} = 6.45$$

The completed table is:

SOURCE	df	SS	MS	F
Industry	2	685,129.34	342,564.67	6.45
Error	21	1,115,232.50	53,106.31	
Total	23	1,800,361.83		

b. It is desired to determine if there is a difference among the means of the 1986 total cash compensations for the three groups of corporate executives, which implies:

H_0: $\mu_1 = \mu_2 = \mu_3$
H_a: At least two treatment means differ

The test statistic is $F = \dfrac{MST}{MSE} = 6.45$

The rejection region requires $\alpha = .01$ in the upper tail of the F distribution with $\nu_1 = k - 1 = 2$ and $\nu_2 = n - k = 21$. From Table 10 of Appendix E, $F_{.01} = 5.78$. The rejection region is $F > 5.78$.

Since the observed value of the test statistic falls in the rejection region ($F = 6.45 > 5.78$), H_0 is rejected. There is sufficient evidence to indicate at least two of the mean cash compensations are different at $\alpha = .01$.

c. The form of the confidence interval for μ_1 is $\bar{x}_1 \pm t_{\alpha/2} s/\sqrt{n_1}$ where $s = \sqrt{MSE}$. For confidence coefficient .90, $\alpha = 1 - .90 = .10$ and $\alpha/2 = .10/2 = .05$. From Table 6 of Appendix E, $t_{.05} = 1.721$ with df $= n - k = 21$. From part (a), MSE $= 53,106.31 \Rightarrow s = \sqrt{53,106.31} = 230.448$. The point estimate for μ_1 is

$$\bar{x}_1 = \frac{\sum x_1}{n_1} = \frac{755 + 712 + \ldots + 1189}{8} = \frac{7662}{8} = 957.75$$

The 90% confidence interval for μ_1 is

$$957.75 \pm 1.721\frac{230.448}{\sqrt{8}}$$

$\Rightarrow 957.75 \pm 140.220$

$\Rightarrow (817.53, 1097.97)$

12.7 a. It is desired to determine if the mean R o P differs for at least two of the three drill bits, which implies

H_0: $\mu_1 = \mu_2 = \mu_3$
H_a: At least two treatment means differ

The test statistic is $F = \dfrac{MST}{MSE} = 9.50$ (from MINITAB output).

The rejection region requires $\alpha = .05$ in the upper tail of the F distribution with $\nu_1 = k - 1 = 2$ and $\nu_2 = n - k = 9$. From Table 8, Appendix E, $F_{.05} = 4.26$. The rejection region is $F > 4.26$.

Since the observed value of the test statistic falls in the rejection region ($F = 9.50 > 4.26$), H_0 is rejected. There is sufficient evidence to indicate that mean R o P differs for at least two of the three drill bits at $\alpha = .05$.

b. The form of the confidence interval for μ_1 is $\bar{x}_1 \pm t_{\alpha/2} s/\sqrt{n_1}$ where $s = \sqrt{MSE}$. For confidence coefficient .95, $\alpha = 1 - .95 = .05$ and $\alpha/2 = .05/2 = .025$. From Table 6 of Appendix E, $t_{.025} = 2.262$ with df $= n - k = 9$. From the MINITAB output, MSE $= 19.3$ $\Rightarrow s = \sqrt{19.3} = 4.393$. The point estimate for μ_1 is

$$\bar{x}_1 = \frac{\sum x_1}{n_1} = \frac{35.2 + 30.1 + 37.6 + 34.3}{4} = \frac{137.2}{4} = 34.3$$

The 95% confidence interval is

$$34.3 \pm 2.262 \, \frac{4.393}{\sqrt{4}}$$

$$\Rightarrow 34.3 \pm 4.968$$

$$\Rightarrow (29.332, 39.268)$$

We are 95% confident this interval encloses the true mean rate of penetration for the new PS-1 drill bit.

c. The form of the confidence interval for $\mu_1 - \mu_2$ is

$$(\bar{x}_1 - \bar{x}_2) \pm t_{\alpha/2} s \sqrt{\frac{1}{n_1} + \frac{1}{n_2}} \text{ where } s = \sqrt{MSE} = 4.393$$

The $t_{\alpha/2}$ value is the same as for part (b). The point estimate for μ_2 is

$$\bar{x}_2 = \frac{\sum x_2}{n_2} = \frac{25.8 + 29.7 + 26.6 + 30.1}{4} = \frac{112.2}{4} = 28.05$$

The 95% confidence interval for $\mu_1 - \mu_2$ is

$$(34.3 - 28.05) \pm 2.262(4.393) \sqrt{\frac{1}{4} + \frac{1}{4}}$$

$$\Rightarrow 6.25 \pm 7.026$$

$$\Rightarrow (-.776, 13.276)$$

Since the interval contains both negative and positive numbers, we cannot conclude that the mean R o P for the PD-1 and IADC 1-2-6 drill bits differ. The difference in mean R o P values ranges from the PD-1 drill bit being .776 slower to 13.276 faster than the IADC 1-2-6 bit.

12.9   a.   The key elements appearing on this printout are:

df(Treatments) = D.F. (Between Groups) = 2
df(Error) = D.F. (Within Groups) = 15
df(Total) = D.F. (Total) = 17
SST = SUM OF SQUARES (Between Groups) = 4.4271
SSE = SUM OF SQUARES (Within Groups) = 2.5535
SS(Total) = SUM OF SQUARES (Total) = 6.9806
MST = Mean Squares (Between Groups) = 2.2136
MSE = MEAN SQUARES (Within Groups) = .1702
F = F RATIO = 13.0032
p-value (observed significance level) = F PROB. = .0005

   b.   It is desired to determine if there is evidence of a difference among the mean starting wages of engineers at Theory X-, Y- and Z-style firms, which implies:

H_0: $\mu_1 = \mu_2 = \mu_3$
H_a: At least two treatment means differ

The test statistic is $F = \dfrac{MST}{MSE} = 13.0032$

The p-value from the printout is .0005. This implies that H_0 will be rejected at any chosen level of α larger than .0005. Since $\alpha = .025$ for this problem, H_0 is rejected. There is sufficient evidence to indicate a difference in mean salaries among at least two of the three theory style firms.

12.11   a. $MST = \dfrac{SST}{k - 1} \Rightarrow SST = MST(k - 1) = 7.3(2) = 14.6$

$MSE = \dfrac{SSE}{n - k} \Rightarrow SSE = MSE(n - k) = 1.265(89) = 112.585$

$SSE = SS(Total) - SST \Rightarrow SS(Total) = SST + SSE = 14.6 + 112.585$

$= 127.185$

$F = \dfrac{MST}{MSE} = \dfrac{7.3}{1.265} = 5.77$

The completed table is:

SOURCE	df	SS	MS	F
Groups	2	14.6	7.3	5.77
Error	89	112.585	1.265	
Total	91	127.185		

b. It is desired to determine if there is a difference among the mean earnings per day of the three groups, which implies:

H_0: $\mu_1 = \mu_2 = \mu_3$
H_a: At least two treatment means differ

The test statistic is $F = \dfrac{MST}{MSE} = 5.77$

The rejection region requires $\alpha = .01$ in the upper tail of the F distribution with $v_1 = k - 1 = 2$ and $v_2 = n - k = 89$. From Table 10, Appendix E, $F_{.01} \approx 4.79$. The rejection region is $F > 4.79$.

Since the observed value of the test statistic falls in the rejection region ($F = 5.77 > 4.79$), H_0 is rejected. There is sufficient evidence to indicate a difference among the mean earnings per day of the three groups at $\alpha = .01$.

12.13 a. $MST = \dfrac{SST}{k - 1} = \dfrac{27.1}{3} = 9.033$

$MSB = \dfrac{SSB}{b - 1} \Rightarrow SSB = MSB(b - 1) = 14.90(5) = 74.50$

$n = b(k) = (5 + 1)(3 + 1) = 24 \Rightarrow df(Error) = n - b - k + 1$
$= 24 - (5 + 1) - (3 + 1) + 1 = 15$

$df(Total) = n - 1 = 24 - 1 = 23$

$SS(Total) = SST + SSB + SSE = 27.1 + 74.5 + 33.4 = 135$

$MSE = \dfrac{SSE}{n - b - k + 1} = \dfrac{33.4}{15} = 2.227$

$F(Treatments) = \dfrac{MST}{MSE} = \dfrac{9.033}{2.227} = 4.06$

$F(Blocks) = \dfrac{MSB}{MSE} = \dfrac{14.90}{2.227} = 6.69$

The completed table is:

SOURCE	df	SS	MS	F
Treatments	3	27.1	9.033	4.06
Blocks	5	74.5	14.90	6.69
Error	15	33.4	2.227	
Total	23	135.0		

b. To see if a difference exists among the treatment means, we test:

H_0: $\mu_1 = \mu_2 = \mu_3 = \mu_4$
H_a: At least two treatment means differ

The test statistic is $F = \dfrac{MST}{MSE} = 4.06$

The rejection region requires $\alpha = .01$ in the upper tail of the F distribution with $\nu_1 = k - 1 = 3$ and $\nu_2 = n - k - b + 1 = 24 - 4 - 6 + 1 = 15$. From Table 10, Appendix E, $F_{.01} = 5.42$. The rejection region is $F > 5.42$.

Since the observed value of the test statistic does not fall in the rejection region ($F = 4.06 \not> 5.42$), H_0 is not rejected. There is insufficient evidence to indicate a difference among the treatment means at $\alpha = .01$.

c. To see if blocking was useful, we test:

H_0: There is no difference among block means
H_a: At least two block means differ

The test statistic is $F = \dfrac{MSB}{MSE} = 6.69$

The rejection region requires $\alpha = .05$ in the upper tail of the F distribution with $\nu_1 = b - 1 = 5$ and $\nu_2 = n - b - k + 1 = 15$. From Table 8, Appendix E, $F_{.05} = 2.90$. The rejection region is $F > 2.90$.

Since the observed value of the test statistic falls in the rejection region ($F = 6.69 > 2.90$), H_0 is rejected. There is sufficient evidence that blocking was useful. There is evidence that there were differences among experimental units in different blocks at $\alpha = .05$.

d. The form of the confidence interval for ($\mu_A - \mu_B$) is

$$(\bar{T}_A - \bar{T}_B) \pm t_{\alpha/2} s \sqrt{\frac{2}{b}} \text{ where } s = \sqrt{MSE}$$

From part (a), MSE = 2.227 => s = $\sqrt{2.227}$ = 1.492. For confidence coefficient .95, α = 1 - .95 = .05 and $\alpha/2$ = .05/2 = .025. From Table 6, Appendix E, $t_{.025}$ = 2.131 with df = n - b - k + 1 = 15.

The 95% confidence interval is

$$(9.7 - 12.1) \pm 2.131(1.492)\sqrt{\frac{2}{6}}$$

=> -2.4 ± 1.836

=> (-4.236, -.564)

e. The form of the confidence interval for $(\mu_B - \mu_D)$ is

$$(\bar{T}_B - \bar{T}_D) \pm t_{\alpha/2}s\sqrt{\frac{2}{b}} \text{ where } s = \sqrt{MSE}$$

From part (d), s = 1.492 and $t_{.025}$ = 2.131.

The 95% confidence interval is

$$(12.1 - 9.3) \pm 2.131(1.492)\sqrt{\frac{2}{6}}$$

=> 2.8 ± 1.836

=> (.964, 4.636)

12.15 a. We would want our blocks (pairs of successive months) to contain matched groups of the 3 treatment periods. This will help remove the variability introduced into the analysis by the month-to-month variation in beer sales.

b. We can only use those blocks for which the data appear across all three periods because each block must be a matched group of k experimental units. The k treatments are then randomly assigned to the experimental units within a block.

To complete the ANOVA table, we need

$$F(\text{Treatments}) = \frac{MST}{MSE} = \frac{4863}{4658} = 1.04$$

$$F(\text{Blocks}) = \frac{MSB}{MSE} = \frac{22,753}{4658} = 4.88$$

The completed table is

SOURCE	df	SS	MS	F
Period	2	9,726	4,863	1.04
Month	3	68,258	22,753	4.88
Error	6	27,947	4,658	
Total	11	105,932		

c. To determine if a difference exists among the three period means, we test:

H_0: $\mu_1 = \mu_2 = \mu_3$
H_a: At least two treatment means differ

The test statistic is $F = \dfrac{MSB}{MSE} = 1.04$

The rejection region requires $\alpha = .10$ in the upper tail of the F distribution with $\nu_1 = k - 1 = 2$ and $\nu_2 = n - b - k + 1 = 6$. From Table 7, Appendix E, $F_{.10} = 3.46$. The rejection region is $F > 3.46$.

Since the observed value of the test statistic does not fall in the rejection region ($F = 1.04 \not> 3.46$), H_0 is not rejected. There is insufficient evidence to indicate that the mean bimonthly beer sales differ among the three periods at $\alpha = .10$.

d. For this randomized block design, $s = \sqrt{MSE} = \sqrt{4658} = 68.250$. For the completely randomized design, $s = 85.30$ (from Exercise 12.6). It appears that the variability has been decreased a significant amount by blocking on months.

e. To determine if blocking was effective, we test

H_0: There is no difference among block means
H_a: At least two block means differ

The test statistic is $F = \dfrac{MSB}{MSE} = 4.88$

The rejection region requires $\alpha = .10$ in the upper tail of the F distribution with $\nu_1 = b - 1 = 3$ and $\nu_2 = n - b - k + 1 = 6$. From Table 7, Appendix E, $F_{.10} = 3.29$. The rejection region is $F > 3.29$.

Since the observed value of the test statistic falls in the rejection region ($F = 4.88 > 3.29$), H_0 is rejected. There is sufficient evidence to indicate at least two block means differ at $\alpha = .10$. As we intuitively decided in part (d), blocking was effective in reducing variability in beer sales.

12.17 a.   df(Cars) = b - 1 = 6 - 1 = 5
            df(Error) = n - k - b + 1 = 12 - 2 - 6 + 1 = 5

$$MST = \frac{SST}{k - 1} \Rightarrow SST = MST(k - 1) = .521(1) = .521$$

$$MSE = \frac{SSE}{n - k - b + 1} = \frac{.044}{5} = .0088$$

$$F(Shocks) = \frac{MST}{MSE} = \frac{.521}{.0088} = 59.20$$

$$F(Cars) = \frac{MSB}{MSE} = \frac{6.365}{.0088} = 723.295$$

The completed table is

SOURCE	df	SS	MS	F
Shocks	1	.521	.521	59.20
Cars	5	31.824	6.3648	723.27
Error	5	.044	.0088	
Total	11	32.389		

   b.   To determine if there is a difference among shock absorber types,
        we test:

H_0: $\mu_1 = \mu_2$
H_a: The two treatment means differ

The test statistic is $F = \frac{MSB}{MSE} = 59.20$

The rejection region requires $\alpha = .05$ in the upper tail of the F
distribution with $\nu_1 = k - 1 = 1$ and $\nu_2 = n - k - b + 1 = 5$. From
Table 8, Appendix E, $F_{.05} = 6.61$. The rejection region is
$F > 6.61$.

Since the observed value of the test statistic falls in the
rejection region ($F = 59.20 > 6.61$), H_0 is rejected. There is
sufficient evidence to indicate a difference in mean strength
among the two types of shock absorbers at $\alpha = .05$.

c. For matched pairs:

PAIR	DIFFERENCE (Manufacturer's - Competitor's)	d^2
1	.4	.16
2	.4	.16
3	.5	.25
4	.4	.16
5	.6	.36
6	.2	.04
	2.5	1.13

$$\bar{d} = \frac{\sum d}{n} = \frac{2.5}{6} = .417$$

$$s_d^2 = \frac{\sum d^2 - \frac{(\sum d)^2}{n}}{n - 1} = \frac{1.13 - \frac{(2.5)^2}{6}}{5} = \frac{.0083}{5} = .0177$$

$$s_d = \sqrt{.0177} = .1329$$

To compare the treatment means, we test:

H_0: $\mu_1 - \mu_2 = 0$
H_a: $\mu_1 - \mu_2 \neq 0$

The test statistic is $t = \dfrac{\bar{d} - D_0}{s_d/\sqrt{n}} = \dfrac{.417 - 0}{.1329/\sqrt{6}} = 7.686$

The rejection region requires $\alpha/2 = .05/2 = .025$ in each tail of the t distribution with df = $n_d - 1 = 5$. From Table 6, Appendix E, $t_{.025} = 2.571$. The rejection region is $t > 2.571$ or $t < -2.571$.

Since the observed value of the test statistic falls in the rejection region ($t = 7.686 > 2.571$), H_0 is rejected. There is sufficient evidence to indicate a difference in mean strength among the two types of shock absorbers at $\alpha = .05$.

d. From part (b),

$F = 59.20$, $F_\alpha = 6.61$

From part (c),

$t = 7.686$, $t_{\alpha/2} = 2.571$

Notice that

$$t^2 = (7.686)^2 = 59.07 \approx F \text{ and}$$

$$t^2_{\alpha/2} = (2.571)^2 = 6.61 = F_\alpha$$

Thus, the F test for a randomized block design is equivalent to the t test for matched pairs when there are k = 2 treatments.

e. Let μ_1 = mean strength for the manufacturer's shock absorber and μ_2 = mean strength for the competitor's shock absorber. The form of the confidence interval for $\mu_1 - \mu_2$ is

$$(\bar{T}_1 - \bar{T}_2) \pm t_{\alpha/2} s \sqrt{\frac{2}{b}} \quad \text{where } s = \sqrt{MSE}$$

From part (a), MSE = .0088 = s = $\sqrt{.0088}$ = .0938

$$\bar{T}_1 = \frac{\sum x_1}{b} = \frac{8.8 + 10.5 + \ldots + 13.2}{6} = \frac{64.3}{6} = 10.717$$

$$\bar{T}_2 = \frac{\sum x_2}{b} = \frac{8.4 + 10.1 + \ldots + 13.0}{6} = \frac{61.8}{6} = 10.3$$

For confidence coefficient .95, $\alpha = 1 - .95 = .05$ and $\alpha/2 = .05/2 = .025$. From Table 6, Appendix E, $t_{.025} = 2.571$ with df = n - b - k + 1 = 5.

The 95% confidence interval is

$$(10.717 - 10.3) \pm 2.571(.0938) \sqrt{\frac{2}{6}}$$

=> .417 ± .139

=> (.278, .556)

f. The form of the confidence interval for matched pairs is $\bar{d} \pm t_{\alpha/2} s_d / \sqrt{n_d}$. From part (c), $\bar{d}$ = .417, s_d = .1329, n_d = 6 and $t_{.025}$ = 2.571.

The 95% confidence interval is

$$.417 \pm 2.571 \frac{.1329}{\sqrt{6}}$$

=> .417 ± .139

=> (.278, .556)

This is the same interval found in part (e).

COMPARING MORE THAN TWO POPULATION MEANS: AN
ANALYSIS OF VARIANCE

12.19 To determine if a difference exists among the mean preference scores
       for the seven color combinations, we test:

H_0: $\mu_1 = \mu_2 = \ldots = \mu_7$
H_a: At least two treatment means differ

The test statistic is $F = \dfrac{MST}{MSE} = \dfrac{70.22}{1.33} = 52.80$

The rejection region requires $\alpha = .05$ in the upper tail of the F
distribution with $\nu_1 = k - 1 = 6$ and $\nu_2 = n - b - k + 1 = 54$. From
Table 8, Appendix E, $F_{.05} \approx 2.25$. The rejection region is $F > 2.25$.

Since the observed value of the test statistic falls in the rejection
region ($F = 52.80 > 2.25$), H_0 is rejected. There is sufficient
evidence to indicate a difference among mean preference scores for the
seven video display color combinations at $\alpha = .05$.

12.21 a. $df(A) = a - 1 = 3 - 1 = 2$
          $df(Error) = ab(r - 1) = 3(2)(4 - 1) = 18$
          $df(Total) = abr - 1 = 3(2)(4) - 1 = 23$

$MS(AB) = \dfrac{SS(AB)}{(a - 1)(b - 1)} \Rightarrow SS(AB) = MS(AB)[(a - 1)(b - 1)]$

$$= 2.5(2) = 5$$

$MSE = \dfrac{SSE}{ab(r - 1)} \Rightarrow SSE = MSE[ab(r - 1)] = 2.0(18) = 36$

$SS(B) = SS(Total) - SS(A) - SS(AB) - SSE = 700 - 100 - 5 - 36$
$\quad\quad = 559$

$MS(A) = \dfrac{SS(A)}{a - 1} = \dfrac{100}{2} = 50$

$MS(B) = \dfrac{SS(B)}{b - 1} = \dfrac{559}{1} = 559$

$F(A) = \dfrac{MS(A)}{MSE} = \dfrac{50}{2} = 25$

$F(B) = \dfrac{MS(B)}{MSE} = \dfrac{559}{2} = 279.5$

$F(AB) = \dfrac{MS(AB)}{MSE} = \dfrac{2.5}{2} = 1.25$

The completed table is:

SOURCE	df	SS	MS	F
A	2	100	50	25
B	1	559	559	279.5
AB Interaction	2	5	2.5	1.25
Error	18	36	2	
Total	23	700		

b. To determine if interaction exists, we test:

H_0: No interaction between factors A and B
H_a: Factors A and B interact

The test statistic is $F = \dfrac{MS(AB)}{MSE} = 1.25$

The rejection region requires $\alpha = .05$ in the upper tail of the F distribution with $\nu_1 = (a - 1)(b - 1) = 2$ and $\nu_2 = ab(r - 1) = 18$. From Table 8, Appendix E, $F_{.05} = 3.55$. The rejection region is $F > 3.55$.

Since the observed value of the test statistic does not fall in the rejection region ($F = 1.25 \not> 3.55$), H_0 is not rejected. There is insufficient evidence to indicate an interaction exists between factors A and B at $\alpha = .05$.

c. To test for the main effects of factor A, we test:

H_0: There are no differences among the means for main effect A
H_a: At least two of the main effect A means differ

The test statistic is $F = \dfrac{MS(A)}{MSE} = 25$

The rejection region requires $\alpha = .05$ in the upper tail of the F distribution with $\nu_1 = a - 1 = 2$ and $\nu_2 = ab(r - 1) = 18$. From Table 8, Appendix E, $F_{.05} = 3.55$. The rejection region is $F > 3.55$.

Since the observed value of the test statistic falls in the rejection region ($F = 25 > 3.55$), H_0 is rejected. There is sufficient evidence to indicate a difference among at least two of the main effect means for factor A at $\alpha = .05$.

d. To test for the main effects of factor B, we test:

H_0: There are no differences among the means for main effect B
H_a: At least two of the main effect B means differ

The test statistic is $F = \dfrac{MS(B)}{MSE} = 279.5$

The rejection region requires $\alpha = .05$ in the upper tail of the F distribution with $\nu_1 = b - 1 = 1$ and $\nu_2 = ab(r - 1) = 18$. From Table 8, Appendix E, $F_{.05} = 4.41$. The rejection region is $F > 4.41$.

Since the observed value of the test statistic falls in the rejection region ($F = 279.5 > 4.41$), H_0 is rejected. There is sufficient evidence to indicate a difference among at least two of the main effect means for factor B at $\alpha = .05$.

12.23   a. $df(V) = b - 1 = 2 - 1 = 1$
$df(VP) = (a - 1)(b - 1) = 1 \times 1 = 1$
$df(Error) = ab(r - 1) = 2(2)(5 - 1) = 16$
$df(Total) = abr - 1 = 2(2)(5) - 1 = 19$

$F = \dfrac{MS(VP)}{MSE} \Rightarrow MS(VP) = F \times MSE = 11.39 \times 15 = 170.85$

$SS(VP) = MS(VP) \times df(VP) = 170.85 \times 1 = 170.85$

$F = \dfrac{MS(V)}{MSE} \Rightarrow MS(V) = F \times MSE = 4.61 \times 15 = 69.15$

$SS(V) = MS(V) \times df(V) = 69.15 \times 1 = 69.15$

$SSE = MSE \times df(Error) = 15 \times 16 = 240$

No further entries can be computed with the information given.

b.

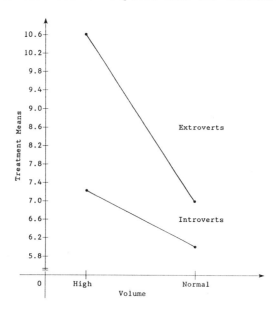

This figure implies interaction is present. At high volume, extroverts have a much higher mean than do the introverts. At normal volume, the extroverts have a higher mean than the introverts, but the difference is much smaller than at the high volume.

c. H_0: No interaction between Personality and Volume
   H_a: Personality and Volume interact

The test statistic is $F = \dfrac{MS(AB)}{MSE} = 11.39$

The rejection region requires $\alpha = .05$ in the upper tail of the F distribution with $\nu_1 = k - 1 = 1$ and $\nu_2 = n - k = 16$. From Table 8, Appendix E, $F_{.05} = 4.49$. The rejection region is $F > 4.49$.

Since the observed value of the test statistic falls in the rejection region ($F = 11.39 > 4.49$), H_0 is rejected. There is sufficient evidence to indicate an interaction between personality type and commercial volume at $\alpha = .05$.

12.25 a. $F(\text{Period}) = \dfrac{MS(P)}{MSE} = \dfrac{5.33}{5.96} = .89$

$F(\text{Ratio}) = \dfrac{MS(R)}{MSE} = \dfrac{16.00}{5.96} = 2.68$

$F(\text{Interaction}) = \dfrac{MS(PR)}{MSE} = \dfrac{23.83}{5.96} = 4.00$

The completed table is

SOURCE	df	SS	MS	F
Length, L	2	10.67	5.33	.89
Ratio, R	2	32.00	16.00	2.68
LR	4	95.33	23.83	4.00
Error	27	161.00	5.96	
Total	35	299.00		

b. The customer satisfaction means are found by summing over each level of period length and ratio and dividing by the number of observations in each level

$\bar{x}_{L_1 R_1} = \dfrac{\sum x_{L_1 R_1}}{r} = \dfrac{25 + 28 + 26 + 27}{4} = 26.5$

$\bar{x}_{L_1 R_2} = \dfrac{31 + 29 + 26 + 27}{4} = 28.25$

$$\bar{x}_{L_1R_3} = \frac{24 + 28 + 25 + 26}{4} = 25.75$$

$$\bar{x}_{L_2R_1} = \frac{26 + 27 + 29 + 30}{4} = 28.0$$

$$\bar{x}_{L_2R_2} = \frac{25 + 24 + 30 + 26}{4} = 26.25$$

$$\bar{x}_{L_2R_3} = \frac{33 + 28 + 25 + 27}{4} = 28.25$$

$$\bar{x}_{L_3R_1} = \frac{22 + 20 + 25 + 21}{4} = 22.0$$

$$\bar{x}_{L_3R_2} = \frac{33 + 27 + 25 + 27}{4} = 28.0$$

$$\bar{x}_{L_3R_3} = \frac{30 + 31 + 26 + 27}{4} = 28.5$$

c.

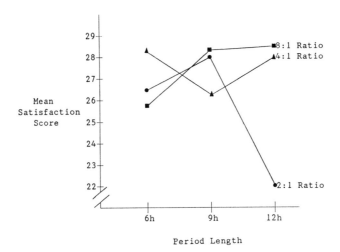

The figure shows a situation where an interaction appears to exist. The effect of the pricing ratio depends on the peak period length.

d. To determine if interaction exists, we test:

H_0: No interaction between period length and ratio exists
H_a: Period and ratio interact

The test statistic is $F = \dfrac{MS(LR)}{MSE} = 4.00$

The rejection region requires $\alpha = .05$ in the upper tail of the F distribution with $\nu_1 = (a - 1)(b - 1) = 4$ and $\nu_2 = ab(r - 1) = 27$. From Table 8, Appendix E, $F_{.05} = 2.73$. The rejection region is $F > 2.73$.

Since the observed value of the test statistic falls in the rejection region ($F = 4.00 > 2.73$), H_0 is rejected. There is sufficient evidence to indicate an interaction between period length and ratio exists at $\alpha = .05$.

e. Note: The results of this test may not be valid since an interaction exists between the two main effects.

To test for the main effects of factor L, we test:

H_0: There are no differences among the means for peak period length

H_a: At least two of the peak period length means differ

The test statistic is $F = \dfrac{MS(L)}{MSE} = .89$

The rejection region requires $\alpha = .05$ in the upper tail of the F distribution with $\nu_1 = a - 1 = 2$ and $\nu_2 = ab(r - 1) = 27$. From Table 8, Appendix E, $F_{.05} = 3.35$. The rejection region is $F > 3.35$.

Since the observed value of the test statistic does not fall in the rejection region ($F = .89 \not> 3.35$), H_0 is not rejected. There is insufficient evidence to indicate a difference among at least two of the peak period length means at $\alpha = .05$.

f. Tests for main effects are only appropriate when no interaction exists between the main effects.

g. The form of the confidence interval for the mean customer satisfaction rating at L_2 and R_1 is

$$\bar{x}_{L_2 R_1} \pm t_{\alpha/2} \dfrac{s}{\sqrt{r}} \text{ where } s = \sqrt{MSE}$$

From part (a), MSE = 5.96 => $s = \sqrt{5.96} = 2.441$. For confidence coefficient .90, $\alpha = 1 - .90 = .10$ and $\alpha/2 = .10/2 = .05$. From Table 6, Appendix E, $t_{.05} = 1.703$ with df = $ab(r - 1) = 27$.

The 90% confidence interval is

$$28.0 \pm 1.703 \frac{2.441}{\sqrt{4}}$$

$$\Rightarrow 28.0 \pm 2.079$$

$$\Rightarrow (25.921, 30.079)$$

h. The form of the confidence interval for the difference in mean customer satisfaction ratings for L_2 and L_1 at R_3 is

$$(\bar{x}_{L_2 R_3} - \bar{x}_{L_1 R_3}) \pm t_{\alpha/2} s \sqrt{\frac{2}{r}} \text{ where } s = \sqrt{MSE}$$

From part (g), s = 2.441. For confidence coefficient .95, $1 - \alpha$ = .05 and $\alpha/2$ = .05/2 = .025. From Table 6, Appendix E, $t_{.025}$ = 2.052 with df = ab(r − 1) = 27.

The 95% confidence interval is

$$(28.25 - 25.75) \pm 2.052(2.441)\sqrt{\frac{2}{4}}$$

$$\Rightarrow 2.50 \pm 3.542$$

$$\Rightarrow (-1.042, 6.042)$$

12.27 a. df(U) = DF for UNION = 1
df(P) = DF for PLAN = 2
df(UP) = DF for UNION × PLAN = 2
df(Error) = DF for Residual = 30
df(Total) = DF for Total = 35

SS(U) = Sum of Squares for UNION = 7168.444
SS(P) = Sum of Squares for PLAN = 5425.167
SS(UP) = Sum of Squares for UNION × PLAN = 159.389
SSE = Sum of Squares for Residual = 8165.000
SS(Total) = Sum of Squares for Total = 20918.000

MS(U) = Mean Square for UNION = 7168.444
MS(P) = Mean Square for PLAN = 2712.583
MS(UP) = Mean Square for UNION × PLAN = 79.694
MSE = Mean Square for Residual = 272.167

F(U) = F for UNION = 26.338
F(P) = F for PLAN = 9.967
F(UP) = F for UNION × PLAN = .293

The ANOVA table is

SOURCE	df	SS	MS	F
Union, U	1	7168.444	7168.444	26.338
Plan, P	2	5425.167	2712.583	9.967
UP	2	159.389	79.694	.293
Error	30	8165.000	272.167	
Total	35	20918.000		

b. In the presence of a UP interaction, the selection of an incentive plan for a particular plant will depend on the union affiliation of its workers.

c. To determine if an interaction exists, we test:

H_0: No interaction between union affiliation and incentive plan exits

H_a: Union affiliation and incentive plan interact

The test statistic is $F = \dfrac{MS(UP)}{MSE} = .293$

The rejection region requires $\alpha = .05$ in the upper tail of the F distribution with $\nu_1 = (a - 1)(b - 1) = 2$ and $\nu_2 = ab(r - 1) = 30$. From Table 8, Appendix E, $F_{.05} = 3.32$. The rejection region is $F > 3.32$.

Since the observed value of the test statistic does not fall in the rejection region ($F = .293 \not> 3.32$), H_0 is not rejected. There is insufficient evidence to indicate an interaction between union affiliation and incentive plan exists at $\alpha = .05$.

12.29 a. For k = 3 means, the number of pairwise comparisons to be made is

$$g = \frac{k(k - 1)}{2} = \frac{3(2)}{2} = 3$$

Thus, we need to find $t_{\alpha/(2g)} = t_{.06/2(3)} = t_{.01}$ with $\nu = n - k = 15 - 3 = 12$. From Table 6, Appendix E, $t_{.01} = 2.681$.

b. For k = 5 means, the number of pairwise comparisons to be made is

$$g = \frac{k(k - 1)}{2} = \frac{5(4)}{2} = 10$$

Thus, we need to find $t_{\alpha/(2g)} = t_{.10/2(10)} = t_{.005}$ with $\nu = n - k = 20 - 5 = 15$. From Table 6, Appendix E, $t_{.005} = 2.947$.

c. For k = 4 means, the number of pairwise comparisons to be made is

$$g = \frac{k(k - 1)}{2} = \frac{4(3)}{2} = 6$$

Thus, we need to find $t_{\alpha/(2g)} = t_{.06/2(6)} = t_{.005}$ with $\nu = n - k$ = 40 - 4 = 36. From Table 6, Appendix E,

$$t_{.005} \approx \frac{2.750 + 2.704}{2} \approx 2.73$$

d. For k = 5 means, the number of pairwise comparisons to be made is

$$g = \frac{k(k-1)}{2} = \frac{5(4)}{2} = 10$$

Thus, we need to find $t_{\alpha/(2g)} = t_{.05/2(10)} = t_{.0025}$ with $\nu = n - k$ = 25 - 5 = 20. From Table 6, Appendix E,

$$t_{.0025} \approx \frac{2.845 + 3.552}{2} \approx 3.20$$

12.31 For a 2 × 2 factorial experiment, there will be k = 4 means. The number of pairwise comparisons to be made is

$$g = \frac{k(k-1)}{2} = \frac{4(3)}{2} = 6$$

a. We need to find $t_{\alpha/(2g)} = t_{.06/2(6)} = t_{.005}$ with $\nu = ab(r-1)$ = 2(2)(1) = 4. From Table 6, Appendix E, $t_{.005}$ = 4.604.

b. We need to find $t_{\alpha/(2g)} = t_{.03/2(6)} = t_{.0025}$ with $\nu = ab(r-1)$ = 2(2)(3) = 12. From Table 6, Appendix E, $t_{.0025} \approx 3.50$.

c. We need to find $t_{\alpha/(2g)} = t_{.05/2(6)} = t_{.0042}$ with $\nu = ab(r-1)$ = 2(2)(9) = 36. From Table 6, Appendix E, $t_{.0042} \approx 2.85$.

12.33 From Exercise 12.12, we have $s = \sqrt{MSE} = \sqrt{.917} = .958$, $\nu = n - b - k + 1 = 6$ df for error and $n_i = n_j = 4$ observations for all treatment pairs (i, j). For k = 3 means, the number of pairwise comparisons to be made is

$$g = \frac{k(k-1)}{2} = \frac{3(2)}{2} = 3$$

Thus, we need to find $t_{\alpha/(2g)} = t_{.06/2(3)} = t_{.01}$ with $\nu = 6$. From Table 6, Appendix E, $t_{.01} = 3.143$. Substituting these values into the equation for Bonferroni's critical difference, we obtain

$$B_{ij} = (t_{.01})s\sqrt{\frac{1}{n_i} + \frac{1}{n_j}} = 3.143(.958)\sqrt{\frac{1}{4} + \frac{1}{4}} = 2.129$$

for any treatment pair (i, j).

12.35 From Exercise 12.9, we have $s = \sqrt{MSE} = \sqrt{.1702} = .4126$, $\nu = n - k$ = 18 - 3 = 15 df for error, and $n_i = n_j = 6$ observations for all treatment pairs (i, j). For k = 3 means, the number of pairwise comparisons to be made is

$$g = \frac{k(k-1)}{2} = \frac{3(2)}{2} = 3$$

Thus, we need to find $t_{\alpha/(2g)} = t_{.06/2(3)} = t_{.01}$ with $\nu = 15$. From Table 6, Appendix E, $t_{.01} = 2.602$. Substituting these values into the equation for Bonferroni's critical difference, we obtain

$$B_{ij} = (t_{.01})s\sqrt{\frac{1}{n_i} + \frac{1}{n_j}} = 2.602(.4126)\sqrt{\frac{1}{6} + \frac{1}{6}} = .620$$

for any treatment pair (i, j). Therefore, population means corresponding to pairs of sample means that differ by more than .620 will be judged to be significantly different. The three treatment means are:

$$\bar{x}_X = \frac{\sum x_X}{n_X} = \frac{57.85}{6} = 9.642$$

$$\bar{x}_Y = \frac{\sum x_Y}{n_Y} = \frac{63.67}{6} = 10.612$$

$$\bar{x}_Z = \frac{\sum x_Z}{n_Z} = \frac{59.96}{6} = 9.493$$

The treatment means are ranked as follows:

Sample means	$\overline{9.493 \qquad 9.642}$	10.612
Treatments	Z X	Y

Using $B_{ij} = .620$ as a yardstick to determine differences between pairs of treatments, we have placed connecting horizontal bars over those means that do not significantly differ.

It appears that firms subscribing to Theory Y have a significantly higher mean starting hourly wage rate than Theory X or Theory Z firms. Theory X and Theory Z firms do not significantly differ.

12.37   From Exercise 12.14, we have $s = \sqrt{MSE} = \sqrt{.0246} = .1568$, $\nu = n - b - k + 1 = 28 - 7 - 4 + 1 = 18$ and $n_i = n_j = 7$ observations for all treatment pairs (i, j). For k = 4 means, the number of pairwise comparisons to be made is

$$g = \frac{k(k-1)}{2} = \frac{4(3)}{2} = 6$$

Thus, we need to find $t_{\alpha/(2g)} = t_{.05/2(6)} = t_{.0042}$ with $\nu = 18$. From Table 6, Appendix E, $t_{.0042} \approx 2.90$. Substituting these values into the equation for Bonferroni's critical difference, we obtain

$$B_{ij} = (t_{.0042})s\sqrt{\frac{1}{n_i} + \frac{1}{n_j}} \approx 2.90(.1568)\sqrt{\frac{1}{7} + \frac{1}{7}} \approx .24$$

for any treatment pair (i, j). Therefore, population means corresponding to pairs of sample means that differ by more than .24 will be judged to be significantly different. The four treatment means are:

$$\bar{T}_A = \frac{\Sigma x_A}{b} = \frac{4.85}{7} = .69$$

$$\bar{T}_K = \frac{\Sigma x_K}{b} = \frac{5.55}{7} = .79$$

$$\bar{T}_P = \frac{\Sigma x_P}{b} = \frac{6.83}{7} = .98$$

$$\bar{T}_F = \frac{\Sigma x_F}{b} = \frac{5.08}{7} = .73$$

The treatment means are ranked as follows:

Sample means	.69	.73	.79	.98
Treatments	A	F	K	P

Using $B_{ij} = .24$ as a yardstick to determine differences between pairs of treatments, we have placed connecting horizontal bars over those means that do not significantly differ. The Publix stores have a significantly higher mean price per item than Albertson's and Food 4 Less.

12.39   a.   The mean profits are computed below.

$$\bar{x}_{1/2, 15} = \frac{\Sigma x_{1/2, 15}}{r} = \frac{64}{3} = 21.333$$

$$\bar{x}_{1/2, 18} = \frac{\Sigma x_{1/2, 18}}{r} = \frac{61}{3} = 20.333$$

$$\bar{x}_{1/2, 21} = \frac{\Sigma x_{1/2, 21}}{r} = \frac{58}{3} = 19.333$$

$$\bar{x}_{1, 15} = \frac{\Sigma x_{1, 15}}{r} = \frac{61}{3} = 20.333$$

$$\bar{x}_{1, 18} = \frac{\Sigma x_{1, 18}}{r} = \frac{71}{3} = 23.667$$

$$\bar{x}_{1,21} = \frac{\sum x_{1,21}}{r} = \frac{61}{3} = 20.333$$

$$\bar{x}_{2,15} = \frac{\sum x_{2,15}}{r} = \frac{52}{3} = 17.333$$

$$\bar{x}_{2,18} = \frac{\sum x_{2,18}}{r} = \frac{64}{3} = 21.333$$

$$\bar{x}_{2,21} = \frac{\sum x_{2,21}}{r} = \frac{66}{3} = 22.000$$

b. From Exercise 12.24, we have $s = \sqrt{MSE} = \sqrt{2.407} = 1.551$, $\nu = ab(r - 1) = 3(3)(2) = 18$ and $n_i = n_j = 3$ observations for all treatment pairs (i, j). For $k = 3$ treatments within each level of ratio, the number of pairwise comparisons to be made is

$$g = \frac{k(k - 1)}{2} = \frac{3(2)}{2} = 3$$

Thus, we need to find $t_{\alpha/(2g)} = t_{.03/2(3)} = t_{.005}$ with $\nu = 18$. From Table 6, Appendix E, $t_{.005} = 2.878$. Substituting these values into the equation for Bonferroni's critical difference, we obtain

$$B_{ij} = (t_{.005})s\sqrt{\frac{1}{n_i} + \frac{1}{n_j}} = 2.878(1.551)\sqrt{\frac{1}{3} + \frac{1}{3}} = 3.645$$

for any treatment pair (i, j). Therefore, population means corresponding to pairs of sample means that differ by more than 3.645 will be judged to be significantly different.

The treatment means within ratio = 1/2 are ranked as follows:

Sample means	19.333	20.333	21.333
Treatments (Supply)	21	18	15

Using $B_{ij} = 3.645$ as a yardstick to determine differences between pairs of treatments, we have placed connecting horizontal bars over those means that do not significantly differ. There are no significant differences in mean profit among the three supply groups at ratio = 1/2.

The treatment means within ratio = 1 are ranked as follows:

Sample means	20.333	20.333	23.667
Treatments (Supply)	15	21	18

There are no significant differences in mean profit among the three supply groups at ratio = 1

The treatment means within ratio = 2 are ranked as follows:

Sample means	17.333	21.333	22.000
Treatments (Supply)	15	18	21

At ratio = 2, the mean profit for supply = 15 is significantly lower than for supply = 18 or supply = 21. There are no other significant differences.

c. From part (b), $s = 1.551$, $t_{.005} = 2.878$ with df = 18, $n_i = n_j = 3$ and $B_{ij} = 3.645$ for any treatment pair (i, j).

The treatment means for supply = 15 are ranked as follows:

Sample means	17.333	20.333	21.333
Treatments (Ratio)	2	1	1/2

At supply = 15, the mean profit for ratio = 1/2 significantly exceeds that for ratio = 2. There are no other significant differences.

The treatment means for supply = 18 are ranked as follows:

Sample means	20.333	21.333	23.667
Treatment(Ratio)	1/2	2	1

There are no significant differences in mean profit among the three ratios for supply = 18.

The treatment means for supply = 21 are ranked as follows:

Sample means	19.333	20.333	22.000
Treatment(Ratio)	1/2	1	2

There are no significant differences in mean profit among the three ratios for supply = 21.

12.41 The following quantities are calculated from the data:

$$CM = \frac{(\sum x)^2}{n} = \frac{(2.1 + 3.3 + \ldots + 2.0)^2}{10} = \frac{(20.8)^2}{10} = 43.264$$

$$SS(Total) = \sum x^2 - CM = (2.1)^2 + (3.3)^2 + \ldots + (2.0)^2 - 43.264$$
$$= 59.32 - 43.264 = 16.056$$

$$SST = \frac{T_1^2}{n_1} + \frac{T_2^2}{n_2} + \frac{T_3^2}{n_3} - CM = \frac{(5.6)^2}{3} + \frac{(11.9)^2}{4} + \frac{(3.3)^2}{3} - 43.264$$

$$= 49.486 - 43.264 = 6.222$$

$$SSE = SS(Total) - SST = 16.056 - 6.222 = 9.834$$

$$MST = \frac{SST}{k-1} = \frac{6.222}{3-1} = 3.111$$

$$MSE = \frac{SSE}{n-k} = \frac{9.834}{10-3} = 1.405$$

$$F = \frac{MST}{MSE} = \frac{3.111}{1.405} = 2.214$$

The ANOVA table is:

SOURCE	df	SS	MS	F
Samples	2	6.222	3.111	2.214
Error	7	9.834	1.405	
Total	9	16.056		

12.43 The following quantities are calculated from the data:

$$CM = \frac{(\sum x)^2}{n} = \frac{(3 + 6 + \ldots + 2)^2}{12} = \frac{(43)^2}{12} = 154.083$$

$$SS(Total) = \sum x^2 - CM = (3)^2 + (6)^2 + \ldots + (2)^2 - 154.083$$

$$= 197 - 154.083 = 42.917$$

$$SST = \frac{T_1^2 + T_2^2 + T_3^2}{b} - CM = \frac{(12)^2 + (22)^2 + (19)^2}{4} - 154.083$$

$$= 177.25 - 154.083 = 23.167$$

$$SSB = \frac{B_1^2 + B_2^2 + B_3^2 + B_4^2}{k} - CM = \frac{(10)^2 + (16)^2 + (7)^2 + (10)^2}{3} - 154.083$$

$$= 168.333 - 154.083 = 14.250$$

$$SSE = SS(Total) - SST - SSB = 42.917 - 23.167 - 14.250 = 5.500$$

$$MST = \frac{SST}{k-1} = \frac{23.167}{3-1} = 11.584$$

$$MSB = \frac{SSB}{b-1} = \frac{14.250}{4-1} = 4.750$$

$$MSE = \frac{SSE}{n - b - k + 1} = \frac{5.500}{12 - 4 - 3 + 1} = .917$$

$$F(\text{Treatments}) = \frac{MST}{MSE} = \frac{11.584}{.917} = 12.63$$

$$F(\text{Blocks}) = \frac{MSB}{MSE} = \frac{4.750}{.917} = 5.18$$

The ANOVA table is:

SOURCE	df	SS	MS	F
Treatments	2	23.167	11.584	12.63
Blocks	3	14.250	4.750	5.18
Error	6	5.500	.917	
Total	11	42.917		

12.45 The following quantities are calculated from the data:

$$CM = \frac{(\sum x)^2}{n} = \frac{(5 + 7 + \ldots + 8 + 5)^2}{24} = \frac{(161)^2}{24} = 1080.0417$$

$$SS(\text{Total}) = \sum x^2 - CM = (5)^2 + (7)^2 + \ldots + (8)^2 + (5)^2 - 1080.0417$$
$$= 1157 - 1080.0417 = 76.9583$$

$$SS(A) = \frac{A_1^2 + A_2^2 + A_3^2}{br} - CM = \frac{(48)^2 + (58)^2 + (55)^2}{(4)(2)} - 1080.0417$$

$$= 1086.6250 - 1080.0417 = 6.5833$$

$$SS(B) = \frac{B_1^2 + B_2^2 + B_3^2 + B_4^2}{ar} - CM = \frac{(37)^2 + (48)^2 + (37)^2 + (39)^2}{3(2)}$$

$$- 1080.0417 = 1093.8333 - 1080.0417 = 13.7916$$

$$SS(AB) = \sum_{ij} \frac{(AB_{ij})^2}{r} - SS(A) - SS(B) - CM$$

$$= \frac{[(5 + 4)^2 + (7 + 9)^2 + \ldots + (5 + 8)^2 + (6 + 5)^2]}{2}$$

$$- 6.5833 - 13.7916 - 1080.0417$$

$$= \frac{2271}{2} - 6.5833 - 13.7916 - 1080.0417 = 35.0834$$

$$SSE = SS(\text{Total}) - SS(A) - SS(B) - SS(AB)$$

$$= 76.9583 - 6.5833 - 13.7916 - 35.0834 = 21.500$$

$$MS(A) = \frac{SS(A)}{a - 1} = \frac{6.5833}{3 - 1} = 3.2917$$

$$MS(B) = \frac{SS(B)}{b - 1} = \frac{13.7916}{4 - 1} = 4.5972$$

$$MS(AB) = \frac{SS(AB)}{(a - 1)(b - 1)} = \frac{35.0834}{2(3)} = 5.8472$$

$$MSE = \frac{SSE}{ab(r - 1)} = \frac{21.5000}{3(4)(2 - 1)} = 1.7917$$

$$F(A) = \frac{MS(A)}{MSE} = \frac{3.2917}{1.7917} = 1.84$$

$$F(B) = \frac{MS(B)}{MSE} = \frac{4.5972}{1.7917} = 2.57$$

$$F(AB) = \frac{MS(AB)}{MSE} = \frac{5.8472}{1.7917} = 3.26$$

The ANOVA table is:

SOURCE	df	SS	MS	F
A	2	6.5833	3.2917	1.84
B	3	13.7916	4.5972	2.57
AB	6	35.0834	5.8472	3.26
Error	12	21.5000	1.7917	
Total	23	76.9583		

12.47   a.   The ANOVA table is:

SOURCE	df	SS	MS	F
Plan	3	154.11	51.37	10.21
Error	13	65.42	5.03	
Total	16	219.53		

b.   To determine if a difference exists among the mean travel times for the four plans, we test:

H_0: $\mu_1 = \mu_2 = \mu_3 = \mu_4$
H_a: At least two treatment means differ

The test statistic is $F = \dfrac{MST}{MSE} = 10.21$

The rejection region requires α = .05 in the upper tail of the F distribution with ν_1 = k - 1 = 3 and ν_2 = n - k = 13. From Table 8, Appendix E, $F_{.05}$ = 3.41. The rejection region is F > 3.41.

Since the observed value of the test statistic falls in the rejection region (F = 10.21 > 3.41), H_0 is rejected. There is sufficient evidence to indicate a difference in mean travel times among at least two of the plans at α = .05.

c. From part (a), we have s = $\sqrt{MSE}$ = $\sqrt{5.03}$ = 2.243 and ν = n - k = 13. For k = 4 means, the number of pairwise comparisons to be made is

$$g = \frac{k(k-1)}{2} = \frac{4(3)}{2} = 6$$

Thus, we need to find $t_{\alpha/(2g)}$ = $t_{.06/2(6)}$ = $t_{.005}$ with ν = 13. From Table 6, Appendix E, $t_{.005}$ = 3.012. Substituting these values into the equation for Bonferroni's critical difference, we obtain

$$B_{ij} = (t_{.005})s\sqrt{\frac{1}{n_i} + \frac{1}{n_j}} = 3.012(2.243)\sqrt{\frac{1}{4} + \frac{1}{5}} = 4.532$$

for any treatment pair (i, j) = (1, 2) and (1, 3)

We obtain

$$B_{ij} = (t_{.005})s\sqrt{\frac{1}{n_i} + \frac{1}{n_j}} = 3.012(2.243)\sqrt{\frac{1}{4} + \frac{1}{3}} = 5.160$$

for any treatment pair (i, j) = (1, 4)

We obtain

$$B_{ij} = (t_{.005})s\sqrt{\frac{1}{n_i} + \frac{1}{n_j}} = 3.012(2.243)\sqrt{\frac{1}{5} + \frac{1}{5}} = 4.273$$

for any treatment pair (i, j) = (2, 3)

Finally, we obtain

$$B_{ij} = (t_{.005})s\sqrt{\frac{1}{n_i} + \frac{1}{n_j}} = 3.012(2.243)\sqrt{\frac{1}{5} + \frac{1}{3}} = 4.934$$

for any treatment pair (i, j) = (2, 4) and (3, 4)

The sample means are computed as follows:

$$\bar{x}_1 = \frac{\sum x_1}{n_1} = \frac{107}{4} = 26.75$$

$$\bar{x}_2 = \frac{\sum x_2}{n_2} = \frac{134}{5} = 26.80$$

$$\bar{x}_3 = \frac{\sum x_3}{n_3} = \frac{112}{5} = 22.40$$

$$\bar{x}_4 = \frac{\sum x_4}{n_4} = \frac{94}{3} = 31.33$$

The treatment means are ranked as follows:

Sample mean	22.40	26.75	26.80	31.33
Treatment (Plan)	3	1	2	4

The mean travel time (in minutes) for plans 2 and 4 are significantly greater than for plan 3. No other pairs are significantly different.

d. The form of the confidence interval for $\mu_1 - \mu_4$ is

$$(\bar{x}_1 - \bar{x}_4) \pm t_{\alpha/2}s\sqrt{\frac{1}{n_1} + \frac{1}{n_4}} \text{ where } s = \sqrt{MSE} = 2.243$$

For confidence coefficient .95, $\alpha = 1 - .95 = .05$ and $\alpha/2 = .05/2 = .025$. From Table 6 of Appendix E, $t_{.025} = 2.160$ with df $= n - k = 13$.

The 95% confidence interval is

$$(26.75 - 31.33) \pm 2.160(2.243)\sqrt{\frac{1}{4} + \frac{1}{3}}$$

$$\Rightarrow -4.58 \pm 3.700$$

$$\Rightarrow (-8.28, -0.88)$$

12.49 a. The following quantities are calculated from the data;

$$CM = \frac{(\sum x)^2}{n} = \frac{(213.84)^2}{18} = 2540.4192$$

$$SS(Total) = \sum x^2 - CM = 2620.2528 - 2540.4192 = 79.8336$$

$$SST = \frac{T_A^2}{n_A} + \frac{T_B^2}{n_B} + \frac{T_C^2}{n_C} + \frac{T_D^2}{n_D} + \frac{T_E^2}{n_E} + \frac{T_F^2}{n_F} - CM$$

$$= \frac{37.33^2}{3} + \frac{41.85^2}{3} + \frac{32.27^2}{3} + \frac{34.83^2}{3} + \frac{26.49^2}{3} + \frac{41.07^2}{3}$$

$$- 2540.4192 = 2595.9661 - 2540.4192 = 55.5469$$

SSE = SS(Total) - SST = 79.8336 - 55.5469 = 24.2867

$$MST = \frac{SST}{k - 1} = \frac{54.5469}{6 - 1} = 11.1094$$

$$MSE = \frac{SSE}{n - k} = \frac{24.2867}{18 - 6} = 2.0239$$

$$F = \frac{MST}{MSE} = \frac{11.1094}{2.0239} = 5.49$$

The ANOVA table is:

SOURCE	df	SS	MS	F
Treatment	5	55.5469	11.1094	5.49
Error	12	24.2867	2.0239	
Total	17	79.8336		

b. To determine if a difference among the mean wears exists, we test:

H_0: $\mu_1 = \mu_2 = \ldots = \mu_6$
H_a: At least two treatment means differ

The test statistic is $F = \dfrac{MST}{MSE} = 5.49$

The rejection region requires $\alpha = .05$ in the upper tail of the F distribution with $\nu_1 = k - 1 = 5$ and $\nu_2 = n - k = 12$. From Table 8, Appendix E, $F_{.05} = 3.11$. The rejection region is $F > 3.11$.

Since the observed value of the test statistic falls in the rejection region ($F = 5.49 > 3.11$), H_0 is rejected. There is sufficient evidence to indicate a difference in mean wear among at least two treatments at $\alpha = .05$.

c. The form of the confidence interval for $\mu_B - \mu_E$ is

$$(\bar{x}_B - \bar{x}_E) \pm t_{\alpha/2} s \sqrt{\frac{1}{n_B} + \frac{1}{n_E}} \text{ where } s = \sqrt{MSE} = \sqrt{2.0239} = 1.4226$$

For confidence coefficient .95, $\alpha = 1 - .95 = .05$ and $\alpha/2 = .05/2 = .025$. From Table 6, Appendix E, $t_{.025} = 2.179$ with $\nu = n - k = 12$.

The point estimates of μ_B and μ_E are:

$$\bar{x}_B = \frac{T_B}{n_B} = \frac{41.85}{3} = 13.95$$

$$\bar{x}_E = \frac{T_E}{n_E} = \frac{26.49}{3} = 8.83$$

The 95% confidence interval is

$$(13.95 - 8.83) \pm 2.179(1.4226)\sqrt{\frac{1}{3} + \frac{1}{3}}$$

$$\Rightarrow 5.13 \pm 2.531$$

$$\Rightarrow (2.589, 7.651)$$

d. The form of the confidence interval for μ_A is $\bar{x}_A \pm t_{\alpha/2}s/\sqrt{n_A}$ where $s = \sqrt{MSE} = 1.4226$. From part (c), $t_{.025} = 2.179$ with $\nu = n - k = 12$.

The point estimate for μ_A is

$$\bar{x}_A = \frac{T_A}{n_A} = \frac{37.33}{3} = 12.443$$

The 95% confidence interval is

$$12.443 \pm 2.179 \frac{1.4226}{\sqrt{3}}$$

$$\Rightarrow 12.443 \pm 1.790$$

$$\Rightarrow (10.653, 14.233)$$

12.51 a. SST = .0992. It is a measure of the total variation among the three drugs' concentrations.

MST = .0496 and is a measure of the average variation among the three drugs' concentrations.

SSE = .0451. It is a measure of the total concentration variation within the three drugs.

MSE = .0021 and is a measure of the average concentration variation within the three drugs.

F = 23.12. F is the ratio of average concentration variation among drugs to that within drugs.

b. To determine if there is a difference among the three drug means, we test:

H_0: $\mu_1 = \mu_2 = \mu_3$
H_a: At least two treatment means differ

The test statistic is $F = \dfrac{MST}{MSE} = 23.1223$

COMPARING MORE THAN TWO POPULATION MEANS: AN
ANALYSIS OF VARIANCE

The p-value from the printout is approximately 0. This implies that H_0 will be rejected at any chosen level of α larger than ~ 0. Since $\alpha = .10$ for this problem, H_0 is rejected. There is sufficient evidence to indicate a difference in mean concentration among at least two of the three drugs.

c. From part (a), we have $s = \sqrt{MSE} = \sqrt{.0021} = .0458$, $\nu = n - k = 24 - 3 = 21$ df for error, and $n_i = n_j = 8$ observations for all treatment pairs (i, j). For $k = 3$ means, the number of pairwise comparisons to be made is

$$g = \frac{k(k - 1)}{2} = \frac{3(2)}{2} = 3$$

Thus, we need to find $t_{\alpha/(2g)} = t_{.10/2(3)} = t_{.0167}$ with $\nu = 21$. From Table 6, Appendix E, $t_{.0167} \approx (2.080 + 2.518)/2 \approx 2.30$. Substituting these values into the equation for Bonferroni's critical difference, we obtain

$$B_{ij} = (t_{.0167})s\sqrt{\frac{1}{n_i} + \frac{1}{n_j}} = 2.30(.0458)\sqrt{\frac{1}{8} + \frac{1}{8}} = .053$$

for any treatment pair (i, j).

The treatment means are:

$$\bar{x}_1 = \frac{\sum x_1}{n_1} = \frac{14.01}{8} = 1.751$$

$$\bar{x}_2 = \frac{\sum x_2}{n_2} = \frac{14.07}{8} = 1.759$$

$$\bar{x}_3 = \frac{\sum x_3}{n_3} = \frac{12.95}{8} = 1.619$$

The treatment means are ranked as follows:

Sample mean	1.619	1.751	1.759
Treatment (Drug)	3	1	2

The mean concentrations for drugs 1 and 2 are significantly higher than that for drug 3. The mean concentrations for drugs 1 and 2 do not differ from each other.

d. The form of the confidence interval for $\mu_1 - \mu_3$ is

$$(\bar{x}_1 - \bar{x}_3) \pm t_{\alpha/2}s\sqrt{\frac{1}{n_1} + \frac{1}{n_3}} \text{ where } s = \sqrt{MSE} = .0458$$

For confidence coefficient .90, $1 - \alpha = .10$ and $\alpha/2 = .10/2 = .05$. From Table 6, Appendix E, $t_{.05} = 1.721$ with $\nu = n - k = 21$.

The 90% confidence interval is

$$(1.751 - 1.619) \pm 1.721(.0458)\sqrt{\frac{1}{8} + \frac{1}{8}}$$

$$\Rightarrow .132 \pm .039$$

$$\Rightarrow (.093, .171)$$

12.53   a.   The following quantities are calculated from the data:

$$CM = \frac{(\sum x)^2}{n} = \frac{(5417)^2}{24} = 1,222,662.042$$

$$SS(Total) = \sum x^2 - CM = 1,229,881 - 1,222,662.042 = 7218.958$$

$$SST = \frac{T_A^2 + T_B^2 + T_C^2}{b} - CM = \frac{1805^2 + 1862^2 + 1750^2}{8} - 1,222,662.042$$

$$= 1,223,446.125 - 1,222,662.042 - 784.083$$

$$SSB = \frac{B_1^2 + B_2^2 + \ldots + B_8^2}{k} - CM$$

$$= \frac{686^2 + 685^2 + 637^2 + 664^2 + 721^2 + 637^2 + 756^2 + 631^2}{3}$$

$$- 1,222,662.042 = 1,227,264.333 - 1,222,662.042 = 4602.291$$

$$SSE = SS(Total) - SST - SSB = 7218.958 - 784.083 - 4602.291$$

$$= 1832.584$$

$$MST = \frac{SST}{k - 1} = \frac{784.083}{3 - 1} = 392.042$$

$$MSB = \frac{SSE}{b - 1} = \frac{4602.291}{8 - 1} = 657.470$$

$$MSE = \frac{SSE}{n - k - b + 1} = \frac{1832.584}{24 - 3 - 8 + 1} = 130.899$$

$$F(Treatments) = \frac{MST}{MSE} = \frac{392.042}{130.899} = 2.99$$

$$F(Blocks) = \frac{MSB}{MSE} = \frac{657.470}{130.899} = 5.02$$

The ANOVA table is:

SOURCE	df	SS	MS	F
Display	2	784.083	392.042	2.99
Period	7	4602.291	657.470	5.02
Error	14	1832.584	130.899	
Total	23	7218.958		

b. To determine if a difference among mean sales for the three displays exists, we test:

H_0: $\mu_1 = \mu_2 = \mu_3$
H_a: At least two treatment means differ

The test statistic is $F = \dfrac{MST}{MSE} = 2.99$

The rejection region requires $\alpha = .05$ in the upper tail of the F distribution with $\nu_1 = k - 1 = 2$ and $\nu_2 = n - k - b + 1 = 14$. From Table 8, Appendix E, $F_{.05} = 3.74$. The rejection region is $F > 3.74$.

Since the observed value of the test statistic does not fall in the rejection region ($F = 2.99 \ngtr 3.74$), H_0 is not rejected. There is insufficient evidence to indicate a difference in mean sales among at least two of the three display types at $\alpha = .05$.

c. To determine if a difference exists among the block means, we test:

H_0: There is no difference among the 8 block means
H_a: At least two block means differ

The test statistic is $F = \dfrac{MSB}{MSE} = 5.02$

The rejection region requires $\alpha = .05$ in the upper tail of the F distribution with $\nu_1 = b - 1 = 7$ and $\nu_2 = n - k - b + 1 = 14$. From Table 8, Appendix E, $F_{.05} = 2.76$. The rejection region is $F > 2.76$.

Since the observed value of the test statistic falls in the rejection region ($F = 5.02 > 2.76$), H_0 is rejected. There is sufficient evidence to indicate the mean sales among at least two of the eight weeks differ at $\alpha = .05$. Blocking was necessary in this experiment.

d. It is not necessary to compare the three display mean sales using Bonferroni's procedure since the test in part (b) revealed no significant differences in mean sales among the three display types.

12.55 a. df(Group) = $k - 1 = 3 - 1 = 2$
df(Error) = $n - k = 93 - 3 = 90$
df(Total) = $n - 1 = 93 - 1 = 92$

SSE = SS(Total) $-$ SST = $12,769.830 - 509.871 = 12,259.959$

$$MST = \frac{SST}{k - 1} = \frac{509.871}{2} = 254.936$$

$$MST = \frac{SSE}{n - k} = \frac{12,259.959}{90} = 136.222$$

$$F = \frac{MST}{MSE} = \frac{254.936}{136.222} = 1.87$$

The completed ANOVA table is:

SOURCE	df	SS	MS	F
Group	2	509.871	254.936	1.87
Error	90	12,259.959	136.222	
Total	92	12,769.830		

b. To determine if a difference among treatment means exists, we test:

H_0: $\mu_1 = \mu_2 = \mu_3$
H_a: At least two treatment means differ

The test statistic is $F = \dfrac{MST}{MSE} = 1.87$

The rejection region requires $\alpha = .05$ in the upper tail of the F distribution with $v_1 = k - 1 = 2$ and $v_2 = n - k = 90$. From Table 8, Appendix E, $F_{.05} \approx (3.15 + 3.07)/2 \approx 3.11$. The rejection region is $F > 3.11$.

Since the observed value of the test statistic does not fall in the rejection region ($F = 1.87 \not> 3.11$), H_0 is not rejected. There is insufficient evidence to indicate a difference in mean risk-taking propensities among at least two of the three groups at $\alpha = .05$.

c. It is not necessary to compare the three group means using Bonferroni's procedure since the test in part (b) revealed no significant differences in means among the three groups.

12.57 a. $F(\text{Treatments}) = \dfrac{MST}{MSE} = \dfrac{.10}{1.30} = .08$

$F(\text{Blocks}) = \dfrac{MSB}{MSE} = \dfrac{121.14}{1.30} = 93.18$

The ANOVA table is:

SOURCE	df	SS	MS	F
Method	2	.19	.10	.08
Brand	5	605.70	121.14	93.18
Error	10	13.05	1.30	
Total	17	618.94		

b. To determine if a difference among treatment means exists, we test:

H_0: $\mu_1 = \mu_2 = \mu_3$
H_a: At least two treatment means differ

The test statistic is $F = \dfrac{MST}{MSE} = .08$

The rejection region requires $\alpha = .05$ in the upper tail of the F distribution with $v_1 = k - 1 = 2$ and $v_2 = n - k + b + 1 = 10$. From Table 8, Appendix E, $F_{.05} = 4.10$. The rejection region is $F > 4.10$.

Since the observed value of the test statistic does not fall in the rejection region ($F = .08 \not> 4.10$), H_0 is not rejected. There is insufficient evidence to indicate a difference in mean estimates of market share among at least two of the three auditing methods at $\alpha = .05$.

c. It is not necessary to compare the three auditing method means using Bonferroni's procedure since the test in part (b) revealed no significant differences in means among the three methods.

12.59 a. To determine if a difference among the mean CO contents of the three types of cigarettes exists, we would test:

H_0: $\mu_R = \mu_L = \mu_E$
H_a: At least two treatment means differ

b. SST = 574.8934. It is a measure of the total variation among the three different cigarettes' CO contents.

MST = 287.4467 and is a measure of the average variation among the three different cigarettes' CO contents.

SSE = 4944.2667. It is a measure of the total CO content variation within the three cigarettes.

MSE = 26.8710 and is a measure of the average CO content variation within the three cigarettes.

F = 10.70. F is the ratio of average CO content variation among cigarettes to that within cigarettes.

c. The test statistic to test the hypotheses in part (a) is

$$F = \frac{MST}{MSE} = 10.70$$

The p-value from the printout is .0001. This implies that H_0 will be rejected at any chosen level of α larger than .0001. This is a very small chance of Type I error if H_0 is rejected; therefore, we will reject H_0. There is sufficient evidence to indicate a difference in mean CO rankings among at least two of the three types of cigarettes.

CASE STUDIES

12.1 a. Visually inspecting the data is not sufficient to determine if a significant difference exists among the three store locations. A statistical test is needed because figure 12.13 does not give a clear vision of whether the difference between the sample means is small relative to the variability within the sample observations.

b. To determine if a difference exists among the mean price indexes for the three store locations, we would test:

H_0: $\mu_I = \mu_S = \mu_R$
H_a: At least two treatment means differ

c. We would use the Analysis of Variance for a completely randomized design since we wish to compare the means of more than 2 treatments for one factor with no blocking variable present.

d. SOURCE   df
    Location   k - 1 = 3 - 1 = 2
    Error   n - k = 14 - 3 = 11
    _____
    Total   n - 1 = 14 - 1 = 13

12.3 a. For Seller's Initial Offer ($ thousands), the following quantities
are calculated:

We must first obtain factor-level sums from the means given.

BUYER CONDITION

		BC	BNC		
Seller	SC	$B_1S_1 = 160.3(20) = 3206$	$B_2S_1 = 173.05(20) = 3461$	$S_1 =$	6667
Condition	SNC	$B_1S_2 = 155.5(20) = 3110$	$B_2S_2 = 149.50(20) = 2990$	$S_2 =$	6100
		$B_1 = 6316$	$B_2 = 6451$	$\sum x =$	12,767

$$CM = \frac{(\sum x)^2}{n} = \frac{(12,767)^2}{2(2)(20)} = 2,037,453.6125$$

$$SS(B) = \frac{B_1^2 + B_2^2}{sr} - CM = \frac{(6316)^2 + (6451)^2}{2(20)} - 2,037,453.6125$$

$$= 2,037,681.425 - 2,037,453.6125 = 227.8125$$

$$SS(S) = \frac{S_1^2 + S_2^2}{br} - CM = \frac{(6667)^2 + (6100)^2}{2(20)} - 2,037,453.6125$$

$$= 2,041,472.225 - 2,037,453.6125 = 4018.6125$$

$$SS(BS) = \frac{B_1S_1^2 + B_1S_2^2 + B_2S_1^2 + B_2S_2^2}{r} - SS(B) - SS(S) - CM$$

$$= \frac{(3206)^2 + (3110)^2 + (3461)^2 + (2990)^2}{20} - 227.8125$$

$$- 4018.6125 - 2,037,453.6125$$

$$= 2,043,457.85 - 227.8125 - 4018.6125 - 2,037,453.6125$$

$$= 1757.8125$$

$$s = 21 \Rightarrow s^2 = MSE = 21^2 = 441$$

$$MSE = \frac{SSE}{bs(r - 1)} \Rightarrow SSE = MSE[bs(r - 1)] = 441[2(2)(19)]$$

$$= 33,516.0000$$

$$SS(Total) = SS(B) + SS(S) + SS(BS) + SSE$$

$$= 227.8125 + 4018.6125 + 1757.8125 + 33,516.0000$$

$$= 39,520.2375$$

$$MS(B) = \frac{SS(B)}{b - 1} = \frac{227.8125}{2 - 1} = 227.8125$$

$$MS(S) = \frac{SS(S)}{s - 1} = \frac{4018.6125}{2 - 1} = 4018.6125$$

$$MS(BS) = \frac{SS(BS)}{(b - 1)(s - 1)} = \frac{1757.8125}{(2 - 1)(2 - 1)} = 1757.8125$$

$$F(B) = \frac{MS(B)}{MSE} = \frac{227.8125}{441.0000} = .52$$

$$F(S) = \frac{MS(S)}{MSE} = \frac{4018.6125}{441.0000} = 9.11$$

$$F(BS) = \frac{MS(BS)}{MSE} = \frac{1757.8125}{441.0000} = 3.99$$

The ANOVA table is:

SOURCE	df	SS	MS	F
Buyer, B	1	227.8125	227.8125	.52
Seller, S	1	4,018.6125	4018.6125	9.11
BS	1	1,757.8125	1757.8125	3.99
Error	76	33,516.0000	441.0000	
Total	79	39,520.2375		

For Buyer's Initial Offer ($ thousands), the following quantities are calculated:

We must first obtain factor-level sums from the means given.

		BUYER CONDITION		
		BC	BNC	
Seller	SC	$B_1S_1 = 114.15(20) = 2283$	$B_2S_1 = 117.944(20) = 2358.88$	$S_1 = 4641.88$
Condition	SNC	$B_1S_2 = 110.895(20) = 2217.9$	$B_2S_2 = 118.278(20) = 2365.56$	$S_2 = 4583.46$
		$B_1 = 4500.9$	$B_2 = 4724.44$	$\sum x = 9225.34$

$$CM = \frac{(\sum x)^2}{n} = \frac{(9225.34)^2}{2(2)(20)} = 1,063,836.2264$$

$$SS(B) = \frac{B_1^2 + B_2^2}{sr} - CM = \frac{(4500.9)^2 + (4724.44)^2}{2(20)} - 1,063,836.2264$$

$$= 1,064,460.853 - 1,063,836.2264 = 624.6266$$

$$SS(S) = \frac{S_1^2 + S_2^2}{br} - CM = \frac{(4641.88)^2 + (4583.46)^2}{2(20)} - 1,063,836.2264$$

$$= 1,063,878.8876 - 1,063,836.2264 = 42.6612$$

COMPARING MORE THAN TWO POPULATION MEANS: AN
ANALYSIS OF VARIANCE

$$SS(BS) = \frac{B_1S_1^2 + B_1S_2^2 + B_2S_1^2 + B_2S_2^2}{r} - SS(B) - SS(S) - CM$$

$$= \frac{(2283)^2 + (2217.9)^2 + (2358.88)^2 + (2365.56)^2}{20} - 624.6266$$

$$- 42.6612 - 1,063,836.2264$$

$$= 1,064,567.9188 - 614.6266 - 42.6612 - 1,063,836.2264$$

$$= 64.4046$$

$$s = 15.13 \Rightarrow s^2 = MSE = (15.13)^2 = 228.9169$$

$$MSE = \frac{SSE}{bs(r-1)} \Rightarrow SSE = MSE[bs(r-1)] = 228.9169[2(2)(19)]$$

$$= 17,397.6840$$

$$SS(Total) = SS(B) + SS(S) + SS(BS) + SSE$$

$$= 624.6266 + 42.6612 + 64.4046 + 17,397.6840$$

$$= 18,129.3764$$

$$MS(B) = \frac{SS(B)}{b-1} = \frac{624.6266}{2-1} = 624.6266$$

$$MS(S) = \frac{SS(S)}{s-1} = \frac{42.6612}{2-1} = 42.6612$$

$$MS(BS) = \frac{SS(BS)}{(b-1)(s-1)} = \frac{64.4046}{(2-1)(2-1)} = 64.4046$$

$$F(B) = \frac{MS(B)}{MSE} = \frac{624.6266}{228.9169} = 2.73$$

$$F(S) = \frac{MS(S)}{MSE} = \frac{42.6612}{228.9169} = .19$$

$$F(BS) = \frac{MS(BS)}{MSE} = \frac{64.4046}{228.9169} = .28$$

The ANOVA table is:

SOURCE	df	SS	MS	F
Buyer, B	1	624.6266	624.6266	2.73
Seller, S	1	42.6612	42.6612	.19
BS	1	64.4046	64.4046	.28
Error	76	17,397.6840	228.9169	
Total	79	18,129.3764		

For Agreed Price ($ thousands), the following quantities are calculated:

We must first obtain factor-level sums from the means given.

BUYER CONDITION

		BC	BNC	
Seller	SC	$B_1S_1 = 129.607(14) = 1814.498$	$B_2S_1 = 135.446(14) = 1896.244$	$S_1 = 3710.742$
Condition	SNC	$B_1S_2 = 128.019(14) = 1792.266$	$B_2S_2 = 132.036(14) = 1848.504$	$S_2 = 3640.770$
		$B_1 = 3606.764$	$B_2 = 3744.748$	$\sum x = 7351.512$

$$CM = \frac{(\sum x)^2}{n} = \frac{(7351.512)^2}{2(2)(14)} = 965,084.4408$$

$$SS(B) = \frac{B_1^2 + B_2^2}{sr} - CM = \frac{(3606.764)^2 + (3744.748)^2}{2(14)} - 965,084.4408$$

$$= 965,424.4334 - 965,084.4408 = 339.9926$$

$$SS(S) = \frac{S_1^2 + S_2^2}{br} - CM = \frac{(3710.742)^2 + (3640.770)^2}{2(14)} - 965,084.4408$$

$$= 965,171.8708 - 965,084.4408 = 87.4300$$

$$SS(BS) = \frac{B_1S_1^2 + B_1S_2^2 + B_2S_1^2 + B_2S_2^2}{r} - SS(B) - SS(S) - CM$$

$$= \frac{(1814.498)^2 + (1792.266)^2 + (1896.244)^2 + (1848.504)^2}{14}$$

$$- 339.9926 - 87.4300 - 965,084.4408$$

$$= 965,523.4823 - 339.9926 - 87.4300 - 965,084.4408$$

$$= 11.6189$$

$$s = 11.8 \Rightarrow s^2 = MSE = (11.8)^2 = 139.2400$$

$$MSE = \frac{SSE}{bs(r - 1)} \Rightarrow SSE = MSE[bs(r - 1)] = 139.24[2(2)(13)]$$

$$= 7240.4800$$

$$SS(Total) = SS(B) + SS(S) + SS(BS) + SSE$$

$$= 339.9926 + 87.4300 + 11.6189 + 7240.4800$$

$$= 7679.5215$$

$$MS(B) = \frac{SS(B)}{b - 1} = \frac{339.9926}{2 - 1} = 339.9926$$

$$MS(S) = \frac{SS(S)}{s - 1} = \frac{87.4300}{2 - 1} = 87.4300$$

$$MS(BS) = \frac{SS(BS)}{(b - 1)(s - 1)} = \frac{11.6189}{(2 - 1)(2 - 1)} = 11.6189$$

$$F(B) = \frac{MS(B)}{MSE} = \frac{339.9926}{139.2400} = 2.44$$

$$F(S) = \frac{MS(S)}{MSE} = \frac{87.4300}{139.2400} = .63$$

$$F(BS) = \frac{MS(BS)}{MSE} = \frac{11.6189}{139.2400} = .08$$

The ANOVA table is:

SOURCE	df	SS	MS	F
Buyer, B	1	339.9926	339.9926	2.44
Seller, S	1	87.4300	87.4300	.63
BS	1	11.6189	11.6189	.08
Error	52	7,240.4800	139.2400	
Total	55	7,679.5215		

For Number of Counteroffers, the following quantities are calculated:

We must first obtain factor-level sums from the means given.

BUYER CONDITION

Seller Condition		BC	BNC	
	SC	$B_1S_1 = 5.79(14) = 81.06$	$B_2S_1 = 5.93(14) = 83.02$	$S_1 = 164.08$
	SNC	$B_1S_2 = 4.43(14) = 62.02$	$B_2S_2 = 4.00(14) = 56.00$	$S_2 = 118.02$
		$B_1 = 143.08$	$B_2 = 139.02$	$\sum x = 282.10$

$$CM = \frac{(\sum x)^2}{n} = \frac{(282.10)^2}{2(2)(14)} = 1421.0788$$

$$SS(B) = \frac{B_1^2 + B_2^2}{sr} - CM = \frac{(143.08)^2 + (139.02)^2}{2(14)} - 1421.0788$$

$$= 1421.3731 - 1421.0788 = .2943$$

$$SS(S) = \frac{S_1^2 + S_2^2}{br} - CM = \frac{(164.08)^2 + (118.02)^2}{2(14)} - 1421.0788$$

$$= 1458.9631 - 1421.0788 = 37.8843$$

$$SS(BS) = \frac{B_1S_1^2 + B_1S_2^2 + B_2S_1^2 + B_2S_2^2}{r} - SS(B) - SS(S) - CM$$

$$= \frac{(81.06)^2 + (62.02)^2 + (83.02)^2 + (56.00)^2}{14}$$

$$- .2943 - 37.8843 - 1421.0788$$

$$= 1460.3946 - .2943 - 37.8843 - 1421.0788$$

$$= 1.1372$$

$$s = 2.80 \Rightarrow s^2 = MSE = (2.80)^2 = 7.8400$$

$$MSE = \frac{SSE}{bs(r - 1)} \Rightarrow SSE = MSE[bs(r - 1)] = 7.8400[2(2)(13)]$$

$$= 407.6800$$

$$SS(Total) = SS(B) + SS(S) + SS(BS) + SSE$$

$$= .2943 + 37.8843 + 1.1372 + 407.6800$$

$$= 446.9958$$

$$MS(B) = \frac{SS(B)}{b - 1} = \frac{.2943}{2 - 1} = .2943$$

$$MS(S) = \frac{SS(S)}{s - 1} = \frac{37.8843}{2 - 1} = 37.8843$$

$$MS(BS) = \frac{SS(BS)}{(b - 1)(s - 1)} = \frac{1.1372}{(2 - 1)(2 - 1)} = 1.1372$$

$$F(B) = \frac{MS(B)}{MSE} = \frac{.2943}{7.8400} = .04$$

$$F(S) = \frac{MS(S)}{MSE} = \frac{37.8843}{7.8400} = 4.83$$

$$F(BS) = \frac{MS(BS)}{MSE} = \frac{1.1372}{7.8400} = .15$$

The ANOVA table is:

SOURCE	df	SS	MS	F
Buyer, B	1	.2943	.2943	.04
Seller, S	1	37.8843	37.8843	4.83
BS	1	1.1372	1.1372	.15
Error	52	407.6800	7.8400	
Total	55	446.9958		

For Elapsed Time (minutes), the following quantities are calculated:

We must first obtain factor-level sums from the means given.

		BUYER CONDITION		
		BC	BNC	
Seller	SC	$B_1S_1 = 20.07(14) = 280.98$	$B_2S_1 = 16.57(14) = 231.98$	$S_1 = 512.96$
Condition	SNC	$B_1S_2 = 17.14(14) = 239.96$	$B_2S_2 = 14.79(14) = 207.06$	$S_2 = 447.02$
		$B_1 = 520.94$	$B_2 = 439.04$	$\sum x = 959.98$

$$CM = \frac{(\sum x)^2}{n} = \frac{(959.98)^2}{2(2)(14)} = 16,456.4572$$

$$SS(B) = \frac{B_1^2 + B_2^2}{sr} - CM = \frac{(520.94)^2 + (439.04)^2}{2(14)} - 16,456.4572$$

$$= 16,576.2359 - 16,456.4572 = 119.7787$$

$$SS(S) = \frac{S_1^2 + S_2^2}{br} - CM = \frac{(512.96)^2 + (447.02)^2}{2(14)} - 16,456.4572$$

$$= 16,534.1015 - 16,456.4572 = 77.6443$$

$$SS(BS) = \frac{B_1S_1^2 + B_1S_2^2 + B_2S_1^2 + B_2S_2^2}{r} - SS(B) - SS(S) - CM$$

$$= \frac{(280.98)^2 + (239.96)^2 + (231.98)^2 + (207.06)^2}{14}$$

$$- 119.7787 - 77.6443 - 16,456.4572$$

$$= 16,658.5090 - 119.7787 - 77.6443 - 16,456.4572$$

$$= 4.6288$$

$$s = 5.8 \Rightarrow s^2 = MSE = (5.8)^2 = 33.64$$

$$MSE = \frac{SSE}{bs(r - 1)} \Rightarrow SSE = MSE[bs(r - 1)] = 33.64[2(2)(13)]$$

$$= 1749.2800$$

$$SS(Total) = SS(B) + SS(S) + SS(BS) + SSE$$

$$= 119.7787 + 77.6443 + 4.6288 + 1749.2800$$

$$= 1951.3318$$

$$MS(B) = \frac{SS(B)}{b - 1} = \frac{119.7787}{2 - 1} = 119.7787$$

$$MS(S) = \frac{SS(S)}{s - 1} = \frac{77.6443}{2 - 1} = 77.6443$$

$$MS(BS) = \frac{SS(BS)}{(b - 1)(s - 1)} = \frac{4.6288}{(2 - 1)(2 - 1)} = 4.6288$$

$$F(B) = \frac{MS(B)}{MSE} = \frac{119.7787}{33.6400} = 3.56$$

$$F(S) = \frac{MS(S)}{MSE} = \frac{77.6443}{33.6400} = 2.31$$

$$F(BS) = \frac{MS(BS)}{MSE} = \frac{4.6288}{33.6400} = .14$$

The ANOVA table is:

SOURCE	df	SS	MS	F
Buyer, B	1	119.7787	119.7787	3.56
Seller, S	1	77.6443	77.6443	2.31
BS	1	4.6288	4.6288	.14
Error	52	1749.2800	33.6400	
Total	55	1951.3318		

b. For Seller's Initial Offer ($ thousands)

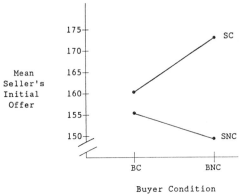

It appears that Buyer Condition and Seller Condition interact.
The lines are not parallel.

For Buyer's Initial Offer ($ thousands)

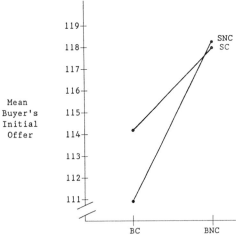

There does not appear to be an interaction between Buyer Condition
and Seller Condition. The lines are fairly parallel.

For Agreed Price ($ thousands)

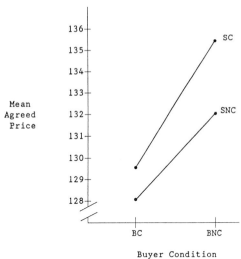

There does not appear to be an interaction between Buyer Condition
and Seller Condition. The lines are fairly parallel.

For Number of Counteroffers

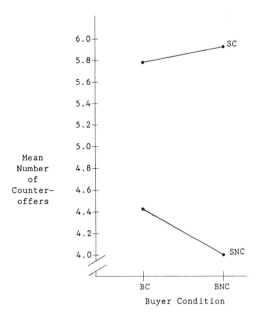

There appears to be an interaction between Buyer Condition and
Seller Condition. The lines are not parallel.

For Elapsed Time (minutes)

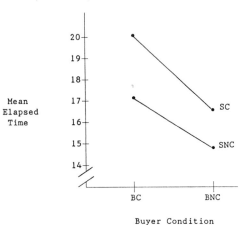

Buyer Condition

There does not appear to be an interaction between Buyer Condition
and Seller Condition. The lines are fairly parallel.

c. The following hypotheses will be used for all five variables:

H_0: There is no interaction between buyer condition and seller
        condition
H_a: Buyer condition and seller condition interact

Seller's Initial Offer: The test statistic is $F = \dfrac{MS(AB)}{MSE} = 3.99$

Buyer's Initial Offer: The test statistic is $F = .28$.

Agreed Price: The test statistic is $F = .08$.

Number of Counteroffers: The test statistic is $F = .15$.

Elapsed Time: The test statistic is $F = .14$

Sellers Initial Offer: The rejection region requires $\alpha = .10$ in
the upper tail of the F distribution with $\nu_1 = (a - 1)(b - 1) = 1$
and $\nu_2 = ab(r - 1) = 76$. From Table 7, Appendix E, $F_{.10} \approx 2.79$.
The rejection region is $F > 2.79$.

Buyer's Initial Offer: Same as above.

Agreed Price: The rejection region requires α = .10 in the upper tail of the F distribution with v_1 = (a - 1)(b - 1) = 1 and v_2 = ab(r - 1) = 52. From Table 7, Appendix E, $F_{.10}$ ≈ 2.79. The rejection region is F > 2.79.

Number of Counteroffers: Same as above.

Elapsed Time: Same as above.

Since the observed value of the test statistic falls in the rejection region only for Seller's Initial Offer (F = 3.99 > 2.79, F = .28 ≯ 2.79, F = .08 ≯ 2.79, F = .15 ≯ 2.79, F = .14 ≯ 2.79), H_0 is only rejected in that case. For the variable 'Seller's Initial Offer,' there appears to be a significant interaction between Buyer and Seller Condition at α = .10. None of the other four variables show a significant interaction between the two factors.

d. 1. Let μ_1 = mean seller's initial offer for BC/SC and μ_2 = mean seller's initial price for BNC/SC. To see if a difference exists between the means of the two groups, we test:

H_0: $\mu_1 - \mu_2 = 0$
H_a: $\mu_1 - \mu_2 \neq 0$

The test statistic is $t = \dfrac{(\bar{x}_1 - \bar{x}_2) - D_0}{s\sqrt{\dfrac{1}{n_1} + \dfrac{1}{n_2}}}$ where $s = \sqrt{MSE} = 21$

$$= \frac{(160.3 - 173.05) - 0}{21\sqrt{\dfrac{1}{20} + \dfrac{1}{20}}} = \frac{-12.75}{6.6408}$$

$$= -1.920$$

For a small sample, two-tailed test, $\alpha/2$ = .05/2 = .025 is in each tail of the t distribution with df = ab(r - 1) = 76. From Table 6, Appendix E, $t_{.025}$ ≈ (2.000 + 1.980)/2 ≈ 1.99. The rejection region is t < -1.99 or t > 1.99.

Since the observed value of the test statistic does not fall in the rejection region (t = -1.920 ≮ -1.99), H_0 is not rejected. There is insufficient evidence to indicate a difference in the mean seller's initial offer for the groups BC/SC and BNC/SC at α = .05.

2. Let μ_1 = mean buyer's initial offer for BC/SC and μ_2 = mean buyer's initial price for BC/SNC. To see if a difference exists between the means of the two groups, we test:

$H_0: \mu_1 - \mu_2 = 0$
$H_a: \mu_1 - \mu_2 \neq 0$

The test statistic is $t = \dfrac{(\bar{x}_1 - \bar{x}_2) - D_0}{s\sqrt{\dfrac{1}{n_1} + \dfrac{1}{n_2}}}$ where $s = \sqrt{MSE} = 15.13$

$$= \frac{(114.15 - 110.895) - 0}{15.13\sqrt{\dfrac{1}{20} + \dfrac{1}{20}}} = \frac{3.255}{4.7845} = .68$$

For a small sample, two-tailed test, $\alpha/2 = .05/2 = .025$ is in each tail of the t distribution with df $= ab(r - 1) = 76$. From Table 6, Appendix E, $t_{.025} \approx (2.000 + 1.980)/2 \approx 1.99$. The rejection region is $t < -1.99$ or $t > 1.99$.

Since the observed value of the test statistic does not fall in the rejection region ($t = .68 \not> 1.99$), H_0 is not rejected. There is insufficient evidence to indicate a difference in the mean buyer's initial offer for the groups BC/SC and BC/SNC at $\alpha = .05$.

3. Let μ_1 = mean agreed price for BC/SNC and μ_2 = mean agreed price for BNC/SC. To see if the mean of BNC/SC is higher than the mean of BC/SNC, we test:

$H_0: \mu_1 - \mu_2 = 0$
$H_a: \mu_1 - \mu_2 < 0$

The test statistic is $t = \dfrac{(\bar{x}_1 - \bar{x}_2) - D_0}{s\sqrt{\dfrac{1}{n_1} + \dfrac{1}{n_2}}}$ where $s = \sqrt{MSE} = 11.8$

$$= \frac{(128.019 - 135.446) - 0}{11.8\sqrt{\dfrac{1}{14} + \dfrac{1}{14}}} = \frac{-7.427}{4.4600}$$

$$= -1.67$$

For a small sample, lower tailed test, $\alpha = .05$ is in the lower tail of the t distribution with df $= ab(r - 1) = 52$. From Table 6, Appendix E, $t_{.05} \approx (1.684 + 1.671)/2 \approx 1.68$. The rejection region is $t < -1.68$.

Since the observed value of the test statistic does not fall in the rejection region ($t = -1.67 \not< -1.68$), H_0 is not rejected. There is insufficient evidence to indicate the mean agreed price for BNC/SC is higher than for BC/SNC at $\alpha = .05$.

4. Let μ_1 = mean number of counteroffers for BC/SC and μ_2 = mean number of counteroffers for BNC/SNC. To see if the mean of BC/SC is higher than the mean of BNC/SNC, we test:

$H_0:$ $\mu_1 - \mu_2 = 0$
$H_a:$ $\mu_1 - \mu_2 > 0$

The test statistic is $t = \dfrac{(\bar{x}_1 - \bar{x}_2) - D_0}{s\sqrt{\dfrac{1}{n_1} + \dfrac{1}{n_2}}}$ where $s = \sqrt{MSE} = 2.80$

$$= \frac{(5.79 - 4.00) - 0}{2.80\sqrt{\dfrac{1}{14} + \dfrac{1}{14}}} = \frac{1.79}{1.0583} = 1.69$$

For a small sample, upper tailed test, $\alpha = .05$ is in the upper tail of the t distribution with df = $ab(r - 1) = 52$. From Table 6, Appendix E, $t_{.05} \approx (1.684 + 1.671)/2 \approx 1.68$. The rejection region is $t > 1.68$.

Since the observed value of the test statistic falls in the rejection region ($t = 1.69 > 1.68$), H_0 is rejected. There is sufficient evidence to indicate the mean number of counteroffers in the BC/SC cell is higher than in the BNC/SNC cell at $\alpha = .05$.

5. Let μ_1 = mean elapsed time for BC/SC and μ_2 = mean elapsed time for BNC/SNC. To see if the mean of BC/SC is higher than the mean of BNC/SNC, we test:

$H_0:$ $\mu_1 - \mu_2 = 0$
$H_a:$ $\mu_1 - \mu_2 > 0$

The test statistic is $t = \dfrac{(\bar{x}_1 - \bar{x}_2) - D_0}{s\sqrt{\dfrac{1}{n_1} + \dfrac{1}{n_2}}}$ where $s = \sqrt{MSE} = 5.80$

$$= \frac{(20.07 - 14.79) - 0}{5.80\sqrt{\dfrac{1}{14} + \dfrac{1}{14}}} = \frac{5.28}{2.1922} = 2.41$$

For a small sample, upper tailed test, $\alpha = .05$ is in the upper tail of the t distribution with df = $ab(r - 1) = 52$. From Table 6, Appendix E, $t_{.05} \approx (1.684 + 1.671)/2 \approx 1.68$. The rejection region is $t > 1.68$.

Since the observed value of the test statistic falls in the rejection region ($t = 2.41 > 1.68$), H_0 is rejected. There is sufficient evidence to indicate the mean elapsed time for the BC/SC group is higher than for the BNC/SNC group at $\alpha = .05$.

COMPARING MORE THAN TWO POPULATION MEANS: AN
ANALYSIS OF VARIANCE

THIRTEEN INTRODUCTION TO PROCESS AND QUALITY CONTROL

13.1 a. For n = 5, A_2 = .577 and d_2 = 2.326

b. For n = 12, A_2 = .266 and d_2 = 3.258

c. For n = 15, A_2 = .223 and d_2 = 3.472

d. For n = 23, A_2 = .162 and d_2 = 3.858

13.3 The necessary calculations are tabulated below.

SAMPLE NUMBER	SAMPLE MEASUREMENTS			SAMPLE MEAN $\bar{x}$	RANGE R
1	8	6	9	7.667	3
2	10	2	5	5.667	8
3	1	4	4	3.000	3
4	7	3	8	6.000	5
5	5	4	9	6.000	5
6	6	11	4	7.000	7
7	3	3	6	4.000	3
8	4	1	10	5.000	9
9	11	10	8	9.667	3
10	2	7	7	5.333	5
11	6	0	5	3.667	6
12	12	9	15	12.000	6
13	4	8	6	6.000	4
14	3	7	3	4.333	4
15	6	5	7	6.000	2
16	4	5	6	5.000	2
17	8	3	9	6.667	6
18	7	5	2	4.667	5
19	2	1	8	3.667	7
20	8	8	6	7.333	2
				118.668	95

a. The values of $\bar{x}$ for each sample are tabulated above.

b. The values of R for each sample are tabulated above.

c. $\bar{\bar{x}} = \dfrac{\sum \bar{x}_i}{k} = \dfrac{118.668}{20} = 5.93$

d. $\bar{R} = \dfrac{\sum R}{k} = \dfrac{95}{20} = 4.75$

e. The lower control limit is LCL $= \bar{\bar{x}} - A_2\bar{R}$ and the upper control limit is UCL $= \bar{\bar{x}} + A_2\bar{R}$. From Table 11, Appendix E, for $n = 3$, $A_2 = 1.023$. The control limits are:

LCL $= \bar{\bar{x}} - A_2\bar{R} = 5.93 - 1.023(4.75) = 5.93 - 4.859 = 1.071$

UCL $= \bar{\bar{x}} + A_2\bar{R} = 5.93 + 1.023(4.75) = 5.93 + 4.859 = 10.789$

f.

The process does not appear to be in control. The mean for sample 12 is outside the control limits.

g. $s^2 = \dfrac{\sum x^2 - \dfrac{(\sum x)^2}{n}}{n - 1} = \dfrac{2664 - \dfrac{356^2}{60}}{60 - 1} = 9.3514, \quad s = \sqrt{9.3514} = 3.058$

h. The control limits are:

LCL $= \bar{\bar{x}} - 3\hat{\sigma}_{\bar{x}} = 5.93 - 3\left(\dfrac{3.058}{\sqrt{3}}\right) = 5.93 - 5.297 = .633$

UCL $= \bar{\bar{x}} + 3\hat{\sigma}_{\bar{x}} = 5.93 + 3\left(\dfrac{3.058}{\sqrt{3}}\right) = 5.93 + 5.297 = 11.227$

These control limits are wider than those in part (f).

13.5   a.   Some preliminary calculations are:

HOUR	$\bar{x}$	R
1	5.00000	.15
2	4.97625	.22
3	4.99375	.11
4	4.98250	.13
5	5.00750	.18
6	4.94875	.20
7	4.99875	.13
8	4.98625	.12
9	5.01250	.09
10	4.98000	.10
11	5.00250	.04
12	5.00500	.20
	59.89375	1.67

The center line is

$$\bar{\bar{x}} = \frac{\sum \bar{x}_i}{k} = \frac{59.89375}{12} = 4.99114$$

b. $\bar{R} = \dfrac{\sum R_i}{k} = \dfrac{1.67}{12} = .139167$

The lower and upper control limits are:

$$LCL = \bar{\bar{x}} - A_2 \bar{R} \text{ and } UCL = \bar{\bar{x}} + A_2 \bar{R}$$

From Table 11, Appendix E, with n = 8, A_2 = .373. The control limits are:

$$LCL = \bar{\bar{x}} - A_2 \bar{R} = 4.99114 - .373(.139167) = 4.99114 - .051909$$
$$= 4.93923$$

$$UCL = \bar{\bar{x}} + A_2 \bar{R} = 4.99114 + .373(.139167) = 4.99114 + .051909$$
$$= 5.04305$$

c.

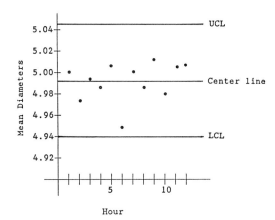

The process appears to be in control since all points are within the control limits.

13.7 a. Some preliminary calculations are:

HOUR	$\bar{x}$	R
1	.40340	.0004
2	.40316	.0004
3	.40308	.0002
4	.40330	.0003
5	.40350	.0005
6	.40322	.0002
7	.40330	.0005
8	.40326	.0013
9	.40338	.0013
10	.40378	.0006
11	.40358	.0004
12	.40384	.0004
13	.40340	.0014
14	.40350	.0004
15	.40338	.0007
16	.40316	.0005
17	.40330	.0005
18	.40282	.0003
19	.40318	.0009
20	.40356	.0006
	8.06710	.0124

The center line is $\bar{\bar{x}} = \dfrac{\sum \bar{x}_i}{k} = \dfrac{8.06710}{20} = .40336$

$$\bar{R} = \frac{\Sigma R_i}{k} = \frac{.0124}{20} = .00062$$

The upper and lower control limits are

$$LCL = \bar{\bar{x}} - A_2\bar{R} \text{ and } UCL = \bar{\bar{x}} + A_2\bar{R}$$

From Table 11, Appendix E, with n = 5, A_2 = .577. The control limits are:

$$LCL = \bar{\bar{x}} - A_2\bar{R} = .40336 - .577(.00062) = .40336 - .00036 = .40300$$

$$UCL = \bar{\bar{x}} + A_2\bar{R} = .40336 + .577(.00062) = .40336 + .00036 = .40372$$

b.

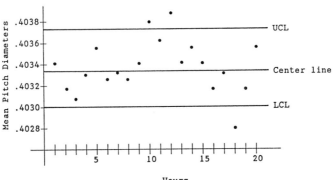

c. The process does not appear to be in control. Three means (for hours 10, 12, and 18) are outside the control limits.

d. Eliminating samples 10, 12, and 18:

$$\bar{\bar{x}} = \frac{\Sigma \bar{x}_i}{k} = \frac{6.85660}{17} = .40333$$

$$\bar{R} = \frac{\Sigma R_i}{k} = \frac{.0111}{17} = .00065$$

The control limits are:

$$LCL = \bar{\bar{x}} - A_2\bar{R} = .40333 - .577(.00065) = .40333 - .00038 = .40295$$

$$UCL = \bar{\bar{x}} + A_2\bar{R} = .40333 + .577(.00065) = .40333 + .00038 = .40371$$

We would recommend using the new control limits in the future. The outlying observations have been eliminated, giving us a better estimate of the true process.

13.9   a. For n = 2, D_3 = 0 and D_4 = 3.276

        b. For n = 10, D_3 = .223 and D_4 = 1.777

        c. For n = 15, D_3 = .348 and D_4 = 1.652

        d. For n = 22, D_3 = .434 and D_4 = 1.566

13.11   The control limits for an R chart are

            LCL = $\bar{R}D_3$ and UCL = $\bar{R}D_4$

        From Table 11, Appendix E, with n = 3, D_3 = 0 and D_4 = 2.575.

        From Exercise 13.3, $\bar{R}$ = 4.75. The control limits are

            LCL = $\bar{R}D_3$ = 4.75(0) = 0
            UCL = $\bar{R}D_4$ = 4.75(2.575) = 12.23125

13.13   From Exercise 13.5, $\bar{R}$ = .139167 and n = 8. The control limits are
        LCL = $\bar{R}D_3$ and UCL = $\bar{R}D_4$.

        From Table 11, Appendix E, with n = 8, D_3 = .136 and D_4 = 1.864. The
        control limits are:

            LCL = $\bar{R}D_3$ = .139167(.136) = .018927
            UCL = $\bar{R}D_4$ = .139167(1.864) = .259407

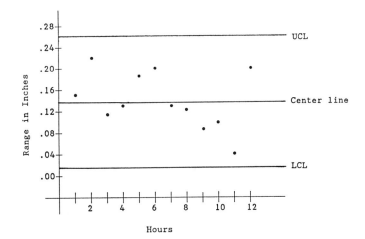

        The process appears to be in control since no range values fall
        outside the control limits.

13.15 From Exercise 13.7, $\bar{R}$ = .00062 and n = 5. The control limits are

$$LCL = \bar{R}D_3 \text{ and } UCL = \bar{R}D_4$$

From Table 11, Appendix E, with n = 5, D_3 = 0 and D_4 = 2.115. The control limits are:

$$LCL = \bar{R}D_3 = .00062(0) = 0$$
$$UCL = \bar{R}D_4 = .00062(2.115) = .001311$$

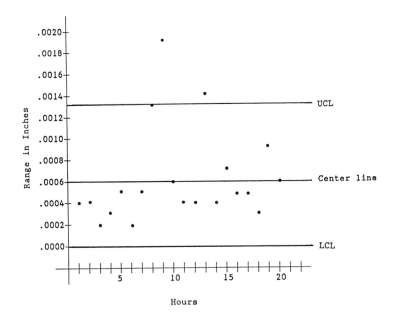

Since there are two samples (9 and 13) with values outside the control limits, it appears the process is not in control.

13.17 From Exercise 13.8, $\bar{R}$ = .00867 and n = 5. The control limits are
$$LCL = \bar{R}D_3 \text{ and } UCL = \bar{R}D_4.$$

From Table 11, Appendix E, with n = 5, D_3 = 0 and D_4 = 2.115. The control limits are:

$$LCL = \bar{R}D_3 = .00867(0) = 0$$
$$UCL = \bar{R}D_4 = .00867(2.115) = .01834$$

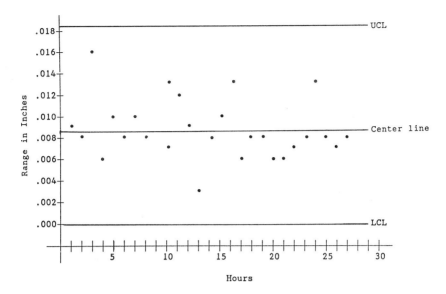

The process variation appears to be in control. There are no sample range values outside the control limits.

13.19 a. No trend is apparent. There are at most 5 consecutive points on the same side of the center line. Since there are only 11 data points, the last two conditions do not apply.

b. No trend is apparent. There are at most 4 consecutive points on the same side of the center line. Since there are only 12 data points, the last two conditions do not apply.

c. No trend is apparent. There are at most 5 consecutive points on the same side of the center line. Since there are only 12 data points, the last two conditions do not apply.

d. A trend appears to be present. Seven consecutive data points fall above the center line.

e. No trend is apparent. There are at most 3 consecutive data points on the same side of the center line. Since there are only 10 data points, the last two conditions do not apply.

f. A trend appears to be present. Nine consecutive data points fall above the center line.

13.21 From the $\bar{x}$-chart in Exercise 13.5, the runs are

```
+  -  +  -  +  -  +  -  +  -  ++
└┘ └┘ └┘ └┘ └┘ └┘ └┘ └┘ └┘ └┘ └─┘
1  2  3  4  5  6  7  8  9  10  11
```

The longest run is two points. There is no evidence of a trend.

From the R-chart in Exercise in 13.13, the runs are

```
++   --   ++   -----   +
└─┘ └─┘ └─┘ └────┘ └┘
 1    2    3     4     5
```

The longest run is 5 points. There is no evidence of a trend.

13.23 From the $\bar{x}$-chart in Exercise 13.7, the runs are:

```
+   ---   +   ---   +++++++   ----   +
└┘ └──┘ └┘ └──┘ └─────┘ └───┘ └┘
1    2    3    4       5       6    7
```

The longest run is 7 points. This indicates evidence of a trend.

From the R-chart in Exercise 13.15, the runs are

```
+  -  +  -  +  -  +  --  +++  --  ++  -------  +  ---
└┘ └┘ └┘ └┘ └┘ └┘ └┘ └─┘ └─┘ └┘ └─┘ └─────┘ └┘ └─┘
1  2  3  4  5  6  7  8   9   10  11     12     13  14
```

The longest run is 7 points. This indicates evidence of a trend.

13.25 a. $\bar{p} = \dfrac{\Sigma \hat{p}_i}{k} = \dfrac{.91}{25} = .0364$

b. The lower and upper control limits are

$$\text{LCL} = \bar{p} - 3\sqrt{\frac{\bar{p}(1 - \bar{p})}{n}} = .0364 - 3\sqrt{\frac{.0364(.9636)}{100}} = .0364 - .0562$$

$$= -.0198 \approx 0$$

$$\text{UCL} = \bar{p} + 3\sqrt{\frac{\bar{p}(1 - \bar{p})}{n}} = .0364 + 3\sqrt{\frac{.0364(.9636)}{100}} = .0364 + .0562$$

$$= .0926$$

c.

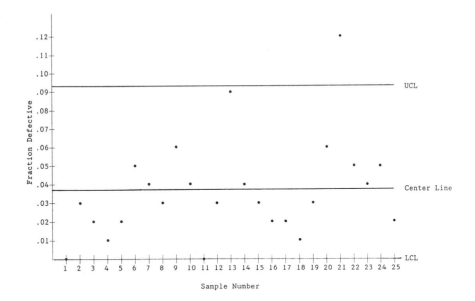

There is one data point (sample 21) that lies outside the control limits. This indicates the process is out of control.

13.27 a. The six sample proportions are computed by dividing the number of defectives each week by the sample size, 20. The sample proportions are:

WEEK	$\hat{p}_i$
1	1/20 = .05
2	0/20 = .00
3	2/20 = .10
4	2/20 = .10
5	3/20 = .15
6	1/20 = .05
	.45

$$\bar{p} = \frac{\Sigma \hat{p}_i}{k} = \frac{.45}{6} = .075$$

The lower and upper control limits are

$$LCL = \bar{p} - 3\sqrt{\frac{\bar{p}(1 - \bar{p})}{n}} = .075 - 3\sqrt{\frac{.075(.925)}{20}} = .075 - .17669$$

$$= -.10169 \approx 0$$

$$LCL = \bar{p} + 3\sqrt{\frac{\bar{p}(1 - \bar{p})}{n}} = .075 + 3\sqrt{\frac{.075(.925)}{20}} = .075 + .17669$$

$$= .25169$$

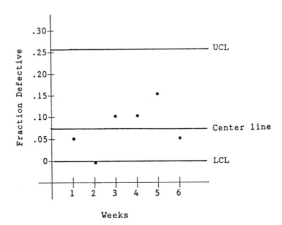

b.   See the p-chart in part (a) for the center line, which is $\bar{p} = .075$.

c.   See the p-chart in part (a) for the upper and lower control limits, which are LCL = 0 and UCL = .25169.

   Since no points lie outside the control limits, the process appears to be in control.

13.29   From Exercise 13.28, the control limits are LCL = 0 and UCL = .09398.

   The next sample has a sample proportion of $\hat{p} = 11/100 = .11$.   Since this value lies above the upper control limit, there is evidence the process is out of control.

13.31   a. $\bar{c} = \dfrac{\sum c_i}{k} = \dfrac{75}{30} = 2.5$

b. The lower and upper control limits are

$$LCL = \bar{c} - 3\sqrt{\bar{c}} = 2.5 - 3\sqrt{2.5} = 2.5 - 4.74342 = -2.24342 \approx 0$$

$$UCL = \bar{c} + 3\sqrt{\bar{c}} = 2.5 + 3\sqrt{2.5} = 2.5 + 4.74342 = 7.24342$$

c.

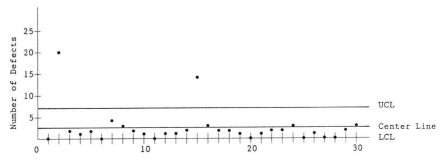

There are two points (samples 2 and 15) that lie above the upper control limit. This indicates the process is out of control.

13.33 a. $\bar{c} = \dfrac{\sum c_i}{k} = \dfrac{72}{15} = 4.8$

The lower and upper control limits are

$$LCL = \bar{c} - 3\sqrt{\bar{c}} = 4.8 - 3\sqrt{4.8} = 4.8 - 6.57267 = -1.77267 \approx 0$$

$$UCL = \bar{c} + 3\sqrt{\bar{c}} = 4.8 + 3\sqrt{4.8} = 4.8 + 6.57267 = 11.37267$$

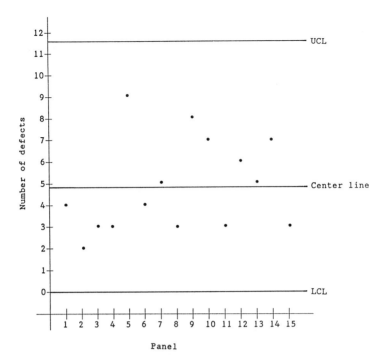

Panel

b. The center line, $\bar{c} = 4.8$, is shown on the chart in part (a).

c. The upper and lower control limits (UCL = 11.37267 and LCL = 0) are shown on the chart in part (a).

   Since no points fall outside the control limits, the process appears to be in control.

d. The runs are

   ```
   ----    +    -    +    -    ++    -    +++    -
   ```
   1   2   3   4   5   6   7   8   9

   Since the longest run is 4 points, there is no evidence of a trend.

13.35 a. $\bar{c} = \dfrac{\sum c_i}{k} = \dfrac{200}{25} = 8$

   The lower and upper control limits are

   $LCL = \bar{c} - 3\sqrt{\bar{c}} = 8 - 3\sqrt{8} = 8 - 8.48528 = -.48528 \approx 0$

   $UCL = \bar{c} + 3\sqrt{\bar{c}} = 8 + 3\sqrt{8} = 8 + 8.48528 = 16.48528$

b.

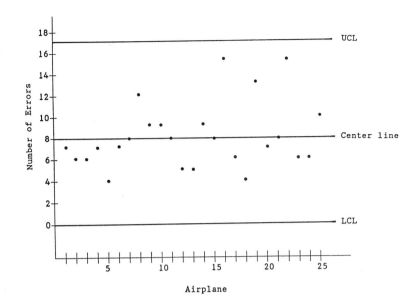

Airplane

c. Since no points lie outside the control limits, the process appears to be in control. Since all points are inside the control limits, we would recommend these limits be used in the future.

13.37 a. For α = .05, γ = .99, and n = 10, K = 4.433.

b. For α = .05, γ = .99, and n = 100, K = 2.934.

c. For α = .01, γ = .95, and n = 40, K = 2.677.

d. For α = .01, γ = .99, and n = 40, K = 3.518.

e. For α = .05, γ = .95, and n = 5, K = 5.079.

f. For α = .01, γ = .95, and n = 5, K = 7.855.

13.39 a. The tolerance interval for the measurements in a normal population is

$\bar{x} \pm Ks$

From Table 12, Appendix E, with n = 130, α = .01, and γ = .95, K $\approx$ 2.355. The tolerance interval is

$\bar{x} \pm Ks$ => 68.2 $\pm$ 2.355(11.5) => 68.2 $\pm$ 27.025
=> (41.175, 95.225)

b. If the population is nonnormal, the sample size required to form a 99% tolerance interval for 95% of the population can be found in Table 13, Appendix E. For $\gamma = .95$, $\alpha = .01$, $n = 130$, the tolerance interval is $(x_{min}, x_{max}) => (25,107)$ since the sample size was 130.

13.41 a. From Exercise 13.7, $\bar{x} = .40336$

$$s^2 = \frac{\sum x^2 - \frac{(\sum x)^2}{n}}{n - 1} = \frac{16.26953793 - \frac{40.3355^2}{100}}{99} = .000000124$$

$$s = \sqrt{.000000124} = .0003529$$

The tolerance interval is

$$\bar{x} \pm Ks$$

From Table 12, Appendix E, with $n = 100$, $\alpha = .05$, and $\gamma = .99$, $K = 2.934$. The tolerance interval is

$$.40336 \pm 2.934(.0003529) => .40336 \pm .00104$$
$$=> (.40232, .40440)$$

b. The specification interval is $.4037 \pm .0013 => (.4024, .4050)$. The lower limit of the specification interval is just smaller than the lower tolerance limit, while the upper limit of the specification interval is larger than the upper tolerance limit. This implies the specifications are being met.

c. From Table 13, Appendix E, with $\alpha = .05$ and $\gamma = .95$, $n = 93$. Since $n = 100$ in this example, we can form the tolerance interval. It is

$$(x_{min}, x_{max}) => (.4023, .4043)$$

13.43 a. Since μ and σ are known, the tolerance interval for 99% of the complaint rates is

$$\mu \pm z_{.005}\sigma => 26 \pm 2.576(11.3) => 26 \pm 29.1088$$
$$=> (-3.1088, 55.1088)$$

This is a 100% tolerance interval. Since μ and σ are known and the population is assumed normal, we know that 99% of the data will fall within 2.576 standard deviations of the mean.

b. Since 93.12 falls outside the tolerance interval, the observed rate is probably due to a specific cause.

13.45 a. Some preliminary calculations are:

HOUR	$\bar{x}$	R
1	12.875	.4
2	13.050	1.1
3	13.075	.4
4	12.525	.9
5	12.450	.9
6	13.175	.7
7	13.200	.8
8	13.150	1.3
	103.500	6.5

$$\bar{\bar{x}} = \frac{\sum \bar{x}_i}{k} = \frac{103.500}{8} = 12.9375$$

$$\bar{R} = \frac{\sum R_i}{k} = \frac{6.5}{8} = .8125$$

The lower and upper control limits are

$$LCL = \bar{\bar{x}} - A_2\bar{R} \text{ and } UCL = \bar{\bar{x}} + A_2\bar{R}$$

From Table 11, Appendix E, for n = 4, A_2 = .729. The control limits are

$$LCL = \bar{\bar{x}} - A_2R = 12.9357 - .729(.8125) = 12.9375 - .5923$$
$$= 12.3452$$

$$UCL = \bar{\bar{x}} + A_2R = 12.9357 + .729(.8125) = 12.9375 + .5923$$
$$= 13.5298$$

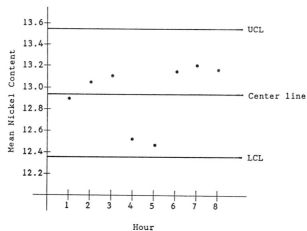

b. The control limits are shown in the chart in part (a).

c. $s^2 = \dfrac{\sum x^2 - \dfrac{(\sum x)^2}{n}}{n-1} = \dfrac{5362.06 - \dfrac{414^2}{32}}{32-1} = .191451612$

$s = \sqrt{.191451612} = .43755$

The control limits using the standard deviation are

$$LCL = \bar{\bar{x}} - 3\hat{\sigma}_{\bar{x}} = 12.9375 - 3\left(\dfrac{.43755}{\sqrt{4}}\right) = 12.9375 - .6563 = 12.2812$$

$$UCL = \bar{\bar{x}} + 3\hat{\sigma}_{\bar{x}} = 12.9375 + 3\left(\dfrac{.43755}{\sqrt{4}}\right) = 12.9375 + .6563 = 13.5938$$

These limits are outside the limits found in part (a).

d. All the sample means fall within the control limits. This implies the process is in control.

e. The tolerance interval is $\bar{x} \pm Ks$

From Table 12, Appendix E, for $n = 4 \times 8 = 32$, $y = .99$ and $\alpha = .01$, $K = 3.733$. The tolerance interval is

$$12.9375 + 3.733(.43755) \Rightarrow 12.9375 \pm 1.6334$$
$$\Rightarrow (11.3041, 14.5709)$$

13.47 a. $\bar{c} = \dfrac{\sum c_i}{k} = \dfrac{119}{12} = 9.9167$

The lower and upper control limits are

$$LCL = \bar{c} - 3\sqrt{\bar{c}} = 9.9167 - 3\sqrt{9.9167} = 9.9167 - 9.4472 = .4695$$

$$UCL = \bar{c} + 3\sqrt{\bar{c}} = 9.9167 + 3\sqrt{9.9167} = 9.9167 + 9.4472 = 19.3639$$

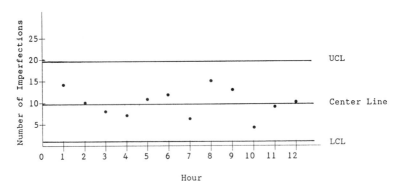

b. The center line and control limits are shown in the chart in part (a).

c. Since none of the data points lie outside the control limits, the process appears to be in control.

13.49 a. For an approximate normal distribution, the tolerance interval is

$$\bar{x} \pm Ks$$

From Table 12, Appendix E, with n = 100, γ = .99, and α = .05, K = 2.934. The tolerance interval is

$$1,312 \pm 2.934(422) \Rightarrow 1,312 \pm 1238.148 \Rightarrow (73.852, \ 2550.148)$$

b. We are 95% confident that 99% of the observations will fall between 73.852 and 2550.148.

c. If the data are not normally distributed, we could use Table 13, Appendix E, to determine the sample size necessary for a particular tolerance interval. Once the sample is taken, the tolerance interval is

$$(x_{min}, \ x_{max})$$

CASE STUDIES

13.1   a.   Some preliminary calculations

SAMPLE	$\bar{x}$	R
1	48.0	110
2	89.8	194
3	42.0	64
4	41.4	86
5	76.6	71
6	47.2	72
7	45.0	112
8	15.8	20
9	27.8	37
10	87.6	201
11	28.6	66
12	48.8	118
13	59.4	103
14	57.2	140
15	35.6	43
16	97.0	217
17	70.0	235
18	52.0	89
19	69.4	135
20	36.2	54
21	31.2	36
22	58.0	157
23	49.0	98
24	19.6	24
25	16.8	25
26	30.8	53
27	40.4	102
28	75.2	127
29	34.6	68
30	39.2	72
	1,470.2	2929

b. $\bar{\bar{x}} = \dfrac{\sum \bar{x}_i}{k} = \dfrac{1470.20}{30} = 49.0067$

$\bar{R} = \dfrac{\sum R_i}{k} = \dfrac{2929}{30} = 97.6333$

The lower and upper control limits are

$$LCL = \bar{\bar{x}} - A_2\bar{R} \quad \text{and} \quad UCL = \bar{\bar{x}} + A_2\bar{R}$$

From Table 11, Appendix E, for n = 5, A_2 = .577. The control limits are

$$LCL = \bar{\bar{x}} - A_2R = 49.0067 - .577(97.6333) = 49.0067 - 56.3344$$
$$= -7.3277 \approx 0$$

$$UCL = \bar{\bar{x}} + A_2R = 49.0067 + .577(97.6333) = 49.0067 + 56.3344$$
$$= 105.3411$$

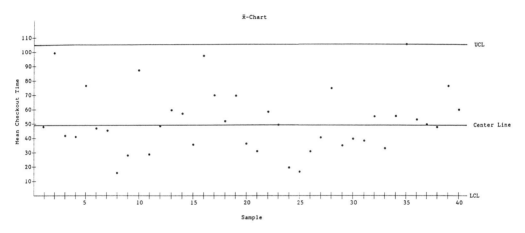

c. The lower and upper control limits for the R-chart are $LCL = \bar{R}D_3$ and $UCL = \bar{R}D_4$.

From Table 11, Appendix E, with n = 5, D_3 = 0, and D_4 = 2.115. The control limits are:

$$LCL = \bar{R}D_3 = 97.6333(0) = 0$$
$$UCL = \bar{R}D_4 = 97.6333(2.115) = 206.4944$$

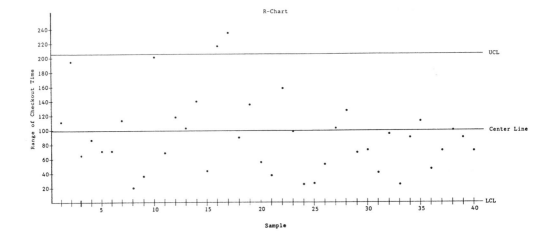

d. Since no points are outside the control limits on the $\bar{x}$-chart (part (b)), the process appears to be in control.

Since two points (samples 16 and 17) lie outside the control limits on the R-Chart (part (c)), the process appears to be out of control.

Thus, we must eliminate samples 16 and 17 and recompute the control limits.

For the $\bar{x}$-chart,

$$\bar{\bar{x}} = \frac{\sum \bar{x}_i}{k} = \frac{1303.2}{28} = 46.5429$$

$$\bar{R} = \frac{\sum R_i}{k} = \frac{2477}{28} = 88.4643$$

The lower and upper control limits for the $\bar{x}$-chart are

$$LCL = \bar{\bar{x}} - A_2 R = 46.5429 - .577(88.4643) = 46.5429 - 51.0439$$
$$= -4.5010 \approx 0$$

$$UCL = \bar{\bar{x}} + A_2 R = 46.5429 + .577(88.4643) = 46.5429 + 51.0439$$
$$= 97.5868$$

The lower and upper control limits for the R-chart are

$$LCL = \bar{R} D_3 = 88.4643(0) = 0$$
$$UCL = \bar{R} D_4 = 88.4643(2.115) = 187.1020$$

e.	SAMPLE	$\bar{x}$	R
	1	28.0	42
	2	54.6	94
	3	33.2	25
	4	54.8	90
	5	105.0	111
	6	52.8	46
	7	49.6	71
	8	47.8	100
	9	76.4	90
	10	59.6	70

f. Sample 5 (with $\bar{x}$ = 105.0) is above the new upper control limit of 97.5868. This indicates the process is out of control.

g. All sample values fall within the new control limits. This indicates the process is in control.

13.3 a. Since μ and σ are known, the tolerance interval for 90% of the fill times is

$\mu \pm z_{.05}\sigma$ => 24 ± 1.645(2.7) => 24 ± 4.4415 => (19.5585, 28.4415)

This is a 100% tolerance interval. Since μ and σ are known and the population is approximately normal, we know that 90% of the data will fall within 1.645 standard deviations of the mean.

b. The tolerance interval is

$\bar{x} \pm Ks$

From Table 12, Appendix E, with n = 30, α = .05, and γ = .90, K = 2.14. The tolerance interval is

25.6 ± 2.14(4.1) => 25.6 ± 8.774 => (16.826, 34.374)

c. For a nonnormal distribution, the necessary sample size is found from Table 13, Appendix E. With α = .05 and γ = .90, n = 46. The tolerance interval is

(x_{min}, x_{max})

d. If the tolerance limits were established when the process was out of control, then the limits would be of little use. Data points that would indicate the process is out of control could fall inside the tolerance limits.

FOURTEEN

SIMPLE LINEAR REGRESSION AND
CORRELATION

14.1   a. $SS_{xy} = \sum xy - \dfrac{\sum x \sum y}{n} = 6 - \dfrac{0(15)}{5} = 6$

b. $SS_{xx}\,` = \sum x^2 - \dfrac{(\sum x)^2}{n} = 10 - \dfrac{0^2}{5} = 10$

c. $SS_{yy} = \sum y^2 - \dfrac{(\sum y)^2}{n} = 49 - \dfrac{15^2}{5} = 4$

d. $r = \dfrac{SS_{xy}}{\sqrt{SS_{xx} SS_{yy}}} = \dfrac{6}{\sqrt{10(4)}} = .949$

14.3   a.

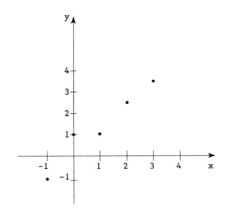

It appears that as x increases, y tends to increase. This
indicates that x and y are positively correlated.

b. $SS_{xy} = \sum xy - \dfrac{\sum x \sum y}{n} = 17.5 - \dfrac{5(7)}{5} = 10.5$

$SS_{xx} = \sum x^2 - \dfrac{(\sum x)^2}{n} = 15 - \dfrac{5^2}{5} = 10$

$$SS_{yy} = \sum y^2 - \frac{(\sum y)^2}{n} = 21.5 - \frac{7^2}{5} = 11.7$$

$$r = \frac{SS_{xy}}{\sqrt{SS_{xx} SS_{yy}}} = \frac{10.5}{\sqrt{10(11.7)}} = .971$$

Since r = .971, there is a strong positive linear relationship between x and y.

c. To determine if x and y are linearly correlated, we test:

H_0: There is no linear correlation between x and y.
H_a: The variables x and y are linearly correlated.

The test statistic is r = .971.

The two-tailed alternative requires a rejection region of $r < -r_{\alpha/2}$ or $r > r_{\alpha/2}$ for n = 5 and $\alpha/2 = .05/2 = .025$. From Table 14, Appendix E, $r_{.025} = .878$. The rejection region is r < -.878 or r > .878.

Since the observed value of the test statistic falls in the rejection region (r = .971 > .878), H_0 is rejected. There is sufficient evidence to indicate that x and y are linearly correlated at $\alpha = .05$.

14.5   a. If all the sample points fall on the same straight line, there is a perfect relationship => r = -1 or r = 1. If there is a positive slope, r = 1.

b. If there is a negative slope, r = -1.

14.7   Yes, the demand for a product is correlated with its price. We would expect the relationship to be negative--as the price increases, the demand would decrease.

14.9   To determine if a negative linear relationship exists between age of marketers and Machiavellianism, we test:

H_0: There is no linear relationship between age and Machiavellianism
H_a: There is a negative linear relationship between age and Machiavellianism

The test statistic is r = -.20.

The one-tailed alternative requires a rejection region of $r < -r_{\alpha}$ for n = 1076 and $\alpha = .05$. From Table 14, Appendix E, $r_{.05} = .164$. (We used n = 102 since it was the largest value in the table.) The rejection region is r < -.164.

Since the observed value of the test statistic falls in the rejection region ($r = -.20 < -.164$), H_0 is rejected. There is sufficient evidence to indicate age and Machiavellianism are negatively correlated at $\alpha = .05$.

14.11 a. To determine if verbal SAT scores and federal spending on education are strongly and negatively correlated, we test:

H_0: Verbal SAT scores and federal spending are not linearly related

H_a: There is a negative linear relationship between verbal SAT scores and federal spending

The test statistic is $r = -.92$.

The one-tailed alternative requires a rejection region of $r < -r_\alpha$ for $n = 10$ and $\alpha = .05$. From Table 14, Appendix E, $r_{.05} = .549$. The rejection region is $r < -.549$.

Since the observed value of the test statistic falls in the rejection region ($r = -.92 < -.549$), H_0 is rejected. There is sufficient evidence to indicate verbal SAT scores and federal spending are negatively correlated at $\alpha = .05$.

b. To determine if math SAT scores and federal spending on education are strongly and negatively correlated, we test:

H_0: There is no linear relationship between math SAT scores and federal spending

H_a: There is a negative linear relationship between math SAT scores and federal spending

The test statistic is $r = -.71$.

The rejection region is $r < -.549$ (see part (a)).

Since the observed value of the test statistic falls in the rejection region ($r = -.71 < -.549$), H_0 is rejected. There is sufficient evidence to indicate the math SAT scores and federal spending are negatively correlated at $\alpha = .05$.

14.13 a. The value of r is $-.1153$. This indicates that there is a negative linear relationship between the average age of corporate boards of directors and the ratio of operating earnings to assets. Since r is close to 0, the relationship is very weak.

b. To determine if the average age of corporate boards of directors is linearly related to ratio of operating earnings to assets, we test:

H_0: There is no linear relationship between average age of corporate boards of directors and ratio of operating earnings to assets

H_a: There is a linear relationship between average age of corporate boards of directors and ratio of operating earnings to assets

The test statistic is $r = -.1153$.

The two-tailed alternative requires a rejection region of $r > r_{\alpha/2}$ or $r < -r_{\alpha/2}$ for n = 399 and $\alpha/2 = .01/2 = .005$. From Table 14, Appendix E, $r_{.005} = .254$. (We used n = 102 since it was the largest value in the table.) The rejection region is $r > .254$ or $r < -.254$.

Since the observed value of the test statistic does not fall in the rejection region (r = -.1153 ≮ -.254), H_0 is not rejected. There is insufficient evidence to indicate the average age of corporate boards of directors is linearly related to ratio of operating earnings to assets at $\alpha = .01$.

14.15 To determine if product quality and market share for capital equipment businesses are positively correlated, we test:

H_0: There is no linear relationship between product quality and market share for capital equipment businesses

H_a: There is a positive linear relationship between product quality and market share for capital equipment businesses

The test statistic is $r = .373$.

The one-tailed alternative requires a rejection region of $r > r_{\alpha}$ for n = 333 and $\alpha = .01$. From Table 14, Appendix E, $r_{.01} = .230$ (We used n = 102 since it was the largest value in the table.) The rejection region is $r > .230$.

Since the observed value of the test statistic falls in the rejection region (r = .373 > .230), H_0 is rejected. There is sufficient evidence to indicate that product quality and market share for capital equipment businesses are positively correlated at $\alpha = .01$.

14.17 a. The y-intercept for the line y = 1.5 + 2x is 1.5. The line crosses the y-axis at the point 1.5.

b. The slope of the line y = 1.5 + 2x is 2. For every unit increase in x, the value of y increases by 2 units.

c. If x increases by 1 unit, y will increase by 2 units.

d. If x decreases by 1 unit, y will decrease by 2 units.

e. When x = 0, y = 1.5 + 2(0) = 1.5.

14.19 a. The y-intercept for the line y = 1.5 - 2x is 1.5. The line crosses the y-axis at the point 1.5.

b. The slope of the line y = 1.5 - 2x is -2. For every unit increase in x, the value of y decreases by 2 units.

c. If x increases by 1 unit, y will decrease by 2 units.

d. When x = 0, y = 1.5 - 2(0) = 1.5

e. The two lines have the same y-intercept 1.5, but have different slopes (+2 and -2).

14.21 Letting the lines follow the form $y = \beta_0 + \beta_1 x$, the corresponding values are:

Line	β_0	β_1
a. y = 1 + 3x	1	3
b. y = 1 - 3x	1	-3
c. y = -1 + 1/2x	-1	1/2
d. y = -1 - 3x	-1	-3
e. y = 2 - 1/2x	2	-1/2
f. y = -1.5 + x	-1.5	1
g. y = 3x	0	3
h. y = -2x	0	-2

14.23 a.

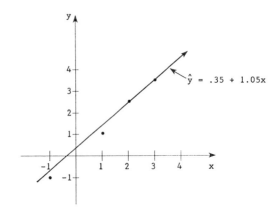

$\hat{y} = .35 + 1.05x$

b. Some preliminary calculations:

$$\sum x = 5 \qquad \sum y = 7 \qquad \sum xy = 17.5$$

$$\sum x^2 = 15 \qquad \sum y^2 = 21.5$$

$$SS_{xy} = \sum xy - \frac{\sum x \sum y}{n} = 17.5 - \frac{5(7)}{5} = 10.5$$

$$SS_{xx} = \sum x^2 - \frac{(\sum x)^2}{n} = 15 - \frac{5^2}{5} = 10$$

$$\hat{\beta}_1 = \frac{SS_{xy}}{SS_{xx}} = \frac{10.5}{10} = 1.05$$

$$\hat{\beta}_0 = \bar{y} - \hat{\beta}_1 \bar{x} = \frac{7}{5} - (1.05)\left(\frac{5}{5}\right) = .35$$

The least squares line is $\hat{y} = .35 + 1.05x$.

14.25   a.

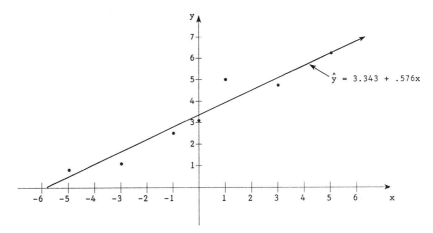

$\hat{y} = 3.343 + .576x$

b. Some preliminary calculations:

$$\sum x = 0 \qquad \sum y = 23.4 \qquad \sum xy = 40.3$$

$$\sum x^2 = 70 \qquad \sum y^2 = 103.24$$

$$SS_{xy} = \sum xy - \frac{\sum x \sum y}{n} = 40.3 - \frac{0(23.4)}{7} = 40.3$$

$$SS_{xx} = \sum x^2 - \frac{(\sum x)^2}{n} = 70 - \frac{0^2}{7} = 70$$

$$\hat{\beta}_1 = \frac{SS_{xy}}{SS_{xx}} = \frac{40.3}{70} = .5757143 \approx .576$$

$$\hat{\beta}_0 = \bar{y} - \hat{\beta}_1\bar{x} = \frac{23.4}{7} - (.5757143)\left(\frac{0}{7}\right) = 3.342857 \approx 3.343$$

The least squares line is $\hat{y} = 3.343 + .576x$

14.27 a.

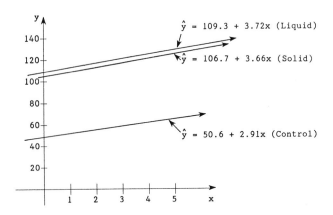

The diet with the largest slope is that associated with the Liquid H diet. The slope is 3.72.

b. For $x = 40$:

      Liquid H: $\hat{y} = 109.3 + 3.72(40) = 258.1$
      Solid H: $\hat{y} = 106.7 + 3.66(40) = 253.1$
      Control: $\hat{y} = 50.6 + 2.91(40) = 167.0$

c. The predicted values will be the same as the estimated mean values found in part (b).

For $x = 40$:

      Liquid H: $\hat{y} = 109.3 + 3.72(40) = 258.1$
      Solid H: $\hat{y} = 106.7 + 3.66(40) = 253.1$
      Control: $\hat{y} = 50.6 + 2.91(40) = 167.0$

14.29 a.

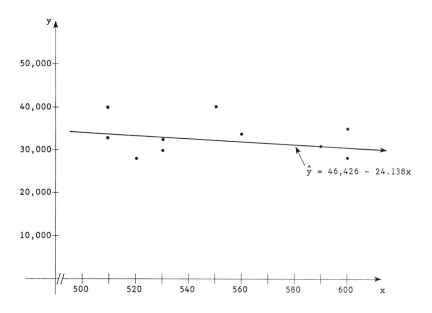

b. Some preliminary calculations:

$\sum x = 5500$ $\qquad\qquad \sum y = 331,500$ $\qquad\qquad \sum xy = 182,045,000$

$\sum x^2 = 3,036,600$ $\qquad\qquad \sum y^2 = 11,155,250,000$

$$SS_{xy} = \sum xy - \frac{\sum x \sum y}{n} = 182,045,000 - \frac{5500(331,500)}{10} = -280,000$$

$$SS_{xx} = \sum x^2 - \frac{(\sum x)^2}{n} = 3,036,600 - \frac{(5,500)^2}{10} = 11,600$$

$$\hat{\beta}_1 = \frac{SS_{xy}}{SS_{xx}} = \frac{-280,000}{11,600} = -24.13793103 \approx -24.138$$

$$\hat{\beta}_0 = \bar{y} - \hat{\beta}_1\bar{x} = \frac{331,500}{10} - (-24.13793103)\frac{5500}{10} = 46,425.862 \approx 46,426$$

The least squares line is $\hat{y} = 46,426 - 24.138x$

d. For $x = 570$, $\hat{y} = 46,426 - 24.138(570) = 32,667.34$

14.31 a.

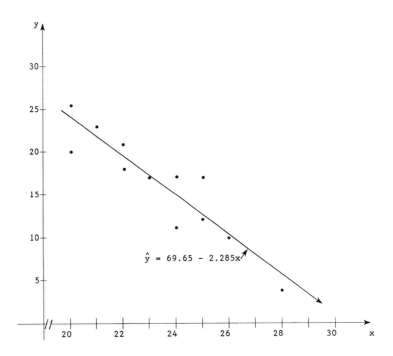

b. Some preliminary calculations:

$\sum x = 280$ $\qquad\qquad\sum y = 196$ $\qquad\sum xy = 4421$

$\sum x^2 = 6600$ $\qquad\quad\sum y^2 = 3618$

$$SS_{xy} = \sum xy - \frac{\sum x \sum y}{n} = 4421 - \frac{280(196)}{12} = -152.3333$$

$$SS_{xx} = \sum x^2 - \frac{(\sum x)^2}{n} = 6600 - \frac{280^2}{12} = 66.6667$$

$$\hat{\beta}_1 = \frac{SS_{xy}}{SS_{xx}} = \frac{-152.3333}{66.6667} = -2.284998358 \approx -2.285$$

$$\hat{\beta}_0 = \bar{y} - \hat{\beta}_1\bar{x} = \frac{196}{12} - (-2.284998358)\frac{280}{12} = 69.64996 \approx 69.65$$

The least squares line is $\hat{y} = 69.65 - 2.285x$

d. For $x = 23$, $\hat{y} = 69.65 - 2.285(23) = 17.095$

14.33 a. From 14.3 and 14.23:

$$SS_{xy} = 10.5$$

$$SS_{xx} = 10.0$$

$$SS_{yy} = \sum y^2 - \frac{(\sum y)^2}{n} = 21.5 - \frac{7^2}{5} = 11.7$$

$$\hat{\beta}_1 = 1.05$$

$$SSE = SS_{yy} - \hat{\beta}_1 SS_{xy} = 11.7 - 1.05(10.5) = .675$$

b. $$s^2 = \frac{SSE}{n-2} = \frac{.675}{5-2} = .225$$

$$s = \sqrt{.225} = .474$$

14.35 a. Some preliminary calculations:

$$\sum x = .958 \qquad \sum y = 190.5 \qquad \sum xy = 10.2915$$

$$\sum x^2 = .061638 \qquad \sum y^2 = 1978.33$$

$$SS_{xy} = \sum xy - \frac{\sum x \sum y}{n} = 10.2915 - \frac{.958(190.5)}{20} = 1.16655$$

$$SS_{xx} = \sum x^2 - \frac{(\sum x)^2}{n} = .061638 - \frac{.958^2}{20} = .0157498$$

$$SS_{yy} = \sum y^2 - \frac{(\sum y)^2}{n} = 1978.33 - \frac{190.5^2}{20} = 163.8175$$

$$\hat{\beta}_1 = \frac{SS_{xy}}{SS_{xx}} = \frac{1.16655}{.0157498} = 74.06760721$$

$$SSE = SS_{yy} - \hat{\beta}_1 SS_{xy} = 163.8175 - 74.06760721(1.16655) = 77.4139$$

$$s^2 = \frac{SSE}{n-2} = \frac{77.4139}{20-2} = 4.301$$

b. $s = \sqrt{4.301} = 2.074$

c. We expect most of the observed values of y to lie within 2s or 2(2.074) or 4.148 units of their respective least squares predicted values, $\hat{y}$.

14.37 a. From Exercise 14.29

$$SS_{xy} = -280,000$$

$$SS_{xx} = 11,600$$

$$SS_{yy} = \sum y^2 - \frac{(\sum y)^2}{n} = 11,155,250,000 - \frac{331,500^2}{10} = 166,025,000$$

$$\hat{\beta}_1 = -24.13793103$$

$$SSE = SS_{yy} - \hat{\beta}_1 SS_{xy} = 166,025,000 - (-24.13793103)(-280,000)$$

$$= 159,266,379.3$$

$$s^2 = \frac{SSE}{n-2} = \frac{159,266,379.3}{10-2} = 19,908,297.41$$

b. $s = \sqrt{19,908,297.41} = 4461.872$

c. We expect most of the observed values of y to lie within 2s or
2(4461.872) or 8923.744 units of their respective least squares
predicted values, $\hat{y}$.

14.39 The degrees of freedom associated with the test statistic is n − 2.
For the following, the degrees of freedom are:

a. df = n − 2 = 6 − 2 = 4

b. df = n − 2 = 10 − 2 = 8

c. df = n − 2 = 25 − 2 = 23

d. df = n − 2 = 50 − 2 = 48

14.41 a. From Exercises 14.3, 14.23, and 14.33,

$$\hat{\beta}_1 = 1.05, \quad s = .474, \quad SS_{xx} = 10$$

$H_0:$ $\beta_1 = 0$
$H_a:$ $\beta_1 \neq 0$

The test statistic is $t = \dfrac{\hat{\beta}_1}{\dfrac{s}{\sqrt{SS_{xx}}}} = \dfrac{1.05}{\dfrac{.474}{\sqrt{10}}} = 7.01$

For the two-tailed test, the rejection region requires $\alpha/2 = .10/2 = .05$ in each tail of the t distribution with df $= n - 2 = 5 - 2 = 3$. From Table 6, Appendix E, $t_{.05} = 2.353$. The rejection region is t < -2.353 or t > 2.353.

Since the observed value of the test statistic falls in the rejection region (t = 7.01 > 2.353), H_0 is rejected. There is sufficient evidence to indicate β_1 is not equal to 0 at $\alpha = .10$.

b. The observed significance level for this test is $2P(t \geq 7.01)$. From Table 6, Appendix E, with df $= n - 2 = 5 - 2 = 3$,

$$2(.001) < 2P(t \geq 7.01) < 2(.005)$$
or $\quad .002 < 2P(t \geq 7.01) < .01$

c. The form of the confidence interval is

$$\hat{\beta}_1 \pm t_{\alpha/2}\frac{s}{\sqrt{SS_{xx}}}$$

For confidence coefficient .90, $\alpha = .10$ and $\alpha/2 = .05$. From Table 6, Appendix E, with df $= n - 2 = 5 - 2 = 3$, $t_{.05} = 2.353$. The 90% confidence interval is

$$1.05 \pm 2.353\left(\frac{.474}{\sqrt{10}}\right) \Rightarrow 1.05 \pm .353 \Rightarrow (.697, 1.403)$$

14.43 From Exercise 14.35, $\hat{\beta}_1 = 74.067$, s = 2.074, $SS_{xx} = .0157498$.

To determine if the R/S ratio contributes information for the prediction of P/E ratio, we test:

H_0: $\beta_1 = 0$
H_a: $\beta_1 \neq 0$

The test statistic is $t = \dfrac{\hat{\beta}_1}{\dfrac{s}{\sqrt{SS_{xx}}}} = \dfrac{74.067}{\dfrac{2.074}{\sqrt{.0157498}}} = 4.48$

For the two-tailed test, the rejection region requires $\alpha/2 = .05/2 = .025$ in each tail of the t distribution with df $= n - 2 = 20 - 2 = 18$. From Table 6, Appendix E, $t_{.025} = 2.101$. The rejection region is t < -2.101 or t > 2.101.

Since the observed value of the test statistic falls in the rejection region (t = 4.48 > 2.101), H_0 is rejected. There is sufficient evidence to indicate that R/S ratio contributes information for the prediction of P/E ratio at $\alpha = .05$.

14.45 a.

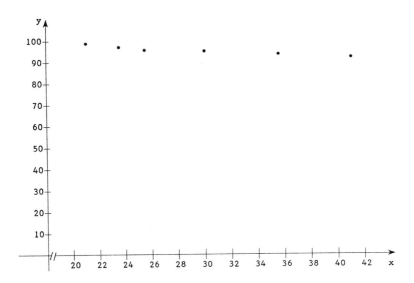

b. Some preliminary calculations:

$\sum x = 177.4$ $\sum y = 574.4$ $\sum xy = 16,885.61$

$\sum x^2 = 5536.24$ $\sum y^2 = 55,022.52$

$$SS_{xy} = \sum xy - \frac{\sum x \sum y}{n} = 16,885.61 - \frac{177.4(574.4)}{6} = -97.48333$$

$$SS_{xx} = \sum x^2 - \frac{(\sum x)^2}{n} = 5536.24 - \frac{177.4^2}{6} = 291.113333$$

$$SS_{yy} = \sum y^2 - \frac{(\sum y)^2}{n} = 55,022.52 - \frac{574.4^2}{6} = 33.29333$$

$$\hat{\beta}_1 = \frac{SS_{xy}}{SS_{xx}} = \frac{-97.48333}{291.113333} = -.334863844 \approx -.3349$$

$$\hat{\beta}_0 = \bar{y} - \hat{\beta}_1 \bar{x} = \frac{574.4}{6} - (-.334863844)\frac{177.4}{6} = 105.634141 \approx 105.634$$

The least squares line is $\hat{y} = 105.634 - .3349x$

c. $SSE = SS_{yy} - \hat{\beta}_1 SS_{xy} = 33.29333 - (-.334863844)(-97.48333)$

$$= .649687$$

$$s^2 = \frac{SSE}{n - 2} = \frac{.649687}{6 - 2} = .1624$$

$$s = \sqrt{.1624} = .403$$

To determine if the network share of revenue decreases as cable penetration increases, we test:

H_0: $\beta_1 = 0$
H_a: $\beta_1 < 0$

The test statistic is $t = \dfrac{\hat{\beta}_1}{\dfrac{s}{\sqrt{SS_{xx}}}} = \dfrac{-.3349}{\dfrac{.403}{\sqrt{291.113333}}} = -14.18$

For a one-tailed test, the rejection region requires $\alpha = .01$ in the lower tail of the t distribution with df $= n - 2 = 6 - 2 = 4$. From Table 6, Appendix E, $t_{.05} = 3.747$. The rejection region is $t < -3.747$.

Since the observed value of the test statistic falls in the rejection region ($t = -14.18 < -2.132$), H_0 is rejected. There is sufficient evidence to indicate the network share of revenue decreases as cable penetration increases at $\alpha = .01$.

d. The form of the confidence is

$$\hat{\beta}_1 \pm t_{\alpha/2} \frac{s}{\sqrt{SS_{xx}}}$$

For confidence coefficient .99, $\alpha = .01$ and $\alpha/2 = .005$. From Table 6, Appendix E, with df $= n - 2 = 6 - 2 = 4$, $t_{.005} = 4.604$. The 99% confidence interval is

$$-.3349 \pm 4.604 \left(\frac{.403}{\sqrt{291.113333}} \right) \Rightarrow -.3349 \pm .1087$$
$$\Rightarrow (-.4436, -.2262)$$

We are 99% confident the true value of β_1 is between $-.4436$ and $-.2262$.

14.47   From Exercises 14.29 and 14.37,

$\hat{\beta}_1 = -24.1379$, $s = 4461.872$, $SS_{xx} = 11,600$

To determine if starting salary and GMAT scores are linearly related, we test:

H_0: $\beta_1 = 0$
H_a: $\beta_1 \neq 0$

The test statistic is $t = \dfrac{\hat{\beta}_1}{\dfrac{s}{\sqrt{SS_{xx}}}} = \dfrac{-24.1379}{\dfrac{4461.872}{\sqrt{11,600}}} = -.583$

For a two-tailed test, the rejection region requires $\alpha/2 = .10/2 = .05$ in each tail of the t distribution with df $= n - 2 = 10 - 2 = 8$. From Table 6, Appendix E, $t_{.05} = 1.860$. The rejection region is $t < -1.860$ or $t > 1.860$.

Since the observed value of the test statistic does not fall in the rejection region ($t = -.583 \not< -1.860$), H_0 is not rejected. There is insufficient evidence to indicate that starting salary and GMAT scores are linearly related at $\alpha = .10$.

14.49   a.   Some preliminary calculations:

$\sum x = 388$ $\sum y = 72.06$ $\sum xy = 2759.66$

$\sum x^2 = 15,192$ $\sum y^2 = 621.8244$

$SS_{xy} = \sum xy - \dfrac{\sum x \sum y}{n} = 2759.66 - \dfrac{388(72.06)}{11} = 217.907273$

$SS_{xx} = \sum x^2 - \dfrac{(\sum x)^2}{n} = 15,192 - \dfrac{388^2}{11} = 1506.18182$

$SS_{yy} = \sum y^2 - \dfrac{(\sum y)^2}{n} = 621.8244 - \dfrac{72.06^2}{11} = 149.7658909$

$\hat{\beta}_1 = \dfrac{SS_{xy}}{SS_{xx}} = \dfrac{217.907273}{1506.18182} = .144675277 \approx .14468$

$\hat{\beta}_0 = \bar{y} - \hat{\beta}_1 \bar{x} = \dfrac{72.06}{11} - (.144675277)\left(\dfrac{388}{11}\right) = 1.4478175 \approx 1.4478$

The least squares line is $\hat{y} = 1.4478 + .14468x$

b. $SSE = SS_{yy} - \hat{\beta}_1 SS_{xy} = 149.7658909 - (.144675277)(217.907273)$

$= 118.240$

$s^2 = \dfrac{SSE}{n - 2} = \dfrac{118.240}{11 - 2} = 13.1378$

$s = \sqrt{13.1378} = 3.6246$

To determine if employment compensation subsidy rate contributes information for the prediction of layoff rate, we test:

$H_0: \quad \beta_1 = 0$
$H_a: \quad \beta_1 \neq 0$

The test statistic is $t = \dfrac{\hat{\beta}_1}{\dfrac{s}{\sqrt{SS_{xx}}}} = \dfrac{.14468}{\dfrac{3.6246}{\sqrt{1506.18182}}} = 1.549$

For the two-tailed test, the rejection region requires $\alpha/2 = .05/2 = .025$ in each tail of the t distribution with $df = n - 2 = 11 - 2 = 9$. From Table 6, Appendix E, $t_{.025} = 2.262$. The rejection region is $t < -2.262$ or $t > 2.262$.

Since the observed value of the test statistic does not fall in the rejection region ($t = 1.5498 \ngtr 2.262$), H_0 is not rejected. There is insufficient evidence to indicate unemployment compensation subsidy rate contributes information for the prediction of layoff rate at $\alpha = .05$.

c. The form of the confidence interval is

$$\hat{\beta}_1 \pm t_{\alpha/2} \frac{s}{\sqrt{SS_{xx}}}$$

For confidence coefficient .95, $\alpha = .05$ and $\alpha/2 = .025$. From Table 6, Appendix E, with $df = n - 2 = 11 - 2 = 9$, $t_{.025} = 2.262$. The 95% confidence interval is

$.14468 \pm 2.262\left(\dfrac{3.6246}{\sqrt{1506.18182}}\right)$ => $.14468 \pm .21126$

=> $(-.06658, .35594)$

We are 95 confident the mean increase in layoff rate for each percentage point increase in salary rate is between $-.06658$ and $.35594$ at $\alpha = .05$.

14.51 $r^2 = \dfrac{SS_{yy} - SSE}{SS_{yy}} = \dfrac{210 - 31}{210} = .852$

14.53   Some preliminary calculations:

$\sum x = 15 \qquad\qquad \sum y = 10 \qquad\qquad \sum xy = 37$

$\sum x^2 = 55 \qquad\qquad \sum y^2 = 26$

a. $SS_{xx} = \sum x^2 - \dfrac{(\sum x)^2}{n} = 55 - \dfrac{15^2}{5} = 10$

b. $SS_{xy} = \sum xy - \dfrac{\sum x \sum y}{n} = 37 - \dfrac{15(10)}{5} = 7$

c. $SS_{yy} = \sum y^2 - \dfrac{(\sum y)^2}{n} = 26 - \dfrac{10^2}{5} = 6$

d. $\hat{\beta}_1 = \dfrac{SS_{xy}}{SS_{xx}} = \dfrac{7}{10} = .7$

e. $SSE = SS_{yy} - \hat{\beta}_1 SS_{xy} = 6 - .7(7) = 1.1$

f. $r^2 = \dfrac{SS_{yy} - SSE}{SS_{yy}} = \dfrac{6 - 1.1}{6} = .8167$

14.55 From Exercise 14.25

$SS_{xy} = 40.3, \ \hat{\beta}_1 = .5757143$

$SS_{yy} = \sum y^2 - \dfrac{(\sum y)^2}{n} = 103.24 - \dfrac{23.4^2}{7} = 25.0171$

$SSE = SS_{yy} - \hat{\beta}_1 SS_{xy} = 25.0171 - (.5757143)(40.3) = 1.8159$

$r^2 = \dfrac{SS_{yy} - SSE}{SS_{yy}} = \dfrac{25.0171 - 1.8159}{25.0171} = .927$

This means that 92.7% of the sum of squares of deviations of the y values about their mean is attributable to the linear relationship between y and x.

14.57 From Exercise 14.35, $SS_{yy} = 163.8175$ and $SSE = 77.4139$.

$r^2 = \dfrac{SS_{yy} - SSE}{SS_{yy}} = \dfrac{163.8175 - 77.4139}{163.8175} = .527$

This means that 52.7% of the sum of squares of deviations of the P/E ratio values about their mean is attributable to the linear relationship between P/E ratio and R/S ratio.

14.59 From Exercise 14.31, $SS_{xy} = -152.3333$ and $\hat{\beta}_1 = -2.284998$

$SS_{yy} = \sum y^2 - \dfrac{(\sum y)^2}{n} = 3618 - \dfrac{196^2}{12} = 416.6667$

$SSE = SS_{yy} - \hat{\beta}_1 SS_{xy} = 416.6667 - (-2.284998)(-152.3333)$

$= 68.58538$

$$r^2 = \frac{SS_{yy} - SSE}{SS_{yy}} = \frac{416.6667 - 68.58538}{416.6667} = .835$$

This means that 83.5% of the sum of squares of deviations of the shrinkage values about their mean is attributable to the linear relationship between shrinkage and number of sales clerks.

14.61　From Exercise 14.45, $SS_{yy} = 33.29333$ and $SSE = .649687$.

$$r^2 = \frac{SS_{yy} - SSE}{SS_{yy}} = \frac{33.29333 - .649687}{33.29333} = .980$$

This means that 98% of the sum of squares of deviations of the network share of television revenues about their mean is attributable to the linear relationship between network share of television revenues and percentage of U.S. Cable TV households.

14.63　a.　$\hat{\beta}_1 = \dfrac{SS_{xy}}{SS_{xx}} = \dfrac{16.22}{4.77} = 3.400419$

$SSE = SS_{yy} - \hat{\beta}_1 SS_{xy} = 59.21 - 3.400419(16.22) = 4.055$

$s^2 = \dfrac{SSE}{n - 2} = \dfrac{4.055}{20 - 2} = .225$

b.　For $x = 2.5$, $\hat{y} = 2.1 + 3.4(2.5) = 10.6$

The form of the 95% confidence interval is

$$\hat{y} \pm t_{\alpha/2} s \sqrt{\frac{1}{n} + \frac{(x - \bar{x})^2}{SS_{xx}}}$$

For confidence coefficient .95, $\alpha = .05$ and $\alpha/2 = .025$. From Table 6, Appendix E, with df = $n - 2 = 20 - 2 = 18$, $t_{.025} = 2.101$. The 95% confidence interval is

$$10.6 \pm 2.101\sqrt{.225} \sqrt{\frac{1}{20} + \frac{(2.5 - 2.5)^2}{4.77}}$$

$\Rightarrow 10.6 \pm .223 \Rightarrow (10.377, 10.823)$

We are 95% confident the mean value of y when x = 2.5 is between 10.377 and 10.823.

c. For x = 2.0, $\hat{y}$ = 2.1 + 3.4(2.0) = 8.9.

The 95% confidence interval is

$$8.9 \pm 2.101\sqrt{.225}\sqrt{\frac{1}{20} + \frac{(2.0 - 2.5)^2}{4.77}}$$

=> 8.9 ± .319 => (8.581, 9.219)

We are 95% confident the mean value of y when x = 2.0 is between 8.581 and 9.219.

d. For x = 3.0, $\hat{y}$ = 2.1 + 3.4(3.0) = 12.3.

The 95% confidence interval is

$$12.3 \pm 2.101\sqrt{.225}\sqrt{\frac{1}{20} + \frac{(3.0 - 2.5)^2}{4.77}}$$

=> 12.3 ± .319 => (11.981, 12.619)

We are 95% confident the mean value of y when x = 3.0 is between 11.981 and 12.619.

e. The width of the interval in (b) is 10.823 - 10.377 = .446
The width of the interval in (c) is 9.219 - 8.581 = .638
The width of the interval in (d) is 12.619 - 11.981 = .638

As the value of x moves away from $\bar{x}$ = 2.5, the width of the confidence interval gets larger.

f. The 95% prediction interval is

$$\hat{y} \pm t_{\alpha/2}s\sqrt{1 + \frac{1}{n} + \frac{(x - \bar{x})^2}{SS_{xx}}}$$

$$12.3 \pm 2.101\sqrt{.225}\sqrt{1 + \frac{1}{20} + \frac{(3.0 - 2.5)^2}{4.77}}$$

=> 12.3 ± 1.046 => (11.254, 13.346)

g. The width of the prediction interval in (f) is 13.346 - 11.254 = 2.092. This is wider than the confidence interval in part (d). The prediction interval is always wider than the confidence interval for the mean because the prediction interval contains both the variability of locating the mean and the variability of y once the mean has been located.

14.65 a. From Exercises 14.3, 14.23, 14.33, 14.41

$$\hat{y} = .35 + 1.05x, \quad SS_{xx} = 10.5, \quad \bar{x} = \frac{5}{5} = 1, \quad s = .474$$

For x = 1, $\hat{y}$ = .35 + 1.05(1) = 1.40

The form of the 90% confidence interval is

$$\hat{y} \pm t_{\alpha/2} s \sqrt{\frac{1}{n} + \frac{(x - \bar{x})^2}{SS_{xx}}}$$

For confidence coefficient .90, α = .10 and $\alpha/2$ = .10/2 = .05.
From Table 6, Appendix E, with df = n - 2 = 5 - 2 = 3,
$t_{.05}$ = 2.353. The 90% confidence interval is

$$1.40 \pm 2.353(.474)\sqrt{\frac{1}{5} + \frac{(1 - 1)^2}{10.5}} \Rightarrow 1.40 \pm .499$$

$$\Rightarrow (.901, 1.899)$$

We are 90% confident the mean value of y when x is equal to 1 is
between .901 and 1.899.

b. The form of the 90% prediction interval is

$$\hat{y} \pm t_{\alpha/2} s \sqrt{1 + \frac{1}{n} + \frac{(x - \bar{x})^2}{SS_{xx}}}$$

The 90% prediction interval is

$$1.40 \pm 2.353(.474)\sqrt{1 + \frac{1}{5} + \frac{(1 - 1)^2}{10.5}} \Rightarrow 1.40 \pm 1.222$$

$$\Rightarrow (.178, 2.622)$$

We are 90% confident the actual value of y when x is 1 is between
.178 and 2.622.

c. The interval in part (b) is wider. The prediction interval for an
actual value of y is always wider than the confidence interval for
the mean value of y.

14.67 a. From Exercise 14.35, $\hat{\beta}_1$ = 74.06760721 $\approx$ 74.0676, SS_{xx} = .0157498,

SS_{xy} = 1.16655, $\bar{x}$ = $\frac{.958}{20}$ = .0479, $\bar{y}$ = $\frac{190.5}{20}$ = 9.525, s = 2.074

$\hat{\beta}_0$ = $\bar{y} - \hat{\beta}_1 \bar{x}$ = 9.525 - (74.06760721)(.0479) = 5.977

$\hat{y}$ = 5.977 + 74.068x

For x = .070, $\hat{y}$ = 5.977 + 74.0676(.070) = 11.1617

The form of the prediction interval is

$$\hat{y} \pm t_{\alpha/2} s \sqrt{1 + \frac{1}{n} + \frac{(x - \bar{x})^2}{SS_{xx}}}$$

For confidence coefficient .99, $\alpha = .01$ and $\alpha/2 = .01/2 = .005$. From Table 6, Appendix E, with df = $n - 2 = 20 - 2 = 18$, $t_{.005} = 2.878$. The 99% prediction interval is

$$11.1617 \pm 2.878(2.074) \sqrt{1 + \frac{1}{20} + \frac{(.07 - .0479)^2}{.0157498}}$$

$$\Rightarrow 11.1617 \pm 6.0260 \Rightarrow (4.9557, 17.3677)$$

We are 99% confident the P/E ratio when the R/S ratio is .070 is between 4.9557 and 17.3677.

b. The form of the 99% confidence interval is

$$\hat{y} \pm t_{\alpha/2} s \sqrt{\frac{1}{n} + \frac{(x - \bar{x})^2}{SS_{xx}}}$$

The 99% confidence interval is

$$11.1617 \pm 2.878(2.074) \sqrt{\frac{1}{20} + \frac{(.07 - .0479)^2}{.0157498}}$$

$$\Rightarrow 11.1617 \pm 1.6989 \Rightarrow (9.4628, 12.8606)$$

We are 99% confident the mean P/E ratio when the R/S ratio is .070 is between 9.4628 and 12.8606.

The prediction interval pertains to an actual value of P/E ratio for a particular R/S ratio while the confidence interval pertains to the mean P/E ratio for a particular R/S ratio.

14.69   Some preliminary calculations from Exercise 14.30 are:

$$\sum x = 115,077 \qquad \sum y = 4.754 \qquad \sum xy = 45,740.475$$

$$\sum x^2 = 1,137,630,209 \qquad \sum y^2 = 1.986222$$

$$SS_{xy} = \sum xy - \frac{\sum x \sum y}{n} = 45,740.475 - \frac{115,077(4.754)}{12} = 150.8035$$

$$SS_{xx} = \sum x^2 - \frac{(\sum x)^2}{n} = 1,137,630,209 - \frac{115,077^2}{12} = 34,070,548$$

$$SS_{yy} = \sum y^2 - \frac{(\sum y)^2}{n} = 1.986222 - \frac{4.754^2}{12} = .102845667$$

$$\hat{\beta}_1 = \frac{SS_{xy}}{SS_{xx}} = \frac{150.8035}{34,070,548} = .000004426$$

$$\hat{\beta}_0 = \bar{y} - \hat{\beta}_1\bar{x} = \frac{4.754}{12} - .000004426\left(\frac{115,077}{12}\right) = .3537$$

The least squares line is $\hat{y} = .3537 + .000004426x$

$$SSE = SS_{yy} - \hat{\beta}_1 SS_{xy} = .1028456679 - .000004426(150.8035) = .10218$$

$$s^2 = \frac{SSE}{n - 2} = \frac{.10218}{12 - 2} = .010218$$

$$s = \sqrt{.010218} = .1011$$

For $x = 8,000$, $\hat{y} = .3537 + .000004426(8000) = .3891$

The form of the prediction interval is

$$\hat{y} \pm t_{\alpha/2}s\sqrt{1 + \frac{1}{n} + \frac{(x - \bar{x})^2}{SS_{xx}}}$$

For confidence coefficient .95, $\alpha = .05$ and $\alpha/2 = .05/2 = .025$. From Table 6, Appendix E, with df = $n - 2 = 12 - 2 = 10$, $t_{.025} = 2.228$.

The 95% prediction interval is

$$.3891 \pm 2.228(.1011)\sqrt{1 + \frac{1}{12} + \frac{(8000 - 9589.75)^2}{34,070,548}}$$

$\Rightarrow .3891 \pm .2423 \Rightarrow (.1468, .6314)$

We are 95% confident the refusal rate for a per capita income of $8,000 is between .1468 and .6314.

14.71   a.   From Exercise 14.31,

$$\hat{y} = 69.65 - 2.285x, \quad SS_{xx} = 66.6667, \quad SS_{xy} = -152.3333,$$

$$\bar{x} = \frac{280}{12} = 23.3333$$

$$SS_{yy} = \sum y^2 - \frac{(\sum y)^2}{n} = 3618 - \frac{196^2}{12} = 416.6667$$

$$SSE = SS_{yy} - \hat{\beta}_1 SS_{xy} = 416.6667 - (-2.284998358)(-152.3333)$$

$$= 68.5853$$

$$s^2 = \frac{SSE}{n - 2} = \frac{68.5853}{12 - 2} = 6.85853$$

$$s = \sqrt{6.85853} = 2.6189$$

The form of the confidence interval is

$$\hat{y} \pm t_{\alpha/2} s \sqrt{\frac{1}{n} + \frac{(x - \bar{x})^2}{SS_{xx}}}$$

For x = 23, $\hat{y}$ = 69.65 - 2.285(23) = 17.095

For confidence coefficient .90, α = .10 and $\alpha/2$ = .10/2 = .05. From Table 6, Appendix E, with df = n - 2 = 12 - 2 = 10, $t_{.05}$ = 1.812. The 90% confidence interval is

$$17.095 \pm 1.812(2.6189) \sqrt{\frac{1}{12} + \frac{(23 - 23.3333)^2}{66.6667}}$$

=> 17.095 ± 1.384 => (15.711, 18.479)

We are 90% confident the mean shrinkage when 23 sales clerks are on duty is between 15.711 and 18.479.

b. The form of the prediction interval is

$$\hat{y} \pm t_{\alpha/2} s \sqrt{1 + \frac{1}{n} + \frac{(x - \bar{x})^2}{SS_{xx}}}$$

The 90% prediction interval is

$$17.095 \pm 1.812(2.6189) \sqrt{1 + \frac{1}{12} + \frac{(23 - 23.3333)^2}{66.6667}}$$

=> 17.095 ± 4.943 => (12.152, 22.038)

We are 90% confident the actual shrinkage when 23 sales clerks are on duty will be between 12.152 and 22.038.

14.73 a.

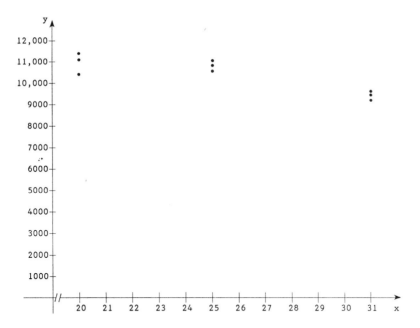

It appears that x and y are negatively correlated.

b. Some preliminary calculations are:

$\sum x = 228$ $\qquad$ $\sum y = 93,762$ $\qquad$ $\sum xy = 2,348,190$

$\sum x^2 = 5958$ $\qquad$ $\sum y^2 = 982,337,764$

$SS_{xy} = \sum xy - \dfrac{\sum x \sum y}{n} = 2,348,190 - \dfrac{228(93,762)}{9} = -27,114$

$SS_{xx} = \sum x^2 - \dfrac{(\sum x)^2}{n} = 5958 - \dfrac{228^2}{9} = 182$

$SS_{yy} = \sum y^2 - \dfrac{(\sum y)^2}{n} = 982,337,764 - \dfrac{93,762^2}{9} = 5,525,248$

$r = \dfrac{SS_{xy}}{\sqrt{SS_{xx}SS_{yy}}} = \dfrac{-27,114}{\sqrt{182(5,525,248)}} = -.855$

This indicates that load and age are negatively linearly related. Since $r = -.855$ is close to -1, the relationship is fairly strong.

c. $\hat{\beta}_1 = \dfrac{SS_{xy}}{SS_{xx}} = \dfrac{-27,114}{182} = -148.978022 \approx -148.978$

SIMPLE LINEAR REGRESSION AND CORRELATION $\qquad$ 335

$$SSE = SS_{yy} - \hat{\beta}_1 SS_{xy} = 5,525,248- (-148.978022)(-27,114)$$

$$= 1,485,857.911$$

$$s^2 = \frac{SSE}{n - 2} = \frac{1,485,857.911}{9 - 2} = 212,265.4159$$

$$s = \sqrt{212,265.4159} = 460.7227$$

To determine if x and y are linearly related, we test:

H_0: There is no linear correlation between x and y
H_a: The variables x and y are linearly related

The test statistic is r = -.855.

The two-tailed alternative requires a rejection region of $r < -r_{\alpha/2}$ or $r > r_{\alpha/2}$ for n = 9 and $\alpha/2 = .05/2 = .025$. From Table 14, Appendix E, $r_{.025} = .666$. The rejection region is $r < -.666$ or $r > .666$.

Since the observed value of the test statistic falls in the rejection region (r = -.855 < -.666), H_0 is rejected. There is sufficient evidence to indicate x and y are linearly related at $\alpha = .05$.

d. $\hat{\beta}_0 = \bar{y} - \hat{\beta}_1 \bar{x} = \dfrac{93,762}{9} - (-148.978022)\left(\dfrac{228}{9}\right) = 14,192.10989$

$$\approx 14,192$$

The least squares line is $\hat{y} = 14,192 - 148.978x$

e. H_0 $\beta_1 = 0$
H_a: $\beta_1 \neq 0$

The test statistic is $t = \dfrac{\hat{\beta}_1}{\dfrac{s}{\sqrt{SS_{xx}}}} = \dfrac{-148.978}{\dfrac{460.7227}{\sqrt{182}}} = -4.36$

For a two-tailed test, the rejection region requires $\alpha/2 = .05/2 = .025$ in each tail of the t distribution with df = n - 2 = 9 - 2 = 7 df. From Table 6, Appendix E, $t_{.025} = 2.365$. The rejection region is t < -2.365 or t > 2.365.

Since the observed value of the test statistic falls in the rejection region (t = -4.36 < -2.365), H_0 is rejected. There is sufficient evidence to indicate that x and y are linearly related at $\alpha = .05$.

f. The form of the prediction interval is

$$\hat{y} \pm t_{\alpha/2} s \sqrt{1 + \frac{1}{n} + \frac{(x - \bar{x})^2}{SS_{xx}}}$$

For x = 35, $\hat{y}$ = 14,192 - 148.978(35) = 8977.735

For confidence coefficient .95, α = .05 and $\alpha/2$ = .05/2 = .025.
From Table 6, Appendix E, with df = n - 2 = 9 - 2 = 7,
$t_{.025}$ = 2.365. The 95% prediction interval is

$$8977.735 \pm 2.365(460.7227) \sqrt{1 + \frac{1}{9} + \frac{(35 - 25.3333)^2}{182}}$$

=> 8977.735 ± 1388.789 => (7588.946, 10,366.524)

We are 95% confident the crack load is between 7588.946 and
10,366.524 when the concrete is 35 days old.

g. Since 35 is outside the observed range of x (20 - 31), we should
use this interval with caution.

14.75 a. The least squares prediction line is $\hat{y}$ = -.0292 + 2.2985x.

b. r^2 = R-SQUARE = .6772. This means that 67.72% of the sum of
squares of deviations of the postmarkdown rate of sale values
about their mean is attributable to the linear relationship
between the postmarkdown rate of sale and the initial rate of
sale.

c. s = ROOT MSE = .1044. We expect most of the observations to fall
within 2s or 2(.1044) or .2088 units of the least squares line.

d. To determine if the postmarkdown rate of sale and initial rate of
sale are linearly related, we test:

H_0: β_1 = 0
H_a: $\beta_1 \neq$ 0

The test statistic is t = 3.83.

The p-value of the test is .0200.

Since the p-value is less than α (.0200 < .05), H_0 is rejected.
There is sufficient evidence to indicate the postmarkdown rate of
sale and initial rate of sale are linearly related at α = .05.

14.77 a. Some preliminary calculations are:

$$\sum x = 20.6 \qquad \sum y = 27 \qquad \sum xy = 412.25$$

$$\sum x^2 = 249.48 \qquad \sum y^2 = 693.34$$

$$SS_{xy} = \sum xy - \frac{\sum x \sum y}{n} = 412.25 - \frac{20.6(27)}{7} = 332.7928571$$

$$SS_{xx} = \sum x^2 - \frac{(\sum x)^2}{n} = 249.48 - \frac{20.6^2}{7} = 188.8571429$$

$$SS_{yy} = \sum y^2 - \frac{(\sum y)^2}{n} = 693.34 - \frac{27^2}{7} = 589.1971429$$

$$\hat{\beta}_1 = \frac{SS_{xy}}{SS_{xx}} = \frac{332.7928571}{188.8571429} = 1.762140695 \approx 1.762$$

$$\hat{\beta}_0 = \bar{y} - \hat{\beta}_1 \bar{x} = \frac{27}{7} - 1.762140695\left(\frac{20.6}{7}\right) = -1.328585 \approx -1.329$$

The least squares line is $\hat{y} = -1.329 + 1.762x$

b. SSE = $SS_{yy} - \hat{\beta}_1 SS_{xy}$ = 589.1971429 - (1.762140695)(332.7928571)

$$= 2.7693$$

$$s^2 = \frac{SSE}{n-2} = \frac{2.7693}{7-2} = .5539$$

$$s = \sqrt{.5539} = .7442$$

Most of the observations will fall within 2s or 2(.7442) or 1.4884 units of the least squares line.

$$r^2 = \frac{SS_{yy} - SSE}{SS_{yy}} = \frac{589.1971429 - 2.7693}{589.1971429} = .995$$

This means that 99.5% of the sum of squares of deviations of the stock rate of return values about their mean is attributable to the linear relationship between stock rate of return and the market rate of return.

c. To determine if the market rate of return is a useful predictor of stock rate of return, we test:

$H_0 \quad \beta_1 = 0$
$H_a: \quad \beta_1 \neq 0$

The test statistic is $t = \dfrac{\hat{\beta}_1}{\dfrac{s}{\sqrt{SS_{xx}}}} = \dfrac{1.762}{\dfrac{.7442}{\sqrt{188.8571429}}} = 32.54$

For a two-tailed alternative, the rejection region requires $\alpha/2 = .01/2 = .005$ in each tail of the t distribution with $n - 2 = 7 - 2 = 5$ df. From Table 6, Appendix E, $t_{.005} = 4.032$. The rejection region is $t < -4.032$ or $t > 4.032$.

Since the observed value of the test statistic falls in the rejection region ($t = 32.54 > 4.032$), H_0 is rejected. There is sufficient evidence to indicate the market rate of return is a useful predictor of stock rate of return at $\alpha = .01$.

d. The form of the confidence interval is

$$\hat{\beta}_1 \pm t_{\alpha/2}\frac{s}{\sqrt{SS_{xx}}}$$

For confidence coefficient .99, $\alpha = .01$ and $\alpha/2 = .01/2 = .005$. From Table 6, Appendix E, with $n - 2 = 7 - 2 = 5$ df, $t_{.005} = 4.032$. The 99% confidence interval is

$$1.762 \pm 4.032 \frac{.7442}{\sqrt{188.8571429}} \Rightarrow 1.762 \pm .218 \Rightarrow (1.544, 1.980)$$

We are 99% confident the mean increase in stock rate of return for every 1% increase in market rate of return is between 1.544 and 1.980.

e. This stock would be considered aggressive. An aggressive stock is defined as one with a slope greater than 1. Since 1 is below the confidence interval, we are confident the slope is greater than 1.

14.79 a. From the printout, the least squares line is

$$\hat{y} = -1180.5 + 6808.1x$$

b. To determine if the model contributes information for the prediction of demand, we test:

H_0 $\beta_1 = 0$
H_a: $\beta_1 \neq 0$

The test statistic is $t = 19.00$ (from printout).

For the two-tailed alternative, the rejection region requires $\alpha/2 = .05/2 = .025$ in each tail of the t distribution with $n - 2 = 8 - 2 = 6$ df. From Table 6, Appendix E, $t_{.025} = 2.447$. The rejection region is $t < -2.447$ or $t > 2.447$.

Since the observed value of the test statistic falls in the
rejection region (t = 19.00 > 2.447), H_0 is rejected. There is
sufficient evidence to indicate the model contributes information
for the prediction of demand at α = .05.

c.

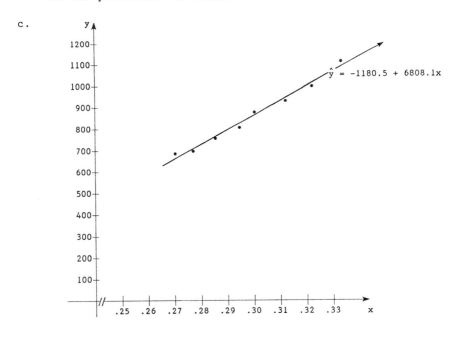

$\hat{y}$ = -1180.5 + 6808.1x

d. r^2 = R-Sq = .984. This means that 98.4% of the sums of squares of
deviations of the demand values about their mean is attributable
to the linear relationship between demand and the inverse of the
price.

14.81   a.   To determine if return on assets and market share are positively
linearly related, we test:

H_0 β_1 = 0
H_a: β_1 > 0

The test statistic is t = 2.51 (from printout).

For a one-tailed alternative, the rejection region requires
$\alpha/2$ = .05 in the upper tail of the t distribution with
n - 2 = 5400 - 2 = 5398 df. From Table 6, Appendix E,
$t_{.05}$ = 1.645. The rejection region is t > 1.645.

Since the observed value of the test statistic falls in the
rejection region (t = 2.51 > 1.645), H_0 is rejected. There is
sufficient evidence to indicate return on assets and market share
are positively linearly related at α = .05.

b. $r^2 = .001$. This means that .1% of the sums of squares of
    deviations of the return on assets value about their mean is
    attributable to the linear relationship between return on assets
    and market share.

c. No. Even though there is a significant positive linear
    relationship between return on assets and market share, the
    relationship is very weak ($r^2 = .001$). Most of the variation in
    return on assets is not identified. One should look for other
    independent variables to include in the model.

CASE STUDIES

14.1 For the Low Parent Education:

For each variable, we want to test:

H_0: The variable and ad exposure are not linearly related
H_a: The variable and ad exposure are linearly related

The test statistic is r.

For a two-tailed alternative, the rejection region is
$r < -r_{\alpha/2}$ or $r > r_{\alpha/2}$. From Table 14, Appendix E, for n = 132 and
$\alpha/2 = .05/2 = .025$, $r_{.025} = .195$. The rejection region is
$r < -.195$ or $r > .195$.

For Belief, r = .06:

Since the observed value of the test statistic does not fall in
the rejection region ($r = .06 \ngtr .195$), H_0 is not rejected. There
is insufficient evidence to indicate Belief and ad exposure are
linearly related at $\alpha = .05$.

For Affect, r = .13:

Since the observed value of the test statistic does not fall in
the rejection region ($r = .13 \ngtr .195$), H_0 is not rejected. There
is insufficient evidence to indicate Affect and ad exposure are
linearly related at $\alpha = .05$.

For Intention, r = .44:

Since the observed value of the test statistic falls in the rejection region (r = .44 > .195), H_0 is rejected. There is sufficient evidence to indicate Intention and ad exposure are linearly related at α = .05.

For Request, r = .39:

Since the observed value of the test statistic falls in the rejection region (r = .39 > .195), H_0 is rejected. There is sufficient evidence to indicate Request and ad exposure are linearly related at α = .05.

For Usage, r = .12:

Since the observed value of the test statistic does not fall in the rejection region (r = .12 $\not>$ .195), H_0 is not rejected. There is insufficient evidence to indicate Usage and ad exposure are linearly related at α = .05.

For the No Self-Administration:

For each variable, we want to test:

H_0: The variable and ad exposure are not linearly related
H_a: The variable and ad exposure are linearly related

The test statistic is r.

For a two-tailed alternative, the rejection region is $r < -r_{\alpha/2}$ or $r > r_{\alpha/2}$. From Table 14, Appendix E, for n = 55 and $\alpha/2$ = .05/2 = .025, $r_{.025} \approx .273$. The rejection region is $r < -.273$ or $r > .273$.

For Belief, r = .29:

Since the observed value of the test statistic falls in the rejection region (r = .29 > .273), H_0 is rejected. There is sufficient evidence to indicate Belief and ad exposure are linearly related at α = .05.

For Affect, r = .26:

Since the observed value of the test statistic does not fall in the rejection region (r = .26 $\not>$ .273), H_0 is not rejected. There is insufficient evidence to indicate Affect and ad exposure are linearly related at α = .05.

For Intention, r = .23:

Since the observed value of the test statistic does not fall in
the rejection region (r = .23 ≯ .273), H_0 is not rejected. There
is insufficient evidence to indicate Intention and ad exposure are
linearly related at α = .05.

For Request, r = .34:

Since the observed value of the test statistic falls in the
rejection region (r = .34 > .273), H_0 is rejected. There is
sufficient evidence to indicate Request and ad exposure are
linearly related at α = .05.

For Usage, r = .23:

Since the observed value of the test statistic does not fall in
the rejection region (r = .23 ≯ .273), H_0 is not rejected. There
is insufficient evidence to indicate Usage and ad exposure are
linearly related at α = .05.

14.3   a.

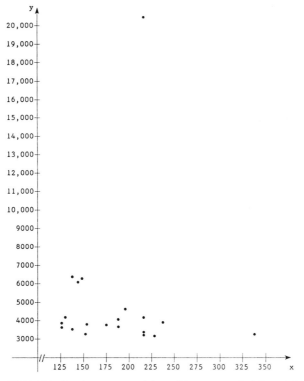

There appears to be a negative linear relationship between total
executive pay and total shareholder return except for the one
extreme data point.

b. Some preliminary calculations are:

$$\sum x = 3654 \qquad \sum y = 99,377 \qquad \sum xy = 18,286,273$$

$$\sum x^2 = 718,118 \qquad \sum y^2 = 767,539,993$$

$$SS_{xy} = \sum xy - \frac{\sum x \sum y}{n} = 18,286,273 - \frac{3654(99,377)}{20} = 130,095.1$$

$$SS_{xx} = \sum x^2 - \frac{(\sum x)^2}{n} = 718,118 - \frac{3654^2}{20} = 50,532.2$$

$$SS_{yy} = \sum y^2 - \frac{(\sum y)^2}{n} = 767,539,993 - \frac{99,377^2}{20} = 273,750,586.5$$

$$\hat{\beta}_1 = \frac{SS_{xy}}{SS_{xx}} = \frac{130,095.1}{50,532.2} = 2.574499032 \approx 2.574$$

$$\hat{\beta}_0 = \bar{y} - \hat{\beta}_1\bar{x} = \frac{99,377}{20} - (2.574499032)\left(\frac{3654}{20}\right) = 4498.489027$$
$$\approx 4498.49$$

$$SSE = SS_{yy} - \hat{\beta}_1 SS_{xy} = 273,750,586.5 - (2.574499032)(130,095.1)$$
$$= 273,415,656.8$$

$$r = \frac{SS_{xy}}{\sqrt{SS_{xx}SS_{yy}}} = \frac{130,095.1}{\sqrt{50,532.2(273,750,586.5)}} = .035$$

c. To determine if a linear relationship exists between the two variables, we test:

H_0: Total cash compensation and total shareholder return are not linearly related
H_a: Total cash compensation and total shareholder return are linearly related

The test statistic is $r = .035$.

For a two-tailed alternative, the rejection region is $r < -r_{\alpha/2}$ or $r > r_{\alpha/2}$. From Table 14, Appendix E, for $n = 20$ and $\alpha/2 = .05/2 = .025$, $r_{.025} = .444$. The rejection region is $r < -.444$ or $r > .444$.

Since the observed value of the test statistic does not fall in the rejection region ($r = .035 \not> .444$), H_0 is not rejected. There is insufficient evidence to indicate total cash compensation and total shareholder return are linearly related at $\alpha = .05$.

c. The least squares line is $\hat{y} = 4498.49 + 2.574x$.

$$s^2 = \frac{SSE}{n-2} = \frac{273,415.656.8}{20-2} = 15,189,758.71$$

$$s = \sqrt{15,189,758.71} = 3897.4041$$

To determine if a linear relationship exists between the two variables, we test:

H_0: $\beta_1 = 0$
H_a: $\beta_1 \neq 0$

The test statistic is $t = \dfrac{\hat{\beta_1}}{\dfrac{s}{\sqrt{SS_{xx}}}} = \dfrac{2.574}{\dfrac{3897.4041}{\sqrt{50,532.2}}} = .15$

For a two-tailed alternative, the rejection region requires $\alpha/2 = .05/2 = .025$ in each tail of the t distribution with $n - 2 = 20 - 2 = 18$ df. From Table 6, Appendix E, $t_{.025} = 2.101$. The rejection region is $t < -2.101$ or $t > 2.101$.

Since the observed value of the test statistic does not fall in the rejection region ($t = .15 \not> 2.101$), H_0 is not rejected. There is insufficient evidence to indicate total cash compensation and total shareholder return are linearly related at $\alpha = .05$.

This is the same conclusion reached in part (b).

d. For $x = 300$, $\hat{y} = 4498.49 + 2.574(300) = 5270.69$.

The form of the prediction interval is

$$\hat{y} \pm t_{\alpha/2}s\sqrt{1 + \frac{1}{n} + \frac{(x - \bar{x})^2}{SS_{xx}}}$$

For confidence coefficient .95, $\alpha = .05$ and $\alpha/2 = .05/2 = .025$. From Table 6, Appendix E, with $n - 2 = 20 - 2 = 18$, $t_{.025} = 2.101$. The 95% prediction interval is

$$5270.69 \pm 2.101(3897.4041)\sqrt{1 + \frac{1}{20} + \frac{(300 - 182.7)^2}{50,532.2}}$$

$\Rightarrow 5270.69 \pm 9415.957 \Rightarrow (-4145.267, 14,686.647)$

We are 95% confident the total cash compensation is between $-4,145.267$ and $14,686.647$ thousand dollars when the total shareholder return is $300.

FIFTEEN MULTIPLE REGRESSION

15.1 a. $E(y) = \beta_0 + \beta_1 x_1 + \beta_2 x_2$

15.3 a. For $x_2 = 0$, $E(y) = 1 + 2x_1 + 0 = 1 + 2x_1$

For $x_2 = 1$, $E(y) = 1 + 2x_1 + 1 = 2 + 2x_1$

For $x_2 = 2$, $E(y) = 1 + 2x_1 + 2 = 3 + 2x_1$

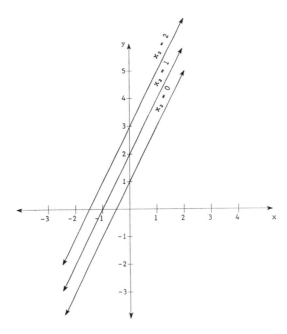

b. The three lines are parallel. Each line has a slope of 2.

c. When $E(y)$ is graphed as a function of one of the independent variables for various values of the other independent variable, the lines will be parallel.

15.5　a.　$s^2 = \dfrac{SSE}{n - \text{number of } \beta's} = \dfrac{.439}{15 - 5} = .0439$

b.　$SS(Model) = SS(Total) - SSE = 1.690 - .439 = 1.251$

$$F = \dfrac{SS(Model)}{SSE} \left[\dfrac{n - (k + 1)}{k} \right] = \dfrac{1.251}{.439} \left[\dfrac{15 - (4 + 1)}{4} \right] = 7.12$$

c.　To determine if the model contributes information for predicting y, we test:

H_0:　$\beta_1 = \beta_2 = \beta_3 = \beta_4 = 0$
H_a:　At least one $\beta_i \neq 0$

The test statistic is $F = 7.12$.

The rejection region requires $\alpha = .05$ in the upper tail of the F distribution with k = 4 numerator degrees of freedom and $n - (k + 1) = 15 - (4 + 1) = 10$ denominator degrees of freedom. From Table 8, Appendix E, $F_{.05} = 3.48$. The rejection region is $F > 3.48$.

Since the observed value of the test statistic falls in the rejection region ($F = 7.12 > 3.48$), H_0 is rejected. There is sufficient evidence to indicate the model contributes information for predicting y at $\alpha = .05$.

15.7　H_0:　$\beta_1 = \beta_2 = \beta_3 = 0$
H_a:　At least one $\beta_i \neq 0$

The test statistic is $F = \left[\dfrac{R^2}{1 - R^2} \right] \left[\dfrac{n - (k + 1)}{k} \right]$

$$= \left[\dfrac{.2623}{1 - .2623} \right] \left[\dfrac{20 - (3 + 1)}{3} \right] = 1.896$$

The rejection region requires $\alpha = .05$ in the upper tail of the F distribution with numerator df = k = 3 and denominator df = $n - (k + 1) = 20 - (3 + 1) = 16$. From Table 8, Appendix E, $F_{.05} = 3.24$. The rejection region is $F > 3.24$.

Since the observed value of the test statistic does not fall in the rejection region ($F = 1.896 \not> 3.24$), H_0 is not rejected. There is insufficient evidence to indicate at least one of the β's is not 0 at $\alpha = .05$.

15.9　a.　For $x_2 = 0$, $\hat{y} = 70.9770 - .2167x_1 - 0 = 70.9770 - .2167x_1$

For $x_2 = 1$, $\hat{y} = 70.9770 - .2167x_1 - 13.2768(1) = 57.7002 - .2167x_1$

For $x_2 = 2$, $\hat{y} = 70.9770 - .2167x_1 - 13.2768(2) = 44.4234 - .2167x_1$

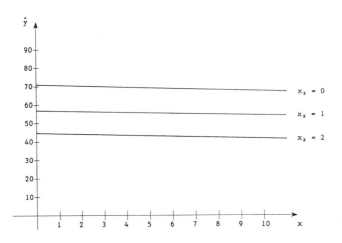

b. To determine if the model is useful for predicting percentage y of metric work performed, we test:

H_0: $\beta_1 = \beta_2 = 0$
H_a: At least one $\beta_i \neq 0$

The test statistic is $F = \left[\dfrac{R^2}{1 - R^2}\right]\left[\dfrac{n - (k + 1)}{k}\right]$

$= \left[\dfrac{.0576}{1 - .0576}\right]\left[\dfrac{350 - (2 + 1)}{2}\right] = 10.604$

The rejection region requires $\alpha = .01$ in the upper tail of the F distribution with numerator df = k = 2 and denominator df = n − (k + 1) = 350 − (2 + 1) = 347. From Table 10, Appendix E, $F_{.01} = 4.61$. The rejection region is F > 4.61.

Since the observed value of the test statistic falls in the rejection region (F = 10.604 > 4.61), H_0 is rejected. There is sufficient evidence to indicate the model is useful for predicting percentage y of metric work performed at $\alpha = .01$.

c. To determine if the percentage y of metric work performed decreases as age x_1 of the company increases, we test:

H_0: $\beta_1 = 0$
H_a: $\beta_1 < 0$

The test statistic is t = −1.56.

The rejection region requires $\alpha = .05$ in the lower tail of the t distribution with df = n − (k + 1) = 350 − (2 + 1) = 347. From Table 6, Appendix E, $t_{.05} = 1.645$. The rejection region is t < −1.645.

Since the observed value of the test statistic does not fall in the rejection region (t = -1.56 $\not<$ -1.645), H_0 is not rejected. There is insufficient evidence to indicate the percentage y of metric work performed decreases as age x_1 of the company increases for companies with the same cost x_2 of conversion at α = .05.

15.11   To determine if the model is useful for predicting the number y of defects in modules of the software product, we test:

H_0: $\beta_1 = \beta_2 = 0$
H_a: At least one $\beta_i \neq 0$

The test statistic is $F = \left[\dfrac{R^2}{1 - R^2} \right] \left[\dfrac{n - (k + 1)}{k} \right]$

$= \left[\dfrac{.78}{1 - .78} \right] \left[\dfrac{253 - (2 + 1)}{2} \right] = 443.18$

The rejection region requires α = .05 in the upper tail of the F distribution with numerator df = k = 2 and denominator df = n - (k + 1) = 253 - (2 + 1) = 250. From Table 8, Appendix E, $F_{.05}$ = 3.00. The rejection region is F > 3.00.

Since the observed value of the test statistic falls in the rejection region (F = 443.18 > 3.00), H_0 is rejected. There is sufficient evidence to indicate the model is useful for predicting the number y of defects in modules of the software product at α = .05.

15.13   a.   To determine if the model is useful for estimating mean bid price, we test:

H_0: $\beta_1 = \beta_2 = 0$
H_a: At least one $\beta_i \neq 0$

The test statistic is F = 120.65.

The p-value = .0001. Since the p-value is less than α = .05, H_0 is rejected. There is sufficient evidence to indicate the model is useful for estimating mean bid price at α = .05.

b.   To determine if the mean bid price increases as the number of bidders increases for road construction projects of the same length, we test:

H_0: $\beta_2 = 0$
H_a: $\beta_2 > 0$

The test statistic is t = 9.86.

The p-value = .0001/2 = .00005. Since the p-value is less than α = .01, H_0 is rejected. There is sufficient evidence to indicate the mean bid price increases as the number of bidders increases for road construction projects of the same length at $\alpha = .01$.

c. R^2 = R-SQUARE = .892713. This implies that 89.27% of the sum of squares of deviations of the bid prices about their mean can be attributed to the regression model.

d. $\hat{\sigma}$ = ROOT MSE = 133.1365. We expect the model with length of road miles (x_1) and number of bidders (x_2) to predict bid price (y) to within 2s or 2(133.1365) or 266.273 thousands of dollars of its true value.

e. The confidence interval is (84.726, 647.18). We are 95% confident the mean bid price will fall between 84.726 and 647.18 thousand dollars when the length of road miles is 100 and the number of bidders is 5.

f. The width of the prediction interval is always wider than the confidence interval for the mean.

15.15 a. $E(y) = \beta_0 + \beta_1 x_1 + \beta_2 x_2 + \beta_3 x_3 + \beta_4 x_4 + \beta_5 x_5 + \beta_6 x_6 + \beta_7 x_7 + \beta_8 x_8 + \beta_9 x_9$

b. To determine if the model is useful for predicting y, we test:

H_0: $\beta_1 = \beta_2 = \beta_3 = \beta_4 = \beta_5 = \beta_6 = \beta_7 = \beta_8 = \beta_9 = 0$
H_a: At least one $\beta_i \neq 0$

The test statistic is F = 4.96.

The p-value = .0001. Since the p-value is less than $\alpha = .01$, H_0 is rejected. There is sufficient evidence to indicate the model is useful for predicting y at $\alpha = .01$.

c. R^2 = R-SQUARE = .3844. This implies 38.44% of the sum of squares of deviations of the call frequency of salespersons per year values around their mean can be attributed to the regression model.

d. s = ROOT MSE = $\sqrt{.104}$ = .3225. We expect the model with the 9 independent variables to predict the call frequency of salespersons per year to within 2s or 2(.3225) or .645 of its actual value.

e. H_0: $\beta_1 = 0$
H_a: $\beta_1 \neq 0$

The p-value = .165. Since the p-value is not less than $\alpha = .01$, H_0 is not rejected. There is insufficient evidence to indicate time in territory is useful in predicting call frequency.

H_0: $\beta_2 = 0$
H_a: $\beta_2 \neq 0$

The p-value = .678. Since the p-value is not less than $\alpha = .01$, H_0 is not rejected. There is insufficient evidence to indicate rebuy customer is useful in predicting call frequency.

H_0: $\beta_3 = 0$
H_a: $\beta_3 \neq 0$

The p-value = .005. Since the p-value is less than $\alpha = .01$, H_0 is rejected. There is sufficient evidence to indicate important purchase decision is useful in predicting call frequency.

H_0: $\beta_4 = 0$
H_a: $\beta_4 \neq 0$

The p-value = .006. Since the p-value is less than $\alpha = .01$, H_0 is rejected. There is sufficient evidence to indicate role consensus is useful in predicting call frequency.

H_0: $\beta_5 = 0$
H_a: $\beta_5 \neq 0$

The p-value = .194. Since the p-value is not less than $\alpha = .01$, H_0 is not rejected. There is insufficient evidence to indicate product shortage is useful in predicting call frequency.

H_0: $\beta_6 = 0$
H_a: $\beta_6 \neq 0$

The p-value = .151. Since the p-value is not less than $\alpha = .01$, H_0 is not rejected. There is insufficient evidence to indicate competition is useful in predicting call frequency.

H_0: $\beta_7 = 0$
H_a: $\beta_7 \neq 0$

The p-value = .013. Since the p-value is not less than $\alpha = .01$, H_0 is not rejected. There is insufficient evidence to indicate disposition is useful in predicting call frequency.

H_0: $\beta_8 = 0$
H_a: $\beta_8 \neq 0$

The p-value = .556. Since the p-value is not less than $\alpha = .01$, H_0 is not rejected. There is insufficient evidence to indicate congeniality is useful in predicting call frequency.

$H_0: \quad \beta_9 = 0$
$H_a: \quad \beta_9 \neq 0$

The p-value = .000. Since the p-value is less than $\alpha = .01$, H_0 is rejected. There is sufficient evidence to indicate important customer is useful in predicting call frequency.

   f.   When several tests are conducted, the probability of Type I error increases above the level of α used for each test.

15.17   To determine if the model is useful for predicting CPU time, we test:

$H_0: \quad \beta_1 = \beta_2 = \ldots = \beta_{18} = 0$
$H_a: \quad$ At least one $\beta_i \neq 0$

The test statistic is $F = \left[\dfrac{R^2}{1 - R^2} \right] \left[\dfrac{n - (k + 1)}{k} \right]$

$\qquad = \left[\dfrac{.95}{1 - .95} \right] \left[\dfrac{20 - (18 + 1)}{18} \right] = 1.056$

The rejection region requires $\alpha = .05$ in the upper tail of the F distribution with numerator df = k = 18 and denominator df = n - (k + 1) = 20 - (18 + 1) = 1. From Table 8, Appendix E, $F_{.05} \approx 245.9$. The rejection region is F > 245.9.

Since the observed value of the test statistic does not fall in the rejection region (F = 1.056 $\not>$ 245.9), H_0 is not rejected. There is insufficient evidence to indicate the model is important for predicting CPU time at $\alpha = .05$.

15.19 $E(y) = \beta_0 + \beta_1 x_1 + \beta_2 x_2 + \beta_3 x_1 x_2$

15.21   a.   For $x_2 = 0$, $E(y) = 1 + 2x_1 + 0 - 3x_1(0) = 1 + 2x_1$

            For $x_2 = 1$, $E(y) = 1 + 2x_1 + 1 - 3x_1(1) = 2 - x_1$

            For $x_2 = 2$, $E(y) = 1 + 2x_1 + 2 - 3x_1(2) = 3 - 4x_1$

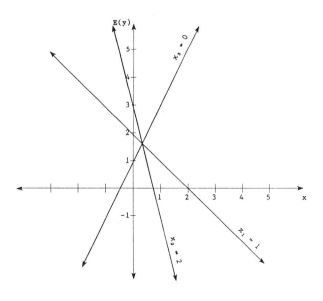

b. In Exercise 15.3, the lines are parallel. In this exercise, the lines are not parallel--the slopes are different.

c. When $x_2 = 0$, the slope is 2.
When $x_2 = 1$, the slope is -1.
When $x_2 = 2$, the slope is -4.

15.23 a. To determine whether the model is adequate for predicting subordinate performance, we test:

H_0: $\beta_1 = \beta_2 = \beta_3 = 0$
H_a: At least one $\beta_i \neq 0$

The test statistic is $F = \left[\dfrac{R^2}{1 - R^2}\right]\left[\dfrac{n - (k + 1)}{k}\right]$

$= \left[\dfrac{.22}{1 - .22}\right]\left[\dfrac{89 - (3 + 1)}{3}\right] = 7.99$

The rejection region requires $\alpha = .10$ in the upper tail of the F distribution with numerator df = k = 3 and denominator df = n − (k + 1) = 89 − (3 + 1) = 85. From Table 7, Appendix E, $F_{.10} \approx 2.18$. The rejection region is F > 2.18.

Since the observed value of the test statistic falls in the rejection region (F = 7.99 > 2.18), H_0 is rejected. There is sufficient evidence to indicate the model is adequate for predicting subordinate performance at $\alpha = .10$.

MULTIPLE REGRESSION

b. For $x_2 = 1$, $\hat{y} = 7.09 - .44x_1 - .01(1) + .06x_1(1) = 7.08 - .38x_1$

For $x_2 = 7$, $\hat{y} = 7.09 - .44x_1 - .01(7) + .06x_1(7) = 7.02 - .02x_1$

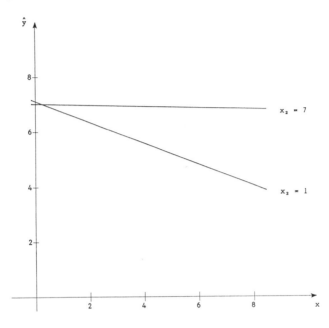

When $x_2 = 1$, as x_1 increases, y decreases at a much greater rate than when $x_2 = 7$.

c. To determine if the relationship between subordinate performance and manager's use of group decision method depends on a manager's legitimization of conflict, we test:

H_0: $\beta_3 = 0$
H_a: $\beta_3 \neq 0$

The test statistic is t = 1.85.

The rejection region requires $\alpha/2 = .10/2 = .05$ in each tail of the t distribution with df = n - (k + 1) = 89 - (3 + 1) = 85. From Table 6, Appendix E, $t_{.05} \approx 1.671$. The rejection region is t < -1.671 or t > 1.671.

Since the observed value of the test statistic falls in the rejection region (t = 1.85 > 1.671), H_0 is rejected. There is sufficient evidence to indicate the relationship between subordinate performance and manager's use of group decision method depends on a manager's legitimization of conflict at α = .10.

d. No. Since the interaction term is significant, the main effects of each of the variables may be covered up. The main effect terms should be included in the model regardless of the magnitude of the p-values.

15.25 a. Nuclear Stocks: $\hat{y} = -17.556 + .519x_1 + 10.889x_2 + .132x_1x_2$

Nonnuclear Stocks: $\hat{y} = -44.682 + 2.880x_1 + 25.062x_2 - .959x_1x_2$

b. To determine if the model is useful for predicting the price of nuclear stocks, we test:

H_0: $\beta_1 = \beta_2 = \beta_3 = 0$
H_a: At least one $\beta_i \neq 0$

The test statistic is F = 13.217.

The p-value = .0018. Since the p-value is less than α = .05, H_0 is rejected. There is sufficient evidence to indicate the model is useful for predicting the price of nuclear stocks at α = .05.

To determine if the model is useful for predicting the price of nonnuclear stocks, we test:

H_0: $\beta_1 = \beta_2 = \beta_3 = 0$
H_a: At least one $\beta_i \neq 0$

The test statistic is F = 60.851.

The p-value = .0001. Since the p-value is less than α = .05, H_0 is rejected. There is sufficient evidence to indicate the model is useful for predicting the price of nonnuclear stocks at α = .05.

c. To determine if interaction exists between return on equity and dividend rate for nuclear stocks, we test:

H_0: $\beta_3 = 0$
H_a: $\beta_3 \neq 0$

The test statistic is t = .118.

The p-value = .9093. Since the p-value is greater than α = .05, H_0 is not rejected. There is insufficient evidence to indicate return on equity and dividend rate interact at α = .05.

To determine if interaction exists between return on equity and dividend rate for nonnuclear stocks, we test:

H_0: $\beta_3 = 0$
H_a: $\beta_3 \neq 0$

The test statistic is t = -1.388.

The p-value = .1904. Since the p-value is greater than α = .05, H_0 is not rejected. There is insufficient evidence to indicate return on equity and dividend rate interact at α = .05.

    d.   The prediction interval is (7.4528, 26.8903).

    e.   We are 95% confident the actual price of a nuclear stock is between 7.4528 and 26.8903 when return on equity is 13.3 and dividend rate is 2.20.

    f.   No. For nuclear stocks, the observed range for dividend rate (x_2) is from 1.40 to 3.00. A dividend rate of 1.10 is outside the observed range. It is very risky to predict values of price per share for values of dividend rate outside the observed range.

15.27 a. $E(y) = \beta_0 + \beta_1 x_1 + \beta_2 x_2 + \beta_3 x_1 x_2$

       b. The graphs in Exercise 15.9 are parallel lines. If the interaction of x_1 and x_2 is significant, the graphs will no longer be parallel lines.

15.29 a. - c.

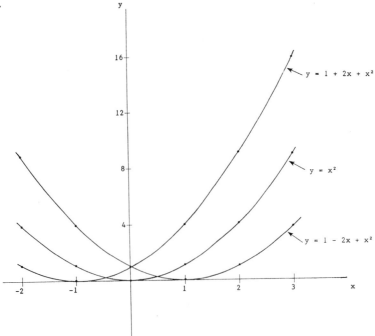

    d. Including 2x shifts the curve to the right or left, but does not change the shape.

    e. If the first-order term is positive, the curve is shifted to the left. If the first-order term is negative, the curve is shifted to the right.

15.31 a. To determine if the model contributes information for predicting y, we test:

H_0: $\beta_1 = \beta_2 = 0$
H_a: At least one $\beta_i \neq 0$

The test statistic is $F = \left[\dfrac{R^2}{1 - R^2}\right]\left[\dfrac{n - (k + 1)}{k}\right]$

$= \left[\dfrac{.91}{1 - .91}\right]\left[\dfrac{20 - (2 + 1)}{2}\right] = 85.94$

The rejection region requires $\alpha = .05$ in the upper tail of the F distribution with numerator df = k = 2 and denominator df = n − (k + 1) = 20 − (2 + 1) = 17. From Table 8, Appendix E, $F_{.05} = 3.59$. The rejection region is F > 3.59.

Since the observed value of the test statistic falls in the rejection region (F = 85.94 > 3.59), H_0 is rejected. There is sufficient evidence to indicate the model contributes information for predicting y at $\alpha = .05$.

    b. H_0: $\beta_2 = 0$
       H_a: $\beta_2 > 0$

    c. H_0: $\beta_2 = 0$
       H_a: $\beta_2 < 0$

15.33 a. For $x_2 = 0$, $E(y) = 1 + x_1 - 0 + x_1(0) + 2x_1^2 + 0^2 = 1 + x_1 + 2x_1^2$

For $x_2 = 1$, $E(y) = 1 + x_1 - 1 + x_1(1) + 2x_1^2 + 1^2 = 1 + 2x_1 + 2x_1^2$

For $x_2 = 2$, $E(y) = 1 + x_1 - 2 + x_1(2) + 2x_1^2 + 2^2 = 3 + 3x_1 + 2x_1^2$

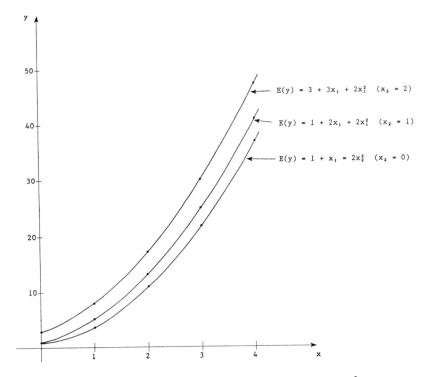

$E(y) = 3 + 3x_1 + 2x_1^2 \quad (x_2 = 2)$

$E(y) = 1 + 2x_1 + 2x_1^2 \quad (x_2 = 1)$

$E(y) = 1 + x_1 = 2x_2^2 \quad (x_2 = 0)$

b. All graphs are second-order because all have an x^2 term.

c. All are curves, but all have different centers and different shapes.

15.35   a.

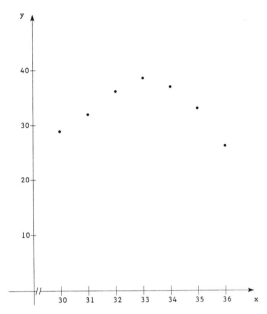

b.   If we were given only the information for x = 30, 31, 32, 33, we
would recommend a linear model. For data for x = 33, 34, 35, 36,
again we would recommend a linear model. For all data, we would
recommend a quadratic model.

15.37   a.

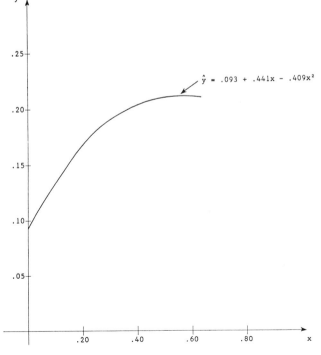

$\hat{y} = .093 + .441x - .409x^2$

b. $R^2 = .002$. This implies .2% of the sum of squares of deviations of the returns on assets about their mean can be attributed to the regression model.

c. To determine if market share is a useful predictor of return on assets, we test:

H_0: $\beta_1 = \beta_2 = 0$
H_a: At least one $\beta_i \neq 0$

The test statistic is $F = \left[\dfrac{R^2}{1 - R^2}\right]\left[\dfrac{n - (k + 1)}{k}\right]$

$= \left[\dfrac{.002}{1 - .002}\right]\left[\dfrac{5400 - (2 + 1)}{2}\right] = 5.41$

The rejection region requires $\alpha = .05$ in the upper tail of the F distribution with numerator df $= k = 2$ and denominator df $= n - (k + 1) = 5400 - (2 + 1) = 5397$. From Table 8, Appendix E, $F_{.05} \approx 3.00$. The rejection region is $F > 3.00$.

Since the observed value of the test statistic falls in the rejection region ($F = 5.41 > 3.00$), H_0 is rejected. There is sufficient evidence to indicate market share is a useful predictor of return on assets at $\alpha = .05$.

d. To test for downward curvature, we test:

H_0: $\beta_2 = 0$
H_a: $\beta_2 < 0$

The test statistic is $t = -2.39$.

The rejection region requires $\alpha = .05$ in the lower tail of the t distribution with df $= n - (k + 1) = 5400 - (2 + 1) = 5397$. From Table 6, Appendix E, $t_{.05} = 1.645$. The rejection region is $t < -1.645$.

Since the observed value of the test statistic falls in the rejection region ($t = -2.39 < -1.645$), H_0 is rejected. There is sufficient evidence to indicate that profits rise with size of market share up to some intermediate level, and taper off thereafter at $\alpha = .05$.

15.39 a. H_0: $\beta_1 = \beta_2 = \beta_3 = \beta_4 = \beta_5 = 0$
H_a: At least one $\beta_i \neq 0$

b. The test statistic is $F = \dfrac{MST}{MSE} = \dfrac{982.31}{53.84} = 18.24$

The rejection region requires α = .05 in the upper tail of the F
distribution with numerator df = k = 5 and denominator
df = n - (k + 1) = 40 - (5 + 1) = 34.   From Table 8, Appendix E,
$F_{.05}$ ≈ 2.53.   The rejection region is F > 2.53.

Since the observed value of the test statistic falls in the
rejection region, (F = 18.24 > 2.53), H_0 is rejected.   There is
sufficient evidence to indicate the complete second-order model
contributes information for the prediction of y, the applicant's
merit rating after 3 years at α = .05.

15.41   a.

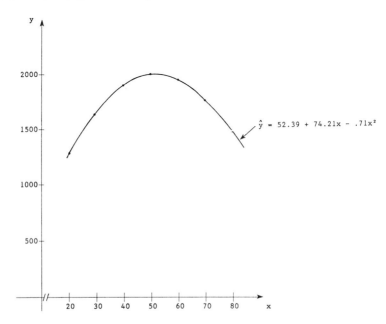

$\hat{y} = 52.39 + 74.21x - .71x^2$

b.   To determine if a quadratic relationship exists, we test:

H_0: β_2 = 0
H_a: β_2 ≠ 0

The test statistic is t = -.15.

The rejection region requires $\alpha/2$ = .10/2 = .05 in each tail of
the t distribution with df = n - (k + 1) > 20,000 - (2 + 1)
> 19,997.   From Table 6, Appendix E, $t_{.05}$ = 1.645.   The rejection
region is t < -1.645 or t > 1.645.

Since the observed value of the test statistic does not fall in
the rejection region (t = -.15 ≮ -1.645), H_0 is not rejected.
There is insufficient evidence to indicate a quadratic
relationship in the wealth-age relationship for the Utah
households during 1860 to 1870 at α = .10.

Even though there is a distinct curve to the fitted regression line, it may be that no one over the age of 60 was surveyed. If $x < 60$, the relationship looks to be rather linear.

15.43   a. $E(y) = \beta_0 + \beta_1 x_1 + \beta_2 x_2 + \beta_3 x_3$

where $x_1 = \begin{cases} 1 \text{ if A} \\ 0 \text{ if not} \end{cases}$ $x_2 = \begin{cases} 1 \text{ if B} \\ 0 \text{ if not} \end{cases}$ $x_3 = \begin{cases} 1 \text{ if C} \\ 0 \text{ if not} \end{cases}$

β_0 = mean response for D, μ_D

β_1 = difference between the mean responses of A and D, $\mu_A - \mu_D$.

β_2 = difference between the mean responses of B and D, $\mu_B - \mu_D$.

β_3 = difference between the mean responses of C and D, $\mu_C - \mu_D$.

15.45   a. $\hat{\beta}_0$ = estimated mean response for level 5, $\bar{x}_5 = 20$

$\hat{\beta}_1$ = estimated difference between the mean responses for levels 1 and 5, $\bar{x}_1 - \bar{x}_5 = -5.6$.

$\hat{\beta}_2$ = estimated difference between the mean responses for levels 2 and 5, $\bar{x}_2 - \bar{x}_5 = 11.2$.

$\hat{\beta}_3$ = estimated difference between the mean responses for levels 3 and 5, $\bar{x}_3 - \bar{x}_5 = -1.7$.

$\hat{\beta}_4$ = estimated difference between the mean responses for levels 4 and 5, $\bar{x}_4 - \bar{x}_5 = -9.0$.

b. $H_0: \mu_1 = \mu_2 = \mu_3 = \mu_4 = \mu_5$
$H_a:$ At least one mean differs

c.   The test statistic is $F = \left[\dfrac{SS(Model)}{SSE}\right]\left[\dfrac{n - (k + 1)}{k}\right]$

where $SS(Model) = SS(Total) - SSE = 1043 - 662 = 381$.

$F = \left[\dfrac{381}{662}\right]\left[\dfrac{20 - (4 + 1)}{4}\right] = 2.16$

The rejection region requires $\alpha = .05$ in the upper tail of the F distribution with numerator df = k = 4 and denominator df = n - (k + 1) = 20 - (4 + 1) = 15. From Table 8, Appendix E, $F_{.05} = 3.06$. The rejection region is F > 3.06.

Since the observed value of the test statistic does not fall in the rejection region (F = 2.16 $\ngtr$ 3.06), H_0 is not rejected. There is insufficient evidence to indicate a difference exists among the 5 level means at $\alpha = .05$.

15.47 a. To determine if the model is adequate for predicting y, we test:

H_0: $\beta_1 = \beta_2 = \beta_3 = \beta_4 = \beta_5 = \beta_6 = \beta_7 = \beta_8 = 0$
H_a: At least one $\beta_i \neq 0$

The test statistic is $F = 53.2$.

The p-value = .001. Since the p-value is less than $\alpha = .05$, H_0 is rejected. (α is not given, so .05 is arbitrarily chosen). There is sufficient evidence to indicate the model is adequate for predicting y at $\alpha = .05$.

The p-value = $P(F \geq 53.2) = .001$. The probability of observing a test statistic of 53.2 or more when H_0 is true is .001. We will reject H_0 for all values of α greater than .001.

b. $s = \sqrt{MSE} = \sqrt{.035} = .187$. We expect the model with the 8 independent variables to predict the natural log of 1977 salary to within 2s or 2(.187) = .374 of its actual value.

c. $R^2 = \dfrac{SS(Model)}{SS(Total)} = \dfrac{14.710}{21.728} = .677$. This implies 67.7% of the sum of squares of deviations of the natural log of 1977 salaries about their means is attributed to the regression model.

d. Confidence coefficient .99 = 1 - α = α = 1 - .99 = .01 and $\alpha/2$ = .01/2 = .005. From Table 6, Appendix E, with df = n - (k + 1) = 212 - (8 + 1) = 203, $t_{.005} = 2.576$. The confidence interval is

$$\hat{\beta}_6 \pm t_{.005}s(\hat{\beta}_6) \Rightarrow -.046 \pm 2.576(.028)$$
$$\Rightarrow -.046 \pm .072 \Rightarrow (-.118, .026)$$

We are 99% confident the difference between the mean natural log of 1977 salaries for whites and blacks is between -.118 and .026.

e. To determine if salary discrimination exists against black baseball players, we test:

H_0: $\beta_6 = 0$
H_a: $\beta_6 > 0$

The test statistic is $t = -1.64$.

The p-value = $P(t \geq -1.64) = 1 - .100/2 = .95$. Since the p-value is greater than $\alpha = .01$, H_0 is not rejected. There is insufficient evidence to indicate salary discrimination exists against black baseball players at $\alpha = .01$.

15.49 a. $\hat{\beta}_0 = \bar{x}_3 = 66.97$

$\hat{\beta}_1 = \bar{x}_1 - \bar{x}_3 = 71.00 - 66.97 = 4.03$

$\hat{\beta}_2 = \bar{x}_2 - \bar{x}_3 = 72.52 - 66.97 = 5.55$

The least squares line is $\hat{y} = 66.97 + 4.03x_1 + 5.55x_2$

b. To determine if differences exist among the mean risk-taking propensities of the three groups of managers, we test:

H_0: $\beta_1 = \beta_2 = 0$
H_a: At least one $\beta_i \neq 0$

15.51 a. The reduced model is $E(y) = \beta_0 + \beta_1x_1 + \beta_2x_2 + \beta_3x_3$

b. The test statistic is $F = \dfrac{(SSE_1 - SSE_2)/(k - g)}{SSE_2/[n - (k + 1)]}$

$= \dfrac{(8500 - 6000)/(6 - 3)}{6000/[25 - (6 + 1)]} = \dfrac{833.3333}{333.3333} = 2.5$

c. The rejection region requires $\alpha = .05$ in the upper tail of the F distribution with $\nu_1 = k - g = 6 - 3 = 3$ and $\nu_2 = n - (k + 1) = 25 - (6 + 1) = 18$. From Table 8, Appendix E, $F_{.05} = 3.16$. The rejection region is $F > 3.16$.

d. Since the observed value of the test statistic does not fall in the rejection region ($F = 2.5 \ngtr 3.16$), H_0 is not rejected. There is insufficient evidence to indicate the complete model is better than the reduced model at $\alpha = .05$.

15.53 a. H_0: $\beta_2 = \beta_3 = 0$
H_a: At least one $\beta_i \neq 0$

b. The test statistic is $F = \dfrac{(SSE_1 - SSE_2)/(k - g)}{SSE_2/[n - (k + 1)]}$

$= \dfrac{(183.2 - 140.5)/(3 - 1)}{140.5/[50 - (3 + 1)]} = \dfrac{21.35}{3.0543} = 6.99$

c. The rejection region requires $\alpha = .05$ in the upper tail of the F distribution with $\nu_1 = k - g = 3 - 1 = 2$ and $\nu_2 = n - (k + 1) = 50 - (3 + 1) = 46$. From Table 8, Appendix E, $F_{.05} \approx 3.23$. The rejection region is $F > 3.23$.

Since the observed value of the test statistic falls in the rejection region ($F = 6.99 > 3.23$), H_0 is rejected. There is sufficient evidence to indicate the mean monthly sales differ for salespeople trained by the three programs at $\alpha = .05$.

15.55 a. β_3, β_4, β_5, β_6, β_7, β_8, β_9, β_{10}, β_{11}

b. H_0: $\beta_3 = \beta_4 = \beta_5 = \beta_6 = \beta_7 = \beta_8 = \beta_9 = \beta_{10} = \beta_{11} = 0$
   H_a: At least one $\beta_i \neq 0$

c. β_2, β_9, β_{10}, β_{11}

15.57 a. The curvilinear trend implies a misspecified model. A quadratic term needs to be added.

b. The spread of the residuals increasing as $\hat{y}$ increases implies unequal variances.

c. A residual lying more than 3 standard deviations form the mean implies an outlier is present.

d. The spread of the residuals increasing and then decreasing as $\hat{y}$ increases implies unequal variances.

e. The histogram indicates nonnormal errors because it is skewed to the right.

15.59 a. First we compute $\hat{y}$ for each value of x using the formula $\hat{y} = -3.179 + 2.491x$. The residual is then found using $y - \hat{y}$. For $x = 2$, $\hat{y} = -3.179 + 2.491(2) = 1.803$. The residual is $5 - 1.803 = 3.197$. The rest of the values for $\hat{y}$ and the residuals are found in a similar manner and are shown in the table:

x	y	$\hat{y}$	$(y - \hat{y})$
2	5	1.803	3.197
4	10	6.785	3.215
7	12	14.258	-2.258
10	22	21.731	.269
12	25	26.713	-1.713
15	27	34.186	-7.186
18	39	41.659	-2.659
20	50	46.641	3.359
21	47	49.132	-2.132
25	65	59.096	5.904

b.

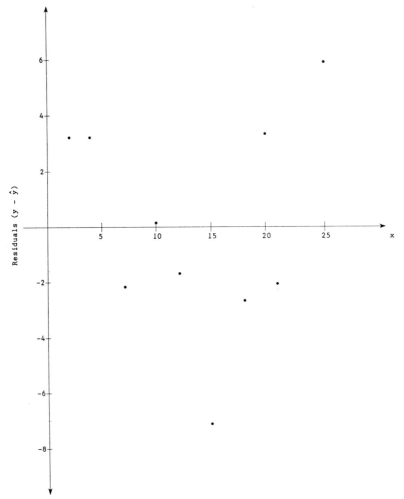

There appears to be a curvature trend to the residual plot. This implies a quadratic term needs to be added.

c.

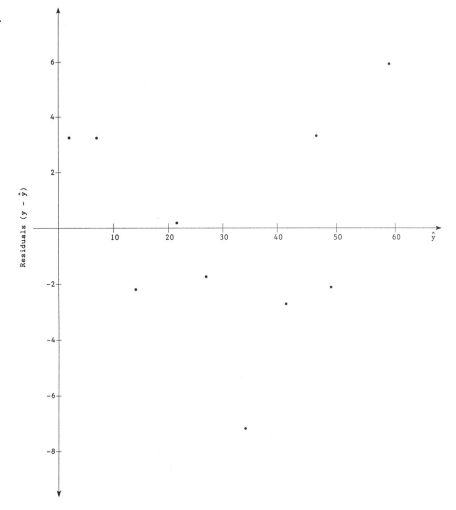

3(s) = 3(4.154) = 12.462. There are no points that lie above
12.462 or below -12.462. Thus, there are no outliers.

d. The shape of the graph in part (c) is similar to that in part (a).
Thus, a quadratic term should be added.

15.61 a. First we compute $\hat{y}$ for each set of values of x_1 and x_2, using the
formula $\hat{y}$ = 9.782 + 1.871x_1 + 1.278x_2. The residual is then found
using $y - \hat{y}$. For x_1 = 23 and x_2 = 5, $\hat{y}$ = 9.782 + 1.871(23)
+ 1.278(5) = 59.205.

The residual is $y - \hat{y}$ = 60.0 - 59.205 = .795. The rest of the
values of $\hat{y}$ and the residuals are found in a similar manner and
are shown in the table:

x_1	x_2	y	$\hat{y}$	$(y - \hat{y})$
23	5	60.0	59.205	.795
11	2	32.7	32.919	-.219
20	9	57.7	58.704	-1.004
17	3	45.5	45.423	.077
15	8	47.0	48.071	-1.071
21	4	55.3	54.185	1.115
24	7	64.5	63.632	.868
13	6	42.6	41.773	.827
19	7	54.5	54.277	.223
25	2	57.5	59.113	-1.613

b.

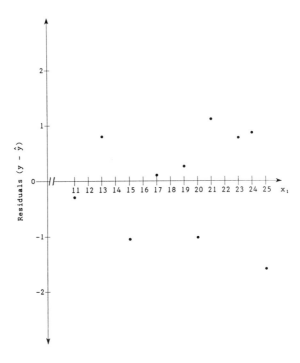

No trends appear in this plot.

c.

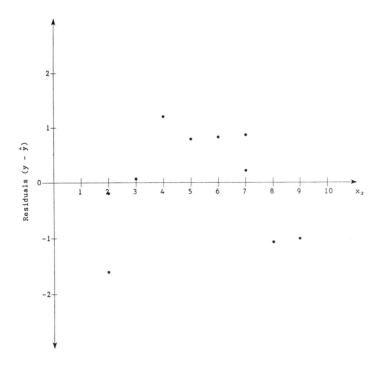

There appears to be a curvature trend to the residual plot. This implies a quadratic term in x_2 needs to be added to the model, $\beta_3 x_2^2$.

15.63 a. The least squares model is $\hat{y} = 200.4 - .78x + .000987x^2$. First we compute $\hat{y}$ for each value of x using the least squares model. The residual is then found using $y - \hat{y}$. For $x = 100$, $\hat{y} = 200.4 - .78(100) + .000987(100^2) = 132.27$. The residual is $y - \hat{y} = 130 - 132.27 = -2.27$. The rest of the values of $\hat{y}$ and the residuals are found in a similar manner and are shown in the table.

x	y	$\hat{y}$	$(y - \hat{y})$
100	130	132.27	-2.27
700	150	138.03	11.97
450	60	49.2675	10.7325
150	120	105.6075	14.3925
500	50	57.15	-7.15
800	200	208.08	-8.08
70	150	150.6363	-.6363
50	160	163.8675	-3.8675
300	50	55.23	-5.23
350	40	48.3075	-8.3075
750	180	170.5875	9.4125
700	130	138.03	-8.03

b.

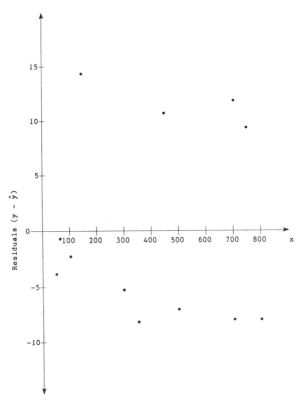

c. No trend is apparent.

d. To determine if the model is useful for predicting demand, we test:

H_0: $\beta_1 = \beta_2 = 0$
H_a: At least one $\beta_i \neq 0$

The test statistic is $F = 171.98$.

The rejection region requires $\alpha = .05$ in the upper tail of the F distributions with $\nu_1 = k = 2$ and $\nu_2 = n - (k + 1) = 12 - (2 + 1) = 9$. From Table 8, Appendix E, $F_{.05} = 4.26$. The rejection region is $F > 4.26$.

Since the observed value of the test statistic falls in the rejection region ($F = 171.98 > 4.26$), H_0 is rejected. There is sufficient evidence to indicate the model is useful for predicting demand at $\alpha = .05$.

The value of R^2 is .975. This indicates 97.5% of the sum of the squares of the deviations of the demand values about their means is attributed to the model. This is very close to 1 which implies this model is quite adequate.

15.65 a. To determine if the model is adequate, we test:

H_0: $\beta_1 = \beta_2 = \beta_3 = \beta_4 = \beta_5 = \beta_6 = \beta_7 = \beta_8 = \beta_9 = \beta_{10} = 0$
H_a: At least one $\beta_i \neq 0$

The test statistic is $F = \left[\dfrac{R^2}{1 - R^2} \right] \left[\dfrac{n - (k + 1)}{k} \right]$

$= \left[\dfrac{.879}{1 - .879} \right] \left[\dfrac{126 - (10 + 1)}{10} \right] = 83.54$

The rejection region requires $\alpha = .05$ in the upper tail of the F distribution with $\nu_1 = k = 10$ and $\nu_2 = n - (k + 1) = 126 - (10 + 1) = 115$. From Table 8, Appendix E, $F_{.05} \approx 1.91$. The rejection region is $F > 1.91$.

Since the observed value of the test statistic falls in the rejection region ($F = 83.54 > 1.91$), H_0 is rejected. There is sufficient evidence to indicate the model is adequate at $\alpha = .05$.

b. The stem-and-leaf plot appears to be fairly mound-shaped. This implies the assumption of normal errors is satisfied.

15.67 a. Some preliminary calculations are:

$$\sum x = 20 \qquad \sum y = 5.12 \qquad \sum xy = 5.96$$

$$\sum x^2 = 60 \qquad \sum y^2 = 3.5648$$

$$SS_{xy} = \sum xy - \frac{\sum x \sum y}{n} = 5.96 - \frac{20(5.12)}{10} = -4.28$$

$$SS_{xy} = \sum x^2 - \frac{(\sum x)^2}{n} = 60 - \frac{20^2}{10} = 20$$

$$\hat{\beta}_1 = \frac{SS_{xy}}{SS_{xx}} = \frac{-4.28}{20} = -.214$$

$$\hat{\beta}_0 = \bar{y} - \hat{\beta}_1 \bar{x} = \frac{5.12}{10} - (-.214)\left(\frac{20}{10}\right) = .94$$

The fitted first-order model is $\hat{y} = .94 - .214x$.

b. First, we find the value of $\hat{y}$ for each value of x using the fitted model. The residual is found using $y - \hat{y}$. For $x = 0$, $\hat{y} = .94 - .214(0) = .94$. The residual is $y - \hat{y} = .94 - .94 = 0$. The rest of the values of $\hat{y}$ and the residuals are found in a similar manner and are shown in the table.

x	y	$\hat{y}$	$(y - \hat{y})$
0	.94	.94	0
0	.96	.94	.02
1	.70	.726	-.026
1	.76	.726	.034
2	.60	.512	.088
2	.40	.512	-.112
3	.24	.298	-.058
3	.30	.298	.002
4	.12	.084	.036
4	.10	.084	.016

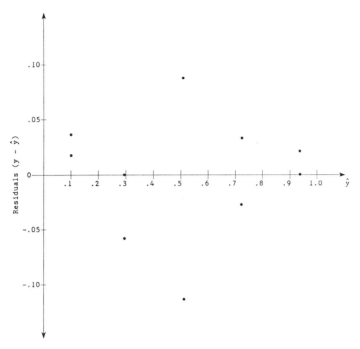

c. The residual plot appears to be football-shaped. This implies the variances are not equal.

d. Since the dependent variable is the proportion of appliance owners who decide to purchase a service contract, we could use a transformation to stabilize the variance. The appropriate transformation is $y^* = \sin^{-1}\sqrt{y}$. We would then fit the model $E(y^*) = \beta_0 + \beta_1 x$.

15.69 a. To determine if the model is adequate for predicting the sale price of a home, we test:

H_0: $\beta_1 = \beta_2 = \beta_3 = \beta_4 = \beta_5 = \beta_6 = 0$
H_a: At least one $\beta_i \neq 0$

The test statistic is $F = \left[\dfrac{R^2}{1 - R^2}\right]\left[\dfrac{n - (k + 1)}{k}\right]$

$= \left[\dfrac{.86}{1 - .86}\right]\left[\dfrac{111 - (6 + 1)}{6}\right] = 106.48$

The rejection region requires $\alpha = .10$ in the upper tail of the F distribution with $v_1 = k = 6$ and $v_2 = n - (k + 1) = 111 - (6 + 1) = 104$. From Table 7, Appendix E, $F_{.10} \approx 1.83$. The rejection region is $F > 1.83$.

Since the observed value of the test statistic falls in the rejection region (F = 106.48 > 1.83), H_0 is rejected. There is sufficient evidence to indicate the model is adequate for predicting the sale price of a home at α = .10.

b. Confidence coefficient .90 = 1 - α => α = 1 - .90 = .10 and $\alpha/2$ = .10/2 = .05. From Table 6, Appendix E, with df = n - (k + 1) = 111 - (6 + 1) = 104, $t_{.05} \approx 1.658$. The 90% confidence interval for β_1 is

$$\hat{\beta}_1 \pm t_{\alpha/2} s_{\hat{\beta}_1} \Rightarrow -725 \pm 1.658(120.8) \Rightarrow -725 \pm 200.29$$
$$\Rightarrow (-925.29, -524.71)$$

We are 90% confident the change in the mean sale price is between -925.29 and -524.71 for each additional year of age, all other variables held constant.

c. $\hat{\beta}_5 = -1450$. The estimated difference in mean sale price between homes conventionally financed and those not conventionally financed is $-1450.

d. To determine if a brokerage commission increases the mean selling price of a home, we test:

H_0: $\beta_6 = 0$
H_a: $\beta_6 > 0$

The test statistic is $t = \dfrac{\hat{\beta}_6}{s_{\hat{\beta}_6}} = \dfrac{.43}{.25} = 1.72$

The rejection region requires α = .10 in the upper tail of the t distribution with df = n - (k + 1) = 111 - (6 + 1) = 104. From Table 6, Appendix E, $t_{.10} \approx 1.290$. The rejection region is t > 1.290.

Since the observed value of the test statistic falls in the rejection region (t = 1.72 > 1.290), H_0 is rejected. There is sufficient evidence to indicate a brokerage commission increases the mean selling price of a home at α = .10.

15.71   a.   Let $x_1 = \begin{cases} 1 \text{ if market concentration is low} \\ 0 \text{ if not} \end{cases}$

$x_2 = \begin{cases} 1 \text{ if market concentration is moderate} \\ 0 \text{ if not} \end{cases}$

The model is $E(y) = \beta_0 + \beta_1 x_1 + \beta_2 x_2$

b.　β_0 = mean excess capacity if the market concentration is high

　　β_1 = difference in mean excess capacity between when the market concentration is low and when it is high.

　　β_2 = difference in mean excess capacity between when the market concentration is moderate and when it is high.

c.　We would test

　　H_0:　$\beta_1 = \beta_2 = 0$
　　H_a:　At least one $\beta_i \neq 0$

15.73　a.　The first-order model is $E(y) = \beta_0 + \beta_1 x_1 + \beta_2 x_2$

b.　The interaction model is $E(y) = \beta_0 + \beta_1 x_1 + \beta_2 x_2 + \beta_3 x_1 x_2$

c.　The second-order model is $E(y) = \beta_0 + \beta_1 x_1 + \beta_2 x_2 + \beta_3 x_1 x_2 + \beta_4 x_1^2 + \beta_5 x_2^2$

d.　R^2 = R-SQUARE = .6004. This implies that 60.04% of the sums of squares of deviations of the refusal rates about their means is attributed to the model.

e.　To determine if the model is adequate for predicting refusal rate, we test:

　　　H_0:　$\beta_1 = \beta_2 = \beta_3 = \beta_4 = \beta_5 = 0$
　　　H_a:　At least one $\beta_i \neq 0$

　　The test statistic is $F = 1.803$ (from printout).

　　The p-value is .2465. Since the p-value is not less than $\alpha = .05$, H_0 is not rejected. There is insufficient evidence to indicate the model is adequate for predicting refusal rate at $\alpha = .05$.

f.　The prediction interval is (.1354, .5774).

　　We are 95% confident the actual refusal rate for per capita income of $10,000 and 29.74% of residents with a college education is between .1354 and .5774. This interval is so wide because the model is inadequate for predicting refusal rate.

15.75　a.　R^2 = R-SQUARE = .9043. This implies 90.43% of the sums of squares of deviations of the projected percentage increases about their means is attributed to the model.

b.　s = ROOT MSE = 4.548548. We would expect most of the observations to fall within 2s or 2(4.548548) or 9.097096 units of the fitted regression line.

c. To determine if the model is adequate, we test:

H_0: $\beta_1 = \beta_2 = 0$
H_a: At least one $\beta_i \neq 0$

The test statistic is F = 33.079.

The p-value = .0003. Since the p-value is less than α = .05, H_0 is rejected. There is sufficient evidence to indicate the model is adequate at α = .05.

d. To determine if the percentage improvement increases more quickly for more costly fleet modifications than for less costly fleet modifications, we test:

H_0: $\beta_2 = 0$
H_a: $\beta_2 > 0$

The test statistic is t = 2.131.

The p-value is .0706/2 = .0353. Since the p-value is less than α = .05, H_0 is rejected. There is sufficient evidence to indicate the percentage improvement increases more quickly for more costly fleet modifications than for less costly fleet modifications at α = .05.

e. First, we find $\hat{y}$ for each value of x using $\hat{y}$ = 10.65903604 − .28160568x + .002671936x^2. The residual is found using y − $\hat{y}$.

For x = 125, $\hat{y}$ = 10.65903604 − .28160568(125) + .002671936(125^2) = 17.2068. The residual is y − $\hat{y}$ = 18 − 17.2068 = .7932.

The rest of the values of $\hat{y}$ and the residuals are found in a similar manner and are shown in the table:

x	y	$\hat{y}$	(y − $\hat{y}$)
125	18	17.2068	.7932
160	32	34.0028	−2.0028
80	9	5.2307	3.7693
162	37	35.1603	1.8397
110	6	12.0124	−6.0124
90	3	6.9569	−3.9569
140	30	23.6035	6.3965
85	10	6.0270	3.9730
150	25	28.5359	−3.5359
50	2	3.2585	−1.2585

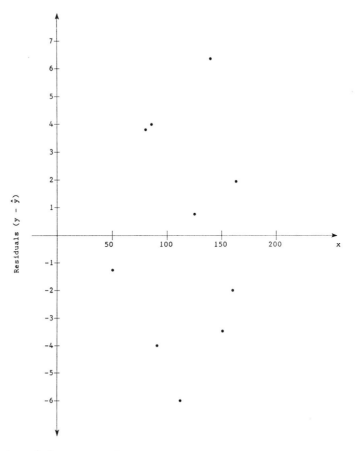

f. No trend is apparent.

   $3s = 3(\text{Root MSE}) = 3(4.548548) = 13.645644$. Since no residuals fall more than 13.645644 units from 0, there is no evidence of outliers.

g. To determine if the type of base is a useful predictor of percentage improvement, we test:

   H_0: $\beta_3 = \beta_4 = 0$
   H_a: At least one $\beta_i \neq 0$

   The test statistic is $F = \dfrac{(\text{SSE}_1 - \text{SSE}_2)/(k - g)}{\text{SSE}_2/[n - (k + 1)]}$

   $= \dfrac{(144.82499 - 97.645)/(4 - 2)}{97.645/[10 - (4 + 1)]} = \dfrac{23.589995}{19.529} = 1.21$

   The rejection region requires $\alpha = .05$ in the upper tail of the F distribution with $\nu_1 = k - g = 4 - 2 = 2$ and $\nu_2 = n - (k + 1)$

$= 10 - (4 + 1) = 5$. From Table 8, Appendix E, $F_{.05} = 5.79$. The rejection region is $F > 5.79$.

Since the observed value of the test statistic does not fall in the rejection region ($F = 1.21 \not> 5.79$), H_0 is not rejected. There is insufficient evidence to indicate the type of base is a useful predictor of percentage improvement at $\alpha = .05$.

15.77   a.   The least square prediction equation is

$\hat{y} = 22.0189 - .1807x_1 - .2498x_2 - 4.6910x_3 + 3.6745x_4 + 22.5201x_5$.

   b. $R^2 = \dfrac{SS(Model)}{SS(Total)} = \dfrac{32,774}{54,660} = .5996$

This implies that 59.96% of the sums of squares of the deviations of the home-origin trip rate values about their mean is attributed to the model.

   c. $s = \sqrt{MSE} = \sqrt{74.95} = 8.657$

We expect most of the observations to fall within 2s or 2(8.657) or 17.314 units of the least squares line.

   d.   To determine if the model is useful for predicting home-origin trip rate, we test:

H_0: $\beta_1 = \beta_2 = \beta_3 = \beta_4 = \beta_5 = 0$
H_a: At least one $\beta_i \neq 0$

The test statistic is $F = 87.45$ (from printout).

The rejection region requires $\alpha = .05$ in the upper tail of the F distribution with $\nu_1 = k = 5$ and $\nu_2 = n - (k + 1) = 298 - (5 + 1) = 292$. From Table 8, Appendix E, $F_{.05} = 2.21$. The rejection region is $F > 2.21$.

Since the observed value of the test statistic falls in the rejection region ($F = 87.45 > 2.21$), H_0 is rejected. There is sufficient evidence to indicate the model is useful for predicting home-origin trip rate at $\alpha = .05$.

   e.   To determine if the home-origin trip rate decreases as in-vehicle travel time increases, we test:

H_0: $\beta_1 = 0$
H_a: $\beta_1 < 0$

The test statistic is $t = \dfrac{\hat{\beta}_1}{s_{\hat{\beta}_1}} = \dfrac{-.1807}{.0389} = -4.645$

The rejection region requires $\alpha = .05$ in the lower tail of the t distribution with df $= n - (k + 1) = 298 - (5 + 1) = 292$. From Table 6, Appendix E, $t_{.05} = 1.645$. The rejection region is $t < -1.645$.

Since the observed value of the test statistic falls in the rejection region ($t = -4.645 < -1.645$), H_0 is rejected. There is sufficient evidence to indicate the home-trip rate decreases as in-vehicle travel time increases at $\alpha = .05$.

f. Confidence coefficient $.95 = 1 - \alpha$; $\alpha = 1 - .95 = .05$ and $\alpha/2 = .05/2 = .025$. From Table 6, Appendix E, with df $= n - (k + 1) = 298 - (5 + 1) = 292$, $t_{.025} = 1.960$. The confidence interval is

$$\hat{\beta}_4 \pm t_{\alpha/2} s_{\hat{\beta}_4} \Rightarrow 3.6745 \pm 1.960(.4027) \Rightarrow 3.6745 \pm .7893$$
$$\Rightarrow (2.8852, 4.4638)$$

We are 95% confident the change in the mean home-trip rate is between 2.8852 and 4.4638 for each additional transit route serving the Sun Tran zone, all other variables held constant.

CASE STUDIES

15.1 a. $R^2 = .54$. This implies that 54% of the sums of squares of the deviations of the natural logarithm of total annual compensation values about their means is attributable to the model with the 11 independent variables.

b. To determine if the overall model is useful for predicting total compensation for business economists, we test:

H_0: $\beta_1 = \beta_2 = \beta_3 = \beta_4 = \beta_5 = \beta_6 = \beta_7 = \beta_8 = \beta_9 = \beta_{10} = \beta_{11} = 0$
H_a: At least one $\beta_i \neq 0$

The test statistic is $F = \left[\dfrac{R^2}{1 - R^2} \right] \left[\dfrac{n - (k + 1)}{k} \right]$

$= \left[\dfrac{.54}{1 - .54} \right] \left[\dfrac{1393 - (11 + 1)}{11} \right] = 147.38$

The rejection region requires $\alpha = .05$ in the upper tail of the F distribution with $\nu_1 = k = 11$ and $\nu_2 = n - (k + 1) = 1393 - (11 + 1) = 1381$. From Table 8, Appendix E, $F_{.05} \approx 1.83$. The rejection region is $F > 1.83$.

Since the observed value of the test statistic falls in the rejection region (F = 147.38 > 1.83), H_0 is rejected. There is sufficient evidence to indicate the overall model is useful for predicting total compensation for business economists at α = .05.

c. For x_1 = log(6) = 1.79176, x_2 = 25, x_3 = 10, x_4 = 0, x_5 = 0, x_6 = 0, x_7 = 1, x_8 = 0, x_9 = 0, x_{10} = 1 and x_{11} = 0,

$$\hat{y} = 9.393 + .224(1.79176) + .019(25) + .049(10) + .194(0)$$
$$+ .245(0) - .180(0) - .281(1) - .266(0) + .067(0)$$
$$+ .078(1) + .122(0) = 10.556354$$

The compensation is $e^{10.556354}$ = \$38,420.80.

15.3 a.

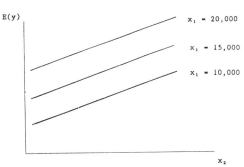

For x_1 = 10,000, E(y) = β_0 + β_1(10,000) + $\beta_2 x_2$

x_1 = 15,000, E(y) = β_0 + β_1(15,000) + $\beta_2 x_2$

x_1 = 20,000, E(y) = β_0 + β_1(20,000) + $\beta_2 x_2$

b. For x_1 = 10,000, x_3 = 0, x_4 = 0, x_5 = 0, x_6 = 0, and x_7 = 0,

E(y) = β_0 + β_1(10,000) + $\beta_2 x_2$

c. For x_1 = 20,000, x_3 = x_4 = x_5 = x_6 = x_7 = 0

(i) E(y) = β_0 + β_1(20,000) + $\beta_2 x_2$

For x_1 = 10,000, x_3 = 1, x_4 = x_5 = x_6 = x_7 = 0,

(ii) E(y) = β_0 + β_1(10,000) + $\beta_2 x_2$ + β_3(1) + β_8(10,000)(1)
$$+ \beta_{13} x_2(1)$$

$$= \beta_0 + \beta_1(10,000) + \beta_3 + \beta_8(10,000) + (\beta_2 + \beta_{13})x_2$$

For $x_1 = 20,000$, $x_3 = 1$, $x_4 = x_5 = x_6 = x_7 = 0$,

(iii) $E(y) = \beta_0 + \beta_1(20,000) + \beta_2 x_2 + \beta_3(1) + \beta_8(20,000)(1)$
$\qquad\qquad + \beta_{13} x_2(1)$

$\qquad = \beta_0 + \beta_1(20,000) + \beta_3 + \beta_8(20,000) + (\beta_2 + \beta_{13})x_2$

d.

The graph might look something like the above.

e.   For $x_1 = 10,000$, $x_3 = x_4 = x_5 = x_6 = x_7 = 0$,

$\qquad E(y) = \beta_0 + \beta_1(10,000) + \beta_2 x_2 + \beta_3(10,000)x_2 + \beta_4(10,000^2)$
$\qquad\qquad + \beta_5 x_2^2$

$\qquad\quad = \beta_0 + \beta_1(10,000) + \beta_4(10,000^2) + [\beta_2 + \beta_3(10,000)]x_2$
$\qquad\qquad + \beta_5 x_2^2$

For $x_1 = 20,000$, $x_3 = x_4 = x_5 = x_6 = x_7 = 0$,

$\qquad E(y) = \beta_0 + \beta_1(20,000) + \beta_2 x_2 + \beta_3(20,000)x_2 + \beta_4(20,000^2)$
$\qquad\qquad + \beta_5 x_2^2$

$\qquad\quad = \beta_0 + \beta_1(20,000) + \beta_4(20,000^2) + [\beta_2 + \beta_3(20,000)]x_2$
$\qquad\qquad + \beta_5 x_2^2$

For $x_1 = 10,000$, $x_3 = 1$, $x_4 = x_5 = x_6 = x_7 = 0$,

$\qquad E(y) = \beta_0 + \beta_1(10,000) + \beta_2 x_2 + \beta_3(10,000)x_2 + \beta_4(10,000^2)$
$\qquad\qquad + \beta_5 x_2^2 + \beta_6(1) + \beta_{11}(1)(10,000) + \beta_{12}(1)x_2$
$\qquad\qquad + \beta_{13}(1)(10,000)x_2 + \beta_{14}(1)(10,000^2) + \beta_{15}(1)x_2^2$

$\qquad\quad = \beta_0 + \beta_1(10,000) + \beta_4(10,000^2) + \beta_6 + \beta_{11}(10,000)$
$\qquad\qquad + \beta_{14}(10,000^2) + [\beta_2 + \beta_3(10,000) + \beta_{12}$
$\qquad\qquad + \beta_{13}(10,000)]x_2 + (\beta_5 + \beta_{15})x_2^2$

For $x_1 = 20,000$, $x_3 = 1$, $x_4 = x_5 = x_6 = x_7 = 0$,

$$
\begin{aligned}
E(y) = &\, \beta_0 + \beta_1(20,000) + \beta_2 x_2 + \beta_3(20,000)x_2 + \beta_4(20,000^2) \\
&+ \beta_5 x_2^2 + \beta_6(1) + \beta_{11}(1)(20,000) + \beta_{12}(1)x_2 \\
&+ \beta_{13}(1)(20,000)x_2 + \beta_{14}(1)(20,000^2) + \beta_{15}(1)x_2^2 \\
= &\, \beta_0 + \beta_1(20,000) + \beta_4(20,000^2) + \beta_6 + \beta_{11}(20,000) \\
&+ \beta_{14}(20,000^2) + [\beta_2 + \beta_3(20,000) + \beta_{12} \\
&+ \beta_{13}(20,000)]x_2 + (\beta_5 + \beta_{15})x_2^2
\end{aligned}
$$

The graphs might look something like the following:

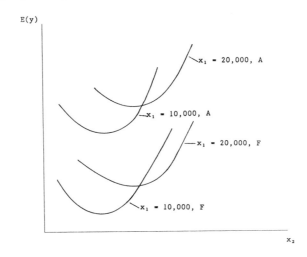

f. H_0: $\beta_3 = \beta_4 = \ldots = \beta_{17} = 0$
H_a: At least one $\beta_i \neq 0$

The test statistic is $F = \dfrac{(SSE_1 - SSE_2)/(k - g)}{SSE_2/[n - (k + 1)]}$

$$
= \frac{(93,233,186,667 - 71,997,720,827)/(17 - 2)}{71,997,720,827/[651 - (17 + 1)]} = \frac{1,415,697,723}{113,740,475.2}
$$

$$
= 12.45
$$

The rejection region requires $\alpha = .01$ in the upper tail of the F distribution with $\nu_1 = k - g = 17 - 2 = 15$ and $\nu_2 = n - (k + 1) = 651 - (17 + 1) = 633$. From Table 10, Appendix E, $F_{.01} \approx 2.04$. The rejection region is $F > 2.04$.

Since the observed value of the test statistic falls in the rejection region ($F = 12.45 > 2.04$), H_0 is rejected. There is sufficient evidence to indicate model 2 is better than model 1 at $\alpha = .01$.

g. H_0: $\beta_3 = \beta_4 = \beta_5 = \beta_{13} = \beta_{14} = \beta_{15} = \beta_{18} = \beta_{19} = \beta_{20} + \beta_{23} = \beta_{24}$
$= \beta_{25} = \beta_{28} = \beta_{29} = \beta_{30} = \beta_{33} = \beta_{34} = \beta_{35} = 0$
H_a: At least one $\beta_i \neq 0$

The test statistic is $F = \dfrac{(SSE_1 - SSE_2)/(k - g)}{SSE_2/[n - (k + 1)]}$

$= \dfrac{(71,997,720,827 - 54,177,821,240)/(35 - 17)}{54,177,821,240/[651 - (35 + 1)]} = \dfrac{989,994,421.7}{88,094,018.28}$

$= 11.24$

The rejection region requires $\alpha = .01$ in the upper tail of the F distribution with $\nu_1 = k - g = 35 - 17 = 18$ and $\nu_2 = n - (k + 1)$ $= 651 - (35 + 1) = 615$. From Table 10, Appendix E, $F_{.01} \approx 2.04$. The rejection region is $F > 2.04$.

Since the observed value of the test statistic falls in the rejection region ($F = 11.24 > 2.04$), H_0 is rejected. There is sufficient evidence to indicate model 3 is better than model 2 at $\alpha = .01$.

h. Since model 2 is better than model 1 and model 3 is better than model 2, model 3 should be used.

i. H_0: $\beta_6 = \beta_7 = \ldots = \beta_{35} = 0$
H_a: At least one $\beta_i \neq 0$

The test statistic is $F = \dfrac{(SSE_1 - SSE_2)/(k - g)}{SSE_2/[n - (k + 1)]}$

$= \dfrac{(76,356,480,863 - 54,177,821,240)/(35 - 5)}{54,177,821,240/[651 - (35 + 1)]} = \dfrac{739,288,654}{88,094,018.28}$

$= 8.39$

The rejection region requires $\alpha = .01$ in the upper tail of the F distribution with $\nu_1 = k - g = 35 - 5 = 30$ and $\nu_2 = n - (k + 1)$ $= 651 - (35 + 1) = 615$. From Table 10, Appendix E, $F_{.01} = 1.70$. The rejection region is $F > 1.70$.

Since the observed value of the test statistic falls in the rejection region ($F = 8.39 > 1.70$), H_0 is rejected. There is sufficient evidence to indicate model 3 is better than model 4 at $\alpha = .01$. This implies the second-order relationships differ from neighborhood to neighborhood.

j. R^2 = R-SQUARE = .9412. This implies 94.12% of the sums of squares of the deviations of the sale prices about their means is attributed to the variables in model 3.

k. To determine if model 3 is a useful predictor of sale price, we test:

H_0: $\beta_1 = \beta_2 = \ldots = \beta_{35} = 0$
H_a: At least one $\beta_i \neq 0$

The test statistic is F = 281.04   (from printout).

The p-value = .0001. Since the p-value is less than α = .01, H_0 is rejected. There is sufficient evidence to indicate that model 3 is a useful predictor of sale price at α = .01.

1. s = ROOT MSE = 9385.841. Most of the observations will fall within 2s or 2(9385.841) or 18,771.682 units of the fitted regression line.

SIXTEEN
TIME SERIES: DESCRIPTIVE TECHNIQUES

16.1   a.

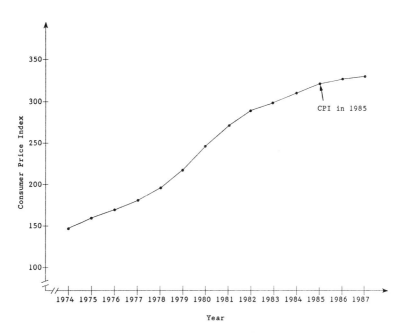

Year

b.   The Consumer Price Index value for 1985 is 322.2.   The CPI in 1985 is 322.2% of what it was in the base year 1967.   It has increased 222.2%.

16.3   a.   The base period is t_0 = January 1984.

The simple index is $I_t = \dfrac{Y_t}{Y_{t_0}} \times 100\%$

For t = Jan 1984: $I_{Jan\ 1984} = \dfrac{Y_{Jan\ 1984}}{Y_{Jan\ 1984}} \times 100\% = \dfrac{9.7}{9.7}(100)$

$= 100.00$

$$t = \text{Feb 1984: } I_{\text{Feb 1984}} = \frac{Y_{\text{Feb 1984}}}{Y_{\text{Jan 1984}}} \times 100\% = \frac{10.3}{9.7}(100)$$

$$= 106.19$$

The rest of the index values are found in a similar manner and are shown in the table.

	1984 APPL.	1984 INDEX	1986 APPL.	1986 INDEX	1985 APPL.	1985 INDEX
Jan.	9.7	100.00	11.1	114.43	24.1	248.45
Feb.	10.3	106.19	11.5	118.56	24.8	255.67
Mar.	12.9	132.99	12.9	132.99	39.1	403.09
Apr.	11.4	117.53	15.8	162.89	51.0	525.77
May	11.1	114.43	15.2	156.70	41.0	422.68
June	8.2	84.54	16.6	171.13	26.9	277.32
July	8.0	82.47	17.6	181.44	24.7	254.64
Aug.	7.8	80.41	17.1	176.29	20.2	208.25
Sept.	7.4	76.29	16.3	168.04	21.7	223.71
Oct.	9.7	100.00	17.1	176.29	18.9	194.85
Nov.	9.8	101.03	14.8	152.58	16.2	167.01
Dec.	9.2	94.85	14.8	152.58	16.7	172.16

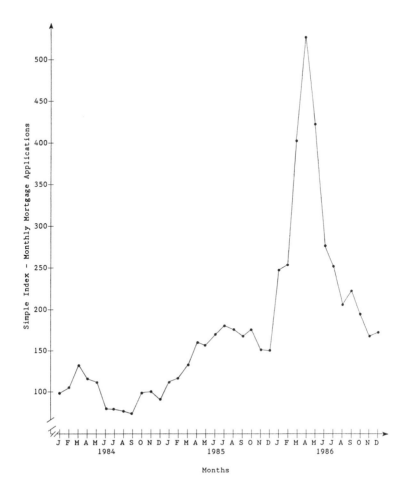

Months

b. The index value in July 1985 is 181.44. This means that the number of monthly mortgage applications in July 1985 is 181.44% of the number of monthly mortgage applications in January 1984, the base period. This is an increase of 81.44%.

16.5 a. The February 1984 Consumer Confidence Index is 95.4. This means that the Consumer Confidence is 95.4% of what it was in the base period, 1970. The Consumer Confidence has decreased by 4.6% since 1970.

b. The January 1984 Consumer Confidence Index is 98.4. This means that the Consumer Confidence is 98.4% of what it was in the base period, 1970. The Consumer Confidence has decreased by 1.6% since 1970.

16.7   a.   The base period is t_0 = January 1983.

The simple index is $I_t = \dfrac{Y_t}{Y_{t_0}} \times 100\%$

For t = Jan 1983: $I_{Jan\ 1983} = \dfrac{Y_{Jan\ 1983}}{Y_{Jan\ 1983}} \times 100 = \dfrac{59}{59}(100) = 100.00$

t = Feb 1983: $I_{Feb\ 1983} = \dfrac{Y_{Feb\ 1983}}{Y_{Jan\ 1983}} \times 100 = \dfrac{63}{59}(100) = 106.78$

The rest of the values of the index are found in a similar manner and are shown in the table.

| | | ATLANTA | | |
| | 1983 | | 1984 | |
	%	INDEX	%	INDEX
Jan.	59	100.00	64	108.47
Feb.	63	106.78	69	116.95
Mar.	68	115.25	73	123.73
Apr.	70	118.64	67	113.56
May	63	106.78	68	115.25
June	59	100.00	71	120.34
July	68	115.25	67	113.56
Aug.	64	108.47	71	120.34
Sept.	62	105.08	65	110.17
Oct.	73	123.73	72	122.03
Nov.	62	105.08	63	106.78
Dec.	47	79.66	47	79.66

b.   The base period is t_0 = January 1983.

The simple index is $I_t = \dfrac{Y_t}{Y_{t_0}} \times 100\%$

For t = Jan 1983: $I_{Jan\ 1983} = \dfrac{Y_{Jan\ 1983}}{Y_{Jan\ 1983}} \times 100 = \dfrac{67}{67}(100) = 100.00$

t = Feb 1983: $I_{Feb\ 1983} = \dfrac{Y_{Feb\ 1983}}{Y_{Jan\ 1983}} \times 100 = \dfrac{85}{67}(100) = 126.87$

The rest of the values of the index are found in a similar manner and are shown in the table.

		PHOENIX			
		1983		1984	
	%	INDEX		%	INDEX
Jan.	67	100.00		72	107.46
Feb.	85	126.87		91	135.82
Mar.	83	123.88		87	129.85
Apr.	69	102.99		75	111.94
May	63	94.03		70	104.48
June	52	77.61		61	91.04
July	49	73.13		46	68.66
Aug.	49	73.13		44	65.67
Sept.	56	83.58		63	94.03
Oct.	69	102.99		73	108.96
Nov.	63	94.03		71	105.97
Dec.	48	71.64		51	76.12

 c.

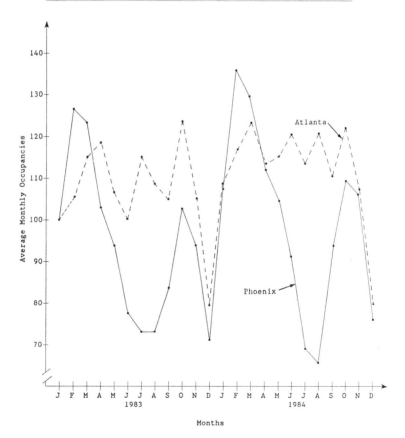

For Atlanta, the average monthly occupancy for all months except December in both years was greater than it was in January 1983.

For Phoenix, the average monthly occupancies for February through April 1983, October 1983, January through May 1984, and October and November 1984, were greater than that in January 1983. The average monthly occupancies for all the other months were below that in January 1983.

16.9 To compute a simple composite index, first select a base period t_0. For this problem, the base period is t_0 = May 1983.

Next, for each time period, sum the values of the k times series, Y_t.

The simple composite index is $I_t = \dfrac{Y_t}{Y_{t_0}} \times 100$.

For Jan 1983: $Y_{\text{Jan 1983}} = 1.47 + 1.15 + .32 = 2.94$

Feb 1983: $Y_{\text{Feb 1983}} = 1.47 + 1.10 + .33 = 2.90$

$\vdots$

May 1983: $Y_{\text{May 1983}} = 1.36 + 1.18 + .33 = 2.87$

The rest of the sums are computed in a similar manner and are shown in the table.

For Jan 1983: $I_{\text{Jan 1983}} = \dfrac{Y_{\text{Jan 1983}}}{Y_{\text{May 1983}}} \times 100 = \dfrac{2.94}{2.87}(100) = 102.44$

Feb 1983: $I_{\text{Feb 1983}} = \dfrac{Y_{\text{Feb 1983}}}{Y_{\text{May 1983}}} \times 100 = \dfrac{2.90}{2.87}(100) = 101.05$

The rest of the index values are found in a similar manner and are shown in the table.

	COFFEE	GAS	SUGAR	TOTAL	INDEX
Jan.	1.47	1.15	0.32	2.94	102.44
Feb.	1.47	1.10	0.33	2.90	101.05
Mar.	1.47	1.06	0.32	2.85	99.30
Apr.	1.39	1.13	0.33	2.85	99.30
May	1.36	1.18	0.33	2.87	100.00
June	1.36	1.20	0.34	2.90	101.05
July	1.36	1.21	0.34	2.91	101.39
Aug.	1.36	1.20	0.34	2.90	101.05
Sept.	1.36	1.19	0.34	2.89	100.70
Oct.	1.36	1.17	0.34	2.87	100.00
Nov.	1.36	1.16	0.33	2.85	99.30
Dec.	1.36	1.15	0.33	2.84	98.95

The simple composite indexes for March, April, November, and December are below that for May. For all other months the simple composite index is above that for May.

16.11   To compute the simple composite index, first select a base period. For this problem, the base period is $t_0 = 1972$.

Next, for each time period, sum the values of the k times series, Y_t.

The simple composite index is $I_t = \dfrac{Y_t}{Y_{t_0}} \times 100$.

For 1972: $Y_{1972} = 7790.52 + 5593.04 + 2192.00 = 15,575.56$

1973: $Y_{1973} = 8683.80 + 5871.00 + 2423.00 = 16,977.80$

The rest of the sums are computed in a similar manner and are shown in the table.

For 1972: $I_{1972} = \dfrac{Y_{1972}}{Y_{1972}} \times 100 = \dfrac{15,575.56}{15,575.56}(100) = 100.00$

1973: $I_{1973} = \dfrac{Y_{1973}}{Y_{1972}} \times 100 = \dfrac{16,977.80}{15,575.56}(100) = 109.00$

The rest of the index values are computed in a similar manner and are shown in the table.

	GM	FORD	CHRYSLER	TOTAL	INDEX
1972	7790.52	5593.04	2192.00	15575.56	100.00
1973	8683.80	5871.00	2423.00	16977.80	109.00
1974	6690.00	5258.93	2015.00	13963.93	89.65
1975	6629.00	4577.77	1773.00	12979.77	83.33
1976	8568.00	5304.44	2371.00	16243.44	104.29
1977	9068.00	6422.30	2328.00	17818.30	114.40
1978	9482.00	6462.06	2212.00	18156.06	116.57
1979	8993.00	5810.30	1796.00	16599.30	106.57
1980	7101.00	4328.45	1225.00	12654.45	81.25
1981	6762.00	4313.18	1283.00	12358.18	79.34
1982	6244.00	4254.90	1182.00	11680.90	75.00
1983	7769.00	4934.23	1493.96	14197.19	91.15
1984	8256.35	5584.65	2034.35	15875.35	101.92
1985	9305.00	5550.50	2157.37	17012.87	109.23

The plot of the index is

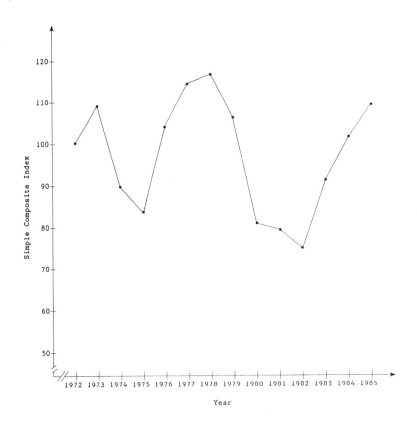

The total car production by Ford, GM, and Chrysler for the years 1974, 1975, and 1980 through 1983 was below the total production in 1972. In all other years from 1972 through 1985, the total car production was above that in 1972.

16.13   a.   First, select the base period, t_0. For this problem, the base period is t_0 = January 1982.

Next, sum the values of the k times series for each time period, Y_t.

The simple composite index is $I_t = \dfrac{Y_t}{Y_{t_0}} \times 100$.

For Jan 1982: $Y_{Jan\ 1982} = 213 + 1683 + 652.5 = 2548.5$

Feb 1982: $Y_{Feb\ 1982} = 213 + 1683 + 635.4 = 2531.4$

The rest of the sums are found in a similar manner and are shown in the table.

For Jan 1982: $I_{Jan\ 1982} = \dfrac{Y_{Jan\ 1982}}{Y_{Jan\ 1982}} \times 100 = \dfrac{2548.5}{2548.5}(100) = 100.00$

Feb 1982: $I_{Feb\ 1982} = \dfrac{Y_{Feb\ 1982}}{Y_{Jan\ 1982}} \times 100 = \dfrac{2531.4}{2548.5}(100) = 99.33$

The rest of the values are computed in a similar manner and are shown in the table.

	IRON	ALUMINUM	PRICES LEAD	TOTAL	INDEX
Jan.	213	1683	652.5	2548.5	100.00
Feb.	213	1683	635.4	2531.4	99.33
Mar.	213	1683	643.9	2539.9	99.66
Apr.	213	1683	615.6	2511.6	98.55
May	213	1683	602.7	2498.7	98.05
June	213	1683	562.4	2458.4	96.46
July	213	1683	604.2	2500.2	98.10
Aug.	213	1683	575.3	2471.3	96.97
Sept.	213	1683	571.1	2467.1	96.81
Oct.	213	1672	556.7	2441.7	95.81
Nov.	213	1672	537.9	2422.9	95.07
Dec.	213	1672	526.1	2411.1	94.61

b. For October 1982, the simple composite index is 95.81. This means that in October 1982 the total price for iron, aluminum, and lead is 95.81% of the total price in January 1982. The total price has decreased 4.19%.

c. First, select the base period. For this problem, the base period is t_0 = January 1982.

Next, sum the values of the k times series for each time period, Y_t.

The simple composite index is $I_t = \dfrac{Y_t}{Y_{t_0}} \times 100$.

For Jan 1982: $Y_{Jan\ 1982}$ = 4489 + 350.5 + 44.6 = 4884.1

  Feb 1982: $Y_{Feb\ 1982}$ = 4169 + 311.4 + 44.8 = 4525.2

The rest of the sums are found in a similar manner and are shown in the table.

For Jan 1982: $I_{Jan\ 1982} = \dfrac{Y_{Jan\ 1982}}{Y_{Jan\ 1982}} \times 100 = \dfrac{4884.1}{4884.1}(100) = 100.00$

  Feb 1982: $I_{Feb\ 1982} = \dfrac{Y_{Feb\ 1982}}{Y_{Jan\ 1982}} \times 100 = \dfrac{4525.2}{4884.1}(100) = 92.65$

The rest of the values of the index are found in a similar manner and are shown in the table.

	IRON	ALUMINUM	PRODUCTION LEAD	TOTAL	INDEX
Jan.	4489	350.5	44.6	4884.1	100.00
Feb.	4169	311.4	44.8	4525.2	92.65
Mar.	4622	336.3	45.3	5003.6	102.45
Apr.	3967	318.6	45.9	4331.5	88.69
May	3909	320.9	46.4	4276.3	87.56
June	3516	299.9	46.9	3862.8	79.09
July	3595	296.9	40.8	3932.7	80.52
Aug.	3277	287.1	47.3	3611.4	73.94
Sept.	3160	271.1	46.0	3477.1	71.19
Oct.	3077	275.3	49.6	3401.9	69.65
Nov.	2648	266.3	46.4	2960.7	60.62
Dec.	2712	275.1	50.0	3037.1	62.18

16.15 First, select the base period, t_0. For this problem, the base period is $t_0 = 1975$. Next, select the weights for each of the k time series. For this problem, the weight for ordinary policies is 200, the weight for group certificates is 102.6, and the weight for industrial policies is 6.7. The sum of the product of the weight times the time series for each of the k time series is computed for each time period, Y_t. The weighted composite index is

$$I_t = \frac{Y_t}{Y_{t_0}} \times 100$$

For 1975: $Y_{1975} = 200(1083.4) + 102.6(904.7) + 6.7(39.4) = 309{,}766.2$

1976: $Y_{1982} = 200(1177.7) + 102.6(1002.6) + 6.7(39.2) = 338{,}669.4$

The rest of the sums are found in a similar manner and are shown in the table.

For 1975: $I_{1975} = \frac{Y_{1975}}{Y_{1975}} \times 100 = \frac{309{,}766.2}{309{,}766.2}(100) = 100.00$

1976: $I_{1976} = \frac{Y_{1976}}{Y_{1975}} \times 100 = \frac{338{,}669.4}{309{,}766.2}(100) = 109.33$

The rest of the values of the index are found in a similar manner and are shown in the table.

	ORDINARY POLICIES	GROUP CERTIFICATES	INDUSTRIAL POLICIES	WEIGHTED TOTALS	INDEX
1975	1083.4	904.7	39.4	309,766.2	100.00
1976	1177.7	1002.6	39.2	338,669.4	109.33
1977	1289.3	1115.0	39.0	372,520.3	120.26
1978	1425.1	1244.0	38.1	412,909.6	133.30
1979	1586.0	1419.0	37.8	463,042.6	149.48
1980	1761.0	1579.0	36.0	514,446.6	166.08
1981	1978.0	1889.0	34.5	589,642.5	190.35
1982	2217.0	2066.0	32.8	655,591.3	211.64
1983	2544.3	2219.6	31.4	736,801.3	237.86
1984	2887.6	2392.4	30.1	823,181.9	265.74
1985	3247.3	2561.6	28.3	912,469.7	294.57

The values of the index increase every year. This implies that the amount of life insurance in force has been increasing every year since 1975.

16.17 a. First, select a base period, t_0. For this problem, the base period is $t_0 = 1980$. Next, select the weights for each of the k time series. For this problem, the weight for automobiles is 40,000, the weight for mobile homes is 10,000, and the weight for revolving credit is 100,000. The sum of the product of the weight times the time series value for each of the k time series is computed for each time period, Y_t. The weighted composite index is

$$I_t = \frac{Y_t}{Y_{t_0}} \times 100$$

For 1975: Y_{1975} = 40,000(57.0) + 10,000(15.4) + 100,0000(14.5)

$\qquad\qquad$ = 3,884,000

$\qquad$ 1976: Y_{1976} = 40,000(66.8) + 10,000(15.7) + 100,0000(16.6)

$\qquad\qquad$ = 4,489,000

$\qquad$ 1980: Y_{1980} = 40,000(112.3) + 10,000(19.1) + 100,0000(54.9)

$\qquad\qquad$ = 10,173,000

The rest of the sums are computed in a similar manner and are shown in the table.

For 1975: $I_{1975} = \dfrac{Y_{1975}}{Y_{1980}} \times 100 = \dfrac{3,884,000}{10,173,000}(100) = 38.18$

$\qquad$ 1976: $I_{1976} = \dfrac{Y_{1976}}{Y_{1980}} \times 100 = \dfrac{4,489,000}{10,173,000}(100) = 44.13$

The rest of the values of the index are found in a similar manner and are shown in the table.

	AUTOMOBILE	MOBILE HOMES	REVOLVING CREDIT	WEIGHTED TOTAL	INDEX
1975	57.0	15.4	14.5	3,884,000	38.18
1976	66.8	15.7	16.6	4,489,000	44.13
1977	80.9	16.4	36.7	7,070,000	69.50
1978	98.7	16.9	45.2	8,637,000	84.90
1979	112.5	18.2	53.4	10,022,000	98.52
1980	112.3	19.1	54.9	10,173,000	100.00
1981	120.0	20.4	60.8	11,084,000	108.96
1982	125.4	21.0	66.0	11,826,000	116.25
1983	146.0	22.2	78.4	13,902,000	136.66
1984	173.1	24.2	98.5	17,016,000	167.27
1985	206.5	25.5	118.3	20,345,000	199.99

b.

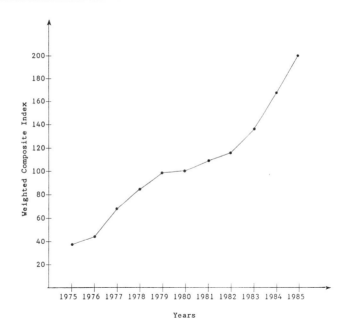

Since the index is always increasing, the total amount of credit extended has been increasing yearly since 1975.

16.19 a. From the graph of Exercise 16.1, the long term trend appears to be increasing.

b. To compute a 3-point moving average, first find the sum of the time series values from one period before, the current period, and one period after. The sum is $S_t = Y_{t-1} + Y_t + Y_{t+1}$. The moving average is found by dividing the sum by 3.

For 1975: $S_{1975} = Y_{1974} + Y_{1975} + Y_{1976} = 147.7 + 161.2 + 170.5$

$$= 479.4$$

1976: $S_{1976} = Y_{1975} + Y_{1976} + Y_{1977} = 161.2 + 170.5 + 181.5$

$$= 513.2$$

The rest of the sums are found in a similar manner and are shown in the table.

For 1975: $M_{1975} = \dfrac{S_{1975}}{3} = \dfrac{479.4}{3} = 159.80$

1976: $M_{1976} = \dfrac{S_{1976}}{3} = \dfrac{513.2}{3} = 171.07$

The rest of the values are found in a similar manner and are shown in the table.

YEAR	CPI	3-POINT MOVING TOTAL, S_t	3-POINT MOVING AVERAGE, M_t
1974	147.7		
1975	161.2	479.4	159.80
1976	170.5	513.2	171.07
1977	181.5	547.4	182.47
1978	195.4	594.3	198.10
1979	217.4	659.6	219.87
1980	246.8	736.6	245.53
1981	272.4	808.3	269.43
1982	289.1	859.9	286.63
1983	298.4	898.6	299.53
1984	311.1	931.7	310.57
1985	322.2	961.7	320.57
1986	328.4	981.1	327.03
1987	330.5		

b.

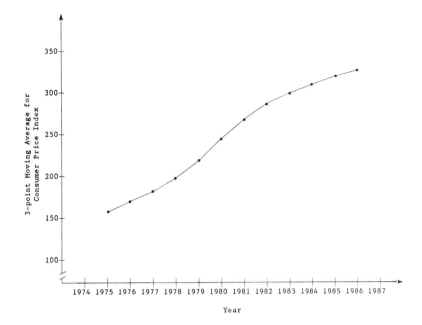

This graph is smoother than the one in Exercise 16.1.   Moving
averages tend to smooth out a time series curve.

16.21 a. To compute a 4-point moving average, first find the sum of the
time series values from two periods before, one period before, the
current period, and from one period ahead.   The sum is
$S_t = Y_{t-2} + Y_{t-1} + Y_t + Y_{t+1}$.   The moving average is found by
dividing the sum by 4.

For 1975,III: $S_{1975,III} = Y_{1975,I} + Y_{1975,II} + Y_{1975,III} + Y_{1975,IV}$

$= 83.36 + 95.19 + 83.87 + 98.13 = 360.61$

1975,IV: $S_{1975,IV} = Y_{1975,II} + Y_{1975,III} + Y_{1975,IV} + Y_{1976,I}$

$= 95.19 + 83.87 + 98.13 + 102.77 = 380.02$

The rest of the sums are found in a similar manner and are shown
in the table.

For 1975,III: $M_{1975,III} = \dfrac{S_{1975,III}}{4} = \dfrac{360.61}{4} = 90.15$

For 1975,IV: $M_{1975,IV} = \dfrac{S_{1975,IV}}{4} = \dfrac{380.02}{4} = 95.01$

The rest of the moving average values are found in a similar manner and are shown in the table.

YEAR	QUARTER	S&P 500	4-POINT MOVING TOTAL, S_t	4-POINT MOVING AVERAGE, M_t
1975	I	83.36		
	II	95.19		
	III	83.87	360.61	90.15
	IV	98.19	380.02	95.01
1976	I	102.77	389.11	97.28
	II	104.28	410.48	102.62
	III	105.24	419.75	104.94
	IV	107.46	415.40	103.85
1977	I	98.42	411.60	102.90
	II	100.48	402.89	100.72
	III	96.53	390.53	97.63
	IV	95.10	381.32	95.33
1978	I	89.21	376.37	94.09
	II	95.53	382.38	95.60
	III	102.54	383.39	95.85
	IV	96.11	395.77	98.94
1979	I	101.59	403.15	100.79
	II	102.91	409.93	102.48
	III	109.32	421.76	105.44
	IV	107.94	425.53	106.38
1980	I	105.36	436.34	109.09
	II	113.72	454.16	113.54
	III	127.14	477.66	119.42
	IV	131.44	507.24	126.81
1981	I	134.94	522.58	130.65
	II	129.06	514.21	128.55
	III	118.77	501.90	125.48
	IV	119.13	484.05	121.01
1982	I	117.09	464.81	116.20
	II	109.82	467.76	116.94
	III	121.72	487.42	121.86
	IV	138.79	521.40	130.35
1983	I	151.07	576.69	144.17
	II	165.11	623.63	155.91
	III	168.66	648.96	162.24
	IV	164.12	657.07	164.27
1984	I	159.18	645.14	161.29
	II	153.18	642.58	160.65
	III	166.10	645.70	161.43
	IV	167.24	667.18	166.80
1985	I	180.66	705.85	176.46
	II	191.85	721.83	180.46
	III	182.08	765.87	191.47
	IV	211.28	817.54	204.39
1986	I	232.33	870.99	217.75
	II	245.30	927.18	231.80
	III	238.27	964.51	241.13
	IV	248.61		

b.

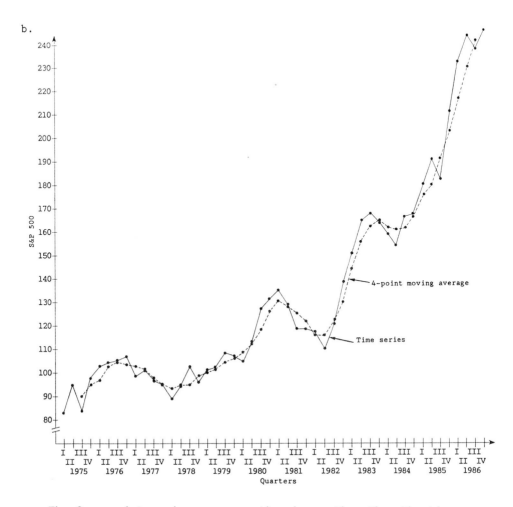

The four-point moving average, though smoother than the time
series, still has many peaks and valleys making the long-term
trend difficult to identify.

16.23 The first value of the exponentially smoothed series is equal to the
first value of the time series. The rest of the values of the
exponentially smoothed series are found using the following:

$$E_t = \omega Y_t + (1 - \omega)E_{t-1} \qquad \text{where } \omega \text{ is the smoothing constant}$$

1982,I: $E_1 = Y_1 = 165.4$

1982,II: $E_2 = \omega Y_2 + (1 - \omega)E_1 = .2(274.0) + (1 - .2)(165.4) = 187.12$

1983,III: $E_3 = \omega Y_3 + (1 - \omega)E_2 = .2(284.3) + (1 - .2)(187.12) = 206.56$

The rest of the values are computed in a similar manner and are found
in the table.

YEAR	QUARTER	HOUSING STARTS	E_t
1982	I	165.4	165.40
	II	274.0	187.12
	III	284.3	206.56
	IV	286.2	222.48
1983	I	296.5	237.29
	II	443.7	278.57
	III	347.4	292.34
	IV	373.1	308.49
1984	I	367.6	320.31
	II	492.4	354.73
	III	418.2	367.42
	IV	349.4	363.82
1985	I	326.1	356.27
	II	509.2	386.86
	III	469.1	403.31
	IV	408.6	404.37
1986	I	357.5	394.99
	II	550.0	425.99
	III	465.5	433.90
	IV	384.6	424.04

16.25   The first value of the exponentially smoothed series is equal to the
first value of the time series. The rest of the values of the
exponentially smoothed series are found using the following:

$$E_t = \omega Y_t + (1 - \omega)E_{t-1} \qquad \text{where } \omega \text{ is the smoothing constant}$$

Jan. 1984: $E_1 = Y_1 = 114.10$

Feb. 1984: $E_2 = \omega Y_2 + (1 - \omega)E_1 = .5(110.2) + (1 - .5)(114.1)$
$= 112.15$

Mar. 1984: $E_3 = \omega Y_3 + (1 - \omega)E_2 = .5(114.0) + (1 - .5)(112.15)$
$= 113.08$

The rest of the values are found in a similar manner and are shown in
the table.

	1984		1985		1986	
	Price	E_t	Price	E_t	Price	E_t
Jan.	114.1	114.10	136.3	129.45	151.4	147.96
Feb.	110.2	112.15	134.0	131.73	150.7	149.33
Mar.	114.0	113.08	127.0	129.36	149.1	149.21
Apr.	113.6	113.34	126.4	127.88	156.2	152.71
May	107.6	110.47	128.5	128.19	152.3	152.50
June	105.6	108.03	123.6	125.90	146.4	149.45
July	110.7	109.37	131.3	128.60	132.4	140.93
Aug.	123.7	116.53	126.5	127.55	138.6	139.76
Sept.	124.3	120.42	123.7	125.62	134.4	137.08
Oct.	124.6	122.51	129.7	127.66	123.5	130.29
Nov.	121.7	122.10	139.6	133.63	127.1	128.70
Dec.	123.1	122.60	155.4	144.52	120.0	124.35

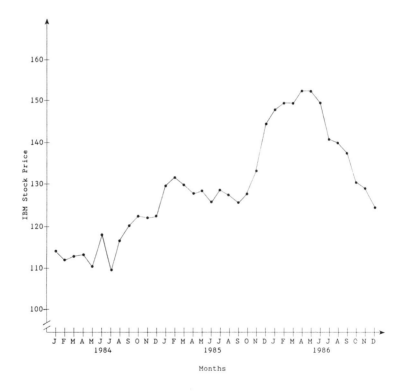

Again, there are many peaks and valleys in the plot of the exponentially smoothed series. This makes detecting a long-term trend very difficult.

16.27 a. First, select the base period, t_0. For this problem, the base period is $t_0 = 1980$. To compute the simple index, divide the time series value for each time period by the time series value in the base period and multiply by 100.

For 1980: $I_{1980} = \dfrac{Y_{1980}}{Y_{1980}} \times 100 = \dfrac{13.77}{13.77}(100) = 100.00$

1981: $I_{1981} = \dfrac{Y_{1981}}{Y_{1980}} \times 100 = \dfrac{16.63}{13.77}(100) = 120.77$

The rest of the values are computed in a similar manner and are shown in the table.

	Interest Rate	Simple Index
1980	13.77	100.00
1981	16.63	120.77
1982	16.09	116.85
1983	13.23	96.08
1984	13.87	100.73
1985	12.43	90.27
1986	10.18	73.93
1987	9.55	69.35

The simple index value for 1986 is 73.93. This means that the interest rate in 1986 is 73.93% of what it was in the base period, 1980. The interest rate has decreased 26.07%.

b. To compute the 3-point moving average, first compute the 3-point moving sum. This sum is found by adding the time series values from the previous time period, from the current time period, and from the next time period. The moving average is found by dividing the moving total by 3.

For 1981: $S_{1981} = Y_{1980} + Y_{1981} + Y_{1982} = 13.77 + 16.63 + 16.09$
$$= 46.49$$

1982: $S_{1982} = Y_{1981} + Y_{1982} + Y_{1983} = 16.63 + 16.09 + 13.23$
$$= 45.95$$

The rest of the sums are found in a similar manner and are shown in the table.

CHAPTER 16

For 1981: $M_{1981} = \dfrac{S_{1981}}{3} = \dfrac{46.49}{3} = 15.50$

1982: $M_{1982} = \dfrac{S_{1982}}{3} = \dfrac{45.95}{3} = 15.32$

The rest of the values are found in a similar manner and are shown in the table.

	Interest Rate	S_t	M_t
1980	13.77		
1981	16.63	46.49	15.50
1982	16.09	45.95	15.32
1983	13.23	43.19	14.40
1984	13.87	39.53	13.18
1985	12.43	36.48	12.16
1986	10.18	32.16	10.72
1987	9.55		

The long-term trend appears to be decreasing. Over the time period from 1980 to 1987, the interest rates are decreasing.

c. The first value of the exponentially smoothed series is equal to the first value of the time series. The rest of the values of the exponentially smoothed series are found using the following:

$E_t = \omega Y_t + (1 - \omega)E_{t-1}$ where ω is the smoothing constant

For 1980: $E_1 = Y_1 = 13.77$

1981: $E_2 = \omega Y_2 + (1 - \omega)E_1 = .2(16.63) + (1 - .2)(13.77)$
$= 14.34$

1982: $E_3 = \omega Y_3 + (1 - \omega)E_2 = .2(16.09) + (1 - .2)(14.34)$
$= 14.69$

The rest of the values are found in a similar manner and are shown in the table.

	Interest Rate	E_t
1980	13.77	13.77
1981	16.63	14.34
1982	16.09	14.69
1983	13.23	14.40
1984	13.87	14.29
1985	12.43	13.92
1986	10.18	13.17
1987	9.55	12.45

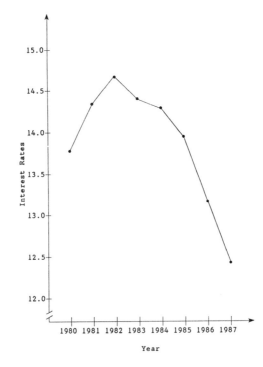

After an increase for 2 years, the interest rates then begin to decrease for the rest of the observed time period.

16.29 a. First, the base period, t_0, is selected. For this problem the base period is t_0 = January 1987. Next, the values of the 2 times series are summed for each time period, Y_t. The simple composite index is found using

$$I_t = \frac{Y_t}{Y_{t_0}} \times 100$$

For January 1987: $Y_{Jan\ 1987} = 52.1 + 193 = 245.1$

February 1987: $Y_{Feb\ 1987} = 46.4 + 202 = 248.4$

The rest of the sums are found in a similar manner and are shown in the table.

For January 1987: $I_{Jan\ 1987} = \dfrac{Y_{Jan\ 1987}}{Y_{Jan\ 1987}} \times 100 = \dfrac{245.1}{245.1}(100)$

$$= 100.00$$

February 1987: $I_{Feb\ 1987} = \dfrac{Y_{Feb\ 1987}}{Y_{Jan\ 1987}} \times 100 = \dfrac{248.4}{245.1}(100)$

$$= 101.35$$

The rest of the values are found in a similar manner and are shown in the table.

	Cotton	Wool	Y_t	Index
Jan.	52.1	193	245.1	100.00
Feb.	46.4	202	248.4	101.35
Mar.	47.5	216	263.5	107.51
Apr.	50.4	260	310.4	126.64
May	60.0	270	330.0	134.64
June	66.2	270	336.2	137.17
July	68.3	270	338.3	138.03
Aug.	65.3	300	365.3	149.04
Sept.	64.9	295	359.9	146.84
Oct.	64.1	300	364.1	148.55
Nov.	65.0	300	365.0	148.92

b. First, the base period, t_0, is selected. For this problem the base period is $t_0 =$ January 1987. Next, the weights for each of the time series are selected. For this problem, the weight of the cotton time series is 546 million and the weight of the wool time series is 13.1. For each time period, the sum of the products of the weight times the value of the time series is computed, Y_t. The index is

$$I_t = \dfrac{Y_t}{Y_{t_0}} \times 100$$

For January 1987: $Y_{Jan\ 1987} = 546(52.1) + 13.1(193) = 30,974.9$

February 1987: $Y_{Feb\ 1987} = 546(46.4) + 13.1(202) = 27,980.6$

The rest of the sums are found in a similar manner and are shown in the table.

For January 1987: $I_{Jan\ 1987} = \dfrac{Y_{Jan\ 1987}}{Y_{Jan\ 1987}} \times 100 = \dfrac{30,974.9}{30,974.9}(100)$

$$= 100.00$$

February 1987: $I_{Feb\ 1987} = \dfrac{Y_{Feb\ 1987}}{Y_{Jan\ 1987}} \times 100 = \dfrac{27,980.6}{30,974.9}(100)$

$$= 90.33$$

The rest of the values are found in a similar manner and are shown in the table.

	Cotton	Wool	Y_t	Index
Jan.	52.1	193	30,974.9	100.00
Feb.	46.4	202	27,980.6	90.33
Mar.	47.5	216	28,764.6	92.86
Apr.	50.4	260	30,924.4	99.84
May	60.0	270	36,297.0	117.18
June	66.2	270	39,682.2	128.11
July	68.3	270	40,828.8	131.81
Aug.	65.3	300	39,583.8	127.79
Sept.	64.9	295	39,299.9	126.88
Oct.	64.1	300	38,928.6	125.68
Nov.	65.0	300	39,420.0	127.26

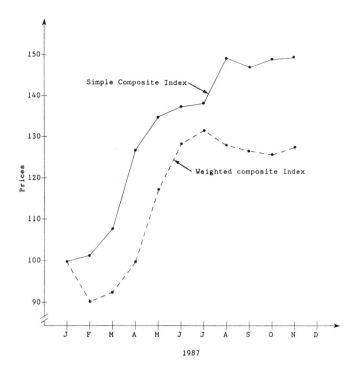

1987

The weighted composite index is always lower than the simple
composite index. Since wool is so much more expensive than
cotton, but the quantity sold is much lower, the weighted
composite index probably better characterizes the increase in
price of textile products. Without the weights, the wool prices
tend to dominate the index.

16.31 a. To compute a 12-point moving average, first compute the 12-point
moving sum. The sum is found by adding the time series values
from the 6 previous time periods, from the current time period,
and from the next 5 time periods. The moving average is found by
dividing the moving sum by 12.

For July 1982: $S_{July\ 1982} = Y_{Jan\ 1982} + Y_{Feb\ 1982} + \cdots$

$$+ Y_{July\ 1982} + \cdots + Y_{Dec\ 1982}$$

$$= 77.34 + 76.21 + 86.57 + 87.96 + 90.81$$

$$+ 88.97 + 91.21 + 89.64 + 88.16$$

$$+ 91.41 + 94.19 + 113.10$$

$$= 1075.57$$

Aug 1982: $S_{\text{Aug 1982}} = Y_{\text{Feb 1982}} + \cdots + Y_{\text{Aug 1982}} + \cdots$

$$+ Y_{\text{Dec 1982}} + Y_{\text{Jan 1983}}$$

$$= 76.21 + 86.57 + \cdots + 113.10 + 81.34$$

$$= 1079.57$$

The rest of the sums are computed in a similar manner and are shown in the table.

For July 1982: $M_{\text{July 1982}} = \dfrac{S_{\text{July 1982}}}{12} = \dfrac{1075.57}{12} = 89.63$

Aug 1982: $M_{\text{Aug 1982}} = \dfrac{S_{\text{Aug 1982}}}{12} = \dfrac{1079.57}{12} = 89.96$

The rest of the values are computed in a similar manner and are shown in the table.

		Retail Sales	St	Mt	Et
1982	Jan.	77.34			77.34
	Feb.	76.21			76.66
	Mar.	86.57			82.61
	Apr.	87.96			85.82
	May	90.81			88.81
	June	88.97			88.91
	July	91.21	1075.57	89.63	90.29
	Aug.	89.64	1079.57	89.96	89.90
	Sept.	88.16	1082.24	90.19	88.86
	Oct.	91.41	1089.42	90.79	90.39
	Nov.	94.19	1095.43	91.29	92.67
	Dec.	113.10	1102.46	91.87	104.93
1983	Jan.	81.34	1114.10	92.84	90.78
	Feb.	78.88	1122.45	93.54	83.64
	Mar.	93.75	1133.04	94.42	89.71
	Apr.	93.97	1142.85	95.24	92.26
	May	97.84	1151.82	95.99	95.61
	June	100.61	1161.95	96.83	98.61
	July	99.56	1174.00	97.83	99.18
	Aug.	100.23	1185.29	98.77	99.81
	Sept.	97.97	1199.87	99.99	98.71
	Oct.	100.38	1210.32	100.86	99.71
	Nov.	104.32	1220.75	101.73	102.48
	Dec.	125.15	1234.51	102.88	116.08
1984	Jan.	92.63	1245.90	103.83	102.01
	Feb.	93.46	1252.34	104.36	96.88
	Mar.	104.20	1262.91	105.24	101.27
	Apr.	104.40	1268.54	105.71	103.15
	May	111.60	1277.26	106.44	108.22
	June	112.00	1285.94	107.16	110.49
	July	106.00	1292.29	107.69	107.80
	Aug.	110.80	1298.13	108.18	109.60
	Sept.	103.60	1300.01	108.33	106.00
	Oct.	109.10	1305.71	108.81	107.86
	Nov.	113.00	1314.31	109.53	110.94
	Dec.	131.50	1322.91	110.24	123.28
1985	Jan.	98.47	1325.71	110.48	108.39
	Feb.	95.34	1334.91	111.24	100.56
	Mar.	109.90	1344.91	112.08	106.16
	Apr.	113.00	1355.11	112.93	110.27
	May	120.20	1361.81	113.48	116.23
	June	114.80	1366.91	113.91	115.37
	July	115.20	1374.11	114.51	115.27
	Aug.	120.80	1381.24	115.10	118.59
	Sept.	113.80	1385.56	115.46	115.71
	Oct.	115.80	1389.86	115.82	115.77
	Nov.	118.10	1392.56	116.05	117.17
	Dec.	138.70	1397.76	116.48	130.09
1986	Jan.	105.60	1403.36	116.95	115.39
	Feb.	99.66	1408.86	117.41	105.95
	Mar.	114.20	1412.16	117.68	110.90
	Apr.	115.70	1422.96	118.58	113.78
	May	125.40	1430.26	119.19	120.75
	June	120.40	1432.96	119.41	120.54
	July	120.70	1445.56	120.46	120.64
	Aug.	124.10			122.71
	Sept.	124.60			123.85
	Oct.	123.10			123.40
	Nov.	120.80			121.84
	Dec.	151.30			139.52

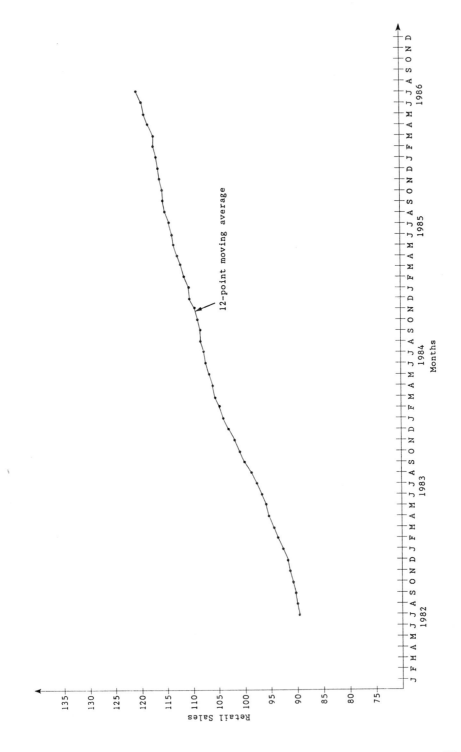

There appears to be a long-term trend. The retail sales are increasing over time.

b. The first value of the exponentially smoothed series is equal to the first value of the time series. The rest of the values of the exponentially smoothed series are found using the formula:

$$E_t = \omega Y_t + (1 - \omega)E_{t-1}$$ where ω is the smoothing constant

For Jan 1982: $E_1 = Y_1 = 77.34$

Feb 1982: $E_2 = \omega Y_2 + (1 - \omega)E_1 = .6(76.21) + (1 - .6)(77.34)$
$= 76.66$

Mar 1982: $E_3 = \omega Y_3 + (1 - \omega)E_2 = .6(86.57) + (1 - .6)(76.66)$
$= 82.61$

The rest of the values are found in a similar manner and are shown under the E_t column in the table in part (a).

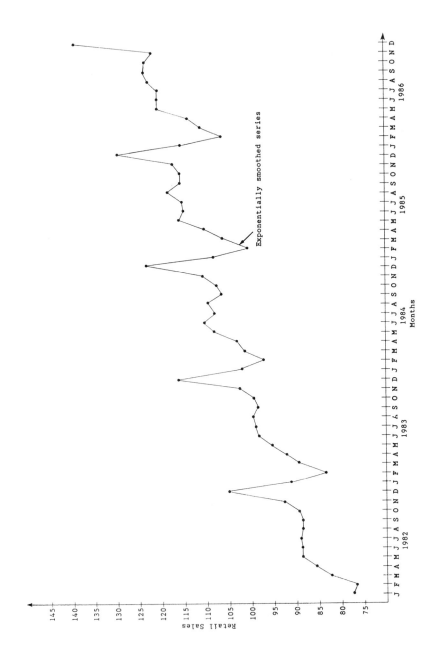

Although not quite so obvious as the 12-point moving average, there appears to be a long-term trend. The retail sales are tending to increase over time.

SEVENTEEN   TIME SERIES MODELS: FORECASTING

17.1   One problem with using a moving average to forecast values of a time series is that values at the ends of the series are "lost," thus requiring that we subjectively extend the graph of the moving average into the future. No exact calculation of a forecast is available. Finally, no measures of reliability are available for this technique.

17.3   No, the reliability of the forecasts obtained using a smoothing technique cannot be measured. This is a problem because we cannot put confidence limits on the forecasts.

17.5   From Exercise 16.23, the exponentially smoothed value for Quarter IV, 1986 is $E_n = 4240$. For any future value, the forecast is

$$F_t = wY_n + (1 - w)E_n \quad \text{for } t > n$$

The forecast for Quarter I, 1987 is

$$F_1 = .2(384.6) + (1 - .2)424.0 = 416.12$$

17.7   a.   From the graph in the solution to Exercise 16.21, the plot of the 4-point moving average is very close to the plot of the original time series. Therefore, there is no seasonal variation. To forecast the quarterly S & P 500 values for 1987, we just extend the graph of the 4-point moving average to the quarters in 1987. Thus, the forecasts are approximately:

$$F_{1987, I} = 253$$

$$F_{1987, II} = 259$$

$$F_{1987, III} = 265$$

$$F_{1987, IV} = 271$$

b. From Exercise 16.26, $Y_n = 248.61$ and $E_n = 229.50$.

The forecasts, using the exponentially smoothed series, are:

$$F_t = wY_n + (1 - w)E_n \qquad \text{for } t = 1, 2, 3, 4$$

$$F_1 = .3(248.61) + (1 - .3)(229.50) = 235.233$$

$$F_2 = F_3 = F_4 = 235.233$$

17.9 a. Extending the general trend of the 12-point moving average graph, the forecast for January 1987 is approximately 138.

b. From Exercise 16.25, $Y_n = 120.00$ and $E_n = 124.35$.

The forecast, using the exponentially smoothed series, is:

$$F_1 = wY_n + (1 - w)E_n = .5(120.0) + (1 - .5)(124.35) = 122.175$$

17.11 a.

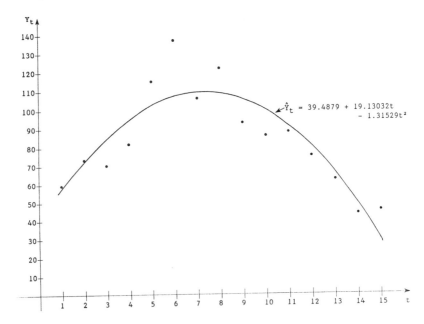

$$\hat{Y}_t = 39.4879 + 19.13032t - 1.31529t^2$$

There appears to be a quadratic trend.

b. Using SAS to fit the model, the output is:

DEP VARIABLE: Y

ANALYSIS OF VARIANCE

SOURCE	DF	SUM OF SQUARES	MEAN SQUARE	F VALUE	PROB>F
MODEL	2	8162.80795	4081.40398	21.599	0.0001
ERROR	12	2267.59205	188.96600		
C TOTAL	14	10430.40000			

ROOT MSE	13.74649	R-SQUARE	0.7826	
DEP MEAN	83.8	ADJ R-SQ	0.7464	
C.V.	16.40393			

PARAMETER ESTIMATES

VARIABLE	DF	PARAMETER ESTIMATE	STANDARD ERROR	T FOR HO: PARAMETER=0	PROB > ¦T¦
INTERCEP	1	39.48791209	12.24446298	3.225	0.0073
T	1	19.13031674	3.52154451	5.432	0.0002
TSQ	1	-1.31528765	0.21402392	-6.146	0.0001

OBS		ACTUAL	PREDICT VALUE	STD ERR PREDICT	LOWER95% PREDICT	UPPER95% PREDICT	RESIDUAL
	1	59.0000	57.3029	9.3709	21.0546	93.5512	1.6971
	2	73.0000	72.4874	7.1173	38.7599	106.2	0.5126
	3	70.0000	85.0413	5.5953	52.7042	117.4	-15.0413
	4	82.0000	94.9646	4.8705	63.1891	126.7	-12.9646
	5	115.0	102.3	4.7908	70.5394	134.0	12.7427
OBS		ACTUAL	PREDICT VALUE	STD ERR PREDICT	LOWER95% PREDICT	UPPER95% PREDICT	RESIDUAL
	6	137.0	106.9	5.0150	75.0374	138.8	30.0805
	7	106.0	109.0	5.2506	76.8895	141.0	-2.9510
	8	122.0	108.4	5.3440	76.2173	140.5	13.6480
	9	93.0000	105.1	5.2506	73.0609	137.2	-12.1225
	10	86.0000	99.2623	5.0150	67.3803	131.1	-13.2623
	11	88.0000	90.7716	4.7908	59.0537	122.5	-2.7716
	12	75.0000	79.6503	4.8705	47.8749	111.4	-4.6503
	13	62.0000	65.8984	5.5953	33.5613	98.2355	-3.8984
	14	44.0000	49.5160	7.1173	15.7885	83.2434	-5.5160
	15	45.0000	30.5029	9.3709	-5.7454	66.7512	14.4971
	16	.	8.8593	12.2445	-31.2506	48.9693	.

SUM OF RESIDUALS	5.79092E-13
SUM OF SQUARED RESIDUALS	2267.592
PREDICTED RESID SS (PRESS)	3525.982

The fitted model is $\hat{Y}_t = 39.4879 + 19.13032t - 1.31529t^2$.

c. The least squares line is shown on the graph in part (a). It appears to fit the data fairly well.

d. From the printout the 95% prediction interval for home sales in week 16 is (-31.2506, 48.9693).

17.13 a. From the data, there appear to be secular trends for all modes of transportation. As time increases, the percentages for railroads and buses tend to decrease. For air carriers, as time increases, the percentage tends to increase.

b. For Railroads:

$$\sum t = 55 \qquad\qquad \sum y = 292.1 \qquad\qquad \sum ty = 926.8$$

$$\sum t^2 = 385 \qquad\qquad \sum y^2 = 14,759.19$$

$$SS_{ty} = \sum ty - \frac{\sum t \sum y}{n} = 926.8 - \frac{55(292.1)}{10} = -679.75$$

$$SS_{tt} = \sum t^2 - \frac{(\sum t)^2}{n} = 385 - \frac{55^2}{10} = 82.5$$

$$\hat{\beta}_1 = \frac{SS_{ty}}{SS_{tt}} = \frac{-679.75}{82.5} = -8.239393939 \approx -8.239$$

$$\hat{\beta}_0 = \bar{y} - \hat{\beta}_1 \bar{t} = \frac{292.1}{10} - (-8.239393939)\left(\frac{55}{10}\right) = 74.526666 \approx 74.527$$

The least squares line is $\hat{Y}_t = 74.527 - 8.239t$

For Buses:

$$\sum t = 55 \qquad\qquad \sum y = 218.3 \qquad\qquad \sum ty = 999.2$$

$$\sum t^2 = 385 \qquad\qquad \sum y^2 = 5557.01$$

$$SS_{ty} = \sum ty - \frac{\sum t \sum y}{n} = 999.2 - \frac{55(218.3)}{10} = -201.45$$

$$SS_{tt} = \sum t^2 - \frac{(\sum t)^2}{n} = 385 - \frac{55^2}{10} = 82.5$$

$$\hat{\beta}_1 = \frac{SS_{ty}}{SS_{tt}} = \frac{-201.45}{82.5} = -2.44181818 \approx -2.442$$

$$\hat{\beta}_0 = \bar{y} - \hat{\beta}_1 \bar{t} = \frac{218.3}{10} - (-2.44181818)\left(\frac{55}{10}\right) = 35.260$$

The least squares line is $\hat{Y}_t = 35.260 - 2.442t$

For Air Carriers:

$$\sum t = 55 \qquad\qquad \sum y = 468.6 \qquad\qquad \sum ty = 3477.8$$

$$\sum t^2 = 385 \qquad\quad \sum y^2 = 32,054$$

$$SS_{ty} = \sum ty - \frac{\sum t \sum y}{n} = 3477.8 - \frac{55(468.6)}{10} = 900.5$$

$$SS_{tt} = \sum t^2 - \frac{(\sum t)^2}{n} = 385 - \frac{55^2}{10} = 82.5$$

$$\hat{\beta}_1 = \frac{SS_{ty}}{SS_{tt}} = \frac{900.5}{82.5} = 10.91515152 \approx 10.915$$

$$\hat{\beta}_0 = \bar{y} - \hat{\beta}_1 \bar{t} = \frac{468.6}{10} - 19.91515152\left(\frac{55}{10}\right) = -13.173333 \approx -13.173$$

The least squares line is $\hat{Y}_t = -13.173 + 10.915t$

c.

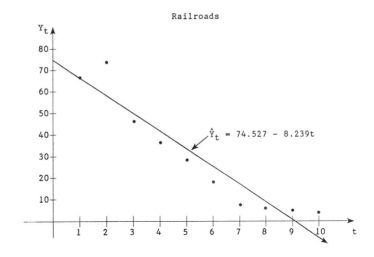

Railroads

$\hat{Y}_t = 74.527 - 8.239t$

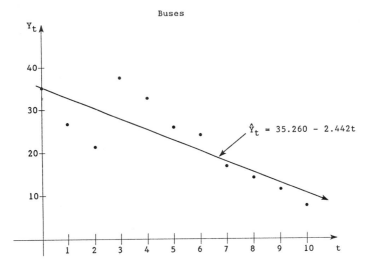

Buses

$$\hat{Y}_t = 35.260 - 2.442t$$

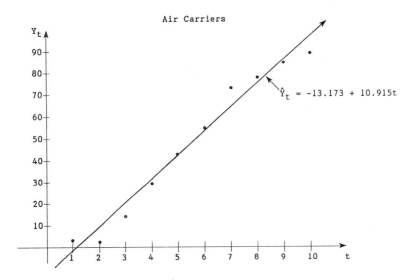

Air Carriers

$$\hat{Y}_t = -13.173 + 10.915t$$

For all three modes of transportation, the models fit the secular trend fairly well. We might want to try a quadratic model for railroads.

d. For Railroads, for t = 11, $\hat{Y}_t$ = 74.527 − 8.239(11) = −16.102

For Buses, for t = 11, $\hat{Y}_t$ = 35.260 − 2.442(11) = 8.40

For Air Carriers, for t = 11, $\hat{Y}_t$ = −13.173 + 10.915(11) = 106.89

Using SAS, the prediction intervals can be found on the following printouts:

DEP VARIABLE: RR

ANALYSIS OF VARIANCE

SOURCE	DF	SUM OF SQUARES	MEAN SQUARE	F VALUE	PROB>F
MODEL	1	5600.72803	5600.72803	71.550	0.0001
ERROR	8	626.22097	78.27762121		
C TOTAL	9	6226.94900			

ROOT MSE	8.847464	R-SQUARE	0.8994	
DEP MEAN	29.21	ADJ R-SQ	0.8869	
C.V.	30.28916			

PARAMETER ESTIMATES

VARIABLE	DF	PARAMETER ESTIMATE	STANDARD ERROR	T FOR HO: PARAMETER=0	PROB > |T|
INTERCEP	1	74.52666667	6.04396861	12.331	0.0001
T	1	-8.23939394	0.97407374	-8.459	0.0001

OBS	ACTUAL	PREDICT VALUE	STD ERR PREDICT	LOWER95% PREDICT	UPPER95% PREDICT	RESIDUAL
1	67.1000	66.2873	5.2001	42.6217	89.9529	0.8127
2	74.3000	58.0479	4.4103	35.2510	80.8447	16.2521
3	46.3000	49.8085	3.7092	27.6856	71.9314	-3.5085
4	36.5000	41.5691	3.1564	19.9071	63.2310	-5.0691
5	28.6000	33.3297	2.8399	11.9019	54.7575	-4.7297
6	17.9000	25.0903	2.8399	3.6625	46.5181	-7.1903
7	7.3000	16.8509	3.1564	-4.8110	38.5129	-9.5509
8	5.8000	8.6115	3.7092	-13.5114	30.7344	-2.8115
9	4.7000	0.3721	4.4103	-22.4247	23.1690	4.3279
10	3.6000	-7.8673	5.2001	-31.5329	15.7983	11.4673
11	.	-16.1067	6.0440	-40.8153	8.6020	.

SUM OF RESIDUALS   2.42473E-13
SUM OF SQUARED RESIDUALS   626.221
PREDICTED RESID SS (PRESS)   1084.633

DEP VARIABLE: BUS

ANALYSIS OF VARIANCE

SOURCE	DF	SUM OF SQUARES	MEAN SQUARE	F VALUE	PROB>F
MODEL	1	491.90427	491.90427	13.134	0.0067
ERROR	8	299.61673	37.45209091		
C TOTAL	9	791.52100			

ROOT MSE	6.119811	R-SQUARE	0.6215
DEP MEAN	21.83	ADJ R-SQ	0.5742
C.V.	28.03395		

PARAMETER ESTIMATES

VARIABLE	DF	PARAMETER ESTIMATE	STANDARD ERROR	T FOR HO: PARAMETER=0	PROB > |T|
INTERCEP	1	35.26000000	4.18062704	8.434	0.0001
T	1	-2.44181818	0.67376905	-3.624	0.0067

OBS	ACTUAL	PREDICT VALUE	STD ERR PREDICT	LOWER95% PREDICT	UPPER95% PREDICT	RESIDUAL
1	26.5000	32.8182	3.5969	16.4486	49.1877	-6.3182
2	21.4000	30.3764	3.0506	14.6077	46.1450	-8.9764
3	37.7000	27.9345	2.5656	12.6321	43.2370	9.7655
4	32.4000	25.4927	2.1833	10.5091	40.4763	6.9073
5	25.7000	23.0509	1.9644	8.2293	37.8725	2.6491
6	24.2000	20.6091	1.9644	5.7875	35.4307	3.5909
7	16.9000	18.1673	2.1833	3.1837	33.1509	-1.2673
8	14.2000	15.7255	2.5656	0.4230	31.0279	-1.5255
9	11.4000	13.2836	3.0506	-2.4850	29.0523	-1.8836
10	7.9000	10.8418	3.5969	-5.5277	27.2114	-2.9418
11	.	8.4000	4.1806	-8.6910	25.4910	.

SUM OF RESIDUALS	8.85958E-14
SUM OF SQUARED RESIDUALS	299.6167
PREDICTED RESID SS (PRESS)	495.6202

DEP VARIABLE: AIR

ANALYSIS OF VARIANCE

SOURCE	DF	SUM OF SQUARES	MEAN SQUARE	F VALUE	PROB>F
MODEL	1	9829.09394	9829.09394	295.268	0.0001
ERROR	8	266.31006	33.28875758		
C TOTAL	9	10095.40400			

ROOT MSE	5.769641	R-SQUARE	0.9736	
DEP MEAN	46.86	ADJ R-SQ	0.9703	
C.V.	12.31251			

PARAMETER ESTIMATES

VARIABLE	DF	PARAMETER ESTIMATE	STANDARD ERROR	T FOR H0: PARAMETER=0	PROB > |T|
INTERCEP	1	-13.17333333	3.94141517	-3.342	0.0102
T	1	10.91515152	0.63521657	17.183	0.0001

OBS	ACTUAL	PREDICT VALUE	STD ERR PREDICT	LOWER95% PREDICT	UPPER95% PREDICT	RESIDUAL
1	2.8000	-2.2582	3.3911	-17.6911	13.1747	5.0582
2	2.7000	8.6570	2.8761	-6.2094	23.5233	-5.9570
3	14.3000	19.5721	2.4188	5.1453	33.9990	-5.2721
4	28.9000	30.4873	2.0583	16.3610	44.6135	-1.5873
5	42.1000	41.4024	1.8520	27.4289	55.3760	0.6976
6	54.7000	52.3176	1.8520	38.3440	66.2911	2.3824
7	73.1000	63.2327	2.0583	49.1065	77.3590	9.8673
8	77.7000	74.1479	2.4188	59.7210	88.5747	3.5521
9	83.9000	85.0630	2.8761	70.1967	99.9294	-1.1630
10	88.4000	95.9782	3.3911	80.5453	111.4	-7.5782
11	.	106.9	3.9414	90.7802	123.0	.

SUM OF RESIDUALS   3.08642E-14
SUM OF SQUARED RESIDUALS   266.3101
PREDICTED RESID SS (PRESS)   457.2737

The prediction interval for railroads is: (-40.8153, 8.6020)

The prediction interval for buses is: (-8.6910, 25.4910)

The prediction interval for air carriers is: (90,7802, 123.0)

17.15 a. Some preliminary calculations are:

$$\sum t = 666 \qquad \sum y = 4657.3 \qquad \sum ty = 89{,}501.9$$

$$\sum t^2 = 16{,}206 \qquad \sum y^2 = 609{,}220.85$$

$$SS_{ty} = \sum ty - \frac{\sum t \sum y}{n} = 89{,}501.9 - \frac{666(4657.3)}{36} = 3341.85$$

$$SS_{tt} = \sum t^2 - \frac{(\sum t)^2}{n} = 16{,}206 - \frac{666^2}{36} = 3885$$

$$\hat{\beta}_1 = \frac{SS_{ty}}{SS_{tt}} = \frac{3341.85}{3885} = .86019305 \approx .860$$

$$\hat{\beta}_0 = \bar{y} - \hat{\beta}_1\bar{t} = \frac{4657.3}{36} - (.86019305)\left(\frac{666}{36}\right) = 113.455873$$
$$\approx 113.456$$

The least squares line is $\hat{Y}_t = 113.465 + .860t$

b.

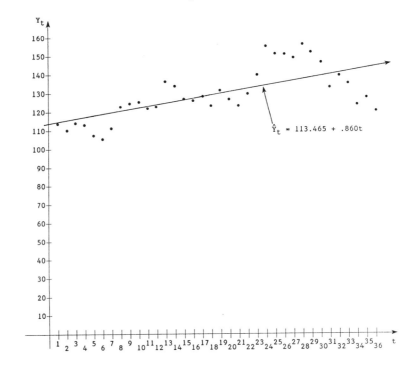

The general trend is fit fairly well by the model.

c. $SS_{yy} = \sum y^2 - \frac{(\sum y)^2}{n} = 609,220.85 - \frac{4657.3^2}{36} = 6708.536389$

$SSE = SS_{yy} - \hat{\beta}_1 SS_{ty} = 6708.536389 - .86019305(3341.85)$
$= 3833.900245$

$s^2 = \frac{SSE}{n-2} = \frac{3833.900245}{36-2} = 112.7618 \qquad s = \sqrt{112.7618} = 10.6189$

To determine if the model is useful for predicting IBM monthly stock price, we test:

H_0: $\beta_1 = 0$
H_a: $\beta_1 \neq 0$

The test statistic is $t = \dfrac{\hat{\beta_1}}{\dfrac{s}{\sqrt{SS_{tt}}}} = \dfrac{.860}{\dfrac{10.6189}{\sqrt{3885}}} = 5.05$

For a two-tailed alternative, the rejection region requires $\alpha/2 = .05/2 = .025$ in each tail of the t distribution with $n - 2 = 36 - 2 = 34$ df. From Table 6, Appendix E, $t_{.025} \approx 2.042$. The rejection region is $t < -2.042$ or $t > 2.042$.

Since the observed value of the test statistic falls in the rejection region (t = 5.05 > 2.042), H_0 is rejected. There is sufficient evidence to indicate the model is useful for predicting IBM monthly stock price at $\alpha = .05$.

d. For t = 37, $\hat{Y}_t = 113.465 + .860(37) = 145.285$

The general form for the prediction interval is

$$\hat{Y} \pm t_{\alpha/2}(s)\sqrt{1 + \frac{1}{n} + \frac{(t - \bar{t})^2}{SS_{tt}}}$$

For confidence coefficient .95, $\alpha = .05$ and $\alpha/2 = .025$. From Table 6, Appendix E, with $n - 2 = 36 - 2 = 34$ df, $t_{.025} \approx 2.042$.

The 95% confidence interval is

$$145.285 \pm 2.042(10.6189)\sqrt{1 + \frac{1}{36} + \frac{(37 - 18.5)^2}{3885}}$$

$\Rightarrow 145.285 \pm 22.906 \Rightarrow (122.379, 168.191)$

The actual value 133.0 does fall in the above interval.

17.17 a. H_0: $\beta_2 = 0$
H_a: $\beta_2 < 0$

The test statistic is $t = -1.39$.

For a one-tailed alternative, the rejection region requires $\alpha = .05$ in the lower tail of the t distribution with $n - 2 = 107 - 2 = 105$ df. From Table 6, Appendix E, $t_{.05} \approx 1.665$. The rejection region is $t < -1.665$.

Since the observed value of the test statistic does not fall in the rejection region (t = -1.39 $\not<$ -1.665), H_0 is not rejected.

There is insufficient evidence that the quarterly number of pension plan qualifications increases at a decreasing rate over time at $\alpha = .05$.

b. For $t = 108$, $\hat{Y}_{108} = 6.19 + .039(108) - .00024(108^2) = 7.603$

Therefore, the forecast is $e^{7.063} = 2003.48$.

c. H_0: $\beta_2 = 0$
   H_a: $\beta_2 < 0$

The test statistic is $t = -1.61$.

For a one-tailed alternative, the rejection region requires $\alpha = .05$ in the lower tail of the t distribution with $n - 2 = 107 - 2 = 105$ df. From Table 6, Appendix E, $t_{.05} \approx 1.665$. The rejection region is $t < -1.665$.

Since the observed value of the test statistic does not fall in the rejection region ($t = -1.61 \not< -1.665$), H_0 is not rejected. There is insufficient evidence that the quarterly number of profit-sharing plan qualifications increases at a decreasing rate over time at $\alpha = .05$.

d. For $t = 108$, $\hat{Y}_{108} = 6.22 + .035(108) - .00021(108^2) = 7.550$

Therefore, the forecast is $e^{7.550} = 1901.81$

17.19 a. From Table 15, $d_L = 1.21$ and $d_U = 1.65$.

b. From Table 16, $d_L = 1.25$ and $d_U = 1.34$.

c. From Table 15, $d_L = 1.16$ and $d_U = 1.80$.

17.21 a. To determine if the model contributes information for the prediction of y, we test:

H_0: $\beta_1 = \beta_2 = \beta_3 = \beta_4 = \beta_5 = 0$
H_a: At least one $\beta_i \neq 0$

The test statistic is $F = \left[\dfrac{R^2}{1 - R^2} \right] \left[\dfrac{n - (k + 1)}{k} \right]$

$= \left[\dfrac{.856}{1 - .856} \right] \left[\dfrac{144 - (5 + 1)}{5} \right] = 164.07$

The rejection region requires $\alpha = .05$ in the upper tail of the F distribution with $\nu_1 = k = 5$ and $\nu_2 = n - (k + 1) = 144 - (5 + 1) = 138$. From Table 8, Appendix E, $F_{.05} \approx 2.29$. The rejection region is $F > 2.29$.

Since the observed value of the test statistic falls in the rejection region (F = 164.07 > 2.29), H_0 is rejected. There is sufficient evidence to indicate the model contributes information for the prediction of y at α = .05.

b. To determine if the regression errors are positively correlated, we test:

H_0: No autocorrelation
H_a: Positive autocorrelation

The test statistic is d = 1.01.

For a one-tailed alternative, the rejection region is $d < d_{L,\alpha}$. From Table 15, Appendix E, with α = .05, n = 144, and k = 5, $d_{L,.05} \approx 1.57$. The rejection region is d < 1.57.

Since the observed value of the test statistic falls in the rejection region (d = 1.01 < 1.57), H_0 is rejected. There is sufficient evidence to indicate the regression errors are positively correlated at α = .05.

c. Since we detected a positive correlation among the regression errors, our conclusion about the model adequacy is suspect. A model that accounts for first-order autocorrelation in the error terms should be considered.

17.23 a. The regression residuals are defined as

$$Y_t - \hat{Y}_t \quad \text{where } \hat{Y}_t = 687.79 - 1.1693t$$

For t = 1, $\hat{Y}_1 = 687.79 - 1.1693(1) = 686.6207$

$$(Y_1 - \hat{Y}_1) = 583.4 - 686.6207 = -103.2207$$

The rest of the values of $\hat{Y}_t$ and $(Y_t - \hat{Y}_t)$ are computed in a similar manner and are shown in the table:

t	Y_t	$\hat{Y}_t$	$(Y_t - \hat{Y}_t)$
1	583.4	686.6207	-103.2207
2	655.0	685.4514	-30.4514
3	756.2	684.2821	71.9179
4	721.1	683.1128	37.9872
5	803.3	681.9435	121.3565
6	727.4	680.7742	46.6258
7	684.1	679.6049	4.4951
8	603.5	678.4536	-74.9356
9	566.7	677.2663	-110.5663
10	689.6	676.0970	13.5030
11	600.7	674.9277	-74.2277
12	560.7	673.7584	-113.0584
13	628.0	672.5891	-44.5891
14	645.2	671.4198	-26.2198
15	768.9	670.2505	98.6495
16	788.2	669.0812	119.1188
17	807.6	667.9119	139.6881
18	676.7	666.7426	9.9574
19	633.5	665.5733	-32.0733
20	744.8	664.4040	80.3960
21	839.4	663.2347	176.1653
22	598.4	662.0654	-63.6654
23	515.8	660.8961	-145.0961
24	558.0	659.7268	-101.7268

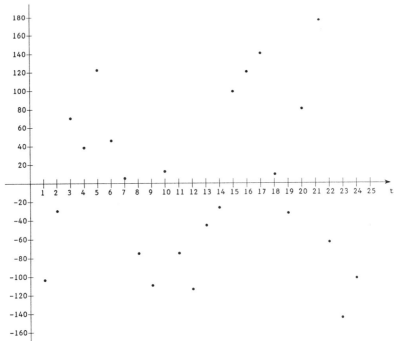

There is a tendency for the residuals to have long positive or negative runs. This indicates the regression errors are correlated.

b. To determine if the residuals are autocorrelated, we test:

H_0: No autocorrelation
H_a: Positive or negative autocorrelation

The test statistic is d = .998.

For a two-tailed alternative, the rejection region is $d < d_{L,\alpha/2}$ or $(4 - d) < d_{L,\alpha/2}$. From Table 15, Appendix E, with n = 24, k = 1, and α = .05, $d_{L,.05}$ = 1.27. (We will use .05 because there is no table for .05/2 = .025.) The rejection region is d < 1.27 or (4 - d) < 1.27.

Since the observed value of the test statistic falls in the rejection region (d = .998 < 1.27), H_0 is rejected. There is sufficient evidence to indicate the residuals are autocorrelated at α = .05.

c. Since we detected the presence of autocorrelation in part (c), the least squares model would not be appropriate. A time series model that accounts for first-order autocorrelation would be a better model.

17.25 a. The regression residuals are defined as $Y_t - \hat{Y}_t$,

where $\hat{Y}_t$ = 74.2 + 1.9165t (from Exercise 17.10)

For t = 1, $\hat{Y}_1$ = 74.2 + 1.9165(1) = 76.1165

$(Y_1 - \hat{Y}_1)$ = 75 - 76.1165 = -1.1165

For t = 2, $\hat{Y}_2$ = 74.2 + 1.9165(2) = 78.033

$(Y_2 - \hat{Y}_2)$ = 78 - 78.033 = -.033

The rest of the values of $\hat{Y}_t$ and $Y_t - \hat{Y}_t$ are found in a similar manner and are shown in the table:

t	Y_t	$\hat{Y}_t$	$(\hat{Y}_t - Y_t)$
1	75	76.1165	−1.1165
2	78	78.0330	−0.0330
3	82	79.9495	2.0505
4	82	81.8660	0.1340
5	84	83.7825	0.2175
6	85	85.6990	−0.6990
7	87	87.6155	−0.6155
8	91	89.5320	1.4680
9	92	91.4485	0.5515
10	92	93.3650	−1.3650
11	93	95.2815	−2.2815
12	96	97.1980	−1.1980
13	101	99.1145	1.8855
14	102	101.0310	0.9690

b. Residuals

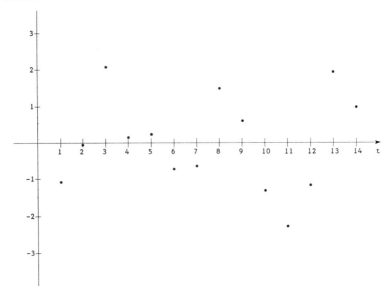

There is some evidence of residual autocorrelation. There are a few positive and negative runs.

c. The output from fitting the model using SAS is:

GENERAL LINEAR MODELS PROCEDURE

DEPENDENT VARIABLE: Y

SOURCE	DF	SUM OF SQUARES	MEAN SQUARE	F VALUE
MODEL	1	835.58681319	835.58681319	459.08
ERROR	12	21.84175824	1.82014652	PR > F
CORRECTED TOTAL	13	857.42857143		0.0001

R-SQUARE	C.V.	ROOT MSE	Y MEAN
0.974526	1.5232	1.34912806	88.57142857

SOURCE	DF	TYPE I SS	F VALUE	PR > F
T	1	835.58681319	459.08	0.0001

SOURCE	DF	TYPE III SS	F VALUE	PR > F
T	1	835.58681319	459.08	0.0001

PARAMETER	ESTIMATE	T FOR HO: PARAMETER=0	PR > ¦T¦	STD ERROR OF ESTIMATE
INTERCEPT	74.19780220	97.42	0.0001	0.76160797
T	1.91648352	21.43	0.0001	0.08944632

OBSERVATION	OBSERVED VALUE	PREDICTED VALUE	RESIDUAL
1	75.00000000	76.11428571	-1.11428571
2	78.00000000	78.03076923	-0.03076923
3	82.00000000	79.94725275	2.05274725
4	82.00000000	81.86373626	0.13626374
5	84.00000000	83.78021978	0.21978022
6	85.00000000	85.69670330	-0.69670330
7	87.00000000	87.61318681	-0.61318681
8	91.00000000	89.52967033	1.47032967
9	92.00000000	91.44615385	0.55384615
10	92.00000000	93.36263736	-1.36263736
11	93.00000000	95.27912088	-2.27912088
12	96.00000000	97.19560440	-1.19560440
13	101.00000000	99.11208791	1.88791209
14	102.00000000	101.02857143	0.97142857

SUM OF RESIDUALS	0.00000000
SUM OF SQUARED RESIDUALS	21.84175824
SUM OF SQUARED RESIDUALS - ERROR SS	-0.00000000
FIRST ORDER AUTOCORRELATION	0.23442486
DURBIN-WATSON D	1.43109853

To determine if the residuals are autocorrelated, we test:

H_0: No autocorrelation

H_a: Positive or negative autocorrelation

TIME SERIES MODELS: FORECASTING

The test statistic is d = 1.431

For a two-tailed alternative, the rejection region is d < $d_{L, \alpha/2}$ or (4 - d) < $d_{L, \alpha/2}$. From Table 15, Appendix E, with n = 14, k = 1, and α = .05, $d_{L, .05} \approx 1.08$ and $d_{U, .05} \approx 1.36$. (Since n = 14 is not given, n = 15 was used. Also, there is no table for α/2 = .025. We will use α = .05 instead.) The rejection region is d < 1.08 or (4 - d) < 1.05. If d > 1.36 or (4 - d) > 1.36, we do not reject H_0.

Since the observed value of the test statistic does not fall in the rejection region (d = 1.431 ≮ 1.08 and d = 1.43 > 1.36), H_0 is not rejected. There is insufficient evidence to indicate the residuals are autocorrelated at α = .05.

17.27 a. To determine if the model is useful for predicting future spot exchange rates, we test:

H_0: $\beta_1 = 0$
H_a: $\beta_1 \neq 0$

The test statistic is t = 47.9

For a two-tailed alternative, the rejection region requires α/2 = .05/2 = .025 in each tail of the t distribution with n - 2 = 81 - 2 = 79 df. From Table 6, Appendix E, $t_{.025} \approx 2.00$. The rejection region is t < -2.00 or t > 2.00.

Since the observed value of the test statistic falls in the rejection region (t = 47.9 > 2.00), H_0 is rejected. There is sufficient evidence to indicate the model is useful for predicting future spot exchange rates at α = .05.

   b. s = .0249. We expect most of the observations to fall within 2s or 2(.0249) or .0498 units of the least squares line.

R^2 = .957. This means that 95.7% of the sums of squares of the deviations of the spot exchange rate values about their means is attributable to the linear relationship between spot exchange rates and the forward rate.

   c. To determine if autocorrelation exists, we test:

H_0: No autocorrelation
H_a: Positive or negative autocorrelation

The test statistic is d = .962.

For a two-tailed alternative, the rejection region is d < $d_{L, \alpha/2}$ or (4 - d) < $d_{L, \alpha/2}$. From Table 15, Appendix E, with n = 81, k = 1, and α = .05, $d_{L, .05} = 1.61$ and $d_{U, .05} = 1.66$. (We used

$\alpha = .05$ instead of $\alpha/2 = .025$ since there is no table for $\alpha/2 = .025$.) The rejection region is $d < 1.61$ or $(4 - d) < 1.61$. If $d > 1.66$ or $(4 - d) > 1.66$, H_0 is not rejected.

Since the observed value of the test statistic falls in the rejection region ($d = .962 < 1.61$), H_0 is rejected. There is sufficient evidence to indicate autocorrelation among the residuals exists at $\alpha = .05$.

d. Because autocorrelation was detected, we should not use the least squares model. A time series model that accounts for first-order autocorrelation should be used.

17.29 For a quadratic secular trend, the regression-autoregressive pair of models would be

$$E(Y_t) = \beta_0 + \beta_1 t + \beta_2 t^2 + R_t$$

and

$$R_t = \phi R_{t-1} + \text{uncorrelated error}$$

17.31 a. The model including a curvilinear relationship would be

$$E(Y_t) = \beta_0 + \beta_1 x_t + \beta_2 x_t^2$$

b. The first-order autoregressive model for R_t is

$$R_t = \phi R_{t-1} + \text{uncorrelated error}$$

c. The full model would be

$$Y_t = \beta_0 + \beta_1 x_t + \beta_2 x_t^2 + R_t$$

or $Y_t = \beta_0 + \beta_1 x_t + \beta_2 x_t^2 + \phi R_{t-1} + \text{uncorrelated error}$

17.33 a. The time series model that includes a straight-line long-term trend and autocorrelated residuals would be

$$Y_t = \beta_0 + \beta_1 t + \phi R_{t-1} + \text{uncorrelated error}$$

b. Using the SAS AUTOREG output, the least squares prediction equation is

$$\hat{Y}_t = 1327.28665 + 61.02839t + .8251\hat{R}_{t-1}$$

c. $\hat{\beta}_0 = 1327.28665$: This is the estimate of where the regression line will cross the Y_t axis.

$\hat{\beta}_1 = 61.02839$: The estimated increase in mean GNP for each additional time period is 61.02839.

$\hat{\phi}$ = .8251. Since $\hat{\phi}$ is positive, it implies that the time series residuals are positively autocorrelated.

d. R^2 = .9976. This means that 99.76% of the sum of squares of the deviation of the GNP values about their means is attributable to the time series model.

ROOT MSE = 39.4595. We would expect most of the observations to fall within 2s or 2(39.4595) or 78.9190 units of their predicted values.

17.35 a. The time series model would be

$$Y_t = \beta_0 + \beta_1 t + \phi R_{t-1} + \text{uncorrelated error.}$$

b. The output from fitting the time series model with SAS is:

AUTOREG PROCEDURE

DEPENDENT VARIABLE = Y

ORDINARY LEAST SQUARES ESTIMATES

SSE	3833.9	DFE	34
MSE	112.7618	ROOT MSE	10.61893
SBC	277.3829	AIC	274.2159
REG RSQ	0.4285	TOTAL RSQ	0.4285
DURBIN-WATSON	0.4111		

VARIABLE	DF	B VALUE	STD ERROR	T RATIO	APPROX PROB
INTERCEPT	1	113.455873	3.61469869	31.387	0.0001
T	1	0.860193	0.17036698	5.049	0.0001

AUTOREG PROCEDURE

ESTIMATES OF AUTOCORRELATIONS

LAG	COVARIANCE	CORRELATION	-1 9 8 7 6 5 4 3 2 1 0 1 2 3 4 5 6 7 8 9 1
0	106.497	1.000000	|********************|
1	76.3198	0.716636	|************** |

PRELIMINARY MSE=   51.80374

ESTIMATES OF THE AUTOREGRESSIVE PARAMETERS

LAG	COEFFICIENT	STD ERROR	T RATIO
1	-0.71663604	0.12141000	-5.902611

YULE-WALKER ESTIMATES

SSE	1527.829	DFE	33
MSE	46.29785	ROOT MSE	6.804252
SBC	248.5658	AIC	243.8153
REG RSQ	0.1089	TOTAL RSQ	0.7723

VARIABLE	DF	B VALUE	STD ERROR	T RATIO	APPROX PROB
INTERCEP	1	116.082830	6.95592436	16.688	0.0001
T	1	0.636159	0.31676531	2.008	0.0529

The fitted model is $\hat{Y}_t = 116.083 + .636t + .7166\hat{R}_{t-1}$

$\hat{\beta}_0 = 116.083$: This is the estimate of where the regression line will cross the Y_t axis.

$\hat{\beta}_1 = .636$: The estimated increase in mean IBM stock price for each additional time period is .636.

$\hat{\phi} = .7166$. Since $\hat{\phi}$ is positive, it implies that the time series residuals are positively autocorrelated.

17.37 a. For $t = 31$:

$$\hat{R}_{30} = Y_{30} - \hat{Y}_{30} = 82 - (10 + 2.5t)$$
$$= 82 - (10 + 2.5(30)) = -3$$

Thus, $\hat{Y}_{31} = 10 + 2.5(31) + .64\hat{R}_{30}$
$$= 87.5 + .64(-3) = 85.58$$

For $t = 32$:

$$\hat{R}_{31} = .64\hat{R}_{30} = .64(-3) = -1.92$$

$$\hat{Y}_{32} = 10 + 2.5(32) + .64\hat{R}_{31}$$
$$= 90 + .64(-1.92) = 88.77$$

For $t = 33$:

$$\hat{R}_{32} = .64\hat{R}_{31} = .64(-1.92) = -1.2288$$

$$\hat{Y}_{33} = 10 + 2.5(33) + .64\hat{R}_{32}$$
$$= 92.5 + .64(-1.2288) = 91.71$$

b. The form of the prediction interval is

$$\hat{Y}_{n+m} \pm 2\sqrt{MSE(1 + \hat{\phi}^2 + \hat{\phi}^4 + \ldots + \hat{\phi}^{2(m-1)})}$$

where m is the number of steps ahead.

For $t = 31$, $m = 1$

The approximate 95% prediction interval is

$$\hat{Y}_{31} \pm 2\sqrt{MSE} \Rightarrow 85.58 \pm 2\sqrt{4.3}$$
$$\Rightarrow 85.58 \pm 4.15$$
$$\Rightarrow (81.43, 89.73)$$

For t = 32, m = 2

The approximate 95% prediction interval is

$$\hat{Y}_{32} \pm 2\sqrt{MSE(1 + \hat{\phi}^2)} \Rightarrow 88.77 \pm 2\sqrt{4.3(1 + .64^2)}$$
$$\Rightarrow 88.77 \pm 4.92$$
$$\Rightarrow (83.85, 93.69)$$

For t = 33, m = 3

The approximate 95% prediction interval is

$$\hat{Y}_{33} \pm 2\sqrt{MSE(1 + \hat{\phi}^2 + \hat{\phi}^4)}$$

$$\Rightarrow 91.71 \pm 2\sqrt{4.3(1 + .64^2 + .64^4)}$$

$$\Rightarrow 91.71 \pm 5.21$$
$$\Rightarrow (86.50, 96.92)$$

17.39   From Exercise 17.33, the fitted time series model is

$$\hat{Y}_t = 1327.29 + 61.03t + .825\hat{R}_{t-1}$$

For quarter 1, 1986, t = 45.

$$\hat{R}_{44} = Y_{44} - \hat{Y}_{44} = 4087.7 - (1327.29 + 61.03(44))$$
$$= 4087.7 - 4012.61 = 75.09$$

$$\hat{Y}_{45} = 1327.29 + 61.03(45) + .825\hat{R}_{44}$$
$$= 4073.64 + .825(75.09) = 4135.6$$

For quarter 2, 1986, t = 46.

$$\hat{R}_{45} = \hat{\phi}\hat{R}_{44} = .825(75.09) = 61.94925$$

$$\hat{Y}_{46} = 1327.29 + 61.03(46) + .825\hat{R}_{45}$$
$$= 4134.67 + .825(61.94925)$$
$$= 4185.8$$

For quarter 3, 1986, t = 47.

$$\hat{R}_{46} = \hat{\phi}\hat{R}_{45} = .825(61.94925) = 51.10813$$

$$\hat{Y}_{47} = 1327.29 + 61.03(47) + .825\hat{R}_{46}$$
$$= 4195.7 + .825(51.10813)$$
$$= 4237.9$$

For quarter 4, 1986, t = 48.

$$\hat{R}_{47} = \hat{\phi}\hat{R}_{46} = .825(51.10813) = 42.16421$$

$$\begin{aligned}\hat{Y}_{48} &= 1327.29 + 61.03(48) + .825\hat{R}_{47}\\&= 4256.73 + .825(42.16421)\\&= 4291.5\end{aligned}$$

The general form of the approximate 95% prediction interval is

$$\hat{Y}_{n+m} \pm 2\sqrt{MSE(1 + \hat{\phi}^2 + \hat{\phi}^4 + \dots + \hat{\phi}^{2(m-1)})}$$

where m is the number of steps ahead.

For quarter 1, 1986, n = 44 and m = 1. The prediction interval is

$$\begin{aligned}\hat{Y}_{45} \pm 2\sqrt{MSE} &=> 4135.6 \pm 2\sqrt{1557.052}\\&=> 4135.6 \pm 78.92\\&=> (4056.68, 4214.52)\end{aligned}$$

This does contain the actual value of 4,149.2

For quarter 2, 1986, n = 44 and m = 2. The prediction interval is

$$\begin{aligned}\hat{Y}_{46} \pm 2\sqrt{MSE(1 + \hat{\phi}^2)} &=> 4185.8 \pm 2\sqrt{1557.052(1 + .825^2)}\\&=> 4185.8 \pm 102.31\\&=> (4083.49, 4288.11)\end{aligned}$$

This does contain the actual value of 4175.6.

For quarter 3, 1986, n = 44, m = 3. The prediction interval is

$$\begin{aligned}\hat{Y}_{47} \pm 2\sqrt{MSE(1 + \hat{\phi}^2 + \hat{\phi}^4)} &=> 4237.9 \pm 2\sqrt{1557.052(1 + .825^2 + .825^4)}\\&=> 4237.9 \pm 115.55\\&=> (4122.35, 4353.45)\end{aligned}$$

Again, this contains the actual value of 4240.7.

For quarter 4, 1986, n = 44, m = 4. The prediction interval is

$$\hat{Y}_{48} \pm 2\sqrt{MSE(1 + \hat{\phi}^2 + \hat{\phi}^4 + \phi^6)}$$

$$\begin{aligned}&=> 4291.5 \pm 2\sqrt{1557.052(1 + .825^2 + .825^4 + .825^6)}\\&=> 4291.5 \pm 123.76\\&=> (4167.74, 4415.26)\end{aligned}$$

Again, this contains the actual value of 4268.4.

17.41 From Exercise 17.35, the fitted model is

$$\hat{Y}_t = 116.083 + .636t + .7166\hat{R}_{t-1}$$

For February, 1987, t = 38

$$\hat{R}_{36} = Y_{36} - \hat{Y}_{36} = 120.0 - (116.083 + .636(36))$$
$$= -18.979$$

$$\hat{R}_{37} = \hat{\phi}\hat{R}_{36} = .7166(-18.979) = -13.600$$

$$\hat{Y}_{38} = 116.083 + .636(38) + .7166\hat{R}_{37}$$
$$= 140.251 + .7166(-13.600)$$
$$= 130.51$$

The form of the prediction interval is

$$\hat{Y}_{n+m} \pm 2\sqrt{MSE(1 + \hat{\phi}^2 + \hat{\phi}^4 + \ldots + \hat{\phi}^{2(m-1)})}$$

where m is the number of steps ahead.

For t = 38 and m = 2.

The approximate 95% prediction interval is

$$\hat{Y}_{38} \pm 2\sqrt{MSE(1 + \hat{\phi}^2)} \Rightarrow 130.51 \pm 2\sqrt{46.29785(1 + .7166^2)}$$
$$\Rightarrow 130.51 \pm 16.74$$
$$\Rightarrow (113.77, 147.25)$$

17.43 a. To determine if the model is useful for predicting annual traffic fatalities, we test:

$H_0: \beta_1 = \beta_2 = \ldots = \beta_7 = 0$
$H_a:$ At least one $\beta_i \neq 0$

The test statistic is F = 217.23.

The rejection region requires $\alpha = .05$ in the upper tail of the F distribution with $\nu_1 = k = 7$ and $\nu_2 = n - (k + 1) = 28 - (7 + 1) = 20$. From Table 8, Appendix E, $F_{.05} = 2.51$. The rejection region is F > 2.51.

Since the observed value of the test statistic falls in the rejection region (F = 217.23 > 2.51), H_0 is rejected. There is sufficient evidence to indicate the model is useful for predicting annual traffic fatalities at $\alpha = .05$.

b. To determine if the residuals are autocorrelated, we test:

$H_0:$ No autocorrelation
$H_a:$ Positive or negative autocorrelation

The test statistic is d = 1.97.

For a two-tailed alternative, the rejection region is $d < d_{L,\alpha/2}$ or $(4 - d) < d_{L,\alpha/2}$. From Table 15, Appendix E, with $n = 28$, $k = 5$, and $\alpha = .05$, $d_{L,.05} = 1.03$ and $d_{U,.05} = 1.85$. (Since there is no table for $\alpha/2 = .025$, I used $\alpha = .05$.) The rejection region is $d < 1.03$ or $(4 - d) < 1.03$. If $d > 1.85$ or $(4 - d) > 1.85$, H_0 is not rejected.

Since the observed value of the test statistic does not fall in the rejection region ($d = 1.97 \nless 1.03$ but $d = 1.97 > 1.85$), H_0 is not rejected. There is insufficient evidence to indicate the residuals are autocorrelated at $\alpha = .05$.

17.45 a. Some preliminary calculations are:

$$\sum t = 91 \qquad \sum y = 2330.1 \qquad \sum ty = 17,068.8$$

$$\sum t^2 = 819 \qquad \sum y^2 = 421,214.73$$

$$SS_{ty} = \sum ty - \frac{\sum t \sum y}{n} = 17,068.8 - \frac{91(2330.1)}{13} = 758.1$$

$$SS_{tt} = \sum t^2 - \frac{(\sum t)^2}{n} = 819 - \frac{91^2}{13} = 182$$

$$\hat{\beta}_1 = \frac{SS_{ty}}{SS_{tt}} = \frac{758.1}{182} = 4.165384615 \approx 4.165$$

$$\hat{\beta}_0 = \bar{y} - \hat{\beta}_1 \bar{t} = \frac{2330.1}{36} - (4.165384615)\left(\frac{91}{13}\right) = 150.080769$$
$$\approx 150.081$$

The least squares line is $\hat{Y}_t$ 150.081 + 4.165t

b.

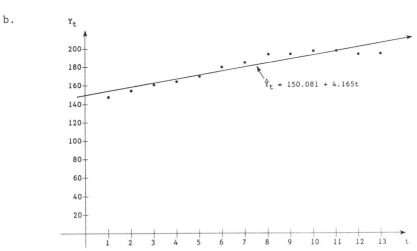

The line appears to fit the data fairly well. However, a quadratic model may fit better. The data are leveling off in the last few time periods while the least squares line continues to increase. This could be a problem.

From the plot, $\hat{Y}_{14} \approx 208.39$

c. The residuals are found using $Y_t - \hat{Y}_t$ where

$$\hat{Y}_t = 150.081 + 4.165t$$

For $t = 1$, $\hat{Y}_1 = 150.081 + 4.165(1) = 154.246$

$$Y_1 - \hat{Y}_1 = 148.6 - 154.246 = -5.646$$

For $t = 2$, $\hat{Y}_2 = 150.081 + 4.165(2) = 158.411$

$$Y_2 - \hat{Y}_2 = 156.2 - 158.411 = -2.211$$

The rest of the residuals are found in a similar manner and are listed in the output in part (d).

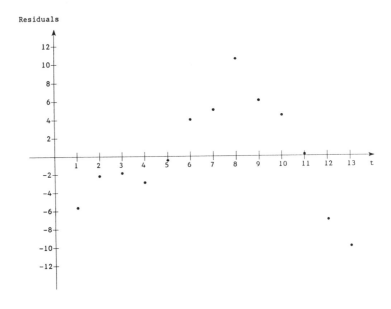

There is significant evidence to indicate autocorrelation. The first 5 residuals are negative, the next 6 are positive, and the last 2 are negative.

d. The output from fitting the model using SAS is:

DEP VARIABLE: Y

ANALYSIS OF VARIANCE

SOURCE	DF	SUM OF SQUARES	MEAN SQUARE	F VALUE	PROB>F
MODEL	1	3157.77808	3157.77808	84.022	0.0001
ERROR	11	413.41269	37.58297203		
C TOTAL	12	3571.19077			

ROOT MSE	6.130495	R-SQUARE	0.8842
DEP MEAN	179.2385	ADJ R-SQ	0.8737
C.V.	3.420301		

PARAMETER ESTIMATES

VARIABLE	DF	PARAMETER ESTIMATE	STANDARD ERROR	T FOR HO: PARAMETER=0	PROB > |T|
INTERCEP	1	150.08077	3.60686711	41.610	0.0001
T	1	4.16538462	0.45442254	9.166	0.0001

OBS	ACTUAL	PREDICT VALUE	STD ERR PREDICT	LOWER95% PREDICT	UPPER95% PREDICT	RESIDUAL
1	148.6	154.2	3.2133	139.0	169.5	−5.6462
2	156.2	158.4	2.8379	143.5	173.3	−2.2115
3	160.6	162.6	2.4890	148.0	177.1	−1.9769
4	163.7	166.7	2.1793	152.4	181.1	−3.0423
5	170.5	170.9	1.9280	156.8	185.1	−0.4077
6	179.1	175.1	1.7600	161.0	189.1	4.0269
7	184.2	179.2	1.7003	165.2	193.2	4.9615
8	194.1	183.4	1.7600	169.4	197.4	10.6962
9	193.7	187.6	1.9280	173.4	201.7	6.1308
10	196.2	191.7	2.1793	177.4	206.1	4.4654
11	196.0	195.9	2.4890	181.3	210.5	0.1000
12	193.0	200.1	2.8379	185.2	214.9	−7.0654
13	194.2	204.2	3.2133	189.0	219.5	−10.0308
14	.	208.4	3.6069	192.7	224.1	.

SUM OF RESIDUALS	0.00000000
SUM OF SQUARED RESIDUALS	413.41269231
SUM OF SQUARED RESIDUALS − ERROR SS	−0.00000000
PRESS STATISTIC	615.06346442
FIRST ORDER AUTOCORRELATION	0.62669572
DURBIN−WATSON D	0.42611675

The Durbin-Watson statistic can be used to test for autocorrelation. To test for this, we use:

H_0: No autocorrelation
H_a: Positive or negative correlation

The test statistic is d = .426 (from printout).

For a two-tailed alternative, the rejection region is $d < d_{L,\alpha/2}$ or $(4 - d) < d_{L,\alpha/2}$. From Table 15, Appendix E, with n = 13, k = 1, and α = .05, $d_{L,.05} = 1.08$ Since n = 13 is not on the table, we used n = 15. Also, for a two-tailed test, we need a table for $\alpha/2 = .025$. We used the table for $\alpha = .05$.) The rejection region is $d < 1.08$ or $(4 - d) < 1.08$.

Since the observed value of the test statistic falls in the rejection region ($d = .426 < 1.08$), H_0 is rejected. There is sufficient evidence to indicate autocorrelation is present at $\alpha = .05$.

e. A possible time series model would be

$$Y_t = \beta_0 + \beta_1 t + \phi R_{t-1} + \text{uncorrelated error.}$$

The output from fitting the time series using SAS is:

AUTOREG PROCEDURE

DEPENDENT VARIABLE = Y

ORDINARY LEAST SQUARES ESTIMATES

SSE	413.4127	DFE	11
MSE	37.58297	ROOT MSE	6.130495
SBC	86.99576	AIC	85.86586
REG RSQ	0.8842	TOTAL RSQ	0.8842
DURBIN-WATSON	0.4261		

VARIABLE	DF	B VALUE	STD ERROR	T RATIO	APPROX PROB
INTERCEPT	1	150.080769	3.60686711	41.610	0.0001
T	1	4.165385	0.45442254	9.166	0.0001

AUTOREG PROCEDURE

ESTIMATES OF AUTOCORRELATIONS

LAG	COVARIANCE	CORRELATION	-1 9 8 7 6 5 4 3 2 1 0 1 2 3 4 5 6 7 8 9 1
0	31.801	1.000000	|********************|
1	19.9295	0.626696	|************* |

PRELIMINARY MSE= 19.31122

ESTIMATES OF THE AUTOREGRESSIVE PARAMETERS

LAG	COEFFICIENT	STD ERROR	T RATIO
1	-0.62669572	0.24642493	-2.543151

YULE-WALKER ESTIMATES

SSE	191.514	DFE	10
MSE	19.1514	ROOT MSE	4.376231
SBC	80.05621	AIC	78.36136
REG RSQ	0.8049	TOTAL RSQ	0.9464

VARIABLE	DF	B VALUE	STD ERROR	T RATIO	APPROX PROB
INTERCEP	1	149.725019	5.22233035	28.670	0.0001
T	1	3.986360	0.62058644	6.424	0.0001

The fitted model is $\hat{Y}_t = 149.725 + 3.986t + .6267\hat{R}_{t-1}$

f. For $\hat{Y}_{14}$, we must find $\hat{R}_{13}$

$$\hat{R}_{13} = Y_{13} - \hat{Y}_{13} = 194.2 - (149.725 + 3.986(13))$$
$$= -7.343$$

$$\hat{Y}_{14} = 149.725 + 3.986(14) + .6267\hat{R}_{13}$$
$$= 205.529 + .6267(-7.343)$$
$$= 200.927$$

17.47 a. First, we graph the moving averages calculated in Exercise 16.27(b)

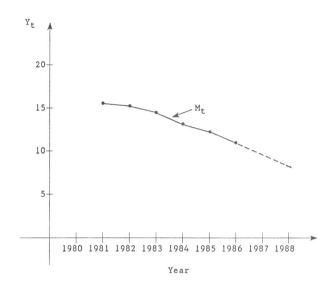

Extending the moving averages to 1988, the estimate for 1988 is approximately 7.0.

b. From Exercise 16.27(c), the exponentially smoothed value for 1987 is $E_n = 12.45$. For any future value, the forecast is

$$F_t = wY_n + (1 - w)E_n \quad \text{for } t > n$$

The forecast for 1988 is

$$F_{1988} = .2(9.55) + (1 - .2)(12.45) = 11.87$$

c. Some preliminary calculations are:

$\sum t = 36$	$\sum y = 105.75$	$\sum ty = 439.81$
$\sum t^2 = 204$	$\sum y^2 = 1441.8075$	

$$SS_{ty} = \sum ty - \frac{\sum t \sum y}{n} = 439.81 - \frac{36(105.75)}{8} = -36.065$$

$$SS_{tt} = \sum t^2 - \frac{(\sum t)^2}{n} = 204 - \frac{36^2}{8} = 42$$

$$SS_{yy} = \sum y^2 - \frac{(\sum y)^2}{n} = 1441.8075 - \frac{105.75^2}{8} = 43.924687$$

$$\hat{\beta}_1 = \frac{SS_{ty}}{SS_{tt}} = \frac{-36.065}{42} = -.858690476 \approx -.857$$

$$\hat{\beta}_0 = \bar{y} - \hat{\beta}_1 \bar{t} = \frac{105.75}{8} - (-.858690476)\left(\frac{36}{8}\right) = 17.082857 \approx 17.083$$

The least squares line is $\hat{Y}_t = 17.083 - .859t$

$$SSE = SS_{yy} - \hat{\beta}_1 SS_{ty} = 43.924687 - (-.858690476)(-36.065)$$

$$= 12.95601498$$

$$s^2 = \frac{SSE}{n - 2} = \frac{12.95601498}{8 - 2} = 2.1593 \qquad s = \sqrt{2.1593} = 1.4695$$

For $t = 9$, $\hat{Y}_9 = 17.083 - .859(9) = 9.352$

The general form of the prediction interval is

$$\hat{Y}_t \pm t_{\alpha/2}(s)\sqrt{1 + \frac{1}{n} + \frac{(t - \bar{t})^2}{SS_{tt}}}$$

For confidence coefficient .95, $\alpha = .05$ and $\alpha/2 = .05/2 = .025$. From Table 6, Appendix E, with $n - 2 = 8 - 2 = 6$ df, $t_{.025} = 2.447$. The 95% prediction interval is

$$9.352 \pm 2.447(1.4695)\sqrt{1 + \frac{1}{8} + \frac{(9 - 4.5)^2}{42}}$$

$$= 9.352 \pm 4.559 \Rightarrow (4.793, 13.911)$$

d. The first-order autoregressive model is

$$Y_t = \beta_0 + \beta_1 t + \phi R_{t-1} + \text{uncorrelated error.}$$

Using SAS to fit the model, the output is:

AUTOREG PROCEDURE

DEPENDENT VARIABLE = Y

ORDINARY LEAST SQUARES ESTIMATES

SSE	12.95602	DFE	6
MSE	2.159336	ROOT MSE	1.469468
SBC	30.71885	AIC	30.55997
REG RSQ	0.7050	TOTAL RSQ	0.7050
DURBIN-WATSON	1.7372		

VARIABLE	DF	B VALUE	STD ERROR	T RATIO	APPROX PROB
INTERCEPT	1	17.0828571	1.14500016	14.920	0.0001
T	1	-0.8586905	0.22674382	-3.787	0.0091

AUTOREG PROCEDURE

ESTIMATES OF AUTOCORRELATIONS

LAG	COVARIANCE	CORRELATION	-1 9 8 7 6 5 4 3 2 1 0 1 2 3 4 5 6 7 8 9 1
0	1.6195	1.000000	| |********************|
1	-0.191151	-0.118031	| **| |

PRELIMINARY MSE= 1.59694

ESTIMATES OF THE AUTOREGRESSIVE PARAMETERS

LAG	COEFFICIENT	STD ERROR	T RATIO
1	0.11803057	0.44408756	0.265782

YULE-WALKER ESTIMATES

SSE	12.64584	DFE	5
MSE	2.529168	ROOT MSE	1.590336
SBC	32.61846	AIC	32.38014
REG RSQ	0.7479	TOTAL RSQ	0.7121

VARIABLE	DF	B VALUE	STD ERROR	T RATIO	APPROX PROB
INTERCEP	1	17.2215858	1.14763512	15.006	0.0001
T	1	-0.8801292	0.22849934	-3.852	0.0120

The fitted model is $\hat{Y}_t = 17.222 - .880t - .118\hat{R}_{t-1}$

To predict Y_9, we must find $\hat{R}_8$.

$$\hat{R}_8 = Y_8 - \hat{Y}_8 = 9.55 - (17.222 - .880(8)) = -.632$$

$$\hat{Y}_9 = 17.222 - .880(9) - .118\hat{R}_8$$
$$= 9.302 - .118(-.632) = 9.3766$$

The approximate 95% prediction interval is

$$\hat{Y}_{n+m} \pm 2\sqrt{MSE(1 + \hat{\phi}^2 + \hat{\phi}^4 + \ldots + \hat{\phi}^{2(m-1)})}$$

where m is the number of steps ahead.

For $t = 9$, $m = 1$

$$\hat{Y}_9 \pm 2\sqrt{MSE} \Rightarrow 9.3766 \pm 2\sqrt{2.5292}$$
$$\Rightarrow 9.3766 \pm 3.1087$$
$$\Rightarrow (6.1959, \ 12.5573)$$

17.49   a.   From the printout, the least squares line is

$$\hat{Y}_t = .4015 + 4.2956t$$

      b.   To determine if the model is useful for predicting yearly sales, we test:

$H_0: \quad \beta_1 = 0$
$H_a: \quad \beta_1 \neq 0$

The test statistic is $t = \dfrac{\hat{\beta}_1}{\dfrac{s}{\sqrt{SS_{tt}}}} = 40.196$ (from printout)

For a two-tailed alternative, the rejection region requires $\alpha/2 = .05/2 = .025$ in each tail of the t distribution with $n - 2 = 35 - 2 = 33$ df. From Table 6, Appendix E, $t_{.025} \approx 2.042$. The rejection region is $t < -2.042$ or $t > 2.042$.

Since the observed value of the test statistic falls in the rejection region ($t = 40.196 > 2.042$), H_0 is rejected. There is sufficient evidence to indicate the model is useful for predicting yearly sales at $\alpha = .05$.

      c.   The residuals do appear to be correlated. There are several positive and negative runs.

      d.   To determine whether positive residual correlation exists, we test:

$H_0: \quad$ No autocorrelation
$H_a: \quad$ Positive autocorrelation

The test statistic is $d = .821$ (from printout)

For a one-tailed alternative, the rejection region is $d < d_{L,\alpha}$. From Table 15, Appendix E, with $n = 35$, $k = 1$, and $\alpha = .05$, $d_{L,.05} = 1.40$. The rejection region is $d < 1.40$.

Since the observed value of the test statistic falls in the rejection region ($d = .821 < 1.40$), H_0 is rejected. There is sufficient evidence to indicate a positive autocorrelation exists at $\alpha = .05$.

e. A first-order autoregressive model is

$$Y_t = \beta_0 + \beta_1 t + \phi R_{t-1} + \text{uncorrelated error.}$$

f. The fitted model is $\hat{Y}_t = .4058 + 4.2959t + .5896\hat{R}_{t-1}$

$\hat{\beta}_0 = .4058$: This is the estimate of where the regression line
will cross the Y_t axis.

$\hat{\beta}_1 = 4.2959$: The estimated increase in sales revenue for each
additional time period is 4.2959.

$\hat{\phi} = .5896$: Since $\hat{\phi}$ is positive, it implies that the time series
residuals are positively autocorrelated.

g. <u>For t = 36</u>:

$$\hat{R}_{35} = Y_{35} - \hat{Y}_{35} = 150.9 - (.4058 + 4.2959(35)) = .1377$$

Thus, $\hat{Y}_{36} = .4058 + 4.2959(36) + .5896\hat{R}_{35}$
$= 155.0582 + .5896(.1377) = 155.139$

The approximate 95% prediction interval is

$$\hat{Y}_{n+m} \pm 2\sqrt{\text{MSE}(1 + \hat{\phi}^2 + \hat{\phi}^4 + \ldots + \hat{\phi}^{2(m-1)})}$$

where m is the number of steps ahead.

For t = 36, m = 1. The prediction interval is

$$155.139 \pm 2\sqrt{27.42767} \Rightarrow 155.139 \pm 10.474 \Rightarrow (144.665, 165.613)$$

<u>For t = 37</u>:

$$\hat{R}_{36} = \hat{\phi}\hat{R}_{35} = .5896(.1377) = .0812$$

$\hat{Y}_{37} = .4058 + 4.2959(37) + .5896\hat{R}_{36}$
$= 159.3541 + .5896(.0812) = 159.4020$

For t = 37, m = 2. The prediction interval is

$$159.402 \pm 2\sqrt{27.42767(1 + .5896^2)} \Rightarrow 159.402 \pm 12.159$$
$$\Rightarrow (147.243, 171.561)$$

For t = 38:

$$\hat{R}_{37} = \hat{\phi}\hat{R}_{36} = .5896(.0812) = .0479$$

$$\hat{Y}_{38} = .4058 + 4.2959(38) + .5896\hat{R}_{37}$$
$$= 163.65 + .5896(.0479) = 163.678$$

For t = 38, m = 3. The prediction interval is

$$163.678 \pm 2\sqrt{27.42767(1 + .5896^2 + .5896^4)}$$

$$\Rightarrow 163.678 \pm 12.693 \Rightarrow (150.985, 176.37)$$

For t = 39:

$$\hat{R}_{38} = \hat{\phi}\hat{R}_{37} = .5896(.0479) = .0282$$

$$\hat{Y}_{39} = .4058 + 4.2959(39) + .5896\hat{R}_{38}$$
$$= 167.9459 + .5896(.0282) = 167.963$$

For t = 39, m = 4. The prediction interval is

$$167.963 \pm 2\sqrt{27.42767(1 + .5896^2 + .5896^4 + .5896^6)}$$

$$\Rightarrow 167.963 \pm 12.873 \Rightarrow (155.090, 180.836)$$

For t = 40:

$$\hat{R}_{39} = \hat{\phi}\hat{R}_{38} = .5896(.0282) = .0166$$

$$\hat{Y}_{40} = .4058 + 4.2959(40) + .5896\hat{R}_{39}$$
$$= 172.2418 + .5896(.0166) = 172.252$$

For t = 40, m = 5. The prediction interval is

$$172.252 \pm 2\sqrt{27.42767(1 + .5896^2 + .5896^4 + .5896^6 + .5896^8)}$$

$$\Rightarrow 172.252 \pm 12.935 \Rightarrow (159.317, 185.187)$$

CASE STUDIES

17.3   a.   For weekdays, $X_{4t} = X_{5t} = 0$.

The model for summer months would include $x_{3t} = 1$, and $x_{2t} = 0$. Substituting, we get:

$$E(Y_t) = \beta_0 + \beta_1(X_{1t} - 59)(0) + \beta_2(X_{1t} - 78)(1) + \beta_3(0) + \beta_4(0)$$
$$= (\beta_0 - 78\beta_2) + \beta_2 X_{1t}$$

The model for non-weather sensitive months would include $x_{2t} = x_{3t} = 0$. Substituting, we get:

$$E(Y_t) = \beta_0 + \beta_1(X_{1t} - 59)0 + \beta_2(X_{1t} - 78)0 + \beta_3(0) + \beta_4(0)$$
$$= \beta_0$$

b.   The model assumes that the difference in mean peak demand between weekdays and weekends/holidays is the same for each of the three temperature ranges.

c.   From part (a) the model for winter months is

$$E(Y_t) = (\beta_0 + 59\beta_1) + \beta_1 X_{1t}$$

The slope of the line is β_1. We would expect β_1 to be negative. As the temperature gets closer to 59° (from below), we would expect demand to decrease.

d.   From part (a), the model for summer months is

$$E(t) = (\beta_0 - 78\beta_2) + \beta_2 X_{1t}$$

The slope of the line is β_2. We would expect β_2 to be positive. As the temperature rises above 78°, we would expect the demand to increase.

e.   The autocorrelation is negative when ϕ is negative and it is positive when ϕ is positive.

f. R^2 = R-SQUARE = .8307. This means that 83.07% of the sums of squares of the deviations of the demand values about their mean is attributable to the model.

F = 441.729. This is the ratio of MS(Model) and MSE. The associated p-value is .0001. This indicates the model contributes to the prediction of demand.

ROOT MSE = 245.585. We would expect most of the observations to fall within 2s or 2(245.585) or 491.170 units of the fitted line.

g. H_0: $\phi = 0$
    H_a: $\phi > 0$

The test statistic is d = .705

For the one-tailed alternative, the rejection region is $d < d_{L,\alpha}$. From Table 15, Appendix E, with n = 365, k = 4, and α = .05, $d_{L,.05} \approx 1.59$. The rejection region is d < 1.59.

Since the observed value of the test statistic falls in the rejection region (d = .705 < 1.59, H_0 is rejected. There is sufficient evidence to indicate a positive autocorrelation at α = .05.

h. R^2 = .9225. This means that 92.25% of the sums of squares for deviations of the demand values about their means is attributable to the model.

ROOT MSE = 166.3943. We would expect most of the observations to fall within 2s or 2(166.3943) or 332.7886 units of the fitted line.

The R^2 value in this part is much higher than that in part (f) (.9225 to .8307). Also, ROOT MSE is 166.3943 in this part and is much smaller than that in part (f) (245.585). These both indicate Model 2 is better.

i. From the plot in Figure 17.10, the value of Y_{365} appears to be about 2750.

Thus, $\hat{R}_{365} = Y_{365} - \hat{Y}_{365} = 2750 - (2812.967) = -60.967$

Note: Day 365 is Monday, October 31 => $X_{2t} = X_{3t} = X_{4t} = X_{5t} = 0$

Thus, $\hat{Y}_{365} = 2,812.967$.

For Tuesday, Nov. 1, $X_{2t} = X_{3t} = X_{4t} = X_{5t} = 0$

$\hat{Y}_{366} = 2,812.967 + .6475\hat{R}_{365} = 2,812.967 + .6475(-60.967)$
$= 2773.49$

For Wednesday, Nov. 2, $X_{2t} = X_{3t} = X_{4t} = X_{5t} = 0$

$\hat{R}_{366} = \hat{\phi}\hat{R}_{365} = .6475(-60.967) = -39.4761$

$\hat{Y}_{367} = 2,812.967 + .6475\hat{R}_{366}$
$= 2,812.967 + .6475(-39.4761) = 2787.41$

For Thursday, Nov. 3, $X_{2t} = X_{3t} = X_{4t} = X_{5t} = 0$

$$\hat{R}_{367} = \hat{\phi}\hat{R}_{366} = .6475(-39.4761) = -25.5608$$

$$\hat{Y}_{368} = 2{,}812.967 + .6475\hat{R}_{367}$$
$$= 2{,}812.967 + .6475(-25.5608) = 2796.42$$

For Friday, Nov. 4, $X_{2t} = X_{3t} = X_{4t} = X_{5t} = 0$

$$\hat{R}_{368} = \hat{\phi}\hat{R}_{367} = .6475(-25.5608) = -16.5506$$

$$\hat{Y}_{369} = 2{,}812.967 + .6475\hat{R}_{368}$$
$$= 2{,}812.967 + .6475(-16.5506) = 2802.25$$

For Saturday, Nov. 5, $X_{2t} = X_{3t} = X_{5t} = 0$, $X_{4t} = 1$

$$\hat{R}_{369} = \hat{\phi}\hat{R}_{368} = .6475(-16.5506) = -10.7165$$

$$\hat{Y}_{370} = 2{,}812.967 - 130.828(1) + .6475\hat{R}_{369}$$
$$= 2{,}682.139 + .6475(-10.7165) = 2675.20$$

For Sunday, Nov. 6, $X_{2t} = X_{3t} = X_{4t} = 0$, $X_{5t} = 1$

$$\hat{R}_{370} = \hat{\phi}\hat{R}_{369} = .6475(-10.7165) = -6.9389$$

$$\hat{Y}_{371} = 2{,}812.967 - 275.551(1) + .6475\hat{R}_{370}$$
$$= 2{,}537.416 + .6475(-6.9389) = 2532.92$$

For Monday, Nov. 7, $X_{2t} = X_{3t} = X_{4t} = X_{5t} = 0$

$$\hat{R}_{371} = \hat{\phi}\hat{R}_{370} = .6475(-6.9389) = -4.4929$$

$$\hat{Y}_{372} = 2{,}812.967 + .6475\hat{R}_{371}$$
$$= 2{,}812.967 + .6475(-4.4929) = 2810.06$$

j. The form of the prediction interval is

$$\hat{Y}_{n+m} \pm 2\sqrt{MSE(1 + \hat{\phi}^2 + \hat{\phi}^4 + \ldots + \hat{\phi}^{2(m-1)})}$$

where m is the number of steps ahead. From the printout, MSE = 27,687.44 and $\hat{\phi} = .6475$.

For t = 366, m = 1. The prediction interval is

$$2787.41 \pm 2\sqrt{27{,}687.44} \Rightarrow 2773.49 \pm 332.79$$
$$\Rightarrow (2440.70, 3106.28)$$

For t = 367, m = 2.

$$2787.41 \pm 2\sqrt{27{,}687.44\ (1 + .6475^2)} \Rightarrow 2787.41 \pm 396.46$$
$$\Rightarrow (2390.95,\ 3183.87)$$

For t = 368, m = 3.

$$2796.42 \pm 2\sqrt{27{,}687.44(1 + .6475^2 + .6475^4)}$$

$$\Rightarrow 2376.42 \pm 420.30$$
$$\Rightarrow (2376.12,\ 3216.72)$$

For t = 369, m = 4.

$$2802.25 \pm 2\sqrt{27{,}687.44(1 + .6475^2 + .6475^4 + .6476^6)}$$

$$\Rightarrow 2802.25 \pm 429.90$$
$$\Rightarrow (2372.35,\ 3232.15)$$

For t = 370, m = 5.

$$2675.20 \pm 2\sqrt{27{,}687.44(1 + .6475^2 + .6475^4 + .6475^6 + .6475^8)}$$

$$\Rightarrow 2675.20 \pm 433.86$$
$$\Rightarrow (2241.34,\ 3109.06)$$

For t = 371, m = 6.

$$2532.92 \pm 2\sqrt{27{,}687.44(1 + .6475^2 + .6475^4 + .6475^6 + .6476^8 + .6475^{10})}$$

$$\Rightarrow 2532.92 \pm 435.51$$
$$\Rightarrow (2097.41,\ 2968.43)$$

For t = 372, m = 7.

$$2810.06 \pm$$
$$2\sqrt{27{,}687.44(1 + .6475^2 + .6475^4 + .6475^6 + .6476^8 + .6475^{10} + .6475^{12})}$$

$$\Rightarrow 2810.06 \pm 436.20$$
$$\Rightarrow (2373.86,\ 3246.26)$$

18.1   a.   For α = .05 and df = 8, $\chi^2_{.05}$ = 15.5073

        b.   For α = .01 and df = 8, $\chi^2_{.01}$ = 20.0902

        c.   For α = .10 and df = 8, $\chi^2_{.10}$ = 13.3616

18.3   a.

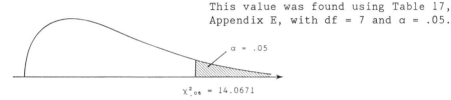

This value was found using Table 17, Appendix E, with df = 7 and α = .05.

$$\alpha = .05$$

$$\chi^2_{.05} = 14.0671$$

        b.

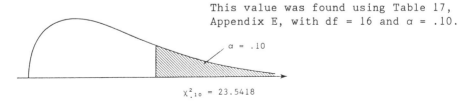

This value was found using Table 17, Appendix E, with df = 16 and α = .10.

$$\alpha = .10$$

$$\chi^2_{.10} = 23.5418$$

        c.

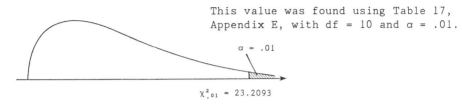

This value was found using Table 17, Appendix E, with df = 10 and α = .01.

$$\alpha = .01$$

$$\chi^2_{.01} = 23.2093$$

d.

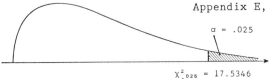

This value was found using Table 17, Appendix E, with df = 8 and α = .025.

$\chi^2_{.025}$ = 17.5346

e.

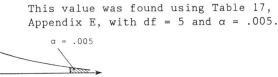

This value was found using Table 17, Appendix E, with df = 5 and α = .005.

$\chi^2_{.005}$ = 16.7496

18.5   a. $e_1 = np_1 = 100(.1) = 10$
$e_2 = np_2 = 100(.3) = 30$
$e_3 = np_3 = 100(.3) = 30$
$e_4 = np_4 = 100(.3) = 30$

b.   From Table 17, Appendix E, with α = .10 and df = k − 1 = 4 − 1 = 3, $\chi^2_{.10}$ = 6.25139.

c. H_a: At least two of the cell probabilities differ from p_1 = .1, $p_2 = p_3 = p_4$ = .3

d.   To determine if the null hypothesis is false, we test:

H_0: p_1 = .1, $p_2 = p_3 = p_4$ = .3
H_a: At least two of the cell probabilities differ from
         p = .1, $p_2 = p_3 = p_4$ = .3

The test statistic is $\chi^2 = \sum \dfrac{(0_i - e_i)^2}{e_i}$

$= \dfrac{(14 - 10)^2}{10} + \dfrac{(35 - 30)^2}{30} + \dfrac{(27 - 30)^2}{30} + \dfrac{(24 - 30)^2}{30} = 3.933$

The rejection region requires α = .10 in the upper tail of the χ^2 distribution with df = k − 1 = 4 − 1 = 3. From part (b), the rejection region is χ^2 > 6.25139.

Since the observed value of the test statistic does not fall in the rejection region (χ^2 = 3.933 $\ngtr$ 6.25139), H_0 is not rejected. There is insufficient evidence to indicate H_0 is false at α = .10.

18.7   a.   If there are no differences in the percentages of marketing
        executives in the four response categories,

$$p_1 = p_2 = p_3 = p_4 = .25$$

b. $e_1 = np_1 = 36(.25) = 9$
      $e_2 = np_2 = 36(.25) = 9$
      $e_3 = np_3 = 36(.25) = 9$
      $e_4 = np_4 = 36(.25) = 9$

c. $$\chi^2 = \sum_{i=1}^{n} \frac{(O_i - e_i)^2}{e_i} = \frac{(8 - 9)^2}{9} + \frac{(18 - 9)^2}{9} + \frac{(8 - 9)^2}{9} + \frac{(2 - 9)^2}{9}$$

$$= 14.667$$

d.   To determine if the percentages of marketing executives differ
        among the categories, we test:

H_0: $p_1 = p_2 = p_3 = p_4 = .25$
H_a: At least two of the cell probabilities are different from
        each other

The test statistic is $\chi^2 = \sum \frac{(O_i - e_i)^2}{e_i} = 14.667$ (from part (c)).

The rejection region requires $\alpha = .05$ in the upper tail of the χ^2
distribution with df = $k - 1 = 4 - 1 = 3$. From Table 17, Appendix
E, $\chi^2_{.05} = 7.81473$. The rejection region is $\chi^2 > 7.81473$.

Since the observed value of the test statistic falls in the
rejection region ($\chi^2 = 14.667 > 7.81473$), H_0 is rejected. There
is sufficient evidence to indicate the percentages of marketing
executives differ among the categories at $\alpha = .05$.

18.9   Some preliminary calculations are:

$$e_1 = e_2 = e_3 = e_4 = e_5 = e_6 = e_7 = e_8 = np_i = 714(.125) = 89.25$$

a.   To determine if the probabilities of worker accidents are higher
        for some time periods, we test:

H_0: $p_1 = p_2 = p_3 = p_4 = p_5 = p_6 = p_7 = p_8 = .125$
H_a: At least two of the cell probabilities differ from each other

The test statistic is $\chi^2 = \sum_{i}^{4} \dfrac{(0_i - e_i)^2}{e_i}$

$= \dfrac{(93 - 89.25)^2}{89.25} + \dfrac{(71 - 89.25)^2}{89.25} + \dfrac{(79 - 89.25)^2}{89.25} + \ldots$

$+ \dfrac{(110 - 89.25)^2}{89.25} = 15.905$

The rejection region requires $\alpha = .10$ in the upper tail of the χ^2 distribution with df $= k - 1 = 8 - 1 = 7$. From Table 17, Appendix E, $\chi^2_{.10} = 12.0170$. The rejection region is $\chi^2 > 12.0170$.

Since the observed value of the test statistic falls in the rejection region ($\chi^2 = 15.905 > 12.017$), H_0 is rejected. There is sufficient evidence to indicate the probabilities of worker accidents are higher in some time periods at $\alpha = .10$.

b. $\hat{p}_1 = \dfrac{98 + 89 + 102 + 110}{714} = \dfrac{399}{714} = .5588$

$H_0: \quad p_1 = .5$
$H_a: \quad p_1 > .5$

The test statistic is $z = \dfrac{\hat{p}_1 - p_{10}}{\sqrt{\dfrac{p_{10}(q_{10})}{n}}} = \dfrac{.5588 - .5}{\sqrt{\dfrac{.5(.5)}{714}}} = 3.14$

The rejection region requires $\alpha = .10$ in the upper tail of the z distribution. From Table 4, Appendix E, $z_{.10} = 1.28$. The rejection region is $z > 1.28$.

Since the observed value of the test statistic falls in the rejection region ($z = 3.14 > 1.28$), H_0 is rejected. There is sufficient evidence to indicate the probability of an accident during the last 4 hours of a shift is greater than during the first 4 hours at $\alpha = .10$.

18.11   Some preliminary calculations:

$e_1 = e_2 = e_3 = np_i = 382(1/3) = 127.333$

To determine if the percentages of job applicants falling into the three response categories differ, we test:

$H_0: \quad p_1 = p_2 = p_3 = 1/3$
$H_a: \quad$ At least two of the cell probabilities differ from $1/3$

The test statistic is $\chi^2 = \sum\limits_{i} \dfrac{(O_i - e_i)^2}{e_i}$

$$= \frac{(152 - 127.333)^2}{127.333} + \frac{(137 - 127.333)^2}{127.333} + \frac{(93 - 127.333)^2}{127.333}$$

$$= 14.77$$

The rejection region requires $\alpha = .05$ in the upper tail of the χ^2 distribution with df $= k - 1 = 3 - 1 = 2$. From Table 17, Appendix E, $\chi^2_{.05} = 5.99147$. The rejection region is $\chi^2 > 5.99147$.

Since the observed value of the test statistic falls in the rejection region ($\chi^2 = 14.77 > 5.99147$), H_0 is rejected. There is sufficient evidence to indicate the percentages of job applicants falling into the three response categories differ at $\alpha = .05$.

18.13   a.   The estimated expected cell counts are computed using

$$e_{ij} = \frac{R_i C_j}{n}$$

$$e_{11} = \frac{R_1 C_1}{n} = \frac{352(334)}{800} = 146.96$$

$$e_{12} = \frac{R_1 C_2}{n} = \frac{352(466)}{800} = 205.04$$

$$e_{21} = \frac{R_2 C_1}{n} = \frac{448(334)}{800} = 187.04$$

$$e_{22} = \frac{R_2 C_2}{n} = \frac{448(466)}{800} = 260.96$$

b. $\chi^2 = \sum\sum \dfrac{(O_{ij} - e_{ij})^2}{e_{ij}} = \dfrac{(133 - 146.96)^2}{146.96} + \dfrac{(219 - 205.04)^2}{205.04}$

$$+ \frac{(201 - 187.04)^2}{187.04} + \frac{(247 - 260.96)^2}{260.96} = 4.065$$

18.15   a.   df $= (r - 1)(c - 1) = (2 - 1)(2 - 1) = 1$

b.   df $= (r - 1)(c - 1) = (4 - 1)(2 - 1) = 3$

c.   df $= (r - 1)(c - 1) = (3 - 1)(3 - 1) = 4$

d.   df $= (r - 1)(c - 1) = (3 - 1)(4 - 1) = 6$

18.17 a. The estimated expected cell counts are found using

$$e_{ij} = \frac{R_i C_j}{n}$$

$$e_{11} = \frac{R_1 C_1}{n} = \frac{88(34)}{210} = 14.25 \qquad e_{12} = \frac{R_1 C_2}{n} = \frac{88(28)}{210} = 11.73$$

$$e_{13} = \frac{R_1 C_3}{n} = \frac{88(50)}{210} = 20.95 \qquad e_{14} = \frac{R_1 C_4}{n} = \frac{88(98)}{210} = 41.07$$

$$e_{21} = \frac{R_2 C_1}{n} = \frac{63(34)}{210} = 10.20 \qquad e_{22} = \frac{R_2 C_2}{n} = \frac{63(28)}{210} = 8.40$$

$$e_{23} = \frac{R_2 C_3}{n} = \frac{63(50)}{210} = 15.00 \qquad e_{24} = \frac{R_2 C_4}{n} = \frac{63(98)}{210} = 29.40$$

$$e_{31} = \frac{R_3 C_1}{n} = \frac{59(34)}{210} = 9.55 \qquad e_{32} = \frac{R_3 C_2}{n} = \frac{59(28)}{210} = 7.87$$

$$e_{33} = \frac{R_3 C_3}{n} = \frac{59(50)}{210} = 14.05 \qquad e_{34} = \frac{R_3 C_4}{n} = \frac{59(98)}{210} = 27.53$$

b. $$\chi^2 = \sum\sum \frac{(O_{ij} - e_{ij})^2}{e_{ij}} = \frac{(18 - 14.25)^2}{14.25} + \frac{(12 - 11.73)^2}{11.73}$$

$$+ \frac{(21 - 20.95)^2}{20.95} + \ldots + \frac{(30 - 27.53)^2}{27.53} = 3.49$$

c. H_0: The two directions of classifications are independent
   H_a: The two directions of classification are dependent

   The test statistic is $\chi^2 = 3.49$ (from part (b)).

   The rejection region requires $\alpha = .01$ in the upper tail of the χ^2 distribution with df $= (r - 1)(c - 1) = (3 - 1)(4 - 1) = 6$. From Table 17, Appendix E, $\chi^2_{.01} = 16.8119$. The rejection region is $\chi^2 > 16.8119$.

   Since the observed value of the test statistic does not fall in the rejection region ($\chi^2 = 3.49 \not> 16.8119$), H_0 is not rejected. There is insufficient evidence to indicate the two directions of classifications are dependent at $\alpha = .01$.

18.19 a. To calculate the percentage of consumers responding in each of the "value" categories, divide each number in a column by the column total and multiply by 100. The column totals for each of the U.S. "Nations" are:

1.	New England	120
2.	The Foundry	750
3.	Dixie	653
4.	The Islands	32
5.	Breadbasket	307
6.	Mex America	150
7.	Empty Quarter	34
8.	Ecotopia	189

The percentages for each of the U.S. "Nations" are:

MOST IMPORTANT VALUE	NEW ENGLAND	THE FOUNDRY	DIXIE	THE ISLANDS	BREAD-BASKET	MEX AMERICA	EMPTY QUARTER	ECOTOPIA
Self-respect	22.5	20.5	22.5	25.0	17.9	22.7	35.3	18.0
Security	21.7	19.6	23.3	15.6	20.2	17.3	17.6	19.6
Warm relationships	14.2	16.7	13.8	9.4	20.5	18.0	5.9	18.5
Sense of accomplishment	14.2	11.7	9.9	9.4	12.4	11.3	8.8	12.2
Self-fulfillment	9.2	9.9	8.4	3.1	7.5	16.0	5.9	12.7
Being well-respected	8.3	8.7	11.0	15.6	10.1	2.7	2.9	4.2
Sense of belonging	5.0	8.4	7.5	12.5	7.8	6.7	17.6	7.9
Fun-enjoyment	5.0	4.5	3.5	9.4	3.6	5.3	5.9	6.9

b. Some of the U.S. "Nations" appear to have similar distributions of percentages, but others appear to have different distributions.

c. We cannot tell whether the differences in the distributions are significant or not without a formal test.

d. The row totals from the table are:

1.	Self-respect	471
2.	Security	461
3.	Warm Relationships	362
4.	Sense of accomplishment	254
5.	Self-fulfillment	214
6.	Being well-respected	196
7.	Sense of belonging	177
8.	Fun-enjoyment	100
		2235

The expected number of consumers is found using the formula

$$e_{ij} = \frac{R_i C_j}{n}$$

For the first cell in the column,

$$e_{11} = \frac{R_1 C_1}{n} = \frac{471(120)}{2235} = 25.3$$

The rest of the expected numbers of consumers are found in a similar manner and are shown in the following table:

MOST IMPORTANT VALUE	U.S. "NATION"							
	1	2	3	4	5	6	7	8
1	25.3	158.1	137.6	6.7	64.7	31.6	7.2	39.8
2	24.8	154.7	134.7	6.6	63.3	30.9	7.0	39.0
3	19.4	121.5	105.8	5.2	49.7	24.3	5.5	30.6
4	13.6	85.2	74.2	3.6	34.9	17.0	3.9	21.5
5	11.5	71.8	62.5	3.1	29.4	14.4	3.3	18.1
6	10.5	65.8	57.3	2.8	26.9	13.2	3.0	16.6
7	9.5	59.4	51.7	2.5	24.3	11.9	2.7	15.0
8	5.4	33.6	29.2	1.4	13.7	6.7	1.5	8.5

e. The difference between the observed and the expected number for each of the cells is shown below:

MOST IMPORTANT VALUE	U.S. "NATION"							
	1	2	3	4	5	6	7	8
1	1.7	-4.1	9.4	1.3	-9.7	2.4	4.8	-5.8
2	1.2	-7.7	17.3	-1.6	-1.3	-4.9	-1.0	-2.0
3	-2.4	3.5	-15.8	-2.2	13.3	2.7	-3.5	4.4
4	3.4	2.8	-9.2	-.6	3.1	0	-.9	1.5
5	-.5	2.2	-7.5	-2.1	-6.4	9.6	-1.3	5.9
6	-.5	-.8	14.7	2.2	4.1	-9.2	-2.0	-8.6
7	-3.5	3.6	-2.7	1.5	-.3	-1.9	3.3	0
8	.6	.4	-6.2	1.6	-2.7	1.3	.5	4.5

f. $\chi^2 = \sum\sum \dfrac{(O_{ij} - e_{ij})^2}{e_{ij}} = \dfrac{1.7^2}{25.3} + \dfrac{(-4.1)^2}{158.1} + \dfrac{9.4^2}{137.6} + \cdots + \dfrac{4.5^2}{8.5} = 68.695$

g. To determine if the distributions of the percentages of responses to the "value" question differ for the eight U.S. "Nations," we test:

H_0: "Value" and "Nation" are independent
H_a: "Value" and "Nation" are dependent

The test statistic is $\chi^2 = 68.695$ (see part (f)).

The rejection region requires $\alpha = .10$ in the upper tail of the χ^2 distribution with df $= (r - 1)(c - 1) = (8 - 1)(8 - 1) = 49$. From Table 17, Appendix E, $\chi^2_{.10} \approx 63.1671$. The rejection region is $\chi^2 > 63.1671$.

Since the observed value of the test statistic falls in the rejection region ($\chi^2 = 68.695 > 63.1671$), H_0 is rejected. There is sufficient evidence to indicate that the distributions of the percentages of responses to the "value" question differ for the eight U.S. "Nations" at $\alpha = .10$. This implies the people from different parts of the country have different values.

18.21   Some preliminary calculations are:

$$e_{11} = \frac{R_1 C_1}{n} = \frac{96(298)}{389} = 73.542 \qquad e_{12} = \frac{R_1 C_2}{n} = \frac{96(91)}{389} = 22.458$$

$$e_{21} = \frac{R_2 C_1}{n} = \frac{62(298)}{389} = 47.496 \qquad e_{22} = \frac{R_2 C_2}{n} = \frac{62(91)}{389} = 14.504$$

$$e_{31} = \frac{R_3 C_1}{n} = \frac{9(298)}{389} = 6.895 \qquad e_{32} = \frac{R_3 C_2}{n} = \frac{9(91)}{389} = 2.105$$

$$e_{41} = \frac{R_4 C_1}{n} = \frac{222(298)}{389} = 170.067 \qquad e_{42} = \frac{R_4 C_2}{n} = \frac{222(91)}{389} = 51.933$$

To determine if the percentages of computer-generated reports not used differ among the four receiver groups, we test:

H_0: Receiver group and use of reports are independent
H_a: Receiver group and use of reports are dependent

The test statistic is $\chi^2 = \sum\sum \dfrac{(O_{ij} - e_{ij})^2}{e_{ij}}$

$$= \frac{(67 - 73.542)^2}{73.542} + \frac{(29 - 22.458)^2}{22.458} + \frac{(42 - 47.496)^2}{47.496} + \cdots$$

$$+ \frac{(42 - 51.933)^2}{51.933} = 10.43$$

The rejection region requires $\alpha = .05$ in the upper tail of the χ^2 distribution with df $= (r - 1)(c - 1) = (4 - 1)(2 - 1) = 3$. From Table 17, Appendix E, $\chi^2_{.05} = 7.81473$. The rejection region is $\chi^2 > 7.81473$.

Since the observed value of the test statistic falls in the rejection region ($\chi^2 = 10.43 > 7.81473$), H_0 is rejected. There is sufficient evidence to indicate the percentages of computer-generated reports not used differ among the four receiver groups at $\alpha = .05$.

18.23 Some preliminary calculations are:

$$e_{11} = \frac{R_1 C_1}{n} = \frac{833(252)}{1400} = 149.94 \qquad e_{21} = \frac{R_2 C_1}{n} = \frac{567(252)}{1400} = 102.06$$

$$e_{12} = \frac{R_1 C_2}{n} = \frac{833(644)}{1400} = 383.18 \qquad e_{22} = \frac{R_2 C_2}{n} = \frac{567(644)}{1400} = 260.82$$

$$e_{13} = \frac{R_1 C_3}{n} = \frac{833(50)}{1400} = 29.75 \qquad e_{23} = \frac{R_2 C_3}{n} = \frac{567(50)}{1400} = 20.25$$

$$e_{14} = \frac{R_1 C_4}{n} = \frac{833(454)}{1400} = 270.13 \qquad e_{24} = \frac{R_2 C_4}{n} = \frac{567(454)}{1400} = 183.87$$

a. To determine if referral source and job success are dependent, we test:

H_0: Referral source and job success are independent
H_a: Referral source and job success are dependent

The test statistic is $\chi^2 = \sum\sum \dfrac{(0_{ij} - e_{ij})^2}{e_{ij}}$

$$= \frac{(167 - 149.94)^2}{149.94} + \frac{(85 - 102.06)^2}{102.06} + \frac{(383 - 383.18)^2}{383.18} + \dots$$

$$+ \frac{(204 - 183.87)^2}{183.87} = 9.374$$

The rejection region requires $\alpha = .05$ in the upper tail of the χ^2 distribution with df $= (r - 1)(c - 1) = (2 - 1)(4 - 1) = 3$. From Table 17, Appendix E, $\chi^2_{.05} = 7.81473$. The rejection region is $\chi^2 > 7.81473$.

Since the observed value of the test statistic falls in the rejection region ($\chi^2 = 9.374 > 7.81473$), H_0 is rejected. There is sufficient evidence to indicate referral source and job success are dependent at $\alpha = .05$.

b. The point estimate for the proportion of employment agency referrals who perform unsatisfactorily is

$$\hat{p} = \frac{33}{50} = .66$$

The form of the confidence interval is

$$\hat{p} \pm z_{\alpha/2} \sqrt{\frac{\hat{p}\hat{q}}{n}}$$

Confidence coefficient $.95 = 1 - \alpha \Rightarrow \alpha = 1 - .95 = .05;$ $\alpha/2$ = $.05/2 = .025$. From Table 4, Appendix E, $z_{.025} = 1.96$. The confidence interval is

$$.66 \pm 1.96\sqrt{\frac{.66(.34)}{50}} \Rightarrow .66 \pm .131 \Rightarrow (.529,\ 791)$$

c. Let p_1 = proportion of employment agency referrals who perform unsatisfactorily and p_2 = proportion of employee referrals who perform unsatisfactorily. To determine if these proportions differ, we test:

H_0: $p_1 = p_2$
H_a: $p_1 \neq p_2$

$$\hat{p}_1 = \frac{33}{50} = .66 \qquad \hat{p}_2 = \frac{167}{252} = .663 \qquad \hat{p} = \frac{33 + 167}{50 + 252} = .662$$

$$\text{The test statistic } z = \frac{\hat{p}_1 - \hat{p}_2}{\sqrt{\hat{p}\hat{q}\left(\frac{1}{n_1} + \frac{1}{n_2}\right)}} = \frac{.66 - .663}{\sqrt{.662(.338)\left(\frac{1}{50} + \frac{1}{252}\right)}}$$

$$= -.04$$

The rejection region requires $\alpha/2 = .025$ in each tail of the z distribution. From Table 4, Appendix E, $z_{.025} = 1.96$. The rejection region is $z < -1.96$ or $z > 1.96$.

Since the observed value of the test statistic does not fall in the rejection region ($z = -.04 \not< -1.96$), H_0 is not rejected. There is insufficient evidence to indicate the proportions of employment agency referrals and employee referrals who perform unsatisfactorily differ at $\alpha = .05$.

18.25 Some preliminary calculations are:

$$e_{11} = \frac{R_1 C_1}{n} = \frac{40(303)}{686} = 17.668 \qquad e_{12} = \frac{R_1 C_2}{n} = \frac{40(383)}{686} = 22.332$$

$$e_{21} = \frac{R_2 C_1}{n} = \frac{182(303)}{686} = 80.388 \qquad e_{22} = \frac{R_2 C_2}{n} = \frac{182(383)}{686} = 101.612$$

$$e_{31} = \frac{R_3 C_1}{n} = \frac{223(303)}{686} = 98.497 \qquad e_{32} = \frac{R_3 C_2}{n} = \frac{223(383)}{686} = 124.503$$

$$e_{41} = \frac{R_4 C_1}{n} = \frac{128(303)}{686} = 56.536 \qquad e_{42} = \frac{R_4 C_2}{n} = \frac{128(383)}{686} = 71.464$$

$$e_{51} = \frac{R_5 C_1}{n} = \frac{113(303)}{686} = 49.911 \qquad e_{52} = \frac{R_5 C_2}{n} = \frac{113(383)}{686} = 63.089$$

To determine if tourist type and education level are independent, we test:

H_0: Tourist type and education level are independent
H_a: Tourist type and education level are dependent

The test statistic is $\chi^2 = \sum\sum \dfrac{(O_{ij} - e_{ij})^2}{e_{ij}}$

$$= \frac{(13 - 17.668)^2}{17.668} + \frac{(27 - 22.332)^2}{22.332} + \frac{(64 - 80.388)^2}{80.388} + \cdots$$

$$+ \frac{(46 - 63.089)^2}{63.089} = 18.906$$

The rejection region requires $\alpha = .01$ in the upper tail of the χ^2 distribution with df $= (r - 1)(c - 1) = (5 - 1)(2 - 1) = 4$. From Table 17, Appendix E, $\chi^2_{.01} = 13.2767$. The rejection region is $\chi^2 > 13.2767$.

Since the observed value of the test statistic falls in the rejection region ($\chi^2 = 18.906 > 13.2767$), H_0 is rejected. There is sufficient evidence to indicate tourist type and educational level are dependent at $\alpha = .01$. This indicates the marketer of tourist information needs to target those in different education levels differently.

18.27   a.   Yes, the sampling appears to satisfy the assumptions for a multinomial experiment.

   1.   There are 400 identical trials.
   2.   There are 6 possible outcomes for each trial.
   3.   The probabilities of the 6 outcomes are constant from trial to trial.
   4.   The trials are independent.

b. $e_{11} = \dfrac{R_1 C_1}{n} = \dfrac{271(256)}{400} = 173.44$ $e_{21} = \dfrac{R_2 C_1}{n} = \dfrac{129(256)}{400} = 82.56$

   $e_{12} = \dfrac{R_1 C_2}{n} = \dfrac{271(111)}{400} = 75.2025$ $e_{22} = \dfrac{R_2 C_2}{n} = \dfrac{129(111)}{400} = 35.7975$

   $e_{13} = \dfrac{R_1 C_3}{n} = \dfrac{271(33)}{400} = 22.3575$ $e_{23} = \dfrac{R_2 C_3}{n} = \dfrac{129(33)}{400} = 10.6425$

c. $\chi^2 = \sum\sum \dfrac{(O_{ij} - e_{ij})^2}{e_{ij}} = \dfrac{(169 - 173.44)^2}{173.44} + \dfrac{(76 - 75.2025)^2}{75.2025} + \cdots$

   $+ \dfrac{(7 - 10.6425)^2}{10.6425} = 2.219$

d. The hypotheses are:

H_0: Employment category and view on new plan are independent
H_a: Employment category and view on new plan are dependent

e. Using the hypotheses in part (d), the test statistic is

$\chi^2 = 2.219$ (from part (c)).

The rejection region requires $\alpha = .10$ in the upper tail of the χ^2 distribution with df $= (r - 1)(c - 1) = (2 - 1)(3 - 1) = 2$. From Table 17, Appendix E, $\chi^2_{.10} = 4.60517$. The rejection region is $\chi^2 > 4.60517$.

Since the observed value of the test statistic does not fall in the rejection region ($\chi^2 = 2.219 \not> 4.60517$), H_0 is not rejected. There is insufficient evidence to indicate that employees' attitudes toward the new pension plan depend on their employment category at $\alpha = .10$.

f. The observed significance level is $P(\chi^2 > 2.219)$. From Table 17, Appendix E, with df $= 2$,

$P(\chi^2 > 2.219) > .10$

g. The estimate of the proportion of all employees who favor the plan is

$$\hat{p} = \frac{271}{400} = .6775$$

Confidence coefficient $.95 = 1 - \alpha \Rightarrow \alpha = .05$; $\alpha/2 = .05/2 = .025$. From Table 4, Appendix E, $z_{.025} = 1.96$. The confidence interval is

$$\hat{p} \pm z_{\alpha/2}\sqrt{\frac{\hat{p}\hat{q}}{n}} \Rightarrow .6775 \pm 1.96\sqrt{\frac{.6775(.3225)}{400}}$$

$$\Rightarrow .6775 \pm .0458 \Rightarrow (.6317, .7233)$$

h. Let p_1 = proportion of production employees who favor the plan and p_2 = proportion of management employees who favor the plan.

$$\hat{p}_1 = \frac{169}{256} = .660 \qquad \hat{p}_2 = \frac{26}{33} = .788$$

Confidence coefficient $.90 = 1 - \alpha \Rightarrow \alpha = 1 - .90 = .10$; $\alpha/2 = .10/2 = .05$. From Table 4, Appendix E, $z_{.05} = 1.645$. The confidence interval is

$$(\hat{p}_1 - \hat{p}_2) \pm z_{\alpha/2} \sqrt{\frac{\hat{p}_1 \hat{q}_1}{n_1} + \frac{\hat{p}_2 \hat{q}_2}{n_2}}$$

$$\Rightarrow (.660 - .788) \pm 1.645 \sqrt{\frac{.66(.34)}{256} + \frac{.788(.212)}{33}}$$

$$\Rightarrow -.128 \pm .1268 \Rightarrow (-.2548, -.0012)$$

18.29 Some preliminary calculations are:

$e_{11} = \dfrac{R_1 C_1}{n} = \dfrac{67(83)}{311} = 17.88$ \qquad $e_{21} = \dfrac{R_2 C_1}{n} = \dfrac{69(83)}{311} = 18.41$

$e_{12} = \dfrac{R_1 C_2}{n} = \dfrac{67(117)}{311} = 25.21$ \qquad $e_{22} = \dfrac{R_2 C_2}{n} = \dfrac{69(117)}{311} = 25.96$

$e_{13} = \dfrac{R_1 C_3}{n} = \dfrac{67(79)}{311} = 17.02$ \qquad $e_{23} = \dfrac{R_2 C_3}{n} = \dfrac{69(79)}{311} = 17.53$

$e_{14} = \dfrac{R_1 C_4}{n} = \dfrac{67(32)}{311} = 6.89$ \qquad $e_{24} = \dfrac{R_2 C_4}{n} = \dfrac{69(32)}{311} = 7.10$

$e_{31} = \dfrac{R_3 C_1}{n} = \dfrac{104(83)}{311} = 27.76$ \qquad $e_{41} = \dfrac{R_4 C_1}{n} = \dfrac{71(83)}{311} = 18.95$

$e_{32} = \dfrac{R_3 C_2}{n} = \dfrac{104(117)}{311} = 39.13$ \qquad $e_{42} = \dfrac{R_4 C_2}{n} = \dfrac{71(117)}{311} = 26.71$

$e_{33} = \dfrac{R_3 C_3}{n} = \dfrac{104(79)}{311} = 26.42$ \qquad $e_{43} = \dfrac{R_4 C_3}{n} = \dfrac{71(79)}{311} = 18.04$

$e_{34} = \dfrac{R_3 C_4}{n} = \dfrac{104(32)}{311} = 10.70$ \qquad $e_{44} = \dfrac{R_4 C_4}{n} = \dfrac{71(32)}{311} = 7.31$

To determine if a relationship exists between length of stay and hospitalization coverage, we test:

H_0: Length of stay and hospitalization coverage are independent
H_a: Length of stay and hospitalization coverage are dependent

The test statistic is $\chi^2 = \sum\sum \dfrac{(O_{ij} - e_{ij})^2}{e_{ij}}$

$$= \frac{(26 - 17.88)^2}{17.88} + \frac{(30 - 25.21)^2}{25.21} + \frac{(6 - 17.02)^2}{17.02} + \dots + \frac{(11 - 7.31)^2}{7.31}$$

$$= 40.70$$

The rejection region requires $\alpha = .01$ in the upper tail of the χ^2 distribution with df $= (r - 1)(c - 1) = (4 - 1)(4 - 1) = 9$. From Table 17, Appendix E, $\chi^2_{.01} = 21.6660$. The rejection region is $\chi^2 > 21.6660$.

Since the observed value of the test statistic falls in the rejection region ($\chi^2 = 40.70 > 21.6660$), H_0 is rejected. There is sufficient evidence to indicate there is a relationship between length of stay and hospitalization coverage at $\alpha = .01$.

18.31   Some preliminary calculations are:

$$e_1 = np_1 = 32(1/3) = 10.67$$
$$e_2 = np_2 = 32(1/3) = 10.67$$
$$e_3 = np_3 = 32(1/3) = 10.67$$

To determine if the proportions of unpromoted managers with low, medium, and high managerial motivation differ, we test:

H_0: $p_1 = p_2 = p_3 = 1/3$
H_a: At least two of the cell probabilities differ from $1/3$

The test statistic is $\chi^2 = \sum \dfrac{(O_i - e_i)^2}{e_i}$

$$= \frac{(3 - 10.67)^2}{10.67} + \frac{(21 - 10.67)^2}{10.67} + \frac{(8 - 10.67)^2}{10.67} = 16.18$$

The rejection region requires $\alpha = .10$ in the upper tail of the χ^2 distribution with df $= k - 1 = 3 - 1 = 2$. From Table 17, Appendix E, $\chi^2_{.10} = 4.60517$. The rejection region is $\chi^2 > 4.60517$.

Since the observed value of the test statistic falls in the rejection region ($\chi^2 = 16.18 > 4.60517$), H_0 is rejected. There is sufficient evidence to indicate the proportions of unpromoted managers with low, medium, and high managerial motivation differ at $\alpha = .10$.

18.33   Some preliminary calculations are:

The contingency table for this problem is:

	Large	Size of Company Medium	Small	
Much Brighter	53	61	17	131
Not Much Brighter	257	244	190	691
	310	305	207	822

$$e_{11} = \frac{R_1C_1}{n} = \frac{131(310)}{822} = 49.40 \qquad e_{21} = \frac{R_2C_1}{n} = \frac{691(310)}{822} = 260.60$$

$$e_{12} = \frac{R_1C_2}{n} = \frac{131(305)}{822} = 48.61 \qquad e_{22} = \frac{R_2C_2}{n} = \frac{691(305)}{822} = 256.39$$

$$e_{13} = \frac{R_1C_3}{n} = \frac{131(207)}{822} = 32.99 \qquad e_{23} = \frac{R_2C_3}{n} = \frac{691(207)}{822} = 174.01$$

To determine if brighter expectations depend on company size, we test:

H_0: Brighter expectations and company size are independent
H_a: Brighter expectations and company size are dependent

The test statistic is $\chi^2 = \sum\sum \dfrac{(O_{ij} - e_{ij})^2}{e_{ij}}$

$$= \frac{(53 - 49.40)^2}{49.40} + \frac{(61 - 48.61)^2}{48.61} + \ldots + \frac{(190 - 174.01)^2}{174.01}$$

$$= 13.288$$

The rejection region requires $\alpha = .10$ in the upper tail of the χ^2 distribution with df $= (r - 1)(c - 1) = (2 - 1)(3 - 1) = 2$. From Table 17, Appendix E, $\chi^2_{.10} = 4.60517$. The rejection region is $\chi^2 > 4.60517$.

Since the observed value of the test statistic falls in the rejection region ($\chi^2 = 13.288 > 4.60517$), H_0 is rejected. There is sufficient evidence to indicate the percentages with a much brighter expectation this year depend on company size at $\alpha = .10$.

18.35   Some preliminary calculations are:

$$e_{11} = \frac{R_1C_1}{n} = \frac{1284(1372)}{1853} = 950.70 \qquad e_{21} = \frac{R_2C_1}{n} = \frac{241(1372)}{1853} = 178.44$$

$$e_{12} = \frac{R_1C_2}{n} = \frac{1284(221)}{1853} = 153.14 \qquad e_{22} = \frac{R_2C_2}{n} = \frac{241(221)}{1853} = 28.74$$

$$e_{13} = \frac{R_1C_3}{n} = \frac{1284(260)}{1853} = 180.16 \qquad e_{23} = \frac{R_2C_3}{n} = \frac{241(260)}{1853} = 33.82$$

$$e_{31} = \frac{R_3C_1}{n} = \frac{328(1372)}{1853} = 242.86$$

$$e_{32} = \frac{R_3C_2}{n} = \frac{328(221)}{1853} = 39.12$$

$$e_{33} = \frac{R_3C_3}{n} = \frac{328(260)}{1853} = 46.02$$

a. To determine if anxiety level depends on flight experience, we test:

H_0: Anxiety level and flight experience are independent
H_a: Anxiety level and flight experience are dependent

The test statistic is $\chi^2 = \sum\sum \dfrac{(O_{ij} - e_{ij})^2}{e_{ij}}$

$$= \dfrac{(1043 - 950.70)^2}{950.70} + \dfrac{(128 - 153.14)^2}{153.14} + \dfrac{(113 - 180.16)^2}{180.16} + \cdots$$

$$+ \dfrac{(141 - 46.02)^2}{46.02} = 313.18$$

The rejection region requires $\alpha = .05$ in the upper tail of the χ^2 distribution with df = $(r - 1)(c - 1) = (3 - 1)(3 - 1) = 4$. From Table 17, Appendix E, $\chi^2_{.05} = 9.48773$. The rejection region is $\chi^2 > 9.48773$.

Since the observed value of the test statistic falls in the rejection region ($\chi^2 = 313.18 > 9.48773$), H_0 is rejected. There is sufficient evidence to indicate the anxiety level with respect to flying depends on flight experience at $\alpha = .05$.

b. Let p_1 = proportion of flyers who have no anxiety toward flying and p_2 = proportion of nonflyers likely to fly who have no anxiety toward flying.

$$\hat{p}_1 = \dfrac{1043}{1372} = .760 \qquad \hat{p}_2 = \dfrac{128}{221} = .579$$

Confidence coefficient $.95 = 1 - \alpha \Rightarrow \alpha = 1 - .95 = .05$; $\alpha/2 = .05/2 = .025$. From Table 4, Appendix E, $z_{.025} = 1.96$. The confidence interval is

$$(\hat{p}_1 - \hat{p}_2) \pm z_{\alpha/2}\sqrt{\dfrac{\hat{p}_1\hat{q}_1}{n_1} + \dfrac{\hat{p}_2\hat{q}_2}{n_2}}$$

$$\Rightarrow (.760 - .579) \pm 1.96\sqrt{\dfrac{.76(.24)}{1372} + \dfrac{.579(.421)}{221}}$$

$$\Rightarrow .181 \pm .069 \Rightarrow (.112, .250)$$

We are 95% confident the difference between the proportions of flyers and nonflyers likely to fly who have no anxiety toward flying is between .112 and .250.

18.37 Some preliminary calculations are:

$$e_{11} = \frac{R_1 C_1}{n} = \frac{24(20)}{43} = 11.16 \qquad e_{12} = \frac{R_1 C_2}{n} = \frac{24(23)}{43} = 12.84$$

$$e_{21} = \frac{R_2 C_1}{n} = \frac{19(20)}{43} = 8.84 \qquad e_{22} = \frac{R_2 C_2}{n} = \frac{19(23)}{43} = 10.16$$

a. To determine if the distributions of the percentages of survivors and deaths are different for infected babies treated with the drug and those left untreated, we test:

  H_0: Survival and treatment are independent
  H_a: Survival and treatment are dependent

The test statistic is $\chi^2 = \sum\sum \dfrac{(O_{ij} - e_{ij})^2}{e_{ij}}$

$$= \frac{(15 - 11.16)^2}{11.16} + \frac{(9 - 12.84)^2}{12.84} + \frac{(5 - 8.84)^2}{8.84} + \frac{(14 - 10.16)^2}{10.16}$$

$$= 5.589$$

The rejection region requires $\alpha = .05$ in the upper tail of the χ^2 distribution with df $= (r - 1)(c - 1) = (2 - 1)(2 - 1) = 1$ From Table 17, Appendix E, $\chi^2_{.05} = 3.84146$. The rejection region is $\chi^2 > 3.84146$.

Since the observed value of the test statistic falls in the rejection region ($\chi^2 = 5.589 > 3.84146$), H_0 is rejected. There is sufficient evidence to indicate the percentages of survivors and deaths are different for infected babies treated with the drug and those left untreated at $\alpha = .05$.

b. To test p_1 is greater than p_2, we test

  H_0: $p_1 = p_2$
  H_a: $p_1 > p_2$

$\hat{p}_1 = \dfrac{15}{20} = .75 \qquad \hat{p}_2 = \dfrac{9}{23} = .391 \qquad \hat{p} = \dfrac{15 + 9}{20 + 23} = .558$

The test statistic $z = \dfrac{\hat{p}_1 - \hat{p}_2}{\sqrt{\hat{p}\hat{q}\left(\frac{1}{n_1} + \frac{1}{n_2}\right)}} = \dfrac{.75 - .391}{\sqrt{.558(.442)\left(\frac{1}{20} + \frac{1}{23}\right)}}$

$$= 2.36$$

The rejection region requires $\alpha = .05$ in each tail of the z distribution. From Table 4, Appendix E, $z_{.05} = 1.645$. The rejection region is $z > 1.645$.

Since the observed value of the test statistic falls in the rejection region ($z = 2.36 > 1.645$), H_0 is rejected. There is sufficient evidence to indicate p_1 is greater than p_2 at $\alpha = .05$.

c. Yes. Both analyses indicate survival rate and treatment are significantly related.

CASE STUDIES

18.1 a. Some preliminary calculations are:

$$e_{11} = \frac{R_1 C_1}{n} = \frac{388(282)}{782} = 139.92 \qquad e_{21} = \frac{R_2 C_1}{n} = \frac{285(282)}{782} = 102.77$$

$$e_{12} = \frac{R_1 C_2}{n} = \frac{388(300)}{782} = 148.85 \qquad e_{22} = \frac{R_2 C_2}{n} = \frac{285(300)}{782} = 109.34$$

$$e_{13} = \frac{R_1 C_3}{n} = \frac{388(200)}{782} = 99.23 \qquad e_{23} = \frac{R_2 C_3}{n} = \frac{285(200)}{782} = 72.89$$

$$e_{31} = \frac{R_3 C_1}{n} = \frac{94(282)}{782} = 33.90 \qquad e_{41} = \frac{R_4 C_1}{n} = \frac{15(282)}{782} = 5.41$$

$$e_{32} = \frac{R_3 C_2}{n} = \frac{94(300)}{782} = 36.06 \qquad e_{42} = \frac{R_4 C_2}{n} = \frac{15(300)}{782} = 5.75$$

$$e_{33} = \frac{R_3 C_3}{n} = \frac{94(200)}{782} = 24.04 \qquad e_{43} = \frac{R_2 C_3}{n} = \frac{15(200)}{782} = 3.84$$

To determine if the likelihood to fire incompetent workers is related to size of firm, we test:

H_0: Likelihood to fire incompetent workers and size of firm are independent

H_a: Likelihood to fire incompetent workers and size of firm are dependent

The test statistic is $\chi^2 = \sum\sum \dfrac{(O_{ij} - e_{ij})^2}{e_{ij}}$

$$= \frac{(166 - 139.92)^2}{139.92} + \frac{(144 - 148.85)^2}{148.85} + \frac{(78 - 99.23)^2}{99.23} + \cdots$$

$$+ \frac{(6 - 3.84)^2}{3.84} = 35.955$$

The rejection region requires $\alpha = .01$ in the upper tail of the χ^2 distribution with df $= (r - 1)(c - 1) = (4 - 1)(3 - 1) = 6$. From Table 17, Appendix E, $\chi^2_{.01} = 16.8119$. The rejection region is $\chi^2 > 16.8119$.

Since the observed value of the test statistic falls in the rejection region ($\chi^2 = 35.955 > 16.8119$), H_0 is rejected. There is sufficient evidence to indicate the distributions of percentages of responses corresponding to the categories "likelihood of firing an incompetent worker" differ among chief executives at large, medium, and small firms at $\alpha = .01$.

b. Some preliminary calculations are:

$$e_{11} = \frac{R_1 C_1}{n} = \frac{476(282)}{782} = 171.65 \qquad e_{21} = \frac{R_2 C_1}{n} = \frac{177(282)}{782} = 63.83$$

$$e_{12} = \frac{R_1 C_2}{n} = \frac{476(300)}{782} = 182.61 \qquad e_{22} = \frac{R_2 C_2}{n} = \frac{177(300)}{782} = 67.90$$

$$e_{13} = \frac{R_1 C_3}{n} = \frac{476(200)}{782} = 121.74 \qquad e_{23} = \frac{R_2 C_3}{n} = \frac{177(200)}{782} = 45.27$$

$$e_{31} = \frac{R_3 C_1}{n} = \frac{87(282)}{782} = 31.37 \qquad e_{41} = \frac{R_4 C_1}{n} = \frac{42(282)}{782} = 15.15$$

$$e_{32} = \frac{R_3 C_2}{n} = \frac{87(300)}{782} = 33.38 \qquad e_{42} = \frac{R_4 C_2}{n} = \frac{42(300)}{782} = 16.11$$

$$e_{33} = \frac{R_3 C_3}{n} = \frac{87(200)}{782} = 22.25 \qquad e_{43} = \frac{R_4 C_3}{n} = \frac{42(200)}{782} = 10.74$$

To determine if the size of firm and likelihood of raises to poor performers are dependent, we test:

H_0: Size of firm and likelihood of raises to poor performers are independent

H_a: Size of firm and likelihood of raises to poor performers are dependent

The test statistic is $\chi^2 = \sum\sum \dfrac{(O_{ij} - e_{ij})^2}{e_{ij}}$

$$= \frac{(195 - 171.65)^2}{171.65} + \frac{(177 - 182.61)^2}{182.61} + \frac{(104 - 121.74)^2}{121.74} + \cdots$$

$$+ \frac{(16 - 10.74)^2}{10.74} = 23.154$$

The rejection region requires α = .05 in the upper tail of the χ² distribution with df = (r – 1)(c – 1) = (4 – 1)(3 – 1) = 6. From Table 17, Appendix E, $\chi^2_{.05}$ = 12.5916. The rejection region is χ² > 12.5916.

Since the observed value of the test statistic falls in the rejection region (χ² = 23.154 > 12.5916), H_0 is rejected. There is sufficient evidence to indicate the size of firm and the likelihood of raises to poor performers are dependent at α = .05.

c. In part (a), the estimated expected cell count for the cell "Don't know/small firm" is 3.84. In order for the test statistic to have a χ² distribution, all expected cell counts should be at least 5.

18.3 a. To find the number of observations in each cell, multiply the proportion in each cell by the row total. The seven tables are:

AGE

| | Performance Quartile | | | | |
	1	2	3	4	
Over 40	74	275	265	53	667
Under 40	192	599	575	96	1462
	266	874	840	149	2129

SEX

| | Performance Quartile | | | | |
	1	2	3	4	
Females	52	183	137	26	398
Males	224	648	349	175	1396
	276	831	486	201	1794

RACE

| | Performance Quartile | | | | |
	1	2	3	4	
Blacks	10	42	40	12	104
Whites	89	305	330	76	800
	99	347	370	88	904

EXPERIENCE

| | Performance Quartile | | | | |
	1	2	3	4	
Inexperienced	198	549	439	110	1296
Experienced	416	1123	749	208	2496
	614	1672	1188	318	3792

EDUCATION	Performance Quartile				
	1	2	3	4	
High School or Less	162	372	356	81	971
College Degree	501	1093	957	273	2824
	663	1465	1313	354	3795

LOW-TURNOVER	Performance Quartile				
	1	2	3	4	
Job-matched	436	950	317	119	1822
Not Job-matched	40	356	832	1386	2614
	476	1306	1149	1505	4436

HIGH-TURNOVER	Performance Quartile				
	1	2	3	4	
Job-matched	829	1832	305	174	3140
Not Job-matched	87	524	1224	1923	3758
	916	2356	1529	2097	6898

b. We will calculate the estimated expected cell counts for each cell using the formula

$$e_{ij} = \frac{R_i C_j}{n}$$

Age:

$$e_{11} = \frac{R_1 C_1}{n} = \frac{667(266)}{2129} = 83.34 \qquad e_{21} = \frac{R_2 C_1}{n} = \frac{1462(266)}{2129} = 182.66$$

$$e_{12} = \frac{R_1 C_2}{n} = \frac{667(874)}{2129} = 273.82 \qquad e_{22} = \frac{R_2 C_2}{n} = \frac{1462(874)}{2129} = 600.18$$

$$e_{13} = \frac{R_1 C_3}{n} = \frac{667(840)}{2129} = 263.17 \qquad e_{23} = \frac{R_2 C_3}{n} = \frac{1462(840)}{2129} = 576.83$$

$$e_{14} = \frac{R_1 C_4}{n} = \frac{667(149)}{2129} = 46.68 \qquad e_{24} = \frac{R_2 C_4}{n} = \frac{1462(149)}{2129} = 102.32$$

The test statistic is $\chi^2 = \sum\sum \dfrac{(O_{ij} - e_{ij})^2}{e_{ij}}$

$$= \frac{(74 - 83.34)^2}{83.84} + \frac{(275 - 273.82)^2}{273.82} + \cdots + \frac{(96 - 102.32)^2}{102.32}$$

$$= 2.795$$

The estimated expected cell counts for the rest of the tables are found in the same manner as for the Age table.

The estimated expected cell counts for Sex are:

	1	2	3	4
Female	61.23	184.36	107.82	44.59
Male	214.77	646.64	378.18	156.41

The test statistic is $\chi^2 = \sum\sum \dfrac{(O_{ij} - e_{ij})^2}{e_{ij}}$

$$= \frac{(52 - 61.23)^2}{61.23} + \frac{(183 - 184.36)^2}{184.36} + \cdots + \frac{(175 - 156.41)^2}{156.41}$$

$$= 21.909$$

The estimated expected cell counts for Race are:

	1	2	3	4
Blacks	11.39	39.92	42.57	10.12
Whites	87.61	307.08	327.43	77.88

The test statistic is $\chi^2 = \sum\sum \dfrac{(O_{ij} - e_{ij})^2}{e_{ij}}$

$$= \frac{(10 - 11.39)^2}{11.39} + \frac{(42 - 39.92)^2}{39.92} + \cdots + \frac{(76 - 77.88)^2}{77.88}$$

$$= .884$$

The estimated expected cell counts for Experience are:

	1	2	3	4
Inexperienced	209.85	571.44	406.03	108.68
Experienced	404.15	1100.56	781.97	209.32

The test statistic is $\chi^2 = \sum\sum \dfrac{(O_{ij} - e_{ij})^2}{e_{ij}}$

$$= \frac{(198 - 209.85)^2}{209.85} + \frac{(549 - 571.44)^2}{571.44} + \ldots + \frac{(208 - 209.32)^2}{209.32}$$

$$= 6.447$$

The estimated expected cell counts for Education are:

	1	2	3	4
High School or less	169.64	374.84	335.95	90.58
College Degree	493.36	1090.16	977.05	263.42

The test statistic is $\chi^2 = \sum\sum \dfrac{(O_{ij} - e_{ij})^2}{e_{ij}}$

$$= \frac{(162 - 169.64)^2}{169.64} + \frac{(372 - 374.84)^2}{374.84} + \ldots + \frac{(273 - 263.42)^2}{263.42}$$

$$= 3.461$$

The estimated expected cell counts for Low-turnover are:

	1	2	3	4
Job-matched	195.51	536.41	471.93	618.15
Not Job-matched	280.49	769.59	677.07	886.85

The test statistic is $\chi^2 = \sum\sum \dfrac{(O_{ij} - e_{ij})^2}{e_{ij}}$

$$= \frac{(436 - 195.51)^2}{195.51} + \frac{(950 - 536.41)^2}{536.41} + \ldots + \frac{(1386 - 886.85)^2}{886.85}$$

$$= 1813.486$$

The estimated expected cell counts for High-turnover are:

	1	2	3	4
Job-matched	416.97	1072.46	696.01	954.56
Not Job-matched	499.03	1283.54	832.99	1142.44

The test statistic is $\chi^2 = \sum\sum \dfrac{(O_{ij} - e_{ij})^2}{e_{ij}}$

$$= \frac{(829 - 416.97)^2}{416.97} + \frac{(1832 - 1072.46)^2}{1072.46} + \ldots + \frac{(1923 - 1142.44)^2}{1142.44}$$

$$= 3309.52$$

c. We will use Table 17, Appendix E, with df = $(r - 1)(c - 1)$
= $(2 - 1)(4 - 1) = 3$.

Age: p-value = $P(\chi^2 > 2.795) > .10$

Sex: p-value = $P(\chi^2 > 21.909) < .005$

Race: p-value = $P(\chi^2 > .884) > .10$

Experience: p-value = $P(\chi^2 > 6.447) => .05 < P(\chi^2 > 6.447) < .10$

Education: p-value = $P(\chi^2 > 3.461) > .10$

Low-turnover: p-value = $P(\chi^2 > 1813.486) < .005$

High-turnover: p-value = $P(\chi^2 > 3309.52) < .005$

The highest χ^2 values are those associated with the low-turnover and high-turnover, job-matched or not job-matched tables. This agrees with the authors' claim.

NINETEEN   NONPARAMETRIC STATISTICS

19.1   a. Using Table 1 with n = 5 and p = .5,

$$\text{p-value} = P(S \geq 2) = 1 - P(S \leq 1) = 1 - .1875 = .8125$$

   b. Using Table 1 with n = 20 and p = .5,

$$\text{p-value} = 2P(S \geq 16) = 2(1 - P(S \leq 15)) = 2(1 - .9941) = .0118$$

   c. Using Table 1 with n = 10 and p = .5,

$$\text{p-value} = P(S \geq 8) = 1 - P(S \leq 7) = 1 - .9453 = .0547$$

19.3   To determine if the manufacturer's sewer pipe meets specifications, we
        test:

$$H_0: \quad M = 2500$$
$$H_a: \quad M > 2500$$

The test statistic is S = 5, the number of observations larger than
2500.

The p-value is $P(S \geq 5)$. From Table 1, Appendix E, with n = 7 and
p = .5,

$$\text{p-value} = P(S \geq 5) = 1 - P(S \leq 4) = 1 - .7734 = .2266.$$

Since the p-value = .2266 $\not< \alpha$ = .05, H_0 is not rejected.   There is
insufficient evidence to indicate the manufacturer's sewer pipe meets
required specifications at α = .05.

19.5   To determine if the median earnings-per-share of all Fortune 500
        companies is less than $5, we test:

$$H_0: \quad M = 5$$
$$H_a: \quad M < 5$$

The test statistic is S = 16, the number of observations less than 5.

The p-value is $P(S \geq 16)$. From Table 1, Appendix E, with n = 20 and p = .5,

$$P(S \geq 16) = 1 - P(S \leq 15) = 1 - .9941 = .0059$$

Since p = .0059 < α = .05. H_0 is rejected. There is sufficient evidence to indicate the median earnings-per-share of all Fortune 500 companies is less than $5 at α = .05.

19.7   a.   The stem will consist of the digits in or to the left of the thousands column and the leaf will consist of the three right most digits. The stem-and-leaf display is:

Stem	Leaf
3	982, 870, 867, 860, 839, 781, 637, 545, 378, 303, 301, 218, 171, 115
4	603, 336, 255, 078, 076
5	
6	355, 295, 079
7	
8	400
9	
10	
11	
12	
13	063
14	
15	
16	
17	
18	
19	
20	542

These data do not follow a normal distribution. We would not be willing to assume they came from a normal distribution.

b.   No. One assumption necessary for a t-statistic is that the population being sampled from is normal. These data do not appear to come from a normal distribution.

c.   To determine if the median total 1986 compensation of the highest-paid corporate executives in the United States exceeds $3,500,000, we test:

H_0:   M = $3,500,000
H_a: M > $3,500,000

The test statistic is S = 19, the number of observations that exceed \$3,500,000.

The p-value is $P(S \geq 19)$. From Table 1, Appendix E, with n = 25 and p = .5,

$$\text{p-value} = P(S \geq 19) = 1 - P(S \leq 18) = 1 - .9927 = .0073$$

Since the p-value = .0073 < α = .10, H_0 is rejected. There is sufficient evidence to indicate the median total 1986 compensation of the highest-paid corporate executives in the United States exceeds \$3,500,000 at α = .10.

19.9 a. The rejection region is $T_1 \leq 24$ or $T_1 \geq 56$. The rejection region was obtained using Table 18, Appendix E, with n_1 = 5, n_2 = 10, and α = .05 for a two-tailed test.

b. The rejection region is $T_1 \geq 84$. The rejection region was obtained using Table 18, Appendix E, with n_1 = 8, n_2 = 8, and α = .05 for a one-tailed test.

c. The rejection region is $T_1 \leq 22$. The rejection region was obtained using Table 18, Appendix E, with n_1 = 5, n_2 = 7, and α = .05 for a one-tailed test.

19.11 a. The test statistic is $z = \dfrac{T_1 - [\dfrac{n_1 n_2 + n_1(n_1 + 1)}{2}]}{\sqrt{\dfrac{n_1 n_2 (n_1 + n_2 + 1)}{12}}}$

$$= \frac{71 - [\dfrac{10(14) + 10(10 + 1)}{2}]}{\sqrt{\dfrac{10(14)(10 + 14 + 1)}{12}}} = \frac{-54}{17.07825} = -3.16$$

The rejection region requires α = .05 in the lower tail of the z distribution. From Table 4, Appendix E, $z_{.05}$ = 1.645. The rejection region is z < -1.645.

b. The test statistic is $z = \dfrac{T_1 - [\dfrac{n_1 n_2 + n_1(n_1 + 1)}{2}]}{\sqrt{\dfrac{n_1 n_2 (n_1 + n_2 + 1)}{12}}}$

$$= \frac{750 - [\dfrac{25(25) + 25(25 + 1)}{2}]}{\sqrt{\dfrac{25(25)(25 + 25 + 1)}{12}}} = \frac{112.5}{51.53882} = 2.18$$

The rejection region requires $\alpha = .10$ in the upper tail of the z distribution. From Table 4, Appendix E, $z_{.10} = 1.28$. The rejection region is $z > 1.28$.

c. The test statistic is $z = \dfrac{T_1 - [\dfrac{n_1 n_2 + n_1 (n_1 + 1)}{2}]}{\sqrt{\dfrac{n_1 n_2 (n_1 + n_2 + 1)}{12}}}$

$= \dfrac{430 - [\dfrac{20(15) + 20(20 + 1)}{2}]}{\sqrt{\dfrac{20(15)(20 + 15 + 1)}{12}}} = \dfrac{70}{30} = 2.33$

The rejection region requires $\alpha/2 = .025$ in each tail of the z distribution. From Table 4, Appendix E, $z_{.025} = 1.96$. The rejection region is $z < -1.96$ or $z > 1.96$.

19.13 We first rank all the data:

BEFORE RIGHT-TURN LAW	RANK	AFTER RIGHT-TURN LAW	RANK
150	3	145	2
500	13	390	10
250	7	680	16
301	9	560	15
242	6	899	18
435	12	1,250	20
100	1	290	8
402	11	963	19
716	17	180	4
200	5	550	14
	$T_1 = 84$		$T_2 = 126$

To determine whether damages tended to increase after the enactment of the law, we test:

H_0: The distributions of damage estimates before and after enactment of the law are identical

H_a: The distribution of damage estimates before enactment of the law is shifted to the left of the distribution of damage estimates after

The test statistic is $T_1 = 84$.

The rejection region is $T_1 \leq 83$. The rejection region was obtained using Table 18, Appendix E, with $n_1 = n_2 = 10$ and $\alpha = .05$ for a one-tailed test.

NONPARAMETRIC STATISTICS

Since $T_1 = 84 \not> 83$, H_0 is not rejected. There is insufficient evidence to indicate the damages tended to increase after the enactment of the law at $\alpha = .05$.

19.15 First, we rank all the data:

70-cm SLAB WIDTH	RANK	100-cm SLAB WIDTH	RANK
6.00	1	6.80	2
7.20	3	9.20	5.5
10.20	7.5	8.80	4
13.20	13.5	13.20	13.5
11.40	11	11.20	9.5
13.60	15	14.90	16
9.20	5.5	10.20	7.5
11.20	9.5	11.80	12
	$T_1 = 66$		$T_2 = 70$

To determine if the locations of the cracking torsion moment distributions differ for the two types of T-beams, we test:

H_0: The locations of the cracking torsion moment distributions for the two types of T-beams are the same

H_a: The locations of the cracking torsion moment distributions for the two types of T-beams are different

The test statistic is $T_1 = 66$.

The rejection region is $T_1 \leq 52$ or $T_1 \geq 84$. The rejection region was obtained using Table 18, Appendix E, with $n_1 = n_2 = 8$ and $\alpha = .10$ for a two-tailed test.

Since $T_1 = 66 \not< 52$ and $T_1 = 66 \not> 84$, H_0 is not rejected. There is insufficient evidence to indicate the locations of the cracking torsion moment distributions differ for the two types of T-beams at $\alpha = .10$.

19.17 First, we rank the data:

MAJOR-LEAGUE BASEBALL	RANK	NATIONAL BASKETBALL ASSOCIATION	RANK
1,102,000	7	1,500,000	13
1,242,000	9	1,800,000	19
1,550,000	15	1,000,000	3.5
1,850,000	20	773,000	1
1,250,000	10	800,000	2
1,300,000	11.5	1,600,000	16.5
1,200,000	8	1,600,000	16.5
1,652,000	18	1,000,000	3.5
1,100,000	6	1,300,000	11.5
1,531,000	14	1,092,000	5
	$T_1 = 118.5$		$T_2 = 91.5$

To determine if there is a difference in the distributions of salaries of the best-paid professional baseball and basketball players, we test:

H_0: The distributions of salaries of the best-paid professional baseball and basketball players are identical

H_a: The distribution of the salaries of the best-paid professional baseball players is shifted to the right or left of that for basketball players

The test statistic is $z = \dfrac{T_1 - [\dfrac{n_1 n_2 + n_1(n_1 + 1)}{2}]}{\sqrt{\dfrac{n_1 n_2(n_1 + n_2 + 1)}{12}}}$

$$= \dfrac{118.5 - [\dfrac{10(10) + 10(10 + 1)}{2}]}{\sqrt{\dfrac{10(10)(10 + 10 + 1)}{12}}} = \dfrac{13.5}{13.22876} = 1.02$$

The rejection region requires $\alpha/2 = .005$ in each tail of the z distribution. From Table 4, Appendix E, $z_{.005} = 2.575$. The rejection region is $z < -2.575$ or $z > 2.575$.

Since $z = 1.02 \not> 2.575$, H_0 is not rejected. There is insufficient evidence to indicate the distributions of salaries of the best-paid professional baseball and basketball players differ at $\alpha = .01$.

19.19 First, we rank the data:

YOUNGER AGE GROUP	RANK	OLDER AGE GROUP	RANK
4	10	1	1
3	5	5	13.5
4	10	4	10
2	2	3	5
3	5	3	5
5	13.5	4	10
4	10	3	5
	$T_1 = 55.5$		$T_2 = 49.5$

H_0: The two sampled populations of age group taste test scores have identical probability distributions

H_a: The probability distribution for population 1 (taste test scores for younger age groups) is shifted to the right of population 2 (taste test scores for older age group)

The test statistic is $T_1 = 55.5$.

The rejection region is $T_1 \geq 66$. The rejection region was obtained using Table 18, Appendix E, with $n_1 = n_2 = 7$ and $\alpha = .05$ for a one-tailed test.

Since $T_1 = 55.5 \not\geq 66$, H_0 is not rejected. There is insufficient evidence to conclude that the new product is more of a "hit" with the younger group than with the older group. (Population 1 is shifted to the right of population 2) at $\alpha = .05$. The new product's advertising campaign should be geared toward both age groups.

19.21 First, we rank the data:

STAYERS	RANK	LEAVERS	RANK
3	7.5	4	13.5
5	17.5	3	7.5
2	2	3	7.5
3	7.5	2	2
4	13.5	3	7.5
4	13.5	5	17.5
3	7.5	5	17.5
2	2	3	7.5
5	17.5	4	13.5
		3	7.5
	$T_1 = 88.5$		$T_2 = 101.5$

To determine if leavers are better performers than stayers, we test:

H_0: The distributions of performance scores for stayers and leavers are identical

H_a: The distribution of performance scores for stayers is shifted to the right of that for leavers

Note: Smaller values indicate better performances. If leavers are better performers than stayers, the stayers should have larger scores.

The test statistic is $T_1 = 88.5$.

The rejection region is $T_1 \geq 114$. The rejection region was obtained using Table 18, Appendix E, with $n_1 = 9$, $n_2 = 10$, and $\alpha = .025$ for a one-tailed test. (We used $\alpha = .025$ since $\alpha = .01$ is not given. If we do not reject H_0 for $\alpha = .025$, we will not reject H_0 at $\alpha = .01$.)

Since $T_1 = 88.5 \ngeq 114$, H_0 is not rejected. There is insufficient evidence to indicate leavers are better performers than stayers at the oil company at $\alpha = .01$.

19.23 a. The rejection region is $T^- \leq 2$. The rejection region was obtained using Table 19, Appendix E, with $n = 8$ and $\alpha = .01$ for a one-tailed test.

b. The rejection region is $T \leq 4$ where T is the smaller of T^- and T^+. The rejection region was obtained using Table 19, Appendix E, with $n = 7$ and $\alpha = .10$ for a two-tailed test.

19.25 a. First, we rank the data:

ECONOMIST	SEPT. 30	DEC. 31	DIFFERENCE	ABSOLUTE VALUE OF DIFFERENCE	RANK OF ABSOLUTE VALUE
1	8.70	8.90	-.20	.20	2.5
2	8.75	8.50	.25	.25	4.5
3	9.35	9.75	-.40	.40	8
4	7.80	6.00	1.80	1.80	15
5	9.25	8.75	.50	.50	10
6	8.25	8.00	.25	.25	4.5
7	9.25	10.00	-.75	.75	12
8	7.70	7.90	-.20	.20	2.5
9	8.50	8.15	.35	.35	6.5
10	8.50	8.50	0	0	—
11	9.50	8.50	1.00	1.00	13.5
12	8.50	8.15	.35	.35	6.5
13	8.50	9.00	-.50	.50	10
14	9.00	8.50	.50	.50	10
15	9.15	9.30	-.15	.15	1
16	9.25	9.25	0	0	—
17	10.00	9.00	1.00	1.00	13.5

$$T^- = 36$$
$$T^+ = 84$$

To determine if the distributions of interest rate forecasts for September 30 and December 31 differ, we test:

H_0: The distributions of interest rate forecasts on 3-month Treasury bills are the same for both Sept. 30, 1983, and Dec. 31, 1983

H_a: The distribution of interest rate forecasts on 3-month Treasury bills for Sept. 30, 1983, is shifted to the left or right of those for Dec. 31, 1983

The test statistic is T = (smaller of T^- = 36 and T^+ = 84) = 36

The rejection region is $T \leq 25$. The rejection region was obtained using Table 19, Appendix E, with n = 15 and α = .05 for a two-tailed test.

Since T = 36 $\nleq$ 25, H_0 is not rejected. There is insufficient evidence to indicate a difference in the distributions of the interest rate forecasts on 3-month Treasury bills for Sept. 30, 1983, and Dec. 31, 1983.

b. First, we rank the data:

ECONOMIST	SEPT. 30	DEC. 31	DIFFERENCE	ABSOLUTE VALUE OF DIFFERENCE	RANK OF ABSOLUTE VALUE
1	10.88	10.95	−.07	.07	1
2	10.80	10.50	.30	.30	11
3	11.40	11.75	−.35	.35	12
4	10.00	9.00	1.00	1.00	17
5	11.25	11.00	.25	.25	7
6	10.75	10.50	.25	.25	7
7	11.25	11.50	−.25	.25	7
8	9.90	10.00	−.10	.10	2
9	10.75	10.30	.45	.45	13
10	10.75	10.50	.25	.25	7
11	11.25	10.50	.75	.75	16
12	10.70	10.50	.20	.20	3
13	10.75	11.00	−.25	.25	7
14	11.00	10.50	.50	.50	14.5
15	10.75	10.50	.25	.25	7
16	10.75	10.50	.25	.25	7
17	11.00	10.50	.50	.50	14.5

$$T^- = 29$$
$$T^+ = 124$$

To determine if the distributions of interest rate forecasts on 30-year Treasury bonds differ for Sept. 30 and Dec. 31, we test:

H_0: There is no difference in the distributions of interest rate forecasts on 30-year Treasury bonds for Sept. 30, 1983, and Dec. 31, 1983

H_a: The distribution of interest rate forecasts on 30-year Treasury bonds for Sept. 30, 1983, is shifted to the right or left of that for Dec. 31, 1983

The test statistic is T = (smaller of $T^- = 29$ and $T^+ = 124$) = 29.

The rejection region is $T \leq 35$. The rejection region was obtained using Table 19, Appendix E, with $n = 17$ and $\alpha = .05$ for a two-tailed test.

Since $T = 29 \leq 35$, H_0 is rejected. There is sufficient evidence to indicate a difference in the distributions of interest rate forecasts on 30-year Treasury bonds for Sept. 30, 1983, and Dec. 31, 1983, at $\alpha = .05$.

19.27 First, we rank the data:

EMPLOYEE	BEFORE FLEXTIME	AFTER FLEXTIME	DIFFERENCE	ABSOLUTE VALUE OF DIFFERENCE	RANK OF ABSOLUTE VALUE
1	54	68	-14	14	7
2	25	42	-17	17	9
3	80	80	0	0	-
4	76	91	-15	15	8
5	63	70	-7	7	5
6	82	88	-6	6	3.5
7	94	90	4	4	2
8	72	81	-9	9	6
9	33	39	-6	6	3.5
10	90	93	-3	3	1

$$T^- = 43$$
$$T^+ = 2$$

To determine if the pilot flextime program is successful, we test:

H_0: The distributions of the attitudes toward their jobs are identical before and after the flextime program

H_a: The distribution of the attitudes toward their jobs before the flextime program is shifted to the left of that after the flextime program

The test statistic is T = (smaller of $T^+ = 2$ and $T^- = 43$) = 2.

The rejection region is $T \leq 8$. The rejection region was obtained using Table 19, Appendix E, with $n = 9$ and $\alpha = .05$ for a one-tailed test.

Since $T = 2 \leq 8$, H_0 is rejected. There is sufficient evidence to indicate the pilot flextime program was a success at $\alpha = .05$.

19.29 Some preliminary calculations:

PROGRAMMER	LINE-EDIT	FULL-SCREEN-EDIT	DIFFERENCE, d	d^2	ABSOLUTE VALUE OF DIFFERENCE	RANK OF ABSOLUTE DIFFERENCES
1	2	3	-1	1	1	2.5
2	1	4	-3	9	3	8
3	3	4	-1	1	1	2.5
4	1	3	-2	4	2	6
5	3	2	1	1	1	2.5
6	4	5	-1	1	1	2.5
7	3	3	0	0	0	-
8	2	4	-2	4	2	6
9	1	5	-4	16	4	9
10	4	2	2	4	2	6
			$\sum d = -11$	$\sum d^2 = 41$		

$$T^- = 36.5$$
$$T^+ = 8.5$$

$$\bar{d} = \frac{\sum d}{n} = \frac{-11}{10} = -1.1$$

$$s_d^2 = \frac{\sum d^2 - \frac{(\sum d)^2}{n}}{n-1} = \frac{41 - \frac{(-11)^2}{10}}{10-1} = 3.2111$$

$$s_d = \sqrt{3.2111} = 1.792$$

a. To determine if the mean ratings of the two types of terminals differ, we test:

$$H_0: \quad \mu_d = 0$$
$$H_a: \quad \mu_d \neq 0$$

The test statistic is $t = \dfrac{\bar{d} - \mu_d}{\dfrac{s_d}{\sqrt{n}}} = \dfrac{-1.1 - 0}{\dfrac{1.792}{\sqrt{10}}} = -1.94$

The rejection region requires $\alpha/2 = .025$ in each tail of the t distribution with $n - 1 = 10 - 1 = 9$ df. From Table 6, Appendix E, $t_{.025} = 2.262$. The rejection region is $t < -2.262$ or $t > 2.262$.

Since $t = -1.94 \nless -2.262$, H_0 is not rejected. There is insufficient evidence to indicate the mean ratings of the two types of terminals differ at $\alpha = .05$.

The necessary assumptions are:

1. The population of differences is normally distributed.
2. The sample paired observations are randomly selected from the population of differences.

The assumption of normality is probably not met.

b. H_0: The distributions of the ratings for the two types of terminals are identical

   H_a: The distribution of the ratings for the Line-Edit terminal is shifted to the right or left of that for the Full-Screen-Edit terminal

The test statistic is T = (smaller of $T^- = 36.5$ and $T^+ = 8.5$) $= 8.5$.

The rejection region is $T \leq 6$. The rejection region was obtained using Table 19, Appendix E, with $n = 9$ and $\alpha = .05$ for a two-tailed test.

Since $T = 8.5 \nleq 6$, H_0 is not rejected. There is insufficient evidence to indicate the distributions of ratings for the two types of terminals differ at $\alpha = .05$.

19.31 a. $\chi^2_{.05} = 18.3070$ with df = 10

b. $\chi^2_{.025} = 38.0757$ with df = 23

c. $\chi^2_{.01} = 15.0863$ with df = 5

d. $\chi^2_{.10} = 15.9871$ with df = 10

e. $\chi^2_{.05} = 7.81473$ with df = 3

f. $\chi^2_{.005} = 12.8381$ with df = 3

19.33 Some preliminary calculations are:

NO TRAINING	RANK	COMPUTER-ASSISTED TRAINING	RANK	COMPUTER TRAINING PLUS WORKSHOP	RANK
16	6.5	19	11.5	12	2
18	9	22	15.5	19	11.5
11	1	13	3	18	9
14	4	15	5	22	15.5
23	17	20	13	16	6.5
		18	9	25	18
		21	14		
$T_1 = \overline{37.5}$		$T_2 = \overline{71}$		$T_3 = \overline{62.5}$	

To determine if the distributions of scores differ in location for the three types of training, we test:

H_0: The 3 distributions of scores are identical
H_a: At least 2 of the distributions of scores differ in location

The test statistic is $H = \dfrac{12}{n(n+1)} \sum \dfrac{T_i^2}{n_i} - 3(n+1)$

$$= \dfrac{12}{18(18+1)}\left(\dfrac{37.5^2}{5} + \dfrac{71^2}{7} + \dfrac{62.5^2}{6}\right) - 3(18+1)$$

$$= .980$$

The rejection region requires $\alpha = .01$ in the upper tail of the χ^2 distribution with $k - 1 = 3 - 1 = 2$ df. From Table 17, Appendix E, $\chi^2_{.01} = 9.21034$. The rejection region is $H > 9.21034$.

Since $H = .980 \ngtr 9.21034$, H_0 is not rejected. There is insufficient evidence to indicate the distributions of scores for the three types of training differ in location at $\alpha = .01$.

19.35 a. H_0: The distributions of changes in bond prices for the four underwriters are identical
H_a: At least two of the four distributions differ in location

b. Some preliminary calculations are:

MORGAN STANLEY	RANK	FIRST BOSTON	RANK	GOLDMAN SACHS	RANK	MERRILL LYNCH	RANK
.037	23	−.128	3	.025	21	−.047	9
−.016	15	−.054	7	−.080	6	.010	19
−.132	2	.007	18	−.031	12	−.003	17
−.148	1	−.011	16	.049	24	−.104	4
.022	20	.031	22	−.019	14	−.082	5
−.049	8	−.042	10	−.027	13	−.039	11
	$T_1 = 69$		$T_2 = 76$		$T_3 = 90$		$T_4 = 65$

The test statistic is $H = \dfrac{12}{n(n+1)} \sum \dfrac{T_i^2}{n_i} - 3(n+1)$

$$= \frac{12}{24(24+1)}\left(\frac{69^2}{6} + \frac{76^2}{6} + \frac{90^2}{6} + \frac{65^2}{6}\right) - 3(24+1)$$

$$= 76.2067 - 75 = 1.2067$$

c. The rejection region requires $\alpha = .01$ in the upper tail of the χ^2 distribution with $k - 1 = 4 - 1 = 3$ df. From Table 17, Appendix E, $\chi^2_{.01} = 11.3449$. The rejection region is $H > 11.3449$.

Since $H = 1.2067 \not> 11.3449$, H_0 is not rejected. There is insufficient evidence to indicate the distributions of bond price changes differ in location among the four investment firms at $\alpha = .01$.

19.37 Some preliminary calculations are:

NEW YORK	RANK	CHICAGO	RANK	ATLANTA	RANK
7.50	10.5	7.25	9	9.25	17.5
6.25	5.5	6.75	7	8.75	14
7.50	10.5	5.75	2.5	9.00	16
4.75	1	8.00	12	9.25	17.5
6.25	5.5	5.75	2.5	8.75	14
7.00	8	6.00	4	8.75	14
	$T_1 = 41$		$T_2 = 37$		$T_3 = 93$

a. To determine if the level of service ratings differ among the three car rental outlets, we test:

> H_0: The distributions of the service ratings for the three car rental outlets are identical
>
> H_a: At least two of the three distributions differ in location

The test statistic is $H = \dfrac{12}{n(n+1)} \sum \dfrac{T_i^2}{n_i} - 3(n+1)$

$$= \dfrac{12}{18(18+1)} \left(\dfrac{41^2}{6} + \dfrac{37^2}{6} + \dfrac{93^2}{6} \right) - 3(18+1)$$

$$= 68.4157 - 57 = 11.415$$

The rejection region requires $\alpha = .10$ in the upper tail of the χ^2 distribution with $k - 1 = 3 - 1 = 2$ df. From Table 17, Appendix E, $\chi^2_{.10} = 4.60517$. The rejection region is $H > 4.60517$.

Since $H = 11.415 > 4.60517$, H_0 is rejected. There is sufficient evidence to indicate the distributions of service ratings for at least two of the car rental outlets differ in location at $\alpha = .10$.

b. In order to use a parametric test, we must assume the data are from normal distributions. It is very unlikely that these data are from normal distributions.

19.39 a. H_0: The distributions of the three populations are identical
H_a: At least two of the three population distributions differ in location

b. The rejection region requires $\alpha = .05$ in the upper tail of the χ^2 distribution with $k - 1 = 3 - 1 = 2$ df. From Table 17, Appendix E, $\chi^2_{.05} = 5.99147$. The rejection region is $F_r > 5.99147$.

c.

BLOCK	A	B	C
1	1	2	3
2	1.5	1.5	3
3	1	2	3
4	1	2	3
5	3	1	2
6	2	1	3
	$T_A = 9.5$	$T_B = 9.5$	$T_C = 17$

d. $F_r = \dfrac{12}{bk(k + 1)} \sum T_i^2 - 3b(k + 1)$

$\quad = \dfrac{12}{6(3)(3 + 1)}(9.5^2 + 9.5^2 + 17^2) - 3(6)(3 + 1)$

$\quad = 78.25 - 72 = 6.25$

e. Since $F_r = 6.25 > 5.99147$, H_0 is rejected. There is sufficient evidence to indicate at least two of the three population distributions differ in location at $\alpha = .05$.

19.41 Some preliminary calculations are:

YEAR	MODEL 1	MODEL 2	MODEL 3	MODEL 4
1977	2	2	4	2
1978	2	1	4	3
1979	1	2.5	4	2.5
1980	4	1	2	3
1981	2.5	1	4	2.5
	$T_1 = 11.5$	$T_2 = 7.5$	$T_3 = 18$	$T_4 = 13$

To determine if the distributions of 1-year-ahead forecast accuracies differ among the four models, we test:

H_0: The distributions of 1-year-ahead forecast accuracies for the four models are identical

H_a: At least two of the four distributions differ in location

The test statistic is $F_r = \dfrac{12}{bk(k + 1)} \sum T_i^2 - 3b(k + 1)$

$\quad = \dfrac{12}{5(4)(4 + 1)}(11.5^2 + 7.5^2 + 18^2 + 13^2) - 3(5)(4 + 1)$

$\quad = 81.78 - 75 = 6.78$

The rejection region requires $\alpha = .10$ in the upper tail of the χ^2 distribution with $k - 1 = 4 - 1 = 3$ df. From Table 17, Appendix E, $\chi^2_{.10} = 6.25139$. The rejection region is $F_r > 6.25139$.

Since $F_r = 6.78 > 6.25139$, H_0 is rejected. There is sufficient evidence to indicate that the distribution of 1-year-ahead forecast accuracies for at least two of the four models differ at $\alpha = .10$.

19.43 Some preliminary calculations are:

STRESS CATEGORY	NONSUPERVISORS	1st LEVEL	2nd LEVEL	3rd LEVEL
1	2	3	1	4
2	1	2.5	4	2.5
3	4	2.5	1	2.5
4	1	2	3.5	3.5
5	2	2	2	4
6	1.5	1.5	3	4
7	1	2	3	4
8	1	3	2	4
9	2.5	2.5	2.5	2.5
10	4	3	2	1
11	4	2	3	1
12	3.5	1.5	3.5	1.5
13	1	3	2	4
14	1.5	3	4	1.5
15	3.5	3.5	2	1
	$T_1 = 33.5$	$T_2 = 37$	$T_3 = 38.5$	$T_4 = 41$

To determine if the rank orderings of the stress categories differ among the four groups, we test:

H_0: The distributions of the rank orderings of the stress categories are identical for the four groups
H_a: At least two of the four distributions differ in location

The test statistic is $F_r = \dfrac{12}{bk(k+1)} \sum_i T_i^2 - 3b(k+1)$

$$= \frac{12}{15(4)(4+1)}(33.5^2 + 37^2 + 38.5^2 + 41^2) - 3(15)(4+1)$$

$$= 226.18 - 225 = 1.18$$

The rejection region requires $\alpha = .01$ in the upper tail of the χ^2 distribution with $k - 1 = 4 - 1 = 3$ df. From Table 17, Appendix E, $\chi^2_{.01} = 11.3449$. The rejection region is $F_r > 11.3449$.

Since $F_r = 1.18 \not> 11.3449$, H_0 is not rejected. There is insufficient evidence to indicate the rank orderings of the stress categories differ among the four groups at $\alpha = .01$.

19.45 Some preliminary calculations are:

MACHINE	ENVIRONMENT 1	2	3	4	5
1	2	3	5	4	1
2	3	4	2	5	1
3	3	1	5	4	2
4	1	3	5	4	2
5	1	3	5	4	2
	$T_1 = 10$	$T_2 = 14$	$T_3 = 22$	$T_4 = 21$	$T_5 = 8$

To determine if the distributions of the number of forms processed per hour differ for at least two environments, we test:

H_0: The distributions of the number of forms processed per hour for the five environments are identical

H_a: At least two of the five distributions differ in location

The test statistic is $F_r = \dfrac{12}{bk(k + 1)} \sum T_i^2 - 3b(k + 1)$

$$= \dfrac{12}{5(5)(5 + 1)}(10^2 + 14^2 + 22^2 + 21^2 + 8^2) - 3(5)(5 + 1)$$

$$= 102.8 - 90 = 12.8$$

The rejection region requires $\alpha = .10$ in the upper tail of the χ^2 distribution with $k - 1 = 5 - 1 = 4$ df. From Table 17, Appendix E, $\chi^2_{.10} = 7.77944$. The rejection region is $F_r > 7.77944$.

Since $F_r = 12.8 > 7.77944$, H_0 is rejected. There is sufficient evidence to indicate the distributions of the number of forms processed per hour differ for at least two of the five environments at $\alpha = .10$.

19.47 a.

PAIR	x	RANK	y	RANK	d_i	d_i^2
1	65	7	59	6	1	1
2	57	6	61	7	-1	1
3	55	5	58	5	0	0
4	38	2	23	1	1	1
5	29	1	34	2	-1	1
6	43	3	38	4	-1	1
7	49	4	37	3	1	1
					$\sum d_i^2 =$	6

b. $r_s = 1 - \dfrac{6\sum d^2}{n(n^2 - 1)} = 1 - \dfrac{6(6)}{7(7^2 - 1)} = 1 - .107 = .893$

c. To determine if the ranked pairs are correlated, we test:

H_0: There is no correlation between the ranked pairs
H_a: The ranked pairs are correlated

The test statistic is $r_s = .893$.

The rejection region is $r_s < -.786$ or $r_s > .786$. The rejection region was obtained using Table 20, Appendix E, with $n = 7$ and $\alpha = .05$ for a two-tailed test.

Since $r_s = .893 > .786$, H_0 is rejected. There is sufficient evidence to indicate the ranked pairs are correlated at $\alpha = .05$.

19.49 a. Some preliminary calculations are:

ECONOMIST	SEPT. 30	RANK, x	DEC. 31	RANK, y	x^2	y^2	xy
1	8.70	8	8.90	11	64	121	88
2	8.75	9	8.50	7.5	81	56.25	67.5
3	9.35	15	9.75	16	225	256	240
4	7.80	2	6.00	1	4	1	2
5	9.25	13	8.75	10	169	100	130
6	8.25	3	8.00	3	9	9	9
7	9.25	13	10.00	17	169	289	221
8	7.70	1	7.90	2	1	4	2
9	8.50	5.5	8.15	4.5	30.25	20.25	24.75
10	8.50	5.5	8.50	7.5	30.25	56.25	41.25
11	9.50	16	8.50	7.5	256	56.25	120
12	8.50	5.5	8.15	4.5	30.25	20.25	24.75
13	8.50	5.5	9.00	12.5	30.25	156.25	68.75
14	9.00	10	8.50	7.5	100	56.25	75
15	9.15	11	9.30	15	121	225	165
16	9.25	13	9.25	14	169	196	182
17	10.00	17	9.00	12.5	289	156.25	212.5
		153		153	1778	1779	1673.5

$SS_{xx} = \sum x^2 - \dfrac{(\sum x)^2}{n} = 1778 - \dfrac{153^2}{17} = 401$

$SS_{yy} = \sum y^2 - \dfrac{(\sum y)^2}{n} = 1779 - \dfrac{153^2}{17} = 402$

$SS_{xy} = \sum xy - \dfrac{\sum x \sum y}{n} = 1673.5 - \dfrac{153(153)}{17} = 296.5$

$r_s = \dfrac{SS_{xy}}{\sqrt{SS_{xx} SS_{yy}}} = \dfrac{296.5}{\sqrt{401(402)}} = .738$

To determine if there is a positive rank correlation, we test:

H_0: $\rho_s = 0$
H_a: $\rho_s > 0$

The test statistic is $r_s = .738$

The rejection region is $r_s > .582$. The rejection region was obtained using Table 20, Appendix E, with n = 17 and $\alpha = .01$ for a one-tailed test.

Since $r_s = .738 > .582$, H_0 is rejected. There is sufficient evidence to indicate a positive rank correlation at $\alpha = .01$.

b. Some preliminary calculations are:

ECONOMIST	SEPT. 30	RANK, x	DEC. 31	RANK, y	x^2	y^2	xy
1	10.88	11	10.95	13	121	169	143
2	10.80	10	10.50	8	100	64	80
3	11.40	17	11.75	17	289	289	289
4	10.00	2	9.00	1	4	1	2
5	11.25	15	11.00	14.5	225	210.25	217.5
6	10.75	6.5	10.50	8	42.25	64	52.0
7	11.25	15	11.50	16	225	256	240
8	9.90	1	10.00	2	1	4	2
9	10.75	6.5	10.30	3	42.25	9	19.5
10	10.75	6.5	10.50	8	42.25	64	52
11	11.25	15	10.50	8	225	64	120
12	10.70	3	10.50	8	9	64	24
13	10.75	6.5	11.00	14.5	42.25	210.25	94.25
14	11.00	12.5	10.50	8	156.25	64	100
15	10.75	6.5	10.50	8	42.25	64	52
16	10.75	6.5	10.50	8	42.25	64	52
17	11.00	12.5	10.50	8	156.25	64	100
		153		153	1765	1724.5	1639.5

$$SS_{xx} = \sum x^2 - \frac{(\sum x)^2}{n} = 1765 - \frac{153^2}{17} = 388$$

$$SS_{yy} = \sum y^2 - \frac{(\sum y)^2}{n} = 1724.5 - \frac{153^2}{17} = 347.5$$

$$SS_{xy} = \sum xy - \frac{\sum x \sum y}{n} = 1639.25 - \frac{153(153)}{17} = 262.25$$

$$r_s = \frac{SS_{xy}}{\sqrt{SS_{xx} SS_{yy}}} = \frac{262.25}{\sqrt{388(347.5)}} = .714$$

To determine if there is a positive rank correlation, we test:

H_0: $\rho_s = 0$
H_a: $\rho_s > 0$

The test statistic is $r_s = .714$

The rejection region is $r_s > .582$. (See part (a).)

Since $r_s = .714 > .582$, H_0 is rejected. There is sufficient evidence to indicate a positive rank correlation at $\alpha = .01$.

19.51 Some preliminary calculations are:

INDUSTRY	SUBSIDY RATE	RANK, x	LAYOFF RATE	RANK, y	x^2	y^2	xy
1	57	10	12.54	11	100	121	110
2	32	6.5	1.78	1	42.25	1	6.5
3	31	5	7.10	6	25	36	30
4	29	4	8.38	8	16	64	32
5	27	2.5	11.72	10	6.25	100	25
6	36	9	5.10	5	81	25	45
7	32	6.5	4.44	4	42.25	16	26
8	61	11	9.82	9	121	81	99
9	23	1	7.34	7	1	49	7
10	27	2.5	1.98	3	6.25	9	7.5
11	33	8	1.86	2	64	4	16
		66		66	505	506	404

$$SS_{xx} = \sum x^2 - \frac{(\sum x)^2}{n} = 505 - \frac{66^2}{11} = 109$$

$$SS_{yy} = \sum y^2 - \frac{(\sum y)^2}{n} = 506 - \frac{66^2}{11} = 110$$

$$SS_{xy} = \sum xy - \frac{\sum x \sum y}{n} = 404 - \frac{66(66)}{11} = 8$$

$$r_s = \frac{SS_{xy}}{\sqrt{SS_{xx} SS_{yy}}} = \frac{8}{\sqrt{109(110)}} = .073$$

To determine if unemployment compensation subsidy rate is positively correlated with layoff rate, we test:

$H_0:$ $\rho_s = 0$
$H_a:$ $\rho_s > 0$

The test statistic is $r_s = .073$.

The rejection region is $r_s > .523$. The rejection region was obtained using Table 20, Appendix E, with $n = 11$ and $\alpha = .05$ for a one-tailed test.

Since $r_s = .073 \not> .523$, H_0 is not rejected. There is insufficient evidence to indicate that unemployment compensation subsidy rate is positively correlated with layoff rate at $\alpha = .05$.

19.53   a.   Some preliminary calculations are:

ASSET	INFLATION	RANK, x	DISINFLATION	RANK, y	x^2	y^2	xy
1	1.1	1	39.0	8	1	64	8
2	30.7	8.5	0.0	2.5	72.25	6.25	21.25
3	9.7	2	3.9	6	4	36	12
4	16.9	6	0.0	2.5	36	6.25	15
5	30.7	8.5	28.6	7	72.25	49	59.5
6	11.6	4	2.1	5	16	25	20
7	16.8	5	1.7	4	25	16	20
8	20.1	7	109.5	10	49	100	70
9	9.8	3	51.8	9	9	81	27
10	32.9	10	−6.2	1	100	1	10
		55		55	384.5	384.5	262.75

$$SS_{xx} = \sum x^2 - \frac{(\sum x)^2}{n} = 384.5 - \frac{55^2}{10} = 82$$

$$SS_{yy} = \sum y^2 - \frac{(\sum y)^2}{n} = 384.5 - \frac{55^2}{10} = 82$$

$$SS_{xy} = \sum xy - \frac{\sum x \sum y}{n} = 262.75 - \frac{55(55)}{10} = -39.75$$

$$r_s = \frac{SS_{xy}}{\sqrt{SS_{xx} SS_{yy}}} = \frac{-39.75}{\sqrt{82(82)}} = -.485$$

   b.   To determine if the annual rate of return during inflation is negatively correlated with the annual rate of return during disinflation, we test:

$$H_0: \quad \rho_s = 0$$
$$H_a: \quad \rho_s < 0$$

The test statistic is $r_s = -.485$.

The rejection region is $r_s < -.564$. The rejection region was obtained using Table 20, Appendix E, with n = 10 and $\alpha = .05$ for a one-tailed test.

Since $r_s = -.485 \not< -.564$, H_0 is not rejected. There is insufficient evidence to indicate the annual rate of return during inflation is negatively correlated with the annual rate of return during disinflation at $\alpha = .05$.

19.55 First we rank the data:

BUY SIGNAL	4 WEEKS	13 WEEKS	26 WEEKS
1	1	2	3
2	2	3	1
3	2	1	3
4	1	2	3
5	2	3	1
6	1	2	3
7	3	2	1
8	1	2	3
	$T_1 = 13$	$T_2 = 17$	$T_3 = 18$

To determine if the distributions of percentage gains differ in location among the three time periods, we test:

H_0: The distributions of the percentage gains for the three time periods are identical

H_a: At least two of the three distributions differ in location

The test statistic is $F_r = \dfrac{12}{bk(k + 1)} \sum T_i^2 - 3b(k + 1)$

$$= \dfrac{12}{8(3)(3 + 1)}(13^2 + 17^2 + 18^2) - 3(8)(3 + 1)$$

$$= 97.75 - 96 = 1.75$$

The rejection region requires $\alpha = .05$ in the upper tail of the χ^2 distribution with $k - 1 = 3 - 1 = 2$ df. From Table 17, Appendix E, $\chi^2_{.05} = 5.99147$. The rejection region is $F_r > 5.99147$.

Since $F_r = 1.75 \not> 5.99147$, H_0 is not rejected. There is insufficient evidence to indicate the distributions of percentage gains differ in location among the three time periods at $\alpha = .05$.

19.57 To determine if the median percentage of iron in bulk specimens differs from 63, we test:

H_0: $M = 63$
H_a: $M \neq 63$

The test statistic is S = (larger of $S_1 = 5$ and $S_2 = 5$) = 5

where S_1 = number of observations greater than 63
and S_2 = number of observations less than 63

The p-value = $2P(S \geq 5)$. From Table 1, Appendix E, with n = 10 and p = .5,

$$\text{p-value} = 2P(S \geq 5) = 1(1 - P(S \leq 4)$$
$$= 2(1 - .3770) = 2(.6230) = 1.2460 \approx 1$$

Since p-value = 1 $\not< \alpha$ = .05, H_0 is not rejected. There is insufficient evidence to indicate the median percentage of iron in bulk specimens differs from 63 at α = .05.

19.59 The following are the ranks of the data:

LENGTH OF HORIZON RANK, x	AGGRESSIVE STOCKS RANK, y	DEFENSIVE STOCKS RANK, z	NEUTRAL STOCKS RANK, w	x^2	y^2	z^2	w^2	xy	xz	xw
1	1	9	3.5	1	1	81	12.25	1	9	3.5
2	2	8	2	4	4	64	4	4	16	4
3	3	7	1	9	9	49	1	9	21	3
4	5	4.5	5.5	16	25	20.25	30.25	20	18	22
5	7.5	6	3.5	25	56.25	36	12.25	37.5	30	17.5
6	4	3	5.5	36	16	9	30.25	24	18	33
7	6	4.5	7	49	36	20.25	49	42	31.5	49
8	9	2	8	64	81	4	64	72	16	64
9	7.5	1	9	81	56.25	1	81	67.5	9	81
45	45	45	45	285	284.5	284.5	284	277	168.5	277

$$SS_{xx} = \sum x^2 - \frac{(\sum x)^2}{n} = 285 - \frac{45^2}{9} = 60$$

$$SS_{yy} = \sum y^2 - \frac{(\sum y)^2}{n} = 284.5 - \frac{45^2}{9} = 59.5$$

$$SS_{zz} = \sum z^2 - \frac{(\sum z)^2}{n} = 284.5 - \frac{45^2}{9} = 59.5$$

$$SS_{ww} = \sum w^2 - \frac{(\sum w)^2}{n} = 284 - \frac{45^2}{9} = 59$$

$$SS_{xy} = \sum xy - \frac{\sum x \sum y}{n} = 277 - \frac{45(45)}{9} = 52$$

$$SS_{xz} = \sum xz - \frac{\sum x \sum z}{n} = 168.5 - \frac{45(45)}{9} = -56.5$$

$$SS_{xw} = \sum xw - \frac{\sum x \sum w}{n} = 277 - \frac{45(45)}{9} = 52$$

For Aggressive stocks,

$$r_s = \frac{SS_{xy}}{\sqrt{SS_{xx}SS_{yy}}} = \frac{52}{\sqrt{60(59.5)}} = .870$$

For Defensive Stocks,

$$r_s = \frac{SS_{xz}}{\sqrt{SS_{xx}SS_{zz}}} = \frac{-56.5}{\sqrt{60(59.5)}} = -.946$$

For Neutral Stocks,

$$r_s = \frac{SS_{xw}}{\sqrt{SS_{xx}SS_{ww}}} = \frac{52}{\sqrt{60(59)}} = .874$$

b. To determine if length of horizon and beta-value are correlated for aggressive stocks, we test:

$H_0: \rho_s = 0$
$H_a: \rho_s \neq 0$

The test statistic is $r_s = .870$.

The rejection region is $r_s < -.683$ or $r_s > .683$. The rejection region was obtained using Table 20, Appendix E, with n = 9 and $\alpha = .05$ for a two-tailed test.

Since $r_s = .870 > .683$, H_0 is rejected. There is sufficient evidence to indicate length of horizon and beta-value are correlated for aggressive stocks at $\alpha = .05$.

For defensive stocks, we test:

$H_0: \rho_s = 0$
$H_a: \rho_s \neq 0$

The test statistic is $r_s = -.946$.

The rejection region is $r_s < -.683$ or $r_s > .683$. (See above.)

Since $r_s = -.946 < -.683$, H_0 is rejected. There is sufficient evidence to indicate length of horizon and beta-value are correlated for defensive stocks at $\alpha = .05$.

For neutral stocks, we test:

$H_0: \rho_s = 0$
$H_a: \rho_s \neq 0$

The test statistic is r_s = .874.

The rejection region is r_s < −.683 or r_s > .683. (See above.)

Since r_s = .874 > .683, H_0 is rejected. There is sufficient evidence to indicate length of horizon and beta-value are correlated for defensive stocks at α = .05.

19.61 First we rank the data:

PERIOD	A	B	C
1	2	3	1
2	3	2	1
3	2	3	1
4	2	3	1
5	2	3	1
	$T_1 = 11$	$T_2 = 14$	$T_3 = 5$

To determine if there is a difference in location among the distributions of sales for the three types of displays, we test:

H_0: The distributions of sales for the three types of displays are identical

H_a: At least two of the three distributions differ in location

The test statistic is $F_r = \dfrac{12}{bk(k + 1)} \sum T_i^2 - 3b(k + 1)$

$$= \frac{12}{5(3)(3 + 1)}(11^2 + 14^2 + 5^2) - 3(5)(3 + 1)$$

$$= 68.4 - 60 = 8.4$$

The rejection region requires α = .10 in the upper tail of the χ^2 distribution with k − 1 = 3 − 1 = 2 df. From Table 17, Appendix E, $\chi^2_{.10}$ = 4.60517. The rejection region is F_r > 4.60517.

Since F_r = 8.40 > 4.60517, H_0 is rejected. There is sufficient evidence to indicate a difference in location among the distributions of sales for the three types of displays at α = .10.

19.63   First we rank the data:

ARRANGEMENT 1	RANK	ARRANGEMENT 2	RANK
9	11.5	6	5.5
4	1.5	13	19
9	11.5	8	8.5
5	3.5	11	15.5
11	15.5	16	20
4	1.5	9	11.5
12	17.5	8	8.5
5	3.5	10	14
7	7	9	11.5
6	5.5	12	17.5
	$T_1 = 78.5$		$T_2 = 131.5$

To determine if arrangement 1 leads to faster reaction times, we test:

H_0:   The distributions of reaction times for the two arrangements are identical

H_a: The distribution of reaction times for arrangement 1 is shifted to the left of that for arrangement 2

The test statistic is $T_1 = 78.5$.

The rejection region is $T_1 \leq 83$. The rejection region was obtained using Table 18, Appendix E, with $n_1 = n_2 = 10$ and $\alpha = .05$ for a one-tailed test.

Since $T_1 = 78.5 \leq 83$, H_0 is rejected. There is sufficient evidence to indicate arrangement 1 leads to faster reaction times at $\alpha = .05$.

19.65   First we rank the data:

THEORY X	RANK	THEORY Y	RANK	THEORY Z	RANK
5.20	2.5	6.25	13	5.50	5
5.20	2.5	6.80	16	5.75	7.5
6.10	12	6.87	17	4.60	1
6.00	11	7.10	18	5.36	4
5.75	7.5	6.30	14	5.85	9
5.60	6	6.35	15	5.90	10
	$T_1 = 41.5$		$T_2 = 93$		$T_3 = 36.5$

To determine if there are differences in location among the distributions of starting hourly wages of engineers at the three types of firms, we test:

H_0: The distributions of starting hourly wages of engineers are identical for the three types of firms

H_a: At least two of the three distributions differ in location

The test statistic is $H = \dfrac{12}{n(n+1)} \sum \dfrac{T_i^2}{n_i} - 3(n+1)$

$$= \dfrac{12}{18(18+1)} \left(\dfrac{41.5^2}{6} + \dfrac{93^2}{6} + \dfrac{36.5^2}{6} \right) - 3(18+1)$$

$$= 68.442 - 57 = 11.442$$

The rejection region requires $\alpha = .025$ in the upper tail of the χ^2 distribution with $k - 1 = 3 - 1 = 2$ df. From Table 17, Appendix E, $\chi^2_{.025} = 7.37776$. The rejection region is $H > 7.37776$.

Since $H = 11.442 > 7.37776$, H_0 is rejected. There is sufficient evidence to indicate a difference in location among the distributions of starting hourly wages of engineers for the three types of firms at $\alpha = .025$.

CASE STUDIES

19.1 a. Let the stems be the digits in the hundreds column and the leaves be the digits in the tens and ones columns. The stem-and-leaf display is:

Stem	Leaf
0	95
1	76, 04, 20, 23, 35, 57
2	70, 40, 88, 05, 68, 50
3	32, 59, 90, 83, 11, 79
4	31

b. Let the stems be the digits in the tens column and the leaves be the digits in the ones column. The stem-and-leaf display is:

Stem	Leaf
-0	2
0	6, 1, 5
1	9, 3, 2
2	1, 6, 4, 5
3	7, 6, 5, 0, 3
4	5
5	8, 4
6	1

c. I would recommend a nonparametric test. Neither set of data appears to be normal.

d. Some preliminary calculations:

COST	RANK, x	POPULATION	RANK, y	d	d^2
332	15	21	8	7	49
176	7	6	4	3	9
431	20	37	16	4	16
104	2	36	15	-13	169
359	16	26	11	5	25
270	12	35	14	-2	4
390	19	61	20	-1	1
240	9	19	7	2	4
120	3	1	2	1	1
95	1	5	3	-2	4
123	4	13	6	-2	4
383	18	58	19	-1	1
288	13	24	9	4	16
311	14	30	12	2	4
205	8	12	5	3	9
379	17	33	13	4	16
268	11	25	10	1	1
135	5	45	17	-12	144
157	6	-2	1	5	25
250	10	54	18	-8	64
					566

$$r_s = 1 - \frac{6\sum d^2}{n(n^2 - 1)} = 1 - \frac{6(566)}{20(20^2 - 1)} = .574$$

e. To determine if the rank correlation coefficient is positive, we test:

$H_0: \rho_s = 0$
$H_a: \rho_s > 0$

The test statistic is $r_s = .574$.

The rejection region is $r_s > .534$. The rejection region was obtained using Table 20, Appendix E, with n = 20 and α = .01 for a one-tailed test.

Since r_s = .574 > .534, H_0 is rejected. There is sufficient evidence to indicate a positive rank correlation at α = .01.

19.3 a. Because the data are ratings or ranks on a scale of 1 to 6, it is very doubtful that the data are normally distributed. This is a necessity for the ANOVA F test. The Friedman's test would be more appropriate.

b. First we rank the data:

CANDIDATE	RATER 1	RATER 2	RATER 3
A	1.5	1.5	3
B	1	2.5	2.5
C	3	1	2
D	1	2.5	2.5
E	1	2	3
F	1	2.5	2.5
G	2	2	2
	T_1 = 10.5	T_2 = 14	T_3 = 17.5

To determine if the raters are in disagreement, we test:

H_0: The distributions of ratings are identical for the three raters

H_a: At least two of the three distributions differ in location

The test statistic is $F_r = \dfrac{12}{bk(k + 1)} \sum T_i^2 - 3b(k + 1)$

$$= \frac{12}{7(3)(3 + 1)}(10.5^2 + 14^2 + 17.5^2) - 3(7)(3 + 1)$$

$$= 87.5 - 84 = 3.5$$

The rejection region requires α = .01 in the upper tail of the χ^2 distribution with k - 1 = 3 - 1 = 2 df. From Table 17, Appendix E, $\chi^2_{.01}$ = 9.21034. The rejection region is $F_r > 9.21034$.

Since F_r = 3.5 $\not>$ 9.21034, H_0 is not rejected. There is insufficient evidence to indicate the three raters are in disagreement on the candidates' overall in-tray performance at α = .01.

TWENTY   ELEMENTS OF DECISION ANALYSIS

20.1   a. Actions - The set of two or more alternatives the decision maker
        has chosen to consider--one of these alternatives must be
        chosen.

       States of Nature - The set of two or more mutually exclusive and
        collectively exhaustive chance events upon which the outcome
        of the decision-maker's chosen action depends.

       Outcomes - Set of all consequences resulting from all possible
        combinations of actions and states of nature.

       Objective Variable - Quantity used to measure and express the
        outcomes of a decision problem.

20.3   Actions: a_1, Settle out of court; a_2, Proceed with court case

      States of Nature: S_1, Win the case; S_2, Lose the case

      Outcomes: Settle out of court and win the case: $-800,000
               Settle out court and lose the case: $-800,000
               Proceed with court case and win: $-50,000
               Proceed with court case and lose: $-2,000,000

      The objective variable is net loss.

20.5   Actions: a_1, Buy restaurant; a_2, Do not buy restaurant

      States of Nature: S_1, Low demand; S_2, Medium demand; S_3, High demand

      Outcomes: Buy restaurant and low demand: $-125,000
               Buy restaurant and medium demand: $50,000
               Buy restaurant and high demand: $200,000
               Do not buy and low demand: $0
               Do not buy and medium demand: $0
               Do not buy and high demand: $0

      The objective variable is the amount of profit.

20.7   Payoffs are the actual rewards to the decision-maker, while the opportunity losses reflect how much a decision-maker stands to lose if a given action is not selected for a given state of nature.

20.9   a.   The payoff table shows the possible payoffs for each action/state of nature combination. The actions are either "make the loan" or "do not make the loan." The states of nature are that the debtor either pays back the loan or defaults. The payoffs for not making the loan are zero for both states of nature--no loan having been made. The payoffs for making the loan are a $3000 profit if the loan is repaid, or a $13,000 loss in case of default. These are shown in the payoff table below.

		STATES OF NATURE	
		Repaid	Default
ACTION	Make Loan	$3000	-$13,000
	Do Not Make Loan	0	0

b.   Each entry in the opportunity loss table is the difference between the payoff for a chosen action and the maximum payoff possible for the state of nature that occurred. For example, if the state of nature were "default," the maximum payoff would be 0, so the opportunity loss for the action "make the loan" is 0 - (-13,000) = 13,000. The calculations are shown in the following table.

The opportunity loss table is tabulated from the results shown in the payoff table.

		STATES OF NATURE	
		Repaid	Default
ACTION	Make Loan	$ 3000 -3000 $ 0	$ 0 -(-13,000) $ 13,000
	Do Not Make Loan	$ 3000 -0 $ 3000	$ 0 -0 $ 0

20.11 a.   The payoff table shows the possible payoffs for each action/state of nature combination. The actions are: to buy 1, 2, 3, 4, or 5 boxes of the cards. The states of nature are: either 1, 2, 3, 4,

or 5 boxes can be sold (manager's belief of demand). The payoff
for each action/state of nature combination is:

$$-\$10(P) + \$20(S) + \$5(B)$$

where

P = Number of boxes purchased (action)

S = Number of boxes that could be sold (demand--state of
nature) if state of nature is $\leq$ P, or P if state of
nature $>$ P.

B = P - S or 0 if S $>$ P

For example, if three boxes are purchased and two could be sold,
then P = 3, S = 2, and B = 3 - 2 = 1.

Payoff is -$10(3) + $20(2) + $5(1) = $15.

If three boxes are purchased and four or five could be sold, then
P = 3, S = 3, and B = 0.

Payoff is -$10(3) + $20(3) + $5(0) = $30.

The payoff table is:

		STATE OF NATURE (NUMBER OF BOXES THAT COULD BE SOLD)				
		1	2	3	4	5
	Buy 1	10	10	10	10	10
	Buy 2	5	20	20	20	20
ACTION	Buy 3	0	15	30	30	30
	Buy 4	-5	10	25	40	40
	Buy 5	-10	5	20	35	50

Note: Entries in the table are dollars profit (payoff).

b. Each entry in the opportunity loss table is the difference between
the payoff for a chosen action and the maximum payoff possible for
the state of nature that occurred. For example, if the state of
nature were "2 boxes could be sold," the maximum payoff would be
$20, so the opportunity loss for buying one box is $20 - $10
= $10, for buying five boxes is $20 - $5 = $15, and so on. The
calculations are shown in the following table.

		STATE OF NATURE (NUMBER OF BOXES THAT COULD BE SOLD)				
		1	2	3	4	5
	Buy 1	10 −10 ⎯⎯ 0	20 −10 ⎯⎯ 10	30 −10 ⎯⎯ 20	40 −10 ⎯⎯ 30	50 −10 ⎯⎯ 40
	Buy 2	10 −5 ⎯⎯ 5	20 −20 ⎯⎯ 0	30 −20 ⎯⎯ 10	40 −20 ⎯⎯ 20	50 −20 ⎯⎯ 30
ACTION	Buy 3	10 −0 ⎯⎯ 10	20 −15 ⎯⎯ 5	30 −30 ⎯⎯ 0	40 −30 ⎯⎯ 10	50 −30 ⎯⎯ 20
	Buy 4	10 −(−5) ⎯⎯ 15	20 −10 ⎯⎯ 10	30 −25 ⎯⎯ 5	40 −40 ⎯⎯ 0	50 −40 ⎯⎯ 10
	Buy 5	10 −(−10) ⎯⎯ 20	20 −5 ⎯⎯ 15	30 −20 ⎯⎯ 10	40 −35 ⎯⎯ 5	50 −50 ⎯⎯ 0

Note: Entries in the table are dollars of opportunity lost.

20.13 a. The payoff table shows the possible payoffs for each action/state
of nature combination. The actions are: (i) increase the
advertising budget and (ii) do not increase the budget. The
states of nature are: (i) the ad campaign is successful or
(ii) the ad campaign is unsuccessful. The payoff for increasing
the ad campaign is $1,600,000 if the campaign is successful, or
$400,000 if the campaign is unsuccessful. The payoffs for not
increasing the campaign budget are $200,000 in each case. These
are shown in the payoff table below.

		STATES OF NATURE	
		Successful	Unsuccessful
ACTION	Increase	$1,600,000	$400,000
	Do Not Increase	200,000	$200,000

b. Each entry in the opportunity loss table is the difference between
the payoff for a chosen action and the maximum payoff possible for
the state of nature that occurred. For example, if the state of

ELEMENTS OF DECISION ANALYSIS

nature were "successful," the maximum payoff would be $1,600,000,
so the opportunity loss for the action "do not increase" is
$1,600,000 - $200,000 = $1,400,000. The calculations are shown in
the following table.

		STATES OF NATURE	
		Successful	Unsuccessful
ACTION	Increase	$1,600,000 - 1,600,000 $0	$400,000 - 400,000 $0
	Do Not Increase	$1,600,000 - 200,000 $1,400,000	$400,000 - 200,000 $200,000

20.15   a.   The payoff table shows the possible payoffs for each action/state
of nature combination. The actions are: (i) market the new wine,
and (ii) not market the new wine. The states of nature are sales
of either 0.5, 10, 15, 20, or 25 million bottles. Each payoff is
0 for the "not market" action because no money will be spent and
none will be made. Each payoff for the "market" action is 30¢
times the number of bottles sold minus the $3 million to produce
and promote the new wine: in millions, these are

$$.3(.5) - 3 = -2.85$$
$$.3(10) - 3 = 0$$
$$.3(15) - 3 = 1.5$$
$$.3(20) - 3 = 3$$
$$.3(25) - 3 = 4.5$$

The table is:

		STATE OF NATURE (SALES IN MILLIONS OF BOTTLES)				
		.5	10	15	20	25
ACTION	Market	-2.85	0	+1.5	+3	+4.5
	Not Market	0	0	0	0	0

Note: The entries in the table are in millions of dollars.

b.   Each entry in the opportunity loss table is the difference between
the payoff for a chosen action and the maximum payoff possible for
the state of nature that occurred. For example, if the state of

nature were 15 million bottles sold, the maximum payoff would be
$1.5 million, so the opportunity loss for the "market" action is
1.5 - 1.5 = 0 and that for the "not market" action is 1.5 - 0
= 1.5. The calculations are shown in the following table.

		STATE OF NATURE (SALES IN MILLIONS OF BOTTLES)				
		.5	10	15	20	25
ACTION	Market	0 -(-2.85) 2.85	0 -0 0	1.5 -1.5 0	3 -3 0	4.5 -4.5 0
	Not Market	0 -0 0	0 -0 0	1.5 -0 1.5	3 -0 3	4.5 -0 4.5

20.17 The decision tree for the opportunity loss of this problem involves a
path for each action followed by a connection to each possible state
of nature. The opportunity loss is shown with each resultant
action/state of nature. The possible actions are either (1) buy or
(2) don't buy. The possible states of nature are (1) high,
(2) medium, or (3) low demand.

The payoffs and opportunity losses are shown in the following decision
tree.

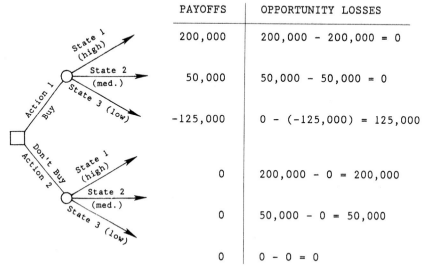

	PAYOFFS	OPPORTUNITY LOSSES
State 1 (high)	200,000	200,000 - 200,000 = 0
State 2 (med.)	50,000	50,000 - 50,000 = 0
State 3 (low)	-125,000	0 - (-125,000) = 125,000
State 1 (high)	0	200,000 - 0 = 200,000
State 2 (med.)	0	50,000 - 0 = 50,000
State 3 (low)	0	0 - 0 = 0

20.19 The decision tree for the opportunity loss of the problem involves a path for each action followed by a connection to each possible state of nature. The opportunity loss is shown with each resultant action/state of nature combination. The possible actions are either a_1, a_2, a_3, or a_4. The states of nature are S_1 and S_2. The payoffs and opportunity losses are shown in the decision tree.

PAYOFFS	OPPORTUNITY LOSSES
100	250 - 100 = 150
10	50 - 10 = 40
28	250 - 28 = 222
42	50 - 42 = 8
0	250 - 0 = 250
50	50 - 50 = 0
250	250 - 250 = 0
-5	50 - (-5) = 55

20.21 The decision tree for the opportunity loss of this problem involves a path for each action followed by a connection to each possible state of nature. The opportunity loss is shown with each resultant action/state of nature combination. The possible actions are either "develop the cancer drug" or "invest in surgical instruments." The states of nature are success in isolating the cancer drug or failure to isolate the cancer drug. The payoffs and opportunity losses (in millions of dollars) are shown in the decision tree.

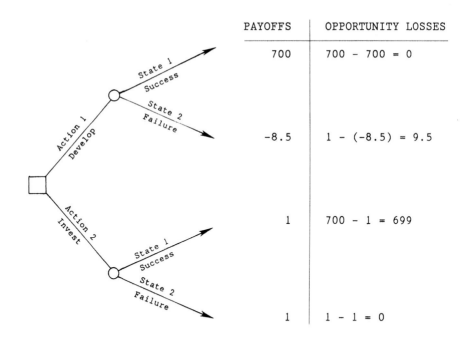

	PAYOFFS	OPPORTUNITY LOSSES
State 1 Success	700	700 - 700 = 0
State 2 Failure	-8.5	1 - (-8.5) = 9.5
State 1 Success	1	700 - 1 = 699
State 2 Failure	1	1 - 1 = 0

20.23   The decision tree for the opportunity loss of the problem involves a
path for each action followed by a connection to each possible state
of nature. The opportunity loss is shown with each resultant
action/state of nature combination. The possible actions are
(1) limited or (2) unlimited. The states of nature are (1) poor,
(2) mediocre, or (3) successful. The payoffs and opportunity losses
are shown in the decision tree below.

	PAYOFFS	OPPORTUNITY LOSSES
State 1	-150,000	-70,000 - (-150,000) = 80,000
State 2	0	20,000 - 0 = 20,000
State 3	200,000	200,000 - 200,000 = 0
State 1	-70,000	-70,000 - (-70,000) = 0
State 2	20,000	20,000 - 20,000 = 0
State 3	95,000	200,000 - 95,000 = 105,000

20.25 The decision tree for the opportunity loss of this problem involves a path for each action followed by a connection to each possible state of nature. The opportunity loss is shown with each resultant action/state of nature. The possible actions are (1) continue with present system, (2) subcontract to another phone company, (3) own a new system, or (4) joint venture with a larger phone company. The possible states of nature are (1) keep present method (study unfavorable) or (2) change to new method (study favorable). The payoffs and opportunity losses are shown in the decision tree below.

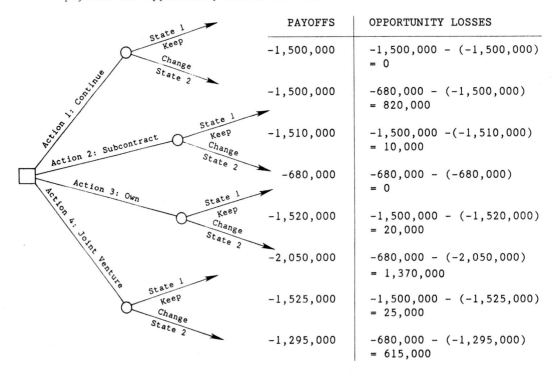

	PAYOFFS	OPPORTUNITY LOSSES
	$-1,500,000$	$-1,500,000 - (-1,500,000) = 0$
	$-1,500,000$	$-680,000 - (-1,500,000) = 820,000$
	$-1,510,000$	$-1,500,000 - (-1,510,000) = 10,000$
	$-680,000$	$-680,000 - (-680,000) = 0$
	$-1,520,000$	$-1,500,000 - (-1,520,000) = 20,000$
	$-2,050,000$	$-680,000 - (-2,050,000) = 1,370,000$
	$-1,525,000$	$-1,500,000 - (-1,525,000) = 25,000$
	$-1,295,000$	$-680,000 - (-1,295,000) = 615,000$

20.27 a. Expected payoffs are

$$EP(a_i) = \sum xp(x)$$

where a_i is action i, x is the payoff for each state of nature, and $p(x)$ is the respective probability.

$EP(a_1) = (-60)(.1) + (-10)(.3) + (40)(.4) + (70)(.2) = 21$
$EP(a_2) = (-90)(.1) + (-40)(.3) + (-10)(.4) + (85)(.2) = -8$
$EP(a_3) = (-50)(.1) + (-25)(.3) + (0)(.4) + (25)(.2) = -7.5$

Since the expected payoff for action a_1, $EP(a_1)$, is the largest, action a_1 should be selected to maximize the expected payoff.

b. Each entry in the opportunity loss table is the difference between the payoff for a chosen action and the maximum payoff possible for the state of nature that occurred. For example, if the state of nature were S_1, the maximum payoff would be -50, so the opportunity loss for action a_1 is $(-50) - (-60) = 10$. The calculations are shown in the opportunity table below.

ACTION	STATE OF NATURE S_1 (.1)	S_2 (.3)	S_3 (.4)	S_4 (.2)
a_1	-50 $- (-60)$ 10	-10 $- (-10)$ 0	40 $- 40$ 0	85 $- 70$ 15
a_2	-50 $- (-90)$ 40	-10 $- (-40)$ 30	40 $- (-10)$ 50	85 $- 85$ 0
a_3	-50 $- (-50)$ 0	-10 $- (-25)$ 15	40 $- 0$ 40	85 $- 25$ 60

$EOL(a_1) = 10(.1) + 0(.3) + 0(.4) + 15(.2) = 4$
$EOL(a_2) = 40(.1) + 30(.3) + 50(.4) + 0(.2) = 33$
$EOL(a_3) = 0(.1) + 15(.3) + 40(.4) + 60(.2) = 32.5$

Since the expected opportunity loss for action a_1 is the smallest, action a_1 should be selected.

c. The expected payoff and expected opportunity loss lead to the same decision.

20.29 The decision is made based on the expected opportunity losses. Expected losses are

$$EOL(a_i) = \sum xp(x)$$

where a_i is the action i, x is the opportunity loss, and p(x) the respective probability.

$EOL(a_1) = (30,000)(.60) + (0)(.40) = 18,000$
$EOL(a_2) = (0)(.60) + (35,000)(.40) = 14,000$

Since the expected opportunity loss for action a_2 is the smallest, action a_2 should be selected to minimize the expected loss.

20.31 a. The decision is made based on the expected payoffs. Expected payoffs are calculated by

$$EP(a_i) = \sum xp(x)$$

where a_i is action i, x is the payoff for each state of nature, and p(x) the respective probability.

$$EP(a_1) = (100,000)(.4) + (-30,000)(.4) + (30,000)(.2) = 34,000$$
$$EP(a_2) = (-50,000)(.4) + (80,000)(.4) + (50,000)(.2) = 22,000$$
$$EP(a_3) = (-50,000)(.4) + (60,000)(.4) + (90,000)(.2) = 22,000$$

Since the expected payoff for action a_1 is the largest, action a_1 should be selected to maximize the expected payoff.

b. Each entry in the opportunity loss table is the difference between the payoff for a chosen action and the maximum payoff possible for the state of nature that occurred. For example, if the state of nature were S_1, the maximum payoff would be 100,000, so the opportunity loss for action a_1 is 100,000 - 100,000 = 0. The calculations are shown in the opportunity table below.

ACTION	STATE OF NATURE		
	S_1 (.4)	S_2 (.4)	S_3 (.2)
a_1	100,000 - 100,000 0	80,000 - (-30,000) 110,000	90,000 - 30,000 60,000
a_2	100,000 - (-50,000) 150,000	80,000 - 80,000 0	90,000 - 50,000 40,000
a_3	100,000 - (-50,000) 150,000	80,000 - 60,000 20,000	90,000 - 90,000 0

The decision is made on the expected opportunity losses, calculated as

$$EOL(a_i) = \sum xp(x)$$

where a_i is the action i, x is the opportunity loss, and p(x) the respective probability.

$$EOL(a_1) = 0(.4) + 110,000(.4) + 60,000(.2) = 56,000$$
$$EOL(a_2) = 150,000(.4) + 0(.4) + 40,000(.2) = 68,000$$
$$EOL(a_3) = 150,000(.4) + 20,000(.4) + 0(.2) = 68,000$$

Since the expected opportunity loss for action a_1 is the smallest, action a_1 should be selected to minimize the expected loss.

20.33 The decision is made based on the expected payoffs, calculated as

$$EP(a_i) = \sum xp(x)$$

where a_i is action i, x is the payoff for each state of nature, and p(x) the respective probability.

The payoff table is shown in the solution to Exercise 20.11.

$EP(a_1) = 10(.15) + 10(.20) + 10(.35) + 10(.25) + 10(.05) = 10$
$EP(a_2) = 5(.15) + 20(.20) + 10(.35) + 20(.25) + 20(.05) = 17.75$
$EP(a_3) = 0(.15) + 15(.20) + 30(.35) + 30(.25) + 30(.05) = 22.5$
$EP(a_4) = (-5)(.15) + 10(.20) + 25(.35) + 40(.25) + 40(.05) = 22$
$EP(a_5) = (-10)(.15) + 5(.20) + 20(.35) + 35(.25) + 50(.05) = 17.75$

Since the expected payoff for action a_3 is the largest, the store manager should order three boxes to maximize the expected payoff.

20.35 a. The maximax criterion selects the action that has the maximum payoff associated with it. The maximum payoff for each action is:

a_1: 100 a_2: 90 a_3: 110 a_4: 195

The action with the maximum payoff is a_4: 195.

b. The maximin criterion selects the action that has the maximum of the minimum payoffs associated with each action. The minimum payoff for each action is:

a_1: 90 a_2: 50 a_3: −25 a_4: 75

The action with the maximum of these minimum payoffs is a_1: 90.

c. Each entry in the opportunity loss table is the difference between the payoff for a chosen action and the maximum payoff possible for the state of nature that occurred. For example, if S_1 occurred, the maximum payoff is 100, so the opportunity loss for action a_3 is 100 − (−25) = 125. The calculations are shown in the following table.

	STATE OF NATURE		
	S_1	S_2	S_3
ACTION a_1	100 − 100 = 0	95 − 95 = 0	195 − 90 = 105
a_2	100 − 50 = 50	95 − 75 = 20	195 − 90 = 105
a_3	100 − (−25) = 125	95 − 25 = 70	195 − 110 = 85
a_4	100 − 75 = 25	95 − 80 = 15	195 − 195 = 0

d. The minimax criterion selects the action with the minimum of the maximum opportunity losses associated with each action. From part (c) above, the maximum opportunity loss for each action is:

a_1: 105 a_2: 105 a_3: 125 a_4: 25

The minimum of these maximum opportunity losses is 25, which is associated with action a_4, thus a_4 is the minimax choice.

20.37 a. The maximax criterion selects the action that has the maximum payoff associated with it. The maximum payoff for each action is:

a_1: 30,000 a_2: 80,000 a_3: 100,000

The action with the maximum payoff is a_3: 100,000.

b. The maximin criterion selects the action with the maximum of the minimum payoffs associated with each action. The minimum payoff for each action is:

a_1: 20,000 a_2: −15,000 a_3: −30,000

The action with the maximum of these minimum payoffs is a_1: 20,000.

20.39 See the solution to Exercise 20.23.

a. The maximax criterion selects the action that has the maximum payoff associated with it. The maximum payoff for each action is:

Limited: 200,000   Unlimited: 95,000

The action with the maximum payoff is limited tickets.

b. The maximin criterion selects the action with the maximum of the minimum payoffs associated with each action. The minimum payoff for each action is:

Limited: −150,000   Unlimited: −70,000

The action with the maximum of these minimum payoffs is unlimited tickets.

c. The minimax criterion selects the action with the minimum of the maximum opportunity losses associated with each action. The maximum opportunity loss for each action is:

Limited: 80,000   Unlimited: 105,000

The action with the minimum of these maximum opportunity losses is limited tickets.

20.41 a. $P(A_1 \text{ and } F) = P(F|A_1)P(A_1) = .02(.3) = .006$

b. $P(A_2 \text{ and } F) = P(F|A_2)P(A_2) = .05(.1) = .005$

c. $P(A_3 \text{ and } F) = P(F|A_3)P(A_3) = .01(.6) = .006$

d. $P(F) = P(F|A_1)P(A_1) + P(F|A_2)P(A_2) + P(F|A_3)P(A_3)$
$= .006 + .005 + .006 = .017$

e. $P(A_1|F) = \dfrac{P(A_1 \text{ and } F)}{P(F)} = \dfrac{.006}{.017} = \dfrac{6}{17} \approx .353$

f. $P(A_2|F) = \dfrac{P(A_2 \text{ and } F)}{P(F)} = \dfrac{.005}{.017} = \dfrac{5}{17} \approx .294$

g. $P(A_3|F) = \dfrac{P(A_3 \text{ and } F)}{P(F)} = \dfrac{.006}{.017} = \dfrac{6}{17} \approx .353$

20.43 $P(A_1) = .3$, $P(A_2) = .2$, and $P(A_3) = .5$

$P(E|A_1) = .01$, $P(E|A_2) = .03$, $P(E|A_3) = .02$

$P(E \text{ and } A_1) = P(E|A_1)P(A_1) = .01(.3) = .003$

$P(E \text{ and } A_2) = P(E|A_2)P(A_2) = .03(.2) = .006$

$P(E \text{ and } A_3) = P(E|A_3)P(A_3) = .02(.5) = .010$

$P(E) = P(E|A_1)P(A_1) + P(E|A_2)P(A_2) + P(E|A_3)P(A_3) = .003 + .006 + .010$
$= .019$

$P(A_1|E) = \dfrac{P(A_1 \text{ and } E)}{P(E)} = \dfrac{.003}{.019} = \dfrac{3}{19}$

$P(A_2|E) = \dfrac{P(A_2 \text{ and } E)}{P(E)} = \dfrac{.006}{.019} = \dfrac{6}{19}$

$P(A_3|E) = \dfrac{P(A_3 \text{ and } E)}{P(E)} = \dfrac{.010}{.019} = \dfrac{10}{19}$

Since $P(A_3|E) = 10/19$ is larger than the others, engineer 3 is most likely to be responsible given a serious error has been made.

20.45 $P(A) = .8$ $P(B) = .2$

Let D = defective part

$P(D|A) = .05$, $P(D|B) = .03$

We first want to find $P(A|D)$ and $P(B|D)$

$P(A \text{ and } D) = P(D|A)P(A) = .05(.8) = .04$

$P(B \text{ and } D) = P(D|B)P(B) = .03(.2) = .006$

$P(D) = P(D|A)P(A) + P(D|B)P(B) = .04 + .006 = .046$

Thus, $P(A|D) = \dfrac{P(A \text{ and } D)}{P(D)} = \dfrac{.04}{.046} = .870$

$P(B|D) = \dfrac{P(B \text{ and } D)}{P(D)} = \dfrac{.006}{.046} = .130$

If an assembled modem selected is found to have a defective part, it is more likely to have come from company A because $P(A|D) > P(B|D)$.

20.47   From Exercise 20.46,

$P(S_1|I) = .316$

$P(S_2|I) = .237$

$P(S_3|I) = .237$

$P(S_4|I) = .210$

Using these posterior probabilities, the expected payoffs are

$EP(a_i) = \sum xp(x)$

where a_i is action i, x is the payoff for each state of nature, and $p(x)$ is the respective posterior probability.

$EP(a_1) = 10(.316) + 20(.237) + 15(.237) + 10(.210) = 13.555$
$EP(a_2) = -10(.316) + 0(.237) + 30(.237) + 15(.210) = 7.100$
$EP(a_3) = 0(.316) + 15(.237) + 20(.237) + 10(.210) = 10.395$

20.49   a.   Expected payoffs are calculated by

$EP(a_i) = \sum xp(x)$

where a_i is action i, x is the payoff for each state of nature, and $p(x)$ the respective prior probability.

$$EP(a_1) = 23(.3) + (-7)(.2) + 14(.5) = 12.5$$
$$EP(a_2) = 16(.3) + 8(.2) + (-5)(.5) = 3.9$$
$$EP(a_3) = 10(.3) + 12(.2) + 9(.5) = 9.9$$
$$EP(a_4) = 31(.3) + (-15)(.2) + 0(.5) = 6.3$$

Since the expected payoff for action a_1 is the largest, this action should be selected to maximize the expected payoff.

b. $P(S_1|I) = \dfrac{P(S_1)P(I|S_1)}{P(S_1)P(I|S_1) + P(S_2)P(I|S_2) + P(S_3)P(I|S_3)}$

$$= \frac{(.3)(.25)}{(.3)(.25) + (.2)(.95) + (.5)(.15)} = \frac{.075}{.34} = \frac{75}{340} = \frac{15}{68}$$

$P(S_2|I) = \dfrac{P(S_2)P(I|S_2)}{P(S_1)P(I|S_1) + P(S_2)P(I|S_2) + P(S_3)P(I|S_3)}$

$$= \frac{(.2)(.95)}{(.3)(.25) + (.2)(.95) + (.5)(.15)} = \frac{.19}{.34} = \frac{19}{34}$$

$P(S_3|I) = \dfrac{P(S_3)P(I|S_3)}{P(S_1)P(I|S_1) + P(S_2)P(I|S_2) + P(S_3)P(I|S_3)}$

$$= \frac{(.5)(.15)}{(.3)(.25) + (.2)(.95) + (.5)(.15)} = \frac{.075}{.34} = \frac{75}{340} = \frac{15}{68}$$

c. Expected payoffs are calculated by

$$EP(a_i) = \sum xp(x)$$

where a_i is action i, x is the payoff for each state of nature, and $p(x)$ the respective posterior probability.

$$EP(a_1) = 23(15/68) + (-7)(19/34) + 14(15/68) = 4.25$$
$$EP(a_2) = 16(15/68) + 8(19/34) + (-5)(15/68) = 6.897$$
$$EP(a_3) = 10(15/68) + 12(19/34) + 9(15/68) = 10.897$$
$$EP(a_4) = 31(15/68) + (-15)(19/34) + 0(15/68) = -1.544$$

d. Since the expected payoff for action a_3 is the largest, this action should be selected to maximize the expected payoff. This is different than what was selected in part (a).

20.51 We need to find the posterior probabilities

$$P(S_1|I), \ P(S_2|I), \ P(S_3|I)$$

where S_1 = product is a failure,
   S_2 = product is moderately successful,
   S_3 = product is very successful,
and   I = survey concludes moderately successful

$$P(S_1|I) = \frac{P(S_1)P(I|S_1)}{P(S_1)P(I|S_1) + P(S_2)P(I|S_2) + P(S_3)P(I|S_3)}$$

$$= \frac{(.6)(.2)}{(.6)(.2) + (.3)(.4) + (.1)(.2)} = \frac{.12}{.26} = \frac{12}{26}$$

$$P(S_2|I) = \frac{P(S_2)P(I|S_2)}{P(S_1)P(I|S_1) + P(S_2)P(I|S_2) + P(S_3)P(I|S_3)}$$

$$= \frac{(.3)(.4)}{(.6)(.2) + (.3)(.4) + (.1)(.2)} = \frac{.12}{.26} = \frac{12}{26}$$

$$P(S_3|I) = \frac{P(S_3)P(I|S_3)}{P(S_1)P(I|S_1) + P(S_2)P(I|S_2) + P(S_3)P(I|S_3)}$$

$$= \frac{(.1)(.2)}{(.6)(.2) + (.3)(.4) + (.1)(.2)} = \frac{.02}{.26} = \frac{2}{26}$$

Expected payoffs are calculated by

$$EP(a_i) = \sum x p(x)$$

where a_i is action i, x is the payoff for each state of nature, and $p(x)$ the respective probability (here the posterior probability).

$$EP(a_1) = (-200,000)(12/26) + (300,000)(12/26) + (600,000)(2/26)$$
$$= 92,308$$
$$EP(a_2) = 0(12/26) + 0(12/26) + 0(12/26) = 0$$

Since the expected payoff for action a_1, market the product, is the largest, this action should be selected to maximize the expected payoff.

20.53 a. The set of actions are either "settle out of court" or "proceed with the legal action in court." The states of nature are two: (1) either win the case or (b) lose the case. Note that these are mutually exclusive and collectively exhaustive. The outcomes are the possible losses the doctor could sustain: $250,000 with an out-of-court settlement; $1,000,000 if he loses in court ($75,000 in court costs, plus $925,000 settlement); and, $0 if he wins (the plaintiff pays $75,000 court costs). The objective variable is the amount of money the doctor could lose.

b. The payoff table shows the possible payoffs for each action/state of nature. The payoffs for settling out of court are $-250,000. If he goes to court and wins, the doctor pays nothing. If he goes to court and loses, the doctor pays $925,000 + $75,000. These are shown in the table below.

		STATE OF NATURE	
		Win	Lose
ACTION	Go to Court	$ 0	$-1,000,000
	Settle	-250,000	-250,000

c. The decision tree for the payoff of this problem involves a path
for each action followed by a connection to each possible state of
nature. The payoff is shown at the right with each resultant
action/state of nature.

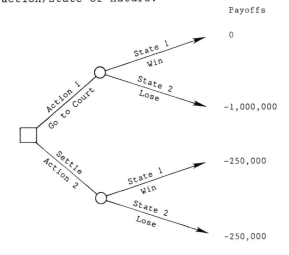

Payoffs

d. Expected payoffs are calculated by

$$EP(a_i) = \sum x p(x)$$

where a_i is action i, x is the payoff for each state of nature,
and $p(x)$ the respective prior probability. In this problem, the
prior probability associated with "win" is .20; with "loss" is
.80.

$$EP(a_1) = 0(.2) + (-1,000,000)(.8) = -800,000$$
$$EP(a_2) = (-250,000)(.2) + (-250,000)(.8) = -250,000$$

Since the expected payoff from action 2, "settle out of court," is
the largest (i.e., the smallest loss), this action should be
selected to maximize the expected payoff.

e. The maximax criterion selects the action that has the maximum payoff associated with it. The maximum payoff for each action is:

a_1: 0 a_2: -250,000

The action with the maximum payoff is a_1: Go to court.

f. The maximin criterion selects the action with the maximum of the minimum payoffs associated with each action. The minimum payoff for each action is:

a_1: -1,000,000 a_2: -250,000

The action with the maximum of these minimum payoffs is a_2: Settle out of court.

g. Each entry in the opportunity loss table is the difference between the payoff and the maximum payoff possible for that state of nature. The calculations are shown in the following table.

		STATE OF NATURE	
		Win	Lose
	Go to Court	0 - 0 0	-250,000 - (-1,000,000) 750,000
ACTION			
	Settle	0 - (-250,000) 250,000	-250,000 - (-250,000) 0

The minimax criterion selects the action with the minimum of the maximum opportunity losses associated with each action. The maximum opportunity loss for each action is:

a_1: 750,000 a_2: 250,000

The action with the minimum of these maximum opportunity losses is a_2: Settle out of court.

20.55 a. The set of actions = buy 3, 4, 5, 6, 7, or 8 dozen dresses.
The states of nature = sell 3, 4, 5, 6, 7, or 8 dozen dresses.

Note that these are mutually exclusive and collectively exhaustive.

The outcomes are: There is a $20 profit on any dress sold in
season. Any dress not sold is a $5 loss. The objective variable
is profit.

b. The payoff table shows the possible payoffs for each action/state
of nature. The payoffs for each action/state of nature
combination is

$$-30(P) + 50(S) + 25(B)$$

where P = number purchased

$$S = \begin{array}{l} \text{number sold if state of nature is} \leq P \text{ or} \\ P \text{ if state of nature} > P \end{array}$$

$$B = \begin{array}{l} P - S \quad \text{if } S \leq P \text{ or} \\ 0 \qquad \text{if } S > P \end{array}$$

For example, if three are purchased and three are sold, then
P = 3, S = 3, and B = P - S = 0.

Payoff = -30(3) + 50(3) + 25(0) = 60

If three are purchased and six could be sold, then P = 3, S = 3,
and B = 0.

Payoff = -30(3) + 50(3) + 25(0) = 60

The payoff table is shown below.

		STATE OF NATURE					
	Sell:	3	4	5	6	7	8
	Buy 3	60	60	60	60	60	60
	Buy 4	55	80	80	80	80	80
	Buy 5	50	75	100	100	100	100
ACTION	Buy 6	45	70	95	120	120	120
	Buy 7	40	65	90	115	140	140
	Buy 8	35	60	85	110	135	160

c. Each entry in the opportunity loss table is the difference between
the payoff for a chosen action and the maximum payoff possible for
the state of nature that occurred. For example, if the state of
nature were four sold, the maximum payoff would be $80, so the
opportunity loss for buying three is 80 - 60 = 20. The
calculations are shown in the opportunity loss table below.

| | STATE OF NATURE | | | | | |
	Sell:	3	4	5	6	7	8

	3	4	5	6	7	8
Buy 3	60	80	100	120	140	160
	−60	−60	−60	−60	−60	−60
	0	20	40	60	80	100
Buy 4	60	80	100	120	140	160
	−55	−80	−80	−80	−80	−80
	5	0	20	40	60	80
Buy 5	60	80	100	120	140	160
	−50	−75	−100	−100	−100	−100
	10	5	0	20	40	60
Buy 6	60	80	100	120	140	160
	45	−70	−95	−120	−120	−120
	15	10	5	0	20	40
Buy 7	60	80	100	120	140	160
	−40	−65	−90	−115	−140	−140
	20	15	10	5	0	20
Buy 8	60	80	100	120	140	160
	−35	−60	−85	−110	−135	−160
	25	20	15	10	5	0

ACTION (label at left, spanning the Buy rows)

d. Expected payoffs are calculated by

$$EP(a_i) = \sum xp(x)$$

where a_i is action i, x is the payoff for each state of nature, and $p(x)$ the respective prior probability.

$EP(a_1) = 60(.05) + 60(.10) + 60(.35) + 60(.40) + 60(.05) + 60(.05)$
$\qquad = 60$
$EP(a_2) = 55(.05) + 80(.10) + 80(.35) + 80(.40) + 80(.05) + 80(.05)$
$\qquad = 78.75$
$EP(a_3) = 50(.05) + 75(.10) + 100(.35) + 100(.40) + 100(.05)$
$\qquad\quad + 100(.05) = 95$
$EP(a_4) = 45(.05) + 70(.10) + 95(.35) + 120(.40) + 120(.05)$
$\qquad\quad + 120(.05) = 102.5$
$EP(a_5) = 40(.05) + 65(.10) + 90(.35) + 115(.40) + 140(.05)$
$\qquad\quad + 140(.05) = 100$
$EP(a_6) = 35(.05) + 60(.10) + 85(.35) + 110(.40) + 135(.05)$
$\qquad\quad + 160(.05) = 96.25$

Since the expected payoff from action a_4, buy 6, is the largest, this action should be selected to maximize the expected payoff.

e. Expected opportunity losses are calculated by

$$EOL(a_i) = \sum xp(x)$$

where a_i is action i, x is the opportunity loss for each state of nature, and p(x) the respective prior probability.

$EP(a_1) = 0(.05) + 20(.10) + 40(.35) + 60(.40) + 80(.05) + 100(.05)$
$\qquad = 49$
$EP(a_2) = 5(.05) + 0(.10) + 20(.35) + 40(.40) + 60(.05) + 80(.05)$
$\qquad = 30.25$
$EP(a_3) = 10(.05) + 5(.10) + 0(.35) + 20(.40) + 40(.05) + 60(.05)$
$\qquad = 14$
$EP(a_4) = 15(.05) + 10(.10) + 5(.35) + 0(.40) + 20(.05) + 40(.05)$
$\qquad = 6.5$
$EP(a_5) = 20(.05) + 15(.10) + 10(.35) + 5(.40) + 0(.05) + 20(.05)$
$\qquad = 9$
$EP(a_6) = 25(.05) + 20(.10) + 15(.35) + 10(.40) + 5(.05) + 0(.05)$
$\qquad = 12.75$

Since the expected opportunity loss for action a_4, buy 6, is the smallest, this action should be selected to minimize the opportunity loss. This selection agrees with part (d).

f. The maximax criterion selects the action that has the maximum payoff associated with it. The maximum payoff for each action is:

$\quad a_1$: 60 $\quad a_2$: 80 $\quad a_3$: 100 $\quad a_4$: 120 $\quad a_5$: 140 $\quad a_6$: 160

The action with the maximum payoff is a_6: Buy 8.

g. The maximin criterion selects the action with the maximum of the minimum payoffs associated with each action. The minimum payoff for each action is:

$\quad a_1$: 60 $\quad a_2$: 55 $\quad a_3$: 50 $\quad a_4$: 45 $\quad a_5$: 40 $\quad a_6$: 35

The action with the maximum of these minimum payoffs is a_1: Buy 3.

h. The minimax criterion selects the action with the minimum of the maximum opportunity losses associated with each action. The maximum opportunity loss for each action is:

$\quad a_1$: 100 $\quad a_2$: 80 $\quad a_3$: 60 $\quad a_4$: 40 $\quad a_5$: 20 $\quad a_6$: 25

The action with the minimum of these maximum opportunity losses is a_5: Buy 7.

20.57 a. The actions are either "issue the flyer" or "do not issue the flyer." The states of nature are (1) favorable, (2) no reaction, or (3) unfavorable. Note that these are mutually exclusive and collectively exhaustive. The outcomes are: Issue with favorable reaction and gain 5 points; Issue with no reaction and remain unchanged; Issue with negative reaction and drop 7 points; Do not issue with each of the three reactions (favorable, no reaction, unfavorable) and remain unchanged. The objective variable is point increase in the poll.

b. The payoff table shows the possible payoffs for each action/state of nature. The payoffs for issuing the flyer are: gain 5 points for a favorable reaction; remain unchanged for no reaction; and lose 7 points for an unfavorable reaction. The payoff for not issuing the flyer is: remain unchanged. These are shown in the payoff table below.

		STATE OF NATURE		
		Favorable (.4)	No Reaction (.3)	Unfavorable (.3)
ACTION	Issue	5	0	-7
	Do Not Issue	0	0	0

The expected payoffs are calculated by

$$EP(a_i) = \sum x p(x)$$

where a_i is the action i, x is payoff for each state of nature, and $p(x)$ the respective prior probability.

$$EP(a_1) = 5(.4) + 0(.3) + (-7)(.3) = -.1$$
$$EP(a_2) = 0(.4) + 0(.3) + 0(.3) = 0$$

Since the expected payoff from action a_2, do not issue the flyer, is the largest, this action should be selected to maximize the expected payoff.

c. The maximax criterion selects the action that has the maximum payoff associated with it. The maximum payoff for each action is:

a_1: 5 a_2: 0

The action with the maximum payoff is a_1: Issue the flyer.

The maximin criterion selects the action with the maximum of the minimum payoffs associated with each action. The minimum payoff for each action is:

a_1: -7 a_2: 0

The action with the maximum of these minimum payoffs is a_2: Do not issue the flyer.

d. Each entry in the opportunity loss table is the difference between the payoff for a chosen action and the maximum payoff possible for the state of nature that occurred. The calculations are shown in the opportunity loss table below.

		STATE OF NATURE		
		Favorable (.4)	No Reaction (.3)	Unfavorable (.3)
ACTION	Issue	5 - 5 = 0	0 - 0 = 0	0 - (-7) = 7
	Do Not Issue	5 - 0 = 5	0 - 0 = 0	0 - 0 = 0

The minimax criterion is that which takes the action with the minimum of the maximum opportunity losses associated with each action. The maximum opportunity loss for each action is:

a_1: 7 a_2: 5

The action with the minimum of the maximum opportunity losses is a_2: Do not issue the flyer.

20.59 a. The payoff table shows the possible payoffs for each action/state of nature combination. The actions are:

a_1: Agreement 1 a_2: Agreement 2

The states of nature are the proportions of seriously defective sets: .00, .05, .10, .15, .20. The payoff (i.e., cost) for a_1 is $-460(100) = -46,000$. The payoff (i.e., cost) for a_2 is $100(400) + 400(S_i \times 100)$. These are shown in the payoff table.

	STATE OF NATURE				
	.00	.05	.10	.15	.20
a_1	-46,000	-46,000	-46,000	-46,000	-46,000
ACTION					
a_2	-40,000	-42,000	-44,000	-46,000	-48,000

b. The expected payoffs are calculated by

$$EP(a_i) = \sum xp(x)$$

where a_i is the action i, x is payoff for each state of nature, and p(x) the respective prior probability.

$$EP(a_1) = (-46,000)(.4) + (-46,000)(.3) + (-46,000)(.1)$$
$$+ (-46,000)(.1) + (-46,000)(.1) = -46,000$$
$$EP(a_2) = (-40,000)(.4) + (-42,000)(.3) + (-44,000)(.1)$$
$$+ (-46,000)(.1) + (-48,000)(.1) = -42,400$$

Since the expected payoff for action a_2 is the largest, this action should be selected to maximize the expected payoff.

c. Let I = {defective set}. The $P(I|S_1) = .00$, $P(I|S_2) = .05$, $P(I|S_3) = .10$, $P(I|S_4) = .15$, and $P(I|S_5) = .20$. Also, we have the prior probabilities, $P(S_1) = .4$, $P(S_2) = .3$, $P(S_3) = P(S_4) = P(S_5) = .1$. Substitution yields the following posterior probabilities:

$$P(S_1|I) =$$

$$\frac{P(S_1)P(I|S_1)}{P(S_1)P(I|S_1) + P(S_2)P(I|S_2) + P(S_3)P(I|S_3) + P(S_4)P(I|S_4) + P(S_5)P(I|S_5)}$$

$$= \frac{(.4)(.00)}{(.4)(.00) + (.3)(.05) + (.1)(.10) + (.1)(.15) + (.1)(.20)}$$

$$= \frac{.00}{.06} = 0$$

$$P(S_2|I) =$$

$$\frac{P(S_2)P(I|S_2)}{P(S_1)P(I|S_1) + P(S_2)P(I|S_2) + P(S_3)P(I|S_3) + P(S_4)P(I|S_4) + P(S_5)P(I|S_5)}$$

$$= \frac{(.3)(.05)}{(.4)(.00) + (.3)(.05) + (.1)(.10) + (.1)(.15) + (.1)(.20)}$$

$$= \frac{.015}{.06} = .250$$

$P(S_3|I) =$

$$\frac{P(S_3)P(I|S_3)}{P(S_1)P(I|S_1) + P(S_2)P(I|S_2) + P(S_3)P(I|S_3) + P(S_4)P(I|S_4) + P(S_5)P(I|S_5)}$$

$$= \frac{(.1)(.10)}{(.4)(.00) + (.3)(.05) + (.1)(.10) + (.1)(.15) + (.1)(.20)}$$

$$= \frac{.010}{.06} = .167$$

$P(S_4|I) =$

$$\frac{P(S_4)P(I|S_4)}{P(S_1)P(I|S_1) + P(S_2)P(I|S_2) + P(S_3)P(I|S_3) + P(S_4)P(I|S_4) + P(S_5)P(I|S_5)}$$

$$= \frac{(.1)(.15)}{(.4)(.00) + (.3)(.05) + (.1)(.10) + (.1)(.15) + (.1)(.20)}$$

$$= \frac{.015}{.06} = .250$$

$P(S_5|I) =$

$$\frac{P(S_5)P(I|S_5)}{P(S_1)P(I|S_1) + P(S_2)P(I|S_2) + P(S_3)P(I|S_3) + P(S_4)P(I|S_4) + P(S_5)P(I|S_5)}$$

$$= \frac{(.1)(.20)}{(.4)(.00) + (.3)(.05) + (.1)(.10) + (.1)(.15) + (.1)(.20)}$$

$$= \frac{.02}{.06} = .333$$

Using these posterior probabilities, the expected payoffs are:

$$EP(a_1) = (-46,000)(0) + (-46,000)(.25) + (-46,000)(.167)$$
$$+ (-46,000)(.25) + (-46,000)(.333) = -46,000$$
$$EP(a_2) = (-40,000)(0) + (-42,000)(.25) + (-44,000)(.167)$$
$$+ (-46,000)(.25) + (-48,000)(.333) = -45,332$$

Since the expected payoff for action a_2 is largest, the decision is to choose Agreement 2 if the sampled set is defective.

Now let I = {nondefective set}. Then $P(I|S_1) = 1.00$, $P(I|S_2) = .95$, $P(I|S_3) = .90$, $P(I|S_4) = .85$, and $P(I|S_5) = .80$. These values are used to calculate the new posterior probabilities:

$P(S_1|I) =$

$$\frac{P(S_1)P(I|S_1)}{P(S_1)P(I|S_1) + P(S_2)P(I|S_2) + P(S_3)P(I|S_3) + P(S_4)P(I|S_4) + P(S_5)P(I|S_5)}$$

$$= \frac{(.4)(1.00)}{(.4)(1.00) + (.3)(.95) + (.1)(.90) + (.1)(.85) + (.1)(.80)}$$

$$= \frac{.40}{.94} = .426$$

$P(S_2|I) =$

$$\frac{P(S_2)P(I|S_2)}{P(S_1)P(I|S_1) + P(S_2)P(I|S_2) + P(S_3)P(I|S_3) + P(S_4)P(I|S_4) + P(S_5)P(I|S_5)}$$

$$= \frac{(.3)(.95)}{(.4)(1.00) + (.3)(.95) + (.1)(.90) + (.1)(.85) + (.1)(.80)}$$

$$= \frac{.285}{.94} = .303$$

$P(S_3|I) =$

$$\frac{P(S_3)P(I|S_3)}{P(S_1)P(I|S_1) + P(S_2)P(I|S_2) + P(S_3)P(I|S_3) + P(S_4)P(I|S_4) + P(S_5)P(I|S_5)}$$

$$= \frac{(.1)(.90)}{(.4)(1.00) + (.3)(.95) + (.1)(.90) + (.1)(.85) + (.1)(.80)}$$

$$= \frac{.09}{.94} = .096$$

$P(S_3|I) =$

$$\frac{P(S_4)P(I|S_4)}{P(S_1)P(I|S_1) + P(S_2)P(I|S_2) + P(S_3)P(I|S_3) + P(S_4)P(I|S_4) + P(S_5)P(I|S_5)}$$

$$= \frac{(.1)(.85)}{(.4)(1.00) + (.3)(.95) + (.1)(.90) + (.1)(.85) + (.1)(.80)}$$

$$= \frac{.085}{.94} = .090$$

$P(S_3|I) =$

$$\frac{P(S_5)P(I|S_5)}{P(S_1)P(I|S_1) + P(S_2)P(I|S_2) + P(S_3)P(I|S_3) + P(S_4)P(I|S_4) + P(S_5)P(I|S_5)}$$

$$= \frac{(.1)(.80)}{(.4)(1.00) + (.3)(.95) + (.1)(.90) + (.1)(.85) + (.1)(.80)}$$

$$= \frac{.08}{.94} = .085$$

Using the new posterior probabilities, the expected payoffs are:

$EP(a_1) = -46,000$
$EP(a_2) = (-40,000)(.426) + (-42,000)(.303) + (-44,000)(.096)$
$\qquad + (-46,000)(.090) + (-48,000)(.085) = -42,210$

Again, the expected payoff for action a_2 is largest. Thus, the decision is to choose Agreement 2 no matter whether the sampled set is defective or nondefective.

20.1   a.   From Tables 20.17 and 20.18, the payoff table is

		STATE OF NATURE				
		Dry S_1	20,000 S_2	40,000 S_3	80,000 S_4	100,000 S_5
ACTION	Drill, a_1	-40,000	50,000	300,000	700,000	800,000
	Farm, a_2	0	12,000	60,000	120,000	130,000
	Back-in option, a_3	0	12,000	145,000	400,000	500,000

b.   The expected payoffs are calculated by

$$EP(a_i) = \sum xp(x)$$

where a_i is the action i, x is payoff for each state of nature, and $p(x)$ the respective prior probability.

$$EP(a_1) = -40,000(.30) + 50,000(.25) + 300,000(.25)$$
$$+ 700,000(.10) + 800,000(.10) = 225,500$$
$$EP(a_2) = 0(.30) + 12,000(.25) + 60,000(.25)$$
$$+ 120,000(.10) + 130,000(.10) = 43,000$$
$$EP(a_3) = 0(.30) + 12,000(.25) + 145,000(.25)$$
$$+ 400,000(.10) + 500,000(.10) = 129,250$$

Since the expected payoff for action a_1, drill, is the largest, this action should be selected to maximize the expected payoff.

c.   The maximax criterion selects the action that has the maximum payoff associated with it. The maximum payoff for each action is

   a_1: \$800,000 a_2: \$130,000 a_3: \$500,000

The action with the maximum payoff is a_1: drill.

The maximin criterion selects the action with the maximum of the minimum payoffs associated with each action. The minimum payoff for each action is

   a_1: -40,000 a_2: 0 a_3: 0

The action with the maximum of these minimum payoffs is either a_2: farm or a_3: back-in option.

d. Each entry in the opportunity loss table is the difference between the payoff for a chosen action and the maximum payoff possible for the state of nature that occurred. For example, if the state of nature is "Dry," the maximum payoff would be 0, so the opportunity loss for the action "Drill" is 0 - (-40,000) = 40,000. The calculations are shown in the following table.

The opportunity loss table is tabulated from the results shown in the payoff table.

		STATE OF NATURE				
		S_1	S_2	S_3	S_4	S_5
		0	50,000	300,000	700,000	800,000
	a_1	-(-40,000)	-50,000	-300,000	-700,000	-800,000
		40,000	0	0	0	0
		0	50,000	300,000	700,000	800,000
ACTION	a_2	-0	-12,000	-60,000	-120,000	-130,000
		0	38,000	240,000	580,000	670,000
		0	50,000	300,000	700,000	800,000
	a_3	-0	-12,000	-145,000	-400,000	-500,000
		0	38,000	155,000	300,000	300,000

The minimax criterion selects the action with the minimum of the maximum opportunity losses associated with each action. The maximum opportunity loss for each action is:

a_1: 40,000 a_2: 670,000 a_3: 300,000

The minimum of these maximum opportunity losses is 40,000, which is associated with action a_1, drill. Thus, the minimax choice is to drill.

20.3 a. Let S_1 = Normal Traffic and S_2 = Additional Traffic

From the problem, $P(S_2)$ = .7. Then $P(S_1)$ = 1 - .7 = .3

The expected payoffs are calculated by

$$EP(a_i) = \sum xp(x)$$

where a_i is the action i, x is the payoff for each state of nature, and p(x) the respective prior probability.

$$EP(a_1) = -8.20(.3) + 20.80(.7) = 12.10$$
$$EP(a_2) = -3.70(.3) + 15.50(.7) = 9.74$$
$$EP(a_3) = 10.50(.3) + 10.50(.7) = 10.5$$

Since the payoff for action a_1, Issue coupons, no limitations, is the largest, this action should be selected to maximize the expected payoff.

b. The maximax criterion selects the action that has the maximum payoff associated with it. The maximum payoff for each action is:

a_1: 20.80 $\quad$ a_2: 15.50 $\quad$ a_3: 10.50

The action with the maximum payoff is a_1, Issue coupons, no limitations.

c. The maximin criterion selects the action with the maximum of the minimum payoffs associated with each action. The minimum payoff for each action is

a_1: -8.20 $\quad$ a_2: -3.70 $\quad$ a_3: 10.50

The action with the maximum of these minimum payoffs is action a_3, Do not issue coupons.

d. Each entry in the opportunity loss table is the difference between the payoff for a chosen action and the maximum payoff possible for the state of nature that occurred. For example, if the state of nature is "Normal traffic," the maximum payoff would be 10.50, so the opportunity loss for the action "Issue coupons, no limitations" is 10.50 − (−8.20) = 18.70. The calculations are shown in the following table.

		STATE OF NATURE	
		Normal Traffic	Additional Traffic
	Issue coupons, no limitations	10.50 −(−8.20) 18.70	20.80 −20.80 0
ACTION	Issue coupons, with limitations	10.50 −(−3.70) 14.20	20.80 −15.50 5.30
	Do not issue coupons	10.50 −10.50 0	20.80 −10.50 10.30

The minimax criterion selects the action with the minimum of the maximum opportunity losses associated with each action. The maximum opportunity loss for each action is:

   a_1: 18.70 a_2: 14.20 a_3: 10.30

The minimum of these maximum opportunity losses is 10.30, which is associated with action "Do not issue coupons." The minimax choice is not to issue coupons.